ADOPTION – THE MODERN LAW

ADOPTION – THE MODERN LAW

Caroline Bridge
Barrister, Senior Lecturer in Law, University of Manchester

Heather Swindells QC
St Philip's Chambers, Birmingham

Family Law

2003

Published by Family Law
a publishing imprint of
Jordan Publishing Limited
21 St Thomas Street
Bristol BS1 6JS

British Library Cataloguing-in-Publication Data
A catalogue record for this book is available from the British Library.

ISBN 0 85308 762 8

Typeset by MFK Mendip, Frome, Somerset
Printed by MPG Books Ltd, Bodmin, Cornwall

v

Foreword

The Rt Hon Lady Justice Hale DBE

Who would have thought it? In 1995 a very modest proposal to improve the procedures for deciding property disputes between unmarried couples proved so controversial that the whole Family Homes and Domestic Violence Bill had to be withdrawn for a rethink. Now only 7 years later we have on the statute book a law permitting unmarried couples to adopt – and not only same-sex couples who cannot get married or register their partnerships but also opposite-sex couples who could get married if they chose.

The 1992 Review of Adoption Law was not so bold. We thought that the security and stability that adopted children need were still more likely to be provided by parents who were publicly committed to their relationship and had legal responsibilities towards one another as well as their children. Bringing up children usually involves considerable financial sacrifice for the primary carer. It can also place added strains on a relationship. If the relationship does break down and the couple have no financial responsibilities towards one another, the child and primary carer will suffer even more. But we also recognised that many of the children now considered for adoption were those whose early experiences had made them particularly needy and challenging. It was important to find the best possible people to meet those needs and rise to those challenges. These might not be the same sorts of people who had traditionally put themselves forward to adopt healthy babies. Even in 1992 many unmarried couples, whether of the same sex or opposite sex, were in fact bringing up adopted children together. So it was that both sides in the debates on the Adoption and Children Bill could rightly claim to be championing the best interests of the children as they saw them.

The Bill had its genesis in the 1992 Review of Adoption Law. Like the Review of Child Care Law in 1985, which had led to the widely welcomed Children Act 1989, this was a joint project between the Department of Health and the Family Law team at the Law Commission. Our aim then was to produce a modern code of adoption law to match the modern code of child law. As with the Children Act 1989, there should be a flexible range of responses to meet the increasingly diverse needs of children separated from their birth families. Adoption had already become one of the options to meet the needs of children who had to be removed from their birth families: compulsory adoptions and adoptions with some contact were increasingly part of the landscape. Other children would need greater security in their new homes while still remaining members of their birth families: for older children, in particular, this can be an important part of their sense of self. Step-children would need a recognised relationship with their step-parents while retaining their relationships with both birth parents and birth families. All of these options have found their way into the Adoption and Children Act 2002.

The parallels with the Children Act 1989 do not end there. Rather as Dame Elizabeth Butler-Sloss's inquiry into child abuse in Cleveland sparked the political will to enact the Children Act 1989, so the revelations of Sir Ronald Waterhouse's tribunal of inquiry into abuse in children's homes in North Wales sparked the political will to enact the Adoption and Children Act 2002.

Some of the Act's other provisions, while provoking less political and public controversy than those about unmarried couples, have been controversial with the organisations and professionals who know most about the children and families themselves. Only time will tell how some of these will be interpreted in the courts or work out in practice. It is very much to be hoped tha the parallels with the Children Act 1989 will continue, with a massive inter-disciplinary training effort before implementation and a rigorous research programme afterwards.

Meanwhile, this timely book will provide a valuable resource in understanding the new law, its background and its context, and some of the controversies which have raged about it. A few of the legal conundrums may come my way in future, so it should not be assumed that my views are always those of the authors, particularly in some of their speculations about the likely outcomes in the courts!

BRENDA HALE
May 2003

Preface

Reform of adoption law has been long overdue and, upon implementation, the Adoption and Children Act 2002 will at last provide a substantial and wide-ranging overhaul of the law. This book is intended not only to provide a detailed guide through a new law but to place this law in both a historical and international context.

— Chapter 1 sets out the evolution of the law of adoption both domestically and internationally.

— Chapters 2 to 5 explore the major themes which have been the power-house driving the reforms in the new Act, with Chapter 6 summarising those principal reforms.

— Chapters 7 to 11 concentrate on the key areas of the new domestic adoption law whilst Chapters 12 to 14 look at the wider perspective of intercountry adoption.

— The Appendix contains the full text of the Adoption and Children Act 2002.

We are grateful to the Right Honourable Lady Justice Hale for her Foreword. Our thanks also go to Tom Inglis for his computer re-mastering of a lekythos by the Achilles Painter for the front cover.

The book is a joint enterprise and we dedicate it to our respective families for their endurance, patience and support.

CAROLINE BRIDGE and
HEATHER SWINDELLS QC
May 2003

Contents

Table of Cases

References are to paragraph numbers.

Table of Statutes

References are to paragraph numbers.

Table of Statutory Instruments

References are to paragraph numbers.

Table of EC/UN Material

References are to paragraph numbers.

Table of Guidance etc

References are to paragraph numbers.

Table of International Materials

References are to paragraph numbers

Table of Abbreviations

the 1926 Act	the Adoption of Children Act 1926
the 1949 Act	the Adoption of Children Act 1949
the 1973 Overseas Order	the Adoption (Designation of Overseas Adoptions) Order 1973
the 1992 Review of Adoption Law	Department of Health and Welsh Office *Review of Adoption Law, Report to Ministers of an Interdepartmental Working Group: A Consultative Document* (HMSO, 1992)
AA 1976	Adoption Act 1976
AA Regs 1983	Adoption Agencies Regulations 1983
ACA 2002	Adoption and Children Act 2002
A(IA)A 1999	Adoption (Intercountry Aspects) Act 1999
ASA	adoption support agency
BAAF	British Agencies for Adoption and Fostering
CA 1989	Children Act 1989
CAFCASS	Children and Family Courts Advisory and Support Services
CRB	Criminal Records Bureau
CSA 2000	Care Standards Act 2000
ECO	Entry Clearance Officer
Foster Placement Regs 1991	Foster Placement (Children) Regulations 1991
Fostering Regs 1991	Children (Private Arrangements for Fostering) Regulations 1991
the Hague Convention	the Hague Convention on Protection of Children and Co-operation in Respect of Intercountry Adoption 1993
ISP	internet service provider
NCSC	National Care Standards Commission
Offenders Regs 1997	Children (Protection from Offenders) (Miscellaneous Amendments) Regulations 1997
Overseas Regs 2001	Adoption of Children from Overseas Regulations 2001
PIU Report	*Prime Minister's Review of Adoption* (Performance and Innovation Unit Report, July 2000)
the UN Convention	the UN Convention on the Rights of the Child 1989
VAA	Voluntary Adoption Agency

Chapter 1

ADOPTION – THE HISTORICAL PERSPECTIVE

FROM THE COMMON LAW TO THE HOUGHTON COMMITTEE

Adoption at common law

1.1 Adoption law in England today involves the complete legal transference of parental responsibility from one set of parents to another. For the child it provides full legal membership of a family other than the one into which he or she was born. But it has not always had such formal legal recognition nor always fulfilled its current major role within the childcare system. A trawl back through the history books provides us with an enlightening glimpse into past legal and social thinking about children who needed alternative homes.

1.2 Prior to the Adoption of Children Act 1926, 'adoption' was a familiar social, albeit informal, phenomenon. In social terms, adoption meant the giving of a home to an orphaned or abandoned child – something that has probably always occurred. But in legal terms, the absence of statutory control meant there was no way that the rights of 'adoptive' parents, let alone those of the child, could be recognised. The English common law had no provision for adoption, and adults were thus free to make whatever arrangements suited them. Such informality came about because parental rights and duties were inalienable at common law. There could be no change of status comparable to the *adoptio* or *adrogatio* of Roman law (inherited by the civil law systems) without court jurisdiction.

1.3 In Roman law, adoption was an ancient institution which had its roots in ancestor worship. The maintenance of family observances in honour of ancestors[1] was of such importance that a man, likely to die without issue, was allowed to 'adrogate' some other person in order to give himself a son. Interestingly, a man without a child born in marriage could always 'adrogate' his own illegitimate child and so early Roman law had no need for a system of legitimation. This form of adoption was controlled by civil and religious authorities and continued throughout Roman history, always under the auspices of the State.[2] However, early in the Republic another form of adoption developed. Like the *paterfamilias*, the *filiifamilias* also brought a child into the family, with the father's consent, to be regarded exactly like any other child (*adoptio naturam imitatur*). Such a child could succeed in the event of the intestacy of the head of the

---

1   The family *sacra*.
2   See generally, WW Buckland and AD McNair *Roman Law & Common Law – A Comparison in Outline* (Cambridge University Press, 1952) at p 42.

adoptive family.[1] Thus Roman adoption, like Greek, Chinese, Hindu,[2] African and Japanese[3] practices, was based on securing succession and long served that purpose. It served its function by meeting the needs of those with land but without children to acquire and perpetuate the family's property rights for successive generations. Thus 'heir' adoption had its origins in the law relating to the ownership and inheritance of property. Its property-based social role was clear and its beneficiaries were wealthy families. Interestingly though, the great English families did not do as the Romans had done and adoption was never associated with the preservation of property for the ruling classes in this country.

1.4   While many European countries were influenced by Roman law, its influence also extended to North American states such as Louisiana and Texas via French and Spanish law. Not unsurprisingly, these states recognised adoption very early on.[4] But here its function was rooted far more in a shortage of human labour and a desire to help homeless children whilst benefiting from their labour in exchange,[5] than in any property or inheritance motive. Such children could nevertheless be given a much more humane upbringing than they would have received in an institution and across the USA and Canada generally, the concept of adoption found its way into the common law jurisdiction from 1851 onwards.[6]

1.5   In 1881, New Zealand became the first country in the Commonwealth to enact adoption legislation after recognising that informal adoption was already taking place.[7] Early statutory adoption in that country had been viewed as a means of lightening the State's burden with respect to the maintenance of destitute people, and many adoptions were of young children ('children of useful years') rather than babies.[8] Adoption here, as in the USA and Canada, thus met an economic need, coupled with a welfare need, and bore no resemblance at all to the property-based adoptions of Roman times. The early New Zealand practice was rather like the English feudal practice of placing a child for 'court service' and, later in the sixteenth and seventeenth centuries, taking the children of poor parents into a wealthy household to become pages and servants. Despite such

---

1   WW Buckland *A Manual of Roman Private Law* (Cambridge University Press, 1953).
2   In both Chinese and Hindu societies, a relative was the preferred adoptee, albeit the motive was a religious or inheritance-based one.
3   KJ O'Halloran in 'Adoption in the Two Jurisdictions of Ireland – A Case Study of Changes in the Balance Between Public and Private Law' [2001] *International Family Law* 43, has noted that in Japan the adoption of non-relatives was 'a traditional means of allying with the fortunes of the ruling family'.
4   Although it should be noted that ethnic groups peripheral to American society had long practised kinship fostering and adoption as a means of strengthening the extended family. See generally, Benet *The Character of Adoption* (Jonathan Cape, 1976).
5   Such children were treated very much as second-class citizens and were expected to work harder than a natural child to repay the debt of gratitude. See generally, B Tizard *Adoption: A Second Chance* (Open Books, 1977).
6   The first modern adoption law was enacted in Massachusetts in that year.
7   Although legislation had been enacted in various Australian states and Canadian provinces between the 1890s and 1920s.
8   *Adoption and its Alternatives: A Different Approach and a New Framework*, New Zealand Law Commission (Wellington, New Zealand, 2000) at para 18.

practices,[1] however, it was clear that by 1883 no such institution as legal adoption existed in English common law.

1.6 As a result, an English couple could bring up the destitute child of another but had no protection from unscrupulous birth parents retrieving him at a later date – possibly with a view to taking his earnings.[2] Such *de facto* adoptions appeared to be common in large industrial towns where charitably minded neighbours would sometimes bring up an orphaned or abandoned child as their own, thus keeping him or her from a childhood in an institution.[3] When the economy changed from a land-based agricultural one to an industrial wage-earning society with a more independent nuclear family, children were at greater risk of becoming simply an extra mouth to feed rather than an extra pair of useful hands. For the unwanted children of unmarried mothers, however, the future was even more bleak. There was a strong social and moral stigma attached to illegitimacy and both the mother and the child were regarded as morally inferior. Such children were often left to the mercy of baby farmers who, although receiving a weekly allowance for their care, were unlikely to spend it appropriately. Instead, the child was often 'so culpably neglected, so ill-treated and so badly nurtured' that he or she was probably dead within a short time.[4] Exploitation was clearly rife.

1.7 Public agitation for recognition of a law of adoption developed as part of the general movement to improve the welfare of children. Perhaps the motive might have been described as a philanthropic one. However, the need for formal legal recognition and thus protection had been somewhat mitigated by the nineteenth century Poor Law[5] which enabled guardians to assume parental rights in some circumstances and then arrange for the child to be 'adopted'.[6] Even though this power was patently inadequate and not always used when it was clearly available, the use of 'adoption' in this context was the first time that the concept had appeared in the statute books.[7] However, there was another reason for the early lack of demand for formal legal recognition. Freedom of testation meant that the property-owning classes were able to arrange financial provision for a child, irrespective of his or her legal parentage. The illegitimate children of the rich could thus be provided for even though they had been brought up outside the legitimate family, but such was not often the lot of the unwanted child.

1.8 What we can conclude is that some children have always been unwanted or unable to be cared for by parents, albeit because of the *social* stigma of illegitimacy, and some couples have always wanted or at least been prepared to bring up the child of another as

---

1   Described by KJ O'Halloran (above) as a 'non-kinship adoption' based on an 'allegiance or service model'.

2   Not that such rewards were the sole province of unscrupulous parents. In the USA early adoption practice involved orphaned children being housed and brought up in return for their labour. (See M Richards *Adoption Law* (Family Law, 1989)).

3   Described by KJ O'Halloran (above) as the adoption of abandoned or neglected children for philanthropic motives, as compared with those adopted for inheritance, kinship or service motives.

4   Report of the Select Committee on the Protection of Infant Life, BPP, 1871, vii, 607, as cited in S Cretney *Principles of Family Law* (4th edn, Sweet & Maxwell, 1988) at p 419.

5   Poor Law Act 1899.

6   For an excellent analysis of the legal background to adoption see 'Adoption – From Contract to Status?' in S Cretney *Law, Law Reform and the Family* (Oxford University Press, 1998).

7   Ibid, at p 186. Although there was no change to the child's legal status, the 'adoptive' parents gained some, but not enough, protection against a claim by the child's natural parents.

their own. In this latter context, Cretney concluded that 'the most powerful single factor influencing demand for more general legal recognition of adoption seems to have been the failure of the legal system to protect those who had undertaken the care of a destitute child'.[1] The ground for commercial and emotional exploitation of 'adoptive' parents was a fertile one in the absence of any formal legal regulation.

The Hopkinson and Tomlin Committees

1.9 Attempts to introduce adoption legislation for the purpose of protecting children as well as the adults caring for them in so-called *de facto* adoptions occurred in both 1889 and 1890.[2] But both attempts at legislation failed. This was because of opposition to any change in the inalienability of parental rights. Even though the evil of deserted children being reclaimed so that parents might take advantage of their earnings was widely recognised, opposition to any breach of such a fundamental principle of law was overwhelming.[3]

1.10 The First World War led to a large increase in the number of orphans needing homes and this in turn led to a large increase in *de facto* adoptions. Further demand for reform followed and in 1920 the Hopkinson Committee[4] recommended that provision ought to be made for legal adoption. The Hopkinson Report[5] clearly recognised that adults often wished to bring up children other than their own and emphasised that the increase in numbers of such people may well have been due to '... the loss that many families have sustained in the war ...'.[6] The Committee noted that a large percentage of these prospective parents wanted to love and care for children despite 'the trouble and expense'.[7] The welfare of children and the desire by some people to bring them up as their own was obviously recognised, yet the Committee was also concerned that these prospective 'adopters' lacked the legal rights to prevent natural parents claiming children back. The Committee duly, and controversially, recommended that binding legal effect should be given to agreements for the adoption of children and numerous unsuccessful attempts to enact legislation followed.[8]

1.11 Finally, and in the wake of pressure that something be done the Tomlin Committee was appointed.[9] It concluded that there ought to be some legal security for people who cared for children as if they were their own, even if the post-World War problem were a transient thing. Although the Tomlin Committee was grudging in its

---

1   See 'Adoption – From Contract to Status?' in S Cretney *Law, Law Reform and the Family* (Oxford University Press, 1998) at p 187.
2   Respectively, the Adoption of Children Bill (No 101) 1889 and the Adoption of Children Bill (No 56) 1890 (both withdrawn at the second reading). These legislative attempts are discussed by Nigel Lowe in 'English Adoption Law: Past, Present, and Future' in S Katz, J Eekelaar and M Mclean (eds) *Cross Currents* (Oxford University Press, 2000) at pp 308–309.
3   See N Lowe's discussion, ibid, at p 309.
4   Under the chairmanship of Sir Alfred Hopkinson KC.
5   *Report of the Committee on Child Adoption*, Cmd 1254 (1921).
6   Ibid, at para 10.
7   Ibid, at para 12.
8   Six unsuccessful Bills were introduced during 1924–1925. See the discussion in N Lowe, op cit, at p 310.
9   Under the chairmanship of Tomlin J, a Chancery Judge, the new committee was asked to examine the problem of child adoption from the point of view of possible legislation.

acceptance of the need for an adoption law, it was nonetheless sympathetic to the concerns of *de facto* adopters. Their 'apprehension' was considered to be 'genuine' and 'based on the possibility of interference at some future time by the natural parent … notwithstanding the incapacity of the legal parent to divest himself of his parental rights and duties'.[1]

1.12 The Committee was finally and reluctantly persuaded of the case for an alteration in the law but warned that, because many saw adoption as 'an evil' tending to 'encourage or increase the separation of mother and child', it should, 'if introduced, [be] operated with caution'.[2] Informed consent of the child's parents was to be a prerequisite unless the parent had disappeared, abandoned the child or become incapacitated from giving consent. In an effort to provide safeguards, the Committee recommended that adoption be a matter of judicial decision and court order. In essence, a natural parent was to be enabled to transfer his parental rights and duties to another person. The Bill as ultimately drafted became the Adoption of Children Act 1926 ('the 1926 Act') and marked the birth of English adoption law.

The Adoption of Children Act 1926

1.13 The 1926 Act provided that the rights and duties of the natural parent would vest in and be exercisable by the adopter '… as though the adopted child was a child born to the adopter in lawful wedlock'.[3] Thus was enacted the first irrevocable legal transfer of parental rights and duties from a natural to an adoptive parent. The adopted child would become the legitimate child of the adopters. The 1926 Act required 'competent independent consideration' of the child's welfare and the real and informed consent of the parents. Consent was crucial and followed the tradition established in Roman law, although in that institution only the father's consent was required – such was the absolute ascendency of the *paterfamilias*. The aim was to ensure that mothers were not compelled by extraneous circumstances into relinquishing their children permanently when a temporary respite was all that was needed in reality.[4] Either parent could adopt, either spouse could adopt separately and only a person aged under 21 could be adopted. The 1926 Act, unlike classical Roman law, was essentially for the adoption of children. But as it affected no rights of property or succession for the adopted child and no rights on the intestacy of the new family, the first adoption law could be viewed as merely suspending the parent–child relationship.[5] The rights transferred were merely those of custody and recovery, with the correlative duties of education and maintenance. The main characteristic and purpose of Roman adoption had not appeared at all. It was not until the Adoption of Children Act 1949 ('the 1949 Act') that the irrevocable legal transfer model of adoption became fully fledged and the English concept brought more in line

---

1   Tomlin *Report of the Child Adoption Committee* (1924–5) Cmd 2401, para 9. For a discussion of the differences between the Hopkinson and Tomlin Reports, see N Lowe, op cit, at pp 311–313.
2   Tomlin *Report of the Child Adoption Committee* (1924–5) Cmd 2401, para 11.
3   Section 5(1).
4   Tomlin *Report of the Child Adoption Committee* (1924–5) Cmd 2401, para 11 recommended some safeguard to prevent advantage being taken of a mother's situation and the consequent complete surrender of the child when all she needed was a temporary respite.
5   N Lowe, op cit, at p 313.

with the Roman.[1] Although the 1949 Act established the principle that adoption changed the child's status in terms of succession rights it was not until the Children Act 1975 that the child's total integration into the adoptive family for succession purposes was achieved.

1.14   The 1926 Act was minimalist in its approach and did not regulate the adoption process. Fear that natural mothers would subsequently seek to disturb the child or blackmail the adopters deterred some from using the process and this resulted in a significant number of *de facto* adoptions remaining outside the law.[2] Ten years after the Act came into force only a third of adoptions organised by one of the three largest adoption agencies in the country were given legal sanction under the 1926 Act.[3] Nonetheless, although *de facto* adoptions were rife, the numbers of legal adoptions rose, and while there were 3000 orders granted in 1927,[4] this number rose to an all-time peak of 24,800 by 1968.

1.15   The First World War and the orphaned children and childless families created by it contributed to the need for legally recognised adoption. Likewise, the surge in adoption numbers in 1946 could be related to the legalising of the many *de facto* adoptions that had probably occurred as a result of the Second World War.[5] But war and its aftermath was only one of the prompts for the increased use of legal adoption. Post-War society had witnessed a rise in white middle-class illegitimacy, and adoption was used to deal with what was perceived as a social problem. The social stigma of illegitimacy and accompanying financial hardship encouraged single mothers to give up their babies for adoption, and the beneficiaries were married childless couples who longed for a baby to call their own. On the face of it there were benefits all round: orphaned or illegitimate children found a permanent home, while couples without children were relieved of the taint of their infertility. Emphasis in practice centred on matching the physical characteristics of healthy babies with those of their adoptive parents. The myth surrounding the child's birth became veiled in secrecy and the fiction that the child had truly been born to the adopters 'in lawful wedlock' was enhanced. Consequently, the stereotype that became an entrenched part of thinking about adoption took hold and, by 1951, baby adoptions comprised 52 per cent of all adoptions. By 1968, this proportion was even greater[6] – amounting to 76 per cent of all adoptions – and in the same year, 91 per cent of all adoptions were of illegitimate children. Adoption of illegitimate babies had become the primary focus of adoption law.

1.16   At the same time as the babies of single mothers were being adopted by strangers, they were also being adopted by natural mothers alone or by step-parents. Although adoption by step-parents had not been expressly contemplated by the 1926 Act, it was not expressly forbidden and such orders were being made in the 1920s and 1930s. By the 1950s they had become common. Section 1(1) of the 1949 Act[7] had made it clear that a

---

1   WW Buckland and AD McNair *Roman Law and Common Law – A Comparison in Outline* (Cambridge University Press, 1952) at p 45.
2   Discussed by S Cretney, op cit, at p 190.
3   S Cretney, op cit, at p 190 cites *Departmental Committee on Adoption Societies and Agencies* Cmd 5499 (1937), paras 3 and 16.
4   In England and Wales.
5   N Lowe, op cit, at p 315. Both during and after the Second World War, the number of adoptions rose sharply and reached a peak of 21,000 in 1946.
6   N Lowe, op cit, at p 316.
7   Introduced as a Private Member's Bill by Sir Basil Nield.

legitimate child could be adopted by the mother or the father either solely or jointly with a spouse and, by 1951, following a steep rise in marital breakdown, the practice was deeply entrenched. This was recognised by the Hurst Committee Report in 1954[1] and in the Adoption Act 1958, which implemented its recommendations, parents and step-parents were in some respects treated less stringently than other would-be adopters.[2] Adoptions of legitimate children after the Divorce Reform Act 1969 took effect in 1971 again rose sharply until they comprised roughly a third of all adoptions.

1.17 Although 'adoption' at common law had evolved primarily from the need to provide homes for orphaned or unwanted children – and presumably many of these were more than babies – there was no major return to the practice of adoption as part of a childcare strategy by local authorities until well into the 1970s. The 1926 Act had been used primarily to provide permanent and traditional homes for the babies of unmarried mothers and to facilitate the creation of new nuclear families after a parent's divorce and remarriage. Its focus was not on finding a permanent alternative family for children in care. At the time when baby and step-parent adoptions were flourishing, the adoption of children already in care amounted to less than 10 per cent of the total. It was not until much later on in the twentieth century that practice began to change dramatically and adoptions became regarded as the primary route out of care.

The changing social climate

1.18 The law was amended in 1939,[3] providing the 'rudimentary foundations'[4] of an adoption service. These provisions only became operative in 1943 and were subsequently expanded by the 1949 Act. That Act was particularly significant in providing that the mother's agreement to the making of an adoption order could be given without knowledge of the applicant's identity, with the child's integration into the new family being complete and natural. The prospective adoptive parents' desire for complete secrecy was a major prompt and the reform marked a decisive shift in emphasis by removing the natural mother's opportunity to make a personal decision about the suitability of the adopters.[5] The overwhelming importance of consent, freely given, was diminished, thus lessening, in Cretney's analysis, the idea of adoption as a contract. The first consolidated statute was passed in 1950[6] and subsequently the Adoption Act 1958 enhanced the provision of adoption services, with local authorities as well as the traditional voluntary societies being empowered to arrange adoptions.

1.19 The 1960s saw immense social changes in Great Britain. In particular, attitudes towards illegitimacy changed and, coupled with the advent of the contraceptive pill controlling fertility and the increased numbers of abortions,[7] the numbers of illegitimate babies available for adoption declined dramatically. By 1970 baby adoptions formed 39 per cent of the total (dropping rapidly to only 4 per cent of the total by 1998).[8] The

---

1   *Report of the Departmental Committee on the Adoption of Children* Cmd 9248 (1954).
2   This is the view of M Richards expressed in *Adoption* (Family Law, 1989) at p 4.
3   Adoption of Children (Regulation) Act 1939.
4   N Lowe, op cit, at p 323.
5   See the discussion by S Cretney, op cit, at p 192.
6   Adoption Act 1950.
7   Abortion Act 1967, which came into force in April 1968.
8   Cited by N Lowe, op cit, at p 319.

reduction in the numbers of babies available for adoption has to be seen alongside the prevailing social view that those unable to have their own children should adopt. The demand for babies remained high, but was no longer able to be met as the supply dwindled and unmarried mothers decided to keep their children. During the same period, change was not quite so evident where step-parent adoptions were concerned. The numbers of these continued to rise and during the 1970s, step-parent adoptions dominated the scene even though they subsequently declined.[1] However, during the late 1960s and early 1970s, the climate of opinion began to change. The realisation that adoption of a legitimate child after the mother's remarriage, for example, effectively cut the child off from one side of its family showed up in stark relief against the growing view that knowledge of biological origins was highly significant. The issue was ripe for legislative review.

1.20 Overall, however, change most noticeably occurred in relation to children in the care of local authorities. A growing realisation that many children were spending an entire childhood in care coincided with the continuing demands from infertile couples for a child in order to complete their family. Agencies revised their notion of an adoptable child and began to use adoption to secure the long-term welfare of older children. The importance of adoption in the context of older children in care had been emphasised by the Curtis Report on the Care of Children in 1946,[2] but the practice was slow in developing. Lowe has pointed out that the work of Goldstein, Freud and Solnit,[3] stressing the importance of psychological as opposed to biological parenthood, contributed to the growing practice of placing older children for adoption. The view that abused and neglected children needed long-term permanency planning in the form of adoption took hold. With adoption numbers at their peak in 1968, yet practice clearly changing, major legislative reform was due.

The Houghton Committee

1.21 The Houghton Committee was set up in 1969 to review the law, policy and practice of adoption.[4] It reported in 1972[5] and its recommendations were enacted by the Children Act 1975. That Act was consolidated in the Adoption Act 1976, but was introduced in a piecemeal fashion due to the restraints on public expenditure.

1.22 The Houghton Report reaffirmed that the child was the focal point in adoption and that providing homes for children who needed them was its primary purpose. In support of this central tenet, the Committee recommended the introduction of a comprehensive service as part of the general functions of local authorities. 'What is needed', said the Committee, 'is a service which is comprehensive in scope and available throughout the country.' A major objective was to encourage the use of adoption as part of a well-supervised and integrated childcare service.[6] This was a resumption of the trend

---

1   See N Lowe, op cit, at p 320 for a detailed analysis of step-parent adoptions of both legitimate and illegitimate children.
2   Cmd 6922 (1946).
3   *Beyond the Best Interests of the Child* (1973).
4   The first chairman was Sir William Houghton, but he died in office and was succeeded by Judge FA Stockdale.
5   *Report of the Departmental Committee on the Adoption of Children*, Cmnd 5107 (1972).
6   Ibid, at para 33.

noted earlier by the Curtis Report which had stressed the importance of adoption as an alternative to normal family care. The Houghton recommendation was that a duty to provide an adoption service or ensure that one was provided by voluntary agencies be imposed on all local authorities.[1] The public and private branches, as it were, were to act in partnership, with voluntary agencies becoming registered nationally. The overall objective was to integrate adoption with other childcare services so that, if adoption were the best course for a particular child, then the facilities were to be available for placement. The comprehensive service was to comprise a social work service to natural parents seeking placement for a child, skills and facilities for assessment of the parents' emotional resources and personal and social situation, short-term accommodation for unsupported mothers, general childcare resources – including facilities pending adoption placement, assessment and adoption placement services, after-care for natural parents, and counselling for adoptive families.[2]

1.23   Further recommendations were that, first, certain basic conditions for eligibility on the part of adopters be prescribed by statute, but that decisions on the suitability of particular adopters should be left to the agencies, and, secondly, that natural parents should be entitled to remain anonymous so far as the adopters were concerned. Would-be adopters were to be regulated in that they first had to be approved by an agency, which included being screened by an adoption panel, they had to wait until a suitable child had been matched to them by the agency, and then, if the placement proved successful, they had to apply to court for an adoption order after a minimum period of 13 weeks.

1.24   Coupled with the recommendation that private placement of children for adoption by non-relatives become an offence[3] and that social workers be fully trained, the Houghton Committee was intent on the 'professionalisation' of adoption work and its complete regulation.

1.25   The Houghton Committee addressed many of the issues that have remained relevant to adoption law reform and, in particular, it expressed disquiet about the 'total transplant' concept of adoption where step-parents and relatives were concerned. Adoption of a legitimate child by a parent and the new spouse following divorce[4] effectively cut off the child, who was likely to be older and have a deep sense of loyalty to both parents, from one side of its family. A 1970 Departmental Committee *Working Paper* (under the chairmanship of Sir William Houghton)[5] sounded the alarm over the potential harm these adoptions could cause and asserted that it was 'not appropriate to use adoption in an attempt to ease the pain or cover up the consequences of divorce'. For one thing, the child may not wish to lose contact with the other parent, change his or her name or, indeed, be adopted. But of course, a step-parent adoption was not always

---

1   At para 35, the Report noted that 'local authority social services departments and voluntary organisations with a range of services for children should be able to offer a better and more comprehensive service for children than purely placement agencies . . .'.

2   *Report of the Departmental Committee on the Adoption of Children*, Cmnd 5107 (1972), at para 38.

3   Ibid, at para 81, where it was pointed out that there was nothing to prevent a mother placing a child with a casual acquaintance such as someone she met at the launderette. Consequently, it was recommended, at para 92, that private placements be unlawful.

4   About half of all adoptions at the time were of legitimate children following divorce or the death of a parent.

5   Departmental Committee on the Adoption of Children *Working Paper* (HMSO, 1970), at paras 92–94.

potentially harmful.[1] Subsequently, in 1972 the Houghton Committee recommended the restriction of step-parent adoptions, although not a complete ban.[2] The Committee also noted the large number of adoptions by other relatives and expressed concern at their potential to distort family relationships by concealing the truth about a child's parentage. The adoption of a child by a grandparent was a vivid example of this distortion. Neither relatives nor long-term foster carers had any legal status in relation to the child, and the law had thus far provided no means whereby they could obtain it without cutting the child's links with his or her natural family. The choice was one of doing without the legal security of adoption or applying for an adoption order.[3] In either case there was potential for harm to the child.

1.26 The Houghton Committee concluded that custodianship would 'provide the more realistic and acceptable solution . . .' in most cases of applications by relatives such as grandparents, as an alternative to adoption by step-parents after divorce, or for those foster parents looking after children whose natural parents were out of the picture. The concept of custodianship was seen as a method of giving legal security to those looking after children on a long-term basis, without the child losing his or her own name and sense of identity.[4] The thinking behind the concept clearly indicated that the need for long-term security and permanence for some children without the full legal transference of adoption had been recognised. The legal position of foster parents was intended to be strengthened by custodianship, given that they might or might not end up being approved as suitable adopters. Their chronic lack of security was thought to impact upon their parenting ability.

1.27 History now illustrates that the search for just such an alternative form of permanence has proved illusory. Custodianship was never successful (not least, it is suggested, because of nomenclature) and, although it was only brought into force on 1 December 1985, it became defunct in 1991 when the Children Act 1989 (CA 1989) came into force. A further reason advanced for its singular lack of success was this lengthy delay in implementation. With the provision not coming into force until 13 years after the Committee's recommendation, adoption practice had proceeded without custodianship. As it was, most applicants were grandparents who had had young children living with them for most of the children's lives and wished to safeguard that arrangement.[5] In the interim, the dividing line between adoption and fostering had become more clear cut and the perceived need for such a half-way house became superficially less compelling.

1.28 Whereas parental wishes had always been at the heart of adoption (the Tomlin Committee, for example, assumed that consent would invariably be required), there remained a persistent fear that a parent who had given agreement might change his or her

---

1   In *Re S* (1974) 5 Fam Law 88, for example, where the children had no recollection of their natural father, the adoption order simply gave legal effect to a situation already existing in fact.
2   Ultimately, the Children Act 1975 introduced statutory discouragement of all types of step-parent adoption.
3   Ibid, at para 116.
4   The Houghton Committee, Cmnd 5107, para 121, considered that custodianship would be appropriate where the child was old enough to have a sense of identity which he or she wished to keep and wanted to retain his or her own name, yet the parents were out of the picture and foster parents wanted to secure their legal relationship.
5   E Bullard and E Malos *Custodianship – A Report to the Department of Health on the Implementation of Part II of the Children Act 1975* (University of Bristol, 1990) at paras 9.31 and 9.32.

mind[1] and that a parent whose child had been taken into care and needed a new home might never agree. It was noted that a child might have been taken into care at birth but that the parent then vacillated for years over the question of adoption, thus depriving the child of a settled home life.[2] Equally, the Committee noted, there was no way of testing whether, for example, a parent was withholding consent unreasonably, without first placing the child with the prospective adopters and awaiting a court decision after at least 3 months.[3] If there were then insufficient grounds for dispensing with the parent's consent, the child had to be returned to the agency.

1.29 The Houghton Committee noted that some believed that the law itself encouraged parental indecisiveness.[4] Consequently, it recommended that a new procedure – to be known as 'freeing a child for adoption' – be introduced.[5] This was an attempt to solve both types of consent problem. First, following a system used in many states of the USA, the Committee recommended that a parent be able to make an irrevocable decision to give the child up for adoption and relinquish parental rights and obligations before placement. Secondly, where a child was in care with no satisfactory long-term plan in mind, the Committee believed that it should be open to a local authority or registered agency to 'apply to a court for the parents' consent to be dispensed with on one of the statutory grounds, for parental rights to be transferred to the agency and the child thus freed for placement for adoption'.[6] A particular perception of child welfare was at the root of the Committee's thinking, albeit the report 'accepted the principle that the natural family should be preserved wherever reasonably possible'.[7] On balance, the rights of natural parents were clearly on the way to being relegated to an inferior position in the adoption triangle.

1.30 The Houghton Committee was resolved to ensure that adoption became a 'total legal transplant' and to this end proposed that the adopted child should have 'exactly the same rights under wills and other instruments as a natural child of the adoptive family'. This thinking was premised on the basis that a complete severance from the natural family would result in the establishment of a new and irrevocable relationship.[8] As Hoggett and Pearl noted, however, 'a total legal transplant [did] not mean a total physical or psychological transplant'.[9] In citing from John Triseliotis' 1973 study,[10] which illustrated the often desperate search of Scottish adopted adults for their real identity,

---

1   Cmnd 5107, at para 168, noted that parental rights and obligations were not terminated at the time the parent signed the consent document but continued until the adoption order was made some time later.
2   Ibid, at para 221.
3   Ibid, at para 223.
4   Ibid, at para 168, noted that there was thus unnecessary strain and confusion for the mother.
5   Ibid, at paras 173–186.
6   Ibid, at para 224.
7   Ibid, at para 224.
8   Ibid, at para 327. Following the implementation of these recommendations in 1975, B Hoggett and D Pearl *The Family, Law and Society – Cases and Materials* (Butterworths, 1991) at p 646 pointed out the three exceptions to the principle that the adopted child was the same as the child born to married parents: he could not succeed to peerages; marriage prohibitions with respect to the birth family remained; and certain rights of nationality and immigration were denied.
9   B Hoggett and D Pearl *The Family, Law and Society – Cases and Materials* (Butterworths, 1991) at p 646.
10   *In Search of Origins: The Experiences of Adopted People* (Routledge and Kegan Paul, 1973).

those authors highlighted the Houghton recommendation that 'probably provoked more public debate and controversy than all the other recommendations in the report':[1] that 'all adopted adults in England and Wales, whenever adopted, should in future be permitted to obtain a copy of their original birth entry'.[2] The Committee noted that, as the climate of public opinion changed, mothers had become less concerned to conceal an illegitimate child and that, as a consequence, there should be freer access to background information and a greater openness about adoption. But greater openness in Houghton Committee terms was a far cry from actual contact with an adopted child. In 1972, it was almost unthinkable that birth parents could retain any links with the child who was the subject of an adoption order.

THE ADOPTION ACT 1976

Some key legal concepts

1.31   The Adoption Act 1976 (AA 1976), consolidating earlier Adoption Acts and the Children Act 1975, received Royal Assent on 22 July 1976, but was not fully implemented until 1 January 1988. Minor amendments were brought about by the CA 1989, but otherwise the Act remained the product of the thinking and research of the late 1960s and early 1970s.

1.32   Although most of the Houghton recommendations were ultimately enacted, the time lag caused by staggered implementation meant that the law had not necessarily kept up with changes in childcare practice and new approaches to such matters as openness in adoption. The legislation had a sense of the past about it almost before it was fully in force and the AA 1976 came to be perceived as meeting the demands of an earlier age while failing to accommodate the changing use to which adoption had been put. Nonetheless, it governed adoption for many years and contained within it many of the key legal concepts upon which the new legislation has built. Understanding the Adoption and Children Act 2002 (ACA 2002) therefore requires a reminder of those key concepts.

The adoption order

1.33   An adoption order under the AA 1976 extinguished the parental responsibility of natural parents and gave it to the new adoptive parents.[3] The transfer was final and irrevocable,[4] with the rights and responsibilities that had originally been possessed by the natural mother being passed to the adopters. For the child, an adoption order created a change of status which remained life-long. He or she was regarded in law as having been born to the adopters in lawful wedlock and was a part of their family for all legal

---

1   B Hoggett and D Pearl, op cit, at p 648 cited the following from the *News of the World* (10 October 1976): 'Thousands of women are facing the fear that a secret shadow from the past may soon knock at their door and wreck their marriages. They are the mothers who have never told their husbands and their families that they had an illegitimate baby whom they gave for adoption'.
2   Cmnd 5107, at para 303.
3   AA 1976, s 12(1) and (2).
4   In *Re B (Adoption Order: Jurisdiction to Set Aside)* [1995] 3 All ER 333, at 343, Sir Thomas Bingham MR noted that 'The act of adoption has always been regarded in this country as possessing a peculiar finality ... It effects a change intended to be permanent and concerning three parties'.

purposes.[1] The relationship between them was almost equivalent to that between a parent and his or her natural legitimate child.[2] Only married couples were able to make joint applications to adopt[3] (thus excluding unmarried cohabiting couples or a brother and sister, for example) and agencies invariably placed children within a married nuclear family in order to replicate, as far as possible, the norm. Single people were able to apply,[4] but in practice sole applications were likely to come from an unmarried parent of the child or a relative and, although the court could make an order in favour of one cohabiting partner with a shared residence order in favour of the two partners,[5] adoption remained within the province of the traditional family.

1.34 The effect of an adoption order was unlike that of any other child order. It could not be varied or discharged and did not contain a time scale. It could be made only with the unconditional agreement of the natural parents or where their consent had been dispensed with under the statute. Its impact was life-long and life-changing and, very often, a last resort in childcare terms. Its psychological benefits were recognised as emotionally significant and gave the child such an important sense of 'belonging' that time and again it '[was] held to outweigh a natural parent's unwillingness to give his or her agreement . . .'.[6] Where the CA 1989 sought to regulate the operation of parental responsibility, an adoption order, in stark contrast, had the effect of extinguishing it and discharging any order that had been made under that Act. The only points of similarity between orders under the CA 1989 and an adoption order were the very broad ones: both were intimately concerned with children and their welfare, although unlike the CA 1989, the AA 1976 did not provide any direct guidance on how welfare should be assessed.

1.35 Not only did an adoption order destroy existing legal relationships and create new ones, but it was the only model of adoption order available under the AA 1976. There was no half-way house, no lesser form of adoption tailored to the child's particular circumstances, and no form of long-term security available to step-parents, relatives or foster parents in order to meet both their needs and those of the child. The AA 1976 maintained the 'one size fits all' form of adoption at a time when the changes in its use, which were to later gather steam, were already evident. Unlike CA 1989 orders, such as residence orders and contact orders, which could be tailored to meet the demands of the situation and ensure that the child's welfare was given paramount consideration,[7] an adoption order was invariably inflexible. Until the amendments in the CA 1989 in relation to the making of contact orders came into force in 1991, only s 12(6) enabled the inclusion of terms and conditions.[8] Although these could be imposed in relation to such matters as religious upbringing and contact,[9] terms and conditions were subject to the

---

1   AA 1976, s 39(1).
2   See *Re H (A Minor) (Adoption)* [1985] FLR 519.
3   AA 1976, s 14.
4   Ibid, s 15.
5   See *Re AB (Adoption: Joint Residence)* [1996] 1 FLR 27.
6   *Re H (Adoption: Non-Patrial)* [1996] 1 FLR 717 at 726, per Holman J.
7   Under s 11(7) of the CA 1989, any s 8 order may contain directions and conditions.
8   The study by M Murch et al, *Pathways to Adoption* (1993) found very little evidence of adoption orders being made with access conditions attached.
9   The House of Lords considered the nature of a condition as to access in *Re C (A Minor) (Adoption Order: Conditions)* [1988] 1 All ER 705, and this was followed by the Court of Appeal in *Re S (A Minor) (Blood Transfusion: Adoption Order Condition)* [1994] 2 FLR 416.

general duty prescribed by AA 1976, s 6 and the court was urged to ensure that it did not impose any term which might be 'fundamentally inconsistent with the principles which underline the making of an adoption order'.[1] The aim of ensuring flexibility and interchangeability of orders, so important to the success of the CA 1989, was anathema to the AA 1976. The very concept of adoption was rigid and inflexible.

Adoption and welfare

1.36 Under the AA 1976, the child's welfare was not the paramount consideration.[2] This, of course, was different from the position under s 1 of the CA 1989, where the child's welfare is paramount whenever the court is considering a matter of upbringing. Section 6 of the AA 1976 provided that:

> 'In reaching any decision relating to the adoption of a child a court or adoption agency shall have regard to all the circumstances, first consideration being given to the need to safeguard and promote the welfare of the child throughout his childhood . . .'

1.37 The difference between the wording of s 6 and the paramountcy principle under what was then s 1 of the Guardianship of Minors Act 1971 (now s 1 of the CA 1989) created a deliberate contrast. Parliament accepted that adoption was conceptually different from custody in that it meant an irrevocable severance between parent and child – although, as commentators noted at the time, the weighting to be given to the child's welfare as opposed to other considerations was unclear.[3] The provision has certainly enabled the court to consider other factors; these have included immigration controls,[4] the status of adoption in a foreign country, and the child's welfare during adulthood,[5] but have not applied to decisions dispensing with the natural parent's agreement on the ground of unreasonableness. This interpretation has meant that a child might benefit from adoption, yet an order be refused where the parent did not agree and that agreement could not be dispensed with on the grounds set out in AA 1976, s 16.[6]

1.38 Adoption agencies also had to give the child's welfare first consideration when determining whether or not to place him or her for adoption and both court and agency were required 'so far as practicable' to ascertain[7] and give due consideration to his or her wishes and feelings[8] and to have regard to religious upbringing.

---

1   *Re C (A Minor) (Wardship and Adoption)* [1981] 2 FLR 177, per Roskill LJ.
2   *Re B (Adoption: Child's Welfare)* [1995] 1 FLR 895.
3   S Cretney *Principles of Family Law* (4th edn, Sweet & Maxwell, 1984) noted at pp 426–427 that the child's welfare was to be given greater weight than other considerations but need not prevail over those other considerations.
4   *Re K (A Minor) (Adoption Order)* [1994] 2 FLR 557.
5   *Re D (Adoption Order: Validity)* [1991] Fam 137.
6   An example is *Re BA (Wardship and Adoption)* [1985] FLR 1008, where the mother's refusal was within the band of reasonable decisions.
7   In *Re D (Minors) (Adoption by Step-Parent)* [1981] 2 FLR 102, the Court of Appeal gave weight to the wishes of two girls, aged 13 and 10, that they be adopted and considered that some fairly clear reason would be needed to refuse an order.
8   AA 1976, s 6.

Agreement to adoption

1.39   The AA 1976 provided that neither an adoption order[1] nor a freeing order[2] could be made unless each parent or guardian[3] 'freely and with full understanding of what is involved' agreed unconditionally[4] to its making or, alternatively, that agreement was dispensed with.[5]

1.40   The term 'parent' referred to the mother and married father, but the unmarried father's agreement was not required unless he had acquired legal custody or parental rights or responsibility for the child.[6] It was also a requirement at the outset that a putative father would be joined as a party where he had acquired an affiliation order and, in other cases where his identity was known, he was to be given information about the adoption. Any unmarried father was entitled to be heard on the merits of the application if he were contributing to the child's maintenance.[7] Agreeing to adoption was very much a right of traditional parenthood and did not pass to the local authority if, for example, a care order were made. The requirement for unconditional agreement marked a further area of difference between the concept of adoption and the granting of legal custody or, subsequently, residence. Where adoption was concerned, the whole parent–child relationship was in issue, whereas in custody proceedings, the issue centred on custody, care and control, with the child's welfare being the paramount consideration.[8] Even if adoption were in the best interests of a child, the court could not make such an order if the parent did not agree. However, the AA 1976 made no provision for requiring the older child's agreement to the adoption even though his or her wishes and feelings were to be ascertained and given weight according to age and understanding.

1.41   The 1926 Act had given the court discretion to dispense with the consent of a person if he or she were 'a person whose consent ought, in the opinion of the court and in all the circumstances to be dispensed with'.[9] Although the discretion was wide, there was little evidence that it was used. Even when the 1976 legislation was enacted, few applications were made without parental agreement and contested adoption was considered very rare.[10] But, as community interest in adoption increased, the requirement of parental consent was gradually modified in that the circumstances in which it could be dispensed with were extended. The formula of withholding agreement unreasonably was introduced by the Adoption Act 1949 and, according to the Hurst Committee,[11] was intended to focus attention on the child's welfare.

---

1   AA 1976, s 16(1).
2   Ibid, s 18(1).
3   Ibid, s 72(1).
4   A parent could no longer impose a condition as to religious upbringing as had been allowed under s 4(2) of the Adoption Act 1958.
5   AA 1976, s 16(2).
6   Ibid, s 72(1).
7   Adoption Rules 1984, r 15(2)(h); the courts also had a general discretion to include the unmarried father as a respondent if he expressed an interest.
8   *Re W (An Infant)* [1971] AC 682 at 693, per Lord Hailsham of St Marylebone.
9   AA 1926, s 2(3).
10 Table D of the First Report to Parliament on the Children Act 1975 (HC 268) illustrates that only 6.3 per cent of applications were so made.
11 Cmnd 9248 (1954), para 117.

1.42   Before 1971 and the authoritative guidance of the House of Lords in *Re W (An Infant)*,[1] 'it was considered an accepted fact that courts would almost always refuse to grant an adoption order if parents refused consent . . .'.[2] Early case-law established that it was not necessarily unreasonable for a parent to withhold consent and, instead, another form of culpability was usually required. However, the AA 1976 clearly envisaged that some parental refusals would be unreasonable, and *Re W (An Infant)* clarified the principles to be applied and established a change in direction. Perhaps the most significant of the changes was that, although it was insufficient to show that adoption would simply be in the child's best interests,[3] the whole approach became more child-centred. A reasonable parent would acknowledge the importance of the child's interests even though there might be more than one reasonably held view about how those interests were to be served. Case-law throughout the 1970s and 1980s confirmed the interpretation that the child's interests were of prime importance.[4]

Freeing for adoption

1.43   The Adoption Act 1958 had provided that parental consent be given only in relation to a specific adoption, and that it could be withdrawn at any time up to the making of the final order. It has been suggested that this led to indecisiveness on the part of natural parents and tension for both themselves and the prospective adopters.[5] Prospective adopters, and often agencies themselves, feared that a parent would withhold agreement at the last minute. The result was that some children were not available for adoption even though it was clear that adoption was the preferred solution. This was clearly not in the interests of children. Consequently, a new procedure, 'freeing for adoption', was recommended by the Houghton Committee,[6] and introduced by the Children Act 1975, although it was not ultimately implemented until 1984.

1.44   The freeing order enabled parents to relinquish their parental rights and responsibilities at an earlier stage in the adoption process – before the child was placed or before a full adoption hearing – and those rights were then transferred to the agency before being passed to the adopters. This meant that on the application of an agency, a child could be 'freed' for adoption and subsequently an adoption order made without any further evidence of parental consent. In each case, the court had to be satisfied that each parent or guardian agreed to the making of an adoption order or, alternatively, that their agreement was to be dispensed with as if for an adoption order, so long as the child was already placed for adoption or the court was satisfied that this was likely to happen.[7] Additionally, the court had to be satisfied that a putative father did not intend to apply for a parental responsibility order or residence order under the CA 1989 or that, if he did so intend, the application were likely to be refused.[8]

---

1   [1971] AC 682.
2   (1981) 103 *Adoption and Fostering* 24.
3   *Re W (An Infant)* [1971] AC 682 at 693.
4   In particular, *Re P (An Infant) (Adoption: Parental Consent)* [1977] Fam 25; *Re F (A Minor) (Adoption: Parental Consent)* [1982] 1 WLR 102; *Re D (An Infant) (Adoption: Parent's Consent)* [1977] AC 602.
5   S Cretney *Principles of Family Law* (4th edn, Sweet & Maxwell, 1984) at p 446.
6   Cmnd 5107, paras 221–224.
7   AA 1976, s 18(3).
8   Ibid, s 18(7).

1.45 Thus, the long-held attraction of parental consent to a specific adoption was removed. In reality, the provision meant that a child remained in a unique legal limbo, with no individual holding parental rights.

Secrecy and access

1.46 The 'legal transplant' concept of adoption inherent in the AA 1976 carried with it the notion that secrecy was vital. The very words of s 39 required that a child be regarded as born to the adopters in 'lawful wedlock', and thus a fiction needed to be maintained. Adoption practice attempted to prevent biological and adoptive parents from knowing each others' identities and the law did not require adoptive parents to tell the child about his or her heritage and background. However, the law changed in England and Wales in 1976, and since that time the child has had the right, on reaching adulthood, to obtain the original birth certificate.[1] Despite concerns that birth parents would suffer distress and embarrassment if their adopted child suddenly confronted them, no clear evidence has emerged that this has been the case. Nonetheless, there was no corresponding provision enabling the natural parents to obtain similar information, thus preventing them from learning the identity of the child.

1.47 This concept of adoption had made it almost unthinkable that birth parents would retain any contact with the adopted child. Nonetheless, the AA 1976 provided that an adoption order could contain such terms and conditions as the court thought fit,[2] subject to the general duty to give first consideration to the welfare of the child. Despite the apparent incompatibility between the concept of adoption and contact, the courts had never denied the possibility that maintenance of a link with the original family could be a condition of an adoption order.[3] During the 1970s and early 1980s, access was incorporated as a term of the adoption order in several reported cases,[4] but the court always expressed itself with hesitancy and dubbed the facts 'exceptional'. Access was only allowed in accordance with terms already agreed by the respective parties.[5] The prime difficulty was the dilemma thrown up by the notion of ongoing contact alongside the complete legal transference of adoption: if it was beneficial for a child to keep up contact with his or her natural mother, then surely an adoption order was inappropriate.[6] That

---

1   AA 1976, s 51.

2   Ibid, s 12(6).

3   In *Re B (MF) (An Infant)* [1972] 1 All ER 898, the Court of Appeal confirmed that there was no hard and fast rule that adoption required a complete 'divorce' of the children from their birth family even though this was normally desirable. This was a case in which the adoptive parents and natural parents agreed that two young boys would benefit from ongoing contact with the original family even though it was in the interests of the boys to be adopted.

4   *Re J (A Minor) (Adoption Order: Conditions)* [1973] 2 All ER 410; *Re S (Adoption Order: Access)* [1975] 1 All ER 109; *Re C (Wardship and Adoption)* [1981] 2 FLR 177.

5   In *Re GR (Adoption: Access)* [1985] FLR 643, an access condition was refused, but the judge still expressed the hope that access would continue with the agreement of the adopters.

6   In *Re V (A Minor) (Adoption: Consent)* [1986] 1 All ER 752, the court found that if the child's welfare was so strengthened by ongoing contact with the natural mother that provision had to be made for it in an adoption order, then this was difficult to reconcile with the avowed purpose of adoption. In *Re M (A Minor) (Adoption Order: Access)* [1986] 1 FLR 51, the Court of Appeal concluded that if a blood relationship was to continue and be acknowledged, then there seemed to be little purpose to the adoption.

issue received some clarification in *Re C (A Minor) (Adoption Order: Conditions)*,[1] when the House of Lords held that the court's jurisdiction under s 12(6) enabled a condition as to access to be imposed where this served the child's interests. The case concerned a strong sibling attachment between a 12-year-old girl and her older brother. As young children, the two had spent several years together in a children's home where their attachment had grown, but when the girl was placed for adoption, contact with her brother was discouraged in readiness for a complete severance with the past. The House of Lords grasped the flexibility inherent in s 12(6) and used it to forge a sensible and welfare-based adoption order providing for access between the siblings to be maintained. The girl needed the security of full integration into an adoptive family, but her welfare required an ongoing relationship with her brother. Although their Lordships stressed that a complete break from the birth family on adoption was normally desirable, the guidance offered allowed the contact issue to emerge. Two additional points made that case a significant one in the history of adoption law.

1.48 First, the court highlighted the notion of flexibility and the need to tailor an order that met (exceptionally) the welfare interests of the child. Besides the acknowledgement this accorded to the idea of adoption and contact co-existing, particularly where an older child was concerned, it foreshadowed the thinking behind the greater flexibility and interchangeability of orders in family proceedings that would be brought about once the CA 1989 came into force. Secondly, and perhaps more tangentially, the case was an acknowledgement that the parental rights which transferred on adoption might not necessarily be 'exclusive', albeit there was a legally absolute transference. The idea that adoption might provide a secure form of long-term childcare, rather than persist as a means of creating a substitute family for adoptive parents, was clearly in the wind. The fact that the original birth family might retain any kind of link with the child, post-adoption, thereby challenged both the philosophy of secrecy under the AA 1976 as well as the exclusivity of the adopters' role.

THE EFFECT OF THE CHILDREN ACT 1989

1.49 Although the CA 1989 made few direct changes to adoption law it was not without impact. Section 34 imposed a presumption of contact with children in care and the inclusion of adoption within the definition of 'family proceedings' in the CA 1989 provided greater flexibility for the courts to consider other orders when hearing an adoption application. This broadened the scope for considering that contact and adoption might co-exist by enabling a s 8 contact application to be heard at the same time as the adoption application or, more rarely, by giving the natural parent leave to apply for such an order subsequent to the adoption. It also enabled other orders, most obviously a residence order, to be made on an adoption application.

Contact and adoption

1.50 The early effect of these changes was an increased expectation of 'open' adoption, seen most noticeably in the use made of concurrent adoption and contact applications (since, of course, once an adoption order was made, the natural parent became a 'former'

---

1   [1989] AC 1.

parent and lost the right to apply for s 8 orders without leave of the court[1]). One manifestation of the increased awareness of 'open' adoption was the practice of natural parents seeking to resume contact with a child who was already with foster parents or future adopters, in the hope of subsequently being awarded a s 8 contact order once the child had been adopted. Such a prospect was perceived as making a future adoption more palatable for the natural parents. In *Re H (A Minor) (Freeing Order)*[2] the Court of Appeal, however, refused a renewal of the mother's contact with the child on the basis that unnecessary and inappropriate interference might be caused to the child as a result. The impact of the new emphasis on contact was seen more clearly in *Re A (A Minor) (Adoption: Contact Order)*.[3] Here, an order for monthly contact was made alongside a freeing order, but 8 months later there were still no suitable adopters prepared to enter what looked inevitably like an 'open' adoption with substantial contact. The Court of Appeal's assessment of the situation was telling: 'the degree of contact … has been the inhibiting factor and for many of us, monthly contact would seem incompatible with the likely view of most prospective adopters … The view of open adoption embraced by experts does not seem to be shared by many prospective adopters'.[4]

1.51   Whilst the CA 1989 had highlighted the idea that adoption and contact might not be incompatible, the reality was different, both for the child and the adopters. Perhaps one of the few exceptions was *Re E (A Minor) (Care Order: Contact)*,[5] where children with no prospect of rehabilitation with their parents were found to be facing the likelihood of damage if contact did not take place. Here, the natural parents did not oppose adoption and the local authority was obliged to attempt to find adopters who would accept the substantial involvement needed to support ongoing face-to-face contact.

1.52   The granting of leave to apply for contact after the adoption of a child was facilitated by s 10(9) of the CA 1989, but in practice 'conventional wisdom' won out over the new progressive ideas in the High Court. In *Re C (A Minor) (Adopted Child: Contact)*,[6] where a mother who had never consented to the adoption sought contact with her child whom she had not seen for 3 years, Thorpe J (as he then was) stressed that adoption orders were intended to be permanent and final and that even indirect contact required some fundamental change in circumstances:[7] it was for Parliament to express any new changes in the understanding of what was best for an adopted child and his or her natural parents. This latter point was significant for although the CA 1989 had brought about new rights of contact with children in care, a change in ideas was also beginning to evolve in the context of post-adoption contact.

---

1   CA 1989, s 10(4).
2   [1993] 2 FLR 325.
3   [1993] 2 FLR 645.
4   Ibid, at 649.
5   [1994] 1 FLR 146.
6   [1993] 2 FLR 431.
7   Similar views were held with respect to wardship in *Re O (A Minor) (Wardship: Adopted Child)* [1978] Fam 196 and *Re C (A Minor) (Wardship: Adopted Child)* [1985] FLR 1114, where there needed to be an 'extremely strong prima facie case' to justify investigating the full merits of a former parent's application to seek care and control of the child.

Residence and adoption

1.53   The CA 1989 abolished custodianship and substituted residence as an alternative to adoption in those situations where the child needed long-term security and stability, yet adoption was inappropriate or natural parents refused their agreement. The s 8 residence order gave the applicants[1] a limited form of parental responsibility[2] for a child until he or she reached the age of 16. Consequently, a child living with foster parents under a residence order, for example, did not undergo a change of status such as would occur on adoption, and the natural parents retained their rights, albeit the exercise of these was curtailed.[3] Unlike an adoption order, a residence order could be varied or revoked but, unlike custodianship which could be revoked by the custodian, it could not be brought to an end by the person in whose favour it was made. Significantly, however, the court could make a residence order instead of an adoption order if it considered that to be more appropriate – where a mother refused her agreement to adoption and the court considered that this was not unreasonable, for example.

1.54   In *Re M (Adoption or Residence Order)*[4] the mother's reasonable refusal of agreement to adoption propelled the court towards residence coupled with a restriction on further applications under s 91(14) of the CA 1989. Here, the Court of Appeal concluded that a residence order 'best balances the necessary security with the maintenance of the cherished family tie',[5] despite the view of Simon Brown LJ (dissenting) that adoption was the best course in the circumstances of the foster parents' refusal to contemplate a less permanent form of arrangement. The key to determining which order should be granted was the child's welfare.[6] Should a child who might be rehabilitated with natural parents in the long term be adopted or would a residence order best serve his or her interests? Where the child was older and/or had particular ethnic or cultural roots, might residence better provide him or her with security without losing touch with his or her origins and community? Increasing openness in adoption, enhanced by the changes under the CA 1989 with respect to contact, meant a greater awareness of alternatives to adoption. In procedural terms, the court's power to make a s 8 order of its own motion[7] provided the legal mechanism to bring about such alternatives.

ADOPTION OF CHILDREN FROM ABROAD

1.55   Historically, the United Kingdom has always welcomed unaccompanied refugee children, separated from their parents and fleeing their country of birth during war. There has always been some adoption of refugee children by British families, primarily on

---

1   CA 1989, s 10(2) allows a range of people with whom the child has a special relationship to apply for a residence order or otherwise obtain leave of the court to do so.

2   Those acquiring parental responsibility by means of a residence order could not change the child's name, remove him or her from the UK for more than a month, agree to adoption, nor appoint a testamentary guardian.

3   CA 1989, s 2(8) prevented a person with parental responsibility from acting in a way which was incompatible with a court order.

4   [1998] 1 FLR 570.

5   Ibid, per Ward LJ, at 596H.

6   AA 1976, s 6 and CA 1989, s 1.

7   CA 1989, s 10(1)(b).

humanitarian grounds,[1] but intercountry adoption only became recognised as such in the immediate post-War years of the 1940s. We have always responded to the plight of child victims of disaster, persecution and intense poverty, often inspired by the current headline-grabbing area of conflict – Korea, Vietnam, the Lebanon and, in more recent years, Romania, China, and South and Central America. Detailed adoption information remains scarce, however, due in large measure to the fact that the Children Act 1975 did not allow for non-agency placements and most intercountry placements were non-agency. The little information available, however, indicated that the numbers of intercountry adoptions in the United Kingdom were low in comparison with countries such as the USA and some Western European nations. We can assume, therefore, that it was not high on the list of social work or legislative priorities, even if it did become increasingly relevant to would-be adopters of British children.

1.56 In historical terms we can trace a shift in the motivation of potential adopters. Early humanitarian responses to the plight of dispossessed children gave way to the more individual enterprise of mainly childless couples unable to adopt a baby in their own country. The decreasing numbers of healthy white babies available for adoption meant that infertile couples increasingly turned their attention abroad when other avenues had failed. Eschewing the plight of special-needs children in the United Kingdom, the latest war-torn country became the focus of attention for such people, thus leading to a reversal of the domestic pattern of adoption. Providing a home for a child in need came second to serving the desires of childless couples – a contrast with developments at home. This phenomenon was particularly notable when Romanian orphanages were opened up to the Western world and in the spring of 1990 the adoption of these children by foreigners began. That is not to say that humanitarian concern did not play a part in inspiring those wanting to complete their families to rush to Romania, but undoubtedly the needs of Romanian orphans took their place alongside the needs of infertile couples. As Bainham has noted, many commentators have expressed the view that such adoptions 'have not been child-centred but have had, instead, as their main objective, the satisfaction of adult needs'.[2]

1.57 By the early 1980s, therefore, it was safe to say that intercountry adoption had become a service for childless couples, albeit some were inspired by the perception that they were rescuing a child, while domestic adoption was well on the way to becoming a service for children in care and needing a permanent home.[3] In other words, modern intercountry adoption, which had increased globally, had its origins in the changing patterns and uses of domestic adoption.

1.58 In terms of regulation, the two most important international instruments were the 1986 UN Declaration on Social and Legal Principles relating to the Protection and Welfare of Children, with special reference to Foster Placement and Adoption Nationally and Internationally, and the 1989 UN Convention on the Rights of the Child which was

---

1   See R Baker 'Parentless Refugee Children: The Question of Adoption' in P Bean (ed) *Adoption* (Tavistock, 1984); J Pearce *The Ockenden Venture UK Programme for Unaccompanied Children* (Working, Ockenden Venture, 1981).

2   A Bainham *Children: The Modern Law* (Family Law, 1998) at p 233.

3   J Thoburn and M Charles *A Review of Research Relevant to Inter-country Adoption*, Background Paper 3, (Interdepartmental Review of Adoption Law, Department of Health, Welsh Office and Scottish Office, 1992) at p 4.

ratified by the United Kingdom. These instruments were influential in shaping the development of government policies and legislative reform in sending and receiving countries, but the UN Convention in particular provided the starting point for consideration of further international initiatives for regulating the phenomenon of intercountry adoption.

1.59 In terms of foreign adoptions, s 17 of the AA 1976 provided that a Convention adoption order would be automatically recognised in the United Kingdom, thus implementing the 1965 Hague Convention on Jurisdiction, Applicable Law and Recognition of Decrees Relating to Adoption. An adoption was also recognised if it was effected under the legislation of one of the mainly European or Commonwealth countries specified in the Adoption (Designation of Overseas Adoptions) Order 1973.[1]

CONCLUSION

1.60 The legal framework of the AA 1976 had rooted adoption firmly in the philosophy and practice of the 1960s and 1970s, but a growing sense that it had passed its sell-by date developed during the late 1990s. The numbers of children languishing in care had grown, the ages of such children had increased, the number of babies available for adoption had dwindled to a trickle and, overall, adoption came to be recognised as serving a markedly different purpose from that envisaged by the 1976 legislation. At the same time, intercountry adoption was receiving more attention from prospective adopters as the need for children to complete a family remained a fundamental one. Such was the state of play before the major review and consultation process that preceded the enactment of the ACA 2002.

---

1   SI 1973/19.

Chapter 2

THE PROCESS OF REFORM

INTRODUCTION

2.1   Adoption law reform came hard on the heels of the CA 1989, which gained Royal Assent in November 1989. It had been intended that a review of adoption would take place as part of the Lord Chancellor's systematic review of family law and it had not therefore been included in the review of childcare law preceding that Act. The process leading up to the enactment of the ACA 2002 began with the establishment of a working group in 1989[1] and was followed by the publication of a discussion paper[2] and two background papers[3] in September 1990 and three further discussion papers and a third background paper over the next 2 years.[4] Wide consultation with voluntary and professional organisations and individuals took place and, in October 1992, the working group reported. The Review of Adoption Law[5] was wide-reaching in scope, and addressed such fundamental elements as the nature and effect of adoption, agreement, agency placements, relative and step-parent applications, adoption services, and post-adoption contact as well as intercountry adoption. The following year, a White Paper[6] set out decisions on a number of different matters and, after further consultation on some of the most problematic areas, a further consultation paper, this time incorporating a 104-clause draft Adoption Bill, was published.[7] No legislation was introduced.[8]

2.2   The reasons for this probably had less to do with the substance of the proposed reforms than with the politics of legislating in family matters. As Cretney has noted,[9] the

---

1   The working group established in 1989 comprised officials from the Department of Health and the Law Commission and was set up to review adoption law and report to the Secretary of State for Health, the Lord Chancellor, the Home Secretary and other Ministers.

2   Inter-departmental Review of Adoption Law, *The Nature and Effect of Adoption* (Department of Health, 1990).

3   Inter-departmental Review of Adoption Law, *International Perspectives* and *Review of Research Relating to Adoption* (Department of Health, 1990).

4   Inter-departmental Review of Adoption Law, *Agreement and Freeing, The Adoption Process, Intercountry Adoption* and Background Paper 3, *Intercountry Adoption* (Department of Health, 1991 and 1992).

5   Department of Health and Welsh Office, *Review of Adoption Law, Report to Ministers of an Interdepartmental Working Group: A Consultative Document* (HMSO, 1992) ('the 1992 Review of Adoption Law').

6   *Adoption: The Future,* Cm 2288 (1993).

7   *Adoption – A Service For Children* (HMSO, 1996).

8   The Conservative Government had initiated the reform process, but was then defeated in the General Election of 1997.

9   S Cretney *Family Law* (Sweet & Maxwell, 2000) at p 357.

Conservative Government of the time had been severely embarrassed by the passage through Parliament of the Bill which became the Family Law Act 1996. To save the Bill from defeat, the Government had had to accept many amendments[1] amid much concern about protecting the institution of marriage by making divorce more difficult. The result was a highly complex divorce procedure and, much later, an announcement by the next Lord Chancellor, Lord Irvine, that it would not be implemented. At the same time it had become clear that the adoption law reform proposals were also controversial. Issues of race, ethnicity, cohabiting and homosexual adopters, the plight of children in care, and the matter of adoption versus fostering all had the potential to create a 'battleground for MPs with strong views on morality and the family'.[2] The introduction of an Adoption Bill would thus have provided further fodder for a debate on family values. As Cretney noted in relation to the absence of such a Bill, 'it would be difficult to find a better example of the truth that reform of any aspect of family law may present and have a significant political impact, causing governments to prefer more immediately attractive legislative projects'.[3] It began to look as if the new Labour Government, elected in 1997, had also learned that message thoroughly, as adoption law reform did not appear to be high on its list of legislative priorities,[4] at least until publication of the Waterhouse Enquiry into Child Abuse in Welsh Children's Homes, *Lost in Care*.[5]

ACTION TAKEN

2.3   In her keynote address to the Solicitors' Family Law Association annual conference in February 2000, the President of the Family Division, the Rt Hon Dame Elizabeth Butler-Sloss DBE, recalled that the most worrying aspect of *Lost in Care* was that children had been moved from their families because their parents' care had not been good enough yet, in care, those same children had become seriously worse off. 'Drift in care' was identified as one of the major failings of the system. The report[6] prompted action. In its wake, the Health Minister announced that standards in local authority adoption service provision were unacceptably variable and that there was an unacceptably bad performance. A new National Care Commission was to be established; one of its key roles would be to help local authorities and other providers improve services and support for children[7] and, in February 2000, the Prime Minister announced that he, personally, would lead a major review of adoption of looked-after children. In July 2000, the Cabinet Office Performance and Innovation Unit published its study of the use of adoption for

---

1   The Bill suffered 137 amendments during its passage through the House of Commons.
2   S Cretney *Family Law* (Sweet & Maxwell, 2000), at p 356.
3   Ibid, at p 357.
4   Although the Adoption (Intercountry Aspects) Act 1999 was introduced.
5   *Lost in Care: Report of the Tribunal of Inquiry into the Abuse of Children in Care in the former County Council Areas of Gwynedd and Clwyd since 1974* (The Stationery Office, 2000).
6   For analysis of some of the themes by a Tribunal member, see E Ryder QC *'Lost and Found'* – *Looking to the Future After North Wales* [2000] Fam Law 406.
7   On 15 February 2000, the Health Secretary, Alan Milburn MP, confirmed the establishment of a national Children's Rights Director as part of the National Care Commission.

children in care,[1] in which the Prime Minister vowed to 'ensure that we were making the best use of adoption as an option to meet the needs of children looked after by local authorities', that the 'Government was committed to modernising adoption', that he wanted '... more children to benefit from adoption', and that 'we know adoption works for children'.[2] Matters advanced swiftly.

2.4   While being decidedly less thorough than the lengthy consultation process carried out by the previous administration, albeit building on that consultation, the July 2000 paper was followed by a White Paper, *Adoption: A New Approach*,[3] in December 2000. Just 3 months later, on 15 March 2001, the Adoption and Children Bill 2001 was introduced in Parliament by the Secretary of State for Health, Mr Alan Milburn and, after its Second Reading on 26 March, was sent to a Commons Select Committee, which was due to report back to Parliament by 12 June 2001. Three public hearings were held and a considerable body of evidence gathered, but the general election in May 2001 brought the whole process to an abrupt end before the Committee was able to present its report to Parliament. Subsequently, in its second term of office, on 19 October 2001, the Labour Government's Secretary of State for Health again introduced the Bill in the House of Commons.

2.5   On 20 November 2001, debate on the Bill began at the second of 24 sittings of the Special Standing Committee, the first sitting of the Committee having been held in private on 6 November. That Committee, chaired by Mr David Hinchcliffe,[4] examined witnesses from the Department of Health and the Lord Chancellor's Department, as well as members of organisations such as British Agencies for Adoption and Fostering, the Association of Directors of Social Services, the Catholic Children's Society, the Children's Society, Barnardo's and the NSPCC, to name just a few. However, the Committee concluded its deliberations on 17 January 2002, with a third of the clauses having had no committee time and therefore no opportunity for debating any detail.[5] Strict programming had effectively curtailed deliberations and a delay of 4 months ensued.

2.6   Things had not remained quiet backstage during the apparent hiatus. By the time of the first Report Day,[6] 20 March 2002, 90 amendments had been tabled and four new clauses added. Of these, one of the most controversial proved to be the extension of the right to adopt to unmarried and same-sex couples.[7] Introduced during the second allotted day of the Report Stage,[8] this particular group of amendments aimed at giving

---

1   An 8-week study was carried out, drawing on existing practice and available research and information gained from discussion with interested parties. A seminar on adoption was held at
    10 Downing Street in April 2000 to help inform the conclusions (Performance and Innovation Unit (PIU) Report, July 2000, para 1.3).
2   Foreword to *Prime Minister's Review of Adoption* (PIU Report, July 2000).
3   Cm 5017.
4   Labour MP for Wakefield.
5   The Bill, as amended by the Special Standing Committee, contained 137 clauses.
6   The Report stage before Parliament was not scheduled to occur on consecutive days, and by the end of the first day, no future dates had been settled. Nonetheless, the second allotted day of the Report stage took place on 16 May and the third day on 20 May 2002.
7   Introduced by the Government back-bencher, Mr David Hinchcliffe, Wakefield, who had chaired the Special Standing Committee.
8   16 May 2002.

'thousands of children hope of adoption and of living in suitable homes with loving families', and insisted that children 'must grow up in the 21st century whether we like it or not . . .'.[1] It was remarked[2] that the reason for the 4-month delay between the end of the Committee stage and the Report Stage was that debate had been raging between No 10 and the rest of the Government over the issue of extending adoption to unmarried couples – an issue that was temporarily resolved by a free vote on the government side. In the event, the particular amendment was made[3] and the Bill[4] proceeded to its Third Reading[5] and went on to the House of Lords on 21 May 2002.

2.7   Controversy did not end there. The Bill, with its new clauses enabling unmarried and same-sex couples to adopt a child jointly, received its Second Reading in the House of Lords on 10 June 2002 and, on the first day of the Grand Committee,[6] Earl Howe signified his hope that members of the Committee would be able to change the Government's mind on at least some of the issues.[7] Even though the Grand Committee itself was not successful in generating unanimity on issues surrounding the characteristics of would-be adopters, Earl Howe's amendment to clause 45, restricting the right to adopt jointly to married couples, was agreed to by 34 votes on 16 October 2002.[8] The 'other place' was asked to think again. The Lords had thus defeated what had come to be seen as the lynch-pin of the Government's strategy for moving children out of public care and into the private care of the nuclear family, albeit the proposal had not, initially, been part of that strategy at all.[9]

2.8   Defeat of the particular government provision brought with it intense media interest. The Bill had become a focus for debate about lifestyle choices and rights for adults, albeit the Conservative Party sought to portray its more traditionalist view as one centred solely on the welfare of children.[10] As ever, family legislation was proving highly controversial and political. However, the substance of the provision was not the only focus of media and political interests. As the Government was poised once again, on 4 November 2002, to vote (and a free vote at that) on whether unmarried couples should have the right to apply jointly to adopt a child, the Conservative Party leader imposed a three-line whip. Tories were thus obliged either to obey the whip and vote against extension of the right to adopt jointly or to absent themselves. In the event, the matter became even more highly politicised when some senior Tories chose to disobey the whip and vote with the Government.[11] The vote went the Government's way, thus confirming

---

1   HC Deb, 16 May 2002, vol 385, no 149, col 969.
2   HC Deb, 16 May 2002, vol 385, no 149, col 997, per Mr Tim Laughton.
3   Ayes numbered 288 and Noes 133.
4   The Bill, as amended on Report, contained 151 clauses.
5   On 20 May 2002.
6   24 June 2002.
7   HL Deb, 24 June 2002, vol 636, no 157, CWH 1.
8   The Contents numbered 196; the Not-Contents, 162.
9   It should be noted, however, that the particular group of amendments had not been included in the Prime Minister's Review, the White Paper or the Bill as first presented to Parliament or returned from the Special Standing Committee.
10   In media interviews and reports, particularly leading up to and following the further vote on the Bill in the House of Commons on 4 November 2002, Conservative Party figures argued that they supported the Lords' amendment because of the stability that married couples could offer to children in need of a new home. Unmarried couples were allegedly less stable.
11   Michael Portillo, Kenneth Clark and Francis Maude, among others, voted with the Government and were thus perceived as issuing a challenge to the party leadership.

its view that adoption by unmarried couples was both right and necessary. But the political focus had developed two prongs: on the one hand, the Bill had come to represent the battle between meeting contemporary needs and retaining conservative values, whilst on the other hand it presented a challenge to the modernising promise of the Conservative Party leadership. The Adoption and Children Bill had seemingly become symbolic of the struggle between left and right, liberal and traditional, different visions of morality, right and wrong. Or perhaps it merely provided a suitable vehicle for launching an attack on the Conservative leadership. Certainly the political fall-out was widespread, whether or not the small band of Tory dissenters was truly in a moral dilemma over adoption law.

2.9 The political, social and moral mixture created was a potent one and the media frenzy gathered strength. But all the while time was running out. With the parliamentary session due to close on 7 November 2002, the Bill went back to the House of Lords on 5 November. Would the Lords retain their previous view in light of the Report from the Joint Committee on Human Rights,[1] which concluded that the amended Bill would violate Art 14 of the European Convention on Human Rights? Would the Labour peers gather the force of numbers in support of the Government? Would the eloquent argument of Lord Hunt of Kings Heath carry the day?[2] After all, the House of Lords was entitled to reject the House of Commons amendments a second time.

CONCLUSION

2.10 In the event, of course, the Government's amendments were supported[3] and the Bill received Royal Assent on 7 November 2002. Although, once again, the political nature of legislating in family matters had been demonstrated, one thing was made very clear: the value of the family and its central place in providing the nation with stability were the key factors in the debate. Whether the lawmakers voted for an extension to the categories of people able to apply to adopt children and thus 'immeasurably improve the life chances of hundreds of our most vulnerable children'[4] or whether they voted for a retention of the marriage-linked category and the fundamental premise that 'the optimum environment for raising children is marriage',[5] the core beliefs were the same. The precious and exclusive nature of the family, however one chose to define it, was the optimum environment for the upbringing of children.

---

1   *Twenty-fourth Report of the Joint Committee on Human Rights on the Adoption and Children Bill* as amended by the House of Lords on Report, published as Paper 177/HL/HC Paper 979, 30 October 2002.
2   Department of Health spokesman in the House of Lords and strong advocate of the Government's amendment.
3   A majority of 31 peers supported the Government's amendment.
4   HL Deb, 5 November 2002, vol 640, no 200, col 569, per Lord Hunt of Kings Heath.
5   Ibid, col 576, per Earl Howe.

Chapter 3

THE NEED FOR REFORM – THE BACKGROUND ISSUES

INTRODUCTION

3.1 What had sparked the need for reform both 10 years ago and more latterly on the Prime Minister's initiative? Was the realisation that 'many children wait in care for far too long'[1] the only prompt? Did the earlier reform initiatives still hold good or had the issues changed between then and now? Is the new legislation the true successor to earlier years of research and consultation, or is it a consequence of a brand new approach dealing with different issues, or perhaps existing issues that have acquired a new prominence? This chapter and the following two will explore the major issues that initiated the drive for an improved and more relevant adoption law. The objective is to enable the reader to place the new Act on a broader canvas and within a wider time frame.

THE CHANGING PATTERNS OF ADOPTION

Social changes

3.2 The last 20 years have seen enormous social changes in the nature of the family and family life, the upbringing of children, attitudes towards unmarried, single and homosexual parenthood, as well as in such matters as marriage, cohabitation and divorce. We have also witnessed the advance of medical technology enabling otherwise infertile couples to have children, the practice of terminating unwanted pregnancies and an increased readiness to award social welfare benefits to support those who need help in keeping a child with them. Broad social changes have occurred within a context of greater liberality, internationalism and rights-based philosophy and an increased recognition of both social and ethnic diversity.

3.3 Such dramatic changes have had an impact on adoption: the way it is perceived, the use to which it has been put, the identity of those who have used it to create their own family and the characteristics of those whose children needed it.

Baby adoptions

3.4 During the 1950s and into the late 1960s, adoption was perceived as a primary method of dealing with the problem of illegitimate babies, and the number of adoptions

---

1   Foreword to *Prime Minister's Review of Adoption* (PIU Report, July 2000).

of children under the age of 12 months rose throughout that period. In 1951 there were 5101 adoptions of babies, that number representing 36 per cent of the total adoptions for the year, and by 1968 the figure had risen to 12,641, being 51 per cent of the total.[1] The AA 1976, which provided a veil of secrecy for both the birth mother and the adopters, was clearly meeting a major social demand. The stigma of illegitimacy and the lack of reliable means to avoid unwanted conception and birth were such that a woman might be compelled to conceal the fact that she had ever borne a child. For their part, an adoptive couple could create a family without revealing the nature of the baby's origins, and the child too could be kept in ignorance of its true identity.[2] By the late 1970s, however, it had become apparent that patterns of adoption were in the process of change. By 1977, 23 per cent of all adoptions were of babies less than a year old and by 1991, that number had fallen to under 900 – just 12 per cent of the total. The decline in the adoption of babies was sustained and progressive and clearly linked to the increased use of contraception and abortion[3] and to changed social attitudes towards children born outside marriage.[4] A general culture of families being reluctant to give up their children had developed.[5] But the decline in baby adoptions had begun even while the Children Act 1975, which introduced the new adoption provisions, was being gradually brought into force. It was soon realised that the new law, consolidated as the AA 1976, was out of date – that it addressed the issues of earlier times and that its target group had dramatically changed.

3.5   The major decline in number of babies offered for adoption was explicitly addressed in the previous administration's 1993 White Paper[6] and had become a widely recognised and acknowledged trend. It rightly received less prominence in the Prime Minister's review in July 2000[7] but even so, one of the 'key messages' of that review was that adoption in the twenty-first century was to be '... less about providing homes for relinquished babies and more concerned with providing secure, permanent relationships for some of society's most vulnerable children'.[8]

Public law adoptions

3.6   This shift away from the adoption of white, healthy and often illegitimate babies to a focus on the adoption of young children in local authority care has already been noted as part of 'the history' of adoption law. Being dubbed 'historical' is, in part, indicative of how long we have been aware of the changing usage and changing nature of adoption, albeit the practice of placing young children for adoption did not really take off until the mid-1970s. Statistical changes have formed part of the picture. Between 1952 and 1968 the number of children adopted out of care increased fivefold, even though such children

---

1   These figures are based on those cited in *Adoption: The Future*, Cm 2288 (1993) and N Lowe 'English Adoption Law: Past, Present and Future' in S Katz, J Eekalaar and M McLean (eds) *Cross Currents* (Oxford University Press, 2000) at p 316.
2   Although Adoption Act 1976, s 51 introduced measures whereby an adopted child was entitled to access original birth records on reaching the age of 18.
3   The Abortion Act 1967 came into force in April 1968.
4   The Houghton Report, Cmnd 5107 (1972), para 20.
5   N Lowe, op cit, at p 320.
6   *Adoption: The Future*, Cm 2288 (1993), at paras 3.4 and 3.5.
7   PIU Report, July 2000.
8   Ibid, at Key Message 4 of the Executive Summary.

still comprised a small percentage of the overall numbers: 3.2 per cent rising to 8.7 per cent in 1968.[1] While the number of adoptions overall had fallen over a 30-year period – from 13,000 in 1977 to just over 7000 in 1991 – the number of baby adoptions had fallen dramatically but the number of young children adopted had fallen less. Between 1977 and 1991, for example, the number of young children being adopted had fallen yet their proportion of the whole had increased from 77 per cent to 88 per cent. The trend looks set to continue as public law adoptions of young children (in 1993–94, 42 per cent of adoptions were of children aged 5 or over) have become the most significant type of adoption in England and Wales today.

3.7   Interestingly, the distinction between the adoptions of babies and those of young children has been noted and categorised somewhat differently in the USA.[2] As adoption developed as a specialised child welfare service in that country, a social class distinction became obvious between infants relinquished voluntarily by mothers at birth and those who were removed from home as a result of termination proceedings.[3] The former tended to be placed with middle-class adoptive parents, and the latter, usually the offspring of poor parents from deprived backgrounds, were more usually adopted by their foster parents. Adoption appeared to be meeting both its traditional, as well as its more modern, function in the USA, although as Thoburn has noted, 'the cushion of universal health and income maintenance systems and family support services keeps the numbers actually coming into state care lower in Europe, Australasia and Canada than in the US'.[4]

3.8   In the United Kingdom, the other part of the public law picture was formed by changing local authority practices. The policy of 'permanency planning' which began in the 1970s encouraged local authorities to secure the long-term future of previously 'unadoptable' children by placing them for adoption.[5] This was a new departure, not previously thought possible, and adoption by a loving and stable family came to be seen as preferable to fostering for special-needs, mixed-race or abused, and sometimes, older children. Consequently, local authorities often made robust use of their interventionist powers[6] to promote their adoption policies. This type of adoption, of course, did not conform to the stereotype of babies being adopted by childless strangers. Children who were no longer babies had their own stories, their own memories and attachments, and their placement with adopters was of necessity a more complex procedure. The matching and preparation of both children and adopters, for example, required a level of expertise not needed to the same extent with baby adoptions. Thus, not only were more young and special-needs children being adopted, but the fact of age or special needs gave a different slant to the whole process. Yet, as in all things, fashions change and, in the case of adoption, that particular mind-set did not continue.

---

1   N Lowe, op cit, at p 318.
2   S Katz 'Dual Systems of Adoption in the United States' in S Katz, J Eekelaar and M Mclean (eds) *Cross Currents* (Oxford University Press, 2000).
3   Katz (above) termed these, respectively, the 'voluntary system' and the 'involuntary system' at p 282.
4   J Thoburn 'Home News and Abroad' in Douglas and Philpot (eds) *Adoption: Changing Families, Changing Times* (Routledge, 2002) at p 228.
5   Ibid, at p 322, Lowe made the point that the work of Goldstein, Freud and Solnit *Beyond the Best Interests of the Child* (1973) stimulated this change in childcare practice by challenging the prevailing notion that biological and legal parenthood should prevail over psychological parenthood.
6   The parental rights resolution under the Child Care Act 1980 removed parental rights without judicial scrutiny and sat comfortably with the growing trend towards finding a permanent home as soon as possible.

3.9   In conceptual terms, the CA 1989 asserted the primary importance of birth families. With the concept of parental responsibility as its cornerstone, the CA 1989 emphasised that parenthood entailed autonomy coupled with responsibility. The private ordering of family relationships was its dominant ideology.[1] As Lord Mackay stated in relation to the CA 1989:[2]

> '... the independence of the family is the basic building block of a free and democratic society and the need to defend it should be clearly perceivable in law. Accordingly, unless there is evidence that a child is being or is likely to be positively harmed because of a failure in the family, the state, whether in the guise of a local authority or a court, should not interfere.'

3.10   The best place for children was thus perceived to be with their parents, albeit supported by the local authority. With a strong emphasis on child protection, the CA 1989 invoked the notion of working in partnership with parents and, to that extent, local authorities directed themselves towards supporting birth parents rather than seeking permanence for some children through adoption. Autonomy and non-intervention was the key and, in relation to adoption, the 1992 Review of Adoption Law recommended that even where an adoption order was appropriate the court should not make such an order unless doing so was better for the child than making no order at all.[3] Consequently, as noted by the PIU Report in 2000, 'the proportion of adoptions from care peaked in the years immediately following the Children Act, before dipping in the mid-1990s'.[4] Child protection, rather than permanence through adoption, became the prime focus and the role of foster care increased.

3.11   The emphasis on foster care persisted in the face of research indicating that children generally preferred the sense of security that adoption gave them over long-term foster placements. Long-term foster children who were subsequently adopted, for example, reported that they much preferred their adopted status,[5] whereas children brought up in long-term foster care were found to be less satisfied and did less well than similar children who were adopted.[6] Further, as the PIU study reported, there was no clear research evidence that the option of returning home was of itself able to deliver a better outcome than fostering or adoption.[7] Nonetheless, adoption continued to be somewhat of a Cinderella area for social services and it received little emphasis from central government. As has already been noted, the 1996 draft Adoption Bill failed to find its way into the legislative agenda and under the new Labour Government the issue became submerged until exposure of the 'drift in care' syndrome identified by the Waterhouse Report finally thrust the matter in front of the politicians.[8]

---

1   A Bainham *The Privatisation of the Public Interest in Children* (1990) 53 MLR 206.
2   Joseph Jackson Memorial Lecture (1989) 139 NLJ 505, at 508.
3   At p 4.
4   PIU Report, July 2000, at p 15.
5   M Hill and J Triseliotis 'The transition from long-term care to adoption' in J Hudson and B Galloway (eds) *The State as Parent* (Kluwer Academic, 1989) cited in J Thoburn, *Review of Research Relating to Adoption* (DoH, 1990) at p 39.
6   J Triseliotis and J Russell *Hard to Place – The outcome of adoption and residential care* (Gower, 1984) and J Rowe et al (1984) cited in Thoburn, op cit, at p 34.
7   Rushton *Adoption as a Placement Choice: Argument and Evidence* (The Maudsley, 1999) cited in PIU Report, July 2000, at box 2.4.
8   Although it took the Waterhouse Report to bring the matter to the attention of the politicians, drift in care had been exposed by J Rowe and J Lambert as long ago as 1973 in *Children Who Wait* (Association of British Adoption Agencies (now British Agencies for Adoption and Fostering), 1973) and had been under discussion by professionals ever since.

3.12   Given impetus by the findings of that Report, the new wave of law reform consultation in 2000 focused primarily on the adoption of older children from care. The PIU study in July 2000 highlighted the already changing profile of such children adopted. Within a context in which the numbers of children being 'looked after' by the local authority were increasing again, the characteristics of those who were adopted from care were distinctive: they were more likely to be young,[1] white, female children, who entered care when young, were unlikely to have returned home before adoption and had more 'challenging backgrounds and complex needs' than the bulk of children in care or voluntary accommodation.[2] The study's response to its findings was fully in line with the Prime Minister's drive for more adoption: more families needed to be found for these rising numbers of 'increasingly vulnerable' children – and quickly. From the premise of this 'more adoption' agenda, the study brought its analysis to its own logical conclusion: that, given the 'improved outcomes associated with placement for adoption at a younger age[3] . . . there is a balance to be struck here between appropriate attempts at rehabilitation with birth families and avoiding drift and delay which damages the child'.[4]

3.13   The key message of the White Paper, *Adoption: A New Approach*,[5] was 'stop the "drift" of children in care and move them into adoption'. Adoption was portrayed as the vehicle for resolving the problem of abused and neglected children languishing in the care system. It was put forward as the solution to an obvious need. With its warming vision of damaged children being taken in by caring families and made a permanent part of those families, adoption was firmly identified as the final step in the childcare system. An alternative family, rather than help for the existing family, was the clear objective. This thinking was in striking contrast with that of other jurisdictions like Denmark, for example, where adoption from care is almost unknown. In that country, the social welfare system is able to pour resources into assistance for underprivileged and damaged parents and children, thus enabling birth families to remain together and intact. Nonetheless, in his foreword to the White Paper, the Prime Minister stated that children who could not live with their birth parents and who were thus already vulnerable were being badly let down. There were, he claimed, 'clear problems with the way the system of adoption now operates' and there was '. . . scope to increase the use of adoption'. The essence of the problem, as the Government saw it, was that too many children were in local authority care with too little chance 'for a long-term family life'. The system – the lack of consistency, quality and clarity in local authority practice, the court delays and the dearth of support for adopters, amongst other things – was perceived as letting children down. The experience of care in the public system whilst waiting to be adopted was too often damaging in itself.[6] A government policy shift was clearly under way. There was to be a return to the notion of permanence and therefore adoption for children in care.

---

1   In 1999 the average age was 4 years and 4 months.
2   For a detailed analysis of the profile of looked-after children currently adopted, see PIU Report, July 2000, paras 2.10–2.12.
3   Ibid, at para 2.16. The report indicated that age at placement had the most crucial influence on the chances of disruption. The younger the child when placed for adoption, the greater the chance of a successful adoption.
4   Ibid.
5   Cm 5017 (December 2000).
6   *Adoption: A New Approach*, Cm 5017 (December 2000).

3.14   This move was marked by a strong 'child-saving' rhetoric.[1] In other words, children were identified as languishing in care, they did badly there (according to the PIU study, being four times more likely to be unemployed, 60 times more likely to be homeless and constituting a quarter of the adult prison population, as compared with the general population)[2] and they needed to be saved from such a fate. The thinking behind this rhetoric, illustrated in the thrust of the PIU Report and subsequently the Government's White Paper, was given impetus by the Waterhouse Report and the identification of 'drift'. Not only were relatively low numbers of children being adopted out of care each year, but those awaiting adoptive families were waiting too long. The PIU Report attributed delay to several key factors: the length of time taken to decide that a child should be placed for adoption, the social worker's focus on rehabilitation with birth parents, the length of time taken to successfully place a child with an adoptive family, and the misplaced attempts of the courts to 'give the "benefit of the doubt" to birth parents and order repeat attempts at rehabilitation'.[3] Too many children were in care for too long, therefore more adoption, more quickly was the preferred policy.

3.15   However, although adoption practice and procedure had already begun to change, it had done so within the confines of an outdated piece of legislation. The law was seen as failing to meet the new objectives required by the more recent changed patterns of adoption. If adoption were truly to provide the permanent route for moving disadvantaged and damaged children out of the public sector and into the private arena – the 'child-saving' scheme – then a new law had to reflect those newly identified objectives. On this, the Government's arguments were persuasive. Children 'rightly want to grow up in a stable loving family'[4] and 'society as a whole has a clear responsibility to provide these children with permanence – a safe, stable and loving family to support them through childhood and beyond – and a fresh start as quickly as possible'.[5] Adoption was the way forward, the White Paper argued, because 'research shows that children who are adopted when they are over six months old generally make very good progress through their childhood and into adulthood and do considerably better than children who have remained in the care system through most of their childhood'.[6] The policy objectives were clearly articulated and the way was set to 'modernise' the law so as to give effect to the 'permanence through more adoption more quickly' agenda.

3.16   This agenda was urged upon Parliament. In introducing the 2001 Adoption and Children Bill at its Second Reading in the House of Commons,[7] the Minister of State for the Department of Health[8] focused exclusively on the relationship between adoption and children in care, stressing that adoption legislation was 'vital to our society, because children get only one chance to grow up', that 'society has paid a heavy price' for the

---

1   A term used by Sonia Harris-Short in 'The Adoption and Children Bill – A Fast Track to Failure' [2001] 4 CFLQ 405.
2   PIU Report, July 2000, box 2.3, which draws on findings published in James, *Strategic Planning in Children's Services* (DoH, 1999).
3   PIU Report, July 2000, at paras 3.28–3.50.
4   *Adoption: A New Approach*, Cm 5017 (December 2000) at 1.2.
5   Ibid, at 1.6.
6   Ibid, at 1.12.
7   26 March 2001. This Bill subsequently fell with the dissolution of Parliament in June 2001 and was resurrected in an amended form later that year.
8   Mr John Hutton.

failure to place children in adoptive families and that 'adoption can often be the best solution for children in care who are unable to return to their birth families'.[1] He stressed both speed and an increase in numbers, urging a 'greater use of adoption, to deliver at least a 40% increase in the number of looked-after children who are adopted ...'.[2]

3.17   The same theme was reiterated, even more forcefully, in the introduction to the Second Reading of the Bill in the House of Lords.[3] In an illustration of the belief in the value of adoption as a 'child-saving' measure, a view supported generally by Parliament, Lord Hunt of Kings Heath stated that 'all too often, adoption has been seen as a last resort, for these children [those looked after by the local authorities] when it should have been considered as a first resort. Too often the adoption system has let children down'.[4] The message was clear: increased adoption was the way forward and 'harmful' delay would be minimised by earlier decisions about adoption; this, of course, was felt to be in the best interests of vulnerable children.

Step-parent adoptions

3.18   One of the major reasons behind the overall increase in the rate of adoption by the late 1960s was the escalation of step-parent adoptions. Whether such adoptions occurred as a result of the remarriage of a parent after divorce or after the death of a spouse, or a first marriage for a single parent of a child,[5] there was a vast rise in these non-agency adoptions. It was generally accepted, however, that the biggest increase was in the adoption of legitimate children by a natural parent and her new husband following an earlier divorce. This was a clear sequel to the increase in divorce that occurred following the Divorce Reform Act 1969; by 1975 step-parent adoptions comprised one-third of all adoptions. Currently, they comprise half of all adoptions.

3.19   The desirability or otherwise of step-parent adoptions has long been controversial. The Houghton Committee[6] questioned the practice of adopting legitimate children following a parent's remarriage by highlighting the fact that this legally severed the child from one side of its genetic inheritance, and the 1992 Review of Adoption Law warned that the benefits to the child of a relationship with grandparents and other relatives could be overlooked.[7] The popularity of step-parent adoptions stemmed from a natural desire to show commitment to the new spouse's child and cement new family relationships. Such adoptions could be perceived as acts of generosity – a taking on of someone else's child and a willingness to share the legal as well as physical and emotional responsibilities. However, while adoption was capable of meeting this objective, it also provided an opportunity for the new family to erase the former spouse and parent from their lives. The natural parent (typically the father) would lose his parental responsibility – and also the requirement that he, as the absent parent, provide financially for the

---

1   HC Deb, 26 March 2001, vol 365, no 59, col 699.
2   Ibid, col 700.
3   HL Deb, 10 June 2002, vol 636, no 148, cols 20–21, per Lord Hunt of Kings Heath.
4   Ibid, col 21.
5   See the three types of step-parent adoption identified in J Masson, D Norbury and S Chatterton *Mine, Yours or Ours?* (HMSO, 1983).
6   *Report of the Departmental Committee on the Adoption of Children*, Cmnd 5107 (1972), paras 103–110.
7   At para 19.2.

child. The 1992 Review of Adoption Law noted that a parent may 'agree to adoption simply because he has no interest in the child, or even where he has such an interest and is keen to retain it but wishes to end the payment of maintenance'. As Thorpe LJ stated in *Re PJ (Adoption: Practice on Appeal)*:[1] '... applications in step-parent adoptions may be driven or complicated by motives or emotions derived from conflict within the triangle of adult relationships. They may also be buoyed up by quite unrealistic hopes and assumptions as to the quality of the marriage replacing that into which the children were born'. The 1992 Review of Adoption Law warned that where the 'prime motivation behind an adoption application is the wish to cement the family unit and put away the past, this may be confusing and lead to identity problems for the child, especially if the new marriage breaks down'.[2] 'Appropriate' usage was thus the ideal but, even where this was the case, the parent (usually the mother) was somewhat absurdly obliged to adopt her own child in a joint application with the step-parent.

3.20   Similar policy considerations were evident in New Zealand more recently, where reformers[3] endorsed the earlier reasoning of Cumming-Bruce J in *Re B (A Minor)*.[4] His Lordship had observed that:

> 'It was quite wrong to use adoption law to extinguish the relationship between the protesting father and the child, unless there is some really serious factor which justifies the use of the statutory guillotine. The courts should not encourage the idea that after divorce the children of the family can be reshuffled and dealt out like a pack of cards in a second rubber of bridge. Often a parent who has remarried and has custody of the children from the first family is eager to achieve just that result, but such parents, often faced with very grave practical problems, are frequently blind to the real long-term interests of their children.'

3.21   In the United Kingdom also, the concept of the step-parent adoption was far removed from the traditional adoption envisaged by earlier legislators and has continued to sit uneasily within the whole legislative framework of adoption. Legislative attempts to diminish the practice[5] by directing the court to dismiss an application if a custody order seemed more appropriate had the effect of reducing the number of step-parent adoptions, but this approach was nonetheless not easy to apply and was later repealed by the CA 1989. However, the prevailing view became established – step-parent adoptions of legitimate children were not a good thing, albeit it was not always appropriate to prevent them.[6] And certainly, the new flexibility and inter-changeability of orders introduced by the CA 1989 enabled the court to consider residence, as opposed to adoption, much more readily. A joint residence order to the natural parent and step-parent would give parental responsibility to the step-parent for the duration of the order, without causing the birth parent to lose his status.

---

1   [1998] 2 FLR 252, at 260.
2   At para 19.2.
3   *Adoption and Its Alternatives – A Different Approach and a New Framework* (Law Commission, Report 65, 2000), at paras 365–375.
4   [1975] Fam 127, at 143.
5   Section 14(3) of the AA 1976, later repealed by CA 1989, Sch 15.
6   1992 Review of Adoption Law, at para 19.2.

3.22   The 1993 White Paper nonetheless recognised that step-parent adoptions formed part of the changing landscape of adoption practice.[1] The way forward, alongside the package of orders introduced by the CA 1989,[2] lay in a proposal for a 'new and simpler alternative to step-parent adoptions'[3] – the 'parental responsibility agreement or order'. In form and structure this was based on the provisions in the CA 1989 for unmarried fathers.[4] The idea was to give step-parents what they wanted, and believed they needed – parental responsibility for the child – without severing former links and without requiring the birth parent to adopt her own child. But if adoption were appropriate – a parent marrying for the first time, for example, or the former spouse/parent having died – the 1996 Bill would have allowed the step-parent alone to adopt the child of his new spouse.[5] Without further analysis, the new proposals took over that position, aiming to amend the CA 1989 to enable a step-parent to acquire parental responsibility for the child of a spouse, either by agreement or court order.[6] With the focus so firmly on moving children in local authority care into adoption, debate on the desirability or otherwise of step-parent adoptions was unsurprisingly absent.

3.23   Similarly, the key objective in both New Zealand and Australian step-parent adoption reform proposals was the maintenance of family links and extended family networks, in the best interests of the child. For the natural parent too, there was recognition that he or she would be left without legal rights of custody or access and, for the step-parent, it was noted that he was unlikely to 'suddenly refuse to act as a parent to the child if the order is not granted'.[7] Consequently, the New Zealand Law Commission considered that enduring guardianship (in English terms, parental responsibility) was likely to be more appropriate than adoption, as the law needed to be cautious about severing the birth parent/child relationship. It recommended that, when considering a step-parent adoption application, the court should consider the effect of the order on the parent/child relationship and on the degree of contact the child might have with that parent and its wider family, then consider whether enduring guardianship would be a more appropriate option and whether the step-parent had lived with the child for not less than 3 years preceding the application.

3.24   Clearly, the nature and extent of the step-parent's relationship with the child was to be a major focus. This was also the case for the Law Reform Commission of New South Wales in its review of the Adoption of Children Act 1965 (NSW). The Commission recommended that a step-parent be able to make a sole application but that there must have been an 'established relationship with the child of at least five years' duration before being allowed to adopt', and that the step-parent must have 'been cohabiting with the child's parent for at least three years, before applying for the order'.[8] Subsequently, the

---

1   *Adoption: The Future*, Cm 2288 (1993), paras 3.8–3.9.
2   The s 8 residence order was the major alternative to adoption.
3   *Adoption: The Future*, Cm 2288 (1993), paras 5.20–5.22.
4   Section 4.
5   Clause 45(1)(a); and the adopted child was then to be treated as a child of the step-parents' marriage (cl 51(2)(a)).
6   Clause 107. It was also proposed to remove the anomaly whereby a parent in a step-parent adoption had to adopt his or her own child (cl 51(2)(a)).
7   Law Commission Report 65, at para 370.
8   Law Reform Commission (NSW) Report 81 (1997) *Review of the Adoption of Children Act 1965 (NSW)*, Executive Summary.

Adoption Act 2000 (NSW) enacted that the court could not make an adoption order in favour of a step-parent unless the child was at least 5 years old and had lived with the step-parent and parent together for at least 3 years; specific consent had been given; and the adoption order was clearly preferable in the best interests of the child to any other action the law could take in relation to the child.[1] In other words, both those countries have endorsed the view that in certain prescribed circumstances a step-parent adoption may be in the child's best interests.

3.25 That such an adoption could enhance a child's welfare was illustrated in the United Kingdom in *Re B (Adoption: Father's Objections)*.[2] The Court of Appeal upheld the judge's decision to dispense with a natural father's agreement to a step-parent adoption in relation to his 12-year-old son. This was a case where the boy's welfare demanded the security and stability of a life-long and final adoption order in favour of his mother and step-father, thus relieving him of the stress and uncertainty caused by his natural father.[3] Although it had become rare for the courts to dispense with a natural parent's objection to a step-parent adoption, *Re B* illustrated that such orders could be used to promote the child's welfare and were, from the reformer's point of view, worthy of retention despite their generally bad press. The European Court, too, concluded that step-parent adoptions could be permitted under the European Convention on Human Rights. In *Söderbäck v Sweden*[4] the adoption of a 5-year-old girl by her mother's husband, without the consent of the natural father, was in accordance with law and pursued the legitimate aim of being in the best interests of the child, albeit the adoption was an interference with the father's right to respect for family life under Art 8 of the Convention.

DIVERSE FAMILIES AND DIVERSE RELATIONSHIPS

The concept of family

3.26 The family in all its changing guises has remained a basic social unit in society. It has traditionally been charged with providing emotional, physical and financial support for its members and instilling particular values in the young and has long been recognised as a powerful social, albeit private, institution.[5] While Victorian England did its best to prescribe the social conventions of family life, it is impossible today to confine any analysis of the family to the stereotype so integral to that period. It has been suggested that now, at the beginning of the twenty-first century, we are witnessing some fundamental changes in the nature of families.[6] Certainly, the decreasing rate of marriage, together with the older age at which it is likely to take place, the increase in divorce, the rise in

---

1   Examples of other action the law could take included a parenting order under the Family Law Act 1975 of the Commonwealth.
2   [1999] 2 FLR 215.
3   *Re PJ (Adoption: Practice on Appeal)* [1998] 2 FLR 252 and *Re EH and MH (Step-parent Adoption)* [1993] Fam Law 187 are also cases in which the court, unusually, dispensed with the natural parent's agreement to a step-parent adoption.
4   [1999] 1 FLR 250.
5   Article 8 of the European Convention for the Protection of Human Rights and Fundamental Freedoms 1950 provides that everyone has the right to respect for 'private and family life'.
6   E Silva and C Smart *The New Family* (Sage, 1999).

cohabitation and increase in the birth of children outside of marriage, are all changes instantly recognisable by the person in the street. Today over one-third of all births are to unmarried mothers and of these, 29 per cent are to women who are cohabiting. The notion of stability and security for so long associated with the married nuclear family can no longer be regarded as confined to such traditional family types. The stable intimate relationship between two parents who live together as a unit with their children, dependent on each other for mutual support in all aspects of their lives, can be as nurturing and fulfilling as that of their married counterparts. Unquestionably, such a domestic arrangement falls within even the most narrow definition of 'family'.

3.27 But of course the concept of 'family' has been and always will be notoriously difficult to define. Is a single-person household a family? Does a homosexual relationship constitute a family? English law has increasingly recognised the diverse nature of family and family forms. The House of Lords decision in *Fitzpatrick v Sterling Housing Association Ltd*,[1] for example, extended the legal definition of family, albeit within the context of landlord and tenant law, to include a homosexual man who had lived with his male partner in a stable and monogamous relationship for 18 years. That relationship was nothing if not stable and permanent. While the nature and composition of what many regard as 'family' may fluctuate over time, the overall significance of this concept remains as great as ever.

3.28 In relation to the reform of adoption law, the focus on the family was nowhere more intense than in the 2000 White Paper. In his foreword, the Prime Minister referred to the need for children to be given the 'opportunity to enjoy the kind of loving family life which most of us take for granted' and that, above all, 'we want to see vulnerable children safe, in permanent families'.[2] The family was portrayed throughout the White Paper as the safe haven, the provider of stability and permanence: 'children unable to live with their birth parents still need a stable and loving family to provide them with the security and love through childhood that they require and deserve'.[3] The adjectives 'stable' and 'permanent' were coupled to references to the family throughout. And certainly, the clear objective in relation to the adoption of older children from care is to find stable and permanent new families for those who can no longer live with their birth parents. But the White Paper also stressed the need to find more of these stable and permanent families – by establishing an adoption register of children and approved adoptive families,[4] by establishing new national Adoption Standards, by taking a decision on prospective adopters within 6 months, by consulting on the right to paid adoption leave and by generally 'overhauling and modernising the legal framework for adoption'. In other words, the White Paper's proposal was to make adoption more attractive to families: yet the family image portrayed in the reform proposals was clearly a traditional, nuclear married couple.

---

1   [2000] 11 FLR 271.
2   Foreword to *Adoption: A New Approach* by the Prime Minister, the Rt Hon Tony Blair (29 December 2000).
3   Ibid, at para 1.5.
4   The idea was to establish a meeting point at which the details of children suitable for adoption and the details of prospective approved adopters might coincide.

Married and cohabiting families

3.29   So who and where are these stable and permanent families likely to be willing to adopt difficult older and possibly special-needs children and sibling groups? Given the search for greater numbers of adopters suitable to adopt children from care could the net be cast more widely than the traditional married couple? The 1992 Review of Adoption Law noted that, although family structures were changing with more children born to parents who were not married but were living in stable unions, unmarried parents still did not have the same legal obligations to one another as did a married couple. They had less financial security, particularly if the relationship broke down, and there was a potential for less commitment to the child from the couple's wider families. The latter was noted as particularly significant, given that adoption had the effect of transferring a child from one family to another.[1] In other words, the Review proposed no change in the law, but did not view that as incompatible with allowing a single person with a partner to adopt (although it recommended that the partner also be assessed with respect to parenting capacity).[2] The 1993 White Paper endorsed that stance. It recognised the 'need to reflect more fully in the law the range of relationships that now widely exist between children and the adults who care for them – for example as step-parents or foster parents'[3] but drew the line at altering the presumption in favour of adoption by married couples.[4] Despite acknowledging the high divorce rates and the decision of many adults to enter alternative types of long-term relationship, the 1993 White Paper concluded that marriage remained the most common permanent relationship in which to bring up children[5] and thereby endorsed the 'general preference' of authorities, adoption agencies, and their staffs for adoption by married couples . . .'.[6] At the same time, the diversity of stable relationships was also recognised by the acknowledgement that 'some children, often with special needs, are successfully adopted by unmarried women, women no longer married or women widowed early' and that in a small number of exceptional circumstances 'adoption by a single person may be sensible'.[7]

3.30   The scope for change in the new law was great. Previous legislation and practice had privileged the traditional private, heterosexual, married family, headed by a man. The AA 1976 had used the language of marriage and wedlock[8] in asserting the superiority of the nuclear married family and had made no provision for joint applications, other than by married couples. The point has been made that this particular family form was portrayed as powerful and protective, offering the greatest chance of stability and permanence and was the model of family life sought by social workers and adoption panels.[9] Recent legislative history added to that perception by directing that the institution of marriage be supported[10] and by a 'damned by faint praise' attitude

---

1   1992 Review of Adoption Law, at para 26.10.
2   Ibid, at para 26.14.
3   *Adoption: The Future*, Cm 2288 (1993) at para 2.3.
4   Ibid, at paras 4.35–4.40.
5   Ibid, at para 4.37.
6   Ibid, at para 4.40.
7   Ibid, at para 4.38.
8   Section 39(1)(a) and (b).
9   C Bridge 'Adoption Law: A Balance of Interests' in J Herring (ed) *Family Law – Issues, Debates, Policy* (Willan Publishing, 2001) at p 206.
10   Family Law Act 1996, s 1(a).

towards cohabiting couples.[1] At the same time, the 2000 White Paper's call for an increase in adoption and the consequent need for more adoptive families required, in philosophical as well as in legal and practical terms, a rethinking of family forms and an acceptance of social change. Did the marriage relationship still warrant the exclusivity granted by the White Paper? Would not maintenance of the status quo effectively continue the notion of adoption as a replication of the traditional married nuclear family when what reality demanded was a huge increase in family-style permanent legal carers? On the basis that adopted children needed stability first and foremost, the arguments for retention of that status quo were highly persuasive. Stability in a child's life required stability and permanence in the relationship of the parents. But could an assessment process, designed to identify the qualities of prospective adopters, be a sure test or at least a reliable predictor of stability and permanence in a couple's relationship?[2] Surely marriage itself provided the most obvious indicator of those particular qualities most needed by adopted children. By contrast, two people who lived together without being prepared to marry were arguably signalling that they regarded their relationship as something which might be less than lifelong.[3] At the same time, if non-traditional or cohabiting couples were again to be actively excluded from making joint applications might that not also blind local authorities from seeing that some married couples were not ideal? A focus on the married 'ideal' family[4] which excluded some suitable adopters must invariably have the effect of including inappropriate adopters – and even more so in a climate in which it was recommended that the Government 'should promote an increase in adoption of looked after children ...' and where the first recommendation related to the 'attracting, recruiting and supporting of many more adopters and their families'.[5]

3.31 It became increasingly obvious that demography, changing social perceptions, acceptance of cohabitation and the well-recognised willingness of many unmarried fathers to shoulder financial and parental responsibility for a child would inevitably lead to the conclusion that a search for a stable and permanent family must extend to the unmarried cohabiting couple. However, the Adoption and Children Bill, even when introduced for the second time in 2001, did not take up that challenge but went instead to the Special Standing Committee in November of that year retaining the same restrictions on joint applications as the AA 1976 had enacted.[6] Despite evidence brought to the Committee in November 2001 by the Department of Health that 'married couples, given the publicly recognised commitment that they had given ... were more likely to provide the child with the stability and security that it needed' and that such a restriction was, on balance, compatible with the European Convention on Human

---

1 Family Law Act 1996, at s 41(2), where it states that cohabitants 'have not given each other the commitment involved in marriage'.

2 Earl Howe, in moving his amendment to defeat the Government amendments on the matter, clearly did not believe that it could. See HL Official Report, vol 639, no 188, col 865.

3 Ibid, at col 866, where Earl Howe noted statistics indicating that 83 per cent of cohabitations broke up within 10 years and that the average length of a cohabiting relationship was 2 years.

4 Note that orders in favour of parents and step-parents conform, in general, to the nuclear married family ideal.

5 Key Messages of the PIU Report, July 2000.

6 Clause 48.

Rights,[1] other witnesses[2] endorsed the view that Parliament should grasp the opportunity for amending the law. British Agencies for Adoption and Fostering (BAAF), in particular, took the view that the exclusion (the 'blanket ban') of some suitable, albeit non-married, couples as prospective adopters was to be condemned, and argued that the relationship between the two adults would always be a critical factor in the assessment process,[3] that a court would always have the final say, and that at a time when debate was ongoing about the possibility of some sort of registration for relationships outside marriage it would be regrettable to omit such changes from the Bill.[4] The arguments for change were compelling, but the Minister of State for Health still concluded that it was the Government's belief that 'the security and stability that is needed for joint adoption is more likely to be provided by a suitably assessed married couple'. She went even further, noting the complex questions that would be raised by a search for a legal definition of an unmarried couple, stating that the Bill would be obliged to create a definition and that such a move would not be right without the necessary consultation and thorough consideration. Clauses 47 and 48 were thus ordered to stand part of the Bill, albeit the Minister of State nodded her agreement to participate in further discussions on the matter before the Bill returned to the floor of the House of Commons at the Report Stage.[5]

3.32   When the Bill thus returned from the Special Standing Committee there was no change. It was only later that the fundamental shift was mooted and a group of amendments[6] tabled to the effect that a 'couple' would mean a married couple or two people living as partners in an enduring family relationship, whether they were of different sexes or the same sex.[7] Argument for the amendments focused on modernity and keeping pace with changes in society, coupled with welfare and good assessment of suitability. The views of BAAF, in contrast to their reception in the Special Standing Committee, were frequently endorsed by the Government.[8] In the twenty-first century, it was claimed, 40 per cent of children were born outside marriage, and children, after all, 'must grow up in the real world'.[9] In total contrast to earlier statements by Government members in Committee, it was stressed that 'in this real world, loving stable families . . .

---

1   HC Special Standing Committee, Second Sitting, 20 November 2001, cols 31–32. Mr James Paton for the Department of Health also noted that joint application solely by married couples was in line with the majority of European countries and that many of those countries who had adopted a partnership registration scheme specifically excluded joint adoption.

2   The Association of the Directors of Social Services (20 November 2001, col 54); the Local Government Association (20 November 2001, col 59).

3   In HC Special Standing Committee, Second Sitting, 20 November 2001, col 73, the Association of Directors of Social Services commented that a number of married couples approved as adopters had had a number of previous relationships and previous marriages, yet only the stability of the current relationship was assessed. In contrast, evidence was given that many couples whose relationships have been ongoing for 10 or 15 years came forward to adopt and underwent an incredibly stringent assessment but, of course, could not adopt jointly.

4   HC Special Standing Committee, Second Sitting, 20 November 2001, col 40.

5   HC Special Standing Committee, Eighth Sitting, 29 November 2001, cols 384–386, per Ms Jacqui Smith.

6   8 May 2002.

7   The notice of amendment was tabled by Mr David Hinchcliffe (who had been co-chairman of the Special Standing Committee), Dr Evan Harris, Ms Sandra Gidley and Mr Hilton Dawson.

8   For example, HC Deb, 16 May 2002, vol 385, no 149, col 979, per Mr Hinchcliffe; col 1000, per Ms Jacqui Smith.

9   HC Deb, 16 May 2002, vol 385, no 149, col 696, per Dr Harris.

come in all shapes and sizes' and that children do not grow up in an idealised world that never was. The welfare argument stressed the enhanced hope of adoption that unmarried couples could bring to children in care, and the Government appeared convinced that there were many such couples just waiting to adopt, who would otherwise be deterred.[1] The point that it was in a child's interests to have two legal parents, rather than being adopted by a single parent only, albeit with a residence order to the other, added to the welfare perspective. Rigorous assessment was to be made on a case-by-case basis so that there was 'no justification for disqualifying a couple from adopting jointly simply because they do not possess a marriage certificate, if they clearly possess all the characteristics that the agencies would otherwise expect from suitable adoptive parents'.[2] Opposition argument centred on the attributes of marriage *per se* – in particular, its greater financial security and its greater apparent stability[3] – but in the end the Government's claim that its amendments were about welfare rather than marriage or the promotion of alternative lifestyles won the day. The U-turn was complete, and those who remained supportive of the Government's original stance and the maintenance of the status quo were accused of attempting to 'spoil the life chance of so many young people'.[4] On 16 May 2002, the House of Commons voted overwhelmingly to extend eligibility to make adoption applications to both unmarried and same-sex couples.[5] The prospective pool of adopters was widened and all talk of 'social engineering' and the 'politically correct social worker brigade' was quashed.[6]

3.33 In the event, as noted in Chapter 2, the particular provisions of the Bill were voted down by the House of Lords, returned to the House of Commons, and finally passed by the Lords at the last minute on 5 November 2002. The overwhelming thrust of the pro-unmarried couples debate in the Lords centred on widening the pool of adopters – that adoption by a couple, whether they be married, unmarried or of the same sex, was superior to a childhood in care.[7] And even more, that a child 'nurtured in a supportive, loving, functional family will tend to have a head start in life and that a child nurtured without love will tend to be at a disadvantage for life'.[8]

3.34 Other Western jurisdictions beginning the process of reviewing their adoption law have not been so caught up in the seemingly moral questions surrounding the nature of prospective adopters' relationships.[9] The New Zealand Law Commission, for example, perceived at the outset that the time had come for cohabiting couples (or 'de

---

1   HC Deb, 16 May 2002, vol 385, no 149, at col 970.
2   Ibid, at col 971. Interestingly, Mr Hinchcliffe proceeded (at col 979) to dissociate stability from marriage, claiming that 'some of the most unstable people that I have met in my life have been married'.
3   Ibid, at col 983, per Ms Widdecombe.
4   HC Deb, 4 November 2002, vol 392, no 200, col 33, per Mr Michael Jabez Foster.
5   By 288 votes to 133.
6   HC Deb, 16 May 2002 at col 1003.
7   HL Deb, 10 June 2002, vol 636, no 148: eg Baroness Howarth of Breckland at col 67; Lord Alli at col 68; The Lord Bishop of Oxford at col 47; Baroness Gould of Potternewton at col 50; Lord Adebowale at col 52. It should be noted that Baroness Young (at col 33) vehemently opposed the extension and concluded that the new clauses would mean the downgrading of marriage once more.
8   Ibid, at col 57, per Lord Northbourne.
9   Although it should be noted that the Republic of Ireland, for example, still tries to ensure that adopters conform closely to the constitutionally approved marital family unit. Only in statutorily specified instances will applications from anyone other than a married couple be accepted.

factos', as they are usually termed in that country) to be eligible to adopt jointly and recommended that they be permitted to apply.[1] Central to the New Zealand debate was the question of what constituted a cohabiting couple – how durable did the relationship have to be, for example, given that the future security of the child would be linked to relationship stability? After considering submissions that between 2 and 3 years of stable relationship should be required, the New Zealand Law Commission eschewed evidence of durability in favour of quality. Would the particular couple, whether married, cohabiting, or of the same sex, be suitable to serve the best interests of the particular child? That was the recommended question, with the answer to be supplied by social workers dealing with the case.[2] Assessment of applicants on their merits, despite the status or nature of their relationship, was thus the recommended New Zealand approach.

3.35 In dealing with the same issue, the New South Wales Law Reform Commission in Australia was mindful of the change in community attitudes towards ex-nuptial births in the 30 years or so since the last adoption law reform process. At the same time it noted that selection of adoptive parents was a controversial area and that flexibility was the key. It therefore recommended that there be very few legislative requirements relating to eligibility to adopt. Beyond prescribed minimum requirements it concluded that 'selection of the best parent for each child should be a matter for the agencies, which, equipped as they are with adoption expertise and experience, are in the best position to determine the more detailed requirements for eligibility'.[3] However, New South Wales did not take its flexibility policy quite as far as New Zealand had done. While recommending that both unmarried and same-sex couples be eligible to adopt, it also recommended that a cohabitation period of at least 3 years become part of the prescribed requirements in the case of joint applications. In the event, the Adoption Act 2000 (NSW) provided that a couple must have been living together for a continuous period of at least 3 years before making the application.[4]

3.36 A further contrast is provided by the law of adoption in the Republic of Ireland.[5] In that country the strength of the marital status has meant that the child of married parents is only available for adoption on a coercive basis (it is not possible for a married parent voluntarily to relinquish a child of the marriage) and virtually all prospective adopters must conform to the approved marital family unit, with applications from anyone other than a married couple being accepted only in statutorily specified instances. The assumption is made that only the married nuclear family will serve the child's best interests.[6] O'Halloran notes that 'the special position of the Roman Catholic Church, religion in general, the legal integrity of the marital family unit . . . and a strong reliance upon extended family networks to substitute for parental responsibilities can all be seen

---

1   The current (New Zealand) Adoption Act 1955 does not permit joint applications from non-married couples.

2   *Adoption and its Alternatives: A Different Approach and a New Framework* Report 65 (The Law Commission, Wellington, New Zealand, 2000) at paras 348 and 349.

3   New South Wales Law Reform Commission, Report 81 (1997) *Review of the Adoption of Children Act 1965* (NSW), Executive Summary.

4   Section 28(4) of the Adoption Act 2000 (NSW).

5   The law is contained in unconsolidated adoption legislation, namely the Adoption Acts of 1952, 1964, 1976, 1988, 1991 and 1998.

6   KJ O'Halloran 'Adoption in the Two Jurisdictions of Ireland – A Case Study of Changes in the Balance between Public and Private Law' [2001] *International Family Law* 43 at 46.

to colour the law and practice of adoption'.[1] Comparison with this aspect of Irish law highlights a more general point than simply the marital status or otherwise of adoption applicants. It illustrates once again the extent to which 'the traditional cultural hallmarks' of a society govern and shape legislative reform.

3.37 In answer to the question posed at the beginning of this chapter – 'is the new legislation a true successor to earlier research and consultation or is it the consequence of a brand new approach …?' – the answer must lie somewhere in between. The need for reform had grown with the change in social patterns of adoption and developing views about the value of maintaining secrecy in all its forms, but by far the greatest prompt was ultimately the Government's response to the Waterhouse Report. The last year of the reform process witnessed an inexorable surge in the view that adoption was the way out of care. But in all the millions of words spoken about adoption law reform there was never any question raised about the desirability of adoption *per se*. No question was asked as to whether there was another route out of care. No mention was made of the need for huge resources to be poured into child welfare and protection in order to assist many parents in keeping their children with them. The whole issue of married and unmarried parents which threatened to hijack the Bill in its passage through Parliament was essentially only about increasing the numbers of adoptions. Widening the pool of adopters by extending eligibility to apply to couples of all persuasions became the perceived *modus operandi* for achieving the Government's 'more adoption' target.

Single and homosexual families

3.38 The AA 1976 had of course made provision for single people to adopt.[2] The PIU Report in 2000 recommended that more single people be encouraged to apply to become adopters.[3] The Lowe and Murch study,[4] however, found that of the approved single adopters across the range of statutory and voluntary agencies, most were actually cohabiting couples and divorcees. In practice, a single cohabitant might be granted an adoption order and a joint residence order might then be made in favour of both parties – a procedure virtually constituting a back-door method for cohabiting couples to adopt a child jointly. In *Re AB (Adoption: Joint Residence)*,[5] for example, a stable, heterosexual, cohabiting couple had fostered a child who subsequently needed a permanent home. The foster father had applied to adopt the child and had made a joint application for a joint residence order with the foster mother. Although the natural mother agreed to the latter order but not to the adoption order, both applications were granted on the basis that the child's welfare positively demanded that he be adopted. The result, however, was that the father and mother each had a different legal relationship with the child – the mother simply acquiring the parental responsibility that accompanies a residence order under the CA 1989.[6] In the event, the outcome for the child was good – the granting of both orders was 'positively for the [child's] benefit'. This was a classic case for the extension of the

---

1   KJ O'Halloran 'Adoption in the Two Jurisdictions of Ireland – A Case Study of Changes in the Balance between Public and Private Law' [2001] *International Family Law* 43 at 51.

2   This had always been the case in New Zealand also, and the recommendations in that country in 2000 reiterated the need to enable single people to continue to adopt.

3   PIU Report, July 2000, para 5.17.

4   N Lowe and M Murch et al *Supporting Adoption – Reframing the Approach* (BAAF, 1999).

5   [1996] 1 FLR 27.

6   Section 12(2).

right to apply jointly. The couple had lived together for 20 years, had two older daughters, and were a 'happy, united and responsible' family with each of the partners 'equally and strongly committed to the other'.[1] Nonetheless, as was mentioned frequently in debate on the Bill, a child could be compromised by the fact that only one parent had a legal relationship with him or her. If the legal parent died, or indeed the parents separated, and statistically, as compared with married couples, that is twice as likely to happen, the child could potentially be thrown into a legal limbo.

3.39   Single-person adoptions have for long involved homosexual adopters and of course there has been no legislative ban on such adopters. Nonetheless, it has remained the case that homosexual applicants are more likely to succeed where the child has already proved difficult to place – either because of extremely disturbed behaviour or special physical or emotional needs. For example, in *Re E (Adoption: Freeing Order)*[2] where a very disturbed girl from a chaotic background was placed with a single lesbian adopter, the Court of Appeal concluded that, although the placement was undesirable in principle, the case was a special one. Indeed, it was special in that without the lesbian adopter the child may have remained adrift. As the judgment made clear, homosexual adopters have been considered second best and only in comparison with a childhood in care will they be perceived as a less detrimental alternative.

3.40   Given that the English law reform process had not recommended that cohabiting couples be permitted to apply jointly for an adoption order or indeed, even considered the issue seriously, the notion of a same-sex couple making a joint application was not even part of the initial equation. Consequently, there was virtually no background discussion or wider consultation on the issues of joint adoption by same-sex couples. That was not the case in New Zealand. There, the Law Commission proposed that same-sex and cohabiting couples would be placed on the same footing: that is, they would not be disqualified from applying, but their suitability to adopt would be judged in accordance with the needs of the particular child. In other words, there was to be no blanket prohibition on same-sex couple applications but, rather, there would simply be an assessment on the merits. The New Zealand question was to be – what is in the child's best interests as a matter of *fact*, rather than making assumptions as to the eligibility of the applicants as a matter of *law*.[3] The same was true in Australia, albeit the enduring nature of the relationship had to be proved by the 3-year cohabitation requirement.[4]

3.41   The European perspective on same-sex adoption was highlighted in February 2002 when the European Court of Human Rights held, by four votes to three, that the ban on adoption by lesbian and gay individuals did not violate Art 14, the non-discrimination provision of the European Convention on Human Rights, combined with Art 8, respect for private life. In *Fretté v France*[5] the European Court found that the State was entitled to draw distinctions between homosexuals and others in the

1   *Re AB (Adoption: Joint Residence)* [1996] 1 FLR 27, at 35.
2   [1995] 1 FLR 382.
3   *Adoption and its Alternatives: A Different Approach and a New Framework*, Report 65 (Law Commission, Wellington, New Zealand, 2000) at para 360.
4   Section 28(4) of the Adoption Act 2000 (NSW).
5   Application No 3651/97, where a homosexual man was discouraged from proceeding with an adoption application once he revealed his sexual orientation, albeit initial reports on his attributes as a prospective parent were favourable.

adoption process. It was noted that, in general and in common with the AA 1976, the majority of Contracting States did not explicitly exclude homosexuals from adoption when they allowed unmarried individuals to adopt,[1] but there was a serious lack of uniform principles on such major social questions.[2]

3.42 A recent case from South Africa, however, provided ammunition for the proponents of joint same-sex adoption.[3] There, the case of *du Toit and de Vos v Minister for Welfare and Population Development and Others*[4] held that it was in the particular children's interests to be adopted by their same-sex carers, as to prevent their doing so would have defeated the very essence of adoption.[5] The exclusion of same-sex adopters in the case was found to be in conflict with Art 28(2) of the Constitution of South Africa, which provides that 'a child's best interests are of paramount importance in every matter concerning the child'.

3.43 In terms of the law reform process in the United Kingdom, the extension of joint application rights to same-sex couples was bound to follow the shift in thinking on the purpose of adoption and the widening of the adoption pool.[6] As the focus of parliamentary debate moved almost exclusively to the characteristics of adopters during the latter stages of the passage through Parliament of the Adoption and Children Bill 2002, same-sex couples were tagged on to the coat tails of unmarried couples more generally. Having only been introduced at the Report Stage, the issues had not been subject to any wider public discussion and instead became primarily subsumed into the debate on marriage.[7] As a result, the term 'unmarried couple' was effectively construed as including both heterosexual and homosexual couples,[8] albeit some rather more focused debate occurred in the closing stages of the Bill. Three major reasons were put forward for extending joint application rights to same-sex couples:[9] first, the legal disadvantages to a child of having only one parent with a full legal relationship with him; secondly, the potential adopters who were deterred from applying to adopt because of the legal restrictions,[10] and, thirdly, the need to end discrimination as between unmarried and same-sex couples. The first and second reasons applied with equal force to unmarried

---

1   In *Fretté* (above), Judge Kuris noted that France excluded homosexuals and that Sweden was about to repeal a judicially created ban.

2   Consequently a wider margin of appreciation ought to be allowed to each state, per Judge Kuris in *Fretté*.

3   This case was cited favourably by the *24th Report of the Joint Committee on Human Rights* (HL Paper 177/HC Paper 979).

4   Case CCT 40/01, 10 September 2002, CC of South Africa.

5   Section 17(a) and (c) of the South African Child Care Act 1983 prevented all unmarried couples from jointly adopting children.

6   It should be noted, however, that at the Report Stage in the House of Lords, Lord Jenkin of Roding tabled an amendment which would have allowed regulations to provide for married and unmarried heterosexual couples and single people to adopt but not couples of the same sex. Once Earl Howe's amendment had been approved, Lord Jenkin's amendment could not be moved.

7   In HC Deb, 4 November 2002, col 26, Mr Hinchcliffe, who proposed the amendment, noted that on Report, his speech on the amendment covered six columns of *Hansard*, but just two paragraphs had dealt with same-sex adoption.

8   Mr Hinchcliffe, in support of the amendment, commented that 'the way forward was to accept the fact that we are dealing with unmarried partners, who may be heterosexual, homosexual or lesbian'.

9   HC Deb, 4 November 2002, vol 392, no 200, col 50, per Dr Harris.

10 By this stage of the debate, Dr Harris referred to the 'tens of thousands of children in care who are waiting for suitable adoptive families', in comparison to the 5,000 mentioned earlier.

couples. Their focus was essentially on the provision of a greater number of adopters and the enhanced legal benefits for the child after adoption. Only the human rights argument based on discrimination was of direct relevance and, even then, the supporters of the amendment were in an uncertain position. On the face of it, they were neither supported by the *Fretté* case nor by the lack of commonality of views on the issue amongst European jurisdictions. Even the present Government's legal advisers confirmed that the stance of the AA 1976, as reproduced in the Adoption and Children Bill as first introduced, was compatible with the European Convention on Human Rights. Subsequently, when the Bill was amended by the House of Commons to allow joint applications from unmarried couples but was further amended by the House of Lords so as to return to the original position, the opinion of the same Joint Committee on Human Rights was to the opposite effect. That original stance was confirmed as incompatible with Convention rights.[1]

3.44   Opponents of the amendment focused their concerns on the issues of whether a homosexual parent would have an adverse influence on the growing sexuality of a child in his or her care, whether the child would be teased or bullied, and whether such a couple could offer stability and security to a vulnerable child given that homosexual relationships were said to be generally less stable and long-lasting than heterosexual relationships. The effect of a parent's homosexuality on the child's physical and psychological well-being has been addressed by the courts, but questions are still raised[2] – in particular, whether the child will be teased and bullied. The joint dissenting opinion in *Fretté* found that homosexuality needed to be accompanied by 'behaviour that was prejudicial to the raising of a child' in order to justify the Art 14 discrimination and noted there had been no explanation by reference to scientific studies as to why and how the interests of a child were contrary to the preliminary approval of the particular applicant.[3] In the House of Lords, however, perhaps the most sanguine and common-sense view was that expressed by the Bishop of Oxford.[4] In supporting the rights of same-sex couples to apply jointly to adopt a child, the Bishop emphasised the welfare of the child. He stated that the issue was, in reality, a simple one – that, as a homosexual single person could already adopt a child, the extension of that right so as to give legal responsibility to both parents, if it were in the

1   However, even Lord Hunt of Kings Heath, supporter of the amended position in the House of Lords, noted that the Government did not necessarily accept the Committee's reasoning, but that in light of developing case-law there was always a risk that current law and the Bill could be found to be incompatible (HL Deb, 5 November 2002, at col 617). A defence of the Report of the Joint Committee on Human Rights was given by Lord Lester of Herne Hill, HL Deb, 5 November 2002, col 606, but at col 580, Earl Howe raised the issue of 'which Report of the Joint Committee do we believe?' and at col 587, Lord Jenkin of Roding concluded that the Report was 'nonsense and full of factual errors'.
2   In *C v C (A Minor) (Custody: Appeal)* [1991] 1 FLR 223, the Court of Appeal held that the nature of the mother's lesbian relationship was an important factor to put in the balance in a custody case. Earlier, in *Re D (An Infant) (Adoption: Parent's Consent)* [1977] AC 602, the adverse consequences for a child of a father's homosexuality were considered so severe that his consent to the boy's adoption was dispensed with. However, the courts developed a more tolerant attitude, and in *G v F (Contact and Shared Residence: Applications for Leave)* [1998] 2 FLR 799 found that there was no basis for discriminating against an applicant because of a lesbian relationship. Recently, in *Re M (Sperm Donor Father)* (unreported), Black J in the Family Division of the High Court held that the court could not ignore the fact that different considerations were present where a child was raised in a lesbian household. These included possible discrimination at school and extra questions by the child about her background.
3   Per Judges Bratza, Fuhrmann and Tulkens.
4   HL Deb, 10 June 2002, vol 636, no 148, col 47.

child's best interests to do so, was a positive step. Unlike much of the debate, the Bishop's view was an informed one based on research. He noted that existing research findings suggested that a mother's sexual orientation was, among other things, of less importance for a child's psychological adjustment than 'warm supportive relationships with parents in a positive family environment'[1] and that it was not clear that children who were brought up in such relationships would be more confused about their sexual identity than children adopted by married or single people. Other findings[2] reach a similar conclusion. Dr Golombok's research suggested that 'whether their mother is lesbian or heterosexual may matter less for children's psychological adjustment than warm and supportive relationships with their parents and a harmonious family environment'.[3]

3.45 In practice, same-sex couples who have been rigorously assessed as suitable parents are likely to fill the family void for some children, albeit these children may be very difficult and hard to place. While such people may not necessarily be placed at the top of the list of prospective adopters – it is likely that a hierarchy will develop – it must surely be right in principle for suitable couples of whatever sexual orientation to have the right to apply jointly, in the best interests of a child.

WHAT OF THE NATURAL PARENT PRESUMPTION?

3.46 Adoption has always severed the legal tie between a child and his birth parents. Birth parents become 'former' parents, having either agreed to cede the upbringing of their child to others or been required to do so despite their protestations. One assumed therefore, particularly where agreement had been dispensed with, that the alternative placement chosen for the child was superior to remaining with parents or in care. A comparison between a child's current situation and that which could be provided by others seemed inevitable. And it seemed inevitable too, that birth parents would not fare well in any contest with stable, well-off, married prospective adopters. But how unsuitable must birth parents be and are charges of social engineering legitimately made? What weight do we place on the biological tie *per se*?

3.47 This section will explore the jurisprudence dubbed the 'natural parent presumption' in an attempt to tease out the current status and value of biological parenthood and discern where parents have been placed in the drive to reform adoption law.

3.48 The move from parental rights to parental responsibility in the CA 1989 was indicative of a resurgence in notions of family autonomy and responsibility. The general philosophy underlying that Act asserted that the rights and responsibilities associated with child-rearing belonged to the natural parents. The implication was that parents had been granted the duty and responsibility to make decisions for the child on the basis of his welfare. Although the unmarried father had yet to acquire parental responsibility automatically, at least he was able to achieve the status via an agreement with the mother

---

1   HL Deb, 10 June 2002, vol 636, no 148, col 47.
2   Notably that by a Professor of Psychology, Dr Susan Golombok 'Lesbian Mother Families' in
     A Bainham, S Day Sclater and M Richards (eds) *What is a Parent?* (Hart Publishing, 2000). At the
     same time, this could be the research that the Bishop of Oxford was citing.
3   Ibid, at p 175.

or, where that was not possible, a court order.[1] But even without the legal baggage of parental responsibility, parenthood *per se* gave him a legally recognised status under the Act.[2] The message of the CA 1989 was one of endorsement for parents and an assertion of their value and stature.

The biological parent

3.49   Case-law too asserted the value of birth parents. In his famous statement in *Re KD (A Minor) (Ward: Termination of Access)*[3] Lord Templeman stated that:

> 'The best person to bring up the child is the natural parent. It matters not whether the parent is wise or foolish, rich or poor, educated or illiterate, provided the child's moral and physical health are not endangered. Public authorities cannot improve on nature.'

Some 10 years later, Jane Fortin[4] described Lord Templeman's statement as a 'stirring reminder of the "naturalness" of the child–parent relationship', and suggested that it was part of the wave of jurisprudence that gave the biological link between parent and child increasingly greater significance during the 1980s and 1990s. In 1990, for example, Butler-Sloss LJ (as she then was) stated that 'the mother must be shown to be entirely unsuitable before another family can be considered, otherwise we are in grave danger of slipping into social engineering'. The appropriate question to be asked by the court, therefore, when foster carers were pitched against birth parents was – is the natural family so unsuitable that the child's welfare positively demands the displacement of their parental responsibility?[5]

3.50   In 1992, in *Re O (A Minor) (Custody: Adoption)*,[6] the Court of Appeal again asserted the primary position of the birth parents in caring for the child. In this case, the father sought custody of his child who had been placed with an adoption society at birth by the mother and had subsequently blossomed with short-term carers. The question for Butler-Sloss LJ again was – is the sole remaining parent a fit and suitable parent to care for the child? Her Ladyship concluded that, as the best person to bring up the child was the natural parent, the alternative of adoption should be considered only where that parent was unfit. A further classic example of the presumption in favour of natural parenthood was *Re M (Child's Upbringing)*.[7] Here, a 10-year-old Zulu boy had come to live in London with the family (his foster family) for whom his mother had worked in South Africa. He had lived with them since he was 18 months old while his mother lived in separate quarters in their household. Once in England, the foster mother applied to adopt him. After lengthy proceedings, the Court of Appeal ordered that the boy be returned to South Africa to his parents. With other things being equal, stated Ward LJ, it was in the child's interests to be brought up by his natural parents.

---

1   CA 1989, s 4.
2   Under s 10(4) of the CA 1989 he is entitled to apply for any s 8 order; is entitled to be informed about the application of an emergency protection order and can apply for its discharge; is liable to make payments under the Child Support Act 1991; is entitled to the presumption of contact with his child in care; and was entitled to be given notice of impending adoption proceedings.
3   [1988] AC 806 at 812.
4   See '*Re D (Care: Natural Parent Presumption)* – Is Blood Really Thicker Than Water?' [1999] CFLQ 435 at 437.
5   In *Re K (A Minor) (Wardship: Adoption)* [1991] 1 FLR 57 at 62.
6   [1992] 1 FLR 77.
7   [1996] 2 FLR 441.

3.51   The Court of Appeal here was effectively equating the child's welfare with an upbringing by natural parents, even in the face of a strong psychological attachment to foster carers. The clear judicial message was that birth parents were best even where the child had flourished with foster carers – the biological, as opposed to the psychological, link was dominant and the superiority of 'naturalness' was thereby endorsed. In the event, in *Re M (Child's Upbringing)*, however, the reunification with the natural parents did not work and the child was returned to the foster mother. Jane Fortin articulated two further factors which she perceived as instrumental in the growth of the natural parent presumption. These were, first, anxiety generated by the fact that comparisons between the homes of relatively well-off foster carers and disadvantaged birth parents would invariably favour the former and lead to decisions which might be criticised as 'social engineering' and, secondly, that the emergence of children's rights embraced the notion that children had a 'right' to be brought up by their birth parents.[1] The first factor may well be explained by reference to the CA 1989 and its ethos of parental rights and responsibilities, albeit overlaid with a reasonable dose of political correctness. The second is consistent with the child's right to respect for private and family life under the European Convention on Human Rights. Yet the strength of both factors as manifested in the jurisprudence which emerged subsequently from the courts has arguably diminished. According to Fortin's analysis, psychological, as opposed to biological, attachments began to regain ascendancy in judicial thinking.[2]

3.52   There are numerous examples. In *Re P (Section 91(14) Guidelines) (Residence and Religious Heritage)*[3] the bonds of psychological and emotional attachment were pitted against the biological and cultural ties of the natural family. Jewish parents sought the return of their Down's Syndrome child who had lived for several years with Roman Catholic foster parents under a residence order. At first instance the critical issues were the child's capacity to understand and appreciate her Jewish heritage, the degree of her attachment to the foster parents and the subsequent risk of harm if she were removed. The Court of Appeal concluded that there was no presumption that natural parents should be preferred over foster parents – here 'the psychological tie outweighs the biological tie'.[4] However, the court's focus was very much on the attachment between the foster parents and the child, and the harm that would be caused if it were broken, rather than on the advantages of an upbringing with the natural parents within their particular religious community. On that basis, one can question whether the importance of psychological attachment to prospective adopters had been elevated in the judicial mind or whether the benefits of an upbringing with the natural family were found wanting. Certainly the natural parents' rights under the European Convention on Human Rights cannot be given effect if they would harm the child's health or development.[5]

---

1   'Re D (Care: Natural Parent Presumption) – Is Blood Really Thicker Than Water?' [1999] CFLQ 435 at 437.
2   Ibid, at 441.
3   [1999] 2 FLR 573.
4   Ibid, per Ward LJ, at 602.
5   See for example the point made in *Olsen v Sweden (No 2) (Reunion with Children in Care)* (1992) 17 EHRR 134.

3.53 A further example of the psychological versus biological dilemma was *Re A (Adoption: Mother's Objections).*[1] In this case, Sumner J confronted the issue of whether the harm that would flow from breaking a one-year-old's attachment to highly suitable adopters would be outweighed by the benefits he would derive from an upbringing with his natural mother – a student who had placed her baby for adoption at birth but later changed her mind.[2] The judge opted for the psychological argument in preference to the supposed benefits of the blood tie. If the child were removed from the prospective adopters, he said, there was a real risk of disturbance and lasting psychological damage and this overrode the significant right the child had to be brought up by his natural mother. Welfare was seen as resting with attachment rather than blood tie, albeit the latter was still important.

3.54 So where did the drive to reform adoption law place the biological tie in relationship to psychological attachments? What was the value of the biological tie *per se*? The 1993 White Paper highlighted one of the key principles of the CA 1989 as 'the importance of keeping children in their birth families whenever possible and of supporting them where necessary'.[3] The role of parents was utterly integral. Even where a child was placed in care, the parents continued to have parental responsibility. As the 1992 Review of Adoption Law had noted, it was anticipated that adoption would continue to have a 'valuable role for some children', significantly for those who were 'unable to return to their families'.[4] Adoption was clearly envisaged as a last resort. The overriding view of the 1993 White Paper was that a reformed law should aim to meet the needs of children first and adoptive parents second. That birth parents could best serve their children's needs unless they were utterly unsuitable could perhaps be said to have been implicit. However, as the reform process evolved, consideration of the significance of the birth family appeared to recede.

3.55 In 2000, the White Paper noted that under the CA 1989 'the first duty of local social services authorities, where children cannot live with their birth parents, is to seek a home for them with their extended family'.[5] From that statement we can construe that, in a hierarchy of potential permanent homes, those within the extended birth family were intended to take precedence over those of strangers. Otherwise the only further explicit reference in the proposals was the concern that 'local authorities may sometimes work to keep a child with an unsatisfactory family for too long when it would be better to apply to the court for an order authorising an alternative family placement with perhaps a view to adoption'.[6] Any other policy objectives were only discernible by reading between the lines – for example, the recognition that severance of a child from birth parents 'should be justified by clear and significant advantage to the child compared with less permanent options' and the later discussions of alternatives to adoption and subsequent contact with birth parents. The stance taken in the 2000 White Paper was stronger in its support for children and adoptive parents than that stated in 1993. While recognising that growing

---

1   [2000] 1 FLR 665.
2   It should be noted here that the maternal grandmother was a highly persuasive influence on the young mother's decision to seek the return of the child.
3   *Adoption: The Future*, Cm 2288 (1993), para 3.14.
4   At paras 3.2–3.3.
5   *Adoption: A New Approach*, Cm 5017 (December 2000), para 5.4.
6   Ibid, at para 3.16.

up within a birth family offered children '... the best prospects of succeeding ...',[1] the strong message was that adoption, and quickly, was the next best option.

3.56   That insistent message, reiterated time and again in debate throughout the passage of the Bill through Parliament, emphasised that children should not linger in care. Drift and delay were to be avoided at all costs. That stream of thinking stressed the rapid movement of children from care to adoption and did not dwell on the extent to which families might be helped to keep their children with them. At no stage did debate focus on what further measures the State might take to help children remain at home with their birth parents, for example. Policy in this respect differs in other Western jurisdictions. In Denmark, for example, the adoption of children from local authority care is virtually unknown and in the whole of 2001 only 53 Danish children were adopted in Denmark by people outside the family. Even more surprisingly, the Danish Adoption Act rule enabling parental consent to adoption to be dispensed with has been used only three times (all between 1994 and 1996) in the last 10 years.[2] The reasons why adoption simply does not figure in Danish child protection policy stem largely from the huge State resources available to help struggling parents.[3] The commitment in that country is to prevention rather than cure, with strenuous efforts made to return all children to their natural parents.[4] Comparison with England and Wales begs the question whether Part III of the CA 1989 really works on anything like the scale it should. In rightly aiming to rescue children from a childhood in care, UK objectives have centred solely on increasing the speed at which a transfer into the private sector – the adoptive home – can be achieved.

3.57   In introducing the Adoption and Children Bill for its Second Reading in the House of Lords on 10 June 2002, Lord Hunt of Kings Heath indicated how far government thinking had travelled in that direction: his Lordship stated in his opening remarks that 'all too often, adoption has been seen as a last resort for these children when it should have been considered as a *first resort*'[5] (emphasis added). If adoption were truly to be considered a first resort, then the interests of birth parents and the value of the biological tie will plummet further and be left floundering as a mere by-product of the race to move children out of care.

Relatives and unmarried fathers

3.58   Article 3 of the UN Declaration on Foster Placement provides that 'the first priority for a child is to be cared for by his or her own parents' but, failing that, '... care by relatives or the child's parents, by another substitute – foster or adoptive – family or, if necessary, by an appropriate institution should be considered'.[6] In relation to grandparents, uncles, aunts and other relatives applying to adopt a child it will be recalled

---

1   *Adoption: A New Approach* Cm 5017 (December 2000) at para 1.3.
2   Information given to the authors by retired Danish Court of Appeal Judge, Svend Danielsen.
3   The *hjemmearbejder* or home worker is a special social worker on hand to help parents; both parents receive parental leave when children are born; and State kindergartens look after children until 6 pm, thus enabling parents to work.
4   Article 8 of the European Convention on Human Rights is taken very seriously. Consequently, there is no policy of trying to move children from care into adoption.
5   HL Deb, 10 June 2002, vol 636, no 148, col 21.
6   Article 4 of the UN Declaration on Foster Placement.

that the Houghton Committee opposed such applications because of the potential for distorting relationships within the family.[1] Fostering, rather than adoption, thus became the preferred means of care within the family[2] and, following the CA 1989 a residence order became the alternative legal means of achieving security for the child.[3] Placing the child with relatives clearly has the advantage of keeping him within his own biological family grouping with the consequent benefits of knowledge of origins and personal identity. A residence order of course grants parental responsibility to those in whose favour the order is made, for as long as it is in force. But perhaps one of the major issues for such children is what happens then – how secure are they within the family in the absence of a long-term or permanent order? How secure might relatives feel where schooling and medical matters are concerned? Parental responsibility is the key but, as every parent knows, childhood, or at least dependency, does not end at age 16 or 18. The need to enhance the legal standing of both children and their relatives in order to maximise the advantages of placement within the extended family was a further prompt to reform adoption law.[4]

3.59   In assessing whether regard should be had to the existence of any blood tie when a child is to be placed for adoption, it should be recalled that under the 1976 legislation there was no duty to consult with, let alone inform, siblings of a natural parent about the upbringing of a child. This was clarified by Holman J in *Z County Council v R*[5] where a mother who had placed her child for adoption was adamant that she did not want her siblings to know of his existence. The High Court ruled against the guardian ad litem contacting them to see if they may be able to care for the child and endorsed the wishes of the mother that she be able to make 'discreet, dignified and humane arrangements' for adoption.[6] Nonetheless, in finding that, in principle, 'family life' within Art 8 of the European Convention on Human Rights existed between a child and the extended family, the court went further than European jurisprudence strictly required. European case-law has suggested that, apart from the mother/child relationship, family life does not exist merely by virtue of the blood tie but, rather, is a question of fact – the 'quality of the relationship and its importance to the relative and, in particular, to the child rather than ... the nominal relationship alone'.[7]

---

1   Cmnd 5107, at para 111.
2   It should be noted that the New Zealand Children, Young Persons and Their Families Act 1989, unlike the New Zealand Adoption Act 1955, provides that wherever possible care and protection issues in relation to children should be resolved by their own family or extended family or tribal group. The law reformers in that country recommend a future legislative requirement to consider 'intra-family care' in order to emphasis how important the family is.
3   Although adoption was preferred in *Re W (A Minor) (Adoption: Custodianship: Access)* [1988] 1 FLR 175 where grandparents had cared for the child since birth and the mother had limited mental abilities and a lack of relationship with the child. The Court of Appeal held that adoption would enable the grandparents to appoint a testamentary guardian.
4   McGill in 'Kinship Care' in A Douglas and T Philpot (eds) *Adoption: Changing Families, Changing Times* (Routledge, 2002) has noted the need to increase the quality of kinship care alongside an extension of the range of placements available to looked-after children.
5   [2001] 1 FLR 365.
6   Gillian Douglas has noted (at [2001] Fam Law 8) that the case confirms that the law does not privilege the child's right to know his identity over the mother's right to respect for her private life.
7   H Swindells et al *Family Law and the Human Rights Act 1998* (Family Law, 1999) para 6.52.

3.60 Of even greater significance than the role of blood relatives is that of the unmarried father, albeit without parental responsibility. Under the AA 1976[1] it was not necessary to obtain his agreement to an adoption, although his interests would later be taken into account at the welfare stage. The 1992 Review of Adoption Law proposed no change and recommended that, where an unmarried father did not have parental responsibility, his agreement should not be a 'pre-requisite to the making of an adoption order'.[2] Some unmarried fathers, said the Review, may have had no actual relationship with the child and displayed no concern for the child's welfare, but where there was a genuine relationship it was suggested that the father have the opportunity to discuss the adoption plan and any possible alternatives to it.[3] Prompted by the coming into force of the Human Rights Act 1998, recent jurisprudence has revisited the unmarried father's legal rights vis-à-vis the child and, by implication, reconsidered the value of the blood tie.

3.61 In *Re R (Adoption: Father's Involvement)*,[4] where the father's involvement with the mother and baby had been erratic and violence had been provoked by the mother's agreement to the adoption, the Court of Appeal preferred to ensure that he had, at least, notice of the proceedings. This was part of a noticeable shift towards according fathers without parental responsibility, even where they were blatantly unmeritorious, a greater involvement in adoption proceedings. But such a finding was prompted, in part, by the caution and pragmatism engendered by hovering human rights considerations. Even though the European Convention on Human Rights did not impact on the court's discretionary balance with respect to joining the father as a respondent, the court considered it was 'wise' to allow the particular father to be heard, rather than 'storing up trouble for the future'.[5]

3.62 A more complex issue in relation to the weight to be accorded natural parenthood arose when two unmarried mothers placed their babies for adoption on the basis that they would not be required to disclose the identity of the fathers. One of the fathers in *Re H; Re G (Adoption: Consultation of Unmarried Fathers)*[6] had cohabited with the mother for a period and they already had an older child with whom he had contact. The mother feared damage to her relationship with the father if the pregnancy were revealed. In the second case, the father, who was from overseas and was training for a profession in the United Kingdom, had never cohabited with the mother and, although they had been engaged, they ultimately lost touch completely. In ordering that the first father be identified and consulted but that no steps be taken to identify the second father, Dame Elizabeth Butler-Sloss P confirmed that the more significant the relationship between the parents had been in the past, the stronger was the father's prima facie case to be given notice.[7] It

---

1   AA 1976, s 16. Under Adoption Rules 1984, SI 1984/265, rr 4(1)(f), 10(1), 15(2)(h) and 23(1) the unmarried father without parental responsibility had the right to be a party to the proceedings if he was contributing to the child's maintenance.
2   At para 9.3.
3   1992 Review of Adoption Law, para 9.3.
4   [2001] 1 FLR 302.
5   Without notice of the application, the father may have been justified in raising a complaint of unfairness and violation of his Art 6 right to a fair trial.
6   [2001] 1 FLR 646.
7   *Keegan v Ireland* (1994) 18 EHRR 342 confirmed that in terms of European jurisprudence the notion of 'family' in Art 8 extended to parents who were no longer cohabiting or whose relationship had ended.

became clear that, in principle, natural fathers should be joined as respondents to freeing and adoption applications, unless it would be entirely unsuitable to do so.[1] Where there had been a significant relationship, the father was entitled to respect for family life with the child under Art 8 and therefore to place the child for adoption without notice would prima facie be in breach of this right.[2] That right prevailed over the mother's desire for confidentiality, thus furthering the notion that the blood tie *per se* did, indeed, carry weight in the adoption process.

3.63   Further evidence of the influence of Arts 6 and 8 on the standing of the natural father in domestic law was highlighted by the Court of Appeal's decision in *Re B (Adoption Order).*[3] In that case, the child was thriving in foster care under a care order and enjoyed regular contact and an excellent relationship with his father. But, encouraged by the local authority, the foster carer applied for adoption rather than abide by the former residence order, and the trial judge found that adoption would be in the child's best interests, thereby dispensing with the father's agreement. The Court of Appeal did not agree. Not only was an adoption order inconsistent with the reality of the child's parentage (and here the father maintained a strong relationship with the child), but the father's rights under Art 8 had not been sufficiently protected.[4] In other words, here was a child thriving with a foster mother and, unquestionably, the arrangement was a permanent one, yet because of the relationship with the natural father, there was to be no adoption. As Hale LJ noted, where there was extensive contact with a birth relative one must question 'the appropriateness of the wholesale transfer in legal terms which adoption brings about'.[5] Her Ladyship stressed that, although living with a foster parent, the child had a family and the only issue was to find the appropriate legal machinery to recognise that undoubted fact – the legal relationship had to reflect the actual relationship. Certainly, that was not by means of adoption.

3.64   In terms of domestic law, the case raised two significant points. First, whilst we all recognise that children need permanence, security, and a stable and loving family, Hale LJ made clear that the child had already been granted those attributes – they were secured by the residence order coupled with the good continuing relationship with the father. In other words, the recognised objectives for all children unable to live with birth families could be achieved in some cases without recourse to the total legal severance of adoption. Permanence could be achieved by other legal mechanisms. This idea had been suggested by the 2000 White Paper, even though adoption remained highly favoured. The intention of the reformers was to 'provide new options for permanence',[6] while at the same time highlighting that adoption had a 'good record in delivering a stable, permanent

---

1   This point was also confirmed in principle by the Court of Appeal in *Re B (Adoption by One Natural Parent to Exclusion of Other)* [2001] 1 FLR 589.

2   See also *Re M (Adoption: Rights of Natural Father)* [2001] 1 FLR 745 where a violent father was denied knowledge of the baby's existence by the mother, and the local authority had sought directions that he need not be given notice. Here, Bodey J held that there had been no established family life and that a decision not to inform the father about the proposed adoption was necessary, just and proportionate.

3   [2001] EWCA Civ 347, [2001] 2 FLR 26.

4   The trial judge had not considered whether the making of an adoption order was necessary and proportionate in accordance with Art 8(2).

5   *Re B* (above) at [24].

6   *Adoption: A New Approach*, Cm 5017 (December 2000), Executive Summary, p 3.

new family for looked after children who cannot return to their birth parents'.[1] Secondly, the case reflected a re-evaluation of the position of the birth family. Will adoption ever be appropriate and in the child's best interests where a good relationship is ongoing with one parent, even where residence with that parent is not an option?

3.65   Lady Justice Hale herself supplied an answer in commenting, as an aside, that 'the ideal solution in this case might have been, were it possible, that an adoption order was made for the foster mother to replace J's mother while leaving the relationship between J and his father intact'.[2] Apart from such a 'wish list', the new law, in s 1(4)(f), has certainly re-emphasised the importance of a continuing relationship with the natural parent and, further, provided another alternative to adoption in the form of a special guardianship order.

3.66   Support for adoption as the preferred means of securing permanence was highly evident in the 2000 White Paper. The point was emphasised that 'The Government believes that more can and should be done to promote the wider use of adoption for looked after children who cannot return to their birth parents'.[3] That position is not inconsistent with the view expressed later in the White Paper that '. . . a safe and caring new home for children with wider family or friends . . . is therefore the preferred choice where it is possible and consistent with the child's welfare'.[4] Permanence and security are concepts closely tied to adoption, yet the White Paper also made clear that other forms of permanence which did not require absolute severance of legal ties with birth families would be explored.

3.67   It must, of course, be remembered that the CA 1989 created a range of orders determining where a child would live, with whom he or she would have contact, and who would exercise parental responsibility. The 1992 Review of Adoption Law had recommended that the court should have a duty to consider those alternatives when deciding whether to make a placement or adoption order. As that Review had stated, 'it [was] important that adoption [was] not seen as the only or best means of providing a child with a permanent home. Permanence [could] be achieved in a number of ways: for instance, working with the child's family to enable the child to return home, care by other relatives, or long-term foster care'.[5] The 1993 White Paper proposed a second alternative for those who cared for children on a long-term basis. This was the *inter vivos* guardianship order and was intended to supplement the residence order by providing that no application to dissolve it could be made without prior leave of the court. Directed primarily at foster parents, the proposed order recognised that long-term security and stability were vital to a child, particularly an older one, yet needed to be available without the full adoption process. In the event, there was no provision for this proposal in the 1996 Bill.

3.68   Both of these earlier proposals were aimed at rectifying problems engendered by the changing patterns of adoption. It had become clear that a 'one size fits all' model of adoption no longer met the demands of the circumstances to which it was directed.

---

1   *Adoption: A New Approach*, Cm 5017 (December 2000), at para 1.14.
2   *Re B (Adoption Order)* [2001] EWCA Civ 347, [2001] 2 FLR 26, at [27].
3   *Adoption: A New Approach*, Cm 5017 (December 2000), at para 1.13.
4   Ibid, at para 5.4.
5   Ibid, at para 6.1.

Alternatives falling short of complete legal transfer were required: first, to meet the relatively straightforward needs of children and step-parents in the increasingly common 'reconstituted' family and, secondly, to meet the long-term emotional and physical needs of older children for whom adoption was either not available or appropriate. The same theme was taken up by the 2000 White Paper. It was recognised that there was no status which gave legal permanence without a complete legal break from birth parents,[1] yet children needed 'a secure stable and loving family to support them through childhood and beyond'.

3.69   Nigel Lowe made the salient point, however, that so long as the current concept of adoption remained, any lesser form of order would invariably be perceived as a second-class adoption. His remedy, given that complete severance may be inappropriate for the current pattern of adopting older children, was to modify the existing concept of adoption itself rather than to create other types of orders.[2] Why, said Lowe, should adoption automatically end the legal relationship between birth siblings or even between children and grandparents? Was there not a case for preserving the child's succession rights from birth parents as well as from those from the adoptive family? 'In other words', said Lowe, 'it is by no means obvious that all connections should be severed and indeed with older children being adopted it makes less sense to do so'.[3] The point has a general application but is also specifically pertinent to step-parent adoptions where, following the pattern of adoption overall, the children are frequently over 10 years old.

3.70   Where, as in *Re B (Adoption Order)*,[4] the child's return home was not possible, the 2000 White Paper made clear that 'a foster carer's application to adopt should be viewed positively and processed in three months – faster than adoptive parents who are not currently foster carers'.[5] While 'special guardianship' was proposed as a means of providing legal permanence short of adoption,[6] the examples given by the White Paper did not suggest that a *Re B* type situation was envisaged as falling within its ambit. Rather, special guardianship impliedly referred to older children who did not want adoption yet would benefit from permanence, children who remained with the wider family and others for whom religious or ethnic beliefs mitigated against adoption. One commentator has already noted that, against the backdrop of human rights legislation, the concept of special guardianship may result in more children in care being placed with permanent foster families or placed under the terms of such an order, and that the growing practice of family group conferences may also lead to more placements with relatives. Special guardianship is likely to be particularly appropriate for relatives.[7] However, reform proposals did not indicate that the existence of meaningful ties with a natural parent *per se* would render adoption in any way inappropriate and it could be concluded that the local authority in *Re B (Adoption Order)* was reflecting that response.

---

1   *Adoption: A New Approach*, Cm 5017 (December 2000) paras 5.1 and 5.2.
2   N Lowe *English Adoption Law: Past, Present and Future* in S Katz, J Eekelaar and M Mclean (eds) *Cross Currents* (Oxford University Press, 2000) at p 337.
3   N Lowe *English Adoption Law: Past, Present and Future*, op cit, at p 338.
4   [2001] 2 FLR 26.
5   *Adoption: A New Approach*, Cm 5017 (December 2000), at para 5.7.
6   Ibid, at para 5.8.
7   J Thoburn 'Home New and Abroad' in A Douglas and T Philpot (eds) *Adoption: Changing Families, Changing Times* (Routledge, 2002) at p 229.

3.71 When such a policy is coupled with the proposal to accord paramount consideration to the child's welfare, the authors feel confirmed in their view that the existence of attachments to a natural father and all that this can mean for the child will not necessarily receive overriding weight under the new law. In European terms, however, it must be noted that the European Court of Human Rights has been keen to recognise the continuing interest of birth parents in the future upbringing of their child.[1]

Exclusion of a natural parent

3.72 Section 15(3) of the AA 1976 provided that a natural parent alone could not adopt his or her own child unless (a) the other natural parent was dead or could not be found or (b) there was some other reason justifying exclusion of the other natural parent. The reasoning behind the provision was articulated in a Working Paper published by the Houghton Committee in 1970 and set out by Hale LJ in *Re B (Adoption by One Parent to Exclusion of Other)*.[2] It indicated that the strength of the concept of exclusion stemmed from the use single parents had made of the ability to adopt their own illegitimate child and thereby 'put the gloss of respectability upon the facts, or even to hide them from the child . . .'. In the long run, that was likely 'to be damaging to [the child] rather than helpful', and was undesirable because it would sever the links between the child and the other parent.[3] However, when the Houghton Committee reported in 1972 it clearly contemplated some exceptional cases where adoption by a natural parent would be in the child's best interests. In such cases, it recommended, the applicant would be required to satisfy the court that there were special circumstances which justified the making of an order, and the court should be required to state the reason for its opinion that there were special circumstances. Thus did s 15(3) evolve, although in its final form it was watered down and did not use the word 'exceptional' or even 'special'. By these means, the child's birth heritage received a measure of protection and the natural parent a measure of security as against the other parent seeking to exclude him (or more unusually, her). But of course that was over 30 years ago. In more recent times, natural parents have received even greater measures of protection[4] and the 1996 Adoption Bill retained the exclusion concept albeit the reasons for doing so were much diminished in comparison with former times. The subsequent failure of the 2000 White Paper to discuss any exclusionary provision such as s 15(3) suggested that there was no longer any need to protect either child or natural parent from the cutting of family links. Was this part of the general movement towards a diminishing of the role of a natural parent and his significance to the lineage of the child?

3.73 Although s 51(4) of the Adoption and Children Act 2002 ultimately reiterated the main thrust of the first two subsections in s 15(3) of the AA 1976, the emphasis has shifted from a requirement for reasons justifying exclusion of a natural parent to reasons justifying an adoption. One might assume from the change that the significance of the natural parent has further diminished. Certainly, the value of heritage and lineage within

---

1   *Johansen v Norway* (1997) 23 EHRR 33.
2   [2001] 1 FLR 589.
3   Paragraphs 82–85 of the Working Paper for consultation published by the Houghton Committee (1970) cited by Hale LJ [2001] 1 FLR 589 at 597.
4   The natural father's position was transformed by the Family Law Reform Act 1987, and later by s 4 of the CA 1989, as amended by s 111 of the ACA 2002.

the context of the provision was watered down by the House of Lords in *Re B (Adoption: Natural Parent)*.[1] In allowing the father's appeal from the Court of Appeal's decision in that case,[2] the House of Lords restored the adoption order in the best interests of the child, and Lord Nicholls suggested a range of circumstances, apart from the statutory ones, that might justify the exclusion of a natural parent. These were abandonment, persistent neglect or ill-treatment of the child. The exclusion of the mother, and thus of her wider family, was subordinated to the father's need to be free from anxiety about her possible interference in the future,[3] in the interests of the child's stability and security. In other words, the House of Lords jurisprudence extended the scope for excluding a natural parent and thus relegated even further the value of knowing and understanding the truth about familial heritage and personal identity. As was noted by Harris-Short,[4] adoption by a sole natural parent does not sit easily with the current social and legal purpose of adoption.

---

1   [2001] UKHL 70, [2002] 1 FLR 196.
2   [2001] 1 FLR 589.
3   Albeit the mother agreed that she would seek no part in the child's life, an issue which was addressed by an order under s 91(14) of the CA 1989.
4   S Harris-Short '*Re B (Adoption Natural Parent)*; Putting the Child at the Heart of Adoption?' [2002] CFLQ 325.

Chapter 4

THE NEED FOR REFORM – ISSUES OF CHILD WELFARE

THE OBJECTIVE OF CONSISTENCY

4.1   One of the key legal issues identified by the second wave of reform proposals in 2000 was the apparent lack of consistency between the AA 1976 and the CA 1989.[1] Whereas the latter placed the child's welfare as the paramount concern whenever upbringing was being considered by the courts,[2] the adoption legislation had required only that welfare be the first consideration in adoption proceedings.[3] In other words, considerations apart from welfare also had a role to play in the determination. The reason for that distinction stemmed from the fact that adoption differed fundamentally from other cases concerned with children's upbringing. It had never been the case that a child's legal relationship with a parent could be severed lightly and parents were therefore able to take their own wishes and welfare reasonably into account alongside the child's welfare when deciding whether or not to agree to adoption.[4] Adoption, more so than upbringing cases, has a long-term significance for both parents as well as children. This long-term significance for the child was well recognised by the 1992 Review of Adoption Law,[5] which urged that the welfare test should refer to the child into adult life as well as throughout childhood.[6] For parents, the sheer irrevocability of adoption had always sustained the view that it was unacceptable completely to override their wishes.

4.2   Reform proposals, however, called for an 'overhaul' and 'modernisation' of the old law and its 'alignment' with the CA 1989 to further the '[promotion of] permanence and adoption of looked after children'.[7] The PIU Report justified a wholesale alignment with the CA 1989 on the basis that a new approach 'should put the needs of the child at the centre of the process'.[8] In a modern adoption law, said the Prime Minister in the White Paper, 'we need to ensure that children's needs come first' and must therefore 'align the Adoption Act 1976 with the Children Act 1989, to make the needs of children

---

1   *Adoption: A New Approach*, Cm 5017 (December 2000), at para 2.11.
2   In *J v C* [1970] AC 668, the child's welfare overrode the wishes and welfare of unimpeachable parents.
3   AA 1976, s 6.
4   See, for example, *Re V (A Minor) (Adoption: Dispensing with Agreement)* [1987] 2 FLR 89.
5   At para 7.2.
6   That view was subsequently reflected in the 1996 draft Adoption Bill which set out in clause 1(2) that 'The paramount consideration of the court or adoption agency must be the child's welfare in childhood and later'.
7   PIU Report (July 2000) at para 8.2.
8   Ibid, at para 4.8.

paramount in making decisions about their future'.[1] The rhetoric was thus strongly child-centred and chimed well with the overall child-saving agenda. It was attractive in its simplicity but its ramifications ran deep.

4.3   The reform objective of consistency with the CA 1989 extended to the idea of a checklist similar to that in s 1(3) of that Act. Just as argument surrounding the establishment of the CA 1989 checklist centred on the fact that it cast the relevant considerations in concrete, albeit they were not to be considered exhaustive, so it was with a checklist for adoption legislation. The 1992 Review of Adoption Law considered that the complexity of the decisions to be made in relation to a proposed adoption militated against establishing any rules to determine exactly how such decisions should be made. Despite that stance, the Review nonetheless considered that it would be helpful to set out the key factors that should always be taken into account.[2] The proposal recommended that the s 1(3) factors of the CA 1989 be incorporated,[3] as they were all equally important in adoption proceedings, together with additional factors which were specifically appropriate to adoption. These latter considerations were (i) the likely affect on the child's adult life of any change in legal status and (ii) the value of his relationships with parents, siblings, other relatives and any other relevant persons continuing, and the likelihood of them continuing if the order was or was not made.[4] Consistently with the CA 1989, the Review recommended that when a court was deciding whether to make an adoption order it should not do so unless the order would be better for the child than no order at all, and that both agencies and the courts should have regard to the principle that delay was likely to be prejudicial to the welfare of the child. The former provision was considered to be important where the outcome of the application was likely to affect the child's legal status but not likely to affect his or her current living situation.[5] With respect to the latter issue, the question of delay had become particularly relevant in the context of children lingering in care. The Review focused on the particular vulnerabilities and insecurities of children awaiting a decision about their future and suggested that a child's perception of time could be very different from that of an adult. Unnecessary delays which could heighten those feelings of insecurity and leave a child unsure what his or her position may be were to be avoided by both agencies and courts.[6]

4.4   By the time the reform process had reached the PIU Report stage in 2000, the Prime Minister in his foreword was stressing the delay factor – 'we know that many children wait in care for far too long'. The Report's key messages included ensuring that local authorities considered all options for children 'as soon as possible' and that 'time scales and performance indicators' avoided 'damaging drift and delay for children'.[7] It identified 'delay and lack of grip' in the court system as a problem and urged that courts

---

1   *Adoption: A New Approach*, Cm 5017 (December 2000) at para 4.14.
2   At para 7.4.
3   Respectively: the child's wishes and feelings; his physical, emotional and educational needs; the likely effect on him of any change in circumstances; his age, sex, background and any characteristics of his which the court considers relevant; any harm which the child has suffered or is at risk of suffering; how capable the child's parents, the applicants and any other relevant persons are of meeting his needs; and the range of powers available to the court under the Act.
4   1992 Review of Adoption Law at para 7.6.
5   For example, an application by a step-parent, relative or foster parent.
6   1992 Review of Adoption Law at para 7.3.
7   PIU Report (July 2000), Executive Summary.

should improve adoption proceedings in order to 'tackle delay and improve the quality and consistency of decision-making'.[1] The damaging effects of delay were again highlighted during the parliamentary debates and it was noted that 'almost every critic of the adoption system had focused on delays' and that it was extremely rare that an adoption went through in the 12-month period that was by then the Government's target.[2] The ideas that there should be consistency with the CA 1989 with respect to welfare and that delay had to be minimised received almost unanimous endorsement during the passage of the Bill through Parliament.

4.5   The broad concept of welfare, including the point that delay was prejudicial to that welfare, was at the heart of the need for adoption law reform. Both elements combined to bolster the Government's view that its underlying policies were truly in the interests of children: that it was in the best interests of children in care who were unable, readily, to be rehabilitated with natural parents, to be moved into adoption quickly. The arguments were simple, straightforward and persuasive. They did, however, carry a moral overtone, making it difficult to advocate for the retention of some consideration for the plight of natural parents and for the notion that many children were fundamentally better off within their own birth families, albeit great assistance might be needed there.

WELFARE AND PARENTAL AGREEMENT

4.6   Earlier reform proposals had also recommended an alignment between the two Acts, but with a qualification. The 1992 Review of Adoption Law noted that responses to its widespread public consultation were unanimous in wanting the paramountcy principle extended to adoption, yet it did not recommend a complete alignment. Rather, it recommended that the principle be applicable across the spectrum of considerations in the adoption process, but that it should stop short of dispensing with the parents' agreement. The welfare principle should thus not apply to the determination of whether to make an adoption order without the agreement of natural parents. The reasoning behind that important exception centred on protection for the parent. After all, it had always been considered a fundamental principle that an adoption order could not be made unless each parent or guardian of the child agreed unconditionally, 'freely, and with full understanding of what [was] involved'[3] to the making of the order. The Tomlin Committee, as long ago as 1925, had treated adoption as a transaction between natural and adoptive parents, in which the court's task was to ensure that their agreement did not prejudice the welfare of the child. But the influence of natural parents decreased over the years and, although under the AA 1976 the agreement of both parents with parental responsibility was required, the court had the power to dispense with that agreement on relatively restrictive grounds.

---

1   PIU Report (July 2000) at paras 7.1 and 7.2.

2   HC Deb, 16 May 2002, vol 385, no 149, col 941, per Mr Julian Brazier. At col 945, Ms Jacqui Smith, however, countered that claim somewhat by noting that the average time a child was looked after before adoption had fallen from 3 years and 4 months in 1996–1997 to 2 years and 9 months in 2000–2001.

3   AA 1976, s 16(1)(b).

4.7   The 1992 Review of Adoption Law had hypothesised that '[i]f the principle of the paramountcy of the child's welfare were to apply in this respect, the court would be able to override completely a parent's wishes, which we would consider unacceptable in relation to an order which irrevocably terminates a parent's legal relationship with a child'.[1] That reasoning was endorsed by academic commentators who, whilst supporting the introduction of the welfare principle into adoption law generally, were much less enthusiastic about its application to dispensing with parental agreement.[2] The Review had expressed concern that insufficient weight was being given to a parent's lack of agreement, that there was little room for parental views in the courtroom once it had been decided that adoption was in the child's interests, and that this was an unsatisfactory state of affairs given the irrevocable nature of adoption.[3] It was also noted, however, that the court was often presented with a *fait accompli* – that, by the time it was asked to resolve the question of parental agreement, the strength of the parent/child relationship had been diminished by the sheer passage of time.

4.8   In reality, throughout the 1990s, parents were not necessarily receiving the protection that had originally been envisaged. When it came to a balance of the three sets of interests within the adoption triangle, the child's welfare had virtually become the paramount consideration when dispensing with parental agreement. The 1992 Review of Adoption Law found that situation to be 'unsatisfactory when dealing with parental wishes and feelings in relation to so important a step as adoption'.[4] This was due in part to the difficult test of determining whether or not a parent was withholding agreement unreasonably.[5] For example, stated the Review, even where the child had not yet been placed, there had developed a tendency to decide that if adoption were in his or her best interests parental agreement should be dispensed with on that basis – that, in terms of s 16 of the AA 1976, agreement was being unreasonably withheld.[6] Consequently, it proposed a new test to apply in all situations where the parent was withholding agreement – that the court be 'satisfied that the advantages to a child of becoming part of a new family and having a new legal status are so significantly greater than the advantages to the child of any alternative option so as to justify overriding the wishes of a parent'.[7] In other words, it was proposed that the birth parents be part of the equation – that on a 'balance of advantage' test the scales would tip in favour of adoption only where that proved to be significantly better for the child than any other option.

---

1   At para 7.1.
2   B Lindley and N Wyld 'The Children Act and the Draft Adoption Bill – Diverging Principles' [1996] CFLQ 327 at 330; J Murphy 'Child Welfare in Transracial Adoptions: Colour-blind Children and Colour-blind Law' in J Murphy (ed) *Ethnic Minorities, Their Families and the Law* (Hart Publishing, 2000) at p 46.
3   At para 12.1.
4   Ibid, at para 12.4.
5   AA 1976, s 16(2)(b).
6   The leading authority is *Re W (An Infant)* [1971] AC 682 which laid down the test of reasonableness in relation to s 16(2)(b). Lord Campbell of Alloway, who acted for the adoptive parents in that case, spoke in the House of Lords (10 June 2002, col 55) expressing his concern at the balance of advantage test which, he said, could work against the best interest of the child by introducing a derivative of the 'blood tie' argument. This argument had been expressly rejected by the House of Lords in *Re W*.
7   1992 Review of Adoption Law at para 12.6.

4.9 The 1996 draft Adoption Bill[1] rejected that proposed qualification. Instead, it provided that in any agency or court decision relating to adoption, the child's welfare would be the paramount consideration, both in childhood and later. The child should not be placed for adoption unless the parents consented, or the court made a placement order,[2] and an adoption order would only be made against a parent's opposition if the 'court [were] satisfied that the welfare of the child require[d] consent to be dispensed with'.[3] Thus the 1996 draft Bill provided that the welfare principle, together with a checklist set out in clause 1, be applied throughout. The 2000 White Paper followed suit, taking the view that if children were the overriding priority then their welfare must be paramount in *all* decisions relating to adoption. The implication was that anything less risked demoting the emphasis on the child. If there were to be casualties during the process, better they be the natural parents than the child. As one commentator explained so succinctly, achievement of the Government's objective required minimising 'to the greatest extent possible, the most common cause of disruption and delay in a child's journey to a new and "better" home: the rights and interests of the natural parents'.[4] Extending the welfare principle to all aspects of the adoption process thus removed any scope for a true balancing of interests.[5]

4.10 Interestingly, the 'balance of advantage' test came up for consideration again during submissions to the Parliamentary Select Committee in relation to the Adoption and Children Bill in October 2001. The British Agencies for Adoption and Fostering (BAAF) indicated that it was 'still inclined to favour the form of words suggested by the Adoption Law Review team', primarily for the purpose of ensuring that parents retained some status and that a distinction remained between parents who agreed to adoption and those who did not.[6] The question of support for this much higher hurdle where children were placed for adoption against parental wishes was duly put to another witness, Professor Sonia Jackson.[7] Her response indicated absolute opposition. Professor Jackson's reasoning centred on the claim that the care system had failed children, that only adoption offered them 'by far the most stable form of substitute placement' and that parents should not be able to stand in the way of achieving such a desirable outcome. If the welfare of children were put above the interests of parents as it should be, she claimed, then raising the threshold, as the 1992 Review of Adoption Law and the BAAF recommended, 'would be a very bad idea' and 'would seriously jeopardise the Government's objective of increasing the number of children being adopted'.[8]

4.11 Throughout the passage of the Bill through Parliament, the issue of dispensing with parental consent was one of those matters not thoroughly debated due to the guillotine. Nonetheless, concern about the simplicity of the welfare test in relation to

---

1 Incorporated in a further White Paper, *Adoption – A Service for Children* (HMSO, 1996).

2 Clause 23(1).

3 Clause 46.

4 S Harris-Short 'The Adoption and Children Bill – A Fast Track to Failure?' [2001] CFLQ 405 at 419.

5 C Bridge 'Adoption Law: A Balance of Interests' in J Herring (ed) *Family Law – Issues, Debates, Policy* (Willan Publishing, 2001) at p 198.

6 HC Official Report, Special Standing Committee, Adoption and Children Bill, Second Sitting, 20 November 2001, at col 39.

7 Evidence given by Professor Sonia Jackson, 21 November 2001, at col 130.

8 Ibid.

dispensing was apparent in the House of Lords. Baroness Howarth of Breckland, in particular, commented that 'it had always been clear to her that most – not all – children would prefer to retain contact with their birth family' and that, as a consequence, she was 'concerned about the dispensation wording in the Bill' as it 'was easy in many circumstances to be convinced that the welfare of the child required consent to be dispensed with'.[1] Baroness David posed some searching questions – the answers to which still hang in the air; how was the wording of the welfare test in relation to dispensing compatible with the Human Rights Act 1998? The Baroness noted that:

> 'the concern was that the simple welfare test ... will be in breach of Art 8 of the European Convention because it was no different from the ground for any other Children Act order, such as a residence or [the new] special guardianship order. Yet, given that adoption was irrevocable, European case law suggested that there needed to be exceptional circumstances to justify the state overturning parental consent.'[2]

4.12   But again, the thrust of the 'child-saving' agenda was in full swing and, again, it was highly persuasive. It was the Government's belief that, first and foremost, adoption was a service for children. It was not a balancing of rights. If adoption provided the only stable alternative to living with birth families, then more adoption, more quickly – and forget the birth parents – was the call in the best interests of the child. Certainly, as the reform process moved forward from 1992, culminating in the new Adoption and Children Act in 2002, that call had become stronger.

RACIAL AND CULTURAL MATCHING

4.13   It is trite to note that a 'new and better home' requires the child to be 'matched' to the adopters, and sociological studies are hardly needed to support the contention that good 'matching' is likely to be the key to the success of the adoption. But does good matching demand same-race placement? Will the child's welfare interests only be served by adoption by a family of the same ethnic and cultural background or will a sound placement, whatever the ethnic mix, be more significant?

4.14   Particular tension has traditionally surrounded social work policy with respect to race and ethnicity. Many agencies having a 'same race' matching policy with the objective being to place children with adopters of the same racial background. The Lowe and Murch study revealed that 31 per cent of the total agencies (ie both statutory and voluntary) involved in placing children for adoption would *not* place a child 'transculturally'.[3] Others agreed that same-race placement was the ideal but was not always possible to achieve in practice, and many said they would 'go to some lengths to achieve the ideal by going all over the country first . . .'.[4] At the same time, white adopters were sometimes discouraged from adopting a black child even when they expressed

---

1   HL Deb, 10 June 2002, vol 636, no 148, col 65.
2   Ibid, at col 63.
3   N Lowe and M Murch *Supporting Adoption – Reframing the Approach* (BAAF, 1999) at pp 164–167.
4   One respondent to the Lowe and Murch study explained that the first preference was for both
        adopters to be of the same race as the child, the second preference was for one partner to be of the
        same race, the third was for some extended family or another sibling same-race match and the fourth
        preference, where there was no possibility in the family, was a match with the nearby community
        (op cit, p 165).

themselves as having awareness of the particular issues and actively sought a mixed-race or black child.

4.15 Delay and subsequent 'drift' may undoubtedly be caused while a same-race placement is sought – in the best interests of the child. But why should local authorities have embraced, so wholeheartedly, the view that placing a child with prospective adopters of the same race was vital to the child's well-being and that not doing so was simply storing up trouble for the future? Hayes and Williams have claimed that 'virtually all social services departments take the view that it is self-evident that the child's interests are best served if he has his home with persons of the same ethnic origin'[1] and have described these beliefs as 'virtually unchallenged orthodoxy'.[2] Murphy,[3] too, has claimed the existence of the false assumption that adoption should 'mirror biology; that matching genetic heritage is a fundamental determinant of successful adoptive placements for minority children'. It stemmed, he claimed, from the 'markedly sociological' objectives, methodology and 'broad considerations of social policy' of the particular studies on which such views were based: studies which were unsuited to assisting the lawyer and the courts in dealing with individual cases of trans-racial adoption.

4.16 In a challenge to the prevailing assumption that ethnically compatible adults provide the best adopters, Murphy's perusal of the relevant literature revealed no basis for the contention.[4] Despite a 1995 policy statement from BAAF that '[i]t is essential for black children to be placed with families who can help them deal with the experience of being black in a racist society ...',[5] Murphy concluded that trans-racial adoptions were neither harmful to the particular child, although they could sometimes be problematic for older children,[6] nor to minority community interests. On the contrary, there could be positive benefits for the child and for the society in terms of integration. Central to his thesis was the concern that a preoccupation with same-race placement denied the paramountcy of the child's welfare – that a less good, but same-race family would be preferred, or that it was better to wait for such a family than be placed in a white-parent home. He concluded that the best outcome for a child, and thus his or her best interests, arose from being placed with dedicated and genuine adopters, given that race-matching was no guarantor of welfare.[7]

4.17 Jurisprudence emerging from the courts over the past decade or so has attempted to answer the question of whether same-race adoption was of such overwhelming significance to the child that it outweighed the bond of attachment that may have developed between an ethnic minority child and white foster parents. The Court of

---

1   M Hayes and C Williams *Family Law: Principles, Policy and Practice* (Butterworths, 1999) at pp 291–295.

2   M Hayes 'The Ideological Attack on Transracial Adoption in the USA and Britain' (1995) 9 *International Journal of Law and the Family* 1.

3   J Murphy 'Child Welfare in Transracial Adoptions: Colour-blind Children and Colour-blind Law' in J Murphy (ed) *Ethnic Minorities – Their Families and the Law* (Hart Publishing, 2000) at p 34.

4   Ibid, at pp 36–39.

5   *Practice Note 13: The Placement Needs of Black Children* (BAAF, 1995).

6   J Murphy, op cit, at p 45.

7   Note that M Parry in 'Local Authority Support for Ethnic Minority Children' in J Murphy (ed), op cit, at p 27 claimed that, whilst same-race placements should be followed as a general principle, where there was a lack of ethnically matched placements that principle should not be upheld at the expense of the welfare of the child.

Appeal in *Re A (A Minor) (Cultural Background)*[1] answered that question in the negative only after hearing powerful expert evidence that, regardless of the length of time the West African child had been with white foster parents, she must be placed back with a West African family. It has been suggested that such views are illustrative of the powerful hold which a particular ideological approach has had over some local authority social workers,[2] whereas the courts have tended to be more balanced. Bush J in *Re N (A Minor) (Adoption)*,[3] for example, described the emphasis on colour as 'dedication to dogma' and 'highly dangerous' and pointed out that there was little real evidence that trans-racial placements were harmful. This should be compared, however, with *Re P (A Minor) (Adoption)*[4] where a mixed-race infant was placed with white foster parents who subsequently sought to adopt. There, the Court of Appeal held that the trial judge was entitled to conclude that the advantages of bringing up a child of mixed race in a black family outweighed the importance of maintaining the status quo.

4.18   The particular issue was also considered in *Re JK (Adoption: Transracial Placement)*, where a Sikh child had been placed with short-term white foster parents while the local authority looked for same-race adopters.[5] Three years later the child was still with the foster parents, had become deeply attached to them and they asked to be considered as prospective adopters. That proposal was rejected in the interests of the local authority's same-race policy, and the issue before the court was whether psychological attachment or racial and cultural identity should determine the matter. As there was no Sikh family available[6] and expert evidence suggested that a move from the foster parents would be likely to cause irreparable psychological damage, leave was granted to the foster carers to start the adoption process with an independent adoption agency. The local authority here appeared to have given too much weight to the guiding principle that a child should be placed with a family of similar ethnic origin and religion.

4.19   However, in what appeared to be a reversal of the significant weight accorded to emotional and psychological attachments over racial characteristics, the Court of Appeal ordered a Zulu child's return to South Africa. In *Re M (Child's Upbringing)*[7] Neill LJ stated that the 10-year-old boy had the 'right to be reunited with his Zulu parents and with his extended family in South Africa',[8] despite expert evidence that he would be deeply traumatised by leaving the foster mother to whom he had been attached since infancy. The outcome of the ruling, unsurprisingly, proved disastrous and the boy eventually returned to his foster mother in England.

4.20   In the context of religious heritage, recent judicial trends have favoured securing the welfare of the child over a strict adherence to religious persuasion. *Re P (Section*

---

1   [1987] 2 FLR 429.
2   M Hayes and C Williams, *Family Law: Principles, Policy and Practice* (Butterworths, 1999) at p 293.
3   [1990] 1 FLR 58.
4   [1990] 1 FLR 96.
5   [1991] 2 FLR 340.
6   Adoption within the Sikh community is very rare and the local authority here was investigating two Hindu families and one Asian Roman Catholic family as potential adopters. Hayes and Williams, op cit, at p 294 have commented that, with none of those families being Sikh, it was hard to see how such an arrangement would have paid regard to the child's religious and cultural heritage.
7   [1996] 2 FLR 441.
8   Ibid, at 454.

91(14) Guidelines (Residence and Religious Heritage)[1] was an example, albeit in the context of fostering rather than adoption and involving a child with the capacity for limited understanding and appreciation of the Jewish religion. There, Orthodox Jewish parents sought the return of their Down's Syndrome child from the Roman Catholic foster parents with whom she had lived for several years. In considering the relevance and importance of religion, Butler-Sloss LJ (as she then was) concluded that the child's religious and cultural heritage could not be an overwhelming factor and could not displace other 'weighty welfare factors'.

4.21 Of even greater relevance to notions of adoption and welfare was *Re C (Adoption: Religious Observance)*,[2] where Wilson J observed that the justice system was a secular one and that his approach to the child's ethnic background (here a mixture of Jewish, Turkish/Cypriot, Irish, Muslim and Roman Catholic) would be a pragmatic one – very much along the lines Wall J adopted in *Re J (Specific Issue Orders: Muslim Upbringing and Circumcision)*.[3] Section 7 of the AA 1976 had provided that an agency placing a child was to have '... regard (so far as is practicable) to any wishes of a child's parents and guardians as to the religious upbringing of the child'. Parliament had thus chosen to invest parental wishes concerning religious upbringing with greater significance than it had accorded to any other aspect of upbringing. Nonetheless, the parliamentary intention was qualified by guidance to the effect that those wishes would be respected '... unless, because of a shortage of adoptive parents in that religion, the child's prospects of having a permanent family would be threatened'.[4] In *Re C (Adoption: Religious Observance)* the guardian had failed in her application for judicial review of the local authority's decision to place the 2-year-old child for adoption with a Jewish couple in the face of what she perceived to be the wishes of the parents. Although somewhat muddled, these appeared to indicate a wish for a secular environment, although there had been half-hearted views about a Jewish home. But, as Wilson J concluded, it was paradoxical to seek to replicate in the adoptive home the religious void (albeit there was a religious heritage) in the parents' own home – a home he characterised as not only physically poor but intellectually and emotionally barren. The guardian had argued that the parental wishes and the child's complex ethnicity should have been reflected in 'a religiously neutral environment' – a view described by Wilson J as 'inflexible and doctrinaire'.

4.22 Those two words – inflexible and doctrinaire – exemplify the very attitudes that need to be avoided in relation to both racial and cultural matching if a child's welfare is to be paramount. The suitability of prospective adopters in psychological and emotional terms are prized attributes. If the racial and cultural/religious match is also apparent, so much the better. In the absence of such factors, however, the approach of the President of the Family Division as illustrated in *Re P (Section 91(14) Guidelines) (Residence and Religious Heritage)*[5] – refusing to allow those considerations to displace the modern, albeit secular, characteristics of security and stability – must be the view that most enhances welfare.

---

1   [1999] 2 FLR 573.
2   [2002] 1 FLR 1119.
3   [1999] 2 FLR 678.
4   Guidance to agencies contained in a Circular of 28 August 1998.
5   [1999] 2 FLR 573.

4.23   In terms of reform, the issues clearly needed to be addressed and guidance given on the weight to be accorded ethnic and cultural matching vis-à-vis existing attachments and the greater likelihood of permanence through adoption. From the very outset of the reform process over 10 years ago, it was recognised that there existed a range of opinions on the significance or otherwise of trans-racial adoption.[1] It was recognised that ideology and doctrinaire attitudes were alive and well, albeit the majority of relevant studies were American. In summary, the fears of black social workers about the dangers of trans-racial placements in England and Wales were not supported, although the generally positive picture of such adoptions needed to be treated with caution. By the time of the White Paper, *Adoption: The Future,* in 1993, the Government had come round to believing it right to consider factors of ethnicity, culture and religion alongside others in matching children even though such factors had sometimes been given an 'unjustifiably decisive influence' and had thereby contributed to a failure in making 'balanced overall judgement of the parents' suitability'. Overall, ethnicity and culture were not to be considered as 'more influential than any other issue'.[2] Such statements indicated a clear movement away from rigidity and the sometimes ideologically driven policies towards the Murphy approach of psychological and emotional well-being rather than ethnic matching.

4.24   By 2000, the reformers were even more decisive. The next White Paper, *Adoption: A New Approach*, stressed that '. . . the child's welfare is paramount and no child should be denied loving adoptive parents solely on the grounds that the child and the parents do not share the same racial or cultural background'.[3] Welfare and safety were the first priority for children and the assessment criteria for potential adopters, as required by the Draft National Standards, urged that it not be 'judgmental in its consideration of potential adopters'.[4] The Government did not vary from that stance. The earlier recognition that the benefits of same-race matching should ideally be balanced against the harmful effects of delay continued to hold sway. The consistent view maintained throughout the passage of the Bill through Parliament was summed up by Lord Hunt of Kings Heath in the House of Lords:

> 'Of course, the best adoptive placement for a child should reflect his/her religious persuasion, racial origin, cultural and linguistic heritage, but only if that can be found without unnecessary or harmful delay. What counts, and what the Bill enshrines, is that the interests of the child must come first.'[5]

4.25   What should also be added is that, given the welfare considerations accorded to a same-race family, all else being equal, greater efforts need to be put into recruitment of ethnic adopters. Theoretical knowledge and research over the past decade has supported the view that black families with religious, cultural and linguistic backgrounds similar to the black child's own, and who are assessed as able to meet the child's developmental

---

1   See J Thoburn *Review of Research Relating to Adoption* (DoH, 1990), where the author noted that arguments for and against trans-racial placement were all well documented: in particular, J Weis *Transracial Adoption: A Black Perspective* (Social Work Monographs, UEA, 1987); D Dale *Denying Homes to Black Children* (Social Affairs Unit, 1987); B Tizard and A Phoenix *Black Identity and Transracial Adoption* (New Community, 1989) at p 15.
2   *Adoption: The Future,* Cm 2288 (1993) at para 4.32.
3   Cm 5017 (December 2000), para 6.15.
4   Ibid, at para 6.18.
5   HL Deb, 10 June 2002, vol 636, no 148, col 22.

needs, are able to offer him or her the optimum adoptive placement.[1] The drive to recruit more carers and adopters will have a twofold benefit if it is also sensitively extended to people from a range of racial, cultural, linguistic and religious backgrounds. In the final analysis, however, to achieve its goal of 'more adoption, more quickly' the Government will have to require agencies to retain flexibility in their recruitment processes and place the child's welfare, in terms of finding an adoptive home, ahead of the niceties of same-race matching.

---

1   For a review of research relating to trans-racial adoption, see A Gupta 'Adoption, Race and Identity' in A Douglas and T Philpot (eds) *Adoption – Changing Families, Changing Times* (Routledge, 2002) at p 208.

Chapter 5

THE NEED FOR REFORM – ISSUES OF CONTACT AND INFORMATION

CONTACT

5.1   In its 2000 White Paper, the Government expressed itself as intent upon placing 'children at the heart of the adoption process'.[1] Their welfare was to be central, the paramount factor across the spectrum of considerations. With one qualification – that of dispensing with parental agreement – few would disagree. Few would also disagree that consideration of post-adoption contact and the whole issue of how 'open' an adoption should be goes hand in hand with welfare.

Why maintain contact?

5.2   Judith Masson described contact as 'the practical demonstration of a continuing relationship'.[2] Whether post-adoption contact is 'direct' by way of face-to-face meetings or telephone calls or 'indirect' by means of the mail-box or an annual report and photograph, it is intended to enhance welfare by maintaining existing relationships and providing the child with a sense of continuity. While face-to-face contact with birth parents may not always be compatible with an adoption order, the maintenance of some lesser form of contact between older children and the parents they already know and have attachments to may enhance the child's welfare and ultimately his adoptive placement. Even though children adopted from care are likely to benefit from integration into a new and stable family, the maintenance of links with their birth family is thought to assist the development of personal identity and sense of family continuity. As Ward LJ noted in *Re G (Adoption: Contact)*,[3] the benefit of contact:

> 'is the benefit that comes from the children simply knowing who the natural parent figures are. It is to remove the sense of the ogre, as they reach adolescence and begin to search for their own identity, with the double crisis not only of adolescence itself but of coming to grips with the fact that they are adopted. That is why the current research is in favour of some contact in adoption.'

5.3   Academic research more generally has indicated that children who are adopted commonly experience a sense of loss and rejection even when they have been placed successfully with an adoptive family.[4] The Lowe and Murch study found that maintenance of links was perceived as important to the long-term welfare of adopted

---

1   *Adoption: A New Approach*, Cm 5017 (2000), Executive Summary.
2   J Masson 'Thinking About Contact – A Social or a Legal Problem?' [2000] CFLQ 15.
3   [2003] 1 FLR 270 at 274.
4   D Casey and A Gibberd 'Adoption and Contact' [2001] Fam Law 39.

children: it enabled children to know that their parents still loved them, that they need not be anxious about the well-being of their birth family[1] and that they had their parents' 'seal of approval' to become emotionally attached to the adopters.[2] An enhanced sense of personal identity gleaned from greater knowledge of family background and heritage flowed from post-adoption contact and it has long been suggested by the courts that contact may well be of singular importance to the long-term welfare of the child.[3]

5.4   The benefits of maintaining links for reasons of racial identity are also significant. In *Re O (Transracial Adoption: Contact)*,[4] for example, post-adoption contact between a Nigerian mother and her child was intended to give the child 'immediate exposure to Nigerianness' which was not otherwise available from the adopters. Contact in that case was intended as a means of countering the fantasies the child harboured about her mother. One of the key advantages of post-adoption contact more generally is that facts are able to replace speculation and fantasy about the birth family, thus promoting a more realistic perception.[5] Ward LJ's comment[6] with respect to removing 'the sense of the ogre' is particularly pertinent.

5.5   Contact and openness are especially relevant to the changed profile of adoption today. As has already been noted, adoption is now primarily concerned with older children from care who already know their birth families and are likely to retain their memories and emotional attachments however inadequate their parenting may have been. Nigel Lowe illustrated the nature of modern adoption particularly well in his construction of a 'contract/services' instead of a closed and exclusive (the traditional adoption of babies) paradigm.[7] The essence of Lowe's new way of seeing adoption lay in understanding it as an informal contract between natural family, adoptive family and child. The contract would create a pattern of reciprocal obligations with ongoing State support, adoption allowances, updated information and post-adoption contact. Adoptive parents would effectively enter a contract to bring up a child, possibly damaged by years in care, as if he or she were their own. Legally, of course, the child would become their own, but if that were coupled by the mind-set of the 'contract/services' model, the new parents would view the adoption very much more as a life-long fostering arrangement rather than a life-long pretence that the child had been 'born to them in lawful wedlock'.[8] In other words, in Lowe's view, it was possible today to view adoption as a new style of childcare which, while severing the legal relationship with birth parents, would nonetheless retain tangible links with them in a way that would allow them to remain part of the background for the child – in the child's interests. Post-adoption contact, even when not direct face-to-face contact, was an integral part of Lowe's theory.

---

1   The need for reassurance was also noted by J Fratter *Adoption with Contact* (BAAF, 1996) at p 234.
2   N Lowe and M Murch et al *Supporting Adoption – Reframing the Approach* (BAAF, 1999) at p 324 and ch 15 more generally.
3   See, for example, *Re E (A Minor) (Care Order: Contact)* [1994] 1 FLR 146 at 154H–155B, per Simon Brown LJ.
4   [1995] 2 FLR 597.
5   M Ryburn 'In Whose Best Interests? – Post Adoption Contact with the Birth Family' [1998] CFLQ 53 at 60, and J Fratter *Adoption with Contact* (BAAF, 1996) at p 19.
6   In *Re G (Adoption: Contact)* [2003] 1 FLR 270 at 274.
7   N Lowe 'The Changing Face of Adoption – The Gift/Donation Model versus the Contract/Services Model' [1997] CFLQ 371.
8   AA 1976, s 39(1).

5.6   As has been seen in other areas of family law, such as paternity disputes and the question of identifying information about anonymous sperm donors in the context of artificial reproduction, the need for knowledge about one's origins is perceived as vital to personal growth and well-being. The significance of these considerations in the context of paternity testing was well illustrated by a recent amendment to the Family Law Reform Act 1969.[1] In response to the concerns expressed by Wall J in *Re O and J (Paternity: Blood Tests)*,[2] legislative intervention was considered necessary so that a parent with care and control of a child could not obstruct a search for the truth about parentage by refusing to give consent for the child's blood to be taken for the purposes of testing. The new s 21(3) of the Family Law Act 1969 enabled the court to override a parent's refusal if it considered that to do so would be in the best interests of the child.[3] In other words, the child's ability to gain knowledge about his or her parentage, his or her roots and thereby his or her identity, was considered overwhelming. A parallel can clearly be drawn with an adopted child's ability either to gain or to retain such personal knowledge.

Research findings on contact

5.7   At the outset it has to be stated that ongoing academic debate about post-adoption contact between children and birth families has been characterised by some disagreement about how far it is vital for children's long-term well-being and therefore how far social policy and law should seek to promote and enforce it.[4] There is, however, a substantial body of literature that discusses the advantages of adoption with contact, albeit the long-term advantages are not entirely substantiated.[5] Quinton et al, for example, have noted that current research has 'not been methodologically sophisticated enough to identify causal relationships between variables associated with contact . . . and indicators of children's development or well-being'.[6] Despite a lack of long-term outcome data, Smith and Logan have highlighted the 'wealth of qualitative research' suggesting that children, adoptive and birth families frequently experience direct contact as beneficial.[7] Smith and Logan's own research found that the vast majority of children valued contact, while also expressing satisfaction and happiness with their adoptive family, but the authors accepted that more needed to be known about the conditions that were likely to promote beneficial consequences.

---

1   By s 21(3) of the Child Support, Pensions and Social Security Act 2000.
2   [2000] 1 FLR 418.
3   In *Re T (Paternity: Ordering Blood Tests)* [2001] 2 FLR 1190, the first case on the new s 21(3), Bodey J held that DNA testing would be in the best interests of the child. Certainty of parentage would be to his advantage and, under Art 8 of the European Convention on Human Rights, his interests in having the possibility of knowing about his roots and identity carried more weight than the interests of the adult parties.
4   C Smith and J Logan 'Adoptive Parenthood as a "Legal Fiction" – Its Consequences for Direct Post-adoption Contact' [2002] CFLQ 281.
5   Ibid, at 282.
6   D Quinton, A Rushton, C Dance and D Mayes 'Contact between Children Placed Away from Home and their Birth Parents: Research Issues and Evidence' (1997) 2(3) *Clinical Child Psychology and Psychiatry* 393. See also D Quinton 'Contact with Birth Parents: A Response to Ryburn' [1998] CFLQ 349.
7   C Smith and J Logan, op cit, at 284. See also Department of Health *Adoption Now: Messages from Research* (Wiley, 1999) for an overview of research findings in this context.

5.8   Contact between older adopted children and members of the birth family was one of the more contentious practice issues explored by the Lowe and Murch study.[1] Of the families in the study, 77 per cent had some form of ongoing contact with the birth family and, in general, it was seen as 'helping children settle in their new family and [was] an important contributing factor to the success of adoptive placements'.[2] While the authors found themselves not committed to the view that contact was always in the child's interests,[3] research nonetheless led them to conclude that, in general, a range of benefits flowed from some form of contact between child and birth family. Contact was, unsurprisingly, found to be 'potentially important for the child's sense of identity and knowledge of their family background'.[4] It could reduce feelings of being rejected and help the child settle in and attach to the adoptive family, relieving any anxiety there may be in relation to the well-being of birth relatives.[5] Even though contact with siblings who had been placed in other families could be complicated, Lowe and Murch found that for many children it was a significant and important source of support.[6] Another analyst, Ryburn, also made positive findings from the wealth of research on post-adoption contact. He concluded that, at least in 1997, the messages from research were sufficiently clear as to warrant a general presumption in favour of contact.[7] Advantages, he claimed, were apparent to all three parties whether the contact was direct or indirect: the child gained a sense of reassurance from direct contact with birth parents (it sent a clear message that the placement was supported by the original family and showed the child that the adopters felt positively about that family) and that strengthened his or her attachment to the adopters; direct contact gave adopters a sense of security and permanence in the parenting role; and contact generally made a significant difference to birth parents.[8] In a major 1991 survey of adoption and permanent foster care placements cited by Ryburn, contact with the birth family was identified as the single factor able to enhance the stability of placements.[9] Other studies, looking specifically at the relationship between contact and outcome in long-term foster placements, also concluded that well-being was higher and breakdown rates either the same or lower if children remained in contact with their natural parents.[10]

5.9   The benefits of post-adoption contact, however, were found to run deeper than those more obvious and direct effects on the child. Lowe and Murch recognised that in some families contact 'actually enhanced the adopters' relationship with the child and

---

1   N Lowe and M Murch, op cit, at p 278.

2   Ibid, at p 280.

3   Ibid, at p 323.

4   Ibid, at p 324.

5   Ibid.

6   Ibid, at p 325.

7   M Ryburn 'In Whose Best Interests? Post Adoption Contact with the Birth Family' [1998] CFLQ 53.

8   Ibid, at 59.

9   J Rowe and J Thoburn, in J Fratter et al *Permanent Family Placement: A Decade of Experience* (BAAF, 1991), chs 1–3.

10   The following research was cited by J Thoburn *Review of Research Relating to Adoption* (DoH, 1990) at p 35: D Fanshel and E Shinn *Children in Foster Care – A Longitudinal Study* (Columbia University Press, 1978); D Berridge and H Cleaver *Foster Home Breakdown* (Blackwell, 1987) and J Thoburn and L Rowe *Evaluating Permanent Substitute Family Placement for Children in Care who have Special Needs* (UEA, 1989).

their feelings of security as parents',[1] although, in others, it enabled birth parents to communicate their disapproval of the adoption and thus risked usurping the parental status of the adopters. Some adopters in the study perceived contact as harmful and a hindrance to the formation of new attachments.[2] Others were against it in order to protect the child from carrying a 'burden of responsibility' for birth parents.[3] Yet others believed that children needed contact with the birth family to assure themselves that siblings who remained with that family were not in danger.[4] Fratter's 1996 study, *Adoption with Contact*, concluded that a majority of adoptive parents felt their identity as parents had been enhanced through greater openness and contact.[5]

5.10 Significant among Lowe and Murch's conclusions were findings as to the several conditions that needed to be in place in order for adopters to feel comfortable with contact and to see the benefits of it for their adopted children. First, birth relatives needed to approve of the adoption and not make destructive comments to the children about it; secondly, adoptive parents needed to accept that the child not only had birth relatives but might need to see them and, to some extent, be prepared to admit them to the family; thirdly, although contact could be threatening where there was already insecurity about the adoption, it could work well where the birth parent agreed to the adoption, believing it in the child's best interests, and was involved in planning for the child; and fourthly, adopters themselves needed to be positive about contact and recognise its value not only for the child but for the family as a whole.[6]

5.11 Further findings by Lowe and Murch indicated that although most families had some degree of contact the types of arrangements varied enormously – from fortnightly visits to annual letters[7] – and the whole issue of maintaining direct contact between birth and adoptive families was a complex one. For many children in the study, direct contact was not deemed appropriate. Instead, letter-box contact was arranged, sometimes in an 'idiosyncratic or ad hoc way', sometimes involving letters written wholly by the adopters on behalf of the children, and sometimes consisting of emotive letters and inappropriate material from birth families.[8] The authors' anecdotal evidence from both social welfare professionals and adopters indicated a web of unresolved problems and varying sets of criteria for the establishment and successful working of contact agreements. The process of negotiating the agreement was a long one and, according to many families, often involved local authority social workers going to some length to 'get a good deal' for birth parents.[9] This was seen as particularly so where the child's social worker was also allocated to the birth family, and led to the claim by some adopters that professionals were overly sympathetic to that family – particularly where children had been removed against the parents' will. Contact was sometimes seen as a means of alleviating that loss and thus

---

1   N Lowe and M Murch, op cit, at p 324, and J Fratter *Adoption with Contact* (BAAF, 1996) at pp 23 and 235.
2   N Lowe and M Murch, op cit, at p 281.
3   Ibid, at p 282.
4   Ibid, at p 285.
5   BAAF, 1996, at p 237.
6   N Lowe and M Murch, op cit, at p 324.
7   Ibid, at p 294.
8   Ibid, at pp 301–311.
9   Ibid, at p 313.

as serving the interests of the birth parents rather than the child.[1] Granting contact for their benefit rather than the child's was found by the authors to have 'negative implications later', to have 'caused conflict at other levels'[2] and to have actually been detrimental to the child.[3]

5.12   Just as significantly, some prospective adopters felt they were pressured to agree to contact plans as a condition of approval[4] (some agencies claimed that once the child was placed the adopters started 'backing off') and others argued that contact was used as a bargaining tool to persuade the birth parents to sign the consent form or to deter them from actively opposing the adoption in court.[5] It appeared from the study that the very concept of ongoing contact was used as a means of encouraging birth parents to accept what would otherwise be unacceptable, with adopters simply going along with it at the outset. Although a picture of agency encouragement and facilitation tended to emerge from the study, all may not have been quite as it appeared. For example, adopters indicated that direct contact with the immediate birth family was less common for families approved by voluntary (as opposed to statutory) agencies, whereas the responses given by agencies revealed the reverse. The authors were led to query whether 'the different pictures given by adopters and practitioners [are] due to chance, or could it be that agencies are saying one thing and doing another?'[6] Anecdotal evidence from legal practitioners is virtually unanimous in concluding that agencies are unwilling to encourage, support or facilitate contact in the great majority of cases. Some support for that position is found in the study's conclusion, where the authors point out that many agencies regarded supervision as a drain on resources or believed in 'normalisation' thus not building supervision into arrangements.[7]

5.13   Be that as it may, it was apparent from the research that agencies had developed a view that contact should be agreed unless there was actual evidence to the contrary, but quite what that evidence was and whether contact was likely to be pursued despite its existence was one of the tensions uncovered. Fewer than half of the adopters in the study had their contact agreements in writing, yet the authors concluded that written contact agreements were very useful. They were not rigid like a contact order, but could encompass the child's changing needs – perhaps needing contact once settled with the adoptive family or starting off with contact but needing it to tail off.[8] The idea of the New Zealand parenting plan for adoption (discussed later in this chapter) is highly relevant here.[9] Lowe and Murch's exploration of the problems and issues surrounding contact led the authors to the significant overall view that contact had to be governed by the welfare of the child as perceived in his or her particular circumstances, albeit those

---

1   N Lowe and M Murch, op cit, at p 313.
2   Ibid, at p 326.
3   Ibid, at p 313.
4   Note that in the USA, lawyers acting for social services agencies or for birth parents use post-adoption visitation rights as a 'strategy for facilitating a settlement of a termination of parental rights'. See S Katz 'Dual Systems of Adoption in the United States', in S Katz, J Eekelaar and M Mclean (eds) *Cross Currents* (Oxford University Press, 2000) at p 303.
5   N Lowe and M Murch, op cit, at pp 314–317.
6   Ibid, at p 295.
7   Ibid, at p 325.
8   Ibid, at pp 324–325.
9   It should be noted that parenting plans have been developed in this country in relation to negotiating contact after parental separation.

may change from time to time, and that what had to be avoided was the imposition of 'inflexible rules based on doctrinaire policies'.[1] Those findings confirmed the conclusions of others[2] that it was not yet possible to make confident assertions about the benefits of contact *regardless of family circumstances and relationships* but it also endorsed the plea for flexibility which emerged as a significant theme in a concurrent survey of adoptive parents.[3]

Post-adoption contact and the courts

5.14   Post-adoption contact is currently a key element of professional activity in adoption work. However, the process of negotiating a contact agreement can raise certain tensions between agencies and prospective adopters at the outset. The presumption that natural parents will have contact with their children in care[4] requires local authorities to plan for contact. As has already been noted, some adopters feel pressured to agree to contact, thus leading to the assumption that in practice it can be used as a 'bargaining tool' to 'facilitate adoption'. Where agreement has not been successfully negotiated or one of the parties cannot be trusted to keep to the deal, the machinery of the CA 1989 has, in the past, enabled the court to make an order for direct or indirect contact concurrently with an adoption or freeing order and enabled a 'former' parent to apply for leave for contact after adoption.[5] As an interesting point of comparison, it should be noted that a birth mother in the USA[6] who entered an open adoption agreement as consideration for relinquishing her baby to an adoptive couple could have that agreement enforced if a state statute specifically allowed visitation rights. Without such a statutory provision, a judge could use his or her discretionary power to enforce an agreement if it advanced the child's best interests.[7]

5.15   Prior to the CA 1989, the House of Lords held that there was power to impose conditions on an adoption order under s 12(6) of the AA 1976.[8] Subsequently, the primary message from the little case-law that has emerged from the courts[9] was that adopters must be agreeable to contact and should not be ordered to do what they do not wish to do.[10] The judicial view was that the child's interests required that the adopters

---

1   N Lowe and M Murch, op cit, at p 323.
2   D Quinton et al 'Contact with Birth Parents in Adoption – A Response to Ryburn' [1998] CFLQ 349 at 350.
3   Morris *The Adoption Experience: Families who give Children a Second Chance* (Adoption UK, 1999) cited by D Casey and A Gibberd 'Adoption and Contact' [2001] Fam Law 39.
4   CA 1989, s 34.
5   Ibid, ss 8 and 10(9) respectively.
6   There are 51 adoption laws in the USA, one in each American state and the District of Columbia.
7   S Katz 'Dual Systems of Adoption in the United States' in S Katz, J Eekelaar and M Mclean *Cross Currents* (Oxford University Press, 2000) at p 290.
8   See *Re C (A Minor) (Adoption Order: Conditions)* [1989] AC 1 (HL).
9   Note the cases cited and analysed by B Lindley in 'Open Adoption – Is the Door Ajar?' [1997] CFLQ 115 at 126–127.
10   That view was expressed in *Re C* (above) and, following the CA 1989, in *Re T (Adopted Children: Contact)* [1995] 2 FLR 792.

remained in control[1] and that a situation of friction with the birth parents be avoided.[2] Judicial reasoning highlighted the philosophical tensions inherent in the notion of contact co-existing with the secret legal transplant concept of adoption.[3] The culture of permanence, stability and security created by adoption was arguably threatened when contact was imposed rather than agreed. Equally, if contact was so desirable for the child that a contact order was required (and a s 8 contact order can be made only if it is in the child's best interests), the circumstances that also required an adoption order for such a child were bound to be exceptional. Perhaps the real dilemma was summed up by Butler-Sloss LJ (as she then was) in *Re A (A Minor) (Adoption: Contact Order)*,[4] when her Ladyship noted that:

> 'We are moving perceptibly into a new and broader perception of adoption ... The view, however, of open adoption embraced by the experts does not seem to be shared by many prospective adopters ...'

5.16   In the absence of a presumption, is the legal process best placed to deal with such a human and emotional issue as post-adoption contact? Rather than interpret the judicial reluctance to order contact simply as a failure to keep up with current social work practice, it has been viewed as evidence that the law is not needed in dealing with the social factors inherent in post-adoption contact.[5] Judith Masson has expressed the view that an absence of regulation, coupled with consideration of contact as a social problem best managed by social workers rather than as a legal problem to be handled by the courts, has created a situation in which all parties benefit. In her view, adoption agencies are better placed than the courts to facilitate and manage post-adoption contact. Ryburn, however, has argued the reverse. He has urged that courts 'ensure that more rigorous investigations are routinely made' and that there be 'a more exacting examination by the courts' (of care plans which include adoption), and that although efforts should be made to achieve negotiated solutions 'there is still a great deal more the courts could do to secure the welfare of children through sensible, negotiated, post-adoption contact arrangements'.[6] These opinions from two leading scholars illustrate a fundamental dilemma afflicting child and family law generally: should the law be geared to answering problems which are primarily human and social rather than legal? In relation to post-adoption contact, a leaf might be taken from both their books in answer to the key findings of the wealth of academic research on the matter. The Masson approach of less doctrinaire, more objective and workable guidelines might well follow a judicial lead if a

1   See, for example, *Re V (A Minor) (Adoption: Consent)* [1987] Fam 57, sub nom *Re V (A Minor: Dispensing with Agreement)* [1987] 2 FLR 89.
2   *Re C (A Minor) (Adoption Order: Conditions)* [1989] AC 1, per Lord Ackner at 17.
3   In the equivalent of public law adoptions in the USA, post-adoption visitation agreements need statutory authority and judicial approval based on the best interests of the child, and certainly have been enforced. There is recognition in that jurisdiction that children who have been placed in the child welfare system may remember their parents and have had contact with them during their foster-care placement.
4   [1993] 2 FLR 645 at 649–650.
5   J Masson 'Thinking About Contact – A Social or a Legal Problem?' [2000] CFLQ 15 at 28.
6   M Ryburn 'In Whose Best Interests? Post-adoption Contact with the Birth Family' [1998] CFLQ 53 at 67–70.

Ryburn(esque) statutory duty were placed on the court at least to consider the issue of contact whenever an adoption order is made.[1]

5.17 But have the reformers adopted such an approach? Have the complex issues surrounding contact been tackled and the somewhat inconclusive research data incorporated into a sound and workable policy – in the best interests of children?

The reformers' approach

1992 Review of Adoption Law

5.18 The lengthy review of adoption law carried out in 1992 addressed the issue of openness and post-adoption contact as a primary concern.[2] It recognised that:[3]

> 'a child's knowledge of his or her background is crucial to the formation of positive self-identity, and that adoptive families should be encouraged to be open about the child's adoptive status and the special nature of the adoptive relationship.'

5.19 It also recognised that adoption practice had moved towards the retention of some form of contact with birth families, whether by an exchange of cards or by meetings between the child and former parents, grandparents or siblings. Above all, it recognised that the extent to which a particular form of openness was appropriate varied according to the needs of the child in the particular circumstances surrounding the adoption, but that the AA 1976 had, to some extent, precluded such considerations because it had assumed a closed model of adoption. There was no inherent reason, stated the Review, why the complete legal severance model of adoption as under the AA 1976 should 'preclude the possibility of some contact being maintained, nor should it preclude the possibility that there is no contact at all'.[4]

5.20 In terms of developing a new legislative underpinning, such statements were very much in line with the significant, yet still inconclusive, body of academic research on post-adoption contact, and the Review concluded that it could not support a blanket policy in relation to contact.[5] There was, and still is, no solid research data that would support such a policy. As the Review concluded, adoption legislation should not 'prescribe the circumstances under which contact should or should not take place after an adoption or placement order has been made, nor the form contact should take'.[6] But, in the authors' view highly significantly, the Review reasoned that it was important for proper consideration to be given to the question of contact at the time an order was made. It thus recommended that:

> 'adoption legislation should re-affirm the court's powers to make contact orders [and] the court should also have a duty to consider making a contact order; this would follow from a duty to consider the range of powers available under the Children Act 1989 and the Adoption

---

1 Note that D Casey and A Gibberd 'Adoption and Contact' [2001] Fam Law 39 at 43 also suggested that the advent of new legislation has provided an opportunity to introduce a statutory obligation to consider the issue of contact.
2 1992 Review of Adoption Law, at paras 4.1–5.8.
3 Ibid, at para 4.1.
4 Ibid, at para 5.1.
5 Ibid, at para 5.2.
6 Ibid, at para 5.3.

Act [with its proposed new section 1, particularly the requirement that the court consider the range of powers available to the court under the Act].'[1]

Adoption: The Future (1993)

5.21   When the Government introduced its 1993 White Paper, those proposals were translated into a need for 'careful judgment about contact' with particular weight given to the views of both the adopters and the child 'so that the prospects of a successful adoption [were] not undermined . . .'.[2] The thrust of argument was clearly in favour of openness, considered both 'sensible and humane', yet only so long as the prospects of a secure and stable adoption were not undermined. It was clearly recognised that the increased average age of children being adopted led to a greater need for consideration of post-adoption contact.

Adoption and a new framework (2000)

5.22   In 2000, the Prime Minister introduced the PIU Report as 'the first step in a long overdue task of reform'. A mere handful of paragraphs was dedicated to the major issue of post-adoption contact and these reiterated, in the main, that research outcomes on contact and adoption were 'mixed and inconclusive',[3] albeit 'adoption with contact [had] become more common' and that local authorities lacked the necessary expertise to deal with the matter, thus leading to inconsistent practice. To gain any real sense of what policy might be in the process of formulation required a reading between the lines. That approach revealed what we can only describe as a retrenchment in relation to contact. Most significantly, the PIU Report voiced concern that 'the prospect of direct contact can adversely impact upon whether a child can be adopted at all', and that while a birth relative might have been unable to work with the local authority there remained 'a belief that they will work with the adoptive family'.[4] The conclusion drawn by the Report in relation to direct contact was that social workers might be setting up contact in the interests of the birth family rather than the long-term interests of the child (a point made in relation to *some* social workers by Lowe and Murch) and that they might be using contact as a negotiating tool (a point also made by the previous authors in relation to *some* social workers). With respect to indirect contact, the PIU Report demonstrated a reluctance to engage with the issues and determinedly focused on some minor negative points (for example, the tensions that could arise between adopted non-siblings in the same household if there were disparate contact arrangements).[5] The complete lack of discussion on the values of *some* form of contact for *some* children in *some* circumstances revealed at best an ambivalence to the value of any form of contact at all.

5.23   The 2000 White Paper did not fare much better, although its rhetoric – 'links with birth families are very important to children'[6] – indicated some awareness that the

---

1   1992 Review of Adoption Law, at para 5.5.
2   *Adoption: The Future*, Cm 2288 (1993) at para 2.6.
3   PIU Report (2000) at para 3.141. It should be noted, however, that neither of the major studies by
     N Lowe and M Murch or J Fratter was cited.
4   Ibid, at para 3.143.
5   Ibid, at para 3.146.
6   *Adoption: A New Approach*, Cm 5017 (December 2000), at para 6.42.

matter was a significant one. But instead of any discussion of proposed policy or legal amendments in relation to contact, the White Paper simply noted that:[1]

> 'draft standards also state that a child's need to maintain links to their birth family including parents, grandparents, brothers, sisters and other significant people should always be considered, and that where appropriate, the local social services authority should make arrangements to meet the lifelong needs of the child.'

In other words, it was proposed to leave one of the most significant issues in adoption today to the realms of regulation.

New Zealand

5.24   It is clearly pertinent to look abroad and compare the Government's approach with that being taken in countries such as New Zealand – described as 'leading Western adoption practice with respect to openness'.[2] That country has embarked upon adoption law reform in an endeavour to bring its 1955 Adoption Act into line with modern life and its very changed attitudes and values. In particular, the reform is seeking to reconcile the widely practised notion of open adoption (in effect, adoption with contact) with the complete legal transference model. In New Zealand 'most adoptions now involve some degree of contact from the beginning of the adoption arrangement',[3] to the extent that birth parents themselves:

> 'select the adoptive parents from a selection of profiles of couples waiting in the pool of prospective adopters. Birth parents are encouraged to meet the adoptive parents, and many make independent arrangements for continuing contact (letters etc) or access (meetings) with the child. A number of community support groups have formed to assist families to maintain open adoption arrangements.'[4]

5.25   In a country where secrecy has become the exception rather than the rule, belief in the benefits of greater openness and contact are widely held. Contact is believed to help the birth mother come to terms with her loss,[5] help the adoptive parents to understand the child and enhance their own security by the knowledge that they have been chosen by the birth parent, and the benefits thus flow on to the child, enhancing his or her psychological security and maintaining knowledge about the original family.[6]

5.26   Consequently, the New Zealand Law Commission recommended that adoption become part of a Care of Children Act (legislation which would encompass the temporary care of children – temporary custody and/or guardianship – at one end of its spectrum, and a reformulated concept of adoption at the other). With an overarching emphasis on the best interests of the child, such a scheme was intended to highlight the availability of all the alternatives to adoption and ease movement between the options. The proposed reformulation of adoption maintains the legal transference concept, albeit in a

---

1   *Adoption: A New Approach*, Cm 5017 (December 2000), at para 6.43.
2   *Adoption and its Alternative – A Different Approach and a New Framework* Report 65 (New Zealand Law Commission, Wellington, New Zealand, 2000) at p 19.
3   Ibid, at p 19.
4   Ibid, at p 39.
5   It is thought that current knowledge about the well-being of the child helps a birth parent to cope with her grief.
6   *Adoption and its Alternative*, op cit, at p 40.

transparent form and highlights that 'the birth family still exists and may have a role in the child's life'.[1] To manifest that in a more concrete way, the scheme proposed that a 'parenting plan' set out the parties' intentions regarding contact at the outset and that an adoption order should, in the future, always be accompanied by such a plan. In that way, the contact issue would always come before the court when an adoption order was being considered. Even so, in the interests of certainty and stability for the child, the Law Commission recommended that the 'parenting plan' not be legally enforceable but, rather, that the resolution of disputes and tensions between the parties over contact should be settled at mediation.[2]

Australia

5.27   In Australia, too, the Law Reform Commission made a primary recommendation that the Adoption of Children Act 1965 (NSW) be rewritten so that adoption would become characterised by openness and thus reflect the contemporary approach to regarding children as individuals with their own rights within the context of adoption.[3] It recommended that legislation should encourage the parties to negotiate a voluntary plan to make arrangements for contact and exchanges of information between the adoptive and birth families[4] and that children 'should have the ability to initiate or sustain contact with their birth parents or members of their family of origin'. Adoption law and practice were to '. . . assist a child in knowing his or her birth family and cultural background, in providing continuing contact with those who are important to his or her well-being, and in accessing and enjoying his or her cultural heritage'.[5] This was translated into the Adoption Act 2000 (NSW) which provided that an adoption plan, agreed to by the parties to the adoption and registered, focus on, *inter alia*, 'the means and nature of contact between the parties and the child', 'the making of arrangements for the exchange of information', and extended to the child's medical background, his or her development and important events in his or her life.[6]

The passage of the Adoption and Children Bill

5.28   The contrast with the UK Government's White Paper is glaring. Where the New Zealand reform proposals and the new Australian law positively embraced the benefits of contact, reform proposals in this country initially addressed the issue both inadequately and negatively. Admittedly, the United Kingdom already had provision for enforcing contact (via a contact order), but, otherwise, by the time the Adoption and Children Bill was ready to be introduced in the House of Commons it was difficult to avoid the view that emphasis on post-adoption contact had been eschewed for pragmatic reasons relating to widening the net of adopters.[7]

---

1   *Adoption and its Alternative*, op cit, at p 45.
2   Ibid, at pp 50–51.
3   Law Reform Commission Report 81 (1997), *Review of the Adoption of Children Act 1965 (NSW)*, Executive Summary.
4   Ibid.
5   Ibid, at paras 2.18 and 2.35.
6   Adoption Act 2000 (NSW), s 46.
7   See the views of S Harris-Short 'The Adoption and Children Bill – A Fast Track to Failure?' [2001] CFLQ 405 at 418–419.

5.29 During the examination of witnesses in the Special Standing Committee on the Bill, the significance of both contact and information was highlighted,[1] although in the end there was little discussion owing to government timetabling.[2] Professor Triseliotis, however, had the opportunity to address two aspects of retaining links with the birth family: he explained these as, first, 'generational continuity' whereby an adopted person had access to their records and, secondly, 'emotional continuity' facilitated by enabling children to maintain some form of contact with family members who may have been emotionally important to them prior to adoption.[3] Such emotional links could not be excised, particularly in older children, and Professor Triseliotis noted that 'some children need to maintain that link and [that] it may have to involve face to face contact periodically . . .'. He opined that 'contact of that sort did not damage the placement or the relationship. Children were aware of the differences between different types of relationships'.[4] In Committee, the Family Rights Group expressed concern that the Bill had failed to recognise the substantial changes that had occurred in knowledge[5] and practice in relation to contact and sought to address MPs on how it might be improved regarding the issue of openness, contact and maintaining connections. In particular, the Group's Memorandum urged that a specific duty be placed on the court to consider, when applying the welfare checklist, whether a contact order should be made at the same time as a placement or adoption order, thus placing contact and openness on the agenda as one of the child's needs.

5.30 Ultimately, little parliamentary time was given over to the issue of post-adoption contact. When raised at all, it was usually in the context of matters such as dispensing with consent,[6] the extension of the definition of harm and access to information, with little discussion of either the amendments introduced on Report or any broader policy directions. It was left to Mr Jonathan Djanogly to note that it needed to be put on record that contact, even in the context of adoption, was the norm – that this was only right and proper and that we should see contact as an issue affecting the vast majority of adopted children and one which it was particularly important to address.[7] In the House of Lords,

---

1   For example, Professors Triseliotis and Jackson, HC Deb, Third Sitting, 21 November 2001, col 134; Memorandum from the Family Rights Group, HC Deb, Fourth Sitting, 21 November 2001, cols 199–200.

2   Mr Jonathan Djanogly noted, on 16 May 2002, at col 954, that contact had been one of the most important matters not discussed at all in Committee despite more letters received on this topic than on any other.

3   HC Deb, 21 November 2001 at col 134. At col 135, Professor Jackson added that this could extend to a wide range of relations and friends. In response, Mr Julian Brazier voiced concern that face-to-face contact could lead to virtually open adoption which, in Australia, he opined, had led to adoptive parents being required to take on occasional face-to-face contact and thus the almost complete collapse of adoption.

4   HC Deb, 21 November 2001, col 134.

5   In HC Deb, 21 November 2001, cols 199–200, the Family Rights Group noted that research was increasingly confirming that the child's relationship with birth parents did not end with adoption, that birth relatives could provide continuity and support for adopted children, and that a child's need for contact would vary over time.

6   In HL Deb, 10 June 2002, col 65, Baroness Howarth of Breckland commented that throughout her career in social services it had always been clear to her that most children would prefer to retain contact with their birth family and that was why she was concerned about the dispensing with consent provisions.

7   HC Deb, 16 May 2002, col 954.

Lord Hunt of Kings Heath gave some indication of broader policy when he drew a distinction between contact orders under s 8 of the CA 1989 in relation to private law cases and those involving children already placed for adoption.[1] In the former situation where there was likely to have been a dispute about contact, Lord Hunt concluded that it was in the child's interests that the leave requirement (in relation to relatives applying for contact[2]) be in place to act as a screening agent. With contact in the context of placement for adoption, however, Lord Hunt described the situation as 'totally different' with 'the end objective [being] separation from his or her family'.[3] Consequently, relatives who had not secured contact to the child via the agency should, he advocated, be enabled to apply for a contact order without the hurdle of the leave requirement.

5.31   In essence, it was envisaged that adoption would continue to operate as a clean break. Tinkering with streamlining leave provisions for relatives and a call to have regard for the child's existing relationships in the context of welfare indicated some recognition that the older child may benefit from some 'emotional continuity' with significant others. Very little in the parliamentary debates, however, indicated a major departure from previous policy. Nonetheless, the mood throughout the passage of the Bill did creep inexorably towards greater openness, albeit accompanied by an undercurrent of fear that too 'open' a policy was not readily reconcilable with attempts to widen the net of potential adopters.

ACCESS TO INFORMATION AND CONFIDENTIALITY

5.32   Post-adoption contact is part of the much wider modern concept of openness in adoption. The term 'open adoption', is now used to describe the many adoptions where there is an exchange of information and/or contact between the birth and adoptive families. It characterises the situation where the child has known from an early age that he or she is adopted; both the child and adoptive parents have identifying information about the natural parents; and they in turn have identifying information about the adoptive parents and child. However, adoption has not always been so open.

Openness and the Children Acts of 1975 and 1989

5.33   Whereas secrecy had once been the key, with legislation formulated on the assumption that there would be no contact at all in the interests of the three parties to the adoption,[4] the Children Act 1975 began the process of openness. That Act introduced measures which enabled an adopted person, on attaining the age of 18, to access original

---

1   HL Deb, 30 October 2002, col 219. Discussion took place in the context of the amendment to the leave provisions enabling relatives to seek contact with a child whom an agency is authorised to place for adoption.

2   Under s 10(9) of the CA 1989.

3   HL Deb, 30 October 2002, col 219. C Smith and J Logan in 'Adoptive Parenthood as a "Legal Fiction" – Its Consequences for Direct Post-Adoption Contact' [2002] CFLQ 281 at 286, noted that the principles governing post-divorce contact were not appropriate to post-adoption contact because of the way in which adoption changes the status of both the child and birth parents.

4   It was considered that the adoptive parents might be harassed by the birth family, that contact would not be in the child's interests, and that the birth mother might have agreed to the adoption on the basis that she could conceal the fact of the birth from everyone.

birth records and thus trace his or her birth parents.[1] This was inspired by the Houghton Committee in 1972, which recognised the need for freer access to background information and greater openness in order to develop an adopted person's positive sense of identity.[2] This peep under the veil of secrecy was also extended to birth parents by the CA 1989, and a legislative framework for an adoption contact register was established, thus enabling birth relatives to have their details recorded and information passed on to the adopted person if he or she had given notice of a wish for contact.[3]

5.34 The days of 'Secrets and Lies'[4] are clearly over. With the majority of children adopted today being older and thus already knowing the identity of their parents, the need for subterfuge and cover-ups has largely gone. An adoption order cuts legal links with the birth family but does not necessarily cut any emotional, psychological or memory links. A substantial number of children adopted from care will be fully aware of their parents' identities and, of course, are very likely to have some form of contact with them. At the same time, the birth mothers of adopted children are highly unlikely today to feel the pressures of a social stigma which previously compelled single mothers to seek to conceal the fact of a birth. But even if that were so, the system under the AA 1976 did not enable birth relatives to express an objection to an adopted person receiving identifying information about them and to have that taken into account. As was noted in the Special Standing Committee on the 2002 Bill, '. . . after 1975, one adopted a child on the basis that at some point the child would find out – whereas before they would not have found out'.[5]

The background to reform

5.35 Access to adoption information is undoubtedly a complex issue. A major overhaul of adoption law in the twenty-first century would have been expected to recommend greater facilitation of information gathering in the interests of a child's right to knowledge of its origins and increased emphasis on openness in practice, albeit the reformed law was to retain its guillotine effect of completely severing legal ties between birth parents and children.

5.36 The 1993 White Paper considered it both 'sensible and humane to encourage an open approach',[6] and the 1992 Review expressed concern that the legal process of adoption was often unnecessarily secretive. There was clearly a 'need to encourage greater disclosure': many adopted people, the Review claimed, retained an interest in their own origins, family history and background, and many birth mothers felt the need to find out what had happened to an adopted child, often to ease the pain and sense of loss they had

---

1   AA 1976, s 51.

2   In this context, see *Gunn-Russo v Nugent Care Society and Secretary of State for Health* [2001] EWHC Admin 566, [2002] 1 FLR 1, where a middle-aged woman, adopted as a baby and with both adoptive and natural parents dead, desperately sought any remaining morsels of information about her birth family and heritage.

3   AA 1976, s 51A, as inserted by CA 1989, Sch 10, para 21.

4   The name of the box office hit film and used by S Cretney in *Family Law* (Sweet & Maxwell, 2000) at pp 328–329.

5   Per Mr Djanogly, HC Special Standing Committee, 20 November 2001, at p 21.

6   *Adoption: The Future*, Cm 2288 (1993) at para 4.20.

experienced.[1] At the same time, some birth mothers could be gravely distressed when a child contacted them. But while the Adoption Contact Register provided a confidential way for birth parents to assure an adopted person that contact would be welcome, it did not enable registration of a wish that they not be contacted. The Review had thus recommended that birth parents and other relatives be given the opportunity to make any objection clear[2] and the 1993 White Paper confirmed that it would include a provision for recording a wish not to be contacted.[3] By those means, it was intended to afford a degree of protection to the birth mothers who maintained their desire for complete confidentiality and who wished the adoption to remain in the past. Their adult adopted children would have had to be content with non-identifying information.

5.37 The reformers of the 1990s also addressed the question of how far agencies should be permitted to assist people in the process of tracing and how access to agencies' records should be further regulated. Their recommendations would have given agencies the power, if not the duty, to assist birth relatives in tracing an adult adopted child,[4] and it was noted as essential that adoptive parents be given as much information as possible and be encouraged to make it available to the child. The 1992 Review and subsequent White Paper regarded the area as one of particular sensitivity, closely linked to questions of rights of access to identifying information about others.[5] A particular problem was that adopted adults often wanted to identify and trace other members of their birth family, such as siblings, yet could be denied the chance of even knowing whether that person would welcome contact.[6] Providing that opportunity had to be set against the assurances of confidentiality given at the time of the adoption. Provision for agencies to have the power to contact an adopted person or birth relative was considered largely to obviate the need for allowing adopted people direct access to identifying information held on agency records, but it was intended to retain the adopted adult's right to apply to the Registrar General for a copy of the full birth certificate containing identifying information about birth parents.[7]

5.38 In contrast, the 2000 reformers did not place review of access to information very highly on their agenda, albeit their remit included building on past research and

---

1   The 1992 Review of Adoption Law at para 31.4 recognised that pain and bitterness was often expressed by mothers who had felt they were given little or no choice about the adoption of their child in the social and economic climate of the time.

2   1992 Review of Adoption Law at para 31.5.

3   *Adoption: The Future*, Cm 2288 (1993) at para 4.22.

4   For example, the Review recommended that agencies have the power to contact the adopted person on the birth relative's behalf, give identifying information about the adopted person to a responsible tracing agency and that the Registrar General have the power to disclose 'no contact' registrations to tracing and intermediary organisations on request (paras 31.7 and 31.8).

5   1992 Review of Adoption Law at para 35.3. The Data Protection Act 1984 and the Access to Personal Files Act 1987, which allowed a person access to information about himself, applied to social work records but not to adoption. The Review recommended that those provisions apply equally to adoption records, subject to the normal restrictions. Both the 1992 Review and the 1993 White Paper had recommended that provisions of the Data Protection Act 1984 and the Access to Personal Files Act 1987 should apply by and large to adoption records.

6   See *Gunn-Russo v Nugent Care Society and Secretary of State for Health* [2001] EWHC Admin 566, [2002] 1 FLR 1.

7   *Adoption: The Future*, Cm 2288 (1993) at para 4.24. The CA 1989 had amended s 51 of the AA 1976 so as to require those who were adopted before 12 November 1975 and who wished to obtain information about birth records to attend a counselling interview before being given information.

recommendations. The Prime Minister's Review (the PIU Report) noted only that counselling about access to information was given a low priority by local authorities[1] and that services in relation to access to birth records were inconsistent on the part of both local authorities and the courts. Nonetheless, the 2000 White Paper's summary of one of its objectives – 'to provide adopted people with access to information about their history'– implied a more thorough overhaul of the law, and recommendations were made.

5.39   The White Paper stated that 'all adopted people should be able to find out about their family history if and when they wish to do so'[2] and that the Government would legislate with respect to what agency files contained and the circumstances in which adopted people would have access to the information. Nothing prepared the public for one of the dramatic changes revealed in the Adoption and Children Bill, albeit the Select Committee ultimately succumbed to pressure and reversed that change. Consideration of some aspects of that the debate is both illuminating and instructive with respect to the current concept of openness in adoption from a governmental perspective.

The passage of the Bill

5.40   While anticipating openness and an exchange of information in the vast majority of cases, the Bill introduced a provision to restrict access to that information which would enable an adopted person to obtain a certified copy of his birth record.[3] Disclosure of this 's 76 information' was to be at the discretion of the adoption agency where it was considered appropriate, and would not occur other than in 'prescribed circumstances', where there was an effective objection in place.[4] In other words, the basic right of an adult adopted person to obtain an accurate copy of his or her birth record had been removed. The rationale was that in a very small minority of cases birth parents were put in danger by an adopted adult intent on causing harm.[5] None of the witnesses appearing before the Special Standing Committee could understand or explain this approach. Professor Triseliotis, giving evidence to the Committee, claimed that the changed position 'came out of the blue' without prior consultation and that it implied that adopted people were second-class citizens. Birth parents, he said, should not have the right to protect their identity from their adopted children.[6] It was claimed that all voluntary organisations opposed the move and considered it a retrograde step,[7] and that no one was really 'for the proposal'.[8] BAAF's memorandum to the Special Standing Committee noted that, although the PIU Report pointed to inconsistencies between agencies with

---

1   Paragraph 3.138. The 2000 White Paper, *Adoption: A New Approach*, Cm 5017, at para 6.46,
     subsequently stated that legislation would allow bodies other than approved voluntary adoption
     agencies to provide birth records counselling for adopted people.
2   *Adoption: A New Approach*, Cm 5017 (December 2000) at para 6.44.
3   Clause 54(4)–(5). At HC Deb, 16 May 2002, col 1011, Mr Tim Loughton noted that 'for some
     extraordinary reason, which we have still not fathomed, the government actually proposed a
     retrogressive step: to deny people the right of access to information to which they had been entitled
     since 1976 under the Adoption Act 1976'.
4   Clause 58.
5   As in *R v Registrar General, ex parte Smith* [1991] 1 FLR 255, where a mentally disordered person
     threatened the birth mother, thus showing that, in some cases, disclosure could be dangerous.
6   HC Special Standing Committee, 21 November 2001, at col 126.
7   Ibid, per Professor S Jackson, at col 129.
8   Ibid, per Professor J Triseliotis, col 129.

respect to information provision, there was 'never any suggestion that the law should be amended to restrict access to birth record information' and that, in light of the fact that adopted people had valued that right and that the majority of birth parents had welcomed an approach,[1] 'it was hard to understand what [had] led to the inclusion in the new provisions in the Bill'.[2] BAAF concluded by strongly recommending that the right of adopted adults to have access to their original birth certificates be retained.

5.41   The weight of all those representations was not in vain. The Government had a change of heart and, by 10 January 2002, adopted adults had regained the right to information enabling them to acquire a copy of their birth certificates, albeit from the adoption agency[3] rather than the Registrar General.[4] In exceptional circumstances the Registrar General would have recourse to the High Court. The U-turn appeared to be complete and the adopted person's right to knowledge of his or her background and origins had won out in the Bill as amended in Committee. But greater change was urged and further debate ensued on the issues of retrospectivity and mandatory 'telling'.

5.42   As has been seen, the post-War years witnessed a tremendous increase in the numbers of mothers pressured by fear of social stigma into giving up an illegitimate child for adoption. During the Report stage of the Bill, the Government was urged to have regard for this 'forgotten generation of birth mothers'[5] by granting them retrospective rights to seek information about their adopted children, but this all-encompassing view was quashed by the Minister, Ms Jacqui Smith, on the basis of the practical difficulties, indeed 'massive problems', it would pose for agencies, and the consequent fear of raising hopes and expectations unrealistically. While the Bill focused generally on older children who already knew their parents before they were adopted, an amendment was urged to ensure that *all* adopted children – particularly those adopted as babies and very young children – would be told of their adoption when they reached adulthood. This would mean imposing a duty on the State to be the information provider for those who had not already been told, in the interests of their human rights, and as a last resort.[6] Again, the Minister remained unimpressed, and while agreeing that information provision was crucial, she assured Parliament that new guidance, to encourage agencies to help birth parents and adopted people, would remedy current inconsistent practices.[7]

---

1   Professor Triseliotis had noted, at col 129, that in a current study, 94 per cent of birth mothers who had been sought by their adopted children were pleased or very pleased that they had done so. Only an insignificant number had doubts.

2   Memorandum from BAAF, HC Special Standing Committee, 20 November 2001, at col 41.

3   Who would have to seek the High Court's permission not to disclose.

4   The Minister of State, Department of Health, Ms Jacqui Smith, on 10 January 2002, at cols 739–740, stated that under the amended clause an adopted adult would retain the right to access to information that he needed to enable him to obtain a copy of his birth certificate. The route of access would be through the adoption agency. The Minister suggested that this provision would broadly replicate yet improve on the legal position under the 1976 Act.

5   HC Deb, 16 May 2002, col 1012, per Mr Tim Laughton, who also noted that women in Canada, New Zealand and Australia had long ago been granted access to birth records and that, in relation to siblings, research indicated that the loss of a sibling could involve the loss of 'support in adversity, the loss of a shared history, the loss of a sense of kinship and the loss of a resource for the individual's development and identity'.

6   HC Deb, 16 May 2002, cols 1012–1015.

7   Ibid, cols 1018–1019.

5.43 That the issues remained contentious and of great significance was evidenced by the ongoing debate in the House of Lords,[1] but ultimately the matter comes down to one of common sense. It is unsurprising that research evidence[2] suggests that discussion about their adoption is both more important, yet more difficult, with older children.[3] It is also unsurprising that good preparation and continued post-adoption support are considered vital if adoptive parents are to maintain an empathy with adopted children and their birth families in order 'to keep open channels of communication that are clear and responsive'.[4] The goals of the reform are clearly to achieve a sense of emotional and generational continuity, with openness across the adoption process being the key to their achievement.

---

1   For example, HL Deb, 16 October 2002, cols 242–249.

2   See Feast and Howe 'Talking and Telling' in A Douglas and T Philpot (eds) *Adoption – Changing Families, Changing Times* (Routledge, 2002) at p 139.

3   Feast and Howe (above) note that difficulties stem from the problems associated with talking about past abuse and neglect and those associated with establishing secure and open relationships with children whose emotional development may have been disturbed and upset in the years prior to their placement.

4   Feast and Howe (above) at p 145.

Chapter 6

THE NEW LAW – AN OVERVIEW

INTRODUCTION

6.1   Cross-matching the recognised need for changes in adoption law and the Government's reform proposals against the legislation that ultimately gained Royal Assent constitutes a fascinating insight into family law-making. The need for legislative reform had been overwhelming, not least because of changing social factors and a changing social climate. Adoption had clearly moved from being a provider of babies and thus a creator of traditional nuclear families to being a central part of childcare strategy. It had become the ultimate provider of stability and permanence for children unable to live with natural parents. The recognition that a growing number of children in care were simply languishing there provided the final prompt to drag adoption law into the twenty-first century.

6.2   But have the stated objectives been met? Do we now have legislation able to 'see vulnerable children safe in permanent families',[1] while at the same time effecting a proper balance between the three sets of interests in the adoption triangle? Does the new legislation address and accommodate the particular needs of those 'vulnerable children' yet sit neatly and consistently within the broad sweep of family and child law? Do we now have a 'new approach to adoption'?[2]

6.3   The answer is: 'yes, in part'. The outcome of over a decade of consultation, Government initiatives, White Papers, and draft Bills has resulted in some substantial changes, but others are tinged with caution and an apparent reluctance to dig deep into the nation's purse. While there is no doubt that some of the changes are welcome – for example, extending the range of orders for permanence, ensuring the enhancement of adoption support services, granting unmarried couples the right to make a joint application for adoption – and that a real attempt has been made at tackling the many pitfalls of inter-country adoption, there remain substantial challenges in ensuring that the ACA 2002 brings about the major changes of emphasis originally envisaged.

---

1   The words of the Prime Minister in his Foreword to *Adoption: A New Approach*, Cm 5017 (December 2000).
2   Ibid.

BRIEF SUMMARY OF THE MAJOR PROVISIONS OF THE ADOPTION AND CHILDREN ACT 2002

Welfare

Paramountcy

6.4 One of the most radical changes is the alignment of the Act with s 1 of the CA 1989. Section 1(1) and (2) of the ACA 2002 provide that whenever a court or adoption agency is coming to a decision regarding adoption, the child's welfare, throughout his or her life, is the paramount consideration. The child's welfare as the paramount consideration thus extends to dispensing with parental consent.

Non-delay and non-intervention

6.5 As in the CA 1989, the non-delay[1] and non-intervention principles[2] are considerations the court must take into account.

Welfare checklist

6.6 A 'welfare checklist' is provided in s 1(4). That list encompasses the child's ascertainable wishes and feelings, his or her particular needs, the life-long effect of becoming an adopted person, characteristics such as age, sex and background including harm (within the meaning of the CA 1989) and his or her relationship with relatives and other significant individuals. Consideration must be given to the ability and willingness of relatives (including the child's mother and father) or others, as carers, their wishes and feelings regarding the child and the likelihood and value of any ongoing relationship they may have with the him or her.

Other characteristics

6.7 Section 1(5) requires the adoption agency to consider the religious, racial, cultural and linguistic factors pertaining to the child, and the court to consider the whole range of orders available to it (including those under the CA 1989).[3]

Alternative options for permanence

Special guardianship order

6.8 In order to provide a new option for permanence for those children for whom adoption is inappropriate, the ACA 2002 amends the CA 1989 by extending that Act's range of orders to include a special guardianship order.[4] Certain individuals are entitled to apply[5] and the effect of the order is to enable the special guardian to exercise a limited form of parental responsibility (to the exclusion of other holders of parental

---

1   Section 1(3).
2   Section 1(6).
3   Ibid.
4   Section 115, inserting s 14A after s 14 of the CA 1989.
5   CA 1989, s 14A(5), as amended.

responsibility, primarily birth parents).[1] Before making a special guardianship order, the court is under a duty to consider whether or not a contact order should also be made.[2] It should also be noted that, when considering making a special guardianship order, the child's welfare will be the court's paramount consideration, and the welfare checklist in s 1 of the CA 1989 will apply.

Extended residence order

6.9　The Act amends the CA 1989 to provide that a residence order, made in favour of any person who is not a parent or guardian of the child, may continue in force until the child reaches the age of 18.[3]

Parental responsibility for step-parents

6.10　The Act amends the CA 1989 by enabling the acquisition of parental responsibility by step-parents, and follows the legislative pattern set out for unmarried fathers in that Act.[4] In order to boost alternatives to adoption, the step-parent (a person married to the child's parent, but not the cohabiting partner of the child's parent) may acquire parental responsibility for the child by agreement with the parent or, if both the natural parents have parental responsibility, then by the agreement of both.[5] In the alternative, the court may make a parental responsibility order in favour of the step-parent.[6]

Local authority foster parents

6.11　Local authority foster parents can now apply for a s 8 order (including residence) after the child has lived with them for one year.[7] This will include requesting an extended residence order. Such foster parents may also apply for a special guardianship order as of right if the child has lived with them for at least a year.[8]

Consent to adoption

Parental consent

6.12　The consent of each parent with parental responsibility is required before the court may place the child for adoption[9] or make an adoption order.[10] Consent[11] can also take the form of 'advance consent',[12] whereby a parent who consents to his or her child being placed for adoption may also consent to the making of a future adoption order. The

---

1　CA 1989, s 14C(1)(b), as amended.
2　Ibid, s 14B(1), as amended.
3　Section 114, amending s 12 of the CA 1989.
4　Section 112, amending s 4 of the CA 1989.
5　CA 1989, s 4A(1)(a), as amended.
6　Ibid, s 4A(1)(b), as amended.
7　Ibid, s 10 is amended by Sch 3 to the ACA 2002 to include a new subsection (5A).
8　Ibid, s 14A(5)(d), as amended.
9　Section 19(1).
10　Section 47(2).
11　Defined in s 52(5).
12　Section 20; this is also subject to the provisions of s 52.

parents may withdraw their consent to the child's placement at any time until the application for the adoption order has been made.

Consent and the unmarried father

6.13   Only a parent with parental responsibility has the right to consent.[1] Thus, the unmarried father will acquire that right only when he gains parental responsibility by being registered as the child's father, either by agreement with the mother or by court order.[2]

Withdrawal of consent

6.14   Once an application for an adoption order has been made, any consent that has been given with respect to the placement of a child for adoption or any advance consent cannot be withdrawn.[3] Leave to oppose the adoption order can then be given only when the court is satisfied that there has been a change of circumstances since the consent was given or the placement order made.[4]

Dispensing with consent

6.15   There are two grounds only for dispensing with a parent's or guardian's consent to the child being placed for adoption or to the making of an adoption order: either that person cannot be found or is incapable of giving consent,[5] or the welfare of the child requires consent to be dispensed with.[6] It should be noted that the welfare checklist in s 1(4) applies to dispensing with parental consent.

Placement for adoption

6.16   There are two routes for placement. The first is placement with consent, and the second is by means of a placement order. The issue of parental consent is now accelerated so as to be secured before the child is placed with prospective adopters.

Placement with consent

6.17   An adoption agency may place a child for adoption once each parent has given consent[7] or 'advanced consent'.[8] Placement may be with the prospective adopters identified in the consent or those chosen by the agency.[9]

---

1   Section 52(6).
2   CA 1989, s 4, as amended by ACA 2002, s 111.
3   Section 52(4).
4   Section 47(7).
5   Section 52(1)(a).
6   Section 52(1)(b).
7   In accordance with s 52.
8   Section 20.
9   Section 19(1)(a) and (b).

The placement order

6.18   A placement order[1] authorises the local authority to place a child for adoption, but only where each parent consents and has not withdrawn consent, or parental consent should be dispensed with,[2] and the child is subject to a care order or the court is satisfied that the conditions in s 31(2) of the CA 1989 are met.[3] The making of the placement order will also require the court's consideration of the s 1 welfare principles.

6.19   Where a child is subject to a care order, or a care order is made at the same time as a placement order, the care order does not have any effect while the placement order is in force.[4] Equally, any s 8 order under the CA 1989 or any supervision order ceases to have effect once a placement order is made.[5]

6.20   A placement order may be revoked.[6]

Parental responsibility during placement

6.21   Parental responsibility for the child is given to the agency[7] or prospective adopters[8] (while the child is placed with them) whether the placement is via s 19 or a placement order is in force.[9] The agency is empowered to determine the extent to which the parental responsibility of the natural parents (which continues until the adoption order is made), or prospective adopters, is to be restricted.[10]

Contact during placement

6.22   Once an agency is authorised to place a child for adoption, any provision for contact under the CA 1989 ceases to have effect[11] and a free-standing application can be made under the ACA 2002.[12] The court may then make a contact order (with any conditions it considers appropriate[13]) or authorise the agency to refuse contact between the child and a named person. Before making a placement order, the court is under a duty to consider arrangements for contact.[14]

Removal

6.23   Where a child is placed for adoption, he may not be removed from the prospective adopters even though the parent may have withdrawn consent.[15] Where the child is being accommodated   pending   a   placement   order,   he   may   be   removed   from   that

---

1   Defined in s 21(1).
2   Section 21(3).
3   Section 21(2)(a) and (b).
4   Section 29(1).
5   Section 29(2).
6   Section 24.
7   Section 25(2).
8   Section 25(3).
9   Section 25(1).
10   Section 25(4).
11   Section 26(1).
12   Section 26(3).
13   Section 27(5).
14   Section 27(4).
15   Section 30.

accommodation only with the court's leave (or by the authority);[1] but where he is being accommodated and consent to placement under s 19 has been withdrawn, he must be returned to the parent (unless an application for a placement order is made or is pending).[2]

6.24   Where a child has been placed for adoption under s 19 and then consent for the placement has been withdrawn, the prospective adopters must return the child to the agency.[3] But where a placement order has been made, only the local authority can remove the child[4] and there is no provision for parents to have the child returned to them as of right. Where the court has refused a placement order, the prospective adopters must return the child on a date determined by the court.[5]

6.25   Where an application for adoption has been made, the child may be removed only with leave of the court.[6]

The adoption order

The applicants – status, age and domicile

6.26   In a fundamental break with the past, applications for adoption may be made jointly by either a married or an unmarried couple (whether of different sexes or the same sex living in an enduring family relationship),[7] or otherwise by a single person,[8] a step-parent, or the partner of a child's parent.[9] The ACA 2002 continues the policy of imposing restrictions as to age and domicile on the eligibility of those who may adopt.[10]

Preliminaries to making an adoption order

6.27   In an agency adoption,[11] the child must have lived with the applicants for 10 weeks before the adoption application is made.[12] In a non-agency case involving a step-parent or partner of the child's parent, the time required is a continuous preceding period of 6 months[13] and, in the case of local authority foster parents, a continuous period of one year is required.[14] In other non-agency cases, where relatives are concerned for example, the child must have made his or her home with them for a cumulative 3 years during the 5 years preceding the application.[15]

---

1   Section 30(2).
2   Section 31(2).
3   Section 32.
4   Section 34.
5   Section 33(2).
6   Section 37(a).
7   Section 49, subject to restrictions in s 50. 'Couple' is defined in s 144(4).
8   Section 49, subject to restrictions in s 51.
9   Section 51(2), and if the two are a couple within the meaning of s 144(4).
10   Sections 49–51.
11   That is, where the child is placed with the applicants by an adoption agency.
12   Section 42(2).
13   Section 42(3).
14   Section 42(4).
15   Section 42(5).

6.28   In an agency case, the adoption agency must submit a report which addresses the suitability of the applicants and welfare issues in relation to the child. Prospective adopters wishing to adopt jointly will have to demonstrate that they have a stable and lasting relationship.

6.29   There are three alternative conditions necessary for the making of an adoption order:[1]

(a)   the consent condition;[2]
(b)   the placement condition;[3] or
(c)   the child in either Scotland or Northern Ireland must be free for adoption.[4]

Contact

6.30   There is an express duty on the court before making an adoption order, to consider whether there should be arrangements for allowing any person contact with the child.[5]

Status of the adopted child

6.31   The adopted child is to be treated as if he or she were born to the adopters or adopter[6] and, if he or she is adopted by a couple or one of a couple, is to be treated as the child of that relationship.[7] This recognises the status of a child in a partner adoption, for example, under s 51(2).

Contact

Contact upon placement

6.32   Once an adoption agency is authorised to place a child for adoption, any provision for contact under the CA 1989 ceases[8] and from then on an application for contact can be made only under s 26 of the ACA 2002. Section 26 confers on the court the power to make an order requiring the person with whom the child lives or is to live to allow the child to visit or stay with the person named in the order, or for the person named in the order and the child otherwise to have contact.[9]

Post-adoption contact

6.33   The court is under a duty, before making an adoption order, to consider whether there should be arrangements for allowing any person contact with the child. For this purpose, the court must consider any existing or proposed arrangements and obtain any

---

1   Section 47.
2   Section 47(2).
3   Section 47(4).
4   Section 47(6).
5   Section 46(6).
6   Section 67(1).
7   Section 67(2).
8   Section 26(1).
9   Section 26(2)(b).

views of the parties to the proceedings.[1] The parents' right to apply for a s 8 contact order, to be heard concurrently with the adoption application, is explicitly preserved.[2]

6.34   Certain factors in the welfare checklist in the ACA 2002[3] pertain specifically to contact in the context of adoption and it is probable that the court will have regard to them even though, strictly, it is applying the CA 1989 welfare checklist when making a s 8 contact order.[4]

Access to information and confidentiality

The registers

6.35   The Registrar General must continue to maintain the Adopted Children Register[5] and an index of that register.[6]

6.36   The Registrar General must also continue to maintain the Adoption Contact Register,[7] Part I of which is to contain prescribed information about adopted persons who have given notice about their wishes to make contact with birth relatives[8] and Part II of which is to contain the prescribed information about relatives and their wishes with respect to making contact.[9]

Connecting information

6.37   The Registrar General is under a duty to make traceable the connections between the register of live births or other adoption records and any corresponding entry in the Adoption Children Register[10] and disclose that, or any other, information which might enable an adopted person to obtain a certified copy of his or her birth record.[11] In relation to a person adopted before the 'appointed day',[12] the Registrar General may, in exceptional circumstances, be ordered by the court to provide the person with such information.[13] The Registrar General is under a duty to give the connecting birth record information to an adoption agency in respect of a person whose birth record is kept by the Registrar General.[14]

---

1   Section 46(6).
2   Section 26(5).
3   Section 1(4)(c) and (f) recognise such factors as the child's membership of his or her original family, relations with his or her parents, the value of this relationship continuing and the wishes and feelings of the child's relatives, including his or her siblings.
4   See the discussion of the respective welfare checklists in relation to contact in Chapter 11.
5   Section 77(1).
6   Section 78(1).
7   Section 80(1).
8   Section 80(2).
9   Section 81(2).
10   Section 79(1).
11   Section 79(3).
12   Meaning the day appointed for the commencement of the relevant sections, ie ss 56–65.
13   Section 79(4).
14   Section 79(5).

6.38   Section 79 thus governs the disclosure of connecting information and, with s 60, has a part to play in relation to information enabling an adult adoptee to obtain his or her birth record.[1]

Disclosure of information

6.39   The single point of access to identifying information, including the information necessary to access a birth record, is now through the adoption agencies. New provisions[2] deal with the information which the agencies must keep, the information which they must disclose to adopted adults on request, that which they must release to adopted adults and adoptive parents and that which that they may release to adopted adults, birth parents and others.

Confidentiality

6.40   As there is no indication of any wholesale revision of the rules relating to confidentiality, the former law and procedure continue to provide guidance relating to the provision of confidential material to natural parents. There is, however, express provision that adoption proceedings in the High Court or county court may be heard and determined in private.

The Adoption Service

The duties of local authorities

6.41   Each local authority must maintain an adoption service designed to meet the needs of adopted children and their parents and guardians, prospective adopters, and adopted persons, as well as their parents and former parents. Local authorities are also under a statutory duty to provide the requisite facilities for making and participating in the arrangements for the adoption of children[3] and for the provision of specified support services, including financial support.[4]

Adoption support services

6.42   There is a new right to request and receive an assessment of needs for adoption support services for adoptive families and others,[5] and an independent review mechanism to review agencies' determinations with respect to the assessment of prospective adopters and the disclosure of protected information.[6] A new regulatory structure for adoption support agencies requires them to register under Part II of the Care Standards Act 2000.

---

1   It should be noted that s 79 draws a distinction between those persons who were adopted before and those adopted after the commencement of the relevant provisions.
2   Sections 54, 56–65.
3   Whether the adoption is domestic, inter-country, relative, step-parent or with respect to foster carers.
4   Section 3(2)(b).
5   Section 4. Adoptive families will not need to wait until after an adoption order is made.
6   Section 12.

6.43   The new structure for the Adoption Service includes the establishment of the Adoption and Children Act Register[1] to encourage the recruitment of prospective adopters and speed up the matching process, and the national Adoption Standards and Practice Guidance.

Adoption and Children Act Register

6.44   The Act provides for the Secretary of State to establish and maintain an Adoption and Children Act Register for the purpose of suggesting matches between children waiting to be adopted and approved prospective adopters.[2]

Intercountry adoption

International regulation of intercountry adoption

6.45   With respect to England and Wales, the Act largely replaces the Adoption (Intercountry Aspects) Act 1999[3] and enables the United Kingdom to ratify the Hague Convention on Protection of Children and Co-operation in respect of Intercountry Adoption 1993. It places a duty on local authorities to provide an intercountry adoption service and provides for voluntary adoption agencies to apply to operate such a service.

6.46   It provides for a review of the 'designated list' so as to ensure that overseas adoptions will only be recognised in the United Kingdom when the systems in the overseas country meet certain prescribed criteria. In addition, it incorporates the restrictions in the Adoption (Intercountry Aspects) Act 1999 on bringing a child into the United Kingdom for the purpose of adoption by a British resident without complying with prescribed procedures and extends the penalties with respect to a person found guilty of bringing in a child without compliance with those procedures.

Recognition of international adoptions

6.47   Adoption is defined as including a Convention adoption. The effect is to enable such adoptions to be recognised automatically by operation of law, and the adopted person's status is thus automatically recognised in England and Wales.[4] An 'overseas adoption' is also automatically recognised as an adoption order in England and Wales[5] (although it does not necessarily confer UK citizenship upon the child; the 'status' conferred by adoption[6] does not apply for the purposes of the British Nationality Act 1981) and does not need to be repeated domestically in the courts.

6.48   The ACA 2002 allows arrangements to be put in place for the recognition in England and Wales of overseas adoptions.[7] The Secretary of State may make an order

---

1   Sections 125–131.
2   Section 125.
3   Other than ss 1, 2 and 7 and Sch 1.
4   Section 66.
5   Section 66.
6   Under s 67.
7   Section 87.

specifying the adoption orders to be included in a 'designated list' and is able to make regulations setting out the criteria that an overseas adoption must meet to be included.[1]

6.49　There is a new legal mechanism[2] for the High Court to give a direction about whether and to what extent a child adopted in a simple adoption under the Hague Convention should be treated as if he were not the child of any person other than the adopters. It must be recalled that the child's welfare is to be treated as the paramount consideration 'throughout his life'.

Illegal transfers, placements and transactions

6.50　The ACA 2002 re-introduces the prohibition on bringing overseas children into the United Kingdom;[3] makes offences[4] indictable (as well as summary) with a maximum penalty on conviction on indictment of 12 months' imprisonment, an unlimited fine or both;[5] extends and reinforces the former prohibitions on illegal placements and on advertising,[6] including tougher penalties for those seeking to circumvent these safeguards, and introduces criminal sanctions in relation to the preparation and submission of reports which fall outside certain prescribed personnel and circumstances.[7]

6.51　The Act strengthens the safeguards permitting only adoption agencies to make arrangements for adoption and to advertise adoption and has expanded the restrictions on advertising to include both traditional media and electronic means including the internet,[8] together with criminal sanctions. It also imposes express restrictions on the preparation and submission of reports.[9]

6.52　The Act also sets out the restrictions in relation to arranging an adoption imposed on persons who are neither an adoption agency nor acting in pursuance of an order of the High Court.[10] Certain payments or rewards[11] are prohibited in connection with the adoption of a child.[12]

1　Section 87(2) and (3).
2　Section 88.
3　Section 83(1)(a); this is extended to include bringing into the UK a child adopted under an external adoption effected within the previous 6 months.
4　Under ss 83 and 85.
5　Sections 83(8) and 85(6).
6　Sections 123–124.
7　Section 94.
8　Section 123(4) (a).
9　Section 94.
10　Section 92.
11　Section 97(b).
12　Section 95.

Chapter 7

WELFARE

THE FRAMEWORK

7.1   Section 1 of the ACA 2002 is the overarching provision of the Act. It introduces the principles which apply to the exercise of powers under the ACA 2002 and thus provides the power house which drives the whole Act. It is, therefore, essential to have an understanding of how each component of the section's engine is interlinked and how these prime movers work together. We shall refer to the principles collectively as 'the s 1 principles'.

The trigger

7.2   Whenever a court or an adoption agency is 'coming to a decision relating to the adoption of the child', the considerations in s 1 are to apply. This is the trigger event, defined in relation to a court in s 1(7) as including:

(i)   where the orders that might be made by the court include an adoption order (or the revocation of such an order), a placement order (or the revocation of such an order) or an order under s 26 (or the revocation or variation of such an order);[1] and

(ii)   the granting of leave in respect of any action (other than the initiation of proceedings in any court) which may be taken by an adoption agency or individual under this Act (but excluding coming to a decision about granting leave in any other circumstances).

7.3   Although s 1(7) does not expressly refer to 'dispensing with parental consent',[2] it is implicit that the s 1 principles apply to any decision by the court whether or not to dispense with parental consent to adoption.

The paramount consideration

7.4   Section 1(2) provides that 'the paramount consideration of the court or adoption agency must be the child's welfare throughout his life'. The paramountcy principle is, therefore, placed in the forefront of the Act and makes the welfare of the child the

---

1   Under the former law in *Re P (An Infant) (Adoption: Parental Consent)* [1977] Fam 25, the court had held that s 6 of the AA 1976 did not apply to the court's decision on an application to dispense with the parent's consent on the ground that it was being withheld unreasonably under AA 1976, s 16(2)(b). The 'unreasonably withholding consent' ground has now been deleted and any former limitation on the application of the welfare test to the dispensation grounds no longer applies.

2   Earlier Bills had expressly stated that 'references to the court making an order include its dispensing with parental consent'.

pre-eminent consideration outweighing all others.[1] It brings the welfare test into line with the CA 1989.

7.5 Furthermore, it is the welfare of the child 'throughout his life' which must be considered and, therefore, the welfare principle is extended beyond childhood into a lifelong perspective.

Delay

7.6 Section 1(3) applies the general principle that delay is prejudicial to the child's welfare to the decisions of the court or adoption agencies relating to adoption. One of the key aims highlighted in the White Paper, *Adoption: A New Approach*,[2] is the quickening of the pace of the legal process to reduce avoidable delay. The focus for adoption is expressed to be 'to make the legal framework and the legal process as swift as possible'. However, although important, the delay principle remains subordinate to the welfare principle in s 1(2).

Welfare checklist

7.7 Section 1(4) sets out the 'welfare checklist' which is to apply to decisions relating to adoption. Although 'welfare' is not defined in the Act, s 1(4) provides the essential factors to be balanced in the scales. None of the factors is allocated any priority weight and the order has no special significance; nor is the list exhaustive. It is modelled on s 1(3) of the CA 1989, but is tailored to address the particular circumstances of adoption.

Religion, race and culture

7.8 Section 1(5) introduces the child's religious persuasion, racial origin and cultural and linguistic background as considerations for the adoption agency when placing the child for adoption.[3] This falls into line with the duty placed on local authorities by s 22(5)(c) of the CA 1989 when they take any decision about a 'looked after' child, including where such a child should be placed.

Range of powers

7.9 Section 1(6) first sets adoption in its place as one of a 'whole range of powers available . . . in the child's case', which includes not only the powers under this Act but also those under the CA 1989 (including CA 1989, s 8 and s 31 orders).

'No order' principle

7.10 Secondly, under s 1(6), when considering whether to make any order under the Act, the court is not to make an order unless it considers that making the order would be

---

1   *In re D (Adoption: Parents' Consent)* [1977] AC 602 at 638E–F, per Lord Simon.
2   Cm 5017 (December 2000).
3   It gives primary force in the context of adoption to the guidance given in the Department of Health *Children Act 1989 Guidance and Regulations* (HMSO, 1991) Vol 3, paras 2.40 and 2.41, and the Local Authority Circular LAC (98) 20 (28 August 1998) *Adoption – Achieving the Right Balance* paras 11–20 where it relates to 'understanding the needs of children from black and minority ethnic communities'.

better for the child than not doing so. This encapsulates the 'least interventionist' approach[1] and is a critical requirement.

7.11 In determining whether to make any orders under the Act, these elements of s 1 must each be considered, but s 1(2) is the pre-eminent subsection, overriding all others.

The Human Rights Act 1998

7.12 Nor can s 1 of the ACA 2002, taken as a whole, be viewed in isolation. Following the implementation of the Human Rights Act 1998, so far as it is possible to do so, s 1 must be read and given effect to in a way which is compatible with the Convention rights set out in the European Convention on Human Rights:[2]

'The courts will consider each case on its merits, applying clause 1 and having regard to Art 8 of the Convention and Strasbourg case law.'[3]

Therefore, it is important to keep Convention rights (in particular the right to respect for family life enshrined in Art 8) and the jurisprudence of the European Court of Human Rights in the forefront of our minds as we tackle each adoption case.

7.13 Article 8 of the European Convention provides:

'(i) Everyone has the right to respect for his private and family life, his home and his correspondence.

(ii) There shall be no interference by a public authority with the exercise of this right except such as is in accordance with the law and is necessary in a democratic society in the interests of national security, public safety or the economic well-being of the country, for the prevention of disorder or crime, for the protection of health or morals or for the protection of the rights and freedoms of others.'

7.14 The essential object of Art 8 is 'to protect the individual against arbitrary action by public authorities'.[4] It is a qualified right: that is, Art 8(1) sets out the right guaranteed under the Convention, and Art 8(2) sets out the justification upon which the State may interfere. There are three elements to that justification.

(i) The first is that the interference is 'in accordance with the law', ie it has a basis in domestic law, which must be adequately accessible and formulated so as to be reasonably foreseeable and there must be adequate and effective safeguards in that

---

1 *Re O (Care or Supervision Order)* [1996] 2 FLR 755 at 759H–760B, per Hale J (as she then was); *Oxfordshire County Council v L (Care or Supervision Order)* [1998] 1 FLR 70 at 74E, per Hale J (as she then was).

2 Section 3 of the Human Rights Act 1998.

3 HC Deb, 26 March 2001, vol 365, no 59, col 704. When moving the second reading of the Adoption and Children Bill (Bill 66), Mr John Hutton, then Minister of State, Department of Health, highlighted the importance of the European Convention in his statement to Parliament above. Although Bill 66 was superseded by the Adoption and Children Bill (Bill 34), there was considerable overlap between the two Bills, and some of the Government thinking behind Bill 66 remains relevant when considering Bill 34.

4 *Kroon v Netherlands* (1994) 19 EHRR 263, para 31.

law to protect against arbitrary interference.[1] The need for flexibility and discretion is recognised, especially in childcare cases.[2]

(ii)   The second element is that the interference is in pursuit of one of the legitimate aims defined in Art 8(2). In the family law context, the usual justification is either the protection of health or morals or the protection of the rights and freedoms of others which encompasses the interests of the child.[3]

(iii)   The third element is that the interference must be 'necessary in a democratic society': that is to say, the reasons given for the intervention must be 'relevant and sufficient; it must meet a pressing social need; and it must be proportionate to that need'.[4] The more serious the intervention, the more compelling must be the justification.[5]

7.15   Generally, the question which arises is whether the proposed interference with the right to respect for family life is proportionate to the need which makes it legitimate. The principle of proportionality is thus a key force.

7.16   Sections 7 and 8 of the Human Rights Act 1998 have conferred extended powers upon our domestic courts. Section 6 makes it unlawful for a public authority to act in a way which is incompatible with a Convention right. Section 7 enables victims of conduct made unlawful by s 6 to bring court proceedings against the public authority in question. Under s 8, the court may grant such relief or remedy or make such order, within its powers, as it considers just and appropriate. Thus, if a local authority conducts itself in a manner which infringes the Art 8 rights of a parent or child, the court may grant appropriate relief on the application of a victim of the unlawful act. An example of this new statutory power in action is to be found in *Re M (Care: Challenging Decisions by Local Authority)*.[6] An application under s 7 for a violation of Art 8 rights should, however, be regarded as a 'longstop' to be used only after other remedies such as judicial review have first been explored.[7]

PARAMOUNTCY

7.17   As foreshadowed in the White Paper, *Adoption: A New Approach*,[8] the ACA 2002 seeks to align the AA 1976 with the CA 1989, 'to make the needs of children paramount in making decisions about their future'. It does this by importing the paramountcy principle in s 1(1) of the CA 1989 as the overriding principle into s 1(2) of the Act and using the word 'must' to convey the imperative. In so doing, it also brings our adoption law into line with Art 21 of the UN Convention on the Rights of the Child 1989, which

---

1   *Sunday Times v UK* (1979) 2 EHRR 245; *Silver v UK* (1983) 5 EHRR 347; *Malone v UK* (1984) 7 EHRR 14; *Halford v UK* (1997) 24 EHRR 523.

2   *Olsson v Sweden (No 1)* (1988) 11 EHRR 259, para 61; *Eriksson v Sweden* (1989) 12 EHRR 183, paras 59, 60; *Andersson v Sweden* (1992) 14 EHRR 615.

3   *Hendriks v Netherlands* (1983) 5 EHRR 223; *Johansen v Norway* (1996) 23 EHRR 33.

4   *Olsson v Sweden (No 1)* (1988) 11 EHRR 259.

5   *Johansen v Norway* (above).

6   [2001] 2 FLR 1300. See also *C v Bury Metropolitan Borough Council* [2002] 2 FLR 868.

7   *Re S (Minors) (Care Order: Implementation of Care Plan); Re W (Minors) (Care Order: Adequacy of Care Plan)* [2002] 1 FLR 815.

8   Cm 5017 (December 2000), para 4.14.

provides that 'States parties that recognise and/or permit the system of adoption shall ensure that the best interests of the child shall be the paramount consideration'.

7.18 Thus, by making the welfare principle the 'paramount consideration' in s 1(2), the ACA 2002 marks a fundamental departure in concept from the historical tradition of English law, including s 6 of the AA 1976 where welfare was the 'first consideration'. A comparison between the former law and the new law highlights the radical nature of the reform.

Comparison with the former law on adoption: s 6 of the AA 1976

7.19 In stating the former law under s 6 of the AA 1976, Lord Simon, in *In re D (Adoption: Parent's Consent)*,[1] encapsulated the material difference between the two tests:

'In adoption proceedings the welfare of the child is not the paramount consideration (ie outweighing all others) as with custody or guardianship; but it is the first consideration (ie outweighing any other): see Children Act 1975, s 3 (now Adoption Act 1976, s 6) ... The judge must have asked himself, as he should, whether continued access to the father throughout childhood would be of benefit to the child. If the answer were "Yes", it would be a most potent (though not, I think, necessarily a clinching) factor to be weighed against any net benefit to the child from adoption. But if the answer is "No", the net benefit to the child from adoption stands counterbalanced; and though the welfare of the child is not a consideration overriding all others, it is the first consideration, outweighing any other.'

7.20 With the advent of the ACA 2002, the welfare of the child is henceforth the paramount consideration 'outweighing all others' in all adoption proceedings.

The test

7.21 The effect of the ACA 2002 is to make the paramountcy principle of universal application in the majority of cases involving children[2] and, in so doing, is aimed at eliminating any tension which may have been created by the differing tests under the AA 1976 and the CA 1989.[3] Under s 1(2), the welfare of the child now reigns supreme as 'the consideration overriding all others'. It is the clinching factor.

7.22 The origins of the welfare principle in children's cases are to be found in s 5 of the Guardianship of Infants Act 1886, which gave the court jurisdiction, on the application of the infant's mother, to make orders as to custody and access 'having regard to the

---

1   [1977] AC 602 at 638E–F.

2   There are notable exceptions: orders for ancillary financial relief; applications for leave to apply for a s 8 order or to be joined as a party to proceedings under the CA 1989; secure accommodation orders; child support injunctions to restrict publicity; international abduction; non-molestation and occupation orders.

3   For example, in *Re T and E (Proceedings: Conflicting Interests)* [1995] 1 FLR 581, Wall J was concerned with two children, one of whom was the subject of an application for the discharge of a care order, and both were the subjects of freeing applications. He held that the welfare of the child who was the subject of the discharge application should be given paramount consideration and the welfare of the child who was subject only to the freeing application should be given first consideration.

welfare of the child'.[1] The 1886 Act was the crucial turning point and, since Lindley LJ's leading judgment in *Re McGrath (Infants)*,[2] 'welfare' has been the touchstone of judicial decisions in relation to children. In *Re McGrath* Lindley LJ said:

> 'The dominant matter for the consideration of the court is the welfare of the child . . . The welfare of the child is the ultimate guide of the court.'[3]

7.23   In *F v F*,[4] Farewell J said: 'The essential requirements of the infant are paramount' and in *Ward v Laverty and Another*,[5] Viscount Cave said:

> 'It is the welfare of the children, which according to the rules, which are now well accepted, forms the paramount consideration in these cases.'

7.24   In the authoritative words of Lord MacDermott in *J v C*[6] (in respect of the scope and meaning of the words '. . . shall regard the welfare of the child as the first and paramount consideration' in s 1 of the now repealed Guardianship of Infants Act 1925):

> 'Reading those words in their ordinary significance and relating them to the various classes of proceedings which the section has already mentioned, it seems to me that they must mean more than that the child's welfare is to be treated as the top item in the list of items relevant to the matter in question. I think they connote a process whereby, when all the relevant facts, relationships, claims and wishes of parents, risks, choices and other circumstances are taken into account and weighed, the course to be followed will be that which is most in the interests of the child's welfare as that term is now understood. That is the first consideration because it is of first importance and the paramount consideration because it rules upon or determines the course to be followed.'[7]

7.25   According to Lord Dermott's formulation of the principle, welfare is the sole consideration. His formulation, which has become the settled interpretation, rendered

---

1   This research of the authorities is to be found in the first instance decision of Munby J in *Re X and Y (Leave to Remove from Jurisdiction: No Order Principle)* [2001] 2 FLR 118 at 123. Although the actual decision on relocation was disapproved in *Re H (Children) (Residence)* [2001] 2 FLR 1277, his historical review of the welfare test (which was not disapproved) remains of considerable value.

2   [1893] 1 Ch 143.

3   Ibid, at 148 and 149.

4   [1902] 1 Ch 688 at 690.

5   [1925] AC 101 at 108.

6   [1970] AC 668 at 710G.

7   At 713F Lord MacDermott further cites with approval a passage from *In re Adoption Application 41/61 (No 2)* [1964] Ch 48 at 53, per Wilberforce J (who was considering the import of the words from s 7(1)(b) of the Adoption Act 1958 'that the order if made shall be for the welfare of the infant'): 'The passage reads:

> "The section . . . does not prescribe what matters have to be considered in this connection, so that it would seem to me that the court must take into account all the merits and demerits of the alternative proposals as they seem likely to bear upon the child's welfare: not limiting itself to purely material factors, but considering, as they may bear upon the welfare of the infant, such matters as the natural ties of blood and family relationship. The tie (if such is shown to exist) between the child and his natural father (or any other relative) may properly be regarded in this connection, not on the basis that the person concerned has a claim that he has a right, but, if at all, and the extent that the conclusion can be drawn that the child will benefit for the recognition of this tie."

Now that passage was not directed to s 1 of the Act of 1925, but it seems to me to be an apt description of the sort of process which s 1 enjoins, for it too calls for an inquiry as to what will be in the infant's welfare'.

the word 'first' unnecessary and it was thus deleted from s 1(1) of the CA 1989 as otiose.[1] Under s 1(2) therefore, in the final analysis, the court has only to determine the single question: 'what is best for the welfare of the child?'[2]

The relationship between ss 1(2) and 52(1): dispensing with parental consent

7.26 There are now only two grounds for dispensation under s 52(1) of the ACA 2002. Section 52(1)(a) retains the ground that the parent or guardian cannot be found or is incapable of giving consent (formerly s 16(2)(a) of the AA 1976). Section 52(1)(b), however, introduces a new ground: 'the welfare of the child requires the consent to be dispensed with'. Unreasonably withholding consent (formerly s 16(2)(b) of the AA 1976) is no longer a ground for dispensation.

7.27 Under the former adoption law it was established that the determination whether to make an adoption order or a freeing for adoption order involved a two-stage process. The first question was whether adoption was in the best interests of the child. The second and separate question was whether there were grounds to dispense with the parents' consent.[3] Where the ground for dispensation was 'withholding agreement unreasonably', the test was reasonableness and nothing else[4] and, while the welfare of the child was to be taken into account, it was not necessarily the paramount criterion.[5] The 'reasonable' withholding of consent[6] was thus the final redoubt of the natural parents facing the prospect of the extinction of their parental responsibility in the event that an adoption order or freeing order were made.

7.28 Under the ACA 2002, however, when considering the welfare ground for dispensation under s 52(1)(b), the reasons for the distinction between the two questions become lost. Once the court, now applying the paramountcy principle in s 1(2), determines that adoption is in the child's best interests, the scales are heavily loaded in favour of a finding that the welfare of the child requires parental consent to be dispensed with under s 52(1)(b). The two-question approach under the former law is replaced

---

1   Law Com No 172 *Review of Child Law: Guardianship and Custody* (HMSO, 1988) at paras 3.12–3.16. See A Bainham *Children: The Modern Law* (2nd edn, Family Law, 1998), pp 34–35.

2   *Re K (Minors) (Children: Care and Control)* [1977] Fam 179 at 191E–F, per
    Sir John Pennycuick; also *S(BD) v S(DJ) (Children: Care and Control)* [1977] Fam 109 at 114F–G, per Ormrod LJ: 'The question is not what the essential justice of the case requires but what the best interests of the children requires'.

3   *Re E (A Minor) (Adoption)* [1989] 1 FLR 126 at 130D–E, per Balcombe LJ; *Re D (A Minor) (Adoption: Freeing Order)* [1991] 1 FLR 48 at 50B–51B, per Butler-Sloss LJ (as she then was).

4   *Re W (An Infant)* [1971] AC 682 at 699, per Lord Hailsham of St Marylebone LC; *In re D (Adoption: Parent's Consent)* [1977] AC 602 at 625G–H, per Lord Wilberforce.

5   *Re W* (above); *O'Connor v A and B* [1971] 1 WLR 1227; *Re L (A Minor) (Adoption: Statutory Criteria)* [1990] 1 FLR 305.

6   In *Re W* (above), Lord Hailsham emphasised that 'two parents can perfectly come to opposite conclusions on the same set of facts without forfeiting their title to be regarded as reasonable. The question in any given case is whether the parental veto comes within the band of possible reasonable decisions and not whether it is right or mistaken ... There is a band of decisions within which no court should seek to replace the individual's judgment with his own'. It followed that a parent who disagreed with a local authority's opinion that adoption was best for the child's welfare was not necessarily being unreasonable: *Re H; Re W (Adoption: Parental Agreement)* (1983) 4 FLR 614; *Re BA (Wardship and Adoption)* [1985] FLR 1008.

under the new law with, in reality, only one: the 'welfare' question. The 'requirement' to consider the welfare of the child before consent can be dispensed with appears to add very little in practice and, arguably, one of the effects of s 52(1)(b) is to remove any real possibility of taking account of parents' rights or interests.[1]

7.29 Thus one of the consequences of s 1(2), taken together with s 52(1), is a significant erosion of the natural parents' standing in the adoption proceedings. By extending the welfare principle to dispensing with parental consent, the court is able to override completely a parent's wishes, even though they may be reasonable, and notwithstanding that 'uniquely amongst interventions available to protect children's upbringing, adoption involves an irreversible legal separation of the child from his birth parents'.[2] Although foreshadowed in the preceding decade's discussions on adoption reform, now that it is here, it marks a stark and fundamental shift in direction in our domestic adoption law.

7.30 The paramountcy principle may, however, also have the effect of bringing to an end the present stultifying practice of permitting proposed adopters to dictate whether contact should take place, which will be considered in more detail in Chapter 9.

A lifetime consideration

7.31 Adoption, unlike orders under the CA 1989, does not cease to have effect when the child reaches 18 years of age. Section 1(2) of the ACA 2002 expressly places the obligation on the court or adoption agency to consider the child's welfare 'throughout his life'. In this it is distinguishable from the welfare principle under the CA 1989 where, in an appropriate case, the court can take a short-term view.[3] This is an important distinction as it underscores the fundamental difference between adoption orders, which are for life and where the legal ties with the natural family are permanently extinguished, and CA 1989 orders, which do not have such characteristics.

DELAY

7.32 The White Paper, *Adoption: A New Approach*,[4] highlighted the damaging delays in deciding about children's futures and the far-reaching consequences for the children concerned, particularly where the delays were compounded by frequent moves from one foster placement to another. The Government's primary concern was that:

> '... children remain in the care system far longer than they should. More than 28,000 children have been in care continuously for more than two years. Too often, despite the best intentions of all involved, they are passed from pillar to post. Nearly one looked-after child in

---

1   SM Cretney and JM Masson *Principles of Family Law* (6th edn, Sweet and Maxwell, 1997), pp 930–931.
2   White Paper *Adoption: The Future*, Cm 2288 (1993), paras 5.2–5.3. It was this irreversibility which led to the suggestion (at para 5.5) of a further test before the court could override parental refusal of consent, namely that the court had to be satisfied that 'adoption is likely to offer a significantly better advantage to the child than any other option'. This proposal, however, failed to make its way into the draft Adoption Bill 1996 and has not re-emerged since.
3   *T v T (Minors: Custody Appeal)* [1987] 1 FLR 374.
4   Cm 5017 (December 2000), at para 1.16.

five has three or more placements in a year. Some have six or more. For those children, the care system frequently fails to provide the stability that they need to build a successful future.'[1]

7.33 Section 1(3) of the ACA 2002 follows s 1(2) of the CA 1989, although worded slightly differently, in putting the general delay principle amongst the foremost mandatory considerations, although still subject to the welfare principle. The obligation on adoption agencies in s 1(3) to have regard to the damaging effects of delay is, therefore, an overarching provision that applies across all decisions relating to the adoption of the child, including the placement decision.[2] The words 'any delay' constitute the widest drafting concept of delay. Some delay might be in the best interests of the child but this is confined to 'exceptional circumstances'.[3] For example, in the case of a group of siblings, it might be beneficial to wait a little longer in order to find adopters who would be willing to take them all, rather than place them with different adopters.

7.34 In making the delay principle an overarching provision, s 1(3) complies with Art 6(1) of the European Convention on Human Rights, which requires that cases be heard within a reasonable time and 'underlines the importance of rendering justice without delays which might jeopardise its effectiveness and credibility'.[4] The obligation is on the State to take appropriate steps to ensure that proceedings are prosecuted expeditiously and to organise its legal system so as to allow the courts to comply with Art 6.[5]

7.35 Section 109(1) of the ACA 2002 further reinforces the general delay principle in s 1(3) by placing the obligation on the court to draw up a timetable with a view to determining the question of whether an adoption order or a placement order should be made without delay and to give appropriate directions to ensure that the timetable is adhered to. Section 109(2) makes provision for rules prescribing periods within which specified steps must be taken in relation to such proceedings. It mirrors similar provisions

---

1   Mr John Hutton, Minister of State, Department of Health, HC Deb, 26 March 2001, vol 365, no 59, col 698.
2   HL Official Report (24 June 2002), CWH 17, per Lord Hunt of Kings Heath.
3   Ibid, CWH 19–20.
4   *H v France* (1987) 12 EHRR 74, para 58; *Paulsen-Medalen and Svensson v Sweden* (1998) 26 EHRR 260. The reasonableness of the length of the proceedings has to be assessed in the light of the particular circumstances and having regard to the criteria laid down in the European Court's case-law, in particular: (i) the complexity of the case; (ii) the conduct of the applicant; (iii) the relevant authorities; and (iv) the importance of what is at stake for the applicant in the litigation: *Konig v FRG* (1978) 2 EHRR 170, paras 99 and 111; *H v UK* (1987) 10 EHRR 96, para 71; *Piran v France* (2002) 34 EHRR 14, para 54; *Davies v UK* (2002) 35 EHRR 720, para 26. In children's cases, special emphasis is placed on the importance of what is at stake for the applicant in the proceedings in question. *H v UK* (above) para 70, states that particular celerity is required in cases concerning the custody of a child: *Johansen v Norway* (1997) 23 EHRR 33, para 88; *En v Italy* (2001) 31 EHRR 17, para 53.
5   *Buchholz v FRG* (1981) 3 EHRR 597, para 51; *Zimmerman and Steiner v Switzerland* (1984) 6 EHRR 17, para 24; *Humen v Poland* (2001) 31 EHRR 1168, para 66. In *Frydlender v France* (2001) 31 EHRR 1152, at para 45, the European Court reiterated that 'it is for the Contracting State to organise their legal systems in such a way that the courts can guarantee to everyone the right to a final decision within a reasonable time in the determination of his civil rights and obligations'. The 'fair trial guarantee' is not limited to the judicial part of the proceedings but includes unfairness at any stage of the litigation process: *Mantovanelli v France* (1997) 24 EHRR 370.

in the CA 1989 and is seen as an important part of the 'drive to cut harmful delays in adoption'.[1]

7.36   The White Paper, *Adoption: A New Approach*, gave prominence to the delivery of National Adoption Standards, which would include 'timescales within which decisions for most children should be reached and action taken, to ensure that children are not kept waiting for a family'.[2]

7.37   The National Adoption Standards, which were developed under the auspices of the AA 1976, have now become an integral part of the adoption landscape. The key aim in introducing the National Adoption Standards is to provide consistent adoption services, which include the production of a plan for permanence for all looked-after children at the 4-monthly statutory review[3] and a decision on prospective adopters within 6 months of application.

7.38   A further 'key part of the drive to reduce delay'[4] in the adoption process has been the establishment of an Adoption and Children Act Register for England and Wales, which holds information on children waiting to be adopted and on approved adoptive families across the country waiting to adopt. The Act places the register on a statutory footing.

WELFARE CHECKLIST

7.39   Section 1(4) of the ACA 2002 provides that:

'The court or adoption agency must have regard to the following matters (among others) –

(a)   the child's ascertainable wishes and feelings regarding the decision (considered in the light of the child's age and understanding);

(b)   the child's particular needs;

(c)   the likely effect on the child (throughout his life) of having ceased to be a member of the original family and become an adopted person;

(d)   the child's age, sex, background and any of the child's characteristics which the court or agency considers relevant;

(e)   any harm (within the meaning of the CA 1989) which the child has suffered or is at risk of suffering;

(f)   the relationship which the child has with relatives, and with any other person in relation to whom the court or agency considers the question to be relevant, including –

(i)   the likelihood of any such relationship continuing and the value to the child of its doing so;

(ii)   the ability and willingness of any of the child's relatives, or of any such person, to provide the child with a secure environment in which the child can develop, and otherwise to meet the child's needs;

---

1   HC Deb, 26 March 2001, vol 354, no 59, col 711.

2   Cm 5017 (December 2000), para 4.6.

3   Which is a new requirement under s 7 of the Local Authority Social Services Act 1970, together with a requirement that agencies must put in place systems to monitor their performance against the time scales set out in the Standards for matching children with adoptive families and taking a decision on prospective adopters.

4   HC Deb, 29 October 2001, col 656, per Mr Alan Milburn, Secretary of State for Health.

(iii) the wishes and feelings of any of the child's relatives, or of any such person, regarding the child.'

Correlation with s 1(3) of the CA 1989

7.40 The 'welfare checklist' in s 1(3) of the CA 1989 was a ground-breaking reform. As 'welfare' and 'best interests' are indeterminate and elastic concepts, the effect of the statutory checklist in s 1(3) was to superimpose a structure upon the exercise of judicial discretion, but without creating a fetter.

7.41 Section 1(4) of the ACA 2002 adopts the format of s 1(3) of the CA 1989 by providing a checklist of 'welfare' factors to be taken into account by the court or adoption agency, rather than attempting a statutory definition of 'welfare'. The criteria in subsections (4)(a), (d) and (e), for example, reproduce those in s 1(3)(a), (d) and (e) of the CA 1989 and, where the ACA 2002 overlaps that Act, the jurisprudence which has arisen over the last decade in interpreting the CA 1989 will be directly relevant to the similar provisions in the new Act. There are, however, some important differences, where the CA 1989 checklist has clearly been adapted to take account of the particular context of adoption.

'Checklist'

7.42 Although it is useful to refer to s 1(4) as 'the checklist', it should be remembered that it is not so called by statute. As Staughton LJ put it in *H v H*[1] in relation to s 1(3) of the CA 1989:

> 'Perhaps one should remember, when one calls it the checklist, that it is not like the checks which an airline pilot has to make with his co-pilot, aloud one to the other before he takes off. The statute does not say that the judge has to read out the seven items in s 1(3) and pronounce his conclusion on each.'

7.43 This equally applies to s 1(4) of the ACA 2002. Although it will not always be necessary for a judge to go through the checklist item by item, the checklist in s 1(4) does represent 'an extremely useful and important discipline in ensuring that all relevant factors are considered and balanced'.[2]

7.44 However, the list of factors in s 1(4) is not exhaustive. The subsection includes, in parentheses, the words 'among others' and therefore the clear implication is that the court may consider other matters relevant to 'welfare' and is not solely confined to the specified factors.

WISHES AND FEELINGS: SECTION 1(4)(a)

7.45 There is a duty under s 1(4)(a) to obtain the wishes and feelings of the child, where they are ascertainable. It remains, however, a matter for the judge's discretion as to what weight and priority he or she gives to those wishes and feelings.

7.46 The cases decided under s 1(3)(a) of the CA 1989 are likely to be relevant under s 1(4)(a) of the ACA 2002. The older the child, the greater the weight that will be given to

---

1   *H v H (Residence Order: Leave to Remove from Jurisdiction)* [1995] 1 FLR 529 at 532.
2   *B v B (Residence Order: Reasons for Decision)* [1997] 2 FLR 602 at 607H–608B, per Holman J.

his or her views,[1] although, in the end, the decision is that of the court and not of the child.[2] In *Re P (A Minor) (Education)*,[3] where the Court of Appeal was dealing with the welfare of a 14-year-old boy, Butler-Sloss LJ (as she then was), anticipating the statutory duty of the court under s 1(3)(a) of the CA 1989, said:

> 'The courts, over the last few years, have become increasingly aware of the importance of listening to the views of older children and taking into account what children say, not necessarily agreeing with what they want nor, indeed, doing what they want, but paying proper respect to older children who are of an age and maturity to make their minds up as to what they think is best for them, bearing in mind that older children very often have an appreciation of their situation which is worthy of consideration by, and the respect of, the adults, and particularly including the courts.'

7.47   Where the older child understands the broad implications of adoption, the court will, therefore, require clear reasons to justify proceeding against his expressed wishes and feelings.[4]

7.48   As the trend is towards the adoption of older children, s 1(4)(a) is likely to become of key importance, particularly in those cases where the child has a strong sense of identity with his or her natural family, as one of the necessary 'checks and balances' in determining whether the adoption option is, in fact, in the best interests of the child concerned 'throughout his life'.

7.49   It is not the current practice for children to give oral evidence at the hearing. However, one of the questions raised by the European Convention is whether children can insist on being heard in court under the Art 6 'right of access to the court'.[5] Present thinking, where older children are concerned, may have to be revisited in the light of Art 6.[6] Furthermore, the importance of giving a voice to a child in adoption proceedings whose wishes and feelings are in conflict with the guardian's assessment of welfare and disposal has long been recognised as one of the areas for reform in adoption law.[7]

7.50   It is of interest that one of the recommendations in the 1992 Review of Adoption was that the court should not be allowed to grant an adoption order relating to a child aged 12 or over, unless the child had agreed to it or the court had dispensed with the child's agreement. This would have been a significant change, clearly aimed at ensuring that older children were properly consulted and involved in the decision-making process. In the event, the Act has simply reproduced the 'familiar formula'[8] of 'ascertaining wishes and feelings', but it is likely that there will be wide consultation in the future as to

---

1   *Gillick v West Norfolk and Wisbech Area Health Authority and Another* [1986] 1 AC 112;
     M v M (Transfer of Custody: Appeal) [1987] 2 FLR 146; *Re S (Minors) (Access: Religious Upbringing)*
     [1992] 2 FLR 313; *Re P (Minors) (Wardship: Care and Control)* [1992] 2 FCR 681; *Re C (A Minor)*
     (Care: Child's Wishes) [1993] 1 FLR 832; *Re B (Change of Surname)* [1996] 1 FLR 791.
2   *Re P (Minors) (Wardship: Care and Control)* (above).
3   [1992] 1 FLR 316 at 321D–F.
4   *Re D (Minors) (Adoption by Step-parent)* (1981) 2 FLR 102 at 105D.
5   *Golder v UK* (1975) 1 EHRR 524, paras 35 and 36.
6   In *A v A (Contact: Representation of Child's Interests)* [2001] Fam Law 241, the Court of Appeal
     anticipated an increase in the use of guardians representing children in private law proceedings as a
     result of the Human Rights Act 1998.
7   *Re O (Transracial Adoption: Contact)* [1995] 2 FLR 597 at 611E–F, per Thorpe J (as he then was).
8   Discussed by Andrew Bainham in *Children: The Modern Law* (2nd edn, Family Law, 1998) at p 216.

the best means of giving the child a voice and, as we shall see in Chapter 9, some steps have already been taken towards providing looked-after children with an advocacy service.

NEEDS: SECTION 1(4)(b)

7.51   Section 1(4)(b) of the ACA 2002 refers to 'the child's particular needs'. It does not expressly identify those needs as 'physical, emotional and educational' as in s 1(3)(b) of the CA 1989, but it is implicit that those needs will be included. Equally, it follows that the 'particular needs' referred to are not confined to 'physical, emotional and educational' needs, but may embrace, for example, social, moral, psychological and health needs. By not particularising 'needs', the intention of the parliamentary draftsman was clearly to give the widest possible scope its interpretation for the purposes of this subsection.

Physical needs

7.52   'Physical needs' are more than just the basics of an adequate diet and satisfactory accommodation and include 'the most fundamental rule of child care, which is that stability is all-important and the maintenance of some kind of routine is crucial'.[1] The material circumstances which the child is likely to enjoy with proposed adopters compared with the material circumstances of the natural family is not an element that should be allowed to weigh too heavily in the scale, if at all. As Griffiths LJ succinctly put it in *Re P (Adoption: Parental Agreement)*,[2] 'Anyone with experience of life knows that affluence and happiness are not necessarily synonymous'.

Emotional needs

7.53   In *Re M (Contact: Welfare Test)*,[3] Wilson J recognised that there is a fundamental emotional need of every child to have an enduring relationship with both parents. When considering 'emotional needs', it is, therefore, important to remember the words of Lord Templeman in *In re KD (A Minor) (Ward: Termination of Access)*:[4]

> 'The best person to bring up a child is the natural parent. It matters not whether the parent is wise or foolish, rich or poor, educated or illiterate, provided the child's moral and physical health are not endangered. Public authorities cannot improve on nature.'

7.54   This echoes the earlier words of Lord Scarman in *Re E (SA) (A Minor)*:[5] 'A home with his natural parents, if circumstances are right and a loving relationship exists, must be best'. Lord Donaldson of Lymington MR encapsulated the approach in *Re H (A Minor) (Custody: Interim Care and Control)*,[6] when he said:

> '... there is a strong supposition that, other things being equal, it is in the interests of the child that it shall remain with its natural parents. But this has to give way to particular needs in particular situations.'[7]

---

1   *Re B (A Minor) (Interim Custody)* (1983) 4 FLR 683 at 684F–G, per Sir Roger Ormrod.
2   [1985] FLR 635 at 637D–E.
3   [1995] 1 FLR 274 at 278G–H.
4   [1988] 1 AC 806 at 812B–C.
5   [1984] 1 WLR 156.
6   [1991] 2 FLR 109 at 113B–D.
7   Cited with approval in *Re W (A Minor) (Residence Order)* [1993] 2 FLR 625; *Re M (Child's Upbringing)* [1996] 2 FLR 441.

7.55   The child's relationship with siblings is often a significant component of his or her emotional needs and requires careful and sensitive consideration under s 1(4)(b) when coming to a decision relating to adoption.

THE LIKELY EFFECT ON THE CHILD (THROUGHOUT HIS LIFE) OF HAVING CEASED TO BE A MEMBER OF THE ORIGINAL FAMILY AND BECOME AN ADOPTED PERSON: SECTION 1(4)(c)

7.56   Whereas s 1(3)(c) of the CA 1989 looks at the likely effect of any change in the child's circumstances and thus gives an emphasis to those cases where the preservation of the status quo is in the child's best interests,[1] s 1(4)(c) of the ACA 2002 also considers the effect of change but in the very different context of adoption.

7.57   First, it looks at the 'life-long' prospects. Section 6 of the AA 1976 placed the obligation on the court to have regard to the 'long-term' welfare of the child by specifying that the need to safeguard and promote the welfare of the child was 'throughout his childhood'. The long-term view was illustrated by the decision in *Re D (A Minor) (Adoption Order: Validity)*,[2] where it was held that a benefit accruing after majority was nevertheless a relevant factor to be taken into account in considering whether or not to make an adoption order.

7.58   As we have seen, s 1(4)(c) takes an even longer perspective and obliges the court to have regard to the likely effect on the child 'throughout his life'. It therefore brings into consideration such issues as succession, interests under inheritance and trust law, nationality and the right of abode.

7.59   Secondly, it has a twofold focus. It considers, on the one hand, the likely effect on the child of having ceased to be a member of the original family and, on the other, the likely effect on the child of becoming an adopted person.

7.60   It is a fundamental right of every child to belong to a family. This is the principle underpinning the UN Convention on the Rights of the Child 1989. In the Preamble to the UN Convention it is recognised that 'the child, for the full and harmonious development of his or her personality, should grow up in a family environment, in an atmosphere of happiness, love and understanding'. Every child also has 'a right to respect for family life' under Art 8 of the European Convention on Human Rights. Therefore the importance of family life for a child cannot be overstated.

Having ceased to be a member of the original family

7.61   The fact of a child's 'having ceased to be a member of the original family' raises important issues such as:

(i)   the extinction of the parents' parental responsibility and the complete severing of all legal ties with the family of birth;
(ii)   the consequent loss of the child's sense of identity with the birth family, together with a corresponding risk of damage to the child's self-esteem and psychological well-being, particularly in circumstances where he or she may have been cared for by

---

1   *D v M (Minor: Custody Appeal)* [1982] 3 All ER 897 at 902J, per Ormrod LJ.
2   [1991] 2 FLR 66 at 3D–E.

the natural parents or extended family for a significant period of time and where the child perceives that he or she belongs;

(ii) the damaging sense of loss to such a child in seeing himself or herself as abandoned or unloved by his or her parents or extended birth family.

7.62 The Art 8 'family life' provisions are relevant in this context. A closed adoption order represents the most complete severance of the family ties between a child and his or her parents and constitutes clear interference by a public authority (which includes the court) with the exercise of the right to respect for family life by the child or by anyone else with whom the child enjoys 'family life'. One of the central issues which arises, therefore, is whether such an interference is justifiable under one of the grounds in Art 8(2).

7.63 The approach of the European Court can be seen in *Johansen v Norway*,[1] where the Norwegian court decided to take the child into care, place her in a foster home with a view to adoption and refuse the applicant mother contact as from the moment of the child's placement, which was to be kept confidential. The European Court first highlighted that:

'... the mutual enjoyment by parent and child of each other's company constitutes a fundamental element of family life and that domestic measures hindering such enjoyment amount to an interference with the right protected by Art 8.'[2]

7.64 The Court went on to hold:

'In the present case the applicant had been deprived of her parental rights and access in the context of a permanent placement of her daughter in a foster home with a view to adoption by the foster parents. *These measures were particularly far reaching in that they totally deprived the applicant of her family life with the child and were inconsistent with the aim of reuniting them. Such measures should only be applied in exceptional circumstances and could only be justified if they were motivated by an overriding requirement pertaining to the child's best interests*'[3] (emphasis added).

7.65 However, the *Johansen* approach may not necessarily apply in every case. In *Söderbäck v Sweden*,[4] the European Court held that the facts of the case were distinguishable from those of *Johansen*. In *Söderbäck*, the father and mother had never cohabited and the father's contact with his daughter had been very limited. The mother's husband, who had lived with the child for over 6 years, applied successfully for an adoption order. The European Court (unlike the Commission) held that there had been no violation of Art 8. It said:

---

1   (1996) 23 EHRR 33.

2   Ibid, para 52; see also *McMichael v UK* (1995) 20 EHRR 205.

3   *Johansen v Norway* (above), para 78; *Andersson v Sweden* (1992) 14 EHRR 615, para 95. See also *Olsson v Sweden (No 1)* (1989) EHRR 259, para 81; *Olsson v Sweden (No 2)* (1994) 17 EHRR 134, para 90; *Hokkanen v Finland* (1995) 19 EHRR 139, para 81, which support the notion that 'the taking of a child into care should normally be regarded as a temporary measure to be discontinued as soon as circumstances permit and that any measures of implementation of temporary care should be consistent with the ultimate aim of reuniting the natural parent and the child. A fair balance has to be struck between the interests of the child in remaining in public care and those of the parent in being reunited with the child. In carrying out this balancing exercise, the court will attach particular importance to the best interests of the child, which, depending on their nature and seriousness, may override those of the parent'.

4   [1999] 1 FLR 250.

'While it is true that the adoption in the present case ... had the legal effect of totally depriving the applicant of family life with his daughter, the context differs significantly. It does not concern the severance of links between a mother and a child taken into public care but rather, of links between a natural father and a child who had been in the care of her mother since she was born. Nor does it concern a parent who had had custody of the child or who in any other capacity had assumed the care of the child ... the contacts between the applicant and the child were infrequent and limited in character and when the adoption was granted he had not seen her for some time ... Moreover, the child had been living with her mother since her birth and with her adoptive father since she was 8 months old. He had taken part in [her] care [and was] regarded as her father. Thus, when the adoption was granted ... "de facto" family ties had existed between the mother and the adoptive father for 5½ years, until they married ... and between him and [the child] for 6½ years. The adoption consolidated and formalised those ties.'[1]

7.66   The European Court drew this clear distinction between a step-parent adoption and an adoption in a public law context, but it should, however, be noted that the *Söderbäck* case was a case which turned very much on its particular facts.

7.67   It should further be noted that, in considering adoption in the light of Art 8, in *Re B (Adoption: Natural Parent)*[2] Lord Nicholls of Birkenhead, albeit in the limited context of interpreting s 15(3) of the AA 1976 where the mother had consented to the making of an adoption order,[3] sought to reconcile the concepts underlying the 'best interests' approach under domestic adoption law with the concepts underlying a justifiable interference (under Art 8(2)) with the family life provisions in Art 8(1):[4]

'Under Art 8 the adoption must meet a pressing social need and be a proportionate response to that need: see, for example, *Silver v United Kingdom* (1983) 5 EHRR 347, 376–377, para 97(c). Inherent in both these Convention concepts is a balancing exercise, weighing the advantages and disadvantages [adoption would have for the child]. But this balancing exercise, required by Art 8, does not differ in substance from the like balancing exercise undertaken by a court when deciding whether, in the conventional phraseology of English law, adoption would be in the best interests of the child. The like considerations fall to be taken into account. Although the phraseology is different, the criteria to be applied in deciding whether an adoption order is justified under Art 8(2) lead to the same result in the conventional tests applied by English law.'[5]

Becoming an adopted person

7.68   'Becoming an adopted person' not only confers upon the child the legal status set out in s 67 and Chapter IV of the ACA 2002, but also – socially and emotionally – provides for the child a permanent substitute family, where the adopters are legally responsible and, therefore, fully committed to fulfilling their parental responsibilities. This brings with it a sense of permanency and security, not only for the child, but also for

---

1   *Söderbäck v Sweden* (above) at 257E–258A, paras 31–33.
2   [2001] UKHL 70, [2002] 1 FLR 196.
3   So there was no question of adoption being a violation of her rights under Art 8: ibid, at [29].
4   Ibid at [31].
5   For a critical review of this decision, see S Harris Short '*Re B (Adoption: Natural Parent)* Putting the child at the heart of adoption?' [2002] CFLQ 325.

the adopters themselves.[1] It is 'absolutely immutable in character'[2] and thus removes the risk of emotional and psychological damage to the child which may arise from multiple changes of foster carers, shifting views of the local authority, changes of social workers and renewed applications by the natural family.

7.69 In *Re O (Adoption: Withholding Agreement)*,[3] Swinton Thomas LJ put it this way:

'Although in recent years views in relation to adoption have, to an extent, altered, there can be no doubt that adoption gives the adoptive parents and the child greater security and confidence in the relationship. After all, if an adoption order is made, the adopters become the child's parents. If there is not an adoption order in place, the people with whom the child is living may always fear that there will be a change of status. There is a risk, unquantified in this case, that the mother might have a change of mind and reappear on the scene …

Although not the most important issue is this case, it is relevant in my judgment that an adoption order is made for life, whereas a residence order ceases to have effect at the age of 16 or 18. There can be no doubt that, in an appropriate case, it is advantageous for a small child to grow up in the knowledge that he remains a child of the family until the adoptive parents die. Furthermore, K, who regards S as his sister, is an adopted child and S might feel, if no adoption order is made, that he is in a less favoured position than K …'

AGE, SEX, BACKGROUND AND CHARACTERISTICS: SECTION 1(4)(d)

7.70 Where the adoption of an older child with strong links with the birth family is being considered as one of the range of options, the factors of 'age' and 'background' in this subsection may carry particular weight, although they will be always subject to the overall welfare principle. It has been held that 'characteristics' may include racial[4] or cultural factors and so there is some overlap between this subsection and s 1(5) of the ACA 2002. It may also include considerations such as special educational needs or physical disability.

HARM: SECTION 1(4)(e)

7.71 Section 1(4)(e) employs the same definition as s 1(3)(e) of the CA 1989, namely the definition in s 31(9) of the CA 1989. However, the definition of 'harm' in s 31(9) ('ill-treatment or the impairment of health or development') is extended by s 120 of the ACA 2002 to include 'for example, impairment suffered from seeing or hearing the ill-treatment of another'.[5] This is a landmark decision in that it gives statutory recognition for the first time to the impact of domestic violence on a child. The definition of harm in the checklist is now to include harm that a child has suffered or is at risk of suffering as the result of witnessing the abuse of others, including domestic violence and violence which, while not domestic, may nevertheless have affected the child, such as a

---

1   In *Re H (Adoption: Parental Agreement)* (1982) 3 FLR 386, Ormrod LJ asked the question: 'What do adoptive parents gain by an adoption order over and above what they have already got in long term fostering? To that the answer is always the same – and it is always a good one – adoption gives us total security and makes the child part of our family and places us in parental control of the child; long-term fostering leaves us exposed to changes of view of the local authority, it leaves us exposed to applications and so on by the natural parent. That is a perfectly sensible approach …'.

2   *Re G (Adoption Order)* [1999] 1 FLR 400 at 404F, per Thorpe LJ.

3   [1999] 1 FLR 451 at 467E–F and 468C–D.

4   *Re M (Section 94 Appeals)* [1995] 1 FLR 546.

5   The amendment to s 31(9) is in italics.

parent continually being harassed or intimidated or a parent harassing or intimidating others.[1] The objective is to ensure that the impact on a child of witnessing abuse is considered in all CA 1989 and adoption proceedings.[2]

7.72 The Government proposes to take a number of steps to reinforce the significance of domestic violence such as amending court application forms to include specific questions about violence and ill-treatment of children. The court rules will also be amended to oblige courts to determine whether violence or ill-treatment has taken place, if an allegation is made, and, if so, what impact that has or is likely to have on the child. The guidelines on parental contact with children in cases of domestic violence produced by the Children Act Sub-Committee of the Lord Chancellor's Advisory Board on Family Law will be a key starting point, and the Government has signalled an intention to disseminate the guidelines more effectively.[3] The 'harm' in s 1(4)(e) is 'any harm' and not the 'significant harm' of s 31 of the CA 1989.

7.73 'Development' is defined as meaning 'physical, intellectual, emotional, social or behavioural development'; 'health' as meaning 'physical or mental health'; and 'ill-treatment' as including 'sexual abuse and forms of ill-treatment which are not physical'.

7.74 In *Re M and R (Child Abuse: Evidence)*[4] the Court of Appeal, applying the decision in *Re H and R (Child Sexual Abuse: Standard of Proof)*,[5] held that under s 1(3)(e) of the CA 1989 there was no justification for the proposition that, because the welfare of the child was paramount, the standard of proof should be less than the balance of probabilities. This applies equally to s 1(4) (e) of the ACA 2002. Butler-Sloss LJ (as she then was) said at 203C–D:

> 'The court must reach a conclusion based on the facts, not on suspicion or mere doubts. If . . . the court concludes that the evidence is insufficient to prove sexual abuse in the past, and if the fact of sexual abuse in the past is the only basis for asserting risk of sexual abuse in the future, then it follows that there is nothing (except suspicion or mere doubts) to show a risk of future sexual abuse . . .
>
> The fact that there might have been harm in the past does not establish the risk of harm in the future. The very highest it can be put is that what might possibly have happened in the past means that there may possibly be a risk of the same thing happening in the future. Section 1(3)(e), however, does not deal with what might possibly have happened or what future risk there may possibly be. It speaks in terms of what has happened or what is at risk of happening. Thus what the court must do (when the matter is at issue) is to decide whether the evidence establishes harm or risk of harm.
>
> We cannot see any justification for the suggestion that the standard of proof in performing this task should be less than the preponderance of probabilities.'

7.75 At 205D–E she went on to say:

---

1   HC Deb, vol 385, no 149, col 947.
2   See *Re L; Re V; Re M & Re H (Contact: Domestic Violence)* [2000] 2 FLR 334 in which the Court of Appeal considered the report by the Children Act Sub-Committee of the Advisory Board on Family Law on parental contact in domestic violence cases and a joint expert report by two child psychiatrists, Dr Sturge and Dr Glaser.
3   HC Deb, vol 385, no 149, col 947.
4   [1996] 2 FLR 195.
5   [1996] 1 FLR 80.

'In our view risk of harm means the real possibility of future harm. Lord Nicholls said in *Re H and R* at 101C:

> "It is, of course, open to a court to conclude there is a real possibility that the child will suffer harm in the future although harm in the past has not been established. There will be cases where, although the alleged maltreatment itself is not proved, the evidence does establish a combination of profoundly worrying features affecting the care of the child within the family. In such cases, it would be open to a court in appropriate circumstances to find that, although not satisfied the child is yet suffering significant harm, *on the basis of such facts as are proved*, there is likelihood that he will do so in the future."

That passage sets out, in our view, the correct approach to the question how to assess any harm the child is at risk of suffering in s 1(3)(e) of the welfare test.'

7.76   Where the court has found that a child has suffered harm which was inflicted by his or her carer, then the court can have regard to such harm when assessing the harm other children, who are being looked after by the carer, are at risk of suffering.[1]

RELATIONSHIP WHICH THE CHILD HAS WITH RELATIVES: SECTION 1(4)(f)

7.77   Under the spotlight of adoption, s 1(4)(f) has cast a distinctive and wider shadow than that under s 1(3)(f) of the CA 1989 (which concentrated upon the capability of the parents and other relevant persons of meeting the child's needs).

7.78   It has widened the focus of capability to consider the ability and willingness of any of the child's relatives to provide the child with a secure environment in which the child can develop and otherwise meet the child's needs. It has further embraced consideration of both the likelihood of a relationship with relatives continuing and the value to the child of the continuation of such a relationship, and the wishes and feelings of any of the child's relatives regarding the child.

7.79   For the purposes of s 1 of the ACA 2002, there is an extended definition of 'relationships'. Under s 1(8)(a), these 'are not confined to legal relationships' and under s 1(8)(b), 'a relative in relation to a child' includes 'the child's mother and father'.

7.80   Sibling relationships fall within the definition of relationships and are an important consideration under s 1(4)(f). This is particularly so because more than 80 per cent of looked-after children have siblings,[2] yet in 1995 it was found that only 43 per cent of children who were adopted had been placed with a sibling. This was notwithstanding that the importance of the relationship has been stressed in case-law under the CA 1989[3] which supports the proposition that it is generally in the best interests of children to be brought up together. For example, in *C v C (Minors: Custody)*,[4] Purchas LJ said:

---

1   *I v Barnsley Metropolitan Borough Council* [1986] 1 FLR 109 at 122C–G, per Fox LJ.

2   See Dance *Focus on Adoption: A Snapshot of Adoption Patterns in England – 1995* (BAAF, 1997) and an interesting article by S Beckett and D Hershman QC 'The Human Rights Implications for Looked After Siblings' [2001] Fam Law 288.

3   Section 23(7) of the CA 1989 imposes a duty on the local authority which is providing accommodation for a looked-after child and also for a sibling to accommodate them together, so far as is reasonably practicable and consistent with the child's welfare. See also *Re E (Care Proceedings: Social Work Practice)* [2001] 2 FLR 254.

4   [1988] 2 FLR 291.

'It is really beyond argument that unless there are strong features indicating a contrary arrangement, brothers and sisters should, wherever possible be brought up together, so that they are an emotional support to each other in the stormy waters of the destruction of their family.'

7.81 A 'sibling relationship' falls within the 'family life' provisions of Art 8(1) of the European Convention.[1] Arguably, a placement which separates siblings would constitute an interference with their right to respect for family life and would have to be justified not only on welfare grounds but also as a proportionate response for the purposes of Art 8(1).

7.82 Section 1(4)(f)(i)–(iii), therefore, gives significant emphasis to those issues, which are especially critical for the older child who has identity links with his or her natural parents and extended birth family. Such issues include whether there is a real possibility of the child being cared for by grandparents, aunts, uncles, older siblings or friends of the natural family, or whether continuing contact with the natural parents or extended family is of a benefit to the child, particularly given that the reach of the welfare test now stretches beyond childhood into a 'life' perspective.

7.83 However, whether this factor, taken together with the first limb of s 1(4)(c), is sufficient to redress the inherent imbalance against the family of birth, which stems from the incorporation of the paramountcy principle coupled with the removal of the 'unreasonableness' ground, is a matter for debate. Whether, together, they are sufficient to steer s 52(1)(b) clear of a European Convention challenge will be considered in Chapter 8, which looks at s 52 in more detail.

RELIGIOUS, RACIAL, CULTURAL AND LINGUISTIC BACKGROUND

Section 1(5) of the ACA 2002

7.84 A springboard for the inclusion of these important factors in the s 1 principles is to be found in the Department of Health Circular LAC (98) 20 'Adoption – Achieving the Right Balance' which tackled 'understanding the needs of children from black and minority ethnic communities'.[2] The Circular was itself a response to the disquiet[3] which had arisen over the doctrinaire approach frequently adopted by local authorities towards trans-racial adoptions, and the Government was at pains to make clear that 'it is unacceptable for a child to be denied loving adoptive parents solely on the grounds that the child and adopters do not share the same racial or cultural background'.[4]

7.85 The guidance highlighted that a principal tenet in the care of children is the importance of a child's family background: 'A child's ethnic origin, culture, language and

---

1   *Moustaquim v Belgium* (1991) 13 EHRR 802, para 36.
2   The White Paper, *Adoption: A New Approach*, Cm 5017 (December 2000) at para 6.15 reinforced that children's birth heritage and religious, cultural and linguistic background are all important factors to consider in finding a new family.
3   *Re N (A Minor) (Adoption)* [1990] 1 FLR 58; *Re JK (Adoption: Trans-racial Placement)* [1991] 2 FLR 340.
4   DoH Circular LAC (98) 20, para 14.

religion are significant factors to be taken into account when adoption agencies are considering the most appropriate placement for a child'.[1] However, it stressed that such consideration has to take account of '*all* the child's needs'.[2] Simply identifying a child's ethnic background was not sufficient in itself. There was a need for adoption agencies to have regard to the implications for the child of 'how the culture of a family, community or society can influence the way a child sees the world; the significance of religion in a child's daily life and the importance of maintaining a knowledge of this history, culture and language'.

7.86 It stated that 'placement with a family of similar ethnic origin and religion is very often most likely to meet the child's needs as fully as possible, safeguarding his welfare most effectively and preparing him for life as a member of a multi-racial society'.[3] It did, however, emphasise that 'These are ... only some among a number of other significant factors and should not themselves be regarded as the decisive ones'.[4]

7.87 The factors in s 1(5), therefore, must be considered by adoption agencies, but not at the expense of harmful delay to the child. This is why the subsection refers to 'due consideration'; it relates to the need to ensure that there is no undue delay.[5] 'Due consideration' is a subjective test and will depend on the circumstances. The guidance in Circular LAC (98) 20 is important in setting the context in which 'due consideration' to the s 1(5) factors should be given and is further backed up by the National Adoption Standards, which set out the benchmark time scales to help agencies weigh up the question of matching versus delay. In particular, under Standard A.8:

---

1   DoH Circular LAC (98) 20, para 11; see also *Re M (Section 94 Appeals)* [1995] 1 FLR 546, a contact case involving a child of mixed race, where the Court of Appeal expressed concern that the magistrates had failed to address the racial issues and remitted the case for consideration of the significance of race.

2   See *Re J (A Minor) (Wardship: Adoption: Custodianship)* [1987] 1 FLR 455 (where a child of mixed race was placed with white foster carers who were Jehovah's Witnesses. The mother's refusal to consent to adoption was held to be reasonable 'as the child was predominantly West Indian in appearance and in later years may grow away from his adoptive family and seek companionship of friends of his ethnic origin and in that event it would be regrettable if his link with his mother had been severed by adoption'); *Re N (A Minor) (Adoption)* [1990] 1 FLR 58 (where the shame and distress that an adoption order would bring the father in his Nigerian culture and the consequences of that for the child were weighed against the security that adoption would give to the foster parents and child); *Re P (A Minor) (Adoption)* [1990] 1 FLR 96 (where a child born of an Afro-Caribbean mother and white father was placed with a white foster mother who later wished to adopt and the Court of Appeal held that the trial judge was entitled to conclude that the advantages of bringing up a child of mixed race in a black family outweighed the importance of maintaining the status quo); *Re JK (Adoption: Trans-racial Placement)* [1991] 2 FLR 340 (where the child was born to a Sikh mother and was placed short-term with white foster parents. As there was no practical possibility of placing her with a Sikh family due to the stigma of her illegitimacy and the psychiatric evidence was that she would suffer lasting psychological scars if she were moved, leave was granted to the foster carers to start the adoption process. Sir Stephen Brown P did not regard the trans-racial issue as the prime issue).

3   DoH Circular LAC (98) 20, para 13.

4   Ibid, para 13.

5   HC Special Standing Committee, 27 November 2001, col 307; HL Deb, 24 June 2002, CWH 17.

'Children will be matched with families who can best meet their needs. They will not be left waiting indefinitely for a "perfect family"[1].'

RANGE OF POWERS AND 'NO ORDER' PRINCIPLE: SECTION 1(6)

7.88 Section 1(6) of the ACA 2002 sets out two key principles, both of which provide the context within which the welfare principle in s 1(2) must operate. This is given particular emphasis under the Act by the conjunction in s 1(6) of the 'range of powers' consideration (s 1(3)(g) in the CA 1989) and the 'no order principle' (s 1(5) in the CA 1989).

The whole range of powers

7.89 Section 1(6) of the ACA 2002 places the obligation on the court or adoption agency 'always' to consider the whole range of powers available not only under the Act (including placement and adoption orders), but also under the CA 1989 (as amended) (including residence orders, care orders, supervision orders and special guardianship orders).

7.90 Before looking at the first limb of s 1(6), it is important to keep in mind the observations of Ward LJ in a case under the former law, *Re M (Adoption or Residence Order),*[2] where he said:[3]

'Two distinct and separate questions have to be asked before deciding whether or not to make an adoption order, viz:

(1) Should the child live with the applicants or with someone else;
(2) Should the child live with that person(s) under the aegis of:
    (i)   an adoption order; or
    (ii) a care order; or
    (iii) a residence order alone; or
    (iv) a residence order coupled with a s 91(14) [of the CA 1989] restriction; or
    (v)   no order at all . . .

In order to decide what form of order is appropriate, it is essential to have regard to the nature and effect of each order and the advantages and disadvantages each brings to the safeguarding and promotion of the welfare of the child throughout his childhood. The legal nature and effect of an adoption order is governed by s 39 of the Adoption Act 1976 [now s 67 of the ACA 2002]. It changes status. The child is treated in law as if she has been born a child of the marriage of the applicants [the proposed adopters]. She ceases in law to be a child of her mother and sister of her siblings. The old family link is destroyed and new family ties are created. The psychological effect is that the child loses one identity and gains another.

---

1   See *Re C (Adoption: Religious Observance)* [2002] 1 FLR 1119 where the child's heritage was very mixed (Jewish mother/Turkish-Cypriot-Irish father), and Wilson J stressed that the justice system was secular and that a pragmatic approach to ethnic background, as was taken by Wall J in *Re J (Specific Issue Orders: Muslim Upbringing and Circumcision)* [1999] 2 FLR 678, should be followed. He approved the plan for the child's adoption by a Jewish couple. This case provides a valuable reminder that searching for an explicit and complex religious and cultural match should not be such as to delay proceedings which are overwhelmingly in the child's best interests.
2   [1998] 1 FLR 570.
3   Ibid, at 588D–F and 589A–D.

Adoption is inconsistent with being a member of both old and new family at the same time. Long-term fostering does enable the child to have the best of both worlds by feeling she belongs to both families though she must reside with and will anyway usually choose to live with only one – the one who gives her the daily love and care.

The significant advantage of adoption is that it can promote much-needed security and stability, the younger the age of placement, the fuller the advantage. The disadvantage is that it is unlike any other decision made by adults during the child's minority because it is irrevocable. The child cannot at a later stage even in adulthood reverse the process. That is a salutary reminder of the seriousness of the decision. The advantage of the care/residence order is the converse – it can be adapted to meet changing needs, but therein lies its disadvantages – it does not provide absolute certainty and security. Section 91(14) minimises, if not eliminates, the uncertainty.'

7.91   The weighing up of the nature and effect of each order and the advantages and disadvantages which each brings to the welfare of the child throughout his life remains a crucial exercise under the new legislation.

Rehabilitation with birth parents

7.92   Under the CA 1989 the duty of the local authority is to promote the upbringing of children in need by their families, so far as is consistent with the duty to promote and safeguard the children's welfare.[1]

7.93   The local authority's first duty, therefore, remains that of making all reasonable efforts to rehabilitate the child with the birth family, wherever possible.

Home with extended family members or friends

7.94   Under the CA 1989,[2] where children cannot live with their birth parents, the duty of the local authority is to seek a home for the child with the extended family or friends. As the White Paper, *Adoption: A New Approach* recognised, 'Finding a safe and caring home for children with their wider family or friends allows them to keep important attachments and connections in their lives and is therefore the preferred choice where it is possible and consistent with the child's welfare'.[3]

Alternative options for permanence

7.95   Chapter 5 of the White Paper highlighted the need to establish a full range of options for permanent families where the child can no longer live with the birth parents. One of the key objectives of the White Paper was to 'set adoption within a context of permanence, with a spectrum of options for finding families for looked after children who need them'[4] ... 'securing it as a mainstream service'.[5] The intention is to encourage the wider use of adoption, particularly of children looked after by local authorities.

7.96   In addition to informal care with wider family and friends, the White Paper looked at the more formal options of residence orders through to adoption. It concluded

---

1   CA 1989, s 17(1)(b); see also s 17(1)(a).
2   Section 17(1).
3   Cm 5017 (December 2001), para 5.4.
4   Ibid, para 3.8.
5   Ibid, para 3.5.

that the list was incomplete as there was no status which provided legal permanence but lacked the complete break with birth parents. It suggested the creation of a new option of 'special guardianship'. This suggestion has resulted in an amendment to the CA 1989 (by s 115 of the ACA 2002) so as to add 'special guardianship orders' to the range of powers available to the court under a new s14A of the CA 1989.

RESIDENCE ORDERS/RESIDENCE ORDERS COUPLED WITH A S 91(14) RESTRICTION

7.97 A residence order is defined in s 8(1) of the CA 1989 as 'an order settling arrangements to be made as to the person with whom a child is to live'. The phrase 'settling the arrangements' gives the court flexibility to impose detailed conditions[1] and directions on those in whose favour an order is made, the parents and those with parental responsibility or with whom the child is living.[2] The court may also make 'such incidental, supplemental or consequential provision as the court thinks fit'.[3]

7.98 Under the AA 1976, residence orders, coupled with a restriction under s 91(14) of the CA 1989, have been employed as a significant alternative option to adoption. This is illustrated by *Re M (Adoption or Residence Order)*,[4] where the child, M, who was aged 12, had been placed with a Dr and Mrs A when she was nearly 9 years old. Dr and Mrs A were always clear that they wished to adopt. In the expectation of all concerned that M would be adopted, contact was arranged with the natural family and a good relationship with the natural mother developed. When Dr and Mrs A applied to adopt, M said that she did not wish to be adopted and the local authority withdrew its support for the adoption. A residence order was at one point acceptable to Dr and Mrs A, provided the mother did not apply for residence, but when the mother applied for residence, notwithstanding that she subsequently withdrew her application and would have agreed to a s 91(14) restriction, Dr and Mrs A became adamant that only an adoption order was acceptable and they were not prepared to keep M without formal adoption.

7.99 The trial judge made an adoption order, and the majority of the Court of Appeal (Simon Brown LJ dissenting) allowed the mother's appeal, making a residence order in favour of Dr and Mrs A subject to a s 91(14) restriction. The majority were of the view that the trial judge did not adequately address the question of adoption as a change of status, nor the question of whether some other order would adequately safeguard M's welfare. Ward LJ said:[5]

---

1   Note, however, *Re E (Residence: Imposition of Conditions)* [1997] 2 FLR 638, where the trial judge sought to impose a condition that the mother should continue to reside at a specified address. The Court of Appeal held this to be an unwarranted imposition on the right of a parent to choose where she should live within the UK and with whom. Also *Re D (Residence: Imposition of Conditions)* [1996] 2 FLR 281 where the court held that orders, which were injunctive in nature, should not be dressed up as conditions under s 11(7). In SM Cretney and JM Masson *Principles of Family Law* (6th edn, Sweet & Maxwell, 1997) at p 675, n 96, a useful illustration is given of a condition 'allowing a child's move to a new carer to be phased over a period' for a child subject to a care order who had had little contact with the parent or relative who wished to care for him. Although the residence order discharges the care order, a condition could be attached to the residence order whereby the child is to remain temporarily with the foster parents (but not in the care of or accommodated by the local authority).
2   CA 1989, s 11(7)(a) and (b).
3   Ibid, s 11(7)(d).
4   [1998] 1 FLR 570.
5   At 590F–G and 591C.

'Throughout the hearing the judge undoubtedly gave the impression that there was only one question, the answer to which decided the whole case, namely where in the best interests of this girl should she live? ... In my judgment the judge was wrong to inhibit, as he clearly did, a full exploration of the important issue of whether or not the desired security could have been adequately achieved by other means ...'

7.100   Again, in *Re B (Adoption Order)*,[1] Hale LJ stressed that:

'It is important, it seems to me, that everyone concerned recognises that there is more than one way of securing legal permanence ... There has been a tendency, it seems to me, to diminish the value of what can be achieved by a residence order. Provided that it is supported by all the extras that in the particular case are found necessary, it can give this little boy everything that he needs – security and stability throughout his childhood, and contact and a continuing relationship with his family; it can be backed up by additional provisions to protect that security in fact; and if needed, the continuing support of the local authority both can and should be made available to them ...'

7.101   In *Re B* the child had been placed with a foster carer whilst maintaining regular contact and an excellent relationship with his father and his father's family. All the parties, with the exception of the local authority, agreed that there should be a residence order to the foster mother buttressed by a s 91(14) order with generous contact to the father. The local authority, however, encouraged the foster mother to apply for adoption, which the judge at first instance granted. Thorpe LJ, allowing the appeal, held:[2]

'To make an adoption order was inconsistent with the reality that [the child] was both a member of his foster-mother's family and a member of his father's family.

Secondly, I have grave doubts as to whether the judge sufficiently considered the father's right to family life ... It seems to me in this case that it is very hard indeed to demonstrate the necessary proportionality given the completely satisfactory arrangement that was open for judicial approval in the confirmation of the status quo for [the child] ...'

7.102   The principal advantages of a residence order, therefore, are that, first, it is flexible and adaptable; secondly, the natural parents, where they are married, and the unmarried natural father, where he has parental responsibility, retain parental responsibility and share it with the residential carer, so that the family link is maintained; and thirdly, it respects the child's right to 'family life' (where it exists) with the family of his or her birth and is 'less interventionist' than an adoption order. The principal disadvantages of a residence order are that (i) there is no guarantee of certainty and (ii) it is not 'for life', which has relevance to the child's sense of belonging to a permanent family where the order is in favour of a carer other than relatives, such as a local authority foster parent. However, the uncertainty of future, unsettling applications by the non-residential parent(s) may be reduced by a s 91(14) order, and the sense of security enhanced by the amendments to s 12 of the CA 1989.

7.103   Residence orders provide an important option for permanence, particularly for relatives and friends, step-parents and local authority foster parents (especially where a relationship has developed with the natural family). One of the main objections to adoption by relatives is the potential for distorting family relationships. For example, where an adoption order is made in favour of grandparents, the legal consequence of the

---

1   [2001] EWCA Civ 347, [2001] 2 FLR 26 at [24]–[27].
2   At [19]–[20].

adoption is that the grandparents are the parents of the child, and the natural parent becomes a sibling. Residence orders, therefore, are generally the more appropriate and proportionate response for placements within the family. Adoption, however, should not be ruled out, as there may be circumstances which justify the making of an adoption order,[1] although such occasions will be rare.

7.104 As residence orders were 'not perceived as being likely to offer a sufficient sense of permanence for a child and his carers',[2] s 114 of the ACA 2002 amends s 12 of the CA 1989 to empower the court to direct that a residence order made in favour of someone who is not a parent or a guardian of a child may be extended until the child reaches the age of 18. Under the former law, a residence order ceased to have effect when the child reached the age of 16 unless the court was satisfied that the circumstances were exceptional.[3] Now where a court has directed that the order may be extended, an application to vary or discharge the order may be made only with the leave of the court.[4] The intention is to provide a further means of delivering enhanced security where the holder of a residence order who is not the child's parent is caring for the child on a long-term basis. The hope is that this amendment will provide greater legal security for foster parents and step-parents while retaining the legal relationship between the natural family and the child, which would be lost on adoption.

7.105 It is also worth noting that s 112 of the ACA 2002 makes a significant amendment to the CA 1989 in the case of step-parents, with the clear intention of boosting alternatives to adoption, by inserting a new s 4A to enable a step-parent to acquire parental responsibility for the child of his spouse. This may be acquired either by agreement between the step-parent and the parents who have parental responsibility for the child or by order of the court.

7.106 Previously[5] local authority foster parents were unable to apply for a s 8 order (including a residence order) without leave and were only able to seek the leave of the court if they had the consent of the local authority, they were a relative of the child or the child had been living with them for 3 years. This position has been transformed by the ACA 2002. Section 10 of the CA 1989 is amended (by Sch 3 to the ACA 2002) to include a new subsection (5A), which entitles a local authority foster parent to apply for a residence order in relation to a child who has lived with him for a period of at least one year immediately preceding the application. Thus the local authority foster parent is now entitled to apply as of right (ie without the court's leave) for a residence order and the

---

1   See *Re O (A Minor) (Adoption by Grandparents)* [1985] FLR 546; *Re S (A Minor) (Adoption or Custodianship)* [1987] Fam 98; *Re W (A Minor) (Adoption: Custodianship: Access)* [1988] 1 FLR 175; *Re W (A Minor) (Guardianship)* [1992] Fam Law 64.
2   1992 Review of Adoption Law (HMSO, 1992), at para 6.4.
3   CA 1989, s 9(6) and (7).
4   Ibid, s 12(6), as inserted by s 114(1) of the ACA 2002.
5   Ibid, s 9(3). For applications by local authority foster parents under the former law, see *Re A and Others (Minors) (Residence Order: Leave to Apply)* [1992] Fam 182, [1992] 2 FLR 154 and *C v Salford City Council and Others* [1994] 2 FLR 926. Prospective adopters who had a child who had been freed for adoption placed with them by a local authority were held to be local authority foster parents and therefore precluded by s 9(3) from applying for leave: *Re C (Adoption Notice)* [1999] 1 FLR 384.

residence requirement is one year.[1] This paves the way for a much earlier decision to be taken where the appropriate permanency option for the child is a residence order to his foster parents. This option not only gives the child and the foster parents the desired security, but also, where regular contact with the birth family has been taking place successfully, enables this to be maintained in the best interests of the child. The ACA 2002 also amends s 9(3) of the CA 1989 (which sets out restrictions on making applications for s 8 orders)[2] by replacing the residence requirement of 3 years with a one-year period.[3]

FOSTERING

7.107 Long-term fostering is one of the range of options available in planning for permanence. The 2000 White Paper recognises that 'long term fostering may also have a role in providing a family for looked after children', particularly where older children have strong links to their birth families and do not wish for or need the formality of adoption or 'special guardianship'.[4] As Ward LJ put it in *Re M (Adoption or Residence Order)*[5] 'long term fostering can provide the best of both worlds in providing the child with the security of a family, whilst maintaining the relationship and identity with the birth parents and extended family'. This is based on the premise that fostering is best viewed as an inclusive arrangement in the sense that the foster carers recognise the value to the child of the links with and contact to their birth family, which they seek to maintain. This is the approach which best accords with the spirit of 'partnership' in the CA 1989.[6]

7.108 However, there is a downside, namely insecurity for the child and for the foster parents which can take various forms from repeated applications by the birth family to changing views of local authorities, together with the indelible imprint of managerial control and continuing statutory involvement by the authority on the fostering relationship.

SPECIAL GUARDIANSHIP ORDERS

7.109 In recommending the creation of the new option of 'special guardianship', the White Paper recognised that adoption was not always appropriate for children who cannot return to their birth families.

> 'Some older children do not wish to be legally separated from their birth families. Adoption may not be best for some children being cared for on a permanent basis by members of their wider birth family. Some minority ethnic communities have religious and cultural difficulties

1   This is to provide consistency with s 42(4) of the ACA 2002, which entitles a local authority foster parent to apply as of right for an adoption order for a child in his or her care, provided that the child has had his or her home with the foster carer for one year preceding the application.
2   This must mean a s 8 order other than a residence order.
3   ACA 2002, s 113. Section 9(4) of the CA 1989 is omitted.
4   Cm 5017 (December 2000), paras 5.12 and 5.13.
5   [1998] 1 FLR 570.
6   See A Bainham *Children: The Modern Law,* (2nd edn, Family Law, 1998) at p 194 for an interesting discussion on 'Exclusive versus inclusive fostering'. As he puts it 'Exclusive parenting is the notion that children are better off if they relate to one set of "parents" who have their care. Outside involvement with other adults is conceived of as undesirable and disruptive of the foster family. Some foster parents have evidently held this view and have not welcomed interaction with natural parents'.

with adoption as it is set out in law. Unaccompanied asylum seeking children may also need secure, permanent homes, but have strong attachments to their families abroad.'[1]

7.110 'Special guardianship orders' are, therefore, intended to meet the needs of these children 'who cannot live with their birth parents, for whom adoption is not appropriate, but who could still benefit from a legally secure placement'. The new order is intended to offer more than a residence order in terms of the security it brings and the support services to be made available, including financial support.[2] It is designed to be flexible enough to work in a range of situations including, for example, where there is extensive and regular contact with the birth family and instances where that would not be appropriate but where, nevertheless, it is desirable to retain the basic link between the child and parent.[3] When considering making a special guardianship order, the child's welfare is the court's paramount consideration and the welfare checklist in s 1 of the CA 1989 applies.[4]

7.111 Under 'special guardianship orders', the special guardian appointed by the order has parental responsibility for the child and (subject to any other order in force with respect to the child under the Act)[5] is entitled to exercise that parental responsibility to the exclusion of any other person with parental responsibility[6] with two exceptions. It does not affect (i) the operation of any rule of law which requires the consent of all those with parental responsibility (for example, the sterilisation or circumcision of the child),[7] nor (ii) any rights which a natural parent has in relation to the child's adoption or placement for adoption.[8] Where a placement order is in force, the special guardian's exercise of parental responsibility may be restricted by the adoption agency under s 25(4) of the ACA 2002.[9]

7.112 The special guardian, therefore, has responsibility for the day-to-day decisions about caring for the child and for taking decisions about his upbringing. The parents, however, retain some limited rights. They have the right to consent or not to the child's placement for adoption or adoption,[10] and, significantly, before making a special guardianship order, an express duty is imposed upon the court to consider whether it should make a contact order,[11] which would enable continued contact with the birth family. The special guardian must also take reasonable steps to inform the parents if the

---

1   *Adoption: A New Approach*, Cm 5017 (December 2000), para 5.9.
2   HL Deb, 23 October 2002, col 1374, per Lord Hunt of Kings Heath.
3   HL Deb, 18 July 2002, CWH 347, Lord Hunt of Kings Heath.
4   ACA 2002, s 115(2) and (3). CA 1989, s 5 is also amended to make provision about the appointment of guardians for children after the death of a special guardian.
5   See the position in relation to placement orders.
6   CA 1989, s 14C(1)(a) and (b), as amended by s 115 of the ACA 2002.
7   *Re J (Specific Issue Orders: Child's Religious Upbringing and Circumcision)* [2000] 1 FLR 571 at 577D, per Dame Elizabeth Butler-Sloss P: 'There is, in my view, a small group of important decisions, which in the absence of agreement of those with parental responsibility, ought not to be carried out or arranged by a one-parent carer although she has parental responsibility under s 2(7) of the Children Act 1989. Such a decision ought not to be made without the specific approval of the court. Sterilisation is one example. The change of a child's surname is another. Some of the examples, including the change of a child's surname, are based upon statute (see s 13(1) of the CA 1989). The issue of circumcision ... in my view ... comes within that group'.
8   CA 1989, s 14C(2).
9   ACA 2002, s 29(7)(a) and CA 1989, s 14C(1)(b).
10 CA 1989, s 14C(2)(b).
11 Ibid, s 14B(1)(a).

child dies.[1] Before making a special guardianship order, the court must also consider whether or not to vary or discharge any other existing s 8 order (such as a contact order or residence order).[2]

7.113 The aim, therefore, is to provide legal security, whilst preserving the 'basic' link between the child and his or her birth family.[3] Unlike adoption, the child's relationship with his or her birth parents is not severed, but preserved. Although their ability to exercise their parental responsibility is circumscribed, they nevertheless remain legally the child's parents.

The application process

7.114 A court may make a special guardianship order in respect of any child on the application of:[4]

(i)   any guardian of the child;[5]
(ii) any individual in whose favour a residence order is in force in respect of the child[6] or who has the consent of all those in whose favour a residence order is in force;[7]
(iii) anyone with whom the child has lived for at least 3 years out of the last 5 years;[8]
(iv) where the child is in the care of a local authority, anyone with the local authority's consent;[9]
(v)   in any other case, anyone who has the consent of all those with parental responsibility for the child;[10]
(vi) a local authority foster parent with whom the child has lived for a period of at least one year immediately preceding the application;[11]
(vii) anyone else, including the child, who has the leave of the court.[12]

7.115 Where a person is applying for leave to make an application for a special guardianship order, the court is under a duty to have particular regard to:[13]

(i)   the nature of the opposed application for the special guardianship order;
(ii) the applicant's connection with the child;
(iii) any risk there might be of that proposed application disrupting the child's life to such an extent that he would be harmed by it; and

---

1   CA 1989, s 14C(5).
2   Ibid, s 14B(1)(b).
3   *Adoption: A New Approach*, Cm 5017 (December 2000), para 5.10; HL Deb, 23 October 2002, cols 1374–1377, per Lord Hunt of Kings Heath.
4   CA 1989, s 14A(3), (5) and (6), as amended by ACA 2002; see also s 10(5)(b) and (c) of the CA 1989.
5   CA 1989, s 14A(5)(a) as amended.
6   Ibid, s 14A(5)(b).
7   Section 14A(5)(c) includes any individual from those listed in s 10(5)(b) or (c) of the CA 1989 who are the persons entitled to apply for a residence order or contact order. Although s 10(5)(a) of the CA 1989 includes a step-parent as a person entitled to apply for a residence order or contact order, a step-parent is not included in the individuals entitled to apply for a special guardianship order.
8   CA 1989, s 14A(5)(c) and s 10(5)(b) and (10).
9   Ibid, s 14A(5)(c) and s 10(5)(c)(ii).
10 Ibid, s 14A(5)(c) and s 10(5)(iii).
11 Ibid, s 14A(5)(d).
12 Ibid, s 14A(3)(b).
13 Ibid, s 14A(12) and s 10(9).

(iv) where the child is being looked after by a local authority: (a) the authority's plans for the future; and (b) the wishes and feelings of the child's parents.

7.116   In the case of a child seeking leave, the court may grant leave only if it is satisfied that he or she has sufficient understanding to make the proposed application.[1]

7.117   The application may be joint[2] and the persons concerned need not be married, but they must be aged 18 or over and must not be the natural parents.[3] The court has the power to make a special guardianship order in any family proceedings (which includes adoption proceedings)[4] concerning the welfare of the child, irrespective of there being an application before the court.[5] Local authority foster parents may apply for a special guardianship order as of right if the child has lived with them for at least one year.[6]

7.118   Applicants have to give 3 months' written notice to the local authority of their intention to apply for an order.[7] The only exception to this is where a person has the leave of the court to make a competing application for a special guardianship order at a final adoption hearing, in which case the 3-month period does not apply.[8] This is to prevent the competing application delaying the adoption order hearing. The local authority is under a duty to investigate and prepare a report (as prescribed by regulations) to the court as to the suitability of the applicants to be special guardians.[9] It is envisaged that statutory guidance will require the results of earlier relevant assessments to be taken into account, for example when the applicants are approved as foster carers. The court may not make a special guardianship order unless it has received such a report.[10]

7.119   The intention is to provide secondary legislation for an officer of the Children and Family Courts Advisory and Support Service (CAFCASS) to be appointed in appropriate special guardianship proceedings. In the run up to the implementation of the special guardianship provisions in the Act, associated rules will set out not only the circumstances in which the CAFCASS officers must be appointed, but also their duties in each case.[11] It is envisaged that a CAFCASS officer is likely to be appointed in most cases where the court is considering making a special guardianship order. However, it might not be appropriate or necessary to appoint the child as a party nor to appoint a children's guardian in cases where the application is for the variation of the terms of the special guardianship order which is agreed by all the parties.[12] Special guardianship orders will be private law proceedings and currently children's views in s 8 proceedings are put before the court within the CAFCASS officer's report. Rule 4.11B of the Family Proceedings Rules 1991 requires the CAFCASS officer (the child and family reporter) to notify the

---

1   CA 1989, s 14A(12) and s 10(8).
2   Ibid, s 14A(1) and (3).
3   Ibid, s 14A(2)(a) and (b).
4   Ibid, s 8(3).
5   Ibid, s 14A(6)(b), as amended.
6   Ibid, s 14A(5)(d).
7   Ibid, s 14A(7), as amended.
8   ACA 2002, s 29(6) and s 14A(7) of the CA 1989, as amended by s 115 of the ACA 2002.
9   CA 1989, s 14A(9).
10   Ibid, s 14A(11), as amended.
11   HL Deb, 18 July 2002, CWH 349. The Government is currently undertaking a scooping exercise before undertaking a wider consultation on how children are represented in private law CA proceedings.
12   HL Deb, 23 October 2002, col 1375.

child of so much of the contents of this report as he or she considers appropriate to the age and understanding of the child, including any reference to the child's own views on the application and the recommendation of the CAFCASS officer. Rule 4.11B also requires the child and family reporter to consider whether it is in the best interests of the child to be made a party to the proceedings.

7.120   While a special guardianship order is in force with respect to a child, no one may cause the child to be known by a new surname or remove him or her from the United Kingdom without either the written consent of every person who has parental authority or the leave of the court.[1] This does not preclude a special guardian from removing a child for a period of less than 3 months.[2] On making a special guardianship order, the court may give leave for the child to be known by a new surname and give permission for the child to be taken out of the jurisdiction for any period longer than 3 months.[3] Where, however, a placement order is in force, s 14C(3) and (4) does not apply.[4]

7.121   A further distinction from an adoption order is that special guardianship orders can be varied or discharged[5] by the court of its own motion during any family proceedings in which the welfare of the child arises,[6] or on the application of:[7]

(i)   the special guardian;
(ii)   the child's parents or guardian, although only with the leave of the court;[8]
(iii) the child, with leave of the court[9] and provided the court is satisfied that he has sufficient understanding to make the application;[10]
(iv)   any individual in whose favour a residence order is in force in respect of the child;[11]
(v)   any individual (other than a special guardian, parent or guardian or a person with a residence order) who has, or immediately before the making of the special guardianship order had, parental responsibility for the child, but only with the court's leave;[12]
(vi)   if a care order is made in respect of the child, the local authority.[13]

7.122   The following, therefore, must obtain leave:[14]

(i)   the child;
(ii)   any parent or guardian;
(iii) any step-parent who has acquired and has not lost parental responsibility for the child;

---

1   CA 1989, s 14C(3)(a) and (b).
2   Ibid, s 14C(4).
3   Ibid, ss 14B(2)(b) and 14C(3)(b). The leave may be general or for specified purposes.
4   Ibid, s 29(7)(b).
5   Ibid, s 14D.
6   Ibid, s 14D(2).
7   Ibid, s 14D(1).
8   Ibid, s 14D(3)(b).
9   Ibid, s 14D(3)(a).
10   Ibid, s 14D(4).
11   Ibid, s 14D(1)(c).
12   Ibid, s 14D(1)(d).
13   Ibid, s 14D(1)(f).
14   Ibid, s 14D(3)(a)–(d).

(iv) any individual[1] who immediately before the making of the special guardianship order had, but no longer has, parental responsibility.

7.123 Save for the case of the child, the court may grant leave only if it is satisfied that there has been a *significant* change in circumstances since the making of the special guardianship order.[2]

7.124 Provisions are also made for: (i) the court to set time scales for proceedings involving special guardianship orders;[3] (ii) the local authority to make arrangements for the provision of support services including counselling, advice, information and financial support;[4] and (iii) establishing a procedure for considering representations including complaints.[5]

7.125 In relation to the support services, regulations will be made prescribing the circumstances where the local authority must, at the request of special guardians, children who are the subject of special guardianship orders and other prescribed persons (including a parent), carry out an assessment of that person's needs for special guardianship support services. The local authority has a discretion as to whether or not to carry out an assessment at the request of other persons.[6] As with adoption support services, the aim is to facilitate a package of support from the various public services.

7.126 Schedule 3 to the ACA 2002 provides that a special guardianship order discharges any existing care order or related contact order. If, however, the need arises, a care order or a residence order may be made while a special guardianship order is in force.[7] In this case, the special guardianship order is not automatically discharged, but the local authority concerned or person in whose favour the residence order is made has the right to apply for discharge or variation of the special guardianship order by virtue of the new s 14D of the CA 1989.

---

1   Other than a special guardian, parent or guardian or individual with a residence order.
2   CA 1989, s 14D(5).
3   Ibid, s 14E. The court may give directions for ensuring that the timetable is adhered to. The special guardianship order or variation order may contain provisions which are to have effect for a specified period.
4   CA 1989, s 14F. Schedule 3 to the ACA 2002 by amendments to the Children (Leaving Care) Act 2000 also places a duty on local authorities to consider whether to provide advice and assistance to former looked-after children aged between 16 and 21 subject to special guardianship orders, including support for employment, education and training and, if the child is in such need, they must advise and befriend and may also provide assistance.
5   CA 1989, s 14G. It is intended to use these powers to require authorities to establish complaints procedures for special guardianship orders modelled on the revised Children Act complaints procedures to be established under s 26 of the CA 1989, as amended by s 117 of the ACA 2002.
6   Where, as a result of an assessment, a local authority decides that a person has needs for special guardianship support services, they must then decide whether to provide such services to that person: CA 1989, s 14F(5). If the local authority so decides and the circumstances fall within the prescribed description, then the local authority must prepare a plan for the provision of the services and keep the plan under review: s 14F(6).
7   Schedule 3 to the ACA 2002 inserts a new subs (7A) into s 10 of the CA 1989 which provides that 'if a special guardianship order is in force with respect to a child, an application for a residence order may only be made with respect to him, if apart from this subsection the leave of the court is not required, with leave'.

7.127   Where a placement order is in force, no special guardianship order may be made in respect of the child unless:[1]

(i)   an application has been made for a final adoption order; and
(ii)   the person applying for the special guardianship order has obtained leave under s 29(5)(b) of the ACA 2002 or if he or she is the guardian of the child, under s 47(5). Written notice of the intention to make the application must be given to the local authority which is looking after the child or in whose area the individual is ordinarily resident but 3 months' notice is not required.[2]

ADOPTION

7.128   Adoption provides an important mainstream option for permanency. For those children who are unable to return to their birth families, it provides a legally permanent new family, to which children will belong all their lives. It is thus a key means of providing a permanent family for these children.[3]

7.129   Hale LJ has suggested obiter[4] that 'in the right circumstances adoption is a most valuable way of supplying an child with the "family for life" to which everyone ought to be entitled and of which some children are most tragically deprived'. This notion chimes with one of the cardinal themes motivating the reforms, namely the unacceptable numbers of children adrift for long periods in the care system. Generally, the intention of the new legislation is to ensure decisions as to whether adoption is the right option are taken earlier in the adoption process than under the former legislation.

7.130   Further, where there are strong attachments to the foster carers and the children wish to adopted by them, subject to it being in the child's best interests to do so, this is to be encouraged and a fast-track procedure is now provided to enable this to take place.[5]

'Twin track planning'

7.131   The concerns over the delays in the care system had been foreshadowed by Bracewell J in *Re D and K (Care Plan: Twin-Track Planning)*:[6]

> 'Local authorities traditionally have exhausted the possibility of rehabilitation to parents or extended family before even beginning to address the possibility of permanency outside the family ... For too long there has been a culture in which adoption has been regarded as the equivalent of failure and therefore a procedure to be considered only as a last resort when all else has been tried and not succeeded. Such sequential planning often promotes delay with serious consequences for the welfare of the child ...
>
> It is now well researched that children deprived of permanent parenting grow up with unmet psychological needs and far too many children have to wait too long before permanent families are found for them when they cannot return to their natural families. The longer the

---

1   CA 1989, s 14A(13) and ACA 2002, s 29(5).
2   Ibid, s 14A(7) and ibid, s 29(6).
3   *Adoption: A New Approach*, Cm 5017 (December 2000), para 5.5.
4   *Re B (Adoption by One Parent to Exclusion of Other)* [2001] 1 FLR 589, which was overruled by the House of Lords on the interpretation of s 15(3) of the AA 1976, but no comment was made on this specific point.
5   Paragraphs 5.6 and 5.7 of the White Paper.
6   [1999] 2 FLR 872 at 874–875.

delay, the more difficult it is to place children who often become progressively more disturbed in limbo, thereby rendering the task of identifying suitable adoptive families a lengthy and uncertain process. The older the child, the greater the risk of breakdown in an adoptive placement. It is therefore incumbent on local authorities and guardians to seek to prevent these delays by identifying clearly the options available for the court by twin track planning as opposed to sequential planning'.

7.132   These concerns led her to make the following recommendations in relation to twin track planning:

(1)   in such cases, it should be made clear to the natural family at the outset that the local authority are considering two options, ie rehabilitation with a strictly limited time scale or adoption outside the family, and that such twin track planning in no way pre-empts the outcome;

(2)   whenever care proceedings are commenced, the court should be proactive at an early directions hearing by inquiring of the local authority whether twin track planning is suitable for the case and giving appropriate directions. Designated care judges should liaise with their director of social services for children, with the chairman of adoption and fostering panels, with panel managers of guardians and with other concerned persons.

Concurrent planning

7.133   Bracewell J further recommended that 'local authorities should consider in each case whether it is suitable for "concurrent planning" within the meaning of the scheme developed by the Lutheran social services in the USA, the state of Washington and now widespread throughout the states of the USA over a period of 20 years' experience'.

7.134   Concurrent planning should not be confused with twin track planning as the two options are quite distinct. 'Concurrent planning' is defined as 'the process of working towards family reunification, while at the same time establishing an alternative permanent plan'. As Bracewell J said:[1]

> 'The aim is to reduce the number of moves a child experiences in care, and to reduce temporary placements. The project involves the recruitment of foster parents who are carefully selected and trained and who are willing to foster children on the basis that they will work with the natural family towards rehabilitation within a strictly timed framework, but, in the event of rehabilitation being ruled out, wish to adopt the children. Contact between carers and birth children is encouraged and there is openness between parties about the primary aim of rehabilitation with the alternative secondary plan of permanent placement. Placement stability is a top priority.'

7.135   The type of cases suitable for such placements are generally babies or young children where there are 'some but by no means optimistic' prospects of rehabilitation to the birth family.

7.136   Two pilot schemes have been established: (i) the Goodman Project, which started life as a collaboration between Manchester Adoption Society and two local authorities, Bury Metropolitan Borough Council and Salford Metropolitan Borough

---

1   *Re D and K (Care Plan: Twin Track Planning)* [1999] 2 FLR 872 at 875.

Council, but has now been extended to all the local authorities in Greater Manchester and (ii) the Thomas Coram Foundation in London, which is currently carrying out research on the scheme. The White Paper, *Adoption: A New Approach*[1] highlighted the Goodman project as improving the pace and planning for children:

> 'The project has received positive responses from the judiciary and legal professionals, and benefits have been found to include a reduction in the number of placements. Potential permanent families are selected early on in the process, reducing the length of time to reach adoption where this becomes the plan. Birth families are constructively engaged in the planning process.'

7.137 Consequently both 'twin track planning' and 'concurrent planning' remain important players in the range of options which local authorities and the courts should consider when planning for children.

'No order' principle

7.138 The 'no order' principle in s 1(6) of the ACA 2002 is in line with s 1(5) of the CA 1989 which encapsulates the 'non-interventionist' or 'least interventionist' approach. In relation to the 'no order principle' in s 1(5) of the CA 1989, in *B v B (A Minor) (Residence Order)*,[2] Johnson J said:

> 'It is inherent to the philosophy underlying the Children Act 1989 that Parliament has decreed that the State, whether in the guise of a local authority or the court, shall not intervene in the life of children and their families, unless it is necessary to do so . . . and it is in accordance with that general philosophy that s 1(5) is in the terms which I have quoted.'

7.139 In the context of care proceedings, in *Re O (Care or Supervision Order)*,[3] Hale J (as she then was), having referred to s 1(5), said:

> '. . . the court should begin with a preference for the least interventionist rather than the more interventionist approach. This should be considered to be in the better interests of the children, again unless there are cogent reasons to the contrary.'

7.140 Again, in *Oxfordshire County Council v L (Care or Supervision Order)*,[4] she said:

> '. . . one should approach these cases on the basis that the less Draconian order was likely to be better for the child than the more Draconian or interventionist one.'

7.141 The 'no order principle' is the embodiment of the principle of proportionality under the European Convention on Human Rights. Since the implementation of the Human Rights Act 1998, the Court of Appeal has demonstrated a rigorous application of the principle of proportionality in child law cases. In *Re C and B (Care Order: Future harm)*[5] two older children had been taken into care under orders based on actual harm and subsequently two younger children were removed from the mother, the 10-month-

---

1   Cm 5017 (December 2000) at para 5.21.
2   [1992] 2 FLR 327 at 328B.
3   [1996] 2 FLR 755 at 760A.
4   [1998] 1 FLR 70 at 74E; for a case where the choice was between a supervision order and no order see *Re K (Supervision Order)* [1999] 2 FLR 303, where Wall J at 318C said: '. . . an order should only be made if the children need more protection than can be given voluntarily . . . In other words, there must be something in the making or operation of a supervision order which makes it better for the children for an order to be made'.
5   [2001] 1 FLR 611.

old child under an interim care order and the newborn baby under an emergency protection order. In respect of the younger children it was held that, although there was a real possibility of future harm, the action taken must be a proportionate response to the nature and gravity of the feared harm and, as there were no long-standing problems which would interfere with the capacity to provide adequate parenting, the local authority could have taken time to explore other options. Hale LJ said:[1]

> 'There is a long line of European Court of Human Rights jurisprudence on that third requirement [ie the interference must be 'necessary in a democratic society'], which emphasises that the intervention has to be proportionate to the legitimate aim. Intervention in the family may be appropriate, but the aim should be to reunite the family when the circumstances enable that, and the effort should be devoted towards that end. Cutting off all contact and relationship between the child or children and their family is only justified by the overriding necessity of the interests of the child.'[2]

7.142   In *Re O (Supervision Order)*, where the Court of Appeal held that a supervision order was the more proportionate solution than a care order, Hale LJ said:[3]

> 'Proportionality ... is the key. It will be the duty of everyone to ensure that in those cases where a supervision order is proportionate as a response to the risk presented, a supervision order can be made to work, as indeed the framers of the Children Act always hoped it would work.'

7.143   It is suggested, therefore, that the court or adoption agency, in working its way through the range of options, should always ask itself whether the option under consideration is a proportionate response to the current needs of the child. The proportionate application of both limbs of s 1(6) of the ACA 2002 is essential to the working of the whole Act. It is the lubrication which enables the components of s 1 to turn. Without this lubrication, there would be a risk of friction between adoption under the Act and Art 8 of the European Convention on Human Rights. The potential for friction arises from the fact that an adoption order is the most serious interference with the right to respect for family life, not only of the parents but more importantly of the child, as it brings to an end the legal relationship between the child and the whole of his family of birth. In *Johansen v Norway*, as we have seen, the European Court held that to deprive the applicant mother of both her parental rights and contact in the context of adoption were measures which were 'particularly far reaching in that they totally deprived the applicant of her family life with the child'. The Court's approach was that such measures should be applied only in 'exceptional circumstances' and only where they were motivated by an overriding requirement pertaining to the child's best interests. Only by a rigorous pruning under both limbs of s 1(6) can these 'exceptional circumstances' which justify the most complete form of severance with 'family life' be flushed out from the factual undergrowth.

7.144   Under the 'no order principle' in s 1(6) of the ACA 2002, the court should 'begin with a preference for the least interventionist approach ... [which] should be considered to be in the better interests of the child unless there are cogent reasons to the

---

1   [2001] 1 FLR 611 at [34].
2   See *Johansen v Norway* (1996) 23 EHRR 33, para 78.
3   [2001] 1 FLR 923 at [28].

contrary'.[1] It follows from this that the court or adoption agency ought to consider the whole range of options, with the least interventionist being considered first. Applying this approach to Ward LJ's second question in *Re M (Adoption or Residence Order)*[2] and re-arranging the list of options (with the addition of a special guardianship order) in order of the 'least interventionist', it would read:

(i) no order at all;
(ii) a residence order alone;
(iii) a residence order coupled with a s 91(14) restriction;
(iv) a supervision order;
(v) a care order;
(vi) a special guardianship order;
(vii) an adoption order.

7.145 It is suggested that this approach may provide some shade from the proportionality spotlight under Art 8(2) of the European Convention on Human Rights. However, this does not mean that the 'least interventionist' options have to be exhausted in turn before adoption can be considered. This would be to fall into the 'last resort' trap referred to by Bracewell J in *Re D and K (Care Plan: Twin Track Planning)*[3] and promote rather than reduce the damage of delay. What it means in practice is that, at the planning stages for the child's future, 'the range' of options should be considered in the light of the facts of the particular case. This consideration must be a carefully weighed and balanced one, in the sense that it requires the advantages and disadvantages for the child between the legal routes for securing his future home to be carefully evaluated before it should be concluded that adoption is the 'best interests' route. It requires a rigorous discipline. If there is no such analysis, or if it becomes routine and perfunctory, then there is a real risk of trespassing over the borders of compatibility with Art 8 of the Convention. It is submitted that to treat adoption as 'the first resort', as has been suggested,[4] would be contrary to the 'no order' principle in the Act, and a prima facie infringement of the Art 8 rights of the child and the parents.

---

1   *Re O (Care or Supervision Order)*[1996] 2 FLR 755 at 759H–760B, per Hale J (as she then was).
2   [1998] 1 FLR 564 at 588D–E.
3   [1999] 2 FLR 872.
4   HC Deb, 26 March 2001, vol 365, no 59, col 699, per Mr John Hutton, Minister of State, Department of Health.

Chapter 8

PARENTAL CONSENT

PARENTAL CONSENT UNDER THE ADOPTION AND CHILDREN ACT 2002

8.1   The Performance and Innovation Unit Report 'Prime Minister's Review of Adoption'[1] ('the PIU Report') highlighted the handling of parental consent, 'this sensitive and central issue', as 'a key driver of both the length and complexity and the quality of the experience for the child and for both sets of parents'.[2] It concluded that the legal framework under the AA 1976 had not allowed parental agreement to be handled in the most effective manner. This conclusion has prompted a radical and fundamental overhaul of the whole issue of consent under the new legislation, perhaps signalled by the change of wording from 'agreement'[3] to 'consent'.

Parental consent and placement

8.2   The ACA 2002 establishes two routes for placing a child for adoption. First, each parent may consent to placing the child for adoption: *the s 19 route*. Secondly, a local authority may secure a placement order from the court authorising it to place a child with adopters whom it selects: *the s 21 route*. A local authority must apply for a placement order where it is satisfied that a child should be adopted but the parents do not consent to placement or have withdrawn such consent. The key to placement is, therefore, consent.

Advance consent

8.3   Section 20 of the ACA 2002, which is subject to the provisions in s 52,[4] introduces a new concept of 'advance consent'. It enables a parent, who consents to his or her child being placed for adoption by an adoption agency under s 19, at the same time or a subsequent time, to give consent to the making of a future adoption order ('advance consent').[5] 'Advance consent' may be given to adoption (i) by the prospective adopters

---

1   Issued for consultation in July 2000.
2   Paragraph 3.47.
3   The word 'agreement' was introduced by the Children Act 1975 to signal a move away from parental rights. Although the re-employment of the word 'consent' is clearly not intended to herald the return of 'parental rights', the authors would like to think that its use is at least a recognition (albeit a semantic one) that the parents have a real and significant interest when the adoption of their child is being considered, which should carry weight in the balancing exercise of the s 1 principles.
4   ACA 2002, s 20(6).
5   Ibid, s 20(1).

identified in the consent or (ii) by *any* prospective adopters who may be chosen by the agency.[1]

8.4 There is, however, protection provided for the parent who gives 'advance consent' and later has a change of mind. The consent may be withdrawn,[2] but the withdrawal of consent must be in the prescribed form or by notice given to the agency.[3] However, under s 52(4), the withdrawal of any consent given under s 20 is ineffective if it is given after an application for an adoption order is made.

8.5 The parent giving advance consent may give notice to the adoption agency stating that he or she does not wish to be informed when an application for an adoption order is made.[4] This provision is intended to enable a parent who wishes to relinquish his or her child for adoption to do so without the need for any further involvement in the adoption proceedings. However, that person has the option to withdraw such a statement at any subsequent time.[5] The notice under s 20(4) may be given at the same time as advance consent or at any subsequent time and takes effect from the time when it is received by the adoption agency.[6]

8.6 If the parent giving advance consent either makes no statement that he or she does not wish to be informed of any adoption application, or makes such a statement but later withdraws it, that parent does have some procedural protection. Under s 141(3) and (4)(c)(ii), he or she is entitled to notification of the date and place where the application will be heard.[7] If a parent 'opts in', these provisions apply so that he or she automatically receives notice. It is then open to the parent to apply for leave to oppose the making of an adoption order under s 47(3). However, under s 47(3) the court cannot give leave unless satisfied that there has been a change of circumstances since the consent was given.[8] The difficulties in overcoming the 'leave' hurdle at that stage should not be underestimated.

8.7 The purpose of the advance consent provision, therefore, is to provide a route for those small number of cases in which the parents wish to relinquish their child and have nothing further to do with the process of adoption. Where, under s 20, the parents combine consent to placement with consent to the making of the adoption order and opt not to be notified of the final adoption hearing, unless they change their minds, the entire process of placement and adoption will proceed without involving them in any way. Unlike freeing orders under the former law, which could be made against the parents' wishes, the advance consent order is voluntary; hence the presumption that they will not want to be notified of the final adoption hearing.[9]

---

1 ACA 2002, s 20(2).
2 Ibid, s 20(3).
3 Ibid, s 52(8)(a) and (b).
4 Ibid, s 20(4)(a).
5 Ibid, s 20(4)(b)
6 Ibid, s 20(5), but this has no effect if the person has withdrawn his or her consent.
7 Ibid, s 141(3)(a). The rules will also require that he be notified of the fact that, unless he wishes or the court requires, he need not attend: s 141(3)(b).
8 Ibid, s 47(7).
9 HC Special Standing Committee, 29 November 2001, col 344, per Ms Jacqui Smith.

Parental consent and adoption

8.8   Consent also has a role in the making of an adoption order; for example, in non-agency cases, such as relative adoptions, and in cases where the parents obtain leave to oppose the making of an adoption order under s 47(5) and (7). In those circumstances s 47(2) of the ACA 2002 provides that the court must be satisfied that (a) each parent consents to the making of the adoption order; or (b) each parent has given advance consent under s 20 and does not oppose the making of the adoption order; or (c) the parents' consent should be dispensed with.

Section 52: parental consent

8.9   Section 52 of the ACA 2002 is of general application to both placement and adoption and is central to the whole adoption process.

Consent

8.10   'Consent' to the placement of a child for adoption or the making of an adoption order[1] means:[2]

> 'consent given unconditionally and with full understanding of what is involved; but a person may consent to adoption without knowing the identity of the persons in whose favour the order will be made.'

Save that 'consent' has replaced 'agreement' and 'freely' has been omitted, the wording is taken from s 16(1)(b)(i) of the AA 1976. 'Freely' has been omitted to reflect the struggle that many parents face in giving their consent, even when they recognise that placement and adoption are in their child's best interests.

8.11   Although the consent is expressed to be unconditional, the adoption agency is under a duty in s 1(4)(f)(iii) to have regard to the wishes and feelings of any of the child's relatives, including the child's mother and father, in coming to a decision relating to the adoption of the child. The natural parents' wishes, for example, with respect to the child's religious persuasion should, therefore, be taken into account by the adoption agency when placing the child, although those wishes remain subordinate to the overall welfare of the child. The definition also makes clear that a person can give consent to adoption without knowing the identity of the person in whose favour the adoption order will be made, thus facilitating, where necessary, the preservation of the confidentiality of the placement.

8.12   The persons who have the right to consent are the parent 'having parental responsibility'[3] or the guardian of the child (which includes a special guardian).[4] Those 'parents' who qualify, are:

(1)   the birth mother;[5]

---

1   Or future adoption order: s 52(2)(b).
2   ACA 2002, s 52(5).
3   Ibid, s 52(6).
4   Ibid, ss 52(2) and 144(1).
5   CA 1989, s 2(1) and (2).

(2) the birth father, where he is married to the child's mother at the time of the child's birth[1] or if he subsequently marries the mother;[2]

(3) an unmarried father[3] if (i) he becomes registered as the child's father under the Births and Deaths Registration Act 1953; or (ii) he makes a parental responsibility agreement with the child's mother; or (iii) he is granted a parental responsibility order by the court;[4]

(4) the child's adoptive parent, where the child has been the subject of a previous adoption.

8.13 Although he may acquire parental authority, the unmarried father[5] may later cease to have that responsibility, but only by order of the court. Notwithstanding that, while a care order is in force, the local authority shares parental responsibility for the child with the natural parents, the authority does not share the right to consent or refuse to consent.

8.14 Under the ACA 2002, therefore, the categories of those who have the right to give or withdraw consent has been extended to include not only an unmarried father who acquires parental responsibility by registration as the child's father, but also a special guardian.

8.15 The inclusion of a special guardian marks a departure from the former law and in relation to the right to consent has the effect of elevating a special guardian to a position comparable with that of an adoptive parent. At first sight, this produces some surprising results. For example, after the child has lived with him or her for only one year, a local authority foster parent may obtain a special guardianship order and thus gain a right to consent to the child's future adoption, notwithstanding that this right continues to be denied to the child's unmarried father where he does not acquire parental responsibility. This inclusion of a special guardian is intended to be a reflection of the fact that a special guardian is entitled to exercise parental responsibility to the exclusion of any other person with parental responsibility for the child.[6] This, however, does not appear to sit easily with the fact that a special guardianship order is intended to preserve the child's links with the birth family and expressly does not affect the rights which a parent has in relation to the child's adoption or placement for adoption. As the parental responsibility of special guardians does not eclipse that of the natural parents, it appears to follow that the consent of the parents *and* the special guardians (ie potentially four individuals) would be required, or need to be dispensed with, before placement and the making of an adoption order. If this is the intended result, it is not made transparent by the wording in ss 21 and 47, which set the consent requirements for making a placement order and an adoption order and specify throughout 'each parent *or* guardian'.

---

1   CA 1989, s 2(1).

2   Legitimacy Act 1976, s 2; Family Law Reform Act 1987.

3   CA 1989, s 2(2)(b) provides that 'where the child's father and mother are not married to each other at the time of his birth the father shall not have parental responsibility for the child unless he acquires it in accordance with the provisions of this Act'.

4   CA 1989, s 4(1), as amended by s 111 of the ACA 2002.

5   Parental responsibility acquired by an unmarried father under s 4(1) of the CA 1989, as amended, may be terminated only by order of the court on the application of any person with parental responsibility for the child, or, with leave, the child (subject, in the case of s 4(1)(c), to s 12(4)): CA 1989, s 4(2A) and (3), as amended.

6   CA 1989, s 14C(1)(b), as amended. HL Deb, 2 July 2002, CWH 143, per Baroness Andrews.

8.16 'Parent' is not defined in either the CA 1989 or the ACA 2002. Under the former law 'parent' did not include a step-parent. Although the status of a step-parent has been enhanced under the new Act, there is nothing to suggest a major shift in the interpretation of 'parent' in s 52(6) so as to embrace a 'step-parent'. The safeguard for step-parents with parental responsibility is to be found in s 1(4)(f), under which the court would have to consider their views about adoption if they had a significant relationship with the child.

8.17 The parent's consent to the placement of the child for adoption and his or her advance consent to the making of an adoption order must be given in the prescribed form.[1] Unlike under the previous law where the parent's agreement could be given orally to the court or in a non-standard written form,[2] the use of a prescribed form for consent under s 19 or s 20 of the ACA 2002 is now mandatory.

8.18 The form is likely to include wording which highlights that the consent is given in the 'best interests of the child'. The PIU Report identified one of the reasons for contested adoption hearings as being the reluctance of birth parents 'to go on record as having consented to adoption, even though they agree it is in the best interests of the child'.[3] The White Paper, *Adoption: The Future*, signalled the Government's intention to amend the consent form, 'so that it better reflects the reality that birth parents have agreed to the adoption on the basis that it is in the best interests of the child. This should mean that more birth parents feel able to sign the consent form, thus reducing the number of contested adoptions. This will reduce delays in court proceedings and make them easier and less distressing for children'.[4] Given that the material effect of adoption is to extinguish the parents' legal status with respect to the child,[5] whether more sensitive wording on the consent form will have the result of reducing contested hearings, as foreshadowed in the White Paper, remains to be seen.

8.19 CAFCASS officers will play an essential role in advising on the implications of giving consent in consent cases and acting as independent witnesses of the parents' consent. They will be able to witness consent before the commencement of court proceedings and it is envisaged that they will advise parents on the implications of giving consent.[6] In recognition of the importance of ensuring that all relevant matters on the child's welfare are brought to the court's attention, the CAFCASS officer will be required to report to the court, on the court's request, on matters relating to the welfare of the child. This is similar to the provision under s 7 of the CA 1989 and ensures that

---

1   Under s 52(7) the consent forms for the purposes of ss 19 and 20 are to be prescribed by rules made by the Lord Chancellor; the intention is to allow the parent to understand the position clearly. The form under the AA 1976 was Form 2 in Sch 1 to the Adoption Rules 1984 and Form 2 in the Magistrates' Courts (Adoption) Rules 1984. The rules may also prescribe forms in which a person giving consent under the other provisions of Chapter 3 of the ACA 2002 may do so (if he wishes).

2   See s 61 of the AA 1976 and *Re D (Adoption: Freeing Order)* [2001] 1 FLR 403.

3   Cm 2288 (1993), at para 3.64.

4   Ibid, at paras 8.27 and 8.28.

5   Of which the birth parents and their extended family are very painfully aware.

6   ACA 2002, s 102. Section 102(1)(b) provides that for the signification by any person of any consent to placement or adoption, rules must provide for the appointment in prescribed cases of a CAFCASS officer. Those rules will include witnessing documents which signify consent to placement or adoption: s 102(3)(c). HC Deb, 20 May 2002, vol 386, no 150, col 45, per Ms Jacqui Smith.

CAFCASS officers' work is underpinned by the paramountcy principle in s 1 of the ACA 2002. It is anticipated that the welfare report will include the views of birth parents.[1]

8.20   Rules will also set out the effect of consent. One of the consequences of consent is that, once the child is placed for adoption by an adoption agency under s 19, it is an offence under s 30 for the birth parents to remove the child from the prospective adopters. The very act of giving consent therefore has an immediate and significant effect upon their rights as parents. There is also a prohibition on making or receiving any payment or reward in respect of the giving of consent.[2] The provisions relating to consent equally apply to inter-country adoptions.

WITHDRAWAL OF CONSENT

8.21   If consent is withdrawn, it must be in the prescribed form or by notice given to the agency.[3] Once an application for an adoption order has been made, any consent that has been given to the placement of a child for adoption or any advance consent under s 20 cannot be withdrawn.[4] There is, therefore, a 'cut off point' by which consent must be withdrawn. If the parents wish to oppose the adoption order once this point is passed, they must seek the court's leave under s 47(3) (where they have consented under s 20) or s 47(5) (where the child has been placed). Leave cannot be given unless the court is satisfied that there has been a change of circumstances since either the consent was given or the placement order made.[5]

MOTHER'S CONSENT WITHIN 6 WEEKS OF THE BIRTH

8.22   Any consent given by the mother to the making of an adoption order is ineffective if it is given less than 6 weeks after the child's birth.[6] This reflects the provisions of the European Convention on the Adoption of Children.[7] However, she may consent to the placement for adoption at any time after the child is born.

UNMARRIED FATHERS

8.23   Where an unmarried mother gives her consent to adoption under s 19 of the ACA 2002 and subsequently the child's father acquires parental responsibility (either by marriage or by re-registration as the father under the Births and Deaths Registration Act 1953 or by a parental responsibility agreement or order under the CA 1989),[8] he is to be treated as having 'at that time' given consent in accordance with s 52 on the same terms as the mother.[9] Without this, authority for the placement would lapse immediately.

8.24   In the case of a placement for adoption, the father would be in the same position as the mother in relation to his ability to withdraw consent. Where the mother has given advance consent under s 20, the father qualifies for notification of any application for an

---

1   HC Deb, 20 May 2002, vol 386, no 150, col 46, per Ms Jacqui Smith.
2   ACA 2002, s 93.
3   Ibid, s 52(8).
4   Ibid, s 52(4).
5   Ibid, s 47(7).
6   Ibid, s 52(3).
7   Strasbourg, 24 April 1967.
8   ACA 2002, s 52(9).
9   Ibid, s 52(10).

adoption order to be given to him under s 141(3) and (4) and would be able to oppose the making of the adoption order, but only with leave of the court under s 47(3).

Dispensing with parental consent

8.25   Section 52(1), which sees the ACA 2002 in its most radical clothing, reads:

> 'The court cannot dispense with the consent of any parent or guardian of a child to the child being placed for adoption or the making of an adoption order in respect of the child unless the court is satisfied that:
>
> (a)   the parent or guardian cannot be found or is incapable of giving consent; or
> (b)   the welfare of the child requires the consent to be dispensed with.'

Paramountcy principle

8.26   Section 1 of the ACA 2002 applies to the decision whether or not to dispense with the consent of the parent to a placement or adoption order. The child's welfare throughout his or her life is, therefore, the paramount consideration in dispensing with parental consent. As we have seen in Chapter 7, this marks a revolutionary departure from the position under previous adoption legislation.

Welfare checklist

8.27   The welfare checklist under s 1(4) applies to dispensing with parental consent. This is crucial, as the checklist of welfare factors recognises the importance of the child's relationship with his or her birth parents and, therefore, goes some way to redressing the imbalance against the family of birth which s 1, taken together with s 52(1)(b), has created. The weighting of such factors in the welfare checklist as the wishes and feelings of the child under s 1(4)(a), the likely effect on the child of having ceased to be a member of the original family and become an adopted person under s 1(4)(c), and particularly the relationship which the child has with his or her parents under s 1(4)(f)(i)–(iii), therefore, becomes of vital significance in the balancing exercise under s 52.

The grounds for dispensation

8.28   Under s 16(2) of the AA 1976 there were seven grounds for dispensing with consent. Under the ACA 2002 there are only two. The first limb of s 52, 'the parent cannot be found or is incapable of giving consent' in subs (1)(a), which derives from s 16(2)(a) of the AA 1976, remains. However, the second limb, 'the welfare of the child requires the consent to be dispensed with' in subs (1)(b) breaks new ground in adoption law.

8.29   Section 52(1)(b) of the ACA 2002 is intended to be a key component of the new system, where the aim is to ensure that decisions as to whether adoption is the right option for the child, whether the parents consent and, if not, whether their consent should be dispensed with, are made earlier in the adoption process.[1]

8.30   The ACA 2002 has deleted the unreasonableness ground under s 16(2)(b) of the AA 1976 and, thus, at a stroke, removed the legal hurdle under the old law whereby an

---

1   *Adoption: A New Approach*, Cm 2288 (December 2000), para 1.21.

adoption considered to be in the child's best interests could nevertheless be prevented by the parent 'reasonably' withholding his or her consent. As discussed earlier, one of the by-products of this change in the law is likely to be the significant diminution in the status of the natural parents in the whole adoption process.

FIRST GROUND FOR DISPENSATION: CANNOT BE FOUND OR INCAPABLE OF GIVING CONSENT

8.31   Section 52(1)(a) of the ACA 2002 provides that the court cannot dispense with the consent of any parent, unless the court is satisfied that the parent (i) cannot be found or (ii) is incapable of giving consent.

Cannot be found

8.32   The authorities under the former law produced two interpretations of the phrase 'cannot be found'. First, in *Re R (Adoption)*[1] it was held that a person 'cannot be found' where there are no practical means of communicating with a person whose agreement to an adoption order is required. Secondly, in *Re S (Adoption)*[2] the Court of Session in Scotland, applying *Re F (R) (An Infant)*,[3] held that the words 'cannot be found' must mean that 'all reasonable steps must be taken, and even if only one reasonable step is omitted, one cannot say that the person cannot be found'.

8.33   In *Re F (R) (An Infant)*, on the separation of the parents, the father had been left with the child. As he was unable to look after him, he handed over the boy to a couple who raised him and later applied for adoption with the father's consent. The proposed adopters were not aware of the whereabouts of the mother and took steps to find her including writing to her at her last known address (the letter was returned as 'gone away') and placing advertisements in the press, which brought no response. An adoption order was made, dispensing with her consent on the ground that she could not be found. Some months after the order had been made, she learned of it and appealed. On appeal, the adoption order was set aside and the matter remitted for reconsideration. The Court of Appeal had before it an affidavit from the mother's father, in which he stated that the applicants knew him and where he lived, as the applicants had written letters to him there 2 or 3 years before the adoption application. Salmon LJ said:[4]

> 'We are in no position to express any view whether or not the facts in the affidavit are correct, but if they are correct, this is not a case where the mother could not be found, because the words in the section "cannot be found" must mean cannot be found by taking all reasonable steps. The respondents indubitably took many steps and very thorough steps to find the mother. If, however, it is true that they knew that the mother's father was in touch with the mother and that they knew his address, there is one reasonable step which they omitted to take and that was to get in touch with the father and ask him to tell the mother what they proposed . . .'

8.34   In *Re A (Adoption of Russian Child)*,[5] Charles J found that the two interpretations of the phrase 'cannot be found' were not in conflict. He said:

---

1   [1967] 1 WLR 34, per Buckley J.
2   [1999] 2 FLR 374 at 379A–D, per Lord Prosser.
3   [1970] 1 QB 385 at 389B, per Salmon LJ.
4   Ibid, at 389B.
5   [2000] 1 FLR 539.

'The first refers to "no *practical* means" and the second to "all *reasonable* steps". It is important to note that in my judgment correctly neither case refers to *possible* means or steps. They are therefore authority that all practical means must be employed and all reasonable steps must be taken to find and communicate with the relevant person. What is "reasonable" and what is "practical" are not necessarily the same but will often overlap. In my judgment any potential difference does not give rise to difficulty.'

8.35 Reasonable steps include: (i) writing to the parent's last known address; (ii) advertising and making enquiries of the Post Office;[1] (iii) advertising in the press; (iv) contacting members of the extended family or friends where their addresses are known;[2] (v) making enquiries of, for example, the DWP (if the parent had been in receipt of benefits), the Passport Office, the Council Tax Register and any relevant housing authority or association (if the parent was in receipt of housing benefit).[3] In the case of an intercountry adoption, where the parent whose consent is required is outside the jurisdiction, practical steps could include investigations by the child's guardian with the assistance of International Social Services or diplomatic channels or with the assistance of the authorities in the country where the parent resides.

8.36 As was seen in *Re F (R)*, should the parent subsequently reappear, then, provided that consent was dispensed with on this sole ground, the order may be set aside and the case remitted for a rehearing.[4]

Incapable of giving consent

8.37 Under the previous law, Buckley J in *Re R (Adoption)*[5] found that, where there are no practical means of communicating with the person whose consent is required, that person was 'incapable of giving agreement'. He therefore applied the same test as he advocated for the first limb of s 52(1)(a) and held that this ground was satisfied where the parents lived in a 'totalitarian' State and any attempt to communicate with them could cause them risk. Although frequently the two limbs overlap, as in *Re R (Adoption)* and *Re A (Adoption of Russian Child)*, there is a distinction. As Charles J recognised in *Re A (Adoption of Russian Child)*,[6] the second limb can be a true alternative, which applies even though there are reasonable and practical steps that could be taken to find the person. For example, 'incapacity' could include a parent's physical or mental impairment.

8.38 Although under the AA 1976 this first ground for dispensation has been used in only a small percentage of cases[7] concerned with domestic adoptions, and thus has generated little in the way of jurisprudence, it has had greater impact in the context of intercountry adoptions.

---

1   *Re F (R) (An Infant)* [1970] 1 QB 358; *Re T (A Minor) (Adoption Order: Leave to Appeal)* [1995] 3 FCR 299.
2   *Re F (R) (An Infant)* (above).
3   D Hershman and A McFarlane *Children Law and Practice* (Family Law), para H[121].
4   *Re F (R) (An Infant)* (above); *Re B (An Infant)* [1958] 1 QB 12.
5   [1967] 1 WLR 34.
6   [2000] 1 PLR 539 at 548B–D.
7   See Review of Adoption Law, Discussion paper no 2, *Agreement & Freeing* (1991), p 26.

SECOND GROUND FOR DISPENSING WITH CONSENT: THE WELFARE REQUIREMENT

8.39   Section 52(1)(b) of the ACA 2002 provides that the court cannot dispense with the consent of any parent, unless the court is satisfied that the welfare of the child requires that consent to be dispensed with. The overwhelming probability is that this will be the ground used for dispensing with consent in the majority of cases.

8.40   Parental consent is the cornerstone of adoption law, not only historically in UK domestic law, but also internationally in such treaties as the European Convention on Human Rights, the European Convention on Adoption 1967 and the Hague Convention on Inter-country Adoption 1993. The objective underlying the requirement for parental consent is to safeguard the rights of the parents. The importance attached to parental consent is underscored by the historical perspective detailed in Chapter 1, of which *Re H (A Minor) (Adoption: Non-Patrial)*[1] provides a brief judicial glimpse:

> 'In their time, welfare was not given by statute the same prominence as it is given [now] ...
> [in] s 7 of the Adoption Act 1958 ... welfare was placed second of the three matters in respect
> of which the court had to be satisfied before making the adoption order. The first was that the
> consents of those whose consent was necessary had been obtained; the second was that the
> order, if made, would be for the welfare of the infant; and the third was that the applicant had
> not received or any other person made or given or agreed to make any payment or reward in
> consideration of adoption.'

8.41   This new ground for dispensation lies at the central core of the reforms driving the new legislation. 'Welfare' now has the predominant position, even in relation to the disposal of parental consent. It is highly unlikely that anyone will miss that imaginary legal paragon, 'the hypothetical reasonable parent', or the intellectual gymnastics he or she required.[2]

8.42   However, giving predominance to the paramountcy principle in dispensing with consent fundamentally shifts the balance between the child's welfare and birth parents' rights. The welfare of the child must always outweigh parental interests. Whereas parents (under the former law) could take a different view of their child's welfare and not be unreasonable, the court will now be able to impose its view on them.[3] The risk is that dispensing with parental consent under s 52(1)(b) will now become merely a 'rubber stamping' exercise by the court, due to the paramountcy principle's predominant role. Unless the courts are vigilant, this principle has the potential for bringing a strong flavour of social engineering against the birth family and gives rise to the question whether the balance has shifted too far.

8.43   Have the parents any voice left to them under the ACA 2002? In the same breath as highlighting the child's welfare as the paramount consideration in all decisions, including whether to dispense with birth parents' consent, the Government has stressed 'the courts will be explicitly obliged to consider the impact of the child ceasing to be a member of his birth family and the change in his relationship with the family that

---

1   [1982] Fam 121 at 130B–C, per Hollings J.
2   *Re W (An Infant)* [1971] AC 682. See *Re C (A Minor) (Adoption: Parental Agreement: Contact)* [1993]
     2 FLR 260 at 272B–H and *Re F (Adoption: Freeing Order)* [2000] 2 FLR 505 at [20]–[21] where
     Thorpe LJ acknowledged the great difficulty which this area of jurisprudence had produced to trial
     judges up and down the country over the years.
3   As adumbrated in SM Cretney and JM Masson *Principles of Family Law* (6th edn, Sweet & Maxwell,
     1997) at p 931.

adoption would inevitably bring'.[1] This is a clear signal that s 1(4)(c) and s 1(4)(f) are intended to 'make up' for the loss of the parental right of 'reasonably withholding consent'. Therefore, some weighting is given to parental rights.

8.44 Further, the court has to be satisfied that 'the welfare of the child *requires* the consent to be dispensed with'.[2] Arguably, the word 'requires' imports an imperative into the subsection as an additional safeguard, ie a further obligation upon the court to be satisfied that the child's welfare interests 'compel' or make it necessary to dispense with parental consent. However, once the court, having had regard to the welfare checklist, has decided that adoption is in the best interests of the child, there is a sense of inevitability that the paramountcy of the child's welfare will 'require' that the consent of the parent be dispensed with.

8.45 Although these factors do go some way in giving parents a voice, they are in reality a pale substitute for the more full-blooded protection historically afforded by English law to the parents' rights and interests. Under the former law, notwithstanding the prominence of the child's welfare,[3] the parental decision (provided it fell within a reasonable band of decisions) could be effective as a veto.

8.46 Does the loss of a potential parental veto, in conjunction with the paramountcy principle, bring the Act into conflict with the Art 8 of the European Convention on Human Rights? In *McMichael v UK*,[4] the European Court held that:

'Whilst Art 8 contains no explicit procedural requirements, the decision making process leading to measures of interference must be fair and such as to afford due respect to the interests safeguarded by Art 8:

"What ... has to be determined is whether having regard to the particular circumstances of the case and notably the serious nature of the decisions to be taken, the parents have been involved in the decision making process, seen as a whole, to a degree sufficient to provide them with the requisite protection of their interests. If they have not, there will have been a failure to respect their family life and the interference resulting from the decision will not be capable of being regarded as 'necessary' within the meaning of Art 8."[5]'

---

1   HC Deb, 26 March 2001, vol 365, no 59, col 703, per Mr John Hutton.

2   Emphasis added: at HL Deb, 11 July 2002, CWH 264, Baroness Andrews said: 'I want to stress the term "requires"'.

3   Which see-sawed in predominance under the former law: see *Re H; Re W (Adoption: Parental Agreement)* [1983] FLR 614, where the Court of Appeal emphasised that a parent could be behaving reasonably in withholding consent, even where the social workers thought adoption to be in the child's best interests and also *Re E (Minors) (Adoption: Parental Agreement)* [1990] 2 FLR 397; in contrast, in *Re C (A Minor) (Adoption: Parental Agreement: Contact)* [1993] 2 FLR 260, the majority took a more 'child centred approach' and Balcombe LJ took a more 'parent centred' approach, and finally *Re M (Adoption or Residence Order)* [1998] 1 FLR 570 where the Court of Appeal were again divided.

4   (1995) 20 EHRR 205 at para 87.

5   *W v UK* (1988) 10 EHRR 29 at paras 62 and 64. See also *Elsholz v Germany* (2002) 34 EHRR 58, [2000] 2 FLR 486 at para 52; *TP and KM v UK* [2001] 2 FLR 549 at para 72; *Sahin v Germany; Sommerfield v Germany; Hoffman v Germany* [2002] 1 FLR 119 (*Sahin* at [44], *Sommerfield* at [42], *Hoffman* at [44]); *Buchberger v Austria* (Application No 32899/96) (unreported) 20 December 2001, ECHR, for more recent statements of this principle.

8.47   As has been seen in *Johansen v Norway*,[1] the European Court seeks to achieve a fair balance between the rights of the parents and the rights of the child.[2] It follows from 'this rights-based approach' that the European Court views the birth parents as having rights and interests to go into the balance to be properly weighed against the rights and interests of the child.[3] When carrying out the balancing exercise under the Convention, the child's welfare does not automatically justify an interference with the parents' rights guaranteed under Art 8(1), as Art 8(2) requires that any interference must be 'necessary in a democratic society'. Inherent in the principle of proportionality is the requirement that the 'more drastic the interference, the greater must be the need to do it'.[4] The paramountcy principle's intrinsic characteristic is, however, to weigh the balance in favour of the child's welfare. Can it be said that the paramountcy principle, combined with a welfare test to dispense with consent, meets the requirements of a 'fair' balance or a sufficient involvement for the parents in the decision-making process to protect their rights and interests?

8.48   It is the duty of the English court under the Human Rights Act 1998 to attempt to find a compatible interpretation so as to prevent the making of a declaration of incompatibility between primary legislation and the Convention rights.[5] If our domestic courts simply treat the child's best interests as the automatic Art 8(2) justification for any interference, this has the real potential for creating a tension between the Convention and the Act which becomes difficult to reconcile, notwithstanding that it is the duty of the English court under the Human Rights Act 1998 to attempt to find a compatible interpretation so as to prevent the making of a declaration of incompatibility between primary legislation and the Convention rights.

8.49   To date, the lead from the House of Lords in steering a course between Art 8 and the welfare principle has been a conservative defence of the 'paramountcy of the child's best interests against any incursion from the rights-based approach of the Convention cases law'.[6] It is arguable that the traditional view that the balancing exercise under Art 8 does not differ in substance from the balancing exercise under the conventional welfare approach fails to give proper accord to the subtlety required in balancing the competing

---

1   (1997) 23 EHRR 33 at para 78.
2   Ibid.
3   J Herring 'The Human Rights Act and the welfare principle in family law – conflicting or complementary?' [1999] CFLQ 223 at 224 and 231; A Bainham 'Taking Children Abroad: Human Rights, Welfare and the Courts' [2001] CLJ 489 at 492.
4   *Re B (Adoption by One Natural Parent to Exclusion of Other)* [2001] 1 FLR 589, per Hale LJ, at 599.
5   *Re K (Secure Accommodation Order: Right to Liberty)* [2001] 1 FLR 526 at 540, per Dame Elizabeth Butler-Sloss P, in which she went on to agree with the extra-judicial observation of Lord Cooke of Thornhill, who said: 'Section 3(1) [of the Human Rights Act 1998] will require a very different approach to interpretation from that to which the United Kingdom courts are accustomed. Traditionally the search has been for the true meaning, now it will be for a possible meaning that prevents the making of a declaration of incompatibility': 582 HL Official Report (5th Series), col 1272 (3 November 1997); *Donoghue v Poplar Housing Regeneration Community Association Ltd* [2001] 2 FLR 284 at [75], per Lord Woolf CJ, and *Re S (Minors) (Care Order: Implementation of Care Plan); Re W (Care Order: Adequacy of Care Plan)* [2002] 1 FLR 815 at [37]–[40], per Lord Nicholls of Birkenhead.
6   S Harris-Short '*Re B (Adoption: Natural Parent)* Putting the child at the heart of adoption?' [2002] CFLQ 325 at 336–337. See *Re B (Adoption: Natural Parent)* [2002] 1 FLR 196 and *Re S (Minors) (Care Order: Implementation of Care Plan); Re W (Minors) (Care Order: Adequacy of Care Plan)* [2002] 1 FLR 815.

Convention rights and meeting the demands of Art 8(2). For example, Andrew Bainham has criticised the decision in *Payne v Payne*[1] for its willingness to assume 'that any Convention rights which the child herself might have had were subsumed in, or coterminus with, the notion of welfare'.[2] The challenges which flow from the subtle differences in the two approaches will require a strong lead and change of direction from our highest court.

---

1   [2001] EWCA Civ 166, [2001] 1 FLR 1052.
2   In 'Taking Children Abroad: Human Rights, Welfare and the Courts' [2001] CLJ 489 at 492.

Chapter 9

PLACEMENT FOR ADOPTION

THE NEW SYSTEM

9.1 Sections 18–29 of the ACA 2002 introduce a new legal process for placing children for adoption. A widely held view[1] was that the former process left too much to be resolved at the final adoption stage. Under the former law there was no legal concept of 'authorisation to place' dependent upon parental consent. There was no requirement at all to seek parental consent before an adoptive placement was made. For example, where a child was in care and the care plan changed from rehabilitation to adoption, no formal process was necessary to place the child for adoption, nor was parental consent required. The local authority could go ahead, saying 'We've changed our minds. Circumstances have changed; therefore, the child is going to be placed for adoption'. The result was that, in many cases, the first formal opportunity for the parents to contest the issue of adoption was at the final hearing, by which time the child had been with the prospective adopters for many months. Equally, the prospective adopters could suffer great anguish when they found themselves faced with a contest at a final hearing after caring for the child for many months.

> 'The new system is intended to provide greater certainty and stability for children by dealing as far as possible with parental consent *before* they have been placed with the prospective new family; to reduce the uncertainty for the prospective adopters, who possibly face a contested hearing at the adoption order stage; and to reduce the extent to which birth families are faced with a fait accompli at the final adoption hearing, if the child has been placed with prospective adopters for some time.'[2]

In the House of Lords, it was claimed that the new system aimed 'to give greater certainty and stability to children by dealing, as far as possible, with the bulk of the issues that are problematic for families around consent to adoption before they have been placed, so that placement occurs not at the end of ... the process'.[3]

9.2 Section 18[4] sets the new process in motion by specifying that an adoption agency (except in the case of a child who is less than 6 weeks old) may place a child for adoption

---

1   1992 Review of Adoption Law.
2   HC Deb, vol 365, no 59, col 708, per Mr John Hutton in respect of Bill 69 (26 March 2001), the forerunner to Bill 34.
3   HL Grand Committee, 2 July 2002, vol 637, CWH 133, per Baroness Andrews.
4   Section 18 is expressly made subject to ss 30–35 which deal with the removal of children placed by adoption agencies.

with prospective adopters 'only ... under s 19 or a placement order'.[1] A child may, therefore, only be placed for adoption either (i) where there is the consent of the parent or (ii) where there is no parental consent, under a placement order of the court ('the two routes').[2]

9.3 CAFCASS officers will hold a pivotal position in the placement process. They will witness birth parents' consent in those cases where they wish to consent, act on behalf of the child in placement proceedings with the duty of safeguarding the interests of the child, and report to the court, on request, on matters relating to the child's welfare.[3] The job of CAFCASS officers 'will be to ensure that the consent is given properly and transparently with full knowledge and understanding of the parents'.[4] In the Act, 'placing a child for adoption' by an adoption agency is defined as 'placing a child for adoption with prospective adopters' and includes 'where it has placed a child with any persons (whether under this Act or not), leaving the child with them as prospective adopters'.[5]

9.4 An adoption agency may place a child who is less than 6 weeks old for adoption (a 'baby placement') with the voluntary agreement of the parent or guardian.[6] As the baby is not placed under s 19 or under a placement order during those first 6 weeks, the agency has, for example, no discretion to determine to what extent the parental responsibility of any parent or of the prospective adopters is to be restricted under s 25(4) of the ACA 2002. The placement regime simply does not apply. However, the child who is placed with the voluntary agreement of the parent or guardian is a 'looked-after' child of the local authority. When the child attains the age of 6 weeks, if adoption continues to be the plan, the agency must then obtain the consent of the parent or a placement order, otherwise there is no authority for the placement to continue.

9.5 Local authority foster parents will be able to seek formal approval from the local authority as prospective adopters of children being fostered by them. If they are approved as prospective adopters and the agency leaves the child with them as such, the placement will be an agency placement and there will be no need for the foster parents to give formal notice under s 44. If the agency does not approve of them as prospective adopters, local authority foster parents can independently give notice of intention to apply to adopt as a non-agency case, subject to satisfying the residence requirement in s 42(4) (ie the child must have had his or her home with the applicants at all times during the period of one year preceding the application).

---

1   ACA 2002, s 18(1). Under s 18(5), references in Chapter 3 of the Act to an agency being or not being authorised to place a child for adoption are to the agency being or not being authorised to do so under s 19 or a placement order.
2   Note that, under s 18(4), the agency may not place the child with prospective adopters where an application for an adoption order has been made by anyone and has not been disposed of, but an agency which placed the child with those persons may leave the child with them until disposal of the application.
3   ACA 2002, s 102.
4   HL Grand Committee, 2 July 2002, vol 637, CWH 135, per Baroness Andrews.
5   ACA 2002, s 18(5)(a) and (b).
6   Regulations will set out the process for obtaining this agreement.

The two routes

9.6   There are two routes for placement. The first route is under s 19 of the Act, where the placement is by parental consent through either a voluntary adoption agency or a local authority. The second route is under s 22 of the Act, where a placement order under s 21 is required; this route is open only to local authorities.

9.7   The two placement routes are connected. Where a local authority considers that a child it is accommodating ought to be placed for adoption, it must either place the child with parental consent or, if the parents do not consent and the authority considers that the child is at risk of significant harm or if the child is already subject to a care order, apply for a placement order.

9.8   This new process accelerates the issue of parental consent to the period *before* the child is placed with the prospective adoptive family. It is seen as an essential part of the overall legal scheme, which is designed to ensure that decisions about whether adoption is the right option, whether the parents have consented and, if not, whether their consent should be dispensed with are taken earlier in the adoption process. Dealing with the issue of parental consent early in the procedure is viewed by the Government as being one of the strongest safeguards in the adoption process.[1]

9.9   Section 18(2) of the ACA 2002 makes explicit that an adoption agency should place a child for adoption only where it is satisfied that the child *should* be placed for adoption. In coming to this decision, the s 1 principles (including the whole range of powers) apply and bind the local authority and the voluntary agency. 'In other words, there must be a conscious and careful decision making process focusing on the needs of the child before a child can be placed for adoption.'[2] The process for decision making by adoption agencies will be set out in regulations. They are likely to set out a similar process[3] as that under the former law, namely:

> 'Where, as a result of a case review, a local authority is considering adoption for a child it is looking after or a voluntary adoption agency is considering placing a child for adoption, the first step is to refer the case to the adoption panel;
> the adoption panel makes a recommendation to the authority or voluntary agency as to whether adoption is in the child's best interests;
> it is then up to the authority or voluntary agency to decide whether to accept that recommendation. If it does, that is the point at which that the authority or agency is satisfied that a child ought to be placed for adoption.'

9.10   However, the new regulations will provide for this decision to be made *before* the child is placed. They will also require that the child be consulted directly throughout the decision-making process to record the child's views, to ensure that these are taken into account (for example, in panel decisions) and, if the child's views are not acted on, to record the reasons for this.[4] The s 1 principles will apply throughout this decision-making process.

---

1   HL Grand Committee, 2 July 2002, vol 637, CWH 136, per Baroness Andrews.
2   HL Deb, 14 October 2002, vol 639, col 663, per Baroness Andrews.
3   HL Grand Committee, 2 July 2002, vol 637, CWH 126.
4   HC Special Standing Committee, 29 November 2001, col 332, per Ms Jacqui Smith, and HL Grand Committee, 2 July 2002, vol 637, CWH 126.

9.11   It should not be overlooked that a significant part of the new placement process also concerns the removal of children (as provided for by ACA 2002, ss 30–40). It is, therefore, important to read the placement and removal provisions together in order to gain a complete understanding of the philosophy underlying the concept of placement.

The demise of 'freeing orders'

9.12   The ACA 2002 has sounded the death knell for the widely criticised 'freeing for adoption orders'.[1] The freeing order process had involved the court in making decisions before a placement for the child was known with no guarantees that suitable adoptive parents would be found. All too frequently it consigned the child to an indefinite legal limbo, as a 'statutory orphan' without any legal parents at all.[2] It was, therefore (rightly) recognised in the PIU Report that freeing orders were 'flawed instruments' in the sense that:

> 'They had originally been designed primarily as a means of allowing consenting parents to make their child available for adoption but were now also being used in conjunction with Children Act mechanisms to expedite adoption for looked after children in the absence of consent ... In addition, they left freed children without a parent which was both generally unsatisfactory (and unpopular with lawyers and judges) and likely to be vulnerable to ECHR challenge.'[3]

9.13   The placement provisions, therefore, replace the former system of freeing orders. However, the crucial difference between these new provisions and freeing orders is that the birth parents remain the child's parents until the final adoption order, irrespective of whether the consensual route or the placement order route is taken. However, although a parent will not lose parental responsibility, he or she will be required to share this with the prospective adopters and the adoption agency and, as we will see later, the parent's share of parental responsibility may be substantially diminished.

THE CONSENSUAL ROUTE: SECTION 19

Placement and consent

9.14   Section 19(1) of the ACA 2002 authorises an adoption agency to place children for adoption where it is satisfied that each parent or guardian has given consent to placement and that this consent has not been withdrawn. 'Placement by consent is meant to be entirely voluntary.'[4] The section is subject to s 52 as to the meaning of parental consent; this aspect is dealt with in more detail in Chapter 8. Briefly, 'consent' means

---

1   Under the former s 18 of the AA 1976.
2   An example of the traumas of 'adoptive limbo' is to be found in *Re C (Adoption: Freeing Order)* [1999] 1 FLR 348. See also *Re G (Adoption: Freeing Order)* [1997] 2 FLR 202 at 206C–F, per Lord Browne-Wilkinson.
3   Paragraph 3.66. This prediction proved to be correct, as the Convention spotlight has indeed been trained upon freeing for adoption orders in *P, C and S v UK* [2002] 2 FLR 631, where the European Court held that the applicants' complaint that the practice of instituting adoption proceedings together with care proceedings in respect of babies and the use of 'draconian and irreversible' freeing orders breached Arts 6 and 8.
4   HL Grand Committee, 2 July 2002, vol 637, CWH 135, per Baroness Andrews.

consent which is given 'unconditionally and with full understanding of what is involved'[1] and includes 'advance consent' to the final adoption order at the same time as giving consent to placement.[2] 'Parent' is defined as someone 'having parental responsibility'.[3]

9.15 There are three safeguards intended for parents. First, it is a key element of consensual placement that the adoption agency will be under a duty (through regulations) to spell out the need to counsel the parents and to explain to them the full implications of the process to which they are agreeing. Secondly, the parents' consent must be given in the prescribed form, which will spell out clearly the agreement; this is a mandatory requirement.[4] Thirdly, it is intended that consent will be witnessed by an officer of CAFCASS, as provided for under rules to be made under s 102.

9.16 The consensual placement may be with the prospective adopters identified in the consent or with any prospective adopters who may be chosen by the agency.[5] The consent to placement with identified prospective adopters may be combined with consent to a subsequent placement with any prospective adopters chosen by the agency, in circumstances where the child is removed from, or returned by, the identified prospective adopters.[6] The intention is to avoid the delay involved when the agency has to return to court for a further order if the specified placement breaks down. The word 'identified', rather than 'named',[7] was deliberately included with the aim of enabling parents to consent to placement with specific adopters whose name they did not know but with whose characteristics and details they might be familiar through, for example, an anonymous profile passed on by the adoption agency.[8]

9.17 Where the placement is consensual, the birth parents can withdraw their consent at any time, until an application for an adoption order is made.[9] Under the removal provisions, where the child is placed for adoption and the consent is withdrawn, the child must be returned to the parent within 14 days. If the consent is withdrawn *before* the child has been placed, the child must be returned to the birth parents within one week.[10] Thus, the parents have the right to have their child returned if they change their minds. However, if, on withdrawal of parental consent, the local authority is under a duty to apply for a placement order under s 22, the child may be removed with the leave of the court only once the local authority has made the application.[11]

9.18 One of the Government's objectives in shifting the substantive issue of consent to a point earlier in the process is to reduce the opportunity to contest.[12] This is achieved by

---

1 ACA 2002, s 52(5). A person may consent to adoption without knowing the identity of the prospective adopters.
2 Ibid, s 20 – 'or at any subsequent time'.
3 Ibid, s 52(6). 'Parental responsibility' has an extended meaning following the amendments by ss 111 and 112 of the ACA 2002 to ss 4 and 4A of the CA 1989.
4 ACA 2002, s 52(7).
5 Ibid, s 19(1).
6 Ibid, s 19(2).
7 Which was the word used in the 1996 draft Bill.
8 HC Special Standing Committee, 29 November 2001, col 334, per Ms Jacqui Smith.
9 ACA 2002, s 52(4).
10 Ibid, s 31.
11 Ibid, s 30(2).
12 HL Grand Committee, 2 July 2002, vol 637, CWH 134, per Baroness Andrews.

imposing a 'leave' fetter upon the parents' ability to contest a final adoption order. Where a parent has continued to consent to the placement of his or her child for adoption, although he or she may still oppose the final adoption order, he or she can do so only with leave of the court and the court may give leave only if there has been a change of circumstances.[1]

9.19   Where a child is placed with prospective adopters and consent is then withdrawn, the child continues to be treated as placed for adoption until he or she is returned to the parents or any application for a placement order is determined.[2]

Effect on other orders/applications

Pending application for care order

9.20   It is important to note that the provisions relating to the placement of children with parental consent do not apply where there is a pending application as a result of which a care order may be made[3] or where a care order or placement order has been made after the consent was given.[4] In these circumstances, if the appropriate local authority is satisfied that the child should be adopted, then it must take the placement order route under s 22(2).

Residence order

9.21   A parent may not apply for a residence order once a child is placed for adoption or the agency has been authorised to place the child under s 19.[5] There is one exception: where an application for adoption has been made and the parent has obtained the court's leave to oppose the adoption order, as this will allow competing applications for residence orders from the parents at contested final adoption hearings. It will not, however, be an easy task for a parent to obtain leave, as he or she will have to establish a change of circumstances.

Special guardianship order

9.22   Where a child is placed for adoption with consent and a special guardianship order is subsequently made, the authority to place the child no longer applies unless the special guardian consents under s 19(1). However, where the child is placed for adoption or the agency is authorised to place the child and an application is then made for an adoption order, a guardian may not apply for a special guardianship order without first obtaining leave to oppose the adoption.

Existing contact order

9.23   As will be seen below in more detail, when an agency is authorised to place a child, contact orders under the CA 1989 cease to have effect and no application may be made

---

1   ACA 2002, s 47(5) and (7).
2   Ibid, s 19(4).
3   Ibid, s 19(3)(a).
4   Ibid, s 19(3)(b).
5   Ibid, s 28(1).

for a contact order under that Act. Again, there is an exception: a s 8 contact application may be heard at the final adoption hearing.

THE 'PLACEMENT ORDER' ROUTE: SECTIONS 21 AND 22

9.24 The making of a placement order by the court is a new concept in adoption law. It brings together under one banner at an early stage in the adoption process both the threshold criteria from s 31(2) of the CA 1989 and the provisions for dispensing with parental consent in s 52 of the ACA 2002.

9.25 One of the objectives of the ACA 2002 in relation to placement orders is to 'provide that a child cannot be compulsorily placed for adoption without the Children Act threshold test of significant harm being met. That test safeguards the rights of birth families and means there is a consistent threshold for compulsory state intervention in family life across adoption legislation and the 1989 Act'.[1] The link to s 31(2) of the CA 1989 is intended as a part of the general design to align adoption law with that Act. The incorporation of the 'significant harm' condition and the 'attributable' condition from s 31(2) of the CA 1989 into s 21 of the ACA 2002, therefore, brings placement orders into line with the policy in Part IV of the CA 1989 that no child should be removed from his or her family before a statutory threshold has been crossed.[2] The linking of the two sections is intended to provide a common gateway through which the State, in the shape of the local authority and the court, must pass before compulsorily removing a child from the birth family by a care order or placement order. It further brings home the necessity for there to be relevant and sufficient reasons to justify such State intervention for the purposes of para 2 of Art 8 of the European Convention on Human Rights.[3]

9.26 In the 1992 Review of Adoption Law there was concern that, where a child had been permitted to live with prospective adopters, sometimes for years, before an adoption application was made, the court at the time of the hearing was presented 'with something approaching a fait accompli'.[4] The recommendation was made that, in non-consensual cases, the court should be able to consider the question of parental consent and all the alternatives to adoption before the child was placed and the status quo took hold.[5] Hence the origins of the concept of 'the placement order' and, as we have seen, the avoidance of 'the fait accompli' have been highlighted as one of the key objectives of the new placement order.

9.27 Only local authorities may apply for placement orders. Initially, it had been intended that this route would also be open to voluntary adoption agencies, but this crucial change to the Act – confining placement orders to local authorities – was made in

---

1   HC Deb, 29 October 2001, col 720, per Ms Jacqui Smith, Minister of State, Department of Health.
2   This marks a change from the original Adoption and Children Bill (69) in response to consultation. 'Several stakeholders in their evidence to the Select Committee had expressed concern that children would be placed for adoption against the parent's wishes without this threshold being met. This was felt to be inappropriate given the widely understood and accepted principles of the Children Act' (HC Special Standing Committee, 20 November 2001, p 6, para 16).
3   *Olsson v Sweden (No 1)* (1989) 11 EHRR 259, para 68; *K and T v Finland* [2001] 2 FLR 707 at [154].
4   At para 14.2.
5   Ibid, at para 14.6.

recognition of the fact that it was inappropriate to allow voluntary organisations to apply to the court to have a child compulsorily placed for adoption against the parents' wishes.[1]

9.28 Placement orders enable the court to decide whether placement for adoption is in the child's best interests, applying the s 1 principles – including a consideration of all the alternative options and the views and wishes of those with significant relationships with the child. Placement orders are general and not specific. Although the identity of the prospective adopters will clearly be relevant if the child is already placed or if a potential match has provisionally been made, the court is essentially being asked to take a decision in principle that the child ought to be placed for adoption.[2]

9.29 Although it is intended to consult before setting out in detail the court rules, it is clearly envisaged that a child will be a party to placement order proceedings.[3] Section 41[4] of the CA 1989 has been amended by s 122 of the ACA 2002 to include an application for the making or revocation of a placement order as a 'specified proceeding', in which the court will appoint a guardian to safeguard the child's interests, unless satisfied that it is not necessary to do so. Further, s 93 of the CA 1989 has been amended (by s 122 of the ACA 2002) to provide that the rules of court may provide 'for children to be separately represented in relevant proceedings'. Rules will, therefore, provide for a CAFCASS officer to act on behalf of the child upon the hearing of applications for making, varying or revoking placement orders or s 26 contact orders. This officer will have a duty to safeguard the child's interests.[5] To avoid any conflict of interest, an employee of the local authority applying for a placement order is expressly precluded from being appointed to safeguard the child's interests.[6] Provision will also be made for a CAFCASS officer to report to the court, on request, on matters relating to the welfare of the child, which is the paramount consideration under s 1. As a protection for parents, it is anticipated that the welfare report will include the views of birth parents, so that their wishes and feelings are represented in the process of making, varying or revoking placement or s 26 contact orders.

Placement order

9.30 Section 21 of the ACA 2002 defines a 'placement order' as 'an order made by the court authorising a local authority to place a child for adoption with any prospective adopters who may be chosen by the authority'.

9.31 The court may not make a placement order unless:

(1) the child is subject to a care order;[7] or
(2) the court is satisfied that the conditions in s 31(2) of CA 1989 are met;[8] or

---

1   HC Special Standing Committee, 20 November 2001, col 5, para 13.
2   HC Special Standing Committee, 29 November 2001, col 347, per Ms Jacqui Smith.
3   HL Grand Committee, 2 July 2002, vol 637, CWH 168, per Lord Hunt of Kings Heath.
4   ACA 2002, s 122(1)(b) also inserts a new subs (6A) into s 41 of the CA 1989 which provides that: 'The proceedings which may be specified under subsection (6)(i) include (for example) proceedings for the making, varying or discharging of a section 8 order'.
5   ACA 2002, s 102(3).
6   Ibid, s 102(5). HC Deb, 20 May 2002, vol 386, no 150, cols 45–46, per Ms Jacqui Smith.
7   ACA 2002, s 21(2)(a).
8   Ibid, s 21(2)(b).

(3) the child has no parent or guardian;[1] *and*

(4) each parent or guardian has consented to the child being placed for adoption with any prospective adopters (who may be chosen by the local authority) and has not withdrawn consent;[2] or

(5) the parent's consent should be dispensed with under s 52 of the ACA 2002.[3]

9.32 As the placement order is general, rather than a specific order, one of the consequences is that, if the placement with the prospective adopters were to break down and the local authority, on review, still considered that the child ought be placed for adoption, the authority would not have to return to court to seek another placement order before it placed the child for adoption again. The intention behind this is to cut down harmful delay where a suitable alternative family is available.

9.33 A placement order remains in force until it is revoked under s 24 or an adoption order is made or the child marries or attains the age of 18 years.[4] The parents or those 'others' concerned (other than the local authority) may not apply to revoke the order unless (i) the court gives leave *and* (ii) the child is not placed for adoption by the authority.[5] The court may give leave only if the parents' or others' circumstances have changed since the order was made.[6] The requirement that there must be a change of circumstances before the parents or others may apply is intended to prevent the court from being invited simply to repeal the deliberations which have previously taken place. In making the placement order, the court will have already been obliged by s 1 to consider all the alternatives and take account of the views of the child's relatives and their capacity to provide a stable and secure environment. The Government's view is that 'in the interests of promoting the security of the child, … minimising disruption and collectively saving time and resources' the court should 'consider whether those circumstances have changed before it looks at whether or not to reverse that [placement order] decision'.[7] Although the Act refers simply to 'a change' in circumstances, it should be noted that the Government referred to a 'significant' change in the birth parents' circumstances.[8]

9.34 New regulations will place an obligation upon local authorities to review placement regularly. They are likely to impose obligations similar to those under the Adoption Agencies Regulations 1983,[9] which required a review after 4 weeks and thereafter at 6-monthly intervals.

9.35 Where a child has not been placed after 2 years, there appears to be no intention to impose a regulatory imperative, but merely 'an expectation' that the local authority will re-apply the s 1 principles and ask itself whether the adoption route continues to be appropriate or whether there are other and better routes for the child. If the local authority decides that the adoption plan is no longer in the child's best interests, again

---

1   ACA 2002, s 21(2)(c).
2   Ibid, s 21(3)(a).
3   Ibid, s 21(3)(b).
4   Ibid, s 21(4). 'Adoption order' also includes a Scottish or Northern Irish adoption order: s 17(3).
5   Ibid, s 24(2).
6   Ibid, s 24(3).
7   HL Grand Committee, 2 July 2002, vol 637, CWH 160, per Baroness Andrews.
8   Ibid.
9   SI 1983/1964.

there is 'an expectation' that it will apply to revoke the placement order under s 24. As there is, however, no guarantee that a local authority will act in this way, s 24 purports to combat local authority inertia by enabling the child or 'someone acting on his behalf'[1] to apply to discharge the order. The Government suggested that the 'someone' could be 'social services, a social care worker or an (unspecified) range of people acting to safeguard the interests of the child'.[2] As the first two categories are, in effect, the local authority by another name, this does not look to be a promising safeguard, especially where the parents' and others' ability to apply for revocation is restricted by the 'leave' fetter and the condition that the child must not have been placed for adoption.

9.36 There is, however, a further safeguard to avoid local authority drift and limbo for the child, namely the new independent reviewing system which is introduced through amendments to the CA 1989 in s 118 of the ACA 2002. If the placement is failing to an extent that the independent reviewing officer becomes concerned and the local authority does not remedy the situation, the reviewing officer can refer the case to a CAFCASS officer. If that officer considers that the child's human rights may be at risk, then CAFCASS can apply on behalf of the child (without the leave or placement fetters) for discharge of the placement order.[3] As in practice this will be the only real safeguard, it is suggested that the damage which local authority drift can cause to the child makes a compelling argument for ensuring the 'independence' of the reviewing officer, otherwise the reviewing system becomes a self-defeating exercise and this essential safeguard for the child is lost.

9.37 Once a placement order has been made, only the local authority may remove the child. Unlike a placement with consent under s 19, there is no provision for the parents to have their children returned to them as of right at their request. Their only option would be to seek to revoke the placement order but, first, they would have to overcome the twin peaks of the 'leave' and 'placement' conditions under s 24(2), which is likely to be a Herculean task for any parent.

9.38 A placement order provides the local authority with considerable protective powers. Under such an order, it has parental responsibility and the power to restrict the parents' and prospective adopters' ability to exercise their parental responsibility. No one other than the local authority may remove the child from the placement unless that removal is made under a specific legal power or the child is arrested. As 'placed' children will be looked-after children, the authority will be under the same general duties as set out in s 22 of the CA 1989 to safeguard and promote the children's welfare (modified for adoption). If a placement order is revoked, any pre-existing care order will automatically revive, so that the child will continue to be protected.

Threshold criteria

9.39 The court may make a placement order only where the child is already subject to a care order under the CA 1989 or where the threshold criteria under s 31(2) of the CA 1989 are met. Section 31 of the CA 1989 empowers the court to make a care order provided that it is satisfied under subs (2) that:

---

1   HL Grand Committee, 2 July 2002, vol 637, CWH 166, per Baroness Andrews.
2   Ibid.
3   Ibid.

(a)   the child concerned is suffering or is likely to suffer significant harm; and

(b)   the harm or likelihood of harm is attributable to:

> (i)   the care given to the child, or likely to be given to him if the order were not made, not being what it would be unreasonable to expect a parent to give him; or
>
> (ii) the child's being beyond parental control.

9.40   In short, the court has to be satisfied of the existence or likelihood of significant harm attributable either to the care the child is receiving or likely to receive or the child being beyond parental control. 'Harm' is defined in s 31(9) of the CA 1989 (as amended by s 120 of the ACA 2002) as 'ill treatment[1] or the impairment of health[2] or development, including, for example, impairment suffered from seeing or hearing the ill-treatment of another'.[3] The extended definition is intended to highlight that 'harm' includes any impairment to the child's health or development as a result of witnessing the ill-treatment of another person, for example by witnessing domestic violence. Any harm a child suffers as a result of a parent being intimidated or harassed is caught by the definition of 'harm'.

9.41   The law relating to s 31(2) of the CA 1989 has been established in a trilogy of decisions by the House of Lords. In *Re M (A Minor) (Care Order: Threshold Conditions)*,[4] the House of Lords determined that the date at which the threshold criteria for the making of a care order must be satisfied was the date of the application or, if temporary protective arrangements had continuously been in place, the date on which those arrangements were initiated.

9.42   In *Re H (Minors) (Sexual Abuse: Standard of Proof)*,[5] the House of Lords focused on the first threshold condition (the 'significant harm condition' under s 31(2)(a)) and established that:

> –   'the legal burden of establishing the existence of the conditions rests on the applicant for a care order';[6]
>
> –   the standard of proof required is the balance of probabilities and is satisfied if the court considers that, on the evidence, the occurrence of the event was more likely than not.[7] The more improbable the event, the stronger must be the evidence that it did occur before, on balance, it is established that the event occurred;[8]
>
> –   'likely', in the second limb of s 31(2)(a), is used in the sense of a real possibility, ie one which cannot reasonably be ignored having regard to the nature and gravity of the feared harm in the particular case;[9]

---

1   'Ill treatment' is defined in s 31(9) of the CA 1989 as including 'sexual abuse and forms of ill-treatment which are not physical'.

2   'Health' is defined in s 31(9) of the CA 1989 as meaning 'physical and mental health'.

3   'Development' is defined in s 31(9) as meaning 'physical, intellectual, emotional, social or behavioural development'.

4   [1994] 2 AC 424, [1994] 2 FLR 577.

5   [1996] AC 563, sub nom *Re H and R (Child Sexual Abuse: Standard of Proof)* [1996] 1 FLR 80.

6   Ibid, at 95G, per Lord Nicholls of Birkenhead.

7   Ibid, at 95H and 96B, per Lord Nicholls of Birkenhead.

8   Ibid, at 96B–F, per Lord Nicholls of Birkenhead ('the cogency test').

9   Ibid, at 95D, per Lord Nicholls of Birkenhead.

–   whether either limb of s 31(2)(a) is satisfied is an issue to be decided by the court on the basis of the facts admitted or proved on a balance of probabilities, and suspicion is not sufficient.[1]

9.43   In *Lancashire County Council v B*,[2] their Lordships' attention turned to the second threshold criteria (the 'attributable' condition) set out in s 31(2)(b) and, in particular, the phrase 'the care given to the child'. It was held that:

–   'attributable to' connotes a causal connection between the harm or likelihood of harm, on the one hand, and the care or likely care or the child being beyond parental control, on the other hand; a contributory causal connection suffices;[3]
–   within s 31(2)(b)(i), the care given or likely to be given must fall below an objectively acceptable level; that level being the care a reasonable parent would provide for the child concerned;[4]
–   the phrase 'the care given to the child' refers primarily to the care given by a parent or parents or other primary carer (the norm), but where the care was shared the phrase was apt to embrace the care given by any of the carers. This interpretation was necessary to allow the court to intervene to protect the child who was clearly at risk, even when it was not possible to identify the source of the risk.[5]

9.44   These principles are likely to be directly translated into the context of s 21(2)(b) of the ACA 2002. For example, the date at which the court must be satisfied that the s 31(2) conditions are met for the purposes of that subsection is likely to be the date of the making of the placement order or the date of the initiation of temporary protective arrangements, if those have been continuously in place.

9.45   However, it has to be remembered that the function of s 21(2) is to define the court's jurisdiction in entertaining an application for a placement order. To use the words of Lord Clyde in the *Lancashire* case, 'the section merely opens up the way to the possibility that an order may be made'.[6] The making of the placement order not only requires the further fulfilment of the 'consent' conditions in s 21(3) of the ACA 2002 but also requires careful consideration of the s 1 principles, in particular the welfare checklist, the range of options and the 'no order' principle in s 1(6), subject always to the paramount consideration of the child's welfare in s 1(2). However, any findings which the court may make regarding the threshold conditions will be carried forward to the consideration of the child's welfare needs under s 1.

---

1   [1996] 1 FLR 80 at 98H–99C, per Lord Nicholls of Birkenhead.
2   [2000] 1 FLR 583.
3   Ibid, at 585C–E, per Lord Nicholls of Birkenhead. The example he gave was: where a parent entrusts a child to a third party without taking the precautionary steps a reasonable parent would take to check the suitability of the third party, and subsequently the third party injures the child, the harm suffered by the child may be regarded as attributable to the care of the parent as well as the third party.
4   Ibid, at 585E–F, per Lord Nicholls of Birkenhead.
5   Ibid, at 589C–E, per Lord Nicholls of Birkenhead.
6   Ibid, at 592H–593C.

Care plans

9.46   The practice of a local authority filing a care plan has long been an essential feature in public law cases under the CA 1989.[1] Sections 31 and 26[2] of the CA 1989 have been amended[3] to place care plans on a statutory basis and to enable regulations to be made requiring local authorities to keep under review s 31A care plans or care plans for children voluntarily looked after under s 20 of the CA 1989.

9.47   Section 31(3A) provides that no care order may be made until the court has considered a plan for the future care of the child prepared under s 31A ('a s 31A plan').[4] The new s 31A places a duty on the local authority in an application where a care order might be made to prepare a care plan within a time scale set by the court. While such an application is pending or a care order is in force, the authority must keep the care plan under review and revise the plan or make a new one, if it is of the opinion that some change is required. Regulations will set out how the plan is to be drawn up and the information to be included.[5] These requirements are not binding on an interim care order.[6]

9.48   The regulations will require the appointment of a reviewing officer, who must be independent of the case and its management.[7] The reviewing officer will be required to chair the review meetings and ensure the implementation of the care plan by speaking to the child before the review.[8] As a remedy where there has been a failure, the reviewing officer will be empowered to refer the case to CAFCASS,[9] who will be able to bring proceedings on behalf of the child. CAFCASS will be able to use existing remedies under the CA 1989 and the Human Rights Act 1998. These are:

–   an application under the CA 1989 to discharge the care order;
–   an application under the CA 1989 for contact between the child and another person;
–   an application under the Human Rights Act 1998 for an injunction to prevent the local authority from taking a particular step, such as removing the child from an established placement; or

---

1   In *Manchester City Council v F (Note)* [1993] 1 FLR 419, Eastham J accepted that it was the duty of the local authority in all public law cases to file a care plan.
2   Section 26 provides for periodic case reviews by the authority, including obtaining the views of parents and children. For example, one of the required reviews is that every 6 months the local authority must actively consider whether it should apply to the court for a discharge of the care order: Review of Children's Cases Regulations 1991, SI 1991/895.
3   By ss 121 and 118 of the ACA 2002.
4   CA 1989, s 31A(6).
5   In the meantime, the care plan should accord with Department of Health, *The Children Act 1989 Guidance and Regulations* (HMSO, 1991), vol 3, para 2.62, as supplemented by the Local Authority Circular of 12 August 1999 (LAC (99) 29) *Care Plans and Care Proceedings under the Children Act 1989*.
6   CA 1989, s 31A(5).
7   Ibid, s 26(2)(k), amended by s 118 of the ACA 2002.
8   Ibid, s 26(2A)(a) and (b), as amended.
9   Ibid, s 26(2A)(c), as amended.

–   an application under the Human Rights Act 1998 for a declaration that the local
    authority's plans are contrary to the child's human rights (which would require
    those plans to be re-thought) and damages in respect of the local authority's action
    or inaction in implementing the care plan.[1]

The requirements will apply both to children who are the subject of care orders and to
those accommodated by the local authority.[2]

9.49   This system is intended to ensure that in those cases where the reviewing function
has not worked and the care plan is not being implemented, there is a route back to court
so as to provide a safety net for the child's rights. It is intended to fill the statutory lacuna
resulting from the absence of any effective machinery for protecting the civil rights of
young children with no parent able or willing to act for them; a lacuna which was
highlighted by the House of Lords in *Re S (Minors) (Care Order: Implementation of Care
Plan); Re W (Minors) (Care Order: Adequacy of Care Plan).*[3] Lord Nicholls of Birkenhead
said:

> 'In the ordinary course a parent ought to be able to obtain effective relief by one or other of
> these means [judicial review or discharge of a care order] against an authority whose
> mishandling of a child in its care has violated a parent's Art 8 rights. More difficult is the case
> ... where there is no parent able and willing to become involved. In this type of case the Art 8
> rights of a young child may be violated by a local authority without anyone outside the local
> authority becoming aware of the violation. In practice such a child may not always have an
> effective remedy.[4]

> ... The guarantee provided by Art 6(1) can hardly said to be satisfied in the case of a young
> child who in practice has no way of initiating judicial review proceedings to challenge a local
> authority's decision affecting his civil rights. (In such a case ... the child would also lack the
> means of initiating s 7 proceedings to protect his Art 8 rights).

> My conclusion is that in these respects circumstances might perhaps arise when English law
> would not satisfy the requirements of Art 6(1) regarding some child care decisions made by
> local authorities. In one or other of the circumstances mentioned above the Art 6 rights of a
> child or a parent are capable of being infringed.'[5]

9.50   The fact that the local authority knows that its care plan is being referred back to
the court for a review of the order is regarded in itself as a more significant sanction than
existed previously.[6] However, the system will fail *in limine* if the interviewing officer is
not able to exercise true independence. Although the Government has said that the
reviewing officer must be independent of the case management and the line management
of the social workers who are conducting the assessment, it has been more equivocal as to
whether the officer should be independent of the social services department of the local

---

1   HC Deb, 20 May 2002, vol 386, no 150, cols 65–67.
2   CA 1989, s 26(2)(f), (k), (2A), (2B) and (2C), as amended by s 118 of the ACA 2002.
3   [2002] UKHL 10, [2002] 1 FLR 815. See HC Deb, 20 May 2002, vol 386, no 150, col 51, per
    Ms Jacqui Smith, who said: 'The amendments respond ... to the issues in the case as *Re S & Re W*
    ... By putting care plans on a statutory footing, establishing a review process that allows for it to
    happen and providing for a reviewing officer to refer cases to CAFCASS, we are ensuring that this
    gap in the law in properly filled and the children's needs will be met effectively as possible through
    the systems provided under the Children Act'.
4   [2002] 1 FLR 815 at [63].
5   Ibid at [82]–[83].
6   HC Deb, 20 May 2002, vol 386, no 150, col 65.

authority.[1] Yet the suggestion has also been floated that other organisations with expertise, or other authorities, can provide reviewing officers. Not until the regulations have been promulgated will the picture become clear.

9.51 An illustration of the court exercising the statutory power under ss 7 and 8 of the Human Rights Act 1998 in the context of a care plan is to be found in the first instance decision of Holman J in *Re M (Care: Challenging Decisions by Local Authority).*[2] In reviewing its care plan for a child in its care, the local authority ruled out any prospect of the child returning to live with either the father or the mother. In proceedings brought by the parents, Holman J set aside the authority's decision on the grounds that the decision-making process had not sufficiently involved the parents so as to protect their interests as required and was, therefore, unfair and a violation of Art 8 of the European Convention on Human Rights. It should, however, be noted that Lord Nicholls of Birkenhead in *Re S; Re W* emphasised that 'one would not expect proceedings to be launched under s 7 of the Human Rights Act 1998 until any other appropriate remedial routes have first been explored'.[3]

Consent

9.52 Two of the key components to the making of a placement order are (i) consent or, alternatively, (ii) dispensing with consent. Section 21 of the ACA 2002 works, therefore, in conjunction with s 52, to which it is subject. As has been seen in Chapter 8, s 52 has two grounds for dispensing with parental consent, of which the second ground, namely that 'the welfare of the child requires the consent to be dispensed with',[4] is the more likely to be employed in domestic adoptions. Thus, the full panoply of the statutory scheme for dispensing with parental consent under the new legislation (contained in ss 1 and 52) is brought forward in the time span of the adoption process to the earlier placement decision. This enables the court to be brought in at this early stage, with a critical part of its role being to consider the essential elements of s 1. This judicial exercise reinforces the duty imposed under ss 18(2) and 22(1)(d) on the authority to be 'satisfied that the child ought to be placed for adoption' which necessarily, as s 1 of the ACA 2002 applies, involves a consideration of all the alternative options. These are not only crucial safeguards for the interests of the birth family, but also essential if the making of a placement order is to be Convention-compliant.

9.53 A court cannot make a placement order unless an effort has been made to notify the parents or guardians with parental responsibility of the application. Section 141 of the ACA 2002 provides that court rules must require certain persons to be notified of the date and place of the placement order application hearing and of the fact that, unless the person wishes or the court requires, the person need not attend. Such notification must be sent to those whose consent is needed for the making of the placement order under

---

1   HC Deb, vol 386, no 50, cols 60 and 61. At cols 60 and 61, Jacqui Smith said: 'They must be independent of the child's case, but not necessarily of the local authority ... It is not impossible to set up a structure in a local authority, whereby employees can maintain their independence'.

2   [2001] 2 FLR 1300, which was approved by the House of Lords in *Re S; Re W* (above) at [46]. See also *C v Bury Metropolitan Borough Council* [2002] 2 FLR 868, where Dame Butler-Sloss P held that human rights challenges to care plans and placement of children should be held in the Family Division of the High Court, preferably by judges with experience in the Administrative Court.

3   [2002] 1 FLR 815 at [62].

4   Section 52(1)(b) of the ACA 2002.

s 21(3)(a) (or those whose consent would be required but for s 21(3)(b)), in so far as they can be found. Such persons are, first, the natural parents who have parental responsibility. Under the CA 1989, mothers and married fathers have automatic parental responsibility. Unmarried fathers can acquire parental responsibility either by marrying the mother or under s 4 of the CA 1989 (as amended) by joint registration of the birth with the mother, by agreement or court order. As has been seen, those whose consent is needed under s 21(3) also includes any guardian appointed under s 5 of the CA 1989 to act in the event of the parents' death and any special guardian.

9.54   If one of the parents cannot be found, the authority will have to take all reasonable steps to find the other parent. If only one or neither parent can be found, then the authority will have to consider 'seriously if it is still in the best interests of the child to be adopted ... [and should] seek the guidance of the court ...'.[1] Court rules will provide a route for agencies to apply to the court for guidance.[2] If none of those persons whose consent is required can be found, then any relative prescribed in the court rules, who can be found, should be notified. 'Relative' is defined in s 144(1) as meaning, in relation to a child, 'a grandparent, brother, sister, uncle or aunt, whether of the full blood or half-blood or by marriage'.

9.55   There may, however, be 'significant others' in the child's life who fall outside the formal notification provisions. They are catered for by the application of the s 1 principles, including the welfare checklist, first, by the authority at the stage when it is considering whether the child ought to be placed for adoption and whether it should apply for a placement order and, secondly, by the court when it is considering whether or not to make the placement order. Section 1(4)(f) of the ACA 2002 places an obligation on the authority and the court to consider the child's relationship with any person 'in relation to whom the agency considers the relationship to be relevant', including that person's wishes and feelings, and ability to care for the child and offer him or her a stable and secure home. The Adoption Agencies Regulations 1983 placed the agency under a duty to establish whether there were any holders of parental responsibility under s 4 of the CA 1989. This duty is likely to be replicated in regulations and guidance under the new Act. In considering placement, the court will also have access to the report on the recommended placement, which will, as did the former Sch 2 report, cover the child's relationship with his or her family and others of significance to him or her and report on any alternatives to adoption for the purposes of s 1(6). As part of the decision-making process, the adoption panel will scrutinise the plan for the child. This will include an examination of whether the agency has properly explored the wider family situation. The fundamental review of the panel is seen as a safeguard to ensure that this happens.[3]

9.56   In addition, all children looked after by a local authority will come under the new independent reviewing system under s 118. This system will include all children accommodated and covered by Chapter 3 of the Act, whether they are voluntarily placed,

---

1   HL Grand Committee, 2 July 2002, vol 637, CWH 155, per Baroness Andrews.
2   HL Deb, 30 October 2002, vol 640, col 208, per Baroness Andrews. It had been initially mooted that recourse could be had to the inherent jurisdiction of the court. This was subject to criticism; hence the resort to rules. Practitioners will have to await these rules to see how in practice agencies can raise these matters with the court. See also HL Deb, 14 October 2002, cols 659–660, per Baroness Andrews.
3   HL Deb, 30 October 2002, vol 640, col 208, per Baroness Andrews.

actually placed with prospective adopters or simply accommodated pending placement. Each child will have a care plan, which will have to be reviewed regularly by the authority, and an independent reviewing officer will take part in every review. That process will include a review of Art 8 rights concerning links with parents and relatives:[1]

> 'If the authority devises or seeks to implement a plan which breaches a child's human rights by, for example, separating him from the wider family members, the reviewing officer will first notify the authority of his concern in the expectation that the plan will be modified to take account of it. If the authority does not do so, the reviewing officer can inform the child's parents who can take action on the child's behalf or he can alert CAFCASS.'

9.57 If there is any doubt as to the capacity of a parent to give consent, it is envisaged that the CAFCASS officer would not certify the consent and would notify the agency of his or her concerns. Where the agency is the local authority, it may apply in these circumstances for a placement order to be made and the placement order hearing could enable the parent's consent to be dispensed with under s 52.

Section 22: relevant circumstances for applying for a placement order

9.58 There is a *mandatory* requirement placed upon a local authority to apply for a placement order in the following circumstances:

(1) where a child is 'placed' for adoption or is being accommodated by the authority; *and*

  – no adoption agency is authorised to place the child for adoption (ie the parent does not consent to the placement for adoption or has withdrawn consent to placement for adoption); *and*
  – either the authority considers that the conditions in s 31(2) of the CA 1989 are met or the child has no parent or guardian; *and*
  – the authority is satisfied that the child ought to be placed for adoption;[2]

(2) where there is (a) a pending application for a care order (which has not been disposed of) or (b) the child is the subject of a care order and the appropriate local authority is not authorised to place the child for adoption (ie the parent does not consent to the child being placed for adoption); *and*

  – the authority is satisfied that the child ought to be placed for adoption.[3]

9.59 The authority has a *discretion* whether or not to apply for a placement order where a child is subject to a care order and it is the appropriate authority authorised to place the child for adoption under s 19 (ie the parent or guardian is prepared to consent to the placement of the child for adoption).[4] Alternatively, it could simply decide to place the child with parental consent under s 19.

9.60 These provisions, however, do not apply (i) where there is a notice of intention to adopt (unless a 4-month period from the giving of notice has expired without an

1   HL Deb, 30 October 2002, vol 640, col 209, per Baroness Andrews.
2   ACA 2002, s 22(1).
3   Ibid, s 22(2).
4   Ibid, s 22(3).

adoption application or the application has been withdrawn or refused) or (ii) if an application for an adoption order has been made but has not been disposed of.[1]

Appropriate local authority

9.61 An 'appropriate local authority' is defined in s 22(7). It is:

(1) in relation to a care order, the authority in whose care the child is placed by the order; and

(2) in relation to an application on which a care order might be made, the authority which makes the application.

Supplementary

'Looked-after' children

9.62 A child is 'looked after' by the local authority under s 22 of the CA 1989[2] where:

– the authority is under a duty to apply for a placement order;[3]
– the authority has applied for a placement order and the application is pending;[4]
– the child is placed or authorised to be placed for adoption with prospective adopters by the authority.[5]

9.63 The intention in extending 'looked-after' status to a child in these circumstances is to make clear that the local authority is to have the continuing responsibility for managing and overseeing the child's progress until a future adoption order is made and, subsequently, for regularly reviewing its progress. This also applies to a child who is less than 6 weeks old and has been placed for adoption.

9.64 Under s 22 of the CA 1989[6] there is a general duty on the authority looking after any child to safeguard and promote that child's welfare and make such use of the services (which are available for children cared for by their own parents) as appears reasonable to the authority.

9.65 Where, however, a child becomes 'looked after' by an authority which is authorised to place the child for adoption or has placed for adoption a child who is less than 6 weeks old, it is proposed to disapply certain of the 'looked-after' provisions in the

---

1   ACA 2002, s 22(5)(a) and (b).
2   See also CA 1989, Sch 2, Part I.
3   ACA 2002, s 22(4)(a).
4   Ibid, s 22(4)(b).
5   Ibid, s 18(3).
6   Section 22, as amended, does not apply to children who are accommodated with their families under s 17 of the CA 1989. Children under s 17 are not 'looked-after' children. Unaccompanied asylum-seeking children supported under s 17 are not looked-after children. Should they need to be accommodated, they will be accommodated by authorities under s 20. Note that s 17(6) of the CA 1989 has been amended by s 116 of the ACA 2002 to permit authorities to provide services in kind, accommodation or in exceptional circumstances, cash, and s 24A of the CA 1989 has likewise been amended to permit authorities to provide, in exceptional circumstances, accommodation or cash to children who are being looked after while aged 16 or 17. Section 116 came into force on 7 November 2002, as did s 136 which amended s 93 of the Local Government Act 2000 in relation to the payment of grants in connection with welfare services.

CA 1989.[1] This is in order to reflect the particular circumstances of placement for adoption. The following examples are given as the likely 'targets' to be disapplied:[2]

– the duty to ascertain and give due consideration to the wishes and feelings of the child's parents or other relatives or those (other than parents) with parental responsibility before taking any decision with respect to the child under s 22(4)(b)–(d) and (5)(b);

– the duty to promote contact between the child and his or her parent unless it is not reasonably practicable or consistent with the child's welfare under para 15 of Sch 2 to the CA 1989;

– the liability of a parent to contribute to the child's maintenance under para 21 of Sch 2 to the CA 1989.[3]

9.66   As to disapplication of s 22(4)(b)–(d) and (5)(b), the thinking is that it may not be appropriate for an authority to be *under a duty* to consult the child's parents or other relative before taking any decision relating to the child, although it is suggested approaching this on a case-by-case basis. In the case of prospective adopters with parental responsibility for the child placed with them, s 22 is regarded as otiose as the authority will be under an obligation to ascertain their views before making a decision relating to the child under the provisions of the ACA 2002.

9.67   The effect of disapplying the duty to promote contact is that the parents whose child is placed for adoption are distinguished from the parents whose children are subject to care orders, although in both cases they continue to retain some parental responsibility. The parents whose child is placed for adoption may still apply for contact under ss 26 and 27 of the ACA 2002, but they lose the very significant protection afforded by the local authority being under a duty to promote contact. In other words, they lose any presumption in favour of contact.

9.68   It should be noted that s 117 of the ACA 2002 amends ss 24D[4] and 26 of the CA 1989 by making further provision for enquiries carried out by local authorities into representations about services provided under the CA 1989. It corrects an anomaly in the complaints procedure involving children. Previously, complaints about the discharge of local authority functions, including care and supervision and child protection, were dealt with through the adult complaints procedure established under the Local Authority Social Services Act 1970.

9.69   Section 117 extends the more child-focused complaints procedure under the CA 1989 to complaints and representations about those services. The intention is to provide a consistent approach to all complaints made by or concerning children.[5] It enables regulations to be made to impose time limits for the making of representations, to provide

---

1   ACA 2002, s 53.

2   Section 53(3) also makes provision to disapply the similar parts of s 61 of the CA 1989 where a registered adoption society is authorised to place a child for adoption or has placed a child for adoption who is less than 6 weeks old.

3   Also, where a child's home is with persons who have given notice of intention to adopt, no contribution is to be payable towards the maintenance of children looked after by authorities under CA 1989, Sch 2, Part 3 for the period specified in s 53(5): s 53(4).

4   Inserted into the CA 1989 by the Children (Leaving Care) Act 2000.

5   HL Deb, 18 July 2002, vol 637, CWH 367, per Lord Hunt of Kings Heath.

an informal resolution stage and to extend the complaints procedure to services provided under Parts IV and V of the CA 1989.[1] The proposal is that an independent person will not be required in any informal resolution stage and that the informal procedure should have a tight 14-day time scale in recognition of the importance of children having their concerns dealt with quickly.[2]

9.70   The duty to establish a procedure for considering representations is also extended to include complaints made to the authority by any person mentioned in s 3(1) of the ACA 2002[3] about the discharge by the authority of such functions under the ACA 2002 as are specified by the Secretary of State in regulations.

9.71   Section 119 of the ACA 2002 also inserts a new s 26A into the CA 1989, which deals with advocacy services. The National Advocacy Standards[4] state that:

> 'Advocacy is about speaking up for children and young persons, in particular and whenever possible, by enabling them to speak up for themselves. It is about helping them to achieve understanding and participate in and influence decisions that affect their lives, particularly about representing their views, wishes and needs to decision-makers and seeking remedies for breaches of their human rights. Advocacy services offer independent and confidential information, advice, advocacy, representation and support.'

9.72   Section 26A(1) provides that local authorities must make arrangements to provide assistance for children and young persons who make or intend to make complaints under the CA 1989 procedures. This covers the standard procedure under s 26 and also the procedure for young people leaving care under s 24D (inserted by the Children (Leaving Care) Act 2000). It enables local authorities to arrange to provide assistance to children and young persons who have not yet complained, but who intend to do so. This is to ensure that children will be given help in initiating complaint procedures. 'Assistance' is intended to cover those kinds of services specified in the National Advocacy Standards.

9.73   Section 26A(2) provides that the assistance that local authorities must put in place must include representation. This is to ensure that the services provide for the needs of children and young people who need or wish to have someone to speak on their behalf. Section 26A(3)(a) provides that advocacy services must not be provided by a person who is prevented from doing so through regulations. This means that, through regulations, local authorities will be required to ensure that assistance is provided only by those with no responsibility for the case of the child or the issues at stake in the complaint. The principles of independence will also be dealt with in the advocacy standards.[5]

9.74   Local authorities may choose either to provide the assistance themselves or to come to an agreement with a national or local advocacy service provider in order to meet

---

1   It implements some of the changes carried forward from the 'Listening to People' consultation exercise on improving social services complaints procedures.

2   HL Deb, 18 July 2002, vol 637, CWH 367.

3   ACA 2002, s 117(4), which inserts a new subs (3B) into s 26 of the CA 1989. The duty extends also to any other person to whom arrangements for the provision of adoption support services extend and such other person as the authority considers has sufficient interest in the child who is or may be adopted to warrant representations being considered.

4   Published October 2002. These standards will be encompassed in s 7 guidance (ie guidance issued under s 7 of the Local Authority Social Services Act 1970).

5   HL Deb, 23 October 2002, cols 1390–1392, per Lord Hunt of Kings Heath.

their responsibilities. Regulations under s 26A(3)(b) will prescribe how the assistance is to be provided; for example, setting out the persons or bodies with whom the local authority may enter into arrangements to provide assistance and the degree of choice that must be provided. Local authorities will be required to fund the service. Section 26A(4) reflects s 26(6) of the CA 1989, which provides for regulations to require a local authority to monitor the provision of assistance to ensure that it complies with the regulations. Section 26A(5) reflects s 26(8) of the CA 1989, which sets out that local authorities should advertise the advocacy service as they see fit. Visibility of these services will be important to ensure that they can be accessed by the children and young persons who need them.

9.75 Arguably, the services can never be entirely independent of the local authority, given that the local authority will be the body commissioning and paying for them. Therefore, the best that can realistically be achieved under the CA 1989 as amended is to ensure that the assistance is not influenced by the local authority, ie by ensuring that no one with a direct interest in the outcome of the complaint is involved in the provision of the assistance to the child or young person.

Directions

9.76 Section 26A(6) enables the court to give directions for the child to undergo medical, psychiatric or other assessment where (i) an application for a placement order is pending or (ii) no interim care order has been made.

9.77 This mirrors, in part, s 38(6) of the CA 1989 and, therefore, similar considerations are likely to apply. In *Re C (Interim Care Order: Residential Assessment)*[1] it was held that the assessment should involve the participation of the child and should be directed to providing the court with material which, in the view of the court, was required to enable it to reach a proper decision at the final hearing for a full care order. In the context of adoption, 'the hearing for a full care order' can be understood as 'a hearing for a placement order'.

9.78 A child who is of sufficient understanding to make an informed decision may refuse to submit to the examination or assessment.[2]

Effect on other orders

Care orders

9.79 Where a child is subject to a care order or where a care order is made at the same time as the placement order, the care order does not have any effect while the placement order is in force.[3] The care order is, therefore, suspended for the duration of the placement order, but it will automatically revive if the placement order is revoked.

---

1   [1997] 1 FLR 1.
2   ACA 2002, s 22(6).
3   Ibid, s 29(1).

Section 8 orders and supervision orders

9.80   On the making of a placement order, any s 8 order (under the CA 1989) or any supervision order ceases to have effect.[1] While it is in force, the court may not make a prohibited steps order, residence order or specific issue order, nor any supervision order or child assessment order[2] nor any contact order under the CA 1989.[3]

9.81   There is, however, an exception in the case of a residence order. Where an application for a final adoption order has been made and the parents (or guardian or any other person with leave) have obtained leave of the court to oppose the making of the order under s 47(3) or (5), then the parents may make an application for a residence order. This is to enable competing applications for residence orders by the parents to be heard at contested final adoption hearings.

Special guardianship orders

9.82   Where a placement order is in force, no special guardianship order may be made in respect of the child until an application for a final adoption order is made, when a person entitled to do so may make a competing application for a special guardianship order with the leave of the court under s 29(5) or, if he or she is the guardian of the child, with leave under s 47(5).[4]

9.83   The making of a special guardianship order does not automatically discharge a placement order. The court will have to take a positive decision to revoke the order, governed by s 1 of the ACA 2002 and the adoption checklist.[5] One of the reasons for this is that, when making the special guardianship order, the court will be looking at s 1 of the CA 1989, which is not specifically tailored to adoption and the issues surrounding it.

Revocation of placement orders

9.84   Section 24 of the ACA 2002 makes provision for the revocation of placement orders. Although a child or a local authority may apply to revoke a placement order at any time, other persons, including the parents, can apply only if they meet each of the following pre-conditions, namely that:[6]

(a)   the court has given leave, which cannot be given unless the court is satisfied that there has been a change of circumstances since the order was made;[7] and

(b)   the child is not yet placed for adoption by the authority.

However, where an application for revocation has been made and not disposed of, and the child is not placed for adoption by the authority, the child may not be placed for adoption without the court's leave.[8]

---

1   ACA 2002, s 29(2).
2   Ibid, s 29(3).
3   Ibid, s 26(2)(a).
4   Ibid, s 29(5).
5   HC Special Standing Committee, 29 November 2001, col 353, per Ms Jacqui Smith.
6   ACA 2002, s 24(2).
7   Ibid, s 24(3).
8   Ibid, s 24(5).

9.85 At the final adoption hearing, if the court decides not to make an adoption order and further considers that the child should not even be placed for adoption, it has the discretion to revoke the placement order.[1] If, however, the court decides that the child should still be placed for a future adoption, then it may order the placement order to continue.

9.86 The ACA 2002 does not spell out the effect on parental responsibility of revocation of a placement order under s 24.[2] It is to be assumed that, whereas formerly the revocation of a freeing order did not operate to revive a care order,[3] revocation of the placement order will now operate to revive the care order[4] and, with it, the shared parental responsibility between the authority and the parents. Similarly, it is assumed that any restrictions which may have been placed upon the parental responsibility of the parents by the authority under s 24(4) are now removed upon revocation.

9.87 In the case of an application for the revocation of a placement order, the rules made under s 144 of the ACA 2002 must require that every person who can be found, whose consent to the placement order was required under s 21(3)(a) (or would have been required but for subs (3)(b)), be notified of the date and place where the application is to be heard and of the fact that, unless the person wishes or the court requires, he or she need not attend.[5]

Variation

9.88 On a joint application by both authorities, the court may vary a placement order so as to substitute another local authority for the authorised authority.[6] The same requirements as to notification apply in relation to variation of a placement order as in relation to a revocation order.[7]

CONSEQUENCES OF PLACEMENT

Parental responsibility

9.89 Section 25 of the ACA 2002 makes provision for who is to have parental responsibility where a child is placed for adoption under s 19 or an agency is authorised to place a child for adoption under s 19[8] or where a placement order is in force.[9] Parental responsibility for the child is given to the agency,[10] which shares this responsibility with

---

1   ACA 2002, s 24(4).
2   Unlike s 20(3) of the AA 1976, which expressly set out the position on parental responsibility on revocation of a s 18 freeing order.
3   AA 1976, s 20(3A). This created difficulties for the child where the parent was 'unsuitable': see *Re G (Adoption: Freeing Order)* [1997] 2 FLR 202, where the House of Lords filled the lacuna which s 20(3) and (3A) of the AA 1976 created, and also *Re C (Adoption Freeing Order)* [1999] 1 FLR 348.
4   The effect of ACA 2002, s 29(1).
5   ACA 2002, s 144(3) and (4)(b).
6   Ibid, s 23(1) and (2).
7   Ibid, s 144(3) and (4)(b).
8   Ibid, s 25(1)(a).
9   Ibid, s 25(1)(b).
10   Ibid, s 25(2).

the parents. While the child is placed with prospective adopters, it is also given to them so that they share parental responsibility with the agency and the birth parents.[1] The assumption of parental responsibility by the prospective adopters is seen as an incremental process of development rather than an assumption of full responsibility from the moment the child is placed. Placement may last several months and, as the child settles in with his or her new family, the prospective adopters will gradually take on parental responsibility: for example, agreeing to medical treatment and consenting to school trips.[2]

9.90   The parents' parental responsibility is not extinguished upon placement for adoption or on the making of a placement order. However, it is left to the agency to determine to what extent the parental responsibility of any parent or guardian or of the prospective adopters is to be restricted.[3] The objective behind the sharing of parental responsibility, once the child is placed, has been stated as 'to help the management of the placement by making it clear that the agency and the prospective adopters have responsibility for the child and can make day-to-day decisions. It is appropriate for the adoption agency which has overall responsibility for managing the placement to be able to determine the extent to which the birth parents may exercise parental responsibility'.[4] It will not be an easy exercise for the agency to determine where the line should be drawn.

9.91   There is, however, a risk that this gives the agency a wide discretion to curtail the parents' parental responsibility to the point that it becomes an illusory rather than a substantive right, thereby losing the essential advantage of the placement provisions over freeing orders. It is important, therefore, to stress that the discipline of s 1 applies just as much to this agency determination as to others under the ACA 2002 and that such factors as the child's relationship with his or her relatives, the likelihood of this continuing and the value to the child of it continuing are a material consideration in that determination, under s 1(4)(f).

9.92   If the birth parents or the prospective adopters are dissatisfied with the manner in which the agency restricts their ability to exercise parental responsibility, the expectation is that this will be discussed with the agency in the first instance and, if they remain dissatisfied, that the relevant complaints procedure will be utilised.[5] Ultimately, in the case of placement with consent, it is open to the parents to withdraw consent and to request that the child be returned to their sole responsibility.

Contact

9.93   One of the consequences of an agency placing a child for adoption either under s 19 or under a placement order (or if the child placed is less than 6 weeks old) is that any contact order under s 8 or s 34 of the CA 1989 ceases to have effect.[6] Nor can any application for a contact order under the CA 1989 be made while the authority remains

---

1   ACA 2002, s 25(3).
2   HL Grand Committee, 2 July 2002, vol 637, CWH 171, per Lord Hunt of Kings Heath.
3   ACA 2002, s 25(4).
4   HC Special Standing Committee, 29 November 2001, col 338, per Ms Jacqui Smith.
5   HL Grand Committee, 2 July 2002, CWH 171, per Lord Hunt of Kings Heath.
6   ACA 2002, s 26(1) and (6).

authorised to place, save at the final adoption hearing when the court may make a s 8 order for post-adoption contact, where appropriate.[1]

9.94 The objective is that the parents, prospective adopters and agency should, if possible, reach an agreement as to whatever new arrangements for contact are appropriate given the adoptive placement. The thinking behind this appears to be that any pre-existing arrangements for contact are probably inappropriate once the child is placed for adoption.[2] As has been seen, unlike the situation under the CA 1989,[3] it is not proposed that the local authority should be under a statutory duty to promote contact between the child and his or her parents and, therefore, the parents do not have the safeguard of a strong presumption in favour of contact.[4]

A s 26 contact order

9.95 Where, however, agreement is not possible, there is provision for a freestanding application for contact[5] to be made for an order under s 26 of the ACA 2002 'requiring the person with whom the child lives, or is to live, to allow the child to visit or stay with the person named in the order or for that person and the child otherwise to have contact with each other'. The application may be made by:

– the child;[6]
– the agency;[7]
– any parent or guardian or relative;[8]
– any person in whose favour there was a CA 1989 contact order (which ceased to have effect by virtue of s 26(1));[9]
– the person with a residence order in force immediately before the adoption agency was authorised to place, or placed, the child for adoption at a time when he was less than 6 weeks old;[10]
– the person who had care of the child by an order under the High Court's inherent jurisdiction before the agency was authorised to place;[11]
– any person with the court's leave.[12]

9.96 The inclusion of 'relatives' in s 26(3)(b) as persons who may apply as of right for a s 26 contact order is in recognition of the potential importance of contact in adoption, in particular between siblings.[13] Other family members, such as grandparents, aunts and uncles, will also be able to apply for contact orders without the need for the leave of the court.

---

1   ACA 2002, s 26(5), which provides that s 26 does not prevent an application for a contact order under s 8 being made where the application is to be heard with an application for an adoption order.
2   HL Grand Committee, 2 July 2002, CWH 174, per Lord Hunt of Kings Heath.
3   CA 1989, Sch 2, para 15.
4   ACA 2002, s 53(2)(b).
5   Ibid, s 26(3).
6   Ibid, s 26(3)(a).
7   Ibid, s 26(3)(a).
8   Ibid, s 26(3)(b).
9   Ibid, s 26(3)(c).
10 Ibid, s 26(3)(d).
11 Ibid, s 26(3)(e).
12 Ibid, s 26(3)(f).
13 HL Deb, 14 October 2002, col 670, per Baroness Andrews.

9.97   The court, when making a placement order, may on its own initiative make a s 26 order.[1] Further, and importantly, a duty is imposed on the court, before making any placement order, (i) to consider the arrangements which the adoption agency has made, or proposes to make, for allowing any person to have contact with the child and (ii) to invite the parties to the proceedings to comment on those arrangements.[2] It may also attach any conditions it considers appropriate.[3] The obligation placed on the court to consider the contact arrangements before making a placement order is of fundamental importance, especially given the absence of any statutory duty on the authority to promote contact. First, it is implicit in the wording of s 26(4) that there is at least an expectation that the authority will consider and put forward proposals for allowing contact. In the event that such expectation fails to materialise, then the court retains the discretion to seize the initiative itself and make a s 26 order. Secondly, the court, in scrutinising any arrangements or proposed arrangements, must have regard to, and apply, the s 1 principles – including the child's discernible wishes and feelings (in the light of his or her age and understanding), together with the first limb of s 1(4)(c) and (f). Thirdly, the parents have a right to comment upon the arrangements. These provisions give some basic safeguards for the maintenance of contact between the child and his or her parents, which is particularly important in those cases where pre-existing contact arrangements have been successfully established.

9.98   The expectation is that the agency, in line with its obligations under s 1, will discuss contact with the child and take his or her views into account in the making of any arrangements, whether formal or informal. If the child is unhappy with the arrangements made for contact, he or she can take the initiative and apply to the court (under s 26(3)) for an order changing them or, provided he or she has capacity to do so, can instruct a solicitor to make the application on his or her behalf. If the child is very unhappy with the contact arrangements, the intention is that the agency would apply on his or her behalf to make new arrangements, rather than placing this burden on the child.[4]

9.99   The wording in s 26(2) is deliberately modelled on that for contact orders under s 8(1) of the CA 1989.[5] Like a s 8 contact order, the order under s 26 can include an order for 'no contact' where that is in the best interests of the child.[6] In addition, the court may make a prohibited steps order under s 8 of the CA 1989, directed at any person considered to be at risk of initiating harmful contact.[7]

9.100   Provision is made for an agency to refuse to allow contact without a court order if (a) it is satisfied that it is necessary to do so in order to safeguard or promote the child's welfare, and (b) the refusal is decided upon as a matter of urgency and does not last for

---

1   ACA 2002, s 26(4).
2   Ibid, s 27(4)(a) and (b).
3   Ibid, s 27(5).
4   HL Grand Committee, 2 July 2002, vol 637, CWH 180, per Lord Hunt of Kings Heath.
5   HL Grand Committee, 2 July 2002, vol 637, CWH 175, per Lord Hunt of Kings Heath. Note also HL Deb, 14 October 2002, col 670, where Baroness Andrews said that the provisions of s 26 were 'similar to those in section 34 of the Children Act, which governs contact with children in care'. There is, however, no equivalent duty in s 26 to that in s 34(1) of the CA 1989 which places a duty on the authority to allow reasonable parental contact.
6   *Nottinghamshire County Council v P* [1994] Fam 18, [1993] 2 FLR 134, CA, affirming [1993] 1 FLR 514.
7   HL Grand Committee, 2 July 2002, vol 637, CWH 175, per Lord Hunt of Kings Heath.

more than 7 days.[1] Regulations will set out: (i) the steps to be taken by the agency where it has exercised such an emergency power; (ii) the circumstances in which the terms of any s 26 contact order may be departed from by agreement; and (iii) the notification which the agency must give of any variation or suspension of contact arrangements.[2]

9.101 A s 26 contact order has effect while the adoption agency is authorised to place the child for adoption (or the child is less than 6 weeks old), but may be varied or revoked by the court on an application by the child, the agency or the person named in the order.[3]

Surname and removal from the United Kingdom

9.102 Where a child is placed for adoption under s 19 or the agency is authorised to place under s 19 or a placement order is in force, no one may cause a child (i) to be known by a new surname or (ii) to be removed from the United Kingdom (save for a period of less than one month)[4] without the court's leave or each parent's or guardian's written consent.[5]

REMOVAL

9.103 The ACA 2002 has not re-instated the status of 'protected child' (which applied once notice was given of an intention to apply for adoption),[6] but has substituted detailed removal measures which ensure that children placed for adoption are not peremptorily removed and the adoption process disrupted. In line with the recommendations in the 1992 Review of Adoption,[7] the ACA 2002 draws a distinction between agency cases (ss 30–35) and non-agency cases (ss 36–40).

Agency placements

9.104 Section 30 of the ACA 2002 sets out the general rules on removal in relation to agency placements and is subject to ss 31–33 (save where the child is subject to a care order),[8] which expand on these rules to cover placements with consent under s 19 and under placement orders. The removal provisions work broadly as follows.

Placement by consent

9.105 Where the placement is consensual, only the agency (whether a voluntary agency or the local authority) can remove the child, even where the parents later withdraw consent. The agency is able to remove the child at any point, irrespective of whether the

---

1   ACA 2002, s 27(2)(a) and (b).
2   Ibid, s 27(3).
3   Ibid, s 27(1)(a) and (b).
4   Ibid, s 28(4) provides that subs (3) does not prevent the removal of a child from the United Kingdom for a period of less than one month by the person who provides the child's home: s 27(4).
5   ACA 2002, s 28(2) and (3).
6   AA 1976, s 32.
7   Paragraphs 17.4–17.6.
8   ACA 2002, s 30(5). This group of sections applies whether or not the child is in England or Wales. They do not prevent the removal of a child who is arrested: s 30(7); nor do they affect the local authority's exercise of any power conferred by any enactment other than s 20(8) of the CA 1989.

parents have requested the return of the child (for example, where the placement is failing).

9.106   Where parental consent is withdrawn, the child must be returned to the parents within 14 days. If the consent is withdrawn before the child has been placed, the child must be returned to the parents within 7 days. Where, however, the local authority views the return of the child to his or her parents as inappropriate because it considers that the significant harm threshold is met, under s 22 it is under a duty to apply for a placement order. Thus, depending on whether the child is waiting for placement or is actually placed, the local authority has either 7 or 14 days within which it must make its application for a placement order. Once the local authority has applied for the placement order, the child may only be removed with the leave of the court unless it is the authority itself which removes the child.

Placement order

9.107   Where a placement order has been made, the restrictions on removal are dealt with by s 34. Again, only the local authority may remove the child and it can do so at any point. There is no provision for the parents to have their child returned to them as of right at their request. The only recourse for parents is revocation of the placement order, which may not be open to them if they cannot obtain the court's leave or if the child has already been placed for adoption.

9.108   There are, therefore, three 'basic' rules to consider. First, only an adoption agency, not the parents, may actually remove a child from placement. Secondly, where consent to placement has been given and the parents subsequently withdraw it with the request for their child to be returned to them, the adoption agency must comply within a set period: (i) 7 days where the child is under 6 weeks of age or is accommodated by the agency, but is not yet placed with the prospective adopters; or (ii) 14 days where the child has been placed with prospective adopters. Thirdly, the only exception to this return is where the agency is a local authority and, despite the fact that the parents have withdrawn consent, it considers that the child should still be adopted. In that case, application must be made for a placement order, but it must be done within the 7- or 14-day period.[1]

9.109   The position of the voluntarily 'placed' child under the ACA 2002 is, therefore, distinguishable from that of the voluntarily accommodated child under the CA 1989. Under the CA 1989, the parents may remove their child forthwith from voluntary accommodation. In contrast, under the ACA 2002, the parents do not have a right to remove their 'placed' child themselves; instead, it is the agency which carries out the physical removal of the child. Secondly, the removal cannot be immediate but must take place over a defined period. This is clearly to give the local authority the opportunity to consider its position under s 22 and the time to make a placement order application where it is necessary to protect the child. This distinction reflects the difference in nature between a temporary foster placement or temporary respite care under the CA 1989 and placement for adoption under the ACA 2002, which is a highly sensitive process. It further marks a difference in the direction being followed: voluntary accommodation for respite or support is travelling towards rehabilitation; whereas placement is heading towards adoption and the extinction of legal ties with the birth family. Where the

---

1   HL Deb, 14 October 2002, cols 660–661, per Baroness Andrews.

direction taken is towards adoption, it is likely that the authority will have spoken to the child when first accommodated and prepared him or her for leaving the birth family. If the parent then requests the return of the child, and the authority does not apply for a placement order, there is provision for a short period of time to prepare the child for return to the parents.[1]

General prohibitions on removal

9.110 Where a child is placed for adoption by an adoption agency under s 19, or where a child is placed for adoption by an adoption agency and either the child is less than 6 weeks old or the agency has at no time been authorised to place that child, only the agency (whether a voluntary agency or the local authority) can remove the child and it is an offence for any other person to remove the child from the prospective adopters.[2] Even where the parents have withdrawn their consent, it is still the adoption agency which removes the child and oversees the return to the parents.

9.111   Where:

– a child is still waiting to be placed for adoption and is being accommodated by an adoption agency (for example, in a foster placement or a children's home); and
– the agency is authorised to place the child under s 19 or would be so authorised if any consent to placement had not been withdrawn,

again, only the agency can remove the child and it is an offence for any other person to remove the child from the accommodation.[3]

9.112   Where:

– the child is being accommodated by a local authority, but has not been placed for adoption; and
– the authority has applied for a placement order which is pending,

only the local authority or a person who has the court's leave may remove the child from the accommodation.[4]

9.113   The penalty for contravention of this section, on summary conviction, is a term of imprisonment not exceeding 3 months or a fine not exceeding level 5 on the standard scale or both.[5] Section 30 is subject to ss 31–33, but those sections do not apply if the child is subject to a care order.[6]

Recovery by a parent where the child is not yet placed or is a baby: s 31

9.114   Where a child is being accommodated by an agency but is not yet placed for adoption and consent to placement by the agency under s 19 has been withdrawn, the agency *must* return the child to any parent within 7 days of his or her request for the

---

1   HC Special Standing Committee, 29 November 2001, col 338, per Ms Jacqui Smith.
2   ACA 2002, s 30(1) and (8).
3   Ibid, s 30(3).
4   Ibid, s 30(2).
5   Ibid, s 30(8).
6   Ibid, s 30(4).

child's return unless an application for a placement order is made within that period or there is a pending application for a placement order.[1]

9.115   Where a child is placed for adoption by an agency and either the child is less than 6 weeks old or the agency has at no time been authorised to place the child for adoption, and the parent informs the agency that he or she wishes the child to be returned to him or her, then the agency must give notice of this wish to the prospective adopters, who must return the child to the agency within 7 days. As soon as this happens, the child must be returned by the agency to the parent.[2] A failure to return the child by the prospective adopters is a summary offence with liability for a term of imprisonment not exceeding 3 months or a fine not exceeding level 5 or both.[3] The only exception to the obligation to return the child is where the agency is the local authority and it applies for a placement order or has applied for a placement order which is still pending.[4]

Recovery by a parent where the child is placed and consent is withdrawn: s 32

9.116   Section 32 applies where:

–   a child is placed by an agency under s 19;[5]
–   consent to placement has been withdrawn;[6]
–   there is no pending placement order application.

If a parent requests the return of the child:

–   the agency must give notice of the parent's wish to the prospective adopters;[7]
–   the prospective adopters must return the child to the agency within 14 days from the date the notice was given,[8] and failure to do so is an offence;[9]
–   as soon as the child is returned to the agency, it must return the child to the parent.[10]

9.117   However, if, before a notice of removal is given, an application for an adoption order, special guardianship order or residence order, or for leave to apply for a special guardianship order or residence order, was made and has not been disposed of, then the prospective adopters are not required to return the child to the agency unless the court makes an order to that effect.[11]

1   ACA 2002, s 31(1)(a) and (b), (2).
2   Ibid, s 31(3), (4) and (6).
3   Ibid, s 31(5).
4   Ibid, s 31(3).
5   Ibid, s 32(1)(a).
6   Ibid, s 32(1)(b).
7   Ibid, s 32(2)(a).
8   Ibid, s 32(2)(b).
9   Ibid, s 32(3); failure to comply with subs 2(b) renders the prospective adopter liable on summary conviction to imprisonment for a term not exceeding 3 months or a fine not exceeding level 5 or both.
10   Ibid, s 32(4).
11   Ibid, s 32(5).

Recovery by a parent where the application for a placement order is refused

9.118   Under s 33 of the ACA 2002, where:[1]

– the child is placed for adoption by a local authority under s 19;
– the authority's application for a placement order has been refused; and
– the parent has informed the authority that he or she wishes the child to be returned,

the prospective adopters *must* return the child to the authority on a date determined by the court[2] and as soon as the child is returned to the local authority, it must return the child to the parent.[3] A failure by the prospective adopters to comply is an offence.[4]

Placement orders: prohibitions on removal[5]

9.119   Where a placement order:

– is in force; or
– has been revoked, but the child has not been returned by the prospective adopters or remains in the accommodation provided by the local authority,

no person (other than the local authority) may remove the child from the prospective adopters or from the accommodation provided by the authority;[6] removal constitutes an offence.[7]

9.120   However, where the placement order is revoked it will be for the court to determine whether the child remains with the prospective adopters or is to be returned to the parent. If the court determines that the child should not remain with the prospective adopters, then they must return the child to the local authority within the period set by the court;[8] a failure to do so is an offence.[9] If the court then goes on to determine that the child is to be returned to the parent, the authority must return the child to the parent:

– as soon as the child is returned to the authority by the prospective adopters;
– at once, where the child is in accommodation provided by the authority.[10]

---

1   ACA 2002, s 33(1)(a)–(c).
2   Which must mean that the local authority or one of the other parties has to bring the matter before the court.
3   ACA 2002, s 33(4).
4   Ibid, s 33(3); the penalty, on summary conviction, is imprisonment for a term not exceeding 3 months or a fine not exceeding level 5 or both.
5   ACA 2002, s 34 does not affect the exercise by any local authority or other person of any power conferred by any enactment other than s 20(8) of the CA 1989: ACA 2002, s 34(6). It does not prevent the removal of a child who is arrested: ibid, s 34(7). It applies whether or not the child is in England or Wales: ibid, s 34(8).
6   ACA 2002, s 34(1).
7   Ibid, s 34(2) and (5); for penalty, see fn 3 above.
8   Ibid, s 34(3).
9   Ibid, s 34(3) and (5); for penalty, see fn 3 above.
10   Ibid, s 34(4).

Return of the child in other agency cases

9.121   Where the child is placed for adoption and the prospective adopters give notice that they wish to return the child, the agency must:

–   receive the child before the end of 7 days; and
–   give notice to any parent of the prospective adopters' wish.[1]

Where the child is placed for adoption and the agency:

–   is of the opinion that the child should not remain with the prospective adopters; and
–   gives them notice of that opinion,

the prospective adopters must return the child not later than the end of 7 days and, if they fail to do so, are guilty of an offence.[2] The agency must also give notice to any parent of the obligation to return the child to the agency.[3]

9.122   If, however, before such notice is given to the prospective adopters, an application for an adoption order,[4] special guardianship order or residence order, or leave to apply for a special guardianship order or residence order, was made and has not been disposed of, then the prospective adopters are not required to return the child to the agency unless the court makes an order to that effect.[5]

Restrictions on removal in non-agency cases

9.123   Section 36 of the ACA 2002[6] provides that a person may only remove children in non-agency cases in accordance with the group of provisions in ss 37–40. A 'child' for the purpose of these sections is one whose home is with persons ('the people concerned') with whom the child was not placed by an adoption agency, where those persons have:

–   applied for an adoption order and the application has not been disposed of;
–   given notice of intention to adopt;
–   applied for leave to apply for an adoption order under s 42(6) and the application has not been disposed of.[7]

9.124   If a person removes a child in contravention of s 36, this is an offence.[8] Where a parent is able to remove his or her child,[9] the people concerned must (at the request of the parent) return the child to the parent at once;[10] again, failure to do so is an offence.[11] It should be noted also that, for this group of sections:

(a)   a notice of intention to adopt is to be disregarded[12] if:

---

1   ACA 2002, s 35(1). Note that s 35 applies whether or not the child is in England or Wales.
2   Ibid, s 35(2) and (4), with the same penalty as before.
3   Ibid, s 35(3).
4   This includes a Scottish or Northern Irish adoption order.
5   ACA 2002, s 35(5).
6   This section does not prevent the removal of a child who is arrested: s 36(4); and the group of provisions in ss 37–40 applies whether or not the child is in England or Wales: s 36(7).
7   ACA 2002, s 36(1).
8   Ibid, s 36(6); penalty as above.
9   By virtue of the group of sections.
10   ACA 2002, s 36(5).
11   Ibid, s 36(6); penalty as above.
12   Ibid, s 36(2)(a) and (b).

- 4 months have expired without the people concerned applying for an adoption order; or
- the notice is a second or subsequent notice of intention to adopt and was given during the period of 5 months from the last of the preceding notices;

(b) if the people concerned apply under s 42(6) for leave which is granted, the application is not to be treated as disposed of until 3 days have expired from the granting of the leave.[1]

9.125 Sections 37–40 consider in detail the powers of removal in respect of the various categories of 'people concerned'.

9.126 Where an application for adoption has been made, the child may only be removed with leave of the court;[2] or by a local authority or other person in the exercise of their statutory powers, other than s 20(8) of the CA 1989[3] (eg for child protection purposes under the CA 1989). Once an application for adoption has been made in respect of a child voluntarily accommodated under s 20 of the CA 1989, the parents may not automatically remove the child.

9.127 Where a local authority foster parent has given notice of intention to adopt and the child has had his or her home with the foster parents for one year, the child may only be removed:

- with leave of the court;[4]
- by a local authority or other person in the exercise of their statutory powers;[5]
- if the child is voluntarily accommodated under s 20 of the CA 1989, by a person with parental responsibility under s 20(8) of the CA 1989,[6] save where the child has been in foster care for 5 years or more and the foster parents have given notice of intention to adopt or an application for leave to make an application is pending.[7]

9.128 Where the child's home is with the partner of a parent, and the partner has given notice of intention to apply to adopt,[8] the child may only be removed in the following circumstances:

(a) if the child's home has been with the partner for not less than 3 years out of the last 5 years:

- with leave of the court;[9] or
- by a local authority or person in the exercise of a statutory power (other than s 20(8) of the CA 1989);[10]

(b) if the child's home has been with the partner for less than 3 years out of the last 5 years:

---

1 ACA 2002, s 36(3).
2 Ibid, s 37(a).
3 Ibid, s 37(b).
4 Ibid, s 38(5)(b).
5 Ibid, s 38(5)(c).
6 Ibid, s 38(5)(a).
7 Ibid, s 38(2) and (3).
8 Ibid, s 39(1).
9 Ibid, s 39(3)(c).
10 Ibid, s 39(3)(b).

- by a parent;[1]
- with leave of the court; or
- by a local authority or person exercising a statutory power (other than s 20(8) of the CA 1989).

9.129   In other non-agency cases where notice of intention to adopt has been given or a leave application under s 42(6) is pending, the child may be removed with the leave of the court,[2] or by a local authority or other person acting under statutory powers.[3]

Recovery orders

9.130   Section 41 of the ACA 2002 applies where it appears to the court that a child has been removed or withheld and not returned in contravention of ss 30–35, or that there are reasonable grounds for believing that a person intends to remove a child in contravention of those provisions,[4] or where there is a failure to comply with ss 31(4), 32(2), 33(3), 34(3) or 35(2).

9.131   In those circumstances, the court may, on the application of any person, by order:[5]

- direct any person who is in a position to do so to produce him or her on request to an authorised person;
- authorise the removal of the child by an authorised person;
- require anyone who has information as to the child's whereabouts to disclose that information to a constable or officer of the court; or
- authorise a constable to enter any premises specified in the order (if there are reasonable grounds for believing that the child is there)[6] and search for the child, using reasonable force if necessary.[7]

Authorised persons

9.132   'Authorised persons' are any person named by the court, any constable or any person who is authorised to exercise any power under the order by the authorised adoption agency.[8]

Obstruction

9.133   A person who intentionally obstructs an authorised person exercising the power of removal is guilty of an offence and liable to fine not exceeding level 3 on the standard scale.[9]

---

1   ACA 2002, s 39(3)(a).
2   Ibid, s 40(2)(a).
3   Ibid, s 40(2)(b).
4   Ibid, s 41(1).
5   Ibid, s 41(2).
6   Ibid, s 41(3).
7   Ibid, s 41(2). Section 41(9) provides for the order having effect in Scotland (as if it were an order of the Court of Session which that court had jurisdiction to make).
8   Ibid, s 41(4).
9   Ibid, s 41(5).

Disclosure of information

9.134 A person must comply with a request for disclosure, even if it might constitute evidence that he or she had committed an offence. In any criminal proceedings (save for perjury offences),[1] however, the prosecution cannot adduce evidence relating to the information provided or ask questions about it unless it is raised by or on behalf of that person.[2]

---

1   ACA 2002, s 41(8) sets out the excluded offences.
2   Ibid, s 41(6)–(8).

Chapter 10

THE MAKING OF ADOPTION ORDERS

ADOPTION ORDER

10.1 An adoption order is defined as an order which gives parental responsibility for a child to the adopters[1] and extinguishes the parental responsibility which any person including the mother and father has for the child immediately before making the order.[2] The effect of an adoption is that the child's legal relationship with his or her birth family is ended and henceforth the child is to be treated legally as if born as a child of the adopters. In law, therefore, the birth parents of the child cease to be his or her parents and the adoptive parents become his or her parents. This legal effect is absolute and irrevocable. Unlike other orders relating to children, it is for life.

10.2 However, as adoption is a legal fiction, there are exceptions to the general principle that an adopted person is to be treated as if born as a child of the adopters, which necessarily acknowledge the genetic reality. An adopted person remains part of his or her natural family for the purposes of the law relating to marriage and incest.[3] Although an adopted person is deemed to be within the prohibited degrees so that he or she cannot marry his or her adoptive parent,[4] there are no other restrictions on marriage within the adoptive family. An adopted person can marry his or her adoptive sibling or other adoptive relative as there is no genetic objection to intermarriage.

10.3 An adoption order also extinguishes any order under the CA 1989[5] and any duty under an agreement or order of the court to make payments for the adopted child's maintenance or upbringing for the period after the making of adoption order.[6] This includes any liability under the Child Support Act 1991, but excludes any duty arising under a trust agreement or an agreement which expressly provides that the duty is not to be extinguished.[7] Any existing maintenance calculation or court order relating to the child's maintenance, therefore, falls away upon the cessation of the parents' parental responsibility.

---

1   ACA 2002, s 46(1). An adoption order can be made even if the child is already an adopted child: s 46(5).
2   Ibid, s 46(2)(a).
3   Ibid, s 74.
4   He falls within the restrictions set out in the table of kindred and affinity in Sch 1 to the Marriage Act 1949.
5   ACA 2002, s 46(2)(b).
6   Ibid, s 46(2)(d).
7   Ibid, s 46(4)(a) and (b).

10.4   It is, however, important to emphasise that parental responsibility for the period before the adoption order is unaffected.[1] The parental responsibility of the parents continues up to the point that an adoption order is made. It should also be noted that a step-parent or partner adoption[2] does not affect the parental responsibility or duties of the partner who is the natural parent of the adopted child.[3]

WHO MAY APPLY FOR AN ADOPTION ORDER

The former law

10.5   Under the former law, a *joint* application for an adoption order could only be made by a married couple. This prohibition against adoption by unmarried joint applicants had been in place under English law since the first statute on adoption, the Adoption of Children Act 1926. It reflected the policy of setting boundaries for adoption within family relationships based on marriage. The 1992 Review of Adoption Law had recommended that the prohibition be maintained.[4] The justification which was given was that 'the security and stability which adopted children need are still more likely to be provided by parents who have made a publicly recognised commitment to their relationship and who have legal responsibilities towards each other'.[5]

10.6   'Joint' applications by unmarried heterosexual couples or homosexual couples were not permitted. This was notwithstanding that the 1992 Review[6] had recognised that there were examples of extremely successful adoptions, particularly of older children and children with disabilities, by single homosexual or lesbian adopters.

10.7   However, this proved a restriction which was 'ingeniously circumvented'[7] by the courts, for example, by making an adoption order in favour of one member of an unmarried couple together with a joint residence order in favour of them both[8] or by allowing one member of a homosexual couple to make an adoption application.[9] In *Re W (Adoption: Homosexual Adopter)*[10] Singer J concluded that:

> '... the Adoption Act 1976 permits an adoption application to be made by a single applicant, whether he or she at that time lives alone or cohabits in a heterosexual, homosexual or even an asexual relationship with another person who it is proposed should fulfil a quasi-parental role towards the child. Any other conclusion would be illogical, arbitrary and inappropriately

---

1   ACA 2002, s 46(3)(a).
2   Under s 51(2)
3   ACA 2002, s 46(3)(b). This includes any duties of that parent under s 46(2)(d).
4   The original Bill (Bill 66) (26 March 2001) and its successor (Bill 34) (19 October 2001) followed the reasoning in the 1992 Review of Adoption Law: Adoption and Children Bill (Bill 66) (26 March 2001), vol 365, no 59, col 709.
5   1992 Review of Adoption Law, paras 26.9 et seq.
6   Ibid, at paras 26.13 and 26.14.
7   A Bainham *Children: The Modern Law* (2nd edn, Family Law, 2000) at pp 211–212.
8   *Re AB (Adoption: Joint Residence)* [1996] 1 FLR 27.
9   *Re W (Adoption: Homosexual Adopter)* [1997] 2 FLR 406.
10   Ibid.

discriminatory in a context where the court's duty is to give first consideration to the need to safeguard and promote the welfare of the child through his childhood.'[1]

10.8   These marital restrictions, therefore, attracted the strong charge of illogicality both from the judiciary and the academics. Andrew Bainham encapsulated the incongruity when he said: '. . . it is illogical that one member of an unmarried couple, whether heterosexual or homosexual, should be allowed to achieve singly what that couple cannot achieve together'. Thus, this was an area which was ripe for 'some fundamental rethinking before any reformed adoption law reaches the statute book'.[2]

Adoption by a couple

10.9   The ACA 2002 marks a fundamental break with the traditional approach. Under this Act, the marital restriction has been deleted and a new concept of 'couple' has been introduced. An application for an adoption order may now be made by a couple or by one person.[3] A 'couple' is defined as:[4]

–   a married couple; or
–   two people (whether of different sexes or the same sex) living in an enduring family relationship.

'Couple' does not include two people where one of them is the other's parent, grandparent, sister, brother, aunt or uncle.[5] The relevant relationships for these purposes are (i) relationships of the full blood or half blood or, in the case of an adopted person, such of those relationships as would exist but for the adoption, and (ii) the relationship of a child with his adoptive or former adoptive parents, but not including any other adoptive relationships.[6]

10.10   By enabling not only a married couple but also an unmarried couple and a same-sex couple to apply jointly for an adoption order, the ACA 2002 recognises that there has been a significant shift in society away from marriage.

> 'Children must grow up in the real world. They must grow up in the 21st century in which 40 per cent of children are born outside marriage and in which many people who are committed to one another choose not to marry. That applies to 15 per cent of households and the figure is expected to rise to 30 per cent.'[7]

10.11   The rationale behind the changes in the law is seen as threefold. First, it cannot be in a child's best interests, when the two members of a couple play equal parts in the child's life, for only one member to have full legal responsibility. The effect is to downgrade the other parent to a secondary status. Problems also arise should the adopter become ill or die, as no legal relationship is left between the child and the other parent. Secondly, many suitable unmarried couples were deterred from applying to adopt, for

---

1   *Re W* (above), at 413H. See also *Re E (Adoption: Freeing Order)* [1995] 1 FLR 382, where the Court of Appeal upheld a freeing order made with a view to adoption by the child's existing foster carer, a woman of lesbian orientation offering to care for the child as a single parent.
2   A Bainham *Children: The Modern Law*, op cit, at p 212.
3   ACA 2002, s 49, subject to certain restrictions contained in ss 50 and 51.
4   Ibid, s 144(4).
5   Ibid, s 144(5).
6   Ibid, s 144(6).
7   HC Deb, 16 May 2002, vol 385, no 149, col 969, per Dr Harris.

example existing foster carers who were unmarried. Thirdly, the former law discrimi-
nated against unmarried and same-sex couples.

> 'Given the stringent application process for adoption and the rigorous assessments that are
> made on a case-by-case basis there is no justification for disqualifying a couple from adopting
> jointly simply because they do not possess a marriage certificate, if they clearly possess all the
> characteristics that the agencies would otherwise expect from suitable adoptive parents'.[1]

10.12   It is, however, clear that one of the key motivations for the fundamental change
in the law is the widening of the pool of potential applicants for adoption to meet the
overall objective of 'giving a child the chance to live in a stable living family rather than
being left in care'.[2]

Adoption by one person

10.13   While retaining the eligibility of an unmarried applicant who has attained the
age of 21 to make an application to adopt alone,[3] the ACA 2002 has further extended the
categories of sole applicants to include a person whom the court is satisfied is the partner
of a parent of the person to be adopted.[4]

10.14   This last provision is new. A person is 'a partner' of a child's parent if the person
and the parent are a couple (within the meaning of s 144(4)) but the person is not the
child's parent. It therefore enlarges the class of sole applicants to include a step-parent or
partner who may now adopt his or her spouse's or partner's child. This removes the
previous anomaly of the birth parent being required to make a joint application with the
step-parent to adopt his or her own child, which was clearly a legislative nonsense.

10.15   As under the former law, the other circumstances in which a married person may
apply as a single applicant are limited.[5] The sole married applicant must satisfy the court
that: (a) the spouse cannot be found; or (b) the couple have separated and are living apart
and the separation is likely to be permanent; or (c) the spouse is incapable by reason of ill
health (physical or mental) of making an application.[6] The common thread running
through these three grounds is that the marriage relationship, although subsisting at law,
is not viable in fact. The policy behind these provisions is clearly 'to avoid creating
limping relationships within marriage, whereby, as a result of an individual adoption
order, the child would become for all purposes a child of one spouse but not at all of the
other'.[7]

10.16   Where a sole application is made by a mother or father, the court must be
satisfied that: (a) the other natural parent is dead or cannot be found; or (b) there is no
other parent by virtue of s 28 of the Human Fertilisation and Embryology Act 1990; or
(c) there is some other reason justifying the child being adopted by the applicant alone.[8]

---

1   HC Deb, 16 May 2002, vol 385, no 149, cols 970 and 971, per Dr Harris.
2   Ibid, col 1002. This radical approach was encouraged by the strong view in favour of the principle of
     unmarried couples being able to adopt jointly, which was vigorously put forward, notably by the
     BAAF.
3   ACA 2002, s 51(1).
4   Ibid, s 51(2).
5   AA 1976, s 15(1)(b) sets out the former law.
6   ACA 2002, s 51(3).
7   *Re W (Adoption: Homosexual Adopter)* [1991] 2 FLR 406 at 409E, per Singer J.
8   ACA 2002, s 51(4)(a)–(c).

The court must record that it is satisfied as to the facts in (a) and (b) and record the reason in the case of (c).[1]

10.17   This rarely visited corner of the law, the exclusion of one of the parents from the child's life, became the focus of judicial scrutiny in the death throes of the AA 1976. In *Re B (Adoption: Natural Parent)*[2] the House of Lords, adopting a wide interpretation of s 15(3) of the AA 1976, held that the three exceptions in s 15(3) were not exhaustive and there could be other situations where the welfare of the child justified the exclusion of the natural parent, such as cases of abandonment or where there had been persistent neglect or ill-treatment of the child.[3] Lord Nicholls of Birkenhead said:[4]

> 'It is not surprising, therefore, that the exception stated in sub para (b) [which reads "there is some other reason justifying exclusion of the other natural parent"] is altogether open-ended ... What is required by sub para (b) and, all that is required, is that the reason, whatever it be, must be sufficient to justify the exclusion of the other parent.'

10.18   The wording of s 51(4)(c) of the ACA 2002, namely 'there is some other reason justifying the child's being adopted by the applicant alone', by deleting the notion of 'exclusion' altogether is even more open-ended than its predecessor. It is, therefore, likely that the new s 51(4) will be given a broad interpretation and that the three exceptions there should not be seen as exhaustive.

10.19   However, it should be noted that Lord Nicholls went on to say:[5]

> '... it is important ... to keep in mind the wide range of powers the court now has under the Children Act 1989 to restrict the possibility of inappropriate intervention in the child's life by the other natural parent. Adoption is not intended to be used simply as the means by which to protect the child's life with one natural parent against inappropriate intervention by the other natural parent.'

The qualifications

10.20   The ACA 2002 continues the policy of imposing certain restrictions on the eligibility of those persons who may adopt.[6] These qualifications relate both to age and to domicile and residence; they must be satisfied before an adoption order can be made.[7]

The age qualifications

10.21   A single adoptive applicant must have attained the age of 21,[8] and a couple can make a joint application only where both are at least 21 years old,[9] save where a father or

---

1   ACA 2002, s 51(4).
2   [2001] UKHL 70, [2002] 1 FLR 196.
3   Ibid, at [23], per Lord Nicholls of Birkenhead.
4   Ibid, at [24].
5   Ibid, at [25].
6   HC Deb (Bill 66), 26 March 2001, vol 365, no 59, col 709, per Mr John Hutton: 'We are changing the law to remove the anomaly by which, for a parent and step-parent to adopt jointly, the birth parent must first adopt his or her child. That is frankly ridiculous'.
7   ACA 2002, ss 49–51.
8   Ibid, ss 50(1), 51(1), (2) and (3).
9   Ibid, s 50(1).

mother is adopting his or her own child, when the parent need only be 18 years of age provided the other partner is at least 21 years old.[1]

10.22   An application for an adoption order can be made only if the person to be adopted has not reached the age of 18 on the date of the application,[2] but may include a person who has attained that age before the conclusion of the proceedings.[3] An adoption order may not be made in relation to a person who has attained the age of 19[4] or in relation to a person who is or has been married.[5]

Domicile and residence qualifications

10.23   In a joint application under s 50, at least one of the couple must be domiciled in a part of the British Islands[6] and both must have been habitually resident in a part of the British Islands for a period of not less than one year ending with the date of the application.[7] Similar domicile and residence conditions apply to a single applicant making a s 51 application.[8] The concepts of 'domicile' and 'habitual residence' are the subject of extensive literature and what follows is no more than a brief outline.[9]

DOMICILE

10.24   The notion which underlies the concept of domicile is that of permanent home.[10] 'Domicile', however, is not the equivalent of 'home', as a person may have two homes but only one domicile. There are three types of domicile:

(1)   the *domicile of origin*, which is attributed by law to a child at birth[11] and may be changed only as a result of adoption;
(2)   the *domicile of choice*, which may be acquired by any independent person by a combination of residence and intention;
(3)   the *domicile of dependency*, which is the domicile of dependent persons (such as children under 16) and is the same as and changes with the domicile of the person upon whom he or she is legally dependent (such as the parent of the child).

10.25   There are four fundamental principles which lie at the root of the concept of 'domicile':

---

1   ACA 2002, s 50(2)(a) and (b).
2   Ibid, s 49(4).
3   Ibid, s 49(5).
4   Ibid, s 47(9).
5   Ibid, s 47(8).
6   Ibid, s 49(2).
7   Ibid, s 49(3).
8   Ibid, s 49(2) and (3).
9   For a full discussion, see *Dicey & Morris on the Conflict of Laws* (13th edn, Sweet & Maxwell, 2001), Chapter 6, and J McClean *Morris: The Conflict of Laws* (5th edn, Sweet & Maxwell, 2000), Chapter 2, from which the above digest is largely taken.
10   *Whicker v Hume* (1858) 7 HLC 124 at 160; *Re Craignish* [1892] 3 Ch 180 at 192; *Winans v A–G* [1904] AC 287 at 288.
11   *Udny v Udny* (1869) LR 1 Sc & Div 441 at 457, per Lord Westbury: 'It is a settled principle that no man shall be without a domicile and to secure this result the law attributes to every individual as soon as he is born the domicile of his father if the child be legitimate, and the domicile of the mother if illegitimate'.

(1)   no person can be without a domicile;

(2)   no one can have more than one domicile for the same purpose[1] at the same time;[2]

(3)   there is a presumption that an existing domicile continues until it is proved that a new domicile has been acquired. The burden of proof rests on those asserting the change.[3] As was observed by Stephen Brown LJ (as he then was) in *Cramer v Cramer*,[4] 'the burden of establishing a change of domicile – from a domicile of origin to a domicile of choice – is … a heavy one';[5] and

(4)   for the purpose of an English rule of conflict of laws, 'domicile' means domicile in the English sense.[6] The domicile of a person for the purposes of adoption law, therefore, is determined by the law of England.

10.26   In order to show a change of residence, it is necessary to establish both factors of 'residence' and 'intention'. As 'residence' is a concept which is difficult to pin down, as much turns upon the particular context, it is dealt with on a case-by-case basis as a question of fact. 'Ordinary' residence 'connotes residence in a place with some degree of continuity and apart from accidental or temporary absences'.[7] It refers 'to a man's abode in a particular place or country which he has adopted voluntarily and for settled purposes as part of the regular order of his life for the time being, whether of short or of long duration'.[8]

10.27   The intention which is required[9] is the intention to reside permanently or indefinitely in a particular county. 'It must be fixed not for a limited period or particular purpose, but general and indefinite in its future contemplation.'[10] The difficulties of establishing the requisite intention can be illustrated by two contrasting cases. In *IRC v Bullock*,[11] which concerned a Canadian with a domicile of origin in Nova Scotia who had lived in England for more than 40 years, the Court of Appeal held that, as he intended to return to Canada after the death of his English wife, he had not acquired an English domicile of choice. However, in *Re Furse*[12] the deceased was a US citizen who, although he had lived for 39 years until his death on a farm in England, had declared an intention to return to the USA should his health fail and he be unable physically to maintain the farm. It was held that the contingency was so vague and indefinite that it did not prevent the acquisition of an English domicile of choice.

---

1   It has been suggested that a person may have different domiciles for different purposes; see *Lawrence v Lawrence* [1985] Fam 106.

2   *Garthwaite v Garthwaite* [1964] P 356 at 378–379 and 393–394.

3   *In the Estate of Fuld (No 3)* [1968] P 675 at 685.

4   [1987] 1 FLR 116 at 120.

5   It was noted in *Morris: The Conflict of Laws*, at p 29 that of the 12 disputed House of Lords decisions since 1860 there is only one in which it was held that the domicile of origin had been lost: *Casdagli v Casdagli* [1919] AC 145 (the other cases are cited at n 67). For two more recent contrasting cases, see *IRC v Bullock* [1976] 1 WLR 1178 and *Re Furse* [1980] 3 All ER 838.

6   Under the *renvoi* doctrine, however, the court applies the conflict rule of a foreign country. If the foreign rule is in terms of 'domicile', this means domicile in the sense of the foreign law.

7   *Levene v IRC* [1928] AC 217 at 225, per Lord Cave.

8   *R v Barnet London Borough Council, ex parte Shah* [1983] 2 AC 309 at 343G–H, per Lord Scarman.

9   Often called the *animus manendi*.

10   *Udny v Udny* (1869) LR 1 Sc & Div 441 at 458, per Lord Westbury. See also *Cramer v Cramer* [1987] 1 FLR 116.

11   [1976] 1 WLR 1178.

12   [1980] 3 All ER 838.

10.28   A domicile of origin can be lost only by the acquisition of a domicile of choice.[1] A domicile of choice is lost only when both the residence and the intention necessary for its acquisition are abandoned[2] and if a new domicile of choice is not acquired at the same time, then the domicile of origin revives.

Married women

10.29   Before 1974 the absolute rule was that the domicile of the married woman was a domicile of dependency, ie it was the same as, and changed with, the domicile of her husband.[3] The rule was abolished by the Domicile and Matrimonial Proceedings Act 1973,[4] which established that with effect from 1 January 1974 a wife's domicile is determined independently of her husband.[5]

10.30   The domicile of a married woman is now decided by referring to the same factors as in the case of any other individual with the capacity for achieving an independent domicile. Although the marriage and the domicile, residence and nationality of her husband remain relevant, these factors are no longer determinative of a wife's domicile. Although there is a strong probability that where married couples are living together, they will have the same domicile, it does not necessarily follow that this is always the case. They may, on the facts, have different domiciles.[6] As a transitional provision, it is provided that, where immediately before 1 January 1974 a woman was married and then had her husband's domicile by dependence, she is to be treated as retaining that domicile (as a domicile of choice, if it is not also her domicile of origin), unless and until it is changed by acquisition or revival of another domicile either on or after that date.[7]

Children[8]

10.31   The domicile of a dependent *legitimate* child is the same as and changes with the father's domicile during his lifetime.[9] As for a *legitimated* child, at the time when the legitimation takes place, the child's domicile becomes dependent upon his or her father's domicile (prior to that, the child's domicile would have depended on his or her mother's

---

1   *Bell v Kennedy* (1868) LR 1 Sc & Div 307.
2   *Udny v Udny* (1869) LR 1 Sc & Div 441 at 450; *IRC v Duchess of Portland* [1982] Ch 314.
3   *Lord Advocate v Jeffrey* [1921] 1 AC 146.
4   Note that from 1 March 2001 the law on jurisdiction in matrimonial causes has changed in relation to divorce, judicial separation and nullity and in relation to parental responsibility for the children of both spouses on the occasion of matrimonial proceedings, where one party is resident in one of 14 EU Member States. There is a new scheme (known as 'Brussels II') which is derived from the Brussels Convention on Jurisdiction and the Recognition and Enforcement of Judgments in Matrimonial Matters 1998. (This scheme falls outside the scope of this book.) There are consequential amendments to s 5(2) and (3) of the Domestic and Matrimonial Proceedings Act 1973.
5   Domestic and Matrimonial Proceedings Act 1973, s 1(1). This subsection is retrospective in the sense that it applies to women who were married before and after 1 January 1974, but not in any other sense. In considering the domicile of a married woman as at any time before 1 January 1974, the old law will apply.
6   For example, in *IRC v Bullock* [1976] 1 WLR 1178, the matrimonial home was in England but the husband remained domiciled in his country of origin to which he intended to return if he survived his English wife.
7   Domicile and Matrimonial Proceedings Act 1973, s 1(2).
8   Although not relevant to the domicile qualification required under s 42 of the ACA 2002, it is useful, for the sake of completeness, to consider the position of children at this point.
9   *Henderson v Henderson* [1967] P 77.

domicile). The domicile of the *illegitimate* child generally depends on that of his or her mother. However, in *Re Beaumont*[1] it was held that a mother has a discretion to abstain from changing her child's domicile:

> 'The change in the domicile of [the child] which … may follow from a change of domicile on the part of a mother, is not to be regarded as a necessary consequence of a change of the mother's domicile, but as a result of an exercise by her of a power vested in her for the welfare of the infants, which, in their interest, she may abstain from exercising, even when she changes her own domicile.'

10.32   Where parents are 'living apart', the domicile of a dependent child is now governed by the Domicile and Matrimonial Proceedings Act 1973. The domicile of a dependent child whose parents are alive but living apart is that of the child's mother if (a) the child has his or her home with her and no home with the father, or (b) the child has at any time had the mother's domicile by virtue of (a) and has not subsequently had a home with his or her father.[2] Where the mother is dead, the dependent child keeps the domicile held by the mother before she died, if at her death he or she had her domicile[3] and has not since had a home with the father.[4]

10.33   'Home' is not defined. 'Living apart' does not imply any breakdown in the relationship of the parents. It is unlikely that 'living apart' would include a parent's temporary absence, say for hospital treatment or on business, where both parents continue to live together in the same household.[5] However, if the parents do separate, it has been suggested that the negative language in which s 4(2) and (3) of the 1973 Act is couched may indicate, in the absence of other factors, that the child's domicile will be that of his or her father.[6] A child becomes capable of having an independent domicile[7] when he attains the age of 16 or marries under that age.[8]

10.34   However, the above statutory rules, where parents are living apart, should be regarded as the exception. Usually where parents are living apart, the domicile of dependency will be the father's domicile. For example, the father's domicile applies when the child's home is with his father or if the child's home is with his grandparents or foster parents or in a residential children's home. Only if the child has a home with his mother and no home with his father is this usual rule displaced; the child's domicile then becomes the same as that of its mother. Once dependent on the mother for domicile, the child remains dependent until he acquires a home with his father. Unlike the situation at common law, the mother has no discretion as to the child's domicile.

10.35   Where the child's domicile is changed following a change in the parents' domicile, the new domicile is one of dependency and not of origin.[9] Thus, on a later

---

1   [1893] 3 Ch 490 at 496–497.
2   Domicile and Matrimonial Proceedings Act 1973, s 4(2)(a), (b).
3   'By virtue of s 4(2)' of the 1973 Act.
4   Domicile and Matrimonial Proceedings Act 1973, s 4(3).
5   See *Dicey & Morris on the Conflict of Laws* (13th edn, Sweet & Maxwell, 2001) at para 6–100.
6   Annotation to Domicile and Matrimonial Proceedings Act 1973, s 4 in *The Family Court Practice* (Family Law).
7   Domicile and Matrimonial Proceedings Act 1973, s 3(1).
8   In English domestic law, a marriage between persons either of whom is under 16 is void: see s 2 of the Marriage Act 1949; however, a child may be regarded as validly married under foreign law, even if under that age.
9   *Henderson v Henderson* [1967] P 77.

abandonment of a domicile of choice without the simultaneous acquisition of a new one, the domicile of origin, rather than the new domicile of dependency, will revive.

10.36   As adopted children are treated in law as if born as children of the adopters or adopter,[1] the domicile of an adopted child under 16 will be determined as if the child were a legitimate child of the adoptive parents, subject to the statutory rules under the 1973 Act (where they apply). As the domicile of an adopted child is deemed to be that of his or her adoptive parents on adoption, this appears to be the one exception to the general principle that a domicile of origin cannot be changed.

10.37   Domicile is 'an idea of law'[2] which, over the years, has become increasingly convoluted so that it is now largely divorced from practical reality. There was an opportunity for reform in 1987,[3] but this was rejected by a former Government in 1996. The result is that in the twenty-first century we remain saddled with a nineteenth-century concept which has long been recognised to be 'well past its sell-by date'.

HABITUAL RESIDENCE

10.38   'Habitual residence' is distinguishable from 'ordinary residence'. 'Habitual' indicates a quality of residence rather than its length,[4] although duration is a relevant factor. In *Re J (A Minor) (Abduction: Custody Rights)*[5] Lord Brandon of Oakbrook said:

> '... the expression ["habitual residence"] is not to be treated as a term of art with some special meaning, but is rather to be understood according to the ordinary and natural meaning of the two words which it contains. The second point is that the question whether a person is or is not habitually resident in a specified country is a question of fact by reference to all the circumstances of any particular case.[6] The third point is that there is a significant difference between a person ceasing to be habitually resident in country A, and his subsequently becoming habitually resident in country B. A person may cease to be habitually resident in country A in a single day if he or she leaves it with a settled intention not to return to it but to take up long term residence in country B instead. Such a person, cannot, however, become habitually resident in country B in a single day. An appreciable period of time and a settled intention will be necessary to enable him or her to become so. During that appreciable period of time the person will have ceased to resident in country A ...'

Habitual residence may continue during temporary absences.[7]

10.39   However, 'settled intention' is not an essential component of 'habitual residence' in every case, as it clearly cannot arise in the case of a young child, for example, whose 'habitual residence' has to be established for purposes of adoption.[8] In the case of a child, where the parents are together, the habitual residence of the child is that of the

---

1   ACA 2002, s 67(1).
2   *Bell v Kennedy* (1868) LR 1 Sc & Div 307 at 320, per Lord Westbury.
3   *Law of Domicile* Law Com No 168 (HMSO, 1987).
4   *Cruse v Chittum* [1974] 2 All ER 940; *Hack v Hack* (1976) Fam Law 177.
5   [1990] 2 AC 562 at 578F–579A, sub nom *C v S (A Minor) (Abduction)*; [1990] 2 FLR 442. See also *M v M (Abduction: England and Scotland)* [1997] 2 FLR 263; *Re A (Abduction: Habitual Residence)* [1998] 1 FLR 497.
6   See also *Re M (Minors) (Residence Order: Jurisdiction)* [1993] 1 FLR 495.
7   *Oundjian v Oundjian* (1980) 1 FLR 198; *Re B-M (Wardship: Jurisdiction)* [1993] 1 FLR 979.
8   For example, s 83(1)(a) of the ACA 2002.

parents, unless there is a settled agreement between them to the contrary.[1] 'This flows logically from the parents' shared parental responsibility which entitles them to determine where the child lives'.[2] There is a strong burden upon anyone wishing to show that the child's habitual residence is different from that of the parents. Where parents are in agreement, however, they may change the habitual residence of the child without changing their own.[3] One parent cannot unilaterally change the child's habitual residence without the agreement of the other, unless circumstances arise which, quite independently, point to a change in the child's habitual residence.[4]

10.40   Where the parents are separated, the child's habitual residence is that of the parent who has the right to determine where the child shall live. This follows from Lord Brandon's 'fourth point' in *Re J*:[5]

> 'The fourth point is that, where a child of J's age is in the sole lawful custody of the mother, his situation with regard to habitual residence will necessarily be the same as hers.'[6]

Where parents separate and the older child goes by agreement to live with the other parent, all the circumstances have to be considered and it is particularly relevant whether the move is permanent or for the indefinite future.[7]

RESTRICTIONS ON MAKING A SECOND APPLICATION FOR AN ADOPTION ORDER

10.41   Where a previous application for adoption has been refused by any court, a second application for an adoption order may not be heard unless it appears to the court that there is a change in circumstances or other reason which makes it proper to hear the application.[8]

REVOCATION ON LEGITIMATISATION

10.42   The ACA 2002 makes provision for the revocation of an adoption order by the court only in the circumstances where any child, adopted by one natural parent as sole adoptive parent, is subsequently legitimised by the marriage of his natural parents.[9] The application may be made by any party concerned. Save for this one statutory exception,

---

1   *Re A (Wardship: Jurisdiction)* [1995] 1 FLR 767 at 771E–F, per Hale J (as she then was).

2   Ibid, at 771E; *Re J (A Minor) (Abduction: Custody Rights)* [1990] 2 AC 562; *Re O (A Minor) (Abduction: Habitual Residence)* [1993] 2 FLR 594.

3   *Re A* (above) at 772H–773A (but an agreement to send a child to a boarding school would not suffice).

4   Ibid, at 771F; see also *Re S (Minors) (Abduction: Wrongful Retention)* [1994] Fam 70, [1994] 1 FLR 82.

5   *Re J (A Minor) (Abduction: Custody Rights)* [1990] 2 AC 562 at 578.

6   Hale J (as she then was) in *Re A* (above) at 772B–C qualified this proposition 'with a query as to whether, where one has an older child, because J was a very small child, and the parent who has the right to determine where the child will live sends the child to a different country from the one in which she lives, that parent can, in effect, change the child's habitual residence so that it is not the same as her own'.

7   *Findlay v Findlay (No 2)* 1994 SLT 709.

8   ACA 2002, s 48(1). This also applies to a Scottish or Northern Irish adoption order or to an order made in the Isle of Man or any of the Channel Islands: s 47(2).

9   Ibid, s 55(1). This replaces s 52 of the AA 1976.

adoption orders are irrevocable, and only a further adoption order[1] can remove the parental responsibility of the adoptive parents.

10.43 The 1992 Review of Adoption Law[2] canvassed the possibility of revocation for step-parent adoptions if the marriage between the natural parent and the step-parent broke down, but reached the conclusion that all adoption orders should be irrevocable. The ACA 2002 has followed this recommendation and made no changes to the law, although it has taken some steps to clarify the position of the natural parent partner should the marriage or partnership subsequently fail. The Act specifies that an adoption order made in favour of a partner of the adopted child's parent does not affect the parental responsibility or duties of that natural parent.[3]

10.44 This does not really address some problems which may arise. For example, a child may become saddled for the rest of his or her life with a legal identity derived from an adoptive step-parent or partner of his or her birth parent who has since faded entirely from his or her life following the breakdown of the marriage or relationship with the natural parent. As has been pointed out, the 'continued imposition of a legal identity on an adult may appear unjust'.[4]

10.45 However, the justification for the irrevocability of adoption orders was expressed in trenchant terms by the Court of Appeal in *Re B (Adoption: Jurisdiction to Set Aside)*, when Swinton Thomas LJ said:[5]

> 'There is no case which has been brought to our attention in which it has been held that the court has an inherent power to set aside an adoption order by reason of a misapprehension or mistake. To allow considerations such as those put forward in this case *to invalidate an otherwise properly made adoption order would, in my view, undermine the whole basis on which adoption orders are made, namely that they are final and for life as regards the adopters, the natural parents and the child . . . it would gravely damage the lifelong commitment of adopters to their adoptive children if there was a possibility of the child, or indeed the parents, subsequently challenging the validity of the order . . .'* (emphasis added).

10.46 There are cases, however, where an adoption order has been set aside by reason of procedural irregularities or a denial of natural justice: see *Re F (R) (An Infant)*,[6] *Re RA (Minors)*,[7] *Re F (Infants) (Adoption Order: Validity)*.[8] Those cases concerned a failure to effect proper service of the adoption proceedings on a natural parent or ignorance of the parent as to the existence of the adoption proceedings. As Swinton Thomas put it in *Re B (Adoption: Jurisdiction to Set Aside)*:[9]

---

1   ACA 2002, s 46(5), which provides for an adoption order to be made even if the child concerned is already an adopted child.
2   At para 3.7.
3   ACA 2002, s 46(3). 'Duties' refers to any duty arising by virtue of an agreement or court order to make payments in respect of the child's maintenance or upbringing: s 46(2)(d).
4   As highlighted in SM Cretney and JM Masson *Principles of Family Law* (6th edn, Sweet & Maxwell, 1997) at p 882. The facts of *Re B (Adoption: Setting Aside)* [1995] 2 FLR 1 are a graphic, if exceptional, illustration of this. Where an adoption fails, a residence order would be available to a natural parent to re-establish a legal link between the child and the birth family.
5   [1995] 2 FLR 1 at 8.
6   [1970] 1 QB 385.
7   (1974) Fam Law 182.
8   [1977] Fam 165.
9   [1995] 2 FLR 1 at 4G–5A.

'It is fundamental to the making of an adoption order that the natural parent should be informed of the application so that she can give or withhold her consent. If she has no knowledge at all of the application then, obviously, a fundamental injustice is perpetrated. I would prefer myself to regard those cases not as cases where the order has been set aside by reason of a procedural irregularity, although that has certainly occurred, but as cases where natural justice has been denied because the natural parent, who may wish to challenge the adoption, has never been told that it is going to happen.'

10.47   In the absence of such irregularities, there is, therefore, no statutory provision for the annulment or revocation of an adoption order. Brief mention should, however, be made of *Re M (Minors) (Adoption)*,[1] where an adoption order was set aside in the circumstances where a father had agreed to a step-parent adoption in ignorance of his wife's fatal illness. Although the Court of Appeal said that this was a classic case of mistake and the father's ignorance vitiated his consent, it was stressed that this was a wholly exceptional case and should not be thought of as setting any precedent – a view which was strongly underlined in *Re B (Adoption: Jurisdiction to Set Aside)*.

PRELIMINARIES TO MAKING AN ADOPTION ORDER

10.48   There are four preliminary requirements which have to be satisfied before an adoption order can be made. They relate to:

(1) probationary periods which are prescribed in both agency adoptions and non-agency adoptions;
(2) reports required by the court;
(3) in the case of non-agency adoptions, notice provisions; and
(4) generally, the suitability of adopters.

10.49   An 'agency' case is a case where the child is placed for adoption with the applicants by an adoption agency. Where local authority foster parents are concerned, an agency case is one in which the adoption results from the local authority's decision to place the child with them for adoption or from the foster placement being later converted by the local authority to an adoptive placement.

10.50   A 'non-agency' case is where prospective adopters wish to adopt a child who is not placed for an adoption with them by an adoption agency. Such a case may include proposed adoptions by relatives, step-parents and private foster parents. It also includes proposed adoptions by local authority foster parents where the local authority has not placed the child with them 'for adoption'.

Probationary period

10.51   In the case of an agency adoption where the child was placed with the applicants by an adoption agency,[2] the child must have had his or her home with the applicants[3] at all times in the 10 weeks before the application for an adoption order is made. The same

---

1   [1991] 1 FLR 458.
2   'Or pursuant to an order of the High Court': ACA 2002, s 42(2).
3   In the case of an application by a married couple, by one or both of them: ibid, s 42(2).

10-week residence period also applies in the rare case of a natural parent applying to adopt his or her own child.[1]

10.52   In a non-agency case involving a step-parent or partner of the child's parent, the time required is a continuous preceding period of 6 months.[2] This applies whether the step-parent or partner has made a single or a joint application to adopt. In the case of a non-agency adoption involving local authority foster parents,[3] they may not apply to adopt unless the child's home has been with them for a continuous period of not less than one year[4] or if the court gives leave.[5]

10.53   In any other non-agency case (for example, a case involving relatives), the prospective adopters may not apply unless the child's home has been with them for a period of not less than 3 years (whether continuous or not) during the period of 5 years ending with the application or unless the court gives leave to make the application.[6]

10.54   The cumulative probationary period of 3 years for non-agency adoptions, where relatives are concerned, has been extended from one of 13 weeks under the previous law.[7] This reflects the thinking that a residence order is generally more appropriate in these cases.[8] The 3-year period is, therefore, intended as a disincentive to relatives considering adoption and a parliamentary prompt to consider all the alternative options, particularly residence orders. The principal concern in cases concerning 'extended family' adoptions has been the potential for distorting family relationships.

10.55   The objective of the requirement for minimum probationary periods is to ensure that the child and the prospective adopters have the opportunity to form a relationship such as to justify an application for adoption[9] and to ensure that the agency or authority has sufficient opportunity to see the applicants with the child.[10] The period runs up to the point of application for the adoption order, rather than the point at which the final order is made (as was the case under the AA 1976[11]). The difference in the residency requirements between agency and non-agency adoptions is explained by the fact that placements through an agency will involve rigorous assessment of the prospective adopters, whereas in non-agency cases there is not the same level of safeguard.[12] The shorter residency period for non-agency cases involving step-parents and partners of parents is justified by the fact that such adoptions involve one of the child's birth parents.

10.56   The phrase 'has his home' was used in the AA 1976[13] and its predecessor, the Children Act 1975.[14] One of the consequences of this wording was to make the position

---

1   ACA 2002, s 42(2)(b).
2   Ibid, 42(3).
3   Where the child was not placed for adoption with the foster parents by the local authority.
4   ACA 2002, s 42(4).
5   Ibid, s 42(6).
6   Ibid, s 42(5) and (6).
7   AA 1976, s 13(1)(a).
8   1992 Review of Adoption Law, at para 20.1.
9   Under s 45 of the ACA 2002.
10   Under s 42(7). HC Special Standing Committee, 29 November 2001, cols 361–362, per Ms Jacqui Smith.
11   AA 1976, s 13(1) and (2).
12   HC Special Standing Committee, 29 November 2001, col 362, per Ms Jacqui Smith.
13   AA 1976, s 13(1).
14   Children Act 1975, s 9.

of proposed adopters domiciled in the United Kingdom, but resident abroad, significantly more difficult and restricted than under the previous law.[1] Indeed the requirement of a probationary period was a matter which caused difficulty at the Hague Conference on Intercountry Adoption.[2] The AA 1976 had expressly provided that, in determining where a child 'has his home', any absence by the child at hospital or boarding school and any other temporary absence was to be disregarded. This definition was felt to be insufficiently flexible to ensure that temporary absences by other parties, in particular the adoptive applicants, could be excepted where appropriate. In consequence, the definition has been removed altogether, so as to allow the court (i) to take account of and disregard, where appropriate, any temporary absence, for whatever reason, by the child or any other party, and (ii) to consider, where appropriate, the impact of any very lengthy absence.[3]

10.57 Where a child 'has had his home' is a question of fact in each case. The concept presumes regular occupation with some degree of permanency, but does not require continuous presence. Sheldon J in *Re Y (Minors) (Adoption: Jurisdiction)* put it this way:[4]

> '... what is to be regarded as a "home" for these purposes ... in my view ... the concept is (not) capable of precise definition. Nor, too, in my opinion, should such definition be attempted beyond indicating the principal features that a "home" may be expected to embody. Subject to that, in my judgment, it must be a question of fact in any particular case whether or not the applicant has a home here ... "Home" is defined thus in the *Shorter Oxford English Dictionary*:
>
>> "A dwelling-house, house, abode: the fixed residence of a family or household; one's own house; the house in which one habitually lives or which one regards as one's proper abode."
>
> It is a definition which, in my judgment, contains the essential elements of a "home" as it is understood for present purposes. I have no doubt that an individual may have two homes, but each, to be properly so called, must comprise some element of regular occupation (whether past, present, or intended for the future, even if intermittent) with some degree of permanency, based upon the right of occupation, whenever it is required ...'[5]

---

1 It is not clear whether this was deliberate or unintentional on the part of Parliament.
2 W Duncan 'Regulatory Intercountry Adoption – an International Perspective' in A Bainham, DS Pearl and R Pickford (eds) *Frontiers of Family Law* (2nd edn, John Wiley & Sons, 1995) at p 47.
3 HC Deb, 20 May 2002, vol 386, no 150, col 91, per Ms Jacqui Smith.
4 [1986] 1 FLR 152 at 157B.
5 He also cited *Beck v Scholz* [1953] 1 QB 570 at 575, per Lord Evershed MR (a Rent Acts case): 'The word "home" itself is not easy of exact definition, but the question posed and to be answered by ordinary commonsense standards, is whether the particular premises are in personal occupation of the tenant as his or her "home", or as one of his or her homes. Occupation merely as a convenience for ... occasional visits ... would not, I venture to think, according to the common sense of the matter, be occupation as a "home"' and also *Herbert v Byrne* [1964] 1 All ER 882 at 887, per Salmon LJ (a Landlord and Tenant Act case): '"Home" is a somewhat nebulous concept incapable of precise definition ... In my view, if the evidence establishes ... a substantial degree of regular personal occupation by the tenant of an essentially residential nature, it would be difficult, if not impossible, for a court to hold that he was not in occupation of the premises as a home.'

It was further established that even where a child was physically absent, he or she may still be held to have his or her home with the applicants, provided they could show that they remained in effective parental control.[1]

10.58   Before an adoption order can be made, the court has to be further satisfied that the placing adoption agency,[2] or the local authority[3] in non-agency cases, has had sufficient opportunities to see the child with the applicants[4] in 'the home environment'.[5] In *Re Y (Minors) (Adoption: Jurisdiction)*[6] Sheldon J said:

> '... the only statutory obligation in this connection would seem to be that they (the applicants) spend sufficient time there to enable the local authority concerned to see all the parties together in "their home environment" ... and properly to investigate the circumstances. What that will involve in terms of residence will be a question to be decided in the light of the facts of the case.'

10.59   On the facts of the case, the applicants and the two children they were proposing to adopt had a home in Hong Kong. On their visits to England, the applicants merely used the husband's daughter's accommodation as a place to stay on the few occasions such accommodation was required. In those circumstances, it was held that the applicants did not have a 'home' in England and, as a result, the court had no jurisdiction to make an adoption order. This type of difficulty will continue to arise under the new law.

10.60   Although the ACA 2002 has taken some significant steps towards addressing those matters which have caused difficulties for adoptive applicants domiciled in the United Kingdom but resident abroad, it has not solved all the problems which arose under the former law from the phrase 'has his home with the applicant'.

Reports

10.61   In an agency case, the adoption agency which places the child for adoption must submit to the court a report on (a) the suitability of the applicants and (b) any relevant welfare issue under s 1, and must assist the court as it may direct.

10.62   The report should, therefore, particularly address the matters in the welfare checklist. Provision was made under the former law for what became known as the 'Sch 2' report.[7] It is very likely that the report required under s 43 of the ACA 2002 will cover similar matters to the Sch 2 report, which included the views of the birth parents. Rules must provide for the appointment of a CAFCASS officer in relation to an application for an adoption order and it is anticipated that that it will be the CAFCASS officer who

---

1   *Re CSC (An Infant)* [1960] 1 WLR 304; *Re B (An Infant) (No 2)* [1964] Ch 1; *Re KT (Adoption Application)* (1992) *Adoption and Fostering* 58. The absence of a child at boarding school or hospital was disregarded.
2   In ACA 2002, s 42(8), references to an agency include a Scottish or Northern Irish adoption agency.
3   The local authority must be the authority within whose area the home is: s 42(7)(b).
4   ACA 2002, s 42(7) – in the case of an application by a married couple, both of them.
5   Ibid, s 42(7). This mirrors s 13(3) of the AA 1976.
6   [1986] 1 FLR 152.
7   Adoption Rules 1984, r 4(4)(b) and Sch 2.

prepares the welfare report.[1] An employee of the adoption agency which placed the child is expressly precluded from being appointed to safeguard the child's interests.[2]

10.63 In intercountry adoptions, permission to bring a child into the United Kingdom for adoption will only be given by the Home Office where the local authority has provided a satisfactory report about the applicants. In cases under the 1993 Hague Convention on Protection of Children and Co-operation in Respect of Intercountry Adoption, receiving countries are responsible for arranging the assessment of applicants.

Notification in non-agency cases

10.64 The proposed adopters in non-agency cases must have given notice to the appropriate local authority of their intention to apply for an adoption order not more than 2 years nor less than 3 months before applying for an order.[3] The notice must be in writing[4] and may be given by post.[5] The 'appropriate authority' means either the local authority prescribed by regulations or the local authority for the area in which, at the time of giving the notice of intention to adopt, they have their home.[6] The regulations will identify which should be the appropriate authority in those cases where the applicant fulfils the domicile requirement in s 49 but does not currently have his or her home in a local authority area in the United Kingdom, eg members of the armed forces or diplomats temporarily stationed abroad.

10.65 Upon receipt of the notice of intention to adopt, the local authority must arrange for the investigation of the matter and submit a report to the court, in particular in respect of the proposed adopters' suitability and any relevant welfare issues under s 1 of the ACA 2002.[7] The local authority may arrange for elements of the investigation to be carried out by other suitable organisations. For example, in the case of a step-parent or partner adoption application by a service family stationed overseas, it is likely that the Service Families Adoption Agency, a registered voluntary agency, would carry out the investigation and visit the family as required by s 42(7) and pass the results to the relevant local authority. If the local authority was satisfied, it could then submit the report to the court.

10.66 Where a person in a non-agency case needs leave to apply for an adoption order under s 42(6),[8] he or she clearly cannot give notice of intention to apply to adopt until that leave has been given.[9] If a local authority has placed a child with a person (but not as a prospective adopter) and that person gives notice of intention to adopt, the local authority is not to be treated as leaving the child with him or her as a prospective adopter for the purposes of s 18(1)(b).[10]

---

1   ACA 2002, s 102(1) and (3).
2   Ibid, s 102(5)(b).
3   Ibid, s 44(2) and (3).
4   Ibid, s 144(1).
5   Ibid, s 110.
6   Ibid, s 44(9).
7   Ibid, s 44(5) and (6).
8   Eg local authority foster parents in a non-agency case: s 42(4).
9   ACA 2002, s 44(4).
10 Ibid, s 44(8).

Suitability of adopters

10.67   Regulations will prescribe the matters which the adoption agency must take into account in determining the suitability of prospective adopters or in making a report in respect of their suitability.[1] They are likely, for example, to provide that adoption agencies must give proper regard to the need for stability and permanence in the relationship of a couple, in determining their suitability to adopt.[2] They may require consideration of the duration of the relationship. The conditions will apply to married couples, single persons and unmarried couples. Only those prospective adopters who can demonstrate that they have a stable and lasting relationship will be approved to adopt jointly.[3]

THE THREE ALTERNATIVE CONDITIONS FOR MAKING AN ADOPTION ORDER

10.68   Section 47 of the ACA 2002 sets out three conditions, *one* of which must have been met before an adoption order can be made. The conditions in s 47(2) and (4), however, are not mutually exclusive. The section as a whole is subject to s 52.

First condition: 'the consent condition'

10.69   Under the consent condition, the court must be satisfied in the case of each parent or guardian:

(a)   that the parent or guardian consents to the making of the adoption order;[4]
(b)   that the parent or guardian has consented under s 20 (and has not withdrawn consent) and does not oppose the making of the adoption order;[5] or
(c)   that the parent's or guardian's consent should be dispensed with.[6]

10.70   The consent to the making of the adoption order must be given 'unconditionally and with full understanding of what is involved'[7] and must be given in the prescribed form where consent under s 19 is given and where advance consent under s 20 is given.[8] If the consent document is witnessed in accordance with the rules, it is admissible without further proof of the signature and is presumed to have been executed and witnessed on the date and at the place specified in the document, unless the contrary is proved.[9]

---

1   ACA 2002, s 45(1). Consideration of the suitability of prospective adopters is not strictly new in the sense that the Adoption Rules 1984, which dealt with reports, required comments upon the a stability of a married couple's relationship.
2   Ibid, s 45(2).
3   HL Grand Committee, 4 July 2002, vol 637, no 164, CWH 218, per Lord Hunt of Kings Heath.
4   ACA 2002, s 47(2)(a): see s 104 relating to documentary evidence for consent.
5   Ibid, s 47(2)(b). He may not oppose the making of an adoption order without the leave of the court which cannot be given unless there is a change of circumstances: s 46(3) and (7).
6   Ibid, s 47(2)(c).
7   Ibid, s 52(5).
8   Ibid, s 52(7). Rules will also prescribe the forms in which a person may give consent under any provisions (other than ss 19 and 20) (if he or she wishes).
9   Ibid, s 104(1) and (2). A consent document which purports to be witnessed in accordance with the rules is presumed to be so witnessed unless the contrary is proved.

10.71 Where a parent has given advance consent under s 20 of the ACA 2002 to the making of an adoption order, he may not oppose the making of the order under s 47(2)(b) without the court's leave,[1] which cannot be given unless the court is satisfied that there has been a change of circumstances since the consent was given.[2] The court cannot dispense with the consent of any parent to the making of an adoption order under s 47(2)(c) unless either of the two grounds under s 52(1) is satisfied.

10.72 This consent condition arises at the stage of the making of the adoption order, for example: (i) where the child falls outside the placement regime (ie the child has *not* been placed for adoption by an agency with consent under s 19 or by a local authority under a placement order (such as in the case of relative adoptions)); or (ii) where consent under s 19 is combined with advance consent under s 20 which has not been withdrawn before the application for an adoption order is made[3] (although, as an agency placement, the conditions in s 20(4) will also have been fulfilled).

Second condition: 'the placement condition'

10.73 The placement condition applies in those cases which fall within the placement regime either by way of the consensual route or the placement order route. In both cases the issue of parental consent relating to placement for adoption has been considered. The condition is itself subdivided into three sub-conditions, *each* of which must be fulfilled to the satisfaction of the court:

(a) the child has been placed for adoption by the agency with the prospective adopters in whose favour the order is proposed to be made;[4]

(b) either:
(i) the child was placed with the consent of each parent or guardian (and the consent of the mother was given when the child was at least 6 weeks old);[5] or
(ii) the child was placed for adoption under a placement order;[6] and

(c) no parent or guardian opposes the making of the adoption order.[7]

10.74 It follows that where parents have given consent to placement in principle under s 19, but have not given consent to the making of an adoption order under s 20, then once the child has been placed with prospective adopters under s 19 and if the parents do not withdraw their consent before the adoption application is made,[8] they could find themselves unable to oppose the final adoption order unless the court grants leave. If the parents are successful in obtaining leave to oppose the making of the adoption order under s 47(5) and (7), then an adoption order cannot be made under s 47(4), but the court could still make an adoption order under s 47(2) where it was satisfied that the child's welfare required that the parents' consent should be dispensed with under ss 47(2)(c) and 52(1)(b).

---

1   ACA 2002, s 47(3).
2   Ibid, s 47(7). See below for the discussion on the leave criteria.
3   Ibid, s 52(4)
4   Ibid, s 47(4)(a).
5   Ibid, s 47(4)(b)(i).
6   Ibid, s 47(4)(b)(ii). Where a child is less than 6 weeks old, a placement order can still be a valid basis upon which to make a later adoption order.
7   Ibid, s 47(4)(c).
8   Ibid, s 52(4).

10.75 If, however, the parents are unsuccessful in obtaining leave, an adoption order could simply be made under s 47(4) without requiring their consent to the actual making of the adoption order, which (unlike placement for adoption) extinguishes their parental responsibility. This would mean that the court itself may never consider whether the parents' consent to the making of the adoption order has been given or should be dispensed with. In other words, the fundamental issue of parental consent to adoption would be determined by an administrative rather than a judicial act. It is suggested that this absence of judicial scrutiny sits uncomfortably with the notion that parental consent to adoption lies at the core of the adoption process (which has been the approach of previous domestic law and remains the approach in international law) and with the Art 8 right for parents to be engaged in the decision-making process leading to the final adoption order.[1]

10.76 The provisions of s 141(3) and (4)(c) provide that parents (and, if they cannot be found, certain prescribed relatives) must be notified of the date and place of the hearing for the making of the final adoption order.[2] 'Parental opposition', for the purposes of the second placement condition, is controlled by the requirement for leave under s 47(5) and (7). A parent may not oppose the making of an adoption order under the second condition without the leave of the court. Leave, however, cannot be given by the court unless it is satisfied that there has been 'a change of circumstances' since the consent was given or the placement order was made. To gain access to the court, therefore, parents must establish 'a change of circumstances'. Examples given of a relevant change of circumstances are: successful and proven rehabilitation where a placement order was made because of parental drug or alcohol abuse; recovery from mental illness to allow the parent to care for the child; or the identification of a previously unknown natural father willing and able to provide a home.[3] The court is, therefore, likely to interpret the 'change' of circumstances as requiring a 'significant' rather than *de minimis* change of circumstances.[4]

10.77 The following considerations, however, argue against setting a higher jurisdictional test for parents to cross, such as a requirement that there should be a 'fundamental' or 'exceptional' change of circumstances.[5] First, it was open to Parliament to specify that

---

1   See *McMichael v UK* (1995) 20 EHRR 205.
2   ACA 2002, s 141(3) and (4)(c) provides that the rules must require the following persons to be notified of the date and place where the application for an adoption order will be heard: (i) every person who can be found whose consent to the making of the order is required under s 47(2) (or whose consent would be required but for s 47(2)(c)) or, if no such person can be found, any relative prescribed by rules who can be found; (ii) every person who has consented to the making of an order under s 20 (and has not withdrawn the consent) unless he has given a notice under s 20(4)(a); (iii) every person who, if leave were given under s 47(5), would be entitled to oppose the making of the order.
3   HC Special Standing Committee, 29 November 2001, col 368, per Ms Jacqui Smith.
4   At HC Special Standing Committee, 29 November 2001, col 368, Jacqui Smith used the word 'significant'; at HL Grand Committee, 4 July 2002, vol 637, no 164, CWH 224, Baroness Andrews also used 'significant'.
5   Such as is set in relation to leave to obtain contact where an adoption order has been made: see *Re C (A Minor) (Adopted Child: Contact)* [1993] Fam 210 at 216A, per Thorpe J (as he then was); *Re S (Contact: Application by Sibling)* [1998] 2 FLR 897 at 912C–D.

the change of circumstances should be 'fundamental' or 'exceptional'[1] and it chose not to do so. Secondly, as has been seen, the status of the birth parents in the adoption process has been emasculated by the loss of the veto which was available to them previously through the vehicle of 'reasonably' withholding their consent. This loss arguably justifies the lower jurisdictional threshold of 'a change in circumstances' for leave under s 47(5), as the right to oppose in s 47(4)(c) has now become the 'last redoubt' for protecting the parents' rights and interests.

10.78   Thirdly, under Art 6 of the European Convention on Human Rights, the parents have a right to effective access to the court in the determination of their civil rights and obligations.[2] Where the individual's access is limited either by operation of law or in fact, the European Court will examine whether the limitation imposed impairs the essence of the right and, in particular, whether it pursues a legitimate aim and there is a reasonable relationship between the means employed and the aim sought to be achieved.[3] If the restriction is incompatible with these principles, a violation of Art 6 will arise. Furthermore, while Art 8 contains no explicit procedural requirements, the decision-making process involved in measures of interference must be fair and such as to afford due respect to the interests safeguarded by Art 8.[4] Under s 3 of the Human Rights Act 1998, s 47(7) has to be read and given effect in a way which is compatible with those Convention rights.

10.79   If the preliminary hurdle set by the leave provisions is at a height which demands a fundamental or exceptional change in circumstances before a crossing can be attempted, it becomes, in effect, a legal and evidential bar. Arguably, therefore, a high jurisdictional test could amount to an excessively severe restriction on the parents' right of access to court and a disproportionate obstacle to their ability to challenge the making of an order, particularly as the order marks the extinction of their parental interests and rights.

Third condition: Scotland and Northern Ireland

10.80   The third condition applies only to Scotland and Northern Ireland. The child must be free for adoption under s 18 of the Adoption (Scotland) Act 1978 or arts 17(1) or 18(1) of the Adoption (Northern Ireland) Order 1987.[5] The provisions in the AA 1976 relating to freeing orders in England and Wales are repealed by the ACA 2002, but under the transitional provisions in para 6(3) of Sch 4 to the Act, where a child is freed for adoption under s 18 of the AA 1976, the third condition is deemed to be satisfied.

---

1   In respect of special guardianship orders, parents seeking leave to vary or discharge the order must satisfy the court that that there has been a *significant* change of circumstances before obtaining leave: s 14D(5) of the CA 1989, as amended by s 115 of the ACA 2002. Hence it is surprising that the word 'significant' has been omitted from s 47(7); perhaps its omission signals a low jurisdictional threshold.

2   *Golder v UK* (1975) 1 EHRR 524 at paras 35 and 36.

3   *Ashingdane v UK* (1985) 7 EHRR 528 at 546–547 and *TP and KM v UK* [2001] 2 FLR 549 at [98].

4   *W v UK* (1988) 10 EHRR 29 at 50; *McMichael v UK* (1995) 20 EHRR 205 at 241; *TP and KM v UK* [2001] 2 FLR 549 at [72].

5   ACA 2002, s 47(6).

CONTACT

10.81   An express duty has been imposed on the court, before making an adoption order, to consider whether there should be arrangements for allowing any person contact with the child.[1] For that purpose, the court must consider any existing or proposed arrangements and obtain any views of the parties to the proceedings. Under the s 1 principles, the court must always have regard to its 'whole range of powers' under s 1(6), which includes a contact order under s 8 of the CA 1989, and may make a s 8 contact order of its own motion. Parents also retain a reserved right to apply for a s 8 contact order at the final adoption hearing.[2] See Chapter 11 for a full discussion on the issues of post-adoption contact.

STATUS OF THE ADOPTED CHILD

Meaning of adoption

10.82   Chapter 4 of Part 1 of the ACA 2002 makes provision for the status of adopted children.[3] 'Adoption'[4] for the purposes of Chapter 4 means adoption orders made in the United Kingdom, the Channel Islands or the Isle of Man, Convention adoptions, overseas adoptions or adoptions recognised by the law of England and Wales and effected under the law of any other country.[5] The definition has been extended to include adoptions effected under the law of a Hague Convention country.[6] References in Chapter 4 to adoption do not include an adoption effected before the appointed day (the day on which the Chapter comes into force).[7] However, any reference in an enactment to an adopted person within the meaning of the Chapter includes a reference to an adopted child within the meaning of Part 4 of the AA 1976.[8]

Status conferred by adoption: s 67

10.83   An adopted person is to be treated in law as if born as the child of the adopters or adopter.[9] An adopted person is the legitimate child of the adopters or adopter and, if adopted by a couple or one of a couple under s 51(2), is to be treated as a child of the relationship of the couple.[10] Further, an adopted person, if adopted by one member of a couple under s 51(2), is to be treated in law as not being the child of any person other than the adopter and the other member of the couple (although this does not affect any

---

1   ACA 2002, s 46(6).
2   Ibid, s 26(5).
3   It replaces the provisions in Part IV of the AA 1976.
4   ACA 2002, s 66(2) provides that, where the context allows, references to 'adoption' do not include an adoption effected *before* the day on which this Chapter comes into force.
5   Ibid, s 66(1).
6   Ibid, s 66(1)(c). Section 66 replaces the definition in s 38 of the AA 1976.
7   Ibid, s 66(2).
8   Ibid, s 66(3).
9   Ibid, s 67(1). It should be noted that, under the Employment Act 2002, employees who have adopted children are now entitled to adoption leave.
10   ACA 2002, s 67(2)(a) and (b).

reference in the Act to a person's natural parent or any other natural relationship).[1] In any other case, an adopted person is to be treated in law as not being the child of any person other than the adopters or adopter (although, again, this does not affect any reference in the Act to a person's natural parent or any other natural relationship).[2] However, in the case of a person adopted by one of his or her natural parents as a sole adoptive parent, the last provision has no effect as respects any entitlement to property which depends on the relationship to that parent or anything else depending on that relationship.[3] Section 67 has effect from the date of adoption[4] and applies to the interpretation of enactments or instruments passed before and after the adoption; it has effect as respects things done or events occurring on or after the adoption.[5] Section 67 marks significant changes from the old law, including recognition of the status of a child in a step-parent or partner adoption under s 51(2).

Adoptive relatives

10.84 A relationship which exists by virtue of s 67 can be referred to as 'an adoptive relationship'.[6] An adopter may be referred to as 'an adoptive parent' or as an 'adoptive father' or 'adoptive mother'.[7] This extends to any other relative in the adoptive relationship.[8] The word 'adoptive', however, need not necessarily be used to qualify the relationships.[9] A reference (however expressed) to the adoptive mother or father of a child adopted by a couple of the same sex or a partner of the child's parent, where the couple are of the same sex, is to be read as a reference to the child's adoptive parents.[10]

Rules of interpretation for instruments concerning property

10.85 Section 69 of the ACA 2002 sets out the rules of interpretation for any instrument concerning the disposition of property. These are subject to any contrary indication and to Sch 4.

Definitions

10.86 In s 73(2), 'disposition' is defined as including 'the conferring of a power of appointment and any other disposition of an interest in or right over property' and a 'power of appointment' as including 'any discretionary power to transfer a beneficial interest in property without the furnishing of valuable consideration'. The Chapter applies equally to oral dispositions.[11]

10.87 For the purposes of Chapter 4:

---

1 ACA 2002, s 67(3)(a).
2 Ibid, s 67(3)(b).
3 Ibid, s 67(4).
4 Ibid, s 67(5).
5 Ibid, s 67(6)(a) and (b). This section is subject to the provisions of Chapter 4 and Sch 4.
6 Ibid, s 68(1).
7 Ibid, s 68(1)(a).
8 Ibid, s 68(1)(b).
9 Ibid, s 68(2).
10 Ibid, s 68(3)(a) and (b).
11 Ibid, s 73(3).

(a) the death of the testator is the date at which a will or codicil is to be regarded as made;[1]

(b) the provisions of the law of intestate succession are to be treated as if contained in the instrument executed by the deceased (while of full capacity) immediately before his or her death.[2]

Summary of the rules

10.88   In summary, the provisions contained in Chapter 4 are as follows.

(1) Where a disposition depends on the date of birth of the child of the adoptive parents,[3] the adopted person is to be treated as having been born on the date of the adoption order.[4] In the case of the adoption of two or more persons, they will be treated as born on the date of the order, but in order of their actual births.[5] This, however, does not affect any reference to a person's age. The objective is to put in place a clear system which endeavours to put the adopted child and any natural children in the adoptive family on as equal a footing as possible in respect of inheritance issues.

(2) Any interests vested in the adopted person before the adoption are not affected.[6]

(3) Where it is necessary to determine for the purposes of the disposition of property whether a woman can have a child, there is a presumption that a woman who has attained 55 years will not adopt a child and, if she does, that person is not treated as her child for the purposes of the property instrument.[7]

(4) Where a disposition depends on the date of birth of a child who was born illegitimate but adopted by one of the natural parents as sole adoptive parent, his entitlement[8] remains unaffected.[9]

(5) An adoption does not affect the descent of any peerage, dignity, title of honour or the devolution of property devolving from such titles.[10]

(6) A trustee or personal representative is not under a duty to enquire whether any adoption has been effected or revoked before conveying or distributing property, nor is he or she liable for so doing.[11] The right to follow the property is, however, unaffected.[12]

---

1   ACA 2002, s 73(4).
2   Ibid, s 73(5).
3   Ibid, s 69. Examples of phrases in wills on which this subsection operates are given in s 69(3).
4   Ibid, s 69(2)(a).
5   Ibid, s 69(2)(b).
6   Ibid, s 69(4). The subsection does not prejudice any qualifying interest (ie an interest vested in possession in the adopted person before the adoption) or any interest expectant (whether immediately or not) upon a qualifying interest. See *Staffordshire County Council v B* [1998] 1 FLR 261, where the court held that a child's contingent interest, arising out of the mother's interest vested in possession, continued after his adoption by virtue of s 42(4) of the AA 1976 (now ACA 2002, s 69(4)). In Bill 66 a provision had been included which made this clear by expressly giving the court a discretion to allow an adopted person to retain a contingent interest (or part of it) in his or her birth family's property after adoption (cl 53(5)). This was, however, deleted in Bill 34.
7   ACA 2002, s 69(5).
8   By virtue of Part 3 of the Family Law Reform Act 1987 (dispositions of property).
9   ACA 2002, s 70(1). Examples of circumstances where subs (1) will apply are set out in subs (2).
10   Ibid, s 71(1) and (2).
11   Ibid, s 72(1) and (2).
12   Ibid, s 72(3).

(7) The entitlement to a pension payable to the adopted person at the time of the adoption is unaffected.[1]

(8) Any rights and liabilities under an insurance policy that the natural parent has effected for the payment of funeral expenses on the death of the child are transferred to the adoptive parents, who are treated as if they took out the policy.[2]

The enactments to which s 67 does not apply

10.89   Section 67 does not apply principally to the following enactments:

(1) the table of kindred and affinity in Sch 1 to the Marriage Act 1949 or ss 10 and 11 of the Sexual Offences Act 1956 (incest) or s 54 of the Criminal Justice Act 1977 (inciting a girl to commit rape).[3] For these purposes, an adopted child remains a part of the natural family. Although an adopted person and the adoptive parents are prohibited from marrying,[4] there are no other bars on marrying within the adoptive family;

(2) the British Nationality Act 1981;[5]

(3) the Immigration Act 1971.[6]

FAMILY RELATIONSHIPS

Step-parents and partners of the child's parent where they live as a couple[7]

10.90   Under the former law, although over 50 per cent of adoptions were step-parent adoptions, it was observed that contested step-parent adoptions were 'exceptionally rare'[8] and, where they were contested, parental consent was rarely dispensed with. In *Re D (Adoption: Parent's Consent)*,[9] the House of Lords said that 'a direction to dispense with consent should be given sparingly, and only in rare and exceptional cases: this was all the more so in cases such as *In Re B* [1975] Fam 127 (a step-parent adoption) ... where the adoption is desired by one natural parent and the other refuses consent'. In *Re PJ (Adoption: Practice on Appeal)*,[10] Thorpe LJ rejected the argument that the leaning against

---

1   ACA 2002, s 75.

2   Ibid, s 76. Subsection (2) makes a modification to the AA 1976 by making clear that references in subs (1) to adoptive parents include the adopter and person to whom he or she is married in step-parent adoptions.

3   Ibid, s 74(1)(a).

4   Marriage Act 1949, Sch 1, Pt 1, as amended.

5   ACA 2002, s 74(2)(a). It also does not apply to any instrument having effect under an enactment within the provisions of the British Nationality Act 1981 or any other provision of law in force which determines British citizenship.

6   ACA 2002, s 74(2)(b). See fn 3 above, which applies equally to the Immigration Act 1971.

7   A person is the partner of a child's parent if the person and the parent are a couple within the meaning of ACA 2002, s 144(4) but the person is not the child's parent: ibid, s 144(7).

8   *Re PJ (Adoption: Practice on Appeal)* [1998] 2 FLR 252 at 262F, per Thorpe LJ. Anecdotal evidence suggests that the release from child support obligations has provided a significant motivation for fathers to consent to step-parent adoptions.

9   [1977] AC 602 at 627E–F, per Lord Wilberforce.

10   [1998] 2 FLR 252.

step-parent adoptions expressed in *Re D (Adoption: Parent's Consent)* was no longer applicable and held that these cautionary *dicta* were still apt.

10.91   The stance of the 1992 Review of Adoption Law[1] was that, where the child has some form of relationship with a parent or a parent's family, adoption would be against his or her best interests and that it was 'likely that in many circumstances a residence order would be a better way of confirming a step-parent's responsibility because it does not alter a child's legal relationship with his or her parents and family'.[2]

10.92   Although the ACA 2002 has made some important amendments to the position of step-parents, the underlying thinking of the Review has clearly pointed the direction of the reforms towards the alternatives to adoption. This is illustrated by the amendments which the ACA 2002 has made to the CA 1989. Under the new s 4A of the CA 1989, a step-parent who is married to the parent with parental responsibility, may acquire parental responsibility for the child of his or her spouse by an agreement between the step-parent and the parents, who have parental responsibility, or by a court order.[3] This measure is intended to provide an alternative to adoption where a step-parent wishes to acquire parental responsibility for his or her step-child. It has the advantage of not removing parental responsibility from the other birth parent and does not legally separate the child from membership of the family.

10.93   However, parental responsibility, whether under a parental responsibility agreement or a court order, is not indefeasible. It may be brought to an end, but only by an order of the court made on the application of any person who has parental responsibility for the child or, with the leave of the court, of the child.[4] This may reflect concerns as to the high breakdown rates for marriages with step-children, which were highlighted by the 1992 Review of Adoption Law.[5]

10.94   Section 12 of the CA 1989 has also been amended[6] to enable the court to direct that a residence order in favour of a step-parent or partner of the child's parent[7] may continue in force until the child reaches the age of 18, as a further means of delivering enhanced security where the step-parent or partner is caring for the child on a long-term basis. An indication that a residence order is the preferred alternative option may be that a step-parent is included in the category of individuals entitled to apply for a residence order,[8] but excluded from those entitled to apply for a special guardianship order.[9] An individual (who happens to be a step-parent) may nevertheless qualify for a right to apply

---

1   At paras 19.1 et seq.
2   1992 Review of Adoption Law, para 19.5.
3   CA 1989, s 4A(1), as inserted by s 112 of the ACA 2002.
4   Ibid, s 4A(3)(a) and (b), as inserted by s 112 of the ACA 2002.
5   At para 19.4. These concerns were expressed, however, in the context of a proposal that a step-parent adoption should be revocable.
6   By s 114 of the ACA 2002.
7   A person is the partner of a child's parent if the person and the parent are a couple but the person is not the child's parent: ACA 2002, s 144(7).
8   CA 1989, s 10(5)(a). This right to apply for a residence order applies only to step-parents who have been *a party to a marriage* (whether subsisting or not) in relation to whom the child is a child of the family. The step-parent is also entitled to apply for any s 8 order if he or she has parental responsibility for the child by virtue of CA 1989, s 4A (ACA 2002, s 112, Sch 3, para 56(b)). The 'unmarried' partner of the child's parent must obtain leave.
9   CA 1989, s 14A(5), as amended by s 115 of the ACA 2002.

for a special guardianship order if, for example, the child has lived with him or her for a period of at least 3 years or he or she has the consent of each of those who have parental responsibility for the child.

10.95 It should be noted that a cohabiting partner of the child's parent falls outside the new parental responsibility provisions under s 4A of the CA 1989. Like the married step-parent, he does not have a right to apply for a special guardianship order. A parental responsibility order, however, would be granted automatically, were a residence order made in his favour.[1]

10.96 There may, however, be circumstances where a step-parent or partner adoption may be in the child's best interests; for example, where one of the natural parents is a stranger to the child, and the child has no knowledge of this parent's extended family. In order to facilitate the adoption process in these cases, the law has been amended to remove some of the anomalies which occurred under the former law in relation to step-parent adoptions. Under s 51(2) of the ACA 2002, an adoption order may now be made on the single application of a partner of the child's parent, rather than a joint application by both the partner and the birth parent. Under s 67, the status of a child adopted by a couple or one of a couple under s 51(2) is expressly recognised.[2]

10.97 As a preliminary requirement for a step-parent or partner of the child's parent to obtain an adoption order, the child must have had his or her home with the step-parent or partner at all times during the period of 6 months preceding the application.[3] The step-parent or partner must also give notice in writing to the appropriate local authority of his or her intention to apply for an adoption order not more than 2 years, or less than 3 months, before applying for an order.[4] This enables the local authority to arrange for an investigation and submit a report to the court, in particular in respect of his or her suitability and any relevant welfare issues under s 1 of the ACA 2002.[5] Before an adoption order can be made, the step-parent or partner must further satisfy the consent condition in s 46(2).

10.98 Where a step-parent or partner has given notice of intention to apply to adopt, if the child has had his or her home with that person for not less than 3 years (whether continuous or not) out of the last 5 years, the child may be removed only (i) with leave of the court or (ii) by a local authority or other person in the exerise of statutory powers.[6] If the child's home has been with the partner for less than the 3 years, then the child may be removed (i) by the child's parent, (ii) with the court's leave or (iii) by a local authority or other person in the exercise of statutory powers.[7]

10.99 The adoption order, once made, is irrevocable. The suggestion in the 1992 Review of Adoption Law[8] that a step-parent adoption should be revocable where the

---

1   CA 1989, s 12(1).
2   See **10.83** (dealing with status under s 67).
3   ACA 2002, s 42(3).
4   Ibid, s 44(2) and (3).
5   Ibid, s 44(5) and (6).
6   Ibid, s 39(1) and (2).
7   Ibid, s 39(3).
8   At para 19.4.

marriage between the step-parent and the birth parents either ends in divorce or death has been rejected.

Unmarried fathers

10.100   Under the former law, the agreement of an unmarried father to adoption was not required before the court made an adoption order, unless the father had acquired parental responsibility. The term 'parent' in the AA 1976 meant 'any parent who has parental responsibility for the child under the Children Act 1989'.[1]

10.101   The CA 1989 does not automatically give unmarried fathers parental responsibility for their children. Instead, it provides the means whereby an unmarried father may acquire parental responsibility, ie by a parental responsibility agreement or a court order. The aim of the legislation is to provide a mechanism for identifying 'meritorious' fathers who might be accorded parental rights, thereby protecting the interests of both the child and the mother.

10.102   In the leading case, *Re S (Parental Responsibility)*,[2] the Court of Appeal set out the principles to be applied when making a parental responsibility order. The factors highlighted by Balcombe LJ in *Re H (Minors) (Local Authority: Parental Rights) (No 3)*,[3] namely: (i) the degree of commitment which the father has shown towards the child; (ii) the degree of attachment which exists between the father and the child; and (iii) the reasons of the father for applying for the order, were adopted as relevant factors (if not exhaustive) under s 4 of the CA 1989. Ward LJ said:[4]

> '. . . in essence, the granting of a parental responsibility order is the granting of status . . . It is wrong . . . not to concentrate on the fact that what is in issue is conferring upon the *committed*[5] father the status of parenthood for which nature has already ordained that he must bear responsibility.'

10.103   Under the ACA 2002, the key to the parental right to give or withdraw consent remains 'parental responsibility'.[6] The CA 1989, as amended by the ACA 2002,[7] now extends the means whereby an unmarried father may acquire parental responsibility to include where he becomes registered as the child's father under s 10(1)(a)–(c) and s 10A(1)(a)–(c) of the Births and Deaths Registration Act 1953.

10.104   Under the 1953 Act, where the parents are not married at the time of birth, the mother alone has the duty to register the birth and the registrar 'shall not enter in the register the name of any person as father of the child'[8] except:

(1)   at the joint request of the mother and the person stating himself to be the father (in which case that person shall sign the register together with the mother);[9]

---

1   AA 1976, s 72(1), as amended.
2   [1995] 2 FLR 648; see also *Re C and V (Contact and Parental Responsibility)* [1998] 1 FLR 392.
3   [1991] Fam 151 at 185D; [1991] 1 FLR 214 at 218F.
4   [1995] 2 FLR 648 at 657C and F.
5   Emphasis added.
6   ACA 2002, s 52(2) and (6).
7   Ibid, s 111.
8   Births and Deaths Registration Act 1953, s 10(1).
9   Ibid, s 10(1)(a).

(2)   at the request of the mother, on production of (i) a declaration in the prescribed form made by the mother stating that that person is the father of the child, and (ii) a statutory declaration made by that person stating himself to be the father of the child;[1]

(3)   at the request of that person, on production of (i) a declaration in the prescribed form by that person stating himself to be the father of the child, and (ii) a statutory declaration made by the mother stating that that person is the father of the child.[2]

10.105   Section 10A(1) of the 1953 Act deals with re-registration where the parents were not married to each other at the time of the child's birth and no one has been registered as the father of the child. The registrar will re-register the birth so as to show a person as the father:

(1)   at the joint request of the mother and that person;[3]
(2)   at the request of the mother, on the production of a declaration by the mother and a statutory declaration by the father that he is the father of the child;[4]
(3)   at the request of the father, on production of a declaration by him and a statutory declaration by the mother that he is the father of the child;[5]
(4)   at the request of the mother and the father, on production of copies of a parental responsibility agreement[6] or an order under s 4 of CA 1989[7] or an order under para 1 of Sch 1 to the CA 1989 which requires the father to make financial provision for the child[8] or any of the orders in s 10(1A).[9]

10.106   Although widening the range of vehicles for the acquisition of parental responsibility, the ACA 2002 has stopped short of conferring full parental responsibility automatically on all unmarried fathers. It follows that the unmarried father without parental responsibility continues to have no right of consent in the adoption process; the tide, which sought to sweep away the distinctions between illegitimacy and legitimacy for the child, has not yet reached the high water mark of eliminating the distinction between the married and unmarried father. The justification for the distinction between the unmarried father and married father is summed up by Balcombe LJ in *Re H (Illegitimate Children: Father: Parental Rights) (No 2)*,[10] where he said:

'The reason why this method was adopted was because the position of the natural father can be infinitely variable; at one end of the spectrum his connection may be only the single act of intercourse (possibly even rape) which led to conception; at the other end of the spectrum he may have played a full part in the child's life from birth onwards, only the formality of marriage to the mother being absent. Considerable social evils might have resulted if the

1   Births and Deaths Registration Act 1953, s 10(1)(b).
2   Ibid, s 10(1)(c).
3   Ibid, s 10A(1)(a).
4   Ibid, s 10A(1)(b).
5   Ibid, s 10A(1)(c).
6   Ibid, s 10A(1)(d); a declaration in the prescribed form that the agreement was made in compliance with s 4 and had not been brought to an end by the order of the court is also required.
7   Ibid, s 10A(1)(e); a declaration that the order has not been brought to an end by the order of the court is also required; as in the case of the order referred to in subparas (f) and (g).
8   Ibid, s 10A(1)(f).
9   Ie orders under s 4 of the Family Law Reform Act 1987, under s 9 or s 11B of the Guardianship of Minors Act 1971 or s 4 of the Affiliation Proceedings Act 1957.
10   [1991] 1 FLR 214 at 218D–E.

father at the bottom end of the spectrum had been automatically granted full parental rights and duties and so Parliament adopted the scheme [in the CA 1989].'

10.107   In *Re W; Re B (Child Abduction: Unmarried Fathers)*[1] Hale J (as she then was) declined to find that the position of the unmarried fathers compared with that of married fathers (in the context of rights of custody in international abduction cases) amounted to discrimination. She went on to say:

> 'There may come a time when the Parliament of this country, having considered the policy matters further, decides to eliminate those differences. Or there may come a time when so many of the Contracting States to the Convention decide to do so that the currently wide margin of appreciation in this area narrows so far as to oblige us to do so.'

10.108   Having had the opportunity to consider the policy again in the context of adoption law, Parliament has tentatively pushed the doors open a little further, but has shrunk from throwing the doors wide open. This caution has been mirrored in Strasbourg, where in *B v UK*[2] the European Court held, in an echo of the words of Balcombe LJ in *Re H (Illegitimate Children: Father: Parental Rights) (No 2)*, that:

> 'It is true that under the Children Act 1989 married fathers have parental responsibility automatically, while unmarried ones need to acquire it in accordance with the provisions of the Act. However, the court has considered that the relationship between unmarried fathers and their children varies from ignorance and indifference to a close stable relationship indistinguishable from the conventional family-based unit (*McMichael v UK*).[3] For this reason the Court has held that there exists an objective and reasonable justification for the difference in treatment between married and unmarried fathers with regard to the automatic acquisition of parental rights.'

As a result, the European Court concluded that the complaint of discrimination between married and unmarried fathers did not disclose the appearance of a violation of Art 14 in conjunction with Art 8 of the European Convention on Human Rights.

10.109   Parental responsibility granted to an unmarried father under these amended provisions may be terminated but only by order of the court.[4] Applications for termination may be made by any person who has parental responsibility for the child or, with leave, by the child.[5] Where parental responsibility is acquired by court order, the court will not bring that order to an end while a residence order remains in force.[6]

10.110   Where the unmarried father acquires parental responsibility and the child has already been placed for adoption under s 19 pursuant to the consent given by the mother, he is treated as having given consent in the same terms as the mother. He is entitled to withdraw his consent, provided he does so in the prescribed form and before an application for adoption has been made.[7] If he wishes to oppose the making of an adoption order after an application for adoption has been made, he must obtain leave under s 46 on the basis that there has been a change of circumstances.

---

1   [1998] 2 FLR 146 at 163D–168G.
2   [2000] 1 FLR 1 at 5D–G.
3   (1995) 20 EHRR 205 at para 98.
4   CA 1989, s 4(2A), as amended by s 111 of the ACA 2002.
5   Ibid, s 4(3)(a) and (b), as amended.
6   Ibid, s 4(3), as amended, and s 12(4) of the CA 1989.
7   ACA 2002, s 52(4).

10.111   The European Convention has had some impact upon the position of unmarried fathers. The Court of Appeal, with an eye on the potential Art 8 right to respect for family life, has increased the involvement of unmarried fathers in the adoption process and has moved them from the backwaters closer to the mainstream. The climate change was highlighted in *Re R (Adoption: Father's Involvement)* where Thorpe LJ said:[1]

> 'The climate has undoubtedly shifted since the mid-1980s and the shift is towards according greater involvement of natural fathers, even though there has been no marriage and even though there has been no formal order of parental responsibility. The arrival of the European Convention ... probably does not greatly impact on this discretionary balance. But it is a factor that the judge was not only entitled to take account of, but wise to take account of ...'

The Court of Appeal held, in respect of fathers without parental responsibility who might wish to be heard in subsequent adoption proceedings, that each case should be decided on its merits on the issue of whether or not it was appropriate that he should be joined as a respondent.[2]

10.112   In *Re H; Re G (Adoption: Consultation of Unmarried Fathers)*[3] Dame Elizabeth Butler-Sloss P went on to establish that, as a matter of general practice, judges giving directions in adoption applications would be expected to inform natural fathers of the proceedings unless for good reason it was inappropriate to do so.

10.113   It is, therefore, likely that the rules and regulations supporting the ACA 2002 will reflect these developments. Section 1(4)(f) requires an adoption agency to consider the wishes and feelings of the child's relatives, including both parents. There is, thus, an expectation that the agency will be required to consult and involve members of the child's family, including unmarried fathers without parental responsibility, in all circumstances unless it would be contrary to the child's welfare.[4] Under reg 7(3) of the Adoption Agencies Regulations 1983 there is an explicit duty on adoption agencies to contact and involve the unmarried father of the child where he is known to them and where that is practicable and consistent. The Government has expressed an explicit commitment that this obligation will be repeated and expanded upon in new regulations to take account of human rights case-law which places further emphasis on the importance of informing, involving and consulting unmarried fathers.[5] It is further envisaged that, where an agency is in any doubt as to whether or not to consult the unmarried father, provision will be made in court rules for the agency to make a direct application to the court for guidance.[6]

10.114   The intention is, therefore, that in the vast majority of cases the unmarried father without parental responsibility will be aware of the proposed plan for adoption before an application for an adoption order is made. Where a child has been placed for adoption with prospective adopters, there will, however, be a minimum period of only 10 weeks within which it will be possible for an unmarried father to apply for an order

---

1   [2001] 1 FLR 302 at [21].
2   See *Z County Council v R* [2001] 1 FLR 365, per Holman J, and *Re M (Adoption: Rights of Natural Father)* [2001] 1 FLR 745, per Bodey J, where the court found that there were circumstances which made it inappropriate to inform the father.
3   [2001] 1 FLR 646.
4   HL Deb, 16 October 2002, vol 639, no 188, col 933, per Baroness Andrews.
5   Ibid, col 934, per Baroness Andrews.
6   Ibid.

giving him parental responsibility under s 4 of the CA 1989. When an application for a parental responsibility order is pending and an application for a placement order or an adoption order is made at the same time, then the expectation is that the court would ensure that the matter of the parental responsibility would be resolved first, so that the father is not left in a state of limbo.[1]

Relatives

10.115   Relatives may not apply to adopt unless the child's home has been with them for a period of not less than 3 years (whether continuous or not) during the 5 years ending with the application[2] or unless the court gives leave to make an application.[3] As has been seen, s 42 has substantially extended the former probationary residence requirement of 13 weeks in order to steer the court towards other options, in particular residence orders, rather than adoption. However, adoption may be appropriate where the parents are dead or where the relative has cared for the child for a number of years and the birth parents have faded from the scene. Relatives must, however, also give notice to the appropriate local authority of their intention to apply for an adoption order not more than 2 years, or less than 3 months, before applying for an order.[4] They must also meet the suitability qualification,[5] and must further satisfy the consent condition in s 47(2) before an adoption order can be made.

10.116   There has been a clear emphasis in favour of residence orders as the preferred alternative to adoption in the case of relatives since the 1992 Review of Adoption Law. The application of the 'least interventionist' principle should mean that residence orders continue to be the preferred option. However, it may be that relatives themselves see advantages in a special guardianship order. They are eligible to apply for a special guardianship order, only if the child has lived with them for at least 3 years, and they also have the consent of those having a residence order or those having parental responsibility for the child, or of the local authority where the child is in its care. They would be able to exercise parental responsibility to the exclusion of the birth parents, but nevertheless the link with the birth parents would remain, thus avoiding the problems of distorted relationships. One of the former objectives of 'custodianship', which was created by the Children Act 1975, was to provide carers such as grandparents with security without the Draconian effects of adoption. Arguably, special guardianship orders provide a similar form of security. Custodianship was, however, not a success and was abolished by the CA 1989. Practitioners will, therefore, have to wait and see as to whether and to what extent there is any 'take up' of special guardianship orders by relatives.

LOCAL AUTHORITY FOSTER CARERS AND ADOPTION

10.117   In relation to local authority foster parents, a distinction has to be drawn between an agency case and a non-agency case.

---

1   HL Deb, 16 October 2001, vol 639, no 188, col 934, per Baroness Andrews.
2   ACA 2002, s 42(5).
3   Ibid, s 42(6).
4   Ibid, s 44(3).
5   Ibid, s 45.

An agency case

10.118   Where the local authority decides to place a child with foster carers for adoption or to convert a foster placement to an adoptive placement, this is an 'agency' case. Local authority foster carers may seek formal approval from the local authority as prospective adopters for their foster children. Once they have been approved by the local authority, the children may be left with them as 'prospective adopters', but only under s 19 or a placement order. Where the child is placed for adoption with them under s 19 or a placement order, no one other than the local authority may remove the child.[1]

10.119   In an agency case, there is no need for local authority foster parents to give formal notice to the local authority under s 44. They will, however, have to satisfy the preliminary requirements, ie that the child has had his or her home with them at all times during the period of 10 weeks preceding the adoption application, and undergo investigation and reports on their suitability. Provided the parents or guardian do not oppose the making of the adoption order (for which they will require the court's leave), the foster carers, as prospective adopters with whom the child has been placed under s 19 or a placement order, will be able to meet the second placement condition in s 47(4) for the making of an adoption order.

A non-agency case

10.120   A 'non-agency' case is where the local authority has not placed the child with the foster carers 'for adoption' and, when they later seek approval, does not approve of them as prospective adopters. The foster carers may still give notice of their intention to apply to adopt as a non-agency case.

10.121   In such a case, the local authority foster carers have to comply with the preliminary requirements as to residence, notice and suitability. The child's home must have been with them for a continuous period of not less than one year unless the court gives leave to waive this requirement.[2] They must give notice of their intention to adopt to the local authority not more than 2 years, or less than 3 months, before the date on which the application is made under s 44. They will further have to satisfy the consent condition in s 47(2).

10.122   Where the local authority foster carers have given notice of their intention to adopt and the child has had his home with them for one year, the child may be removed only: (i) with the leave of the court; (ii) by a local authority; or (iii) by a person with parental responsibility, if the child is voluntarily accommodated under s 20 of the CA 1989.[3] This latter case does not apply, however, where the child has been in their foster care for 5 years or more and the foster parents have given notice of their intention to adopt or an application for leave to make an application is pending.[4] Once they have made an application for adoption, the child may be removed only: (i) with leave of the court or (ii) by the local authority in the exercise of its statutory powers.[5]

---

1   ACA 2002, ss 30 and 34.
2   Ibid, s 42(4) and (6).
3   Ibid, s 38.
4   Ibid, s 38(2).
5   Ibid, s 38(3).

BABY ADOPTIONS

10.123   Under s 18(1) of the ACA 2002, an adoption agency may place for adoption a child under 6 weeks old without needing either a formal consent under s 19 or a placement order. Sections 52(3) and 47(4) provide that any consent given by the mother to a placement under s 19 or to the making of an adoption order is ineffective for the purpose of making an adoption order if it is given less than 6 weeks after the child's birth. A mother, therefore, has 6 weeks to recover from the birth, to receive counselling and to make a proper, informed decision as to whether she wishes her child to be placed for adoption. The mother is not required to consent formally during that 6-week period, but she must formally re-affirm her consent after 6 weeks for there to be a valid basis for the making of an adoption order under s 47(4). Once the child has been placed for adoption under the Act, the child will remain (in law) placed for adoption unless something happens to change that situation, such as the agency or the parent seeking to withdraw the child from the placement.

10.124   What if the mother consents to a baby under 6 weeks old being placed, but then disappears entirely? This would mean that the agency would never be able to obtain formal consent under s 19. However, there would be nothing to stop the adoptive placement proceeding as an agency placement through to the making of the final adoption order. The difference would be that, rather than the final order being made under s 47(4) on the basis of a valid s 19 consent to placement, the adoption would have to be made under s 47(2) on the basis of the mother's consent being dispensed with under s 52(1).

10.125   Where a child under 6 weeks old has been placed for adoption but, after 6 weeks the agency does not have authorisation under s 19, the rules for removal in Part 1, Chapter 3 of the ACA 2002 still apply. Only the adoption agency may remove the child from the placement.[1] However, the mother can request the return of the child and the child must be returned to her within 7 days;[2] the only exception is where the local authority applies for a placement order and the application has not been disposed of.[3]

10.126   The provisions for placement contact orders in ss 26 and 27 cover baby placements which begin when the child is under 6 weeks old but continue after that point without a s 19 consent being obtained. This is in recognition of the importance of sibling contact, so as to ensure that siblings and other relatives who wish to apply for contact are able to make use of the contact provisions so that they are not shut out from the very early weeks of the child's life, especially if there were to be any gap period between the 6 weeks and the giving of the s 19 consent. This is obviously important to grandparents. The aim is to make clear that the benefits of the placement provisions in terms of the rights of return and contact apply in any gap between the 6-week period and formal consent being given under s 19.[4]

---

1   ACA 2002, s 30(1)(b).
2   Ibid, s 31(4) and (6).
3   Ibid, s 31(3)(a) and (4).
4   HL Deb, 30 October 2002, cols 211–212, per Baroness Andrews.

ORPHANS

10.127   Section 21(2)(c) ensures that that the court may make a placement order in respect of a child of any age, where the child has no parent. The conditions for making an adoption order under s 47 do not apply where the child has no parent.[1] In those cases, the court may make an order on application, provided that it is satisfied that it is in the child's best interests and consistent with the obligations placed on the court by s 1.[2]

MAGISTRATES' COURT APPEALS

10.128   Section 100 of the ACA 2002 aligns appeals from magistrates' courts in relation to placement and adoption proceedings with s 94 of the CA 1989. An appeal lies to the High Court.

---

1   ACA 2002, s 47(1) makes it clear that the conditions apply only if the child has a parent or guardian.
2   HL Deb, 14 October 2002, vol 639, no 186, col 668, per Baroness Andrews.

Chapter 11

CONTACT

PREAMBLE

11.1   The benefits to children of continuing contact with the natural family where their welfare requires a permanent placement outside the family were summarised by Simon Brown LJ in *Re E (A Minor) (Care Order: Contact)*:[1]

> '... even when the s 31 criteria are satisfied, contact may well be of singular importance to the long-term welfare of the child: first, in giving the child the security of knowing that his parents love him and are interested in his welfare; secondly, by avoiding any damaging sense of loss to the child in seeing himself abandoned by his parents; thirdly, by enabling the child to commit himself to the substitute family with the seal of approval of the natural parents; and fourthly, by giving the child the necessary sense of family and personal identity. Contact, if maintained, is capable of reinforcing and increasing the chances of success of a permanent placement, whether on a long-term fostering basis or by adoption.'

11.2   Section 34 of the CA 1989 begins with a provision that a local authority shall allow a child in care reasonable contact, with amongst others, his parents. There is, therefore, a presumption of contact, the onus being on the local authority to apply to the court for an order authorising it to refuse contact under s 34(4). As Sir Stephen Brown P highlighted in *Re E*:[2]

> 'The emphasis is heavily placed on the presumption of continuing parental contact.'

11.3   In striking contrast, in the context of adoption under the former law, a natural parent, as former parent, lost the right to apply *as of right* for a contact order under s 8 of the CA 1989 and had to obtain leave to apply for contact. Although the court had power to impose terms and conditions in an adoption order under s 12(6) of the AA 1976, the exercise of this power was such a rarity that, in *Re T (Adoption: Contact)*,[3] Butler-Sloss LJ (as she then was) commented that experience in the Family Division, including her own, had 'not thrown up any case where there had been an order imposed upon adopters with which they were not in agreement'. In *Re V (A Minor) (Adoption: Consent)*[4] Oliver LJ had put the adopters firmly 'in the driving seat'[5] with control over contact, when he said:

---

1   [1994] 1 FLR 146 at 154H–155B.
2   Ibid, at 151D–E; see also *Re B (Minors) (Care: Contact: Local Authority's Plans)* [1993] 1 FLR 543 at 551D.
3   [1995] 2 FLR 251 at 257E–F.
4   [1987] Fam 57, sub nom *Re V (A Minor: Dispensing with Agreement)* [1987] 2 FLR 89 at 107.
5   *Re T (Adoption: Contact)* [1995] 2 FLR 251 at 253D, where Butler-Sloss LJ (as she then was) asked the question whether 'adopters ... should in effect be in the driving seat'. This was a case where the adopters were willing to agree to contact, and it was held unnecessary to make an order binding them to their agreement.

'. . . any such condition, if it is not to be repugnant to the notion of adoption, must recognise that, in the ultimate analysis, the question of access or no access is for the adopters to decide in exercise of their parental rights.'

11.4   Lord Ackner, in *Re C (A Minor) (Adoption Order: Conditions)*,[1] in echoing earlier jurisprudence from the classic period of closed adoptions,[2] stressed that 'in normal circumstances, it is desirable that there should be a complete break'. He went on to say:

'. . . each case must be considered on its own particular facts. No doubt the court will not, *except in the most exceptional case*,[3] impose terms or conditions as to access to members of the child's natural family to which the adopting parents do not agree. To do so would be to create a potentially frictional situation which would be hardly likely to safeguard or promote the welfare of the child.'

11.5   An example of the adopters' ability to control the issue of contact was provided by *Re D (A Minor) (Adoption Order: Conditions)*,[4] where it was held that, except in exceptional circumstances, the court should not attach a condition to an adoption order requiring the sending of cards, when this was not a matter agreed by the adopters.

11.6   Once the adoption order was made, the jurisdictional hurdle for a member of the natural parent in seeking leave to apply for contact under s 10 of the CA 1989 in the face of opposition from the adopters, was set at Himalayan height. In *Re C (A Minor) (Adopted Child: Contact)*[5] the court stated that 'a fundamental question such as contact, even if confined to the indirect, should not be subsequently re-opened, unless there is some *fundamental change*[6] in circumstances'. In *Re S (Contact: Application by Sibling)*[7] the court said:

'. . . the applicant [from the natural family] must satisfy the court . . . that having regard to the relevant changes in circumstances the decision of the adopters is sufficiently contrary to the best interests of the child or sufficiently unreasonable to warrant the court overriding the discretion conferred on the adopters by the adoption order to determine whether what is proposed by the applicant for leave (eg as here contact with a sibling) should be permitted, by giving itself the jurisdiction and discretion to determine this in s 8 proceedings.'

11.7   In *Re S*, an adopted child aged 9 had applied for leave to have contact with her 7-year-old brother. The boy had cystic fibrosis and had been separately adopted by his former foster parent, who was opposed to him being told of his adopted status until he

---

1   [1989] AC 1 at 17, [1988] 2 FLR 159 at 168.
2   *Re DX (An Infant)* [1949] Ch 320; *Re G (DM) (An Infant)* [1962] 1 WLR 730, where Pennycuick J in considering 'the importance to an adopted infant of complete severance from its natural parents' said: 'I understand that adoption societies and local authorities regard such severance as a primary consideration, and I do not doubt that it is normally desirable that the adopted infant should be cut off from its natural mother, but there is no mandatory requirement of this nature in the Adoption Act 1958 . . .'; *Re B (MF) (An Infant)* [1972] 1 WLR 102 at 104, per Salmon LJ.
3   Emphasis added.
4   [1992] 1 FCR 461; see also *Re E (Adopted Child Contact: Leave)* [1995] 1 FLR 57, where the birth parents were promised by a social worker at a hearing (which the adoptive parents did not attend) that photographs would be forwarded. The adopters subsequently refused to supply a photograph and the birth parents applied for leave under s 10(9) which was refused 'as fundamentally inconsistent with the judicial framework for the care and upbringing of the child laid down in the (adoption proceedings)'.
5   [1993] Fam 210 at 216A, [1993] 2 FLR 431, at 436B, per Thorpe J (as he then was).
6   Emphasis added.
7   [1998] 2 FLR 897 at 912C–D.

was much older. His sister was deeply distressed by the lack of contact, and two child psychologists agreed that contact would be in the interests of both children. In rejecting the expert evidence, Charles J said:[1]

> '... the relevant adopters could not have had an adoption order on terms forced upon them and thus the discretion and freedom of action given to them by the adoption order to safeguard and promote the welfare for the child should be respected.'

11.8 There clearly will always remain those cases where confidentiality should be preserved and where contact with the natural family would be inappropriate as disruptive to the adoptive placement and damaging to the child, but the question which has exercised successive governments is whether, as most of the children adopted now are older with emotional ties to their natural family, there is a case for a radical rethinking of the closed model of adoption which has shaped the contours of our domestic legal landscape for so long.

11.9 As has been seen in Chapter 5, the issue of post-adoption contact has been under consideration for over 20 years and a significant subject of academic research. After a number of recommendations for reform were made in the 1992 Review of Adoption Law, which were designed to bring a greater openness at the different stages of the adoption process, the enthusiasm of the early 1990s for such openness began to wane, and, on searching through the new Act, the authors see little which points to any real change in thinking about post-adoption contact.

CONTACT UPON PLACEMENT UNDER THE ADOPTION AND CHILDREN ACT 2002

11.10 Section 26 of the ACA 2002 caters specifically for contact in the context of placement for adoption. Once an adoption agency is authorised to place a child for adoption, any provision for contact under the CA 1989, whether a s 8 order or a s 34 order, ceases to have effect.[2] No application can be made for contact under the CA 1989[3] until the final adoption hearing, when (as under the former law) a s 8 contact application can be heard together with the application for the adoption order, and the court can make a s 8 contact order.[4]

11.11 During the duration of the placement, an application for contact can be made only under s 26 of the ACA 2002. Section 26 confers on the court the power to make an order requiring the person with whom the child lives or is to live, to allow the child to visit or stay with the person named in the order or for the person named in the order, and the child otherwise to have contact.[5] In an echo of s 34(4) of the CA 1989, the court may authorise the agency to refuse to allow contact,[6] from which can arguably be inferred at least an expectation that the agency ought to allow reasonable contact. The word 'expectation' is used advisedly, as there is no equivalent to s 34(1) of the CA 1989, which

1   *Re S (Contact: Application by Sibling)* [1998] 2 FLR 897 at 912.
2   ACA 2002, s 26(1).
3   Ibid, s 26(2)(a).
4   Ibid, s 26(5).
5   Ibid, s 26(4)(a), (5) and (6).
6   Ibid, s 26(4)(b).

imposes a mandatory duty to allow the child in care reasonable contact with his or her parents[1] and, as the care order ceases to have effect while the placement order is in force,[2] the child can no longer be regarded as being in care for the purposes of s 34(1) of the CA 1989. This casts a long shadow over contact post-placement.

11.12   Scratching about amongst the other sections of the Act, provision is made that a child who is authorised to be placed for adoption by a local authority is to be treated as 'looked after by the authority' whether or not he or she is being placed for adoption.[3] It has been suggested[4] that this should trigger the general duty of the local authority under Sch 2, Part II, para 15 of the CA 1989 to promote contact. There is, however, no express cross-referencing to this duty in the ACA 2002, and s 53 throws doubt upon whether para 15 of Sch 2 to the CA 1989 will apply at all in relation to the child. Furthermore, in highlighting the contrast between a s 8 contact order[5] and a s 26 contact order in relation to relatives, the Government has said:[6]

> '... a child placed for adoption is under a totally different situation. The end objective is separation from his or her family. The child is not in a normal family situation. He is under the supervision of the adoption agency, which will oversee any kind of contact. There is no presumption of contact with those persons.'

11.13   Indeed, the absence of a presumption is given as the reason why there is no leave requirement for relatives seeking a s 26 contact order:[7]

> 'There is already a filter for contact in adoption placements because the adoption agency looks after the child's interests. But we still want to allow for relatives to apply to the courts for contact if they are unable to secure it through the agency. That is why we have allowed them to apply for section 26 contact orders and why there is no leave requirement in that situation.'

POST-ADOPTION CONTACT

11.14   Given the changing face of adoption from ready-packaged babies to difficult older children with memories of the birth family, post-adoption contact presents one of the most challenging and pressing issues in this area of law. It is the one issue which urgently needed addressing in the new legislation, which is probably the last chance of reform for another quarter of a century. Notwithstanding its obvious importance, disappointingly there was minimal mention of post-adoption contact in the White Paper, *Adoption: A New Approach*.[8] Thus, on notice that the 'new approach' was not going to embrace wholeheartedly post-adoption contact, it came as little surprise to find contact tucked away in s 46(6) as an afterthought[9] or to find that the former provision

---

1   Hence the need for s 34(4) of the CA 1989.
2   ACA 2002, s 29(1).
3   Ibid, s 18(3).
4   By S Harris-Short in 'The Adoption and Children Bill – a fast track to failure?' [2001] CFLQ 405.
5   Where leave is still required as a 'screening process': HL Deb, 30 October 2002, vol 640, no 196, col 219, per Lord Hunt of Kings Heath.
6   Ibid.
7   Ibid.
8   Cm 5017 (December 2000), paras 6.42 and 6.43.
9   It was only in the latter stages of the progress of the Bill that this express duty on the court emerged.

for an adoption order to contain terms and conditions had been deleted (no doubt as a recognition of how toothless s 12(6) of the AA 1976 really was).

11.15 Under s 46(6) the court is under a duty, before making an adoption order, to consider whether there should be arrangements for allowing any person contact with the child. For this purpose it must consider any existing or proposed arrangements and obtain any views of the parties to the proceedings. Section 26(5) expressly preserves the parents' right to apply for a s 8 contact order where the application is to be heard together with the application for an adoption order. The signpost is clear. The position under the former legislative framework is to be replicated and there is to be no change in direction.

11.16 Consideration of contact at this critical stage of the final adoption hearing, therefore, becomes particularly important for the following reasons. The making of an adoption order, which results in the most complete severance of family ties, is a *prima facie* interference with the child's and the parents' right to respect for family life. It requires scrupulous justification under Art 8(2) of the European Convention on Human Rights.[1] This is especially so because, once an adoption order has been made, the parent loses the right to apply as 'a parent or guardian' for a s 8 order under the CA 1989. Although he or she can apply for leave under s 10(1)(a)(ii) and (9) of the CA 1989, as has been seen, the jurisprudence[2] in respect of 'leave' under s 10 of the CA 1989 sets a formidable jurisdictional threshold for the parent to cross where the adopters oppose contact.

11.17 One of the vital questions which arises is which of the two checklists, 'the CA 1989 welfare checklist' under s 1(3) of the CA 1989 or 'the adoption welfare checklist' under s 1(4) of the ACA 2002, the court should apply when considering the issue of contact at the final adoption hearing. The checklist under s 1(4) of the ACA 2002, although using similar material to that of the CA 1989, has been tailored to fit adoption. It has been specially shaped so as to incorporate s 1(4)(c) and (f), which recognise such factors as the importance of the child's membership of his or her original family, his or her relationship with his or her parents, the value of such relationship continuing and the wishes and feelings of the child's relatives, including his or her siblings. These are all factors which are highly relevant to the consideration of contact at the final adoption hearing. Surely then the court, when enjoined to consider whether there should be arrangements for allowing contact with the child under s 46(6) of the ACA 2002, should apply the adoption welfare checklist? However, the jurisdiction for the parents' contact application and the court's contact order comes from s 8 of the CA 1989 and, therefore, logic would point to the CA 1989 welfare checklist as being the one to apply, notwithstanding that its shape is not adjusted to adoption. If this is the case, then perhaps one way out of the conundrum is to recall that neither checklist is exhaustive and the courts can (and, it is suggested, should) have regard to the factors in s 1(4)(c) and (f) in the adoption welfare checklist, even where they are, in strict logic, applying the CA 1989 checklist.

1   *Johansen v Norway* (1996) 23 EHRR 33.

2   *Re T and E (Proceedings: Conflicting Interests)* [1995] 1 FLR 581; *Re F (Contact: Child in Care)* [1995] 1 FLR 510; *Birmingham City Council v H (No 3)* [1994] 2 AC 124, [1994] 1 FLR 224; *Re C (A Minor) (Adoption Order: Conditions)* [1989] AC 1, [1988] 1 All ER 705, HL; *Re T (Adopted Children: Contact)* [1995] 2 FLR 792; *Re T (Adoption: Contact)* [1995] 2 FLR 251; and *Re S (Contact Application by Sibling)* [1998] 2 FLR 897.

11.18   The ACA 2002 does appear to be giving out the signal that the traditional approach of the clean break under the controlling hands of the adoptive parents is intended to stay. If so, the suspicion is that the Government's 'target' approach to adoption (ie of achieving a 40 per cent increase in the number of children adopted out of care) may have weakened any earlier resolve to change the climate of the closed adoption to a more open approach in the interests of the older child. As Sonia Harris-Short put it:[1]

> 'A fundamental change in the legal nature of adoption to enshrine an open process in which both the adoptive parents and birth family have a continuing role to play in the life of the child, may well undermine the wish of some adopters to raise the child as "their own" and to do so free from the complications and pressures of having to accommodate the demands of the second [birth] family. It may well, therefore, be the case that if a reformed legal framework was to challenge the prevailing "mindset" and force greater openness on unwilling adoptive parents, it would further decrease the number of parents willing to offer homes …'

11.19   On the other hand, the absence of a robust policy on post-adoption contact may simply reflect a perception that the current research is not sufficiently clear-cut as to the significance and long-term value of post-adoption contact for the adopted person as child, adolescent and adult. If this is the case, then it is a 'misperception', as there is nothing in the current research data which suggests that the concept of openness is so treacherous a road as to justify not even starting out on the journey at all. On the contrary, as has been seen, there is academic data to suggest that, in the appropriate case, post-adoption contact may be of real and lasting value. Whatever the reason, the ACA 2002 does not give any new lead on post-adoption contact.

11.20   Do the s 1 principles in the ACA 2002 give sufficient impetus to the court, in an appropriate case, to take the controls from the prospective adopters as to whether contact should take place and change the traditional direction of adoption by imposing a contact order upon them? The prospects, in the absence of any other support or encouragement in the Act, of bringing about such a radical change of judicial thinking do not, at first blush, look promising and it may well be that the law will remain as outlined in the preamble to this Chapter. There is, nevertheless, some scope for judicial creativity, as the ACA 2002 is only one part of the jigsaw. Article 8 of the European Convention on Human Rights is the other piece, which has to be fitted in to make the picture whole. The court must also ensure that the cutting off of all contact and relationships between the child and his natural family is a proportionate response and justified by the overriding necessity of the interests of the child. If it is not, and continuing contact would be in the best interests of the child, then irrespective of the prospective adopters' unwillingness, the court, under its duty to act compatibly with Art 8 of the European Convention on Human Rights, ought to override any discretion given to the adopters under the adoption order.

11.21   Given the importance of post-adoption contact and the Act's reticence in addressing this major issue, it becomes even more essential for the judiciary to explore and deal with the issue fully in every case. The Lowe and Murch study has suggested[2] that in relation to direct contact many local authorities still do not work with an expectation in favour of contact. One of the critical factors in successful post-adoption contact is the positive attitude of the prospective adopters to continuing contact with the natural

---

1   'The Adoption and Children Bill – A Fast Track to Failure?' [2001] CFLQ 405 at 420–421.
2   N Lowe and M Murch et al *Supporting Adoption – Reforming the Approach* (BAAF, 1999) at p 295.

family. A strong judicial lead would send to local authorities the message that they must be in the forefront of encouraging a positive attitude in their prospective adopters, so as to start the process of climate change from closed to open adoptions. It is only by these subtle shifts in direction that the law and practice may finally begin to catch up with the social changes in adoption which have taken place over the last 25 years.

11.22 An order gives arrangements for contact, even where consensual, much greater force than a voluntary agreement. As such, it avoids the risk of the adopters, who may have held out promises of contact to the birth family in their anxiety to obtain consent to the adoption, subsequently drawing back and refusing contact (a common practice under the former law[1] which, given the discretion allowed to adopters under the adoption order, had the sanction of the court). It is to be hoped in the future that if the best interests of the child show that contact, albeit limited to once or twice a year, reassures the child about the well-being of his or her birth family members, or promotes a more realistic perception of the birth family so as to enhance his or her sense of identity, then under s 1 of the ACA 2002 these interests will prevail over the adopters' discretion under the adoption order.

---

1   N Lowe and M Murch, op cit, at pp 314–316, and J Fratter *Adoption with Contact* (BAAF, 1996), at
     p 240.

Chapter 12

ACCESS TO INFORMATION AND CONFIDENTIALITY

PREAMBLE

12.1   As has been seen in Chapter 1, the notion of secrecy lies at the root of domestic adoption. Since the adoption jurisdiction was created in 1926, the Adoption Rules, empowered by successive Adoption Acts, have recognised the essentially confidential nature of proceedings for adoption. For example, the process of confidentiality has been reinforced by the practice which enables proposed adopters to apply for a serial number so as to preclude natural parents from ascertaining the identity of the adopters.[1] This emphasis upon maintaining the anonymity of the adopters led to the cloak of secrecy, preventing the child from having information about or contact with his or her birth family.

12.2   It was not until 1975 that the guarantee of complete confidentiality given to birth parents was removed and, in the AA 1976, an adoptive person over the age of 18 could apply to obtain his or her original birth certificate.[2] He or she could also apply to the court for the name of the agency which arranged the placement and the local authority which supervised it.[3] Under the AA 1976, however, adopted children under 18 years of age had no right of access to birth records unless intending to marry.[4] Only in 'truly' exceptional circumstances was confidential information held by the Registrar General given to the natural parents.[5]

12.3   Other than these tiny cracks, the shutters on access to information remained tightly shut until the CA 1989 created an Adoption Contact Register.[6] The Adoption Contact Register went some way to relaxing the strictures on disclosure by assisting adopted persons who wished to trace and have contact with their birth families.

12.4   These developments reflected the growing openness in adoption practice and the recognition that there was a deep-seated need felt by many adopted persons to know about their origins. It was in this spirit that the practice of the 'life story work' for the

1   Adoption Rules 1984, r 14; also r 23(3).
2   AA 1976, s 51(1). The Registrar General could refuse to allow access to the birth records on grounds of public policy: *R v Registrar General ex parte Smith* [1990] 2 QB 253, [1990] 2 FLR 79: see **12.8**.
3   AA 1976, s 50(5); Adoption Rules 1984, r 53(3)(b)(ii).
4   AA 1976, s 51(2).
5   *D v Registrar General* [1997] 1 FLR 715 at 722G–H, per Sir Stephen Brown P.
6   AA 1976, s 51A, as inserted by Sch 10, para 21 to the CA 1989; also *The Children Act 1989 Guidance and Regulations, vol 9, Adoption* (HMSO, 1991) at ch 3. Now under ss 80–81 of the ACA 2002 (see **12.26–12.30**).

adopted child began, where it was seen to be very beneficial for the child for there to be a body of information about the birth family. In *Gunn-Russo v Nugent Care Society and Secretary of State for Health*[1] Scott-Baker J said:

> 'The balance has continued to shift towards greater freedom of information to adopted people. It is now recognised that many adopted people wish to have information about their history and background including the reasons for their adoption. Many find it important to have a complete personal history in order to develop a positive sense of identity.
>
> The issue will often be how to resolve the tension between on the one hand maintaining the confidentiality under which the information was supplied and on the other providing the information that the adopted person has a real desire, and often need, to have.'

THE REGISTERS

The Adopted Children Register

The former law

12.5   Under the former law, the Registrar General held birth records and basic information about the adoption, such as the child's adoptive name and the names of the adoptive parents. Under the AA 1976, the Registrar General was under a duty to establish and maintain an Adopted Children Register[2] and cause an index to be made.[3] On adoption, the child's birth certificate was replaced with a certified copy of the entry in the Adopted Children Register, which contained a record of the date and place of birth.[4] Every person was entitled to search the index and to have a certified copy of the entry in the Adopted Children Register.[5]

12.6   In *Re X (A Minor) (Adoption Details: Disclosure)*[6] a local authority applied for an order to restrict the information which was to be placed in the index of the Adopted Children Register and the adoption certificate, since there was a real risk that the natural mother, who suffered from a personality disorder, might seek to trace the child and disrupt the adoptive placement. The Court of Appeal held that it was beyond the powers of the court to edit the entry in the register, but that the High Court could exercise its inherent jurisdiction to make an order restricting disclosure of the details on the register.[7]

---

1   [2001] EWHC Admin 566, [2002] 1 FLR 1 at [47]–[48].
2   AA 1976, s 50(1), Sch 1, para 1(1); Adoption Rules 1984, r 52(1).
3   AA 1976, s 50(3).
4   Ibid, Sch 1, para 1, and s 50(2).
5   Ibid.
6   [1994] Fam 174, [1994] 2 FLR 450.
7   An example in practice was provided by *Re W (Adoption Details: Disclosure)* [1998] 2 FLR 625: an aggrieved foster mother who had unsuccessfully applied to adopt a child (who had been placed outside the natural family from birth due to the mother's mental instability) gave the maternal grandparents the telephone number of the adoptive mother. This enabled them to find her name and address and the grandfather to go and sit outside her address. The result was that the adoptive mother moved house, involving a change of job and school for her daughter. Wall J, under his inherent jurisdiction, directed that the information on the Adopted Children Register should not be disclosed to a third party without leave of the court: [1998] 2 FLR 625. See also the *President's Direction (Adopted Children Register: Restriction on Disclosure)* (17 December 1998) [1999] 1 FLR 315.

12.7   Any entries in other registers or books which recorded or made traceable the connection between an entry in the Register of Births marked 'Adoption' and a corresponding entry in the Adopted Children Register were not open to public search, unless ordered by the court.[1] In *D v Registrar-General*[2] the Court of Appeal stated that the court, in the exercise of its discretion, should order disclosure under s 50(5) of the AA 1976 only in truly exceptional circumstances and that something requiring an exceptional need to know the information sought should be established.[3]

12.8   The Registrar General was also under a mandatory duty to provide an adopted person, who had attained the age of 18, on request, with any information that was necessary to enable him or her to obtain a certified copy of his or her birth certificate.[4] Thus the adopted adult had the right, provided by s 51 of the AA 1976, to obtain information direct from the Registrar General that enabled him or her to access a copy of his or her birth certificate, which identified the birth parents and their address at the time of the birth. The only exception to this was when the Registrar General decided to withhold information on public policy grounds, which could only be challenged by recourse to the High Court. In *R v Registrar General, ex parte Smith*[5] the applicant, who had been adopted as a baby and was serving a life sentence for murder, was further convicted of the manslaughter of a fellow prisoner in the mistaken belief that she was his adoptive mother. He applied under s 51 of the AA 1976 for such information as was necessary to obtain access to his birth records. The Registrar General obtained medical reports which indicated that the applicant's natural mother might be at risk if her identity were disclosed and decided on policy grounds not to disclose the information. The Divisional Court dismissed the application for judicial review and the appeal was refused. The Court of Appeal held that an absolute statutory duty would not be enforced on the grounds of public policy, where, on the evidence, there was a significant risk that to enforce the duty would be to facilitate crime resulting in danger to life. Cases such as the *Smith* case, although small in number, highlighted the need for a reconsideration of the law on access to information.

Under the Adoption and Children Act 2002

12.9   The ACA 2002 continues to place a duty upon the Registrar General to continue to maintain the Adopted Children Register.[6] The Adopted Children Register itself is not open to public inspection or search.[7] Every adoption order must contain a direction to the Registrar General to make an entry in the register in the prescribed form.[8] No entries may be made in the Adopted Children Register other than entries directed to be made in

---

1   AA 1976, s 50(5): either in accordance with s 51 of the AA 1976 or by order of the court by which the adoption order was made. See *Re H (Adoption: Disclosure of Information)* [1995] 1 FLR 236.
2   [1997] 1 FLR 715.
3   Ibid, at 722E and 723A, per Sir Stephen Brown P.
4   AA 1976, s 51(1); the application had to be in the form prescribed by the Adopted Persons (Birth Records) Regulations 1991, SI 1991/1981.
5   [1990] 2 QB 253, [1991] 1 FLR 255.
6   ACA 2002, s 77(1).
7   Ibid, s 77(2).
8   Ibid, Sch 1, para 1(1); Sch 1, para 2 deals with the registration of adoption in Scotland, the Isle of Man and the Channel Islands.

it by adoption orders or those required to be made under Sch 1.[1] 'Records' includes certified copies kept by the Registrar General of entries in any register of births and 'registers of live-births' means the registers of live births under the Births and Deaths Registration Act 1953.[2] The system works as follows.

(1) Provision is made for the marking of the register of live births with the word 'Adopted'[3] and, where an adoption order is made in respect of a child who was previously the subject of an adoption order, the previous entry must be marked 'Re-adopted'.[4]

(2) The prescribed officer of the court which made the order must communicate the order to the Registrar General, who must then comply with the directions as to marking.[5]

(3) Provision is also made for the entry to be made in respect of a child adopted under a 'registrable foreign adoption',[6] which means an adoption which satisfies the prescribed requirements and is either an adoption under a Convention adoption or an adoption under an overseas adoption.[7]

(4) Errors in the particulars contained in the adoption order can be corrected by amending the order, on the application of either the adopter or the adopted person,[8] including the substitution or addition of a name, within 12 months from the beginning of the order.[9]

(5) Provision is also made for rectification of the entries and markings in the Adopted Children Register and the register of live births[10] and for re-registration of birth and cancellation in the registers on legitimation.[11]

12.10   A certified copy of an entry on the register is evidence of the adoption to which it relates[12] and where the birth information is contained in the Adopted Children Register, a certified copy of that entry is to be treated as a certified copy of an entry in the register of live births.[13]

12.11   The Registrar General is under a duty to maintain an index[14] of the Adopted Children Register at the General Register Office and any person may search the index of

---

1   ACA 2002, s 77(3).
2   Ibid, s 82(1). Any register, record or index maintained under Chapter 5 of the ACA 2002 may be maintained in any form the Registrar General considers appropriate; and any references to entries in such a register or to their amendment, marking or cancellation are to be read accordingly: s 82(2).
3   ACA 2002, Sch 1, para 1(2).
4   Ibid, Sch 1, para 1(3).
5   Ibid, Sch 1, para 1(4).
6   Ibid, Sch 1, para 3(1) and (2).
7   Ibid, Sch 1, para 3(5).
8   Ibid, Sch 1, para 4(1).
9   Ibid, Sch 1, para 4(2).
10   Ibid, Sch 1, para 4(3)–(10).
11   Ibid, Sch 1, paras 5 and 6.
12   Ibid, s 77(4), if purporting to be sealed or stamped with the seal of the Registrar General, it is to be received as evidence of the adoption without further or other proof.
13   Ibid, s 77(5).
14   Ibid, s 78(1).

the register and have a certified copy of any entry in the Adopted Children Register.[1] However, a person is not entitled to have a certified copy of an entry in the Adopted Children Register relating to an adopted person who has not attained the age of 18 years unless the applicant has provided the Registrar General with the prescribed particulars.[2]

12.12 Under the ACA 2002, the Registrar General must make traceable the connection between any entry in the registers of live births or other records which has been marked 'Adopted' and any corresponding entry in the Adopted Children Register.[3] The information kept by the Registrar General is not to be open to public inspection or search. This information ('the connecting information') and any other information which would enable an adopted person to obtain a certified copy of the record of birth ('the birth record information') may only be disclosed by the Registrar General in accordance with s 79.

12.13 Disclosure by the Registrar General under s 79 is dealt with by reference to three separate sets of circumstances.

(1) First, under s 79(4), where the adoptee was adopted before 'the appointed day' (the day appointed for the commencement of ss 56–65: here referred to as 'commencement') the court may, in exceptional circumstances, order the Registrar General to give the connecting information or birth record information to the adoptee.

(2) Secondly, under s 79(5), on an application by the appropriate adoption agency, a duty is imposed upon the Registrar General to give to that agency the 'connecting/birth record' information. An 'appropriate adoption agency' for these purposes means (i) the placing adoption agency, or (ii) (if different) the agency keeping the information in relation to the adoption, or (iii) (in any other case) the local authority to which notice of intention to adopt was given.[4]

(3) Thirdly, under s 79(7), on an application by an adopted person a record of whose birth is kept by the Registrar General and who is under the age of 18 years and intends to marry, the Registrar General is under an obligation to inform the applicant whether or not it appears from the information contained in the registers of live births or other records that the applicant and the person whom the applicant intends to marry may be within the prohibited degrees of relationship for the purposes of the Marriage Act 1949.

12.14 The Registrar General may through regulations be required to disclose to any person (including an adopted person) at his or her request any information which the person requires to assist him or her to make contact with the adoption agency which is the appropriate agency in the adoptee's case;[5] or disclose to the appropriate adoption agency any information which the agency requires about any entry relating to the adopted person on the Adoption Contact Register.[6]

---

1   ACA 2002, s 78(2); s 78(4) provides that the terms, conditions and regulations as to payment of fees and otherwise applicable under the Births and Deaths Registration Act 1953 and the Registration of Services Act 1953 are to apply in respect of searches and supplies of certified copies.
2   Ibid, s 78(3).
3   Ibid, s 79(1).
4   Ibid, s 65(1).
5   Ibid, s 64(4)(a).
6   Ibid, s 64(4)(b).

The role of s 79

12.15 Thus, s 79 performs a twofold role. First, it governs the disclosure of the 'connecting information'.[1] Secondly, s 79 has a part to play, together with s 60, in relation to the provision of information which would enable an adult adoptee to obtain a certified copy of his or her record of birth.[2] Its role, however, is complicated by the fact that the section draws a distinction between those persons who were adopted before, and those who were adopted after, commencement.[3]

A PERSON ADOPTED BEFORE COMMENCEMENT

'Connecting/birth record' information

12.16 In order to obtain the 'connecting/birth record' information, the adopted adult has to apply to the court and satisfy the 'exceptional circumstances' test. This test gives statutory force to the safeguards which had been previously put in place under the former law. The adopted adult, however, retains the right of direct access to the court and to receive the 'connecting/birth record' information from the Registrar General without the intermediary of an adoption agency.

The birth certificate

12.17 For the pre-commencement adoptee, the disclosure of the information necessary to obtain a certified birth certificate is governed by Sch 2 to the ACA 2002.[4] The Registrar General remains under a mandatory duty to disclose this information to the adult adoptee,[5] provided he or she applies in the manner specified in Sch 2 and subject to certain conditions such as the payment of a fee. Thus, Sch 2 retains *the right* for the adult adoptee[6] to obtain directly a certified copy of the record of his or her birth.[7] Schedule 2 provides as follows.

(1) Before the Registrar General gives any information to an applicant, he or she must inform the applicant that counselling services are available and where they may be obtained.[8]

(2) If the applicant chooses to receive counselling, the Registrar General must send to the person or body providing the counselling the information to which the applicant is entitled.[9]

---

1   ACA 2002, s 79(3). Before any information is provided, a fee must be paid: s 79(8).
2   Ibid, ss 79(3) and 59.
3   Ibid, s 79(9).
4   Ibid, s 79(6).
5   Ibid, Sch 2, para 1.
6   Who has attained the age of 18 and a record of whose birth is kept by the Registrar General: Sch 2, para 1(a) and (b).
7   ACA 2002, Sch 2, para 1.
8   Ibid, Sch 2, para 2.
9   Ibid, Sch 2, para 2; counselling is available at the General Register Office or from a local authority in England, a council constituted under s 2 of the Local Government etc (Scotland) Act 1994 in Scotland, a Board in Northern Ireland, a registered adoption society or an adoption society which is approved under s 3 of the Adoption (Scotland) Act 1978 or registered under Art 4 of the Adoption (Northern Ireland) Order 1987 or a registered support agency. The persons or bodies listed are obliged to provide counselling if asked by the adopted person.

(3)   Where a person applies for information under Sch 2 and was adopted before 12 November 1975, the Registrar General must not give the information to the applicant unless the applicant has attended an interview with a counsellor arranged by a person or body from whom counselling services are available.[1]

(4)   Where the Registrar General is prevented in cases where the person was adopted before 12 November 1975 from giving information to a person who is not living in the United Kingdom, he may give information to any body which he is satisfied is suitable to provide counselling to that person and which has notified the Registrar General that it is prepared to provide such counselling.[2]

A PERSON ADOPTED AFTER COMMENCEMENT

Connecting information

12.18   In the case of the 'post-commencement' adult adoptee, there is no direct route to access the 'connecting' information from the Registrar General. Such an applicant must go through the intermediary of the adoption agency.

The birth certificate

12.19   Although under s 60(2)(a) of the ACA 2002 the adopted adult retains 'a right', at his request, to receive the information which would enable him or her to obtain a certified copy of his birth certificate, again he or she may only do so through the intermediary of the appropriate adoption agency.[3] On the requisite application by the appropriate adoption agency, the Registrar General must (under s 79(5)) give the agency the 'connecting/ birth record' information. It is implicit in s 60(2)(a) that the adoption agency must then pass on the information to the adopted adult. Adoption agencies will be required to obtain information held on the adoptee's birth record from the Registrar General, if they receive a request from the adopted person for the information.[4]

12.20   However, the adopted adult's right to obtain a certified copy of his or her record of birth in s 60(2)(a) is subject to the words 'unless the High Court orders otherwise'. Through this proviso and s 60(3), the High Court is empowered, on the application of the appropriate agency, to make an order denying the adoptee the birth record information where it is satisfied that the circumstances are exceptional. Thus, an adoption agency which wishes to withhold the information which an adopted adult needs to obtain a copy of his or her birth certificate must now apply to the High Court for an order blocking his or her access to the information. Such an order will only be granted where the court is satisfied that the circumstances are exceptional.

12.21   Clearly, the 'post-commencement' adoptee's 'right' to obtain a birth certificate has ceased to have the simplicity of the former right under s 51 of the AA 1976. It is perhaps worthy of note that in the Adoption and Children Bill (Bill 34), as originally drafted, the right had been deleted altogether and replaced by a discretion vested in the adoption agency as to whether to provide the necessary information. Although its revival

---

1   ACA 2002, Sch 2, para 4(1).
2   Ibid, Sch 2, para 4(2).
3   Ibid.
4   Ibid, s 64(3)(b), through regulations which will require adoption agencies to seek prescribed information from or give prescribed information to the Registrar General.

is welcome, in its 'resuscitated' form it has perhaps lost the directness found in s 51 of the AA 1976, whose spirit lingers on in Sch 2 for the 'pre-commencement' adoptee. This is a surprising development as it runs counter to the more relaxed approach to access to information over the last quarter of a century, especially as s 51 of the AA 1976 appeared to have worked well in the vast majority of cases.[1] The thinking behind this approach is dealt with below.

Adoption support agencies

12.22   One of the areas which the ACA 2002 has sought to address is the 'forgotten' generation – those who were adopted and those parents who agreed to their children being adopted before the reforms in 1975. As has been seen in Chapter 5, in many cases mothers were forced to give up their children because of social stigma. This Act represented the last chance for those people in their twilight years to establish contact with their sons and daughters who were given away for adoption, often reluctantly, or for siblings to make contact with a brother or sister lost in the adoption process. Initially, the Government took the view that to make access to information retrospective would cause massive problems. There was potential for a huge volume of applications (875,000 people have been adopted since 1926) and many of those who were adopted years ago would now be very difficult to trace due to sparse record-keeping, particularly in the case of private adoptions.

> 'Our principal policy aim is to help vulnerable and, in some cases, damaged children who need adoptive parents now. If proposals [as to retrospection] were enacted, [there would be] concern about the priorities of adoption agencies being shifted and the possibility that that might draw resources away from our primary aim.'[2]

12.23   In the event, however, the decision was taken that 'on balance, adoption support agencies should be able to get access to information on past adoptions, provided that there are robust safeguards to ensure that the information is protected and is disclosed only if the informed consent of the adopted adult is forthcoming'.[3] It was recognised that if records have been lost or if the adoption was a private one in which no adoption agency was involved, the only probable source of identifying information is the sensitive information contained in the Adopted Children Register maintained by the Registrar General since the Adoption of Children Act 1926.

12.24   Section 98, therefore, makes express provision for regulations to be made under s 9 for the purpose of assisting adults adopted before the appointed day[4] to obtain information in relation to their adoption and facilitating contact between them and their

---

1   HC Special Standing Committee, Second Sitting, 20 November 2001, col 9, para 67: 'Of a sample of birth parents who were contacted by their adopted adult children, no less than 94% were either positive or very positive. Although about 20% of birth parents initially expressed some concerns and nervousness . . . the overwhelming view is that there is something which has been with them probably throughout their lives. The feelings around relinquishing your child through contested court hearings are so fundamental that such parents often harbour a wish to be discovered at some point'.

2   HC Deb, 16 May 2002, vol 385, no 149, cols 1018–1019, per Ms Jacqui Smith, Minister of Health.

3   HL Deb, 16 October 2002, vol 639, no 188, col 945, per Lord McIntosh of Haringey.

4   ACA 2002, s 98(7): 'the day appointed for the commencement of sections 56 to 65'.

relatives.[1] The regulations will confer functions[2] on: (a) registered adoption support agencies[3] (ASAs); (b) the Registrar General; and (c) adoption agencies for the purpose of authorising or requiring them to disclose information.[4] Disclosure will also include information contained in records kept under s 8 of the Public Records Act 1958 (court records).[5] The disclosure of the information will be subject to conditions including restrictions on its further disclosure.[6]

12.25   The intention, therefore, is to use regulations to establish a scheme that provides for registered ASAs to operate an intermediary service for contact between adopted adults and their adult birth relatives. On receiving an application from the birth relatives, the ASA would establish the identity of the adopted person, seek to trace him or her and, if he or she consents, disclose his or her identity to the birth relative and facilitate contact between them. An adopted adult will be able to ask an ASA to provide the same service if he or she wants contact with a birth relative. This provision would apply only in cases of adults adopted before the appointed day.[7] There will be three key elements. First, an ASA will be able to approach an adoption agency or the Registrar General on behalf of the applicant who wishes to have contact with the subject of the application. Secondly, an adoption agency and the Registrar General will have a duty to provide information to the ASA, which may be used to trace the subject and to provide counselling to him or her and inform his or her consent decision. Thirdly, the ASA will be prohibited from disclosing to the applicant any information about the subject of an application without the informed consent of the subject.[8]

The Adoption Contact Register

12.26   The Registrar General remains under a duty to continue to maintain the Adoption Contact Register at the General Register Office.[9] As was the case under the former law,[10] the Adoption Register is in two Parts, designed to facilitate contact between adopted persons and their birth relatives where both parties have expressed a wish for such contact.

12.27   Part 1 is to contain the prescribed information[11] relating to the adopted person who has given the requisite notice expressing a wish to make contact with his or her

---

1   'Relatives' in relation to an adopted person means 'any person who (but for his adoption) would be related to him by blood (including half blood) or marriage'.
2   ACA 2002, s 98(2).
3   'Registered adoption support agency' means an ASA in respect of which a person is registered under Part 2 of the Care Standards Act 2000: s 98(7). The effect of s 8(1)(a) is that if an undertaking provides information for the purpose of s 98, it will need to be a registered adoption support agency. Registration is intended to provide a safeguard and to ensure that intermediary services are provided to an appropriately high standard by staff with the necessary training and expertise: HL Deb, 30 October 2002, vol 640, no 196, col 203, per Lord McIntosh of Haringey.
4   ACA 2002, s 98(3)(a).
5   Ibid, s 98(3)(b).
6   Ibid, s 98(3). Fees may be charged for the disclosure: s 98(4).
7   HL Deb, 16 October 2002, vol 639, no 188, col 946, per Lord McIntosh of Haringey.
8   Ibid. The intention is to set out the details in the regulations after consultation with the adoption stakeholders. The consultation period will probably last into 2004.
9   ACA 2002, s 80(1).
10   AA 1976, s 51A, which was inserted by the CA 1989.
11   Which will include names and addresses.

relatives.[1] There are three pre-requisites for an entry in Part 1.[2] First, a record of the adopted person's birth must be kept by the Registrar General. Secondly, the adopted person must have attained the age of 18 years. Thirdly, the Registrar General has to be satisfied that the adopted person has such information as is necessary to enable him or her to obtain a certified copy of his or her birth.

12.28   Part 2 is to contain the prescribed information[3] relating to the persons who have given the requisite notice expressing their wishes, as relatives of the adopted persons, to make contact with the adoptee. There are two pre-requisites to an entry in Part 2. First, the person must have attained the age of 18 years. Secondly, the Registrar General has to be satisfied that the person is a relative of the adopted person and has such information as is necessary to enable him or her to obtain a certified copy of the record of the adoptee's birth. 'Relative' means 'any person who (but for his adoption) would be related to him by blood (including half-blood) or marriage' (ie parents, siblings, grandparents, great-grandparents, uncles, aunts, cousins, nephews, nieces and relatives by marriage).[4]

12.29   Regulations will provide for the disclosure of information in one Part of the Register to persons included in the other Part of the register. For example, the regulations are likely to provide that information held on the register should only be given to adoptees in order to enable them to make a choice as to whether to initiate contact with their relatives.[5]

12.30   The Adoption Contact Register is not to be open to public inspection or search[6] and the Registrar General must not give any information entered on the register to any person unless in accordance with the regulations made by virtue of s 80(6) or by virtue of s 64(4)(b).[7]

DISCLOSURE OF INFORMATION ABOUT A PERSON'S ADOPTION

12.31   Under the former law, information about adopted persons and those involved in the adoption process was held by three sources: (i) the adoption agency (which held case details and other information); (ii) the Registrar General (who held birth records and basic information about the adoption, such as the adoptive name and the names of the adoptive parents); and (iii) the court (which held reports submitted to it and the records of the adoption proceedings).

12.32   The nature of the information provided by a birth parent and prospective adopter to an adoption agency is by its nature confidential, having been given in circumstances importing an obligation of confidence. 'There is a public interest in

---

1   ACA 2002, s 80(2).
2   Ibid, s 80(3).
3   Which will include names and addresses.
4   ACA 2002, s 81(2).
5   Ibid, s 79(6). Subsection (6) also makes provision for regulations as to the payment of fees for the making or alteration of entries in the register and the disclosure of information.
6   Ibid, s 81(1).
7   Ibid, s 81(3). Section 64(4)(b) provides that regulations may require the Registrar General to disclose to the appropriate adoption agency any information which the agency requires about any entry relating to the adopted person on the Adoption Contact Register.

maintaining confidentiality that goes beyond the interest of the individual supplier of the information. In short, if confidentiality is to work satisfactorily, confidentiality must be available'.[1] It would be clearly unsatisfactory if public confidence in the integrity of the confidential information supplied during the adoption process were to be undermined.

12.33   The Adoption Act 1976, together with its regulations and guidance, gave emphasis to the confidential nature of case records prepared in the course of an adoption and adoption proceedings. In *Gunn-Russo v Nugent Care Society and Secretary of State for Health*[2] the issue was as to whether this confidentiality remained forever, notwithstanding the age of the adopted person, the passage of time and whether or not the person giving the confidential information and those affected by it were still alive. The adoption agency in the case had rigorously maintained a general policy where confidentiality 'trumped everything, regardless of the circumstances'. Scott Baker J said:[3]

> '... Obviously great care is needed before confidential records are disclosed. The problem is not a new one. It is not uncommon for a balance to have to be struck between disclosure and maintaining a confidence. The court was faced with different, but not entirely dissimilar circumstances in *D v National Society for the Prevention of Cruelty to Children* [1978] AC 171. Lord Edmund-Davies said at 245 that where (i) a confidential relationship exists (other than that of lawyer and client) *and* (ii) disclosure would be in breach of some ethical or social value involving the public interest, the court has a discretion to uphold a refusal to disclose relevant evidence provided that it considers that, on balance, the public interests would be better served by excluding such evidence.'

12.34   He concluded that 'in principle, a duty of confidentiality should cease if the information loses the quality of confidence, whether through the passage of time, loss of secrecy or other change of circumstances'.[4] On the facts of the case, he found that the agency had applied its general policy too rigidly. It ought to have gone through the file on a document-by-document basis, conducting for each document the balancing exercise between the arguments in favour of disclosure on the one hand and the arguments in favour of maintaining confidentiality on the other.

12.35   Under the new provisions, as has been seen, the Registrar General retains his duty to maintain the Adopted Children Register and the Adoption Contact Register, but it will be the adoption agency which is the 'main gateway' for access to this information.

12.36   In the light of the *Smith* case and a minority of similar cases, the Government was concerned that the Registrar General did not have sufficient information about the adopted person or his or her birth family to be sufficiently well placed to reach a decision where there was a possibility of a serious crime being committed. Further underlying concerns were (i) the 'private life' provisions of Art 8 of the European Convention in relation to the birth parents who were unable to take legal action to prevent the Registrar General from releasing identifying information unless they became aware that the adopted person was trying to trace them, and (ii) the data protection philosophy.[5]

---

1   *Gunn-Russo v Nugent Care Society and Secretary of State for Health* [2002] 1 FLR 1 at [51], per Scott Baker J.

2   [2002] 1 FLR 1.

3   At [54].

4   Scott Baker J referred, in particular, to Toulson and Phipps *Confidential Information* (Sweet & Maxwell, 1996) which sets out a comprehensive review of the law of confidentiality.

5   HC Special Standing Committee, 20 November 2001, col 19.

12.37   These concerns have led the Government to create a new system[1] for access to information, whereby access is filtered through adoption agencies so as to provide an intermediary safeguard before disclosure is made. The use of the adoption agency as an intermediary marks a significant change in approach and is based upon the view that the adoption agency is best placed to provide identifying information, to contact the interested parties, to deal appropriately with sensitive information and to arrange for the provision of counselling.[2]

12.38   Sections 54 and 56–65 of the ACA 2002 ('the disclosure group of sections') introduce new provisions on:

–   the information that adoption agencies must keep in relation to a person's adoption;
–   the information that agencies must disclose to adopted adults on request;
–   the information that they must release to adoptive parents and to adopted adults on request;
–   the information that adoption agencies may release to adopted adults, birth parents and others.

12.39   These provisions deal with different types of information.

(1)   *Section 56 information*[3] or 'protected' information[4] which an adoption agency must keep in relation to a person's adoption. This will be:

–   information concerning the adoptee and such other persons as his or her birth parents and siblings, adoptive parents and siblings, and other relatives (and will also include social worker's reports);
–   any information kept by the adoption agency: (a) which the agency has obtained from the Registrar General under s 79(5) and any other information which would enable the adopted person to obtain a certified copy of the record of his or her birth; or (b) which is information about an entry relating to an adopted person in the Adoption Contact Register.[5]

(2)   It includes 'identifying' information, which means information, which, whether taken on its own or together with other information disclosed by the adoption agency, identifies the person or enables the person to be identified.[6] This includes names; residential, educational and employment addresses; photographic or audio-visual material; case records; and legal and medical information held by adoption agencies.

---

1   The new system will apply only to adoptions that take place after the Act has come into force. Previous arrangements will continue to apply to those persons adopted prior to the date of implementation of the Act.
2   HC Special Standing Committee, 10 December 2002, col 692, per Ms Jacqui Smith.
3   ACA 2002, ss 56, 57(1), (3). The 's 56 information' is contained in ss 56–65: s 56(2). The information which an adoption agency must keep in relation to a person's adoption and the form and manner in which it must keep the information will be prescribed by Regulations: s 56(1)(a), (b). Regulations will also provide for the transfer of information to another successor adoption agency: s 56(3).
4   ACA 2002, s 56(3).
5   Ibid, s 57(2).
6   Ibid, s 57(1)(b) and (4).

(3) *Section 58 information* or 'background' information (which does not fall into either category) such as the child's birth details, medical history, interests, any special needs and progress. This is the type of information intended to help adopters in the care and upbringing of the child. It is also information which could be disclosed to the birth family without compromising the adoptee's new identity or whereabouts.[1]

12.40   Regulations will set out the circumstances in which certain specified information will be disclosed to prospective adopters during the adoption process. It is likely to include 'background' information under s 58, together with information concerning the circumstances of the adoption, the views of the birth family and whether or not they would like continuing contact. The regulations will ensure that information is available for prospective adopters at three important points.

(1) There is to be a summary about the child at the linking stage, when the prospective adopters are first visited by the child's social worker and the adoption social worker. The report will provide information about, for example, the child's appearance, family circumstances, the part played in his or her life by the birth parents, the home environment, why he or she was taken into care or is being given up for adoption, behaviour, how he or she relates to adults and the current care status.[2] It should not contain identifying information about anyone other than the child, and the adopters will be asked to keep the information confidential.[3]

(2) There is to be a full matching report on the child before the matching recommendations by the adoption panel and the decision by the agency. The report will include information which the prospective adopters should have to enable them to make a decision about the adoption, such as a full description of the child's history, needs, problems, progress at school and in care, personality and behaviour, supported by medical, psychiatric, psychological and educational information.[4]

(3) After time to consider the full matching report, the prospective adopters, if they wish to proceed to preparations for the placement, are to be provided with a written proposal setting out its terms.[5] The proposal will include details of the financial and other support arrangements as well as details about any agreement about contact arrangements. If the child's birth family agrees in writing, life story books which may include birth certificates, photograph albums and family trees may be passed to the prospective adopters, who would be asked to sign an undertaking to keep the information confidential.[6] This proposal is particularly important in those cases where the child to be adopted has complex needs such as learning or behavioural problems, educational difficulties, challenging psychological experiences from a past home environment or physical disabilities. It is also essential that a full medical

---

1   ACA 2002, s 58(2) enables an adoption agency to disclose background information to any person for the purposes of its functions and under s 58(3) it is under a duty to disclose specified information in certain circumstances to prescribed persons.

2   HC Special Standing Committee, 10 January 2002, col 735, per Ms Jacqui Smith.

3   Ibid.

4   Ibid.

5   HC Deb, 16 May 2002, vol 385, no 149, col 1018, per Ms Jacqui Smith.

6   HC Special Standing Committee, 10 January 2002, col 735, per Ms Jacqui Smith.

history is available at the outset so that appropriate precautionary medical treatment or checks can be prepared for.

12.41   Sections 60–62 of the ACA 2002 set out the new system for the disclosure of protected information, which for the first time is subject to criminal sanctions imposed on adoption agencies who contravene the disclosure provisions.[1] However, provision is made for the disclosure of protected information, where there is agreement between the adoption agency, the adoptive parents and the birth parents for the sharing of such information.[2] Regulations will set out the circumstances in which an adoption agency must disclose protected information to someone other than an adopted person (for example, where it would assist an enquiry under s 17).[3]

12.42   Under the new system the adopted adult has a right (save in exceptional circumstances) to obtain through an adoption agency information which would enable him or her to obtain his or her birth certificate and a right to certain information disclosed to the adopters by the agency.[4] A person may also apply to the appropriate adoption agency for protected information about any person involved in an adoption (such as the adopted person, his or her birth parents or an adoption social worker). If the protected information concerns an adult, s 61 applies. If the protected information is about a child or it is impossible to disclose protected information about an adult without also disclosing protected information about a child, s 62 applies.

12.43   The new access system is intended to work as follows. There is to be a single point of access for 'identifying information', including the information necessary to access a birth record, which is now through adoption agencies. Protected information may only be disclosed by the agency pursuant to ss 57–65.[5] Certain background information must be disclosed to adopters[6] and may be disclosed to certain persons for the purposes of the agency's functions.[7] The adopted adult has the right, at his or her request, to receive from the agency the information disclosed to the adopters by the agency under s 54.[8]

12.44   The adopted adult also has the right, on request:

(1)   to receive from the adoption agency the information (such as his or her birth name) which would enable him or her to obtain his or her birth record from the Registrar General unless the High Court orders otherwise (the court will do so only where there is an application by the agency and the court is satisfied that the circumstances

---

1   ACA 2002, s 59, which provides that a registered adoption society which discloses any information in contravention of s 57 is to be guilty of an offence and liable on summary conviction to a fine not exceeding level 5 on the standard scale. Such proceedings may not be brought more than 6 years after the commission of the offence but, subject to that, may be brought within a period of 6 months from the date on which evidence, sufficient in the opinion of the prosecutor to warrant the proceedings, came to his attention: s 138. Under s 99, proceedings for an offence under s 59 may not, without the written consent of the Attorney General, be taken by any person other than the National Care Standards Commission or the Assembly.
2   ACA 2002, s 57(5). Regulations will provide for the recording of such agreements: s 64(2).
3   Ibid, s 57(6).
4   Ibid, s 60.
5   Ibid, s 57(1) and (2).
6   Ibid, s 54 and 58(3).
7   Ibid, s 58(2).
8   Ibid, s 60(2)(b).

are exceptional).[1] The agency, therefore, cannot make a decision depriving the adopted adult of the right to a birth certificate. It can only apply to the High Court for permission not to disclose the information. It will be for the High Court to consider whether it is justifiable to withhold that information and a high hurdle of 'exceptional circumstances' has to be cleared before the court can deny the adoptee this right. 'Exceptional circumstances' are likely to be those, for instance, which might entail a risk of death to the birth parents and are, therefore, envisaged as a rarity; and

(2) to receive from the court which made the adoption order a copy of any prescribed document or order in so far it does not contain any protected information.[2]

12.45 Where a person applies to the agency for the disclosure of protected information,[3] *none of which involves a child*, the agency has a discretion under s 61 whether or not to proceed with the application. It is not required to proceed unless it considers it appropriate to do so.[4] Thus the agency is given a discretion to decide *not* to continue with the process of identifying and obtaining the consent of those persons who would be identified in the information, for example, where the application is clearly an inappropriate approach or vexatious. If it does proceed with the application, it must take all reasonable steps to obtain the views of the persons to whom the information relates, including whether they consent to the release of the information.[5] It may then disclose the information if it considers it is appropriate to do so.[6] This discretion enables the agency, in the light of particular circumstances or information, or despite the fact that the person has consented to the disclosure of the information, still to refuse disclosure if it considers it appropriate to do so. In determining whether is it appropriate to proceed with the application or disclose the information, it must consider all the circumstances,[7] including:

(i)   the welfare of the adopted person;
(ii) the views of the persons to whom the information refers, obtained under s 61(3);
(iii) any prescribed matters.

12.46 Section 61 does not apply to a request for information by an adopted adult for either the information to enable him to obtain his birth certificate or the information

---

1   ACA 2002, s 60(2)(a) and (3).
2   Ibid, s 60(4) and (5).
3   Ibid, s 61(6). Section 61 does not apply to a request for information under s 60(2) (information to enable an adopted person to obtain his or her birth certificate and any prescribed information disclosed to adopters under s 54) or to a request for information which the agency is required or authorised to disclose by virtue of s 57(6).
4   Ibid, s 61(2) and (4).
5   Ibid, s 61(3). This will require the agencies to engage in research work, to contact individuals, to use information that they have and possibly to gather more information, if their current records do not enable them to trace a individual. They will have the discretion to charge a fee to a person, other than an adopted person, who is seeking protected information about a birth relative, to cover only their costs in acting on an application for such information: HC Special Standing Committee, 10 January 2002, col 748.
6   ACA 2002, s 61(4).
7   Ibid, s 61(5). Examples would include where one of the birth parents objects to the release of identifying information, but the other does not. Another might be where an adopted person has asked for identifying information, the birth relative has objected but the interests of the adopted person's health and welfare are such that he or she should have the identifying information.

given to his adopters under s 54. However, applications by an adopted person for disclosure of all other protected information fall within the scope of this section.

12.47   Where the person applies to the agency for protected information[1] to be disclosed to him or her, *any of which involves a child*, the agency again has a discretion whether or not to proceed with the application and is not required to do so unless it considers it appropriate.[2]

12.48   If it decides to proceed with the application, then it must, *in relation to any information about a person who is a child*, take all reasonable steps to obtain the views of (i) any parent or guardian of the child and (ii) the child, if the agency considers it appropriate to do so, having regard to his or her age and understanding.[3] Where the child is adopted, reasonable efforts must be made to contact the adoptive parents to find out their views and establish whether they consent. In deciding whether to proceed with the application or disclose the information, the agency must:

(1)   have regard to the paramountcy principle in respect of an adopted child and, in the case of any other child, have particular regard to the child's welfare;[4] and
(2)   consider all the circumstances of the case,[5] including:

   –   the welfare of the adoptee (where the adoptee is not an adopted child whose welfare is the paramount consideration);
   –   the views obtained under s 62(3) from the parents or guardian and the child;
   –   any prescribed matters.

12.49   When a request for information concerns an adopted child, the agency is, therefore, under an obligation to seek the views of the adoptive parents on a request for identifying information. In coming to any decision, the adopted child's welfare will be the paramount consideration. Where a request is made for information that could identify both a child and an adult, again the principle of the paramountcy of the child's welfare must be applied to the decision. Although the adopted person does not have a veto, the ACA 2002 is explicitly weighted in the interests of those who have been adopted. It appears, therefore, that prospects will be limited for anyone seeking information against the wishes of the adopted person.

12.50   Where the information is about *a person who has attained the age of 18*, the agency must:

(1)   take all reasonable steps to obtain his or her views as to disclosure;[6] and
(2)   consider all the circumstances of the case,[7] including:
   –   his or her views;

---

1   ACA 2002, s 62(8). As with s 61, s 62 does not apply to a request for information under s 60(2) or to a request for information which the agency is authorised or required to disclose under s 57(6).
2   Ibid, s 62(2) and (5).
3   Ibid, s 62(3). In taking into account the child's age and understanding, the agency should have regard to, eg, whether the child is *Gillick*-competent, is aged 16/17 and/or is living away from home.
4   Ibid, s 62(6). As the section relates not only to adopted children but also to other children, it is necessary to lay down the basis on which the interests of an adopted child and a child who has not been adopted need to be considered, if they are covered by the same disclosure of information.
5   Ibid, s 62(7).
6   Ibid, s 62(4).
7   Ibid, s 62(7).

- the welfare of the adoptee (where the adoptee is not an adopted child to whom the paramountcy principle applies);
- any prescribed matters.

12.51 The agency may then disclose the information if it considers it appropriate to do so. If consent is forthcoming from the relevant parties, the expectation is that the information would normally be disclosed. However, the agency retains an important discretion. If, notwithstanding the consent, the agency takes the view that it was not appropriate to disclose, it can withhold disclosure. Where consent was refused or could not be obtained, the agency could still disclose the information if it were safe and appropriate to do so.[1]

12.52 There is, however, a safeguard. If the agency reaches a determination to disclose or withhold information contrary to the expressed view of the relevant party, the decision will be subject to a review by an independent panel constituted under s 12. Thus, where the adoption agency decides not to disclose the requested information, the adopted person or other requesting party has the right to ask for a review. Once the review procedure is exhausted, there remains recourse to judicial review of the decision.

12.53 Regulations will provide for the balancing of the rights of individuals and the operation of new duties for adoption agencies and the Registrar General under ss 56–65.[2] They will include placing adoption agencies under a duty to inform birth parents at the time of the child's placement of the rights of individuals to request protected information.[3]

12.54 As counselling[4] is regarded as of real value in helping adoptees come to terms with sensitive information about their backgrounds, particularly those whose family history includes distressing events, adoption agencies will also be required through regulations:

- to give information about the availability of counselling to persons seeking information or considering whether to object or consent to disclosure or entering into an agreement to share protected information (for the purposes of s 57(5));[5]
- to make arrangements to secure the provision of counselling;[6] and
- to give prescribed information about the rights or opportunities to obtain information.[7]

12.55 The whole system of access to information has become a much more complex and prescriptive process than under the former law. Clearly, one of the objectives of the new process is to put in place a statutory safety net so as to avoid the pitfalls which cases

---

1 HC Special Standing Committee, 10 December 2001, col 694, per Ms Jacqui Smith.
2 ACA 2002, s 64(1).
3 Under s 64(3), which provides a power to make regulations requiring adoption agencies to give prescribed persons prescribed information about their rights or opportunities to obtain information or give their views as to disclosure.
4 As to the standards for counselling, monitoring will be carried out by the National Care Standards Commission, which will be the registration authority for registered adoption societies and ASAs. Monitoring of counselling carried out by local authorities will be part of the performance management and inspection regimes in place.
5 ACA 2002, s 63(1).
6 Ibid, s 63(2).
7 Ibid, s 64(3).

such as *R v Registrar General ex parte Smith*[1] illuminated. It must, however, be remembered that these were only a handful of cases. For the overwhelming majority, an open landscape provided an important opportunity for the discovery of significant relationships which had been lost and which, when found, proved of mutual value to the adoptee and the birth family.

12.56 Another of the underlying objectives is the protection of the claims of third parties to confidentiality, especially the birth parents, so as to ensure that their right to respect for private and family life under Art 8 of the European Convention on Human Rights is not infringed.

12.57 The European Court's general approach to access to information can be discerned in *Gaskin v UK*,[2] which concerned access to records kept by a local authority in a childcare case. The applicant, who had been in care for most of his life, was given access only to information in his file to which the contributors had consented. He claimed in the European Court that the refusal of access to all his case records constituted a breach of Arts 8 and 10 of the European Convention on Human Rights. The European Court held that records containing information concerning highly personal aspects of his childhood, development and history did relate to his 'private and family life' in such a way that the question of his access fell within the ambit of Art 8. It went on to say that:[3]

> '... persons in the situation of the applicant have a vital interest, protected by the Convention, in receiving the information necessary to know and to understand their childhood and early development. On the other hand, it must be borne in mind that confidentiality of public records is of importance for receiving objective and reliable information and that such confidentiality can also be necessary for the protection of third persons. Under the latter aspect, a system ... which makes access to records dependent on the consent of the contributor, can in principle be considered to be compatible with the obligations under Art 8 ... The court considers, however, that under such a system the interests of the individual seeking access to records relating to his private and family life must be secured when a contributor to the records either is not available or improperly refuses consent. Such a system is only in conformity with the principle of proportionality if it provides that an independent authority finally decides whether access has to be granted in cases where a contributor fails to answer or withholds consent.'

12.58 The Court held that the procedures then in place failed to secure the applicant's private and family life.[4] The Court also went on to look at the applicant's right to freedom to receive information under Art 10. It held[5] that although the right to freedom to receive information basically prohibits a Government from restricting a person from receiving information that others wish or may be willing to impart to him, it did not in the circumstances of the case give the applicant the right to obtain, against the will of the local authority, access to the file held by that authority. The court expressly did not decide whether general rights of access to personal data and information could be derived from Art 8(1).

---

1   [1991] 2 QB 393.
2   (1989) 12 EHRR 36, [1990] 1 FLR 167.
3   At para 49.
4   English law relating to access to files in child care cases has changed since the *Gaskin* case and the law is now set out in the Access to Personal Files Act 1987 and the Access to Personal Files (Social Services) Regulations 1989, SI 1989/206.
5   *Gaskin* (above) at paras 51–52.

12.59 The new system makes significant provision for the consent, wishes and interests of those persons to whom the information relates to be at the centre of the decision. It vests an important discretion in the adoption agency to give or withhold protected information (save for birth record information and certain information disclosed to adopters under s 54). Although the exercise of its discretion involves obtaining the views of the persons identified in the information and then considering them, those views are not decisive, but merely one of a number of circumstances to be considered including the welfare of the adopted person. The new system, therefore, attempts to steer a compatible course between the competing rights of adoptees and third parties.

12.60 A surprising absentee from the ACA 2002 is a statutory duty on the adopters to inform the child of his or her adopted status.[1] Although it is to be hoped that, in practice, few adopted children reach the age of 18 without being told of their adoptive status, should such a fundamental right to know be left to 'hope'? As Ward LJ put it in *Re H (Paternity: Blood Tests)*,[2] in the context of a paternity case:

> 'In my judgment every child has the right to know the truth unless his welfare clearly justifies the cover-up. The right to know is acknowledged in the UN Convention on the Rights of the Child 1989 (Cm 1976) which has been ratified by the UK and in particular Art 7 which provides "that a child has, as far as possible, *the right to know* and be cared for by *his or her parents*".'[3]

12.61 In addition, under Art 8 the UN Convention provides that every child has the 'right to *preserve his or her identity*, including nationality, name and *family relations* as recognised by law without lawful interference'.[4] The child's right to know his genetic identity also falls within the private life provisions of Art 8 of the European Convention on Human Rights. In *Gaskin v UK*[5] the European Court affirmed the Commission's view that 'respect for private life requires that everyone should be able to establish details of their identity as individual human beings and that in principle they should not be obstructed by the authorities from obtaining such very basic information without specific justification'.

12.62 As we have seen in Chapter 5, in the 1992 Review of Adoption Law[6] it was recommended that the legislative framework should 'underline an adopted child's *right to know* that he or she is adopted and contain measures to preclude the likelihood of any adopted child being deprived of this information'. These measures included placing an express duty on the adoption agency not only to advise adoptive parents of the importance of telling the child that he or she was adopted but also to make reasonable efforts to contact the child's adoptive parents, as the child approached 16, to remind them that the child should by now be told the truth. It was also recommended that an adopted child of any age should have the right to access basic non-identifying information about his or her background.[7]

---

1   This omission is fully discussed in Sonia Harris-Short 'The Adoption and Children Bill – A Fast Track to Failure?' [2001] CFLQ 405 at 413 et seq.
2   [1996] 2 FLR 65 at 80.
3   Emphasis added.
4   Emphasis added.
5   (1990) 12 EHRR 36, [1990] 1 FLR 167, at para 39.
6   At paras 27.4–27.5.
7   Ibid, at para 27.5.

12.63   The ACA 2002 makes provision[1] for certain background information to be provided to the adopters which is mirrored by a provision for adopted adults to obtain this information.[2] If, as is likely, the information given to adopters includes the views of the birth parents on continuing contact, there is currently no statutory guarantee that adopted children (when of sufficient age and understanding) will have access to that information. Their right to access this background information will have to wait until they are aged 18. Yet much of this information will be material in which the 'adolescent' adoptee arguably has a 'vital interest, protected by the Convention, in receiving' as 'necessary to know and to understand his childhood and early development'. 'A blanket ban' in these circumstances 'seems difficult to justify' as a 'proportionate response' to welfare concerns.

12.64   While conceding that an adopted child should be informed of his or her adoption, the Government expressed concerns 'as to the practical difficulty in giving an adoption agency a legal duty to trace, track down, make contact with and make arrangements to talk to all adopted people at the age of 18'.[3] What is proposed, therefore, is that regulations will make it a point of good practice to encourage prospective adopters to sign a form of contract saying that they will impart the information to the children at the most appropriate time. The guidance to adopters will also point out that when the adopted person reaches the age of 18, he or she will be entitled to a copy of the original birth certificate and will be entitled to access the prescribed information given by the agency to the adopters as part of the adoption process. This is clearly no substitute for a statutory right to know.

CONFIDENTIALITY IN COURT PROCEEDINGS

12.65   Since the adoption jurisdiction was created in 1926, there has been a progressive emphasis upon the confidential nature of the proceedings for adoption. By 1976 the High Court and County Court Rules were providing that that the report of the guardian would be confidential; the information obtained by any person in the course of the adoption process was confidential and would not be disclosed except in certain prescribed circumstances; and the documents relative to the proceedings would be kept in a place of special security and would not be open to inspection except as required by the rules or by statute.[4]

12.66   The regime embodied in the Adoption Rules 1984 continued the process of enlargement by impressing confidentiality on the reports of the reporting officer, the adoption agency and the local authority. However, in the 1984 Rules there was one

---

1   ACA 2002, s 54.
2   Ibid, s 60(2)(b).
3   HC Deb, 16 May 2002, vol 385, no 149, col 1020, per Ms Jacqui Smith.
4   See *Re S (A Minor) (Adoption)* [1993] 2 FLR 204 at 207D–208B, per Butler-Sloss LJ (as she then was).

significant change of direction, in r 53(2),[1] where for the first time the trend towards non-disclosure was qualified by giving the party referred to in a document the specific entitlement to see the relevant part, subject itself to a qualification in the shape of a judicial discretion to direct that disclosure should not be made.

12.67   The procedure for the contested adoption of a child has been recognised as:[2]

'one of the most anxious and difficult in the civil jurisdiction, for it deals with conflicting human needs and wishes which cannot be fully reconciled ... [and the confidentiality of adoption reports is] one aspect of that process, in which the dilemma is particularly acute, since the demands not only of human relationships but also of procedural fairness must be placed in the scales.'

12.68   The difficulties which may arise were exemplified by the case of *Re S (A Minor) (Adoption)*,[3] a confidential serial number case, where the prospective adoptive father was severely disabled and the guardian ad litem wished to reveal that fact to the natural mother on the grounds that it was relevant information and that the guardian should be able to discuss all aspects of the case with her. The question of whether the information should be disclosed was treated as a preliminary issue. Unlike in care proceedings,[4] the mother was not given notice of the application and was unaware of both the application to the judge at first instance and the prospective adopters' appeal to the Court of Appeal. The Court of Appeal took the view that the information should not be given to the mother. Butler-Sloss LJ (as she then was) said:[5]

'Traditionally, natural parents are given some information about the prospective adopters without breaching confidentiality. At the adoption hearing, the natural parents have the right to cross-examine the prospective adopters through their lawyers, even in a confidential adoption application ... I am satisfied that the natural mother has a right to oppose this adoption and not only the concept of adoption and to cross-examine the prospective adopters as far as she is able to do so on the facts available. That right to play a part in the adoption hearing does not, however, entitle the natural mother to receive the information provided to the judge.

Adoption is a most unusual if not unique form of litigation. It is, to my knowledge, the only proceedings where all the information collected in the case is confidential until it is disclosed ...'

---

1   Rule 53(2) reads: 'A party who is an individual and is referred to in a confidential report supplied to the court by an adoption agency, a local authority, a reporting officer or a children's guardian may inspect, for the purposes of the hearing, that part of the report which refers to him, subject to any direction given by the court that: (a) no part of one or any of the reports shall be revealed to that party, or (b) the part of one or any of the reports referring to that party shall be revealed only to that party's legal advisers, or (c) the whole or part of one or any of the reports shall be revealed to that party'.

2   *In re D (Adoption Reports: Confidentiality)* [1996] AC 593 at 602H–603A, [1995] 2 FLR 687 at 688D–E, per Lord Mustill.

3   [1993] 2 FLR 204.

4   *Official Solicitor v K* [1965] AC 201; *Re C (Disclosure)* [1996] 1 FLR 797; *Re M (Disclosure)* [1998] 2 FLR 1028 which at 1031E–1032B approved the procedure advocated by Johnson J in *Re C (Disclosure)* (above) (tailored to the particular circumstances of the case). For disclosure in CA 1989 proceedings see also: *Re X (Disclosure of Information)* [2001] 2 FLR 440, a decision of Munby J which provides a comprehensive summary of the current law on disclosure.

5   [1993] 2 FLR 204 at 207B–E.

12.69   In *Re D (Minors) (Adoption Reports: Confidentiality)*[1] a mother who was opposing an application by her former husband and his new wife for the adoption of her two sons applied to inspect two sections of the guardian ad litem's report that expressed in detail the children's wishes and feelings towards their parents. Save for the guardian, none of the other parties to the adoption application had seen those two sections. The application was refused and the appeal to the Court of Appeal dismissed. The House of Lords allowed the appeal. Lord Mustill highlighted the tension between two fundamental principles,[2] which at first sight appear to be on a collision course:

> '... it is a first principle of fairness that each party to a judicial process shall have an opportunity to answer by evidence and argument any adverse material which the tribunal may take into account when forming its opinion. The principle is lame if the party does not know the substance of what is said against him (or her) for what he does not know he cannot answer. The requirement of openness is particularly important in proceedings for adoption, not only because it may lead to the deprivation of parental rights, in the self-centred meaning of that word, but because a successful application to adopt brings about a total rupture of the mutual relationship of responsibility and dependency which is the essence of the parental bond. The unique character of the relationship, which the parent will lose, and the generally irreversible nature of the loss, make it specially important that in simple fairness to the parent he or she is aware of anything which may tend to bring it about. There is more to it than this, however, since fairness to a parent is a reflection of fairness to the child. The erasure of the bond with the natural parent and the creation of the entirely new set of responsibilities and dependencies shared with the adopters is an event of critical importance in the life of the child, whose paramount welfare demands that such a momentous step is taken only after a process which is as fair and thorough as can be devised.'

And:

> 'Pulling in the other direction is an impulse towards the confidentiality of sensitive personal information. There are two distinct although often cumulative reasons why this impulse is a feature of proceedings for adoption. First, in a process where the judge is dependent to a great extent on second-hand knowledge of the circumstances it is in the interests of all those who are potentially affected by his decision that the information furnished to him shall be as full and candid as possible; and candour is promoted if those who investigate and report their findings and opinions can do so with a degree of confidence that the dispute will not be exacerbated, and hence the welfare of the child imperilled by the disclosure of material which may arouse resentment. Secondly, where the child has made allegations or expressed wishes to the author of the report, there may be circumstances where full disclosure may put at risk the welfare of the child, including ... its physical and psychological security. For these and other reasons adoption has traditionally been regarded as unique or nearly so in the degree of confidentiality maintained ...'

12.70   Lord Mustill went on to say:[3]

> '... I have no hesitation in saying that a strong presumption in favour of disclosing to a party any material relating to him or her is the point at which the judge should start ... the opportunity to know about and respond to adverse materials is at the heart of a fair hearing. Adoption is an unusual process, but it calls for fairness as much as any other and indeed with special intensity ...

---

1   [1996] AC 593, [1995] 2 FLR 687.
2   [1996] AC 593 at 603H–604F, [1995] 2 FLR 687 at 689D–690B.
3   At 609A–B; 694E–H.

Equally, however, there must be some limit to the duty of disclosure ... no formula can be stated which will answer to every case ... Plainly, where it is suggested that disclosure may harm the child, the court will take the matter very seriously, but it should look closely at both the degree of likelihood that harm will occur, and the gravity of the harm if it does occur. To say that harm must be certain would, in my opinion, pitch the test too high, since future events cannot be predicted with complete confidence, but a powerful combination of likelihood and seriousness of harm will be required before the requirements of a fair trial can be overridden.'

12.71   In steering a safe course between the two principles, Lord Mustill tendered a three-stage approach with which their Lordships were all in accord:[1]

(1)   '... the court should first consider whether disclosure of the material would involve a real possibility of significant harm to the child'.

(2)   'If it would, the court should next consider whether the overall interests of the child would benefit from non-disclosure, weighing on the one hand the interest of the child in having the material properly tested and on the other both the magnitude of the risk that harm will occur and the gravity of the harm if it does occur.'[2]

(3)   'If the court is satisfied that the interests of the child point towards non-disclosure, the next and final step is for the court to weigh that consideration, and its strength in the circumstances of the case, against the interest of the parent or other party in having an opportunity to see and respond to the material. In the latter regard the court should take into account the importance of the material to the issues in the case.'

12.72   Flanked on either side of the tripartite test were two further principles:[3]

'It is a fundamental principle of fairness that a party is entitled to the disclosure of all materials which may be taken into account by the court when reaching a decision adverse to that party. This principle applies with particular force to proceedings designed to lead to an order for adoption, since the consequences of such an order are so lasting and far-reaching.'

and

'Non-disclosure should be the exception and not the rule. The court should be rigorous in its examination of the risk and gravity of the feared harm to the child and should order non-disclosure only when the case for doing so is compelling.'

The importance of this principle was highlighted in the Court of Appeal decision of *Re M (Disclosure)*.[4]

---

1   *Re D (Minors) (Adoption Reports: Confidentiality)* [1996] AC 593 at 615D–H, [1995] 2 FLR 687 at 700G–701B.

2   For example, the risk of the identification and destabilisation of a confidential adoptive placement: see *Re S (A Minor) (Adoption)* [1993] 2 FLR 204.

3   *Re D (Minors) (Adoption Reports: Confidentiality)* [1996] AC 593 at 615C and 616A, [1995] 2 FLR 687 at 700F and 701C.

4   [1998] 2 FLR 1028 at 1032G–H, per Thorpe LJ.

12.73   So far as domestic authority is concerned, the *Re D* principles have been applied in a number of adoption cases. In *Re K (Adoption: Disclosure of Information)*,[1] a confidential serial number adoption, the question of disclosure to the natural mother of the fact that one of the prospective adopters had a conviction for a serious offence was transferred to the High Court as a preliminary issue. The mother was not given notice of the hearing, but the Official Solicitor was appointed as a friend of the court to advance points on behalf of the mother. In the event, Wall J applied the three-stage test in *Re D* and ruled that the documents which would give information about the conviction should not be disclosed to the mother.

12.74   In *Re X (Adoption: Confidential Procedure)*[2] a group of siblings were placed under care orders with foster parents with whom the birth parents felt they had a good relationship. The care plan was adoption. In fact, the prospective adopters were the foster parents who wished to keep their identity secret and were proceeding under the confidential serial number procedure. The parents did not consent to adoption. They wanted the children to remain in long-term foster care with the foster carers and for themselves to have limited direct contact. The parents' solicitor inadvertently learnt the true identity of the prospective adopters and applied for permission to disclose the prospective adopters' identity to the parents. The judge at first instance refused the application but directed that all the information before the court, including identifying reports, could be disclosed to the solicitor. He held that there was a real possibility of significant harm to the children from two sources: first, the intervention of the parents in the lives of the adoptive family which would be disastrous if it happened in an unplanned way, and secondly, harm which could result from the increased anxiety of the adopters. On appeal, Hale LJ said:[3]

> 'In the end, the issue still comes down to striking a fair balance between the various interests involved: the interests of all parties, but particularly the birth parents and the children themselves, in a fair trial of the issues, in which the evidence on each side can be properly tested and the relevant arguments properly advanced before the court; the interests of the children, their birth family and their prospective adoptive family, in protecting their family and private lives from unjustified interference; and the interests of the children being protected from harm and damage to their welfare, whether in the short, medium or longer term.
>
> Hence, *the tripartite test in* Re D *is still the appropriate way of approaching this balance, provided that the relevant interests of the adults are also taken into account.*'

12.75   Although the decision in *Re D* pre-dated the Human Rights Act 1998, in arriving at this decision the House of Lords had regard to the jurisprudence of the European Court of Human Rights, in particular *McMichael v UK*.[4] In that case, the European Court held[5] that:

---

1   [1997] 2 FLR 74; see also *Note Re An Adoption Application* [1990] 1 FLR 412, where the issue of an originating summons by a local authority to have the assistance of the court in deciding whether information contained in a confidential adoption file should be disclosed and, if so, under what circumstances and to whom was approved.
2   [2002] EWCA Civ 828, [2002] 2 FLR 476.
3   Ibid, at [15]–[16] (emphasis added).
4   (1995) 20 EHRR 205; see also *Hendricks v Netherlands* (1983) 5 EHRR 223, para 144.
5   (1995) 20 EHRR 205 at para 87.

'whilst Art 8 contains no explicit procedural requirements, the decision making process leading to measures of interference must be fair and such as to afford due respect to the interests safeguarded by Art 8:

> "What ... has to be determined is whether, having regard to the particular circumstances of the case and notably the serious nature of the decisions to be taken, the parents have been involved in the decision making process, seen as a whole, to a degree sufficient to provide them with the requisite protection of their interests. If they have not, there will have been a failure to respect their family life and the interference resulting from the decision will not be capable of being regarded as 'necessary' within the meaning of Art 8."[1]

12.76   Lord Mustill, in dealing with the jurisprudence of the European Court on Human Rights, said:

> '... the conflation in *McMichael* of the remedies under Arts 6 and 8 of the Convention shows that full disclosure will usually advance the interests of a fair trial and of the parties to the parental relationship. On the other hand, there is nothing in these decisions to suggest that disclosure can never be properly withheld if the interests of the child so demand ...'

12.77   Following the implementation of Human Rights Act 1998, in *Re B (Disclosure to Other Parties)*[2] Munby J, in considering the issue of non-disclosure of certain documents in care proceedings, summarised the current jurisprudence of the European Court under Arts 6 and 8.[3] As in *Re D (Minors) (Adoption Reports: Confidentiality)*, he referred to the fact that unfairness in the trial process may involve a violation of the right under Art 8 by depriving parents of the right to participate effectively in the decision-making process about their children: *W v UK*;[4] *McMichael v UK*;[5] *L v UK*;[6] *TP and KM v UK*.[7]

12.78   Munby J further highlighted the rights under Art 6, taking as his starting point the European Court's recognition in *Golder v UK*[8] that what Art 6 confers is an *effective* right of access to a court in the determination of civil rights and obligations. In particular, he noted that the right to an adversarial trial means the opportunity for the parties to have knowledge of, and comment on, the observations filed or evidence adduced by the other

---

1   *W v UK* (1988) 10 EHRR 29 at paras 62 and 64. See also *Elsholz v Germany* (2002) 34 EHRR 58, [2000] 2 FLR 486 at para 52; *TP and KM v UK* [2001] 2 FLR 549 at para 72; *Sahin v Germany; Sommerfield v Germany; Hoffman v Germany* [2002] 1 FLR 119 (*Sahin* at [44], *Sommerfield* at [42], *Hoffman* at [44]); *Buchberger v Austria* (Application No 32899/96) (unreported) 20 December 2001, ECHR, for more recent statements of this principle.

2   [2001] 2 FLR 1017. See also Munby J's decision in *Re L (Care: Assessment: Fair Trial)* [2002] 2 FLR 730 at [84]–[127].

3   Ibid, at [34]–[43]. His summary was described as 'uncontroversial' by Hale LJ in *Re X (Adoption: Confidential Procedure)* [2002] 2 FLR 476 and is a very useful digest of the current Convention jurisprudence on disclosure. For a comprehensive review of the issues relating to disclosure and confidentiality, see also the decisions of Munby J in *Re X (Disclosure of Information)* [2001] 2 FLR 440; *A Health Authority v X (Discovery: Medical Conduct)* [2002] 1 FLR 383; *Clibbery v Allan* [2001] 2 FLR 819; *Re L (Care: Assessment: Fair Trial)* [2002] 2 FLR 730 at [84]–[127], where he considers in detail how to strike a fair balance between competing Convention rights.

4   (1988) 10 EHRR 29 at para 64.

5   (1995) 20 EHRR 205.

6   [2001] 2 FLR 322 at 332G.

7   Application no 28945/95 [2001] 2 FLR 549.

8   (1979–80) 1 EHRR 542 at paras 35–36.

party: *Ruiz-Mateos v Spain*;[1] *Dombo Beheer v The Netherlands*;[2] and *McMichael v UK*.[3] Also, unlike Art 8, the right to a fair trial is absolute and unqualified and cannot be compromised or watered down by a reference to Art 8. Hale LJ in *Re X (Adoption: Confidential Procedure)* added[4] that:

> '... the content of a fair trial in any particular case is more flexible and depends upon the context, as Lord Bingham of Cornhill said in *Brown v Stott (Procurator Fiscal, Dunfermline) and Another*:[5]
>
>> "What a fair trial requires cannot, however, be the subject of a single unvarying rule or collection of rules. It is proper to take account of the facts and circumstances of particular cases, as the European Court has consistently done."
>
> Departures from the usual requirements of an adversarial trial must, of course, be for a legitimate aim and proportionate to that aim. Protecting the welfare of ... very vulnerable children is undoubtedly a legitimate aim.'

12.79   Munby J went on to suggest[6] that:

> '[there is no] warrant for saying that the only interests capable of denying a litigant access to the documents in the proper case are the interests of *child(ren)*. .... There can be cases ... where a litigant's right to see the documents may have to give way not merely in the interests of the children involved but also, or alternatively, to the Art 8 rights of one or more of the adults involved, whether as victim, party or witness ... In my judgment, *Re D* can no longer stand as authority for the proposition that only the child(ren)'s interests can be taken into account.'

12.80   As has been seen, this extension to the *Re D* principles was approved by the Court of Appeal in *Re X (Adoption: Confidential Procedure)*.[7] It is suggested, therefore, that the threefold test in *Re D* should be read as including the rights and interests of one or more of the adults involved and that this test (as extended) should continue to be applied under the new law[8] and, unless there is to be a wholesale revision of the rules relating to confidentiality (of which there is no sign in the ACA 2002), will continue to provide a guide through the dilemmas relating to the disclosure of confidential material to natural parents.

12.81   However, an officer of CAFCASS who has been appointed to the case has the right to examine and take copies of an adoption agency's records relating to a proposed or actual application in respect of the child concerned.[9] Any copy of such document (or any part of a document) will be admissible as evidence of any matter referred to in any evidence that the officer may give in the proceedings or any report he or she may produce to the court in the proceedings.

---

1   (1993) 16 EHRR 505 at para 63.
2   (1994) 18 EHRR 213 at para 33.
3   (1995) 20 EHRR 205.
4   [2002] EWCA Civ 828, [2002] 2 FLR 476 at [13].
5   [2001] 2 WLR 817 at 824D.
6   In *Re B (Disclosure to Other Parties)* [2001] 2 FLR 1017 at [66].
7   [2002] EWCA Civ 828, [2002] 2 FLR 476 at [16], per Hale LJ.
8   See *Re K (Adoption: Disclosure of Information)* [1997] 2 FLR 74, per Wall J; *Re S (Foster Placement (Children) Regulations 1991)* [2000] 1 FLR 648.
9   ACA 2002, s 103.

PRIVACY

12.82   Children applications are determined in private (in the sense that the public can properly be excluded) and information about children is 'indisputably covered by privacy and secrecy and . . . cannot be disclosed after the end of the case without leave of the court'.[1] The ACA 2002 expressly provides that adoption proceedings in the High Court or county court may be heard and determined in private.[2] By using the phrase 'in private' (rather than 'in chambers' or '*in camera*'), the policy intention is to ensure that only those concerned in the case are present and the public are not admitted.[3] It gives both the High Court and county court judges the discretion to hear adoption proceedings in public when they consider it appropriate to do so, for example where it is in the child's best interests or in the public interest (such as a judgment given in public).

12.83   In *Clibbery v Allan*,[4] although the case itself was not concerned with proceedings involving children, the Court of Appeal took the opportunity to look generally at the question of hearings in private in the context of the European Convention. Dame Elizabeth Butler-Sloss P said:[5]

> '. . . there is nothing in Art 6 of the Convention which requires all cases, willy nilly, to be heard in open court. To hear them in private and to debar publication of the proceedings heard in private must be necessary in a democratic society and proportionate to that necessity. The European Court recognised in *B v United Kingdom; P v United Kingdom* [2001] 2 FLR 261 that the Art 6 requirement to hold a public hearing was subject to exceptions. The court said at 271, para 37:
>
> > ". . . the requirement to hold a public hearing is subject to exceptions. This is apparent from the text of Art 6(1) itself, which contains the proviso that the 'press and public may be excluded from all or part of the trial . . . where the interests of juveniles or the private life of the parties so require or to the extent strictly necessary in the opinion of the court in special circumstances where publicity would prejudice the interests of justice' . . ."
>
> The Human Rights Act 1998 and the European jurisprudence underline our own long-established principles of open justice which are entirely in conformity with the Convention and which our exceptions (including children's cases) do not, in my judgment, breach.
>
> . . . It is widely recognised in European jurisprudence that the balance in children's cases is in favour of confidentiality: see *B v United Kingdom; P v United Kingdom* above.'

12.84   The hearing of a case in private does not, of itself, prohibit the publication of information about proceedings or information given in proceedings. Section 12 of the Administration of Justice Act 1960 ('the 1960 Act') sets out the circumstances in which it

---

1   *Clibbery v Allan* [2002] EWCA Civ 45, [2002] 1 FLR 565 at [74], per Dame Elizabeth Butler-Sloss P.

2   ACA 2002, s 101. Section 69(3) of the Magistrates' Courts Act 1980 will continue to apply and is amended consequentially in Sch 3 to the ACA 2002. There will be power to make court rules for magistrates' courts to sit in private in adoption proceedings.

3   HC Deb, 20 May 2002, vol 386, no 150, col 38, per Ms Jacqui Smith. See also *Clibbery v Allan* (above) for the distinction between 'in private', 'in chambers' and '*in camera*'.

4   [2002] EWCA Civ 45, [2002] 1 FLR 565. The case itself did not concern proceedings involving children.

5   Ibid, at [80]–[81].

would be a contempt of court to publish information given in private proceedings.[1] Section 101(2) of the ACA 2002 amends s 12 of the 1960 Act to include adoption proceedings.

12.85 Protection for the privacy of adopted children has further been provided by aligning the ACA 2002 with s 97 of the CA 1989.[2] Section 97 of the CA 1989, which provides for the privacy of children in proceedings under that Act, is to apply equally to adopted children.[3] There is, therefore, an automatic bar on the identification of children in the county court and the High Court. Under s 97(2), children will be protected at all levels of courts by making it an offence to publish any material which is intended to identify or likely to identify any child involved in any CA 1989 or adoption proceedings or their address or school. Breach of s 97 is an offence punishable on summary conviction by a fine not exceeding level 4 on the standard scale.[4] Material includes 'any picture or representation' and 'publish' 'inclusion in a programme service (within the meaning of the Broadcasting Act 1990)'.[5]

1   Section 12 of the 1960 Act is not exhaustive, as any publication which substantially prejudices the administration of justice would also be a contempt. The best known example of confidentiality based on potential prejudice to the proper administration of justice was the implied undertaking in compulsory disclosure of documents not to make use of the documents outside the action: *Clibbery v Allan* [2002] EWCA Civ 45, [2002] 1 FLR 565.
2   ACA 2002, s 101(3).
3   Ibid.
4   CA 1989, s 97(6). For the available defence, see s 97(4) of the CA 1989.
5   Ibid, s 97(5).

Chapter 13

THE ADOPTION SERVICE

PREAMBLE

13.1   The White Paper, *Adoption: A New Approach*,[1] set out the Government's proposals to promote an increase in the use of adoption, especially of children looked after by local authorities. Each year, there are about 4000 adoptions in England and Wales, around half of which are of children who have been looked after by local authorities. The Government has set a target of a 40 per cent increase in adoptions of looked-after children in England by 2004/05.

13.2   The ACA 2002 makes provision for the structure of the adoption service. Although much of the new Act remodels provisions from the AA 1976, there are some significant areas of new policy, which are intended to encourage more people to come forward as adopters and provide the adopters and adoptees with some measure of comfort in the adoption support services. These key new measures include:

–   a duty on local authorities to make arrangements for the provision of specified adoption support services;[2]
–   a new right to request and receive an assessment of needs for adoption support services, which will link in with other local authority, local education and health services so as to provide a co-ordinated package of support;[3]
–   the establishment of an independent body to review qualifying adoption agency determinations.[4] At the prospective adopter's request, an independent review mechanism will review applications which adoption agencies have indicated an intention to turn down. A second important function of the independent review body will be to review adoption agency determinations about the disclosure of information concerning a person's adoption.

13.3   Allied to and supporting these new provisions in the ACA 2002 for the structure of the adoption service are:

(1)   the establishment of the Adoption and Children Act Register[5] to encourage the recruitment of prospective adopters and speed up the matching process and;

---

1   Cm 5017 (December 2000).
2   ACA 2002, s 3(2)(b).
3   Ibid, s 4.
4   Ibid, s 12.
5   Ibid, ss 125–131.

(2) the National Adoption Standards and Practice Guidance,[1] which include time scales within which decisions for permanency for children should be reached and action taken.[2]

DEFINITIONS

13.4 The services maintained by local authorities under s 3 of the ACA 2002 are collectively referred to as 'The Adoption Service'.[3] An 'adoption agency' refers either to a local authority or to a registered adoption society.[4]

13.5 An 'adoption society' is a body whose functions consist of or include making arrangements for the adoption of children[5] and may also include 'adoption support services', which means 'counselling, advice and information in connection with the adoption' and such other adoption services as are prescribed by regulations.[6] The power to make regulations, which will set out the additional services to be included in the definition of 'adoption support services', must be exercised so as to secure that local authorities provide financial support[7] as part of their adoption support package. The likely financial support will include 'travel expenses for introductions and contact visits; settling in expenses including furniture such as a bed and a washing machine; house alterations and adaptations; provision of transport; purchase of toys, clothing or other articles and respite care'.[8] Financial support is intended to cover not only 'one off' and time-limited payments, but also regular adoption allowances. An adoption allowance, for example, may be paid to an adoptive family to cover the costs of maintaining contact with the birth family.[9]

13.6 A 'registered adoption society' is a voluntary organisation[10] which is an adoption society registered under Part 2 of the Care Standards Act 2000[11] and must be a body corporate.[12] The fact that an adoption society is an incorporated body (ie separate and distinct from the individual members of the body) is regarded as a fundamental requirement to the structure of the Act, especially because adoption agencies carry the significant responsibility of having parental responsibility for a child. An agency must be

---

1   Together with the National Standards for England and Practice Guidance in relation to Adopted Adults and their Birth Siblings. The Standards will have the status of s 7 guidance from April 2003, ie guidance issued under s 7(1) of the Local Authority Social Services Act 1970.
2   White Paper: *Adoption: The New Approach*, Cm 5017 (December 2000), paras 4.4–4.8.
3   ACA 2002, s 2(1).
4   Ibid, s 2(1).
5   Ibid, s 2(5).
6   Ibid, s 2(6).
7   Ibid, s 2(7).
8   HL Deb, 14 October 2002, vol 639, no 186, col 616, per Lord Hunt of Kings Heath.
9   Ibid.
10 ACA 2002, s 2(5) defines a 'voluntary organisation' as a body other than a public or local authority, the activities of which are not carried on for profit.
11 Ibid, s 2(2).
12 Ibid, s 2(4). Note s 143, which deals with offences by bodies corporate and unincorporated bodies.

registered as a single body therefore each branch cannot be registered separately.[1] As there is no branch registration, each registration authority under the Care Standards Act 2000 (ie the National Care Standards Commission (NCSC) in England and the National Assembly for Wales) has been given the appropriate level of scrutiny over the activity of agencies operating in its area. They will be able to deal with agencies based in England that have branches in Wales and vice versa. Section 99 of the ACA 2002 provides for either the Commission or the Assembly to bring proceedings against an adoption agency for contravention of regulations under s 9 or for contravention of s 59 (disclosure of information in contravention of s 57).[2]

13.7 A registered adoption society is treated as registered in respect of any facilities of the Adoption Service unless it is a condition of its registration that it may not provide that facility.[3] References to adoption are to the adoption of persons, wherever they may be habitually resident, effected under the law of any country or territory.[4]

Adoption panels

13.8 In considering the structure of the adoption process, consideration should be given to the important role played by the adoption panels, which under the former law had to be established by each adoption agency. The adoption panel was itself a creature of secondary legislation[5] and was set up in order to advise and make recommendations to the adoption agency on whether or not a particular child should be adopted and as to the suitability of prospective adopters.

13.9 The composition of the panel was intended to achieve a measure of independence by providing that at least three of its members should be 'independent persons' because they were not members or employees of the adoption agency, or elected members, where the agency was a local authority. Where reasonably practicable, they were to include an adoptive parent and adopted person who was at least 18 years of age. The other members were social workers, a member of the adoption agency's management committee (or in the case of a local authority, a member of the authority's social services committee) and a medical adviser.

---

1 To remove the inconsistency which arose between s 11(2) of the Care Standards Act 2000 (CSA 2000) (which required each branch of a voluntary adoption agency registering as a separate agency under Part 2) and the ACA 2002, paras 103–106 of Sch 3 to ACA 2002 disapply the s 11(2) requirements in respect of voluntary adoption agencies. A new s 36A is inserted in Part 2 of the CSA 2000 by s 16 of the ACA 2002 which makes provision for the distribution of functions in relation to registered adoption societies to ensure that the National Assembly for Wales has the appropriate level of oversight of branches of voluntary adoption agencies situated in Wales, but registered in England, and the National Care Standards Commission has the appropriate level of oversight of branches of voluntary adoption agencies situated in England, but registered in Wales: HL Deb, 24 June 2002, vol 636, no 157, CWH 36–37.

2 This mirrors the provision in s 29 of the Care Standards Act 2000 and gives greater flexibility in relation to prosecution. If it were deemed appropriate, it would allow the Assembly to bring proceedings against a voluntary adoption agency registered in England, where the offence was committed by a Welsh branch of the agency: HL Deb, 24 June 2002, vol 636, no 157, CWH 38.

3 ACA 2002, s 2(2) and (3).

4 Ibid, s 2(8).

5 Adoption Agencies Regulations 1983 (AA Regs 1983), SI 1983/1964, regs 5, 5A and 5B, as substituted by the Adoption Agencies and Children (Arrangements for Placement and Reviews) (Miscellaneous Amendments) Regulations 1997, SI 1997/649.

13.10 The panel's functions included making recommendations to the adoption agency as to: (a) whether adoption was in the best interests of the child; (b) the suitability of the prospective adopter to be an adoptive parent; and (c) the suitability of the prospective adopter to be an adoptive parent for the particular child.[1] The agency had to take into account the panel's recommendation, for example, in making a decision on the suitability of the prospective adopter,[2] but was not bound to follow the recommendation.[3]

13.11 Neither the natural parents nor the child's guardian[4] were entitled to attend the panel or make oral submissions. However, the adoption agency was required to give the panel a written report containing any information relevant to the proposed placement,[5] which had to include the views of other professionals who had been involved in considering the future of the children.[6] In *Re R (Adoption: Disclosure)*[7] Cazalet J said that a adoption agency should state within its written report to the panel the views of the child's guardian, if formulated, and that the panel can request the adoption agency to provide further information including the views of the guardian.[8] The guardian's report, however, could not be disclosed to the panel without prior authority of the court. This approach could well be replicated in new regulations.

13.12 New regulations will generally set out a similar process for the deployment of adoption panels as under the former law.[9] The panel will also have a new role in the decision-making process as to whether a local authority should apply for a placement order. One area already clarified by the ACA 2002 is that panel members may be remunerated (by modest payments)[10] for their contribution to the work of the agency.[11] This was in recognition that many panels had been experiencing recruitment problems with consequences to their ability to maintain full panel membership and to deal with adoption cases promptly. It is also intended to help agencies to construct panels that are more representative of their local communities.

13.13 The 'panel system' of recommendation is, therefore, set to continue to have a crucial part to play in the structure of the adoption process.

---

1   AA Regs 1983, reg 10(1)(b).
2   Ibid, reg 11A(1).
3   *R v Wokingham District Council ex parte J* [1999] 2 FLR 1136, per Collins J, although Art 6 of the European Convention on Human Rights was not discussed, as he found that the recommendation was a 'non-binding recommendation' which did not necessarily 'determine the parents' civil rights and obligation', so that Art 6 was not engaged.
4   *R v North Yorkshire County Council ex parte M (No 2)* [1989] 2 FLR 79, per Ewbank J.
5   AA Regs 1983, reg 9.
6   *Re R (Adoption: Disclosure)* [1999] 2 FLR 1123 at 1124F–G, per Cazalet J.
7   [1999] 2 FLR 1123.
8   Ibid at 1124G–H and 1125A–B.
9   HC Special Standing Committee, 27 November 2001, col 323. It should be noted that in October 2002 a consultation document, *Adopter Preparation and Assessment and the Operation of Adoption Panels*, was published, which perhaps signals a fresh look being taken at the operation of adoption panels.
10   HL Deb, 14 October 2002, vol 639, no 186, col 643.
11   ACA 2002, s 11(1)(b) provides for regulations under s 9 to prescribe fees which may be paid by adoption agencies to persons providing *or assisting in providing* ... facilities' as part of the Adoption Service.

MAINTENANCE OF THE ADOPTION SERVICE

13.14   Each local authority must continue to maintain within its area an adoption service designed to meet the needs of: (a) children who may be adopted, their parents and guardians; (b) persons wishing to adopt a child; and (c) adopted persons, their parents, natural parents and former guardians ('the s 3 categories of persons').[1] This is a much wider group than that covered by the equivalent provision in the AA 1976, which did not include adopted adults, their birth and adoptive parents or former guardians.

13.15   Local authorities are under a statutory duty to provide the requisite facilities, which include making and participating in arrangements for the adoption of children and providing adoption support services.[2] This duty, therefore, covers all aspects of a local authority's activities in relation to adoption, such as arranging adoption, assessing prospective adopters and providing adoption support services. This is the first time that an Act has placed a clear duty on local authorities to provide adoption support services. The facilities provided by local authorities under s 3 will cover all types of adoptions whether domestic, intercountry, relative, step-parent or foster-carer adoptions. The intention is that everyone listed in s 3(1) (and in regulations made under s 4(1)(b)) should be able to approach their local authority for an assessment of their needs for adoption support services.

13.16   As part of the service, the provision of adoption support services must extend to certain categories of persons prescribed by regulations and may also extend to other persons ('the extended categories of persons').[3] It is, for example, intended to extend the duty on local authorities to cover birth and adoptive siblings of adoptees and children who may be adopted. Such provision will be made in regulations under s 3(3)(a). A consultation document entitled *Providing Effective Adoption Support*[4] has gone so far as to moot the proposition that adoption support services should be made available to birth and adoptive siblings and *to any other extended family members who are significant to the child.*[5] It is proposed that the results of this consultation will inform regulations for introduction in 2004.[6]

13.17   Local authorities may meet their obligation to provide services by ensuring that they are provided by a registered adoption society or such other persons as may be prescribed by regulations.[7] The facilities of the service must be provided in conjunction with the local authority's other social services[8] and with registered adoption societies in its area in a co-ordinated manner without duplication, omission or avoidable delay.[9]

---

1   ACA 2002, s 3(1).
2   Ibid, s 3(2).
3   Ibid, s 3(3)(a) and (b).
4   Published in June 2002.
5   Emphasis added.
6   HL Deb, 14 October 2002, vol 639, no 186, col 620.
7   ACA 2002, s 3(4).
8   'Other social services' are the functions which are the social services functions within the meaning of the Local Authority Social Services Act 1970 which include, in particular, those functions in so far as they relate to children: ACA 2002, s 3(6).
9   ACA 2002, s 3(5).

13.18   The provisions of ss 2 and 3 of the ACA 2002 (together with s 4, which is discussed below), therefore, are intended to pave the way for the new framework for adoption and financial support.[1]

ADOPTION SUPPORT SERVICES

13.19   Section 4 of the ACA 2002 is a new key provision, which imposes upon a local authority a duty to carry out an assessment of the needs for adoption support services at the request of the 's 3 categories of persons' and the 'extended categories' of persons.[2] It gives people affected by adoption a new right to request and receive an assessment of their needs for adoption support services from their local authority.

13.20   In practice, the needs of adoptive families (adopted children, their adoptive parents and any adoptive siblings) will be assessed together, as it would not be appropriate for the child's needs to be assessed in isolation. Where a child is not of sufficient age and understanding to request an assessment, his or her parent may request the assessment on his or her behalf. An older child may choose to request an assessment personally or, alternatively, his or her parent may request the assessment on his or her behalf. In relation to an adult who lacks capacity to request an assessment of needs, a carer may request an assessment on his or her behalf.

13.21   Adoptive families will not need to wait until after an adoption order has been made to request and receive an assessment of their needs for adoption support services. They will be able to request an assessment at any time: for example, when they have been matched with a child or when the child has been placed with them.

13.22   The authority also has a discretionary power to carry out an adoption support service assessment at the request of any person.[3] This will enable the local authority to assess the needs of any other person, such as a grandparent who may have a significant role in the child's life, in order to respond to the individual circumstances of the family. It can enlist the help[4] of registered adoption societies and other designated persons[5] in carrying out an assessment.

13.23   However, the ACA 2002 does not confer a right upon the adopted child or the adopters to receive the assessed adoption support services. Where a person's needs for adoption support services are identified in an assessment, it is for the local authority then to decide whether to provide those services to that person.[6] Once the assessment is carried out, therefore, the local authority is not under any duty to provide the services required to meet those needs. It is merely under an obligation to decide whether or not to

---

1   The consultation document *Providing Effective Adoption Support* (June 2002) referred to evidence from the USA which showed that the availability of adoption allowances and adoption support was a positive influence on adoption figures. It influenced 35 per cent of adoptive parents in their decision to adopt. In the same study, 29 per cent of parents who received an adoption allowance reported that adoption would not have been possible without that allowance.
2   ACA 2002, s 4(1); although in the case of the extended categories, this is subject to s 4(7)(a).
3   Ibid, s 4(2).
4   Ibid, s 4(3).
5   Ibid, s 3(4)(a) and (b).
6   Ibid, s 4(4).

provide the requisite service. The Government has taken the view that 'local authorities are best placed to provide services to individuals and, if they do so, which services those should be, based on need and *on resources available locally*'.[1] If, however, the authority decides to provide the service, in prescribed circumstances it must prepare a plan for the provision of support services and keep that plan under review.[2] The intention is that a plan will be required where a number of different adoption support services are being provided in order to co-ordinate the provision of those services.

13.24   There are some incentives for a local authority to act reasonably in deciding, following an assessment, whether to provide adoption support services. A failure to act reasonably ought to be picked up through monitoring and performance assessments. Council performance will be regularly assessed by the Social Services Inspectorate and, from April 2003, local authority adoption services will be independently inspected by the NCSC. The proposal is that the NCSC will inspect adoption agencies every 3 years, so as to be able to pick up on poor practice and breaches of regulations.[3]

13.25   The assessment for adopted children and their adoptive parents is intended to provide a mechanism to assist them in accessing adoption support services. It is to provide a means of facilitating the provision of a planned and co-ordinated support package drawn from the range of support services to be set in a new national framework. The objective of the assessment is to provide a link with other local authority functions and local education authority and health services, where the needs for such services are identified, with the aim of identifying a co-ordinated package of support to help adoptions succeed. If, therefore, it appears to the local authority, as a result of an assessment carried out under s 4, that there is a need for health or education services, the authority is under a duty under s 4(9) to notify the appropriate primary care trust or local education authority of the need. Following such notification, the primary care trust or local education authority will determine whether to provide services in accordance with its statutory obligations. Some children to be adopted will have very pressing health needs. They may have mental disorders as well as physical health needs which must be considered. This notification ensures that the health service is alerted through the assessment to the issues arising during the process. However, no statutory duty is placed on the health authority or the local education authority to co-operate with the local authority or to provide the requested services. The provisions in the Act simply mean that if persons affected by adoption are entitled to receive services under the statutory frameworks under which the primary care trusts and local education authorities operate, those services must be provided. Guidance and directions to primary care trusts and local

---

1   Emphasis added. HL Deb, 14 October 2002, vol 639, no 186, col 634. Lord Hunt of Kings Heath put it in this way: 'Ultimately local authorities provide the adoption service, so that they must decide who needs what level of support. We cannot get away from the fact that by requiring local authorities to provide the adoption support services to individuals we should be saying in effect that adoption services should have priority over almost every other service provided by the social services department of a local authority. I do not believe that it would be right in principle or in practice to fetter a local authority's discretion in that way'.

2   ACA 2002, s 4(5).

3   HC Special Standing Committee, 4 December 2001, col 406, per Ms Rosie Winterton, Parliamentary Secretary, Lord Chancellor's Department.

education authorities will be issued so as 'to ensure the joined-up planning and provision of adoption support services in the various public services'.[1]

13.26   The National Adoption Standards[2] already address the need for multi-agency work involving health and education providers. The Standards state that:

> 'Councils will plan and deliver adoption services with local health and education bodies (including schools), voluntary adoption agencies, the local courts and other relevant agencies including, where applicable, other councils.'

The Standards also make clear that children are entitled to support services that meet their needs, including advice and counselling, health, education, leisure and cultural services, and that adoptive parents will have access to a range of services before, during and after adoption.

13.27   Regulations, which are intended to underpin the delivery of the new framework for adoption support and financial support, are likely to set out:[3]

–   the circumstances in which prescribed categories of persons have a right to request and receive an assessment;
–   the type of assessment for each of the designated categories or the way in which an assessment is to be carried out;
–   the way in which the plan is to be prepared;
–   the way in which and the time at which a plan or a review is to take place;
–   the considerations to which a local authority is to have regard in carrying out an assessment or review or preparing a plan;
–   the circumstances in which a local authority may provide adoption support services subject to conditions. For example, the regulations may enable the local authority to specify that the financial support must be spent on specified items or services. Where a one-off grant is being paid for a specific purpose, the local authority may specify that the sum may be recouped if it was not spent accordingly. This would, however, be unlikely to be appropriate for a regular adoption allowance;
–   the consequences of the conditions not being met (including the recovery of any financial support provided by the local authority);
–   the circumstances in which assessments may apply to a local authority in respect of persons outside the local authority's area; and
–   the circumstances in which a local authority may recover from another local authority the expenses of providing adoption support services to any person.

This assessment may be carried out at the same time as an assessment of the person's needs under other legislation,[4] as part of an overall assessment package.

13.28   Reciprocal duties are imposed upon local authorities to co-operate in the exercise of the s 4 functions if it is consistent with the exercise of their functions more generally.[5]

---

1   HL Deb, 14 October 2002, vol 639, no 186, col 626.
2   The Standards will have the status of s 7 guidance from April 2003.
3   ACA 2002, s 4(6) and (7)(a)–(i).
4   Ibid, s 4(8).
5   Ibid, s 4(10) and (11).

13.29   This will be particularly important where a child is placed with a family living in another local authority area. The duty to co-operate under s 4(10) and (11) will ensure that local authorities work together to support people receiving adoption support services while they are settling into a new area. Furthermore, s 4(7)(h) enables regulations to be made setting out the arrangements for the assessment of needs and provision of adoption support services where the child is placed with an adoptive family living within a different local authority area.

13.30   It should also be noted that amendments have been made[1] to the CSA 2000 so as to make new provisions for the registration of adoption support agencies by the registration authority.[2] One of the purposes of the amendments is to allow agencies other than adoption agencies[3] to provide support services in connection with adoption (for example, specialist birth records counselling and other services to be set out in a new national framework for adoption support), while ensuring the proper regulation of such organisations.

13.31   An adoption support agency (ASA) is defined as 'an undertaking, the purpose of which, or one of the purposes of which, is the provision of adoption support services'.[4] An undertaking, however, is not an ASA merely because it provides information in connection with adoption.[5] 'Undertaking' has the same meaning as s 121 of the Care Standards Act 2000. It includes any business or profession, whether voluntary or profit-making, but does not extend, for example, to a self-help group meeting in a person's house. Adoption support providers that are already regulated through other means, such as a registered adoption society, a local authority, a local education authority, a special health authority, primary care trust or NHS Trust and the Registrar General, will be exempt from the requirement to register as an ASA.[6] In this way it is hoped to avoid unnecessary duplication of registration.

13.32   An ASA may, therefore, be voluntary or profit-making and both organisations and sole practitioners providing such services will be required to apply for registration as an ASA. Carrying on or managing an ASA without being registered will be an offence under s 11 of the CSA 2000. It is intended that registered ASAs will be able to provide birth record counselling under para 2(1)(b) of Sch 2 to the ACA 2002 and counselling in respect of information disclosed by adoption agencies under s 60 of the ACA 2002.

13.33   The issue of resources is critically important to the long-term prognosis for support services. The Government originally allocated £66.5 million of the Department of Health's Spending Review settlement over the period 2001/2–2003/4 to support the implementation of the work set out in the White Paper, and local authorities were expected to invest a substantial proportion of this funding in developing adoption

---

1   ACA 2002, s 8(3).
2   The NCSC in England and the National Assembly in Wales; see **13.6**.
3   Providers of adoption support services such as local authorities, registered adoption societies, the Registrar General, the local educational authority and health authority are not included in the definition of 'adoption support agency' in s 8, as they are not registered under Part 2 of the CSA 2000, but regulated through other statutory means.
4   ACA 2002, s 8(1).
5   Ibid, s 8(1)(a).
6   Ibid, s 8(1)(b) and (2).

support services. However, this investment was part of the Quality Protects initiative and appeared to cover only the *initial* costs of establishing the appropriate services. In October 2002, the Government announced that it would be providing an extra £70 million over 3 years as a special grant to local authorities for the provision of adoption and special guardianship support services. The grant is in recognition of the need for councils to deliver a step-change in the support services to be provided. This money will be ring-fenced, which means that local authorities will be required to use it only for adoption support and special guardianship support services. Twelve million pounds will be made available in 2003/4, £23 million in 2004/5 and £35 million in 2005/6.[1] This highlights the importance which the Government attaches to this new service.

LOCAL AUTHORITY PLANS FOR ADOPTION SERVICES

13.34   The ACA 2002 imposes a duty upon a local authority to prepare and publish a plan for the provision of adoption services in its area,[2] which must contain information prescribed by regulations,[3] such as requirements for the review of any plan or the circumstances prescribed for its modification or substitution and publication.[4]

13.35   The Secretary of State[5] may direct the form and manner and the time at which the plan is to be published or reviewed by the local authority and may also direct with whom the local authority is to consult in drawing up the plan.[6] The Secretary of State may also direct that the plan be included in a more general plan for the provision of services relating to children within the local authority's area.[7] The directions[8] may relate to a particular local authority or to a class or description of local authorities or to local authorities in general.[9]

FUNCTIONS, MANAGEMENT AND SUPPLEMENTARY POWERS

Functions

13.36   The ACA 2002 provides a general power to make regulations for any purpose relating to the exercise by the local authority and voluntary adoption agencies of their functions in relation to adoption and by the ASAs of their function in relation to the provision of adoption support services.[10] Breaches of the regulations will be an offence liable on summary conviction (prosecuted in the magistrates' court) to a fine not exceeding level 5 on the standard scale (ie £5,000).[11]

---

1   HL Deb, 14 October 2002, vol 639, no 186, col 635, per Lord Hunt of Kings Heath.
2   ACA 2002, s 5(1).
3   Ibid, s 5(2).
4   Ibid, s 5(3).
5   Ibid, s 5(5); the 'appropriate Minister' is defined in s 144(1) as the Secretary of State.
6   Ibid, s 5(5).
7   Ibid, s 5(4).
8   Ibid, s 5(7).
9   Except for a direction under s 5(4)(b): s 5(7)(c).
10   ACA 2002, s 9(1).
11   Ibid, s 9(3).

Management

13.37 The general regulation-making power contained in s 9 is particularised in s 10 in relation to the management and general operation of local authorities, voluntary adoption agencies and ASAs. The regulations will include provisions as to:[1]

– the fitness of the persons who are to work for these bodies;
– the fitness of the premises;
– the management and control of their operations;
– the number of persons or persons of any particular type;
– the management and training of those persons; and
– the keeping of information.[2]

13.38 Regulations may also be made[3] to ensure that voluntary adoption agencies are managed and that ASAs are carried on by persons who are fit to do so, and for the health and welfare of children placed by voluntary adoption agencies (for example, children waiting to be adopted who are placed with private foster parents) to be adequately protected. Requirements may also be imposed regarding the financial position of the agency and the appointment of a manager. The intention is that the agencies should appoint a manager in all cases, including where the agency has a branch, so as to ensure that all the voluntary adoption agencies and ASAs are appropriately managed.[4]

13.39 The conduct of voluntary adoption agencies and ASAs will also be governed by regulations,[5] including:

– the facilities and services to be provided;
– the keeping of accounts;
– the notification to the registration authority of events occurring on the agency's premises;
– the giving of notice to the registration authority of periods during which the manager is absent and arrangements for the running of the agency during his or her absence;
– the notification to the registration authority of changes in the identity of the manager or in the ownership of the agency or the identity of its officers;[6]
– the arrangements for dealing with complaints.

Fees

13.40 Regulations will provide for the payment of fees: (i) to be charged by adoption agencies in respect of the provision of services to persons providing facilities as part of the

---

1 ACA 2002, s 10(1). Provision may be made for prohibiting persons from working in prescribed positions unless they are on a register of social care workers maintained under s 56 of the CSA 2000: s 10(2).
2 The broader term 'information' is used rather than 'record' to reflect the developments in information technology, in particular information sent by e-mail. Section 144(1) defines 'information' as meaning 'information recorded in any form'.
3 ACA 2002, s 10(3)(a)–(e).
4 HL Deb, 14 October 2002, vol 639, no 186, col 642, per Lord McIntosh of Haringey.
5 ACA 2002, s 10(4).
6 Ibid, s 10(4)(h) makes provision for the payment of a prescribed fee to the registration authority in respect of any notification required of changes in the ownership of an agency or the identity of its officers.

Adoption Service;[1] (ii) to be paid by adoption agencies to persons providing or assisting in providing such facilities;[2] and (iii) to be charged by local authorities in respect of the provision of prescribed facilities of the Adoption Service in connection with the adoption of a child brought into the United Kingdom for the purpose of adoption or a Convention adoption, overseas adoption or an adoption effected under the law of a country or territory outside the British Islands.[3] There will also be regulations for the charging of fees by adoption agencies in respect of the provision of counselling, where that counselling is provided in connection with the disclosure of information relating to a person's adoption.[4]

13.41   The powers in s 9 will enable the appropriate minister to require adoption agencies, through regulations, to publish their fees or make them known to the prospective adopters at the start of the assessment process, if necessary. In respect of fees charged between adoption agencies, the level of inter-agency fee is announced annually by the Consortium of Voluntary Adoption Agencies. This is agreed between the voluntary agencies themselves. The intercountry adoption guide produced by the Department of Health makes it clear that all adoption agencies charging fees to adopters and prospective adopters should state clearly what the fee will be prior to the start of the process.

13.42   Agencies are also encouraged to provide applicants with a written statement detailing what is included in the fee. It is a clear legal requirement in ss 95 and 96 that adoption agencies may not derive any profit from this work.

Information

13.43   Each adoption agency must give the Secretary of State statistical or other general information relating to (i) its performance of all or any of its functions relating to adoption, and (ii) the children and other persons in relation to whom it has exercised those functions.[5]

13.44   In addition, the justices' chief executive for each magistrates' court and the relevant officer[6] of each county court and of the High Court must give the Secretary of State any statistical or other general information he requires about proceedings under this Act.[7]

13.45   The information must be given at the times and in the form directed by the Secretary of State, who may from time to time publish abstracts of the information.[8]

---

1   ACA 2002, s 11(1)(a).
2   Ibid, s 11(1)(b). This will include the members of adoption panels.
3   Ibid, s 11(2) and (3).
4   Ibid, s 11(4).
5   Ibid, s 13(1).
6   Ibid, s 13(3) defines 'relevant officer' as the 'officer of that court who is designated to act for the purposes of the subsection by a direction given by the Lord Chancellor'.
7   Ibid, s 13(2).
8   Ibid, s 13(4) and (5).

Inspection of premises and records

13.46   The Secretary of State may arrange for the inspection from time to time of any premises where a child is living (a) who has been placed by an adoption agency, or (b) in respect of whom a notice of intention to adopt has been given under s 44.[1]

13.47   The person conducting the inspection must be authorised by the Secretary of State[2] and an officer of the local authority may only be so authorised with the consent of the authority.[3] The authorised inspector may visit the child at the premises, and make any examination into the state of the premises and the treatment of the child there which he thinks fit.[4] The person authorised to inspect the premises has the power to enter the premises for that purpose at any reasonable time and require any person to give him any reasonable assistance he may require.[5] If required to do so, he must produce a duly authenticated document showing his authority.[6] Intentionally obstructing an authorised person is an offence.[7]

13.48   These are clearly important protections for the child. Although it may be arguable that these wide powers of entry and inspection constitute an infringement of the right to respect for the home under Art 8 of the European Convention on Human Rights,[8] because such entry and search has a statutory basis[9] and is for the protection of the health of the child and for the rights and freedoms of others, including the welfare of the child, it will be justifiable under Art 8(2), provided that on the facts it is shown not to be a disproportionate response.[10]

13.49   The Secretary of State may also require an adoption agency to give him any information or allow him to inspect records (in whatever form) relating to the discharge of its functions in relation to adoption.[11] Provision is made for the inspection of any computer being used in connection with an adoption agency's records,[12] and a right of entry to premises and to request reasonable assistance for the purpose of inspecting records also exist.[13] A duly authenticated document showing the inspector's authority must be shown if requested[14] and an intentional obstruction constitutes an offence.[15]

---

1   ACA 2002, s 15(1).
2   Ibid, s 15(3).
3   Ibid, s 15(4).
4   Ibid, s 15(5).
5   Ibid, s 15(7).
6   Ibid, s 15(8).
7   Ibid, s 15(9): liable on summary conviction to a fine not exceeding level 3 on the standard scale (ie £1,000).
8   *Niemitz v Germany* (1993) 16 EHRR 97.
9   *Chappell v UK* (1990) 12 EHRR 1 (*Anton Piller* order).
10   *McLeod v UK* (1999) 27 EHRR 493, [1998] 2 FLR 1048.
11   ACA 2002, s 15(2).
12   Ibid, s 15(6).
13   Ibid, s 15(7).
14   Ibid, s 15(8).
15   Ibid, s 15(9); the liability on summary conviction is to a fine not exceeding level 3 (ie £1,000).

Inquiries

13.50   The Secretary of State may cause an inquiry to be held into any matter connected with the functions of an adoption agency,[1] which he may direct to be held in private.[2] Where no such direction has been given, the person holding the inquiry may, if he thinks fit, hold it or any part of it in private.[3] The provisions in s 250(2)–(5) of the Local Government Act 1972 are to apply. Section 17 of the ACA 2002 follows the model of s 81 of the CA 1989, which also provides for inquiries.

INDEPENDENT REVIEW OF DETERMINATIONS

13.51   A new provision in the ACA 2002[4] provides for the establishment of a review procedure in respect of certain determinations made by adoption agencies. The intention is to use this provision to provide prospective adopters with a right to request a referral where an adoption agency has indicated that it proposes to turn down the application to adopt. It is also intended to use the independent review mechanism to review determinations made by adoption agencies concerning the disclosure of protected information held by them where, under the ACA 2002, they have a discretion. The agency will be under an obligation to take account of the views of the subject of the information, together with the welfare of the adopted person, as well as the other matters that may be prescribed in regulations determining whether to release that information.

13.52   Where an adoption agency makes a 'qualifying determination' as specified in regulations[5] in respect of any person, that person may apply to a panel constituted by the Secretary of State for a review of that determination. Regulations[6] will deal with:

–   the duties and powers of the panel (including the power to request a contribution towards the cost of a review from the adoption agency which made the original determination);
–   the administration and procedures;
–   the appointment of panel members;
–   the payment of expenses; and
–   the duties of the adoption agencies in connection with reviews and the monitoring of reviews.

13.53   The Secretary of State may, in relation to the panel, delegate functions to an organisation to perform on his behalf[7] and may make payments to it.[8] 'Organisation' is defined as 'including a public body or private or voluntary organisation'.[9] The organisation must perform its functions in accordance with any general or specific

---

1   ACA 2002, s 17(1).
2   Ibid, s 17(2).
3   Ibid, s 17(3).
4   Ibid, s 12(1). See also ibid, Sch 4, para 5, which inserts a new s 9A dealing with independent reviews after s 9 of the AA 1976.
5   Ibid, s 12(2).
6   Ibid, s 12(3).
7   Ibid, s 12(4).
8   Ibid, s 12(6).
9   Ibid, s 12(8).

directions which the Secretary of State may give.[1] This is intended to ensure the independence of the review mechanism.

13.54 The purpose of the review mechanism, therefore, is to make recommendations to the adoption agencies, not to override their decisions. The intention is that the independent body or organisation, appointed by the appropriate minister under s 12(4), will convene a review panel to re-examine the evidence and make a fresh recommendation to the agency. The agency will then be required by regulations made under s 12(3)(e) to consider both its original determination and the recommendation of the review panel before making its final decision. The ultimate responsibility still rests with the adoption agency as the body responsible for the full range of adoption services and accountable for the number and quality of the placements made.[2]

13.55 It has been stressed that the review mechanism is not intended as a means of micro-managing the day-to-day business of adoption agencies. In relation to local authority adoption services, adoption is a mainstream social service function. The majority of complaints about local authority adoption services are, therefore, to be channelled through the existing social services complaints procedure.[3] However, the use of a regulation-making power to set out which determinations will be reviewed by the independent review mechanism is intended to ensure that there is flexibility to consider for which determinations the mechanism can usefully be used and to allow for the list to be reviewed in the light of developing practice. The Government has indicated that it will review the operation of the independent review mechanism after it has been fully operational for 2–3 years. In that review, consideration will be given specifically as to whether the list should be extended.[4]

DEFAULT POWERS

13.56 Where an adoption society has ceased to be registered under Part 2 of the Care Standards Act 2000, the Secretary of State is empowered to direct that the society make appropriate arrangements for the transfer of its functions relating to children.[5]

13.57 Where a registered adoption society is inactive, defunct or has ceased to be registered under Part 2 of the Care Standards Act 2000 and it has not made arrangements for the transfer of its functions, then the Secretary of State is empowered to direct the appropriate local authority to take action.[6] Before giving such a direction, the Secretary of State must, if practicable, consult both the society and the authority.[7] He may also charge the society for the expenses necessarily incurred by him or on his behalf as a result of its failure to make appropriate arrangements.[8]

---

1   ACA 2002, s 12(5).
2   HL Deb, 27 June 2002, vol 636, no 160, CWH 116, per Lord Hunt of Kings Heath.
3   Ibid, CWH 114.
4   HL Deb, 14 October 2002, vol 639, no 186, cols 646 and 649, per Lord Hunt of Kings Heath.
5   ACA 2002, s 6.
6   Ibid, s 7(1) and (2).
7   Ibid, s 7(5).
8   Ibid, s 7(4).

13.58   Where a local authority has failed, without reasonable excuse, to comply with any duties imposed by the ACA 2002 or s 1 or s 2(4) of the Adoption (Intercountry Aspects Act) 1999, the Secretary of State may make an order (with reasons) declaring that authority to be in default. The order may contain directions to ensure that the duty is complied with within the period specified in the order.[1] Any such directions are enforceable by mandatory order.[2]

ADOPTION AND CHILDREN ACT REGISTER[3]

13.59   In the White Paper, *Adoption: A New Approach*, the Government accepted the PIU Report's recommendation to establish a new Adoption Register 'to tackle delays in finding suitable adoptive placements for children'.[4] The proposals were as follows.

(1)   To provide 'a national infrastructure for adoption services', which will 'hold information on approved adoptive families and children for whom adoption is the plan' and will be used 'to suggest families for children where a local family is either not desirable or cannot be found within a reasonable time'.[5]

(2)   'Adoptive families will be placed on the Register as soon as they are approved for adoption and children when the plan for adoption is made. This will enable the Register to produce non-identifying data on the characteristics of the two groups and the success of the matching process'.[6]

(3)   At the end of an agreed period, or immediately where the finding of a family locally is not in the best interests of the child, the register will be used to suggest matches between children and adoptive families.[7]

The Register

13.60   In line with the proposals in the White Paper, one of the new provisions in the ACA 2002 enables the Queen to make an Order in Council enabling the Secretary of State to establish and maintain an Adoption and Children Act Register.[8] The Register will contain details of children who are suitable for adoption and prospective adopters who have been approved to adopt children.[9] This will enable this information to be used as a means of trying to match children with adoptive families in those cases where a local match is not suitable or cannot be found within an agreed period of time.

---

1   ACA 2002, s 14(1)–(3).
2   Ibid, s 14(4).
3   Although not included in Chapter 2 of the ACA 2002 which deals with the Adoption Service, it has been included in the text at this point as being one of the central planks of the Government's new adoption strategy.
4   Cm 5017 (December 2000), at para 6.7.
5   Ibid, at para 6.8.
6   Ibid, at para 6.10.
7   Ibid, at para 6.12.
8   ACA 2002, s 125(1).
9   Ibid, s 125(1)(a).

13.61   The register will contain additional prescribed material about persons included in the register in respect of events occurring to them after their inclusion.[1] For example, this power may be used to record information about the stability of the adoptive placements.

13.62   The Order may apply to any of the provisions in ss 126–131 (with or without modification) for the purpose of finding persons with whom children may be placed for purposes other than adoption.[2] This provision, therefore, extends the use of the register to cover children needing other forms of permanent placement, such as special guardianship.

13.63   Although the information may be kept in any form considered appropriate by the Secretary of State,[3] it is most likely that the information will be held electronically. The register itself will not be open to public inspection or search.[4] The Order will make provision about the retention of information in the register.[5]

Delegation to organisations

13.64   The Secretary of State may delegate his functions of establishing and maintaining the register and disclosing information entered in (or compiled from information entered in) the register to an organisation,[6] which may be either a public body or a private or voluntary organisation[7] and which will operate the register under the Secretary of State's general or special directions.[8] The Secretary of State is empowered to make payments to the organisation in relation to this arrangement.[9]

13.65   An organisation maintaining the register on the Secretary of State's behalf may be authorised to act as agent for the payment or receipt of sums payable by adoption agencies to other adoption agencies.[10] For example, the organisation may manage the payment of 'inter-agency' fees between adoption agencies in respect of matches suggested by the register. The organisation must perform these functions in accordance with the Secretary of State's directions which may be general or special directions.[11]

---

1   ACA 2002, s 125(1)(b).
2   Ibid, s 125(2).
3   Ibid, s 125(5).
4   Ibid, s 125(3).
5   Ibid, s 125(4).
6   Ibid, s 126(1). Where the Secretary of State delegates his function to such an organisation, the references in the remaining provisions dealing with the register are to that organisation: s 126(5).
7   Ibid, s 131(1); 'voluntary organisation providing a registered adoption service' has the same meaning as in s 144(3).
8   Ibid, s 126(4). Where the Secretary of State delegates his function of establishing and maintaining the register or issues general or special directions, he must first obtain the agreement of the Scottish Ministers, if the register applies to Scotland and of the National Assembly for Wales, if the register applies to Wales.
9   Ibid, s 126(2).
10   Ibid, s 127(1).
11   Ibid, s 127(2). If the Secretary of State does issue such directions, he must first obtain the agreement of the Scottish Ministers and of the National Assembly for Wales, if the provisions apply to either: s 128(3).

Supply of information

13.66   Orders in Council under s 125 will set out the type of information which must be passed by adoption agencies to the Secretary of State or registration organisation for inclusion in the register, together with the time, form and manner in which that information must be given.[1] Adoption societies may be required to pay a fee to the Secretary of State or registration organisation in respect of the information to be entered on the register,[2] which would contribute to the administrative costs and not include any element of profit.

13.67   It is important to note that these requirements remain subject to the parties to whom the information relates[3] consenting to the inclusion of the information on the register; otherwise, there would (arguably) be infringements of the provisions under Arts 8 and 10 of the European Convention on Human Rights. An adoption agency may not, therefore, disclose any information to the Secretary of State or the registration organisation:

(a)   about prospective adopters who are suitable to adopt a child, or persons who were included in the register as such prospective adopters, without their consent;[4]

(b)   about children suitable for adoption or persons who were included in the register as such children, without the consent of the prescribed person.[5]

Disclosure of information

13.68   The information on the register[6] may only be disclosed by the Secretary of State or the registration organisation in accordance with the statutory provisions and on prescribed terms and conditions.[7] The prescribed information held on the register may be given either to an adoption agency which is looking for appropriate adoptive parents with whom to place a child suitable for adoption, or to an adoption agency acting on behalf of approved adoptive parents who wish to adopt a child suitable for adoption.[8] The Order will set out the steps which adoption agencies must take upon receipt of this

---

1   ACA 2002, s 128(1) and (2).
2   Ibid, s 128(3).
3   Ibid, s 128(4).
4   Ibid, s 128(4)(a).
5   Ibid, s 128(4)(b). The Order will set out who may consent to the sharing of the information on the child's behalf. It is to be hoped that the 'prescribed person' will include the child where he or she is of an age and understanding to consent.
6   Information either held on the register or compiled from information held on the register may be passed to certain prescribed categories of persons for statistical or research purposes and other prescribed purposes: s 129(3).
7   ACA 2002, s 129(1) and (6). Subsection (1) does not apply to disclosure of information with the authority of the Secretary of State or to disclosure by the registration authority of prescribed information to the Scottish Ministers or the Welsh Assembly: s 129(5).
8   Ibid, s 129(2)(a) and (b).

information.[1] Disclosure of information, otherwise than in accordance with the Act, will be an offence.[2]

13.69　For the purposes of ss 125–131, a child is 'suitable for adoption if an adoption agency is satisfied that the child ought to be placed for adoption' and 'prospective adopters are suitable to adopt a child if an adoption agency is satisfied that they are suitable to have a child placed with them for adoption'.[3] In this group of clauses, 'adoption agency' means a local authority in England or a voluntary adoption agency registered by the NCSC.[4]

THE NATIONAL ADOPTION STANDARDS

13.70　One of the principal changes highlighted in the White Paper, *Adoption: A New Approach*, was the establishment of National Standards for Adoption, which were to 'set out what children, prospective adopters, adoptive parents and birth parents can expect from the adoption process and the responsibilities of the adoption agencies and councils, so that all parties receive a fair and consistent service, wherever they live'.[5]

13.71　An Expert Working Group chaired by Dame Margaret Booth DBE and organised by the BAAF developed draft proposals which were issued for widespread consultation and resulted in National Adoption Standards. The National Adoption Standards will have the status of s 7 guidance from April 2003. Section 7(1) of the Local Authority Social Services Act 1970 provides:

> 'Local authorities shall, in the exercise of their social functions, including the exercise of any discretion conferred by any relevant enactment, act under the general guidance of the Secretary of State.'

13.72　The Government's view of the status of guidance is:[6]

> 'Guidance documents and circulars are usually issued as general guidance of the Secretary of State as described in s 7(1). Local authorities are required to act in accordance with such guidance which is intended to be a statement of what is held to be good practice. Though they are not in themselves law in the way that regulations are law, guidance documents are likely to

---

1　ACA 2002, s 129(4). Fees will be charged in respect of information given to adoption agencies under s 129(2) or in respect of information given for statistical or research purposes under s 129(3): s 129(7).

2　Ibid, s 129(8) and (9), ie punishable on summary conviction by up to 3 months' imprisonment or a fine not exceeding level 5 on the standard scale (£5000) or both. Proceedings may not be brought more than 6 years after the commission of the offence but, subject to that, may be brought within 6 months from the date on which evidence, sufficient in the opinion of the prosecutor to warrant proceedings, came to his knowledge; s 138. Any action taken by the Secretary of State or the registration authority which might otherwise be an offence under ss 93–95 is not an offence where the action was authorised or required to be done by virtue of ss 125–131: s 131(3).

3　Ibid, s 131(2)(a) and (b).

4　Ibid, s 130(1). An Order in Council made under s 125 may provide for any requirements imposed on English adoption agencies to apply to Scottish and/or Welsh local authorities and voluntary adoption agencies. This will enable the Adoption and Children Act Register to be extended to Scotland and/or Wales: s 130(2).

5　Cm 5017 (December 2000), at para 4.5.

6　*The Care of Children – Principles and Practice in Regulations and Guidance, 1989,* p 2.

be quoted or used in court proceedings as well as in local authority policy and practice papers. They could provide the basis for a legal challenge of an authority's action or inaction, including (in extreme cases) default action by the Secretary of State.'

13.73   In *R v Islington London Borough Council, ex parte Rixon*,[1] Sedley J (as he then was) held that in enacting s 7(1), Parliament did not intend local authorities, to whom ministerial guidance was given, to be free, having considered it, to take it or leave it. He said that local authorities were required:[2]

'... to follow the path charted by the Secretary of State's guidance, with liberty to deviate from it, where on admissible grounds, there is reason to do so, but without the freedom to take a substantially different course.'

13.74   Although these important developments relate to the former law under the AA 1976, it is inconceivable that similar initiatives drawing heavily from the experiences in forming the '1976 Act' National Adoption Standards will not equally apply under the ACA 2002. The strong likelihood is that the 'current' National Adoption Standards will either simply be replicated or form the bedrock from which the National Standards for the new Act will be carved.

13.75   The current National Standards deal with (i) children; (ii) prospective adopters; (iii) adoptive parents; (iv) birth parents and birth families; and (v) councils: both corporate and senior management responsibilities. The current Standards have a 'values statement' for domestic adoptions, which sets out the important principles underpinning the standards.

13.76   Some key points in the current National Standards relating to the practice for placing children are set out below as a guide to the probable practice in respect of planning for permanence and time scales under the ACA 2002.

Children

13.77   The child's need for a permanent home will be addressed at the 4-month review and a plan for permanence made. Clear time scales will be set for achieving the plan which will be appropriately monitored and considered at every review. Where adoption has been identified as the plan for the child at a review, the adoption panel will make its recommendation within 2 months.

13.78   Where adoption is the plan, taking into account the child's individual needs, the following actions will be taken.

(1)   A match with suitable adoptive parents will be identified and approved by the panel within 6 months of the agency agreeing that adoption is in the child's best interests.

(2)   In care proceedings, where the plan is adoption, a match with suitable adoptive parents will be identified and approved by the panel within 6 months of the court's decision.

---

1   (1998) 1 CCL Rep 119.
2   A failure to comply with this approach is unlawful: *R v North Yorkshire County Council, ex parte Hargreaves* (1994) 26 BMLR 121.

(3) Where a parent has requested that a child aged under 6 months be placed for adoption, a match with suitable adoptive parents will be identified and approved by the panel within 3 months of the agency agreeing that adoption is in the child's best interest.

13.79 This prescribed time scale for planning for permanence is, on any practical view, extremely tight and so it becomes doubly important not to lose sight of the fact that adoption is only one of a spectrum of options and that the birth parents are still the best prospect for a permanent family for most children. It is important to note that the Department of Health is developing an Integrated Children's System framework to support all aspects of the planning process which will include an 'exemplar permanence plan' and it is to be hoped that this exemplar will reinforce the need to consider all the options for permanence, notwithstanding the Government's target of a 40 per cent increase in adoptions.

ADOPTION AND FOSTERING: CRIMINAL RECORDS AND DISQUALIFICATION

13.80 As a safeguard in recruiting suitable and safe prospective adopters and foster carers, the Police Act 1997 has established a new Criminal Records Bureau (CRB) which provides (amongst other things) for a system of vetting those who are concerned with children, and a 'one-stop shop' to simplify and speed up the process. The objective is that criminal record checks ('standard disclosures') and enhanced criminal record checks ('enhanced disclosures') should be available through the CRB on both prospective foster parents and adoptive parents, together with other adults in the same household. Although such checks are provided for under ss 113 and 115 of the Police Act 1997, s 135 of the ACA 2002 amends both sections to make absolutely clear that adoptive parents, foster parents and other adults in the same household are caught by the checks.

13.81 The criminal record certificates will cover both spent and unspent convictions, together with cautions, reprimands and warnings. Enhanced criminal record certificates will also include 'soft information' from local police records which the Chief Officer of Police considers relevant, for example relevant matters which did not lead to a conviction. The process will involve a check of lists maintained by the Department of Health and Department for Education and Skills of persons considered unsuitable to work with children under the Protection of Children Act 1999. These provisions supplement the stringent checks already in force in respect of the recruitment of foster carers and prospective adopters.

13.82 Approval of foster parents had been governed by the Foster Placement (Children) Regulations 1991 (referred to as 'the Foster Placement Regs 1991') enacted under the provisions of the CA 1989, which required foster parents to be approved in accordance with certain requirements, whereby the local authority had to be satisfied that the foster parents were suitable and that the household was suitable.[1] As we have seen, approval of prospective adopters was governed by the AA Regs 1983, as amended

---

1   Foster Placement Regs 1991, reg 3; the approval included the information specified in Sch 1 to the Regulations.

in 1997. An adoption agency was under a duty to take steps to consider whether a person may be suitable to be an adoptive parent and, if so, to undertake further prescribed enquiries, including the disclosure of any other relevant information which may assist the adoption panel or may be requested by the panel.[1]

13.83   However, in the wake of the case of Roger Saint,[2] the Foster Placement Regs 1991 and the AA Regs 1983 were amended by the Children (Protection from Offenders) (Miscellaneous Amendments) Regulations 1997[3] (referred to as the 'Offenders Regs 1997') which came into force in October 1997. These Regulations (amongst other things) tightened up the requirements for approval of foster parents and prospective adopters, but in so doing stripped away the discretion from the decision-makers, save in some cases where the offender was aged under 20 at the time of the offence.

13.84   The new regulations resulted in a person not being regarded as suitable to act as either a foster parent or a prospective adopter if he or a member of his household *over the age of 18 years*[4] (a) had been convicted of an offence specified in Sch 1 to the Children and Young Persons Act 1933, or (b) had been cautioned by a constable in respect of any such offence, which, at the time the caution was given, he admitted.[5] The Offenders Regs 1997 were mandatory[6] and resulted in a flurry of applications,[7] as local authorities grappled with the anomalies thrown up by these amendments which forced them into disqualifying prospective adopters and previously approved foster carers, where children were well-settled and thriving, thus subjecting those children to detrimental upheaval. In *R v Secretary of State for Health and Kent County Council, ex parte B,*[8] Scott-Baker J, although rejecting the argument that the Offenders Regulations 1997 were *ultra vires* (in not allowing any discretion to be exercised by local authorities in placing children with foster parents (or prospective adopters)), looked forward to amendments which were being then proposed by the Department of Health to 're-instate local authority discretion' in a limited number of cases.[9]

---

1   AA Regs 1983, regs 8(1) and (2).
2   A number of children had been placed with Roger Saint by several local authorities, notwithstanding his conviction for indecent assault on a boy of 12 years old. He was sentenced to 6½ years' imprisonment for serious sexual abuse of several children who had been in his care. The case highlighted the fact that local authorities were failing to identify potential abusers.
3   SI 1997/2308.
4   The words in italics have subsequently been amended; see below.
5   AA Regs 1983, reg 8A(2)(b).
6   *Re RJ (Foster Placement)* [1998] 2 FLR 110 at 113C, per Sir Stephen Brown P; *Re RJ (Fostering: Person Disqualified)* [1999] 1 FLR 605 at 612, where, after citing para 5 of the Guidance to the Offenders Regulations 1997 (LAC (97) 17), Butler-Sloss LJ (as she then was) said that '... the lack of discretion appears to be intentional'. See *Re RJ (Wardship)* [1999] 1 FLR 618 for the final outcome in the *Re RJ* case, in which Cazalet J made orders in wardship proceedings vesting care and control in the foster carers, and also *Re A (Protection from Offenders Regulations)* [1999] 1 FLR 697, per Hogg J, in respect of a private law case.
7   See various cases referred to in *R v Secretary of State for Health ex parte B* [1999] 1 FLR 650 at 658–661.
8   [1999] 1 FLR 650 at 656, per Scott Baker J.
9   Ibid at 662E–H.

13.85   The limited amendments finally came on 1 October 2001. The AA Regs 1983 were amended[1] to read:

> '8A(1) An adoption agency shall, so far as practicable, take steps to obtain any previous criminal convictions and any cautions given by a constable in respect of criminal offences which relate to a prospective adopter and other members of his household *aged 18 or over*[2] when considering ... whether a person may be suitable to be an adoptive parent.
>
> (2) An adoption agency shall not consider a person to be suitable to be an adoptive parent or, as the case may be, shall consider a person no longer to be suitable, if he or any member of his household over the age of 18:
>
> (a)   has been convicted of a specified offence *committed at the age of 18 or over*, or
> (b)   has been cautioned by a constable in respect of a specified offence which, at the time the caution was given, he admitted.'

13.86   Therefore, the position under the Offenders Regs 1997 has been ameliorated to this extent: those who as juveniles were convicted or cautioned in respect of Sch 1 offences or who have as members of their household those who as juveniles were so convicted or cautioned are no longer automatically disqualified as prospective adopters or foster parents. Otherwise, the law remains that there is an absolute prohibition in respect of certain specified offences, as part of the overall strategy 'to protect vulnerable children from the sexual predators who regrettably circulate in our society'.[3]

---

1   The Foster Placement Regs 1991 were amended to the same effect.
2   The words in italics show the amendments.
3   *R v Secretary of State for Health and Kent County Council ex parte B* [1999] 1 FLR 650 at 662E, per Scott Baker J.

Chapter 14

INTERNATIONAL REGULATION OF INTERCOUNTRY ADOPTION

INTRODUCTORY BACKGROUND

14.1   An 'intercountry adoption' is a general term referring to the adoption of a child resident abroad by adopters resident in the United Kingdom and may also refer to the adoption of a child resident in the United Kingdom by adopters resident overseas. Before 1990 there were a few intercountry adoptions, most of which were adoptions by birth relatives. The AA 1976 was passed at the time when intercountry adoption was unusual[1] and, consequently, detailed provisions were not included.[2]

14.2   In the 1990s, the media coverage of the horrifying conditions under which orphaned and other children were living in Eastern European countries, such as Romania and Bosnia, and South American countries, such as Guatemala and El Salvador, led to a sharp increase in intercountry adoptions. In *Re C (Adoption: Legality)*,[3] an adoption case which concerned a Mayan Indian child from Guatemala, Johnson J highlighted how the deplorable conditions in the States of origin of many intercountry adoptees can become a compelling consideration, when he said:

> 'Anyone who has seen the conditions in which some children are brought up in some Central and South American countries, in the shanty towns and favelas alongside the great cities, will feel an urgent desire that children be given the opportunities represented by adoption into an English family.'

14.3   By the year 2000, over 300 applications were being made annually to adopt children resident abroad by adopters living in the United Kingdom. These were applications where the adopters had been approved as suitable to adopt by their local authority or an approved adoption agency. There were, however, about 100 other cases where the adoption procedures were disregarded and the children brought into the United Kingdom without approval. As was further observed by Johnson J in *Re C (Adoption: Legality)*:[4]

---

1   There were as few as 50 per annum: see the White Paper, *Adoption: The Future*, Cm 2288 (1993), para 6.2.

2   Save for the Hague Convention on Jurisdiction, Applicable Law and Recognition of Decrees relating to Adoptions 1965 which concluded at The Hague on 15 November 1965. This Convention was only ever ratified by three countries (UK, Austria and Switzerland), and all three countries have declared their intention to denounce it. The 1965 Convention has been overtaken by the Hague Convention on Protection of Children and Co-operation in respect of Intercountry Adoption 1993.

3   [1999] 1 FLR 370 at 376H–377A.

4   Ibid at 376F–376H.

'Most of those [100 applications] will be made by parents who have previously been rejected as suitable for the adoption of a British child, yet ask the court for an adoption order in respect of an overseas child in disregard of the safeguards laid down to protect a British child.'

THE 1993 HAGUE CONVENTION

14.4   In response to this proliferation of intercountry adoptions, the Hague Convention on Protection of Children and Co-operation in Respect of Intercountry Adoption (henceforth referred to as 'the Hague Convention') was concluded at The Hague on 29 May 1993. Currently 30 countries have ratified this Convention, 12 have signed but not yet ratified it and a further 11 have acceded to it.[1] The United Kingdom signed in 1994 and proposes to ratify the Hague Convention before the implementation of the ACA 2002.

SAFEGUARDS IN THE BEST INTERESTS OF THE CHILD

14.5   The Hague Convention provides a framework of minimum[2] standards for regulating the process of intercountry adoption. The Convention's aims are threefold:

(1)   to establish safeguards to ensure that intercountry adoptions take place in the best interests of the child and with respect for his or her fundamental rights as recognised by international law;[3]
(2)   to establish a system of co-operation amongst Contracting States to ensure that the safeguards are respected and thereby prevent the abduction, the sale of or traffic in children;[4]
(3)   to secure the recognition in Contracting States of adoptions made in accordance with the Convention.[5]

14.6   It is underpinned by the UN Convention on the Rights of the Child 1989 ('the UN Convention').[6] The Preamble to the Hague Convention expressly states that it is designed 'to establish common provisions . . . taking into account the principles set forth in international instruments, in particular the United Nations Convention on the Rights of the Child . . .'.

---

1   'Accession' is in effect ratification by countries who sent no delegates to the final 'diplomatic' session of the Hague Conference in May 1993.
2   William Duncan 'Regulating Intercountry Adoption – an International Perspective' in A Bainham, DS Pearl and R Pickford (eds) *Frontiers of Family Law* (2nd edn, John Wiley & Sons, 1995) at p 51. 'It is important . . . to point out that the Convention will establish a set of minimum standards and procedures, which may be supplemented by additional safeguards thought appropriate or necessary by individual states. For example . . . it will be undoubtedly open to individual states to insist upon "approved-agency" adoptions in their own cases'.
3   Article 1(a).
4   Article 1(b).
5   Article 1(c).
6   Articles 20 and 21. The UK ratified the UN Convention in December 1991. It is not, however, directly enforceable in our domestic law.

14.7   In its Preamble, the Hague Convention also makes specific reference to the UN Declaration on Social and Legal Principles relating to the Protection and Welfare of Children, with Special Reference to Foster Placement and Adoption Nationally and Internationally.[1] These two international agreements are the bedrocks in the general approach to the welfare of the child in intercountry adoptions and together form an important foundation of principle.

UN Convention on the Rights of the Child 1989

14.8   The fundamental principles which underlie the Hague Convention are drawn from the UN Convention, in particular the 'best interests' principle, and it is important, therefore, to have an understanding of the conceptual content of these principles and of how they have been absorbed into the Hague Convention.

14.9   The preamble to the UN Convention in recognising that 'the child, for a full and harmonious development, should grow up in a family environment, in an atmosphere of happiness, love and understanding …' provides the justification for intercountry adoption.

14.10   Where the child's existing family are no longer able to meet the child's needs, Art 20 requires the State to provide 'special protection and assistance to a child'[2] and 'to ensure alternative care for such a child'.[3] The alternative care may include adoption.[4]

14.11   The pivotal provision for the purposes of adoption is Art 21 which requires those Member States which recognise and/or permit adoption to ensure that '*the best interests of the child shall be the paramount consideration*'. In the context of adoption, therefore, the child's 'best interests' are expressly stated to be 'paramount'. Thus Art 21 picks up the 'best interests' baton from Art 3(1), which establishes that 'in all actions concerning children, whether undertaken by public or social welfare institutions, courts of law, administrative authorities or legislative bodies, the best interests of the child shall be the primary consideration' and runs to the 'paramountcy' tape.

14.12   Article 21 goes on to require Member States to:

(a)   ensure that the adoption of the child is authorised only by competent authorities who determine, in accordance with applicable law and procedures and on the basis of all pertinent and reliable information, that adoption is permissible in view of the child's status concerning the parents, relatives and legal guardians and that, if required, the persons concerned have given their informed consent to the adoption on the basis of such counselling as may be necessary;

(b)   recognise that intercountry adoption may be considered as an alternative means of a child's care, *if the child cannot be placed in a foster home or an adoptive home or cannot in any suitable manner be cared for in the child's country of origin*;[5]

---

1   General Assembly Resolution 41/85 (3 December 1986).
2   Article 20(1).
3   Article 20(2).
4   Article 20(3).
5   Emphasis added. This is the principle of 'subsidiarity' which is discussed at **14.24** et seq below.

(c) ensure that the child concerned in intercountry adoption enjoys safeguards and standards equivalent to those existing in the case of national adoption;[1]

(d) take all appropriate measures to ensure that, in intercountry adoption, the placement does not result in improper financial gain for those involved in it;

(e) promote, where appropriate, the objectives of this Article by concluding bilateral or multi-lateral arrangements or agreements, and endeavour, within this framework, to ensure that the placement of the child in another country is carried out by competent authorities or organs.

14.13 The Hague Convention in its Preamble recognises that 'intercountry adoption may offer the advantage of a permanent home to a child *for whom a suitable family cannot be found in his or her State of origin*'[2] and thus (save for some slight changes to the wording) endorses the principle of 'subsidiarity' in Art 21(b) of the UN Convention. Article 4(b) of the Hague Convention, which provides that a Convention adoption 'shall only take place if the competent authorities of the State of origin have determined, *after the possibilities for placement within the State of origin have been given due consideration*,[3] that intercountry adoption is in the child's best interests' derives directly from this principle.[4]

14.14 The 'standards and safeguards' in Art 21(c) of the UN Convention apply both to procedures prior to the adoption order being made, and to the status of the child following the making of the order. It fleshes out the general rule against discrimination set out in Art 2(1) of the UN Convention[5] and recognises that there are differing forms of intercountry adoption which may require different approaches to the protection of children. A prime example is the difference between full and simple adoptions which has resulted in the rules in Art 26 of the Hague Convention dealing with the recognition and effect of such adoptions and Art 27 dealing with conversion. This, in its turn, has spawned the 'conversion section', s 88, in the ACA 2002. One of the overall aims of the ACA 2002 is to set standards for the protection of children, which are to be applied equally to domestic and intercountry adoptions. This is a reflection of the 'equivalence' principle enshrined in Art 21(c) of the UN Convention.

14.15 The principles in Art 21(a) of the UN Convention have been given effect in Art 4(c) of the Hague Convention, which sets out the requirements for consent. Art 12(1) of the UN Convention obliges Member States to 'assure to the child, who is capable of forming his or her views, the right to express those views freely in all matters affecting the child, the views of the child being given due weight in accordance with the age and maturity of the child'. This provides the source for Art 4(d) of the Hague Convention, which specifies the requirements for counselling the child and considering his wishes and feelings.

---

1   This is the 'equivalence' principle which is referred to below.
2   Emphasis added.
3   Emphasis added.
4   See **14.24**.
5   Article 2(1) provides that 'State parties shall respect and ensure the rights set forth in the present Convention to each child within their jurisdiction without discrimination of any kind, irrespective of the child's or his parent's or legal guardian's race, colour, sex, language, religion, political or other opinion, national, ethnic or social origin, property, disability, birth or other status'.

14.16   Article 11(1) of the UN Convention turns the spotlight on the illicit trafficking in children. It places obligations on Member States to take measures to combat the illicit transfer and non-return of children abroad. This goal is translated into the Hague Convention's Preamble which refers to the signatory States' conviction of the necessity to 'prevent the abduction, the sale of, or traffic in children' and is in turn reflected in the transfer and placement prohibitions in ss 83 and 92–97 of the ACA 2002.

14.17   Upon ratification of the Hague Convention, these underlying principles taken from the UN Convention will provide the standard for measuring our domestic law.

'State of origin' and 'receiving State' under the Hague Convention

14.18   Under Art 2, the Hague Convention applies where a child is habitually resident in one Contracting State ('the State of origin') and has been or is being moved to another Contracting State ('the receiving State'). This can be either after his adoption in the State of origin by spouses or a person habitually resident in the receiving State, or for the purposes of such an adoption in the receiving State or in the State of origin.

14.19   Under Art 2(2), the Hague Convention only covers adoptions which create a permanent parent–child relationship. Trans-frontier fostering arrangements and the Islamic institution of *kafala*, which provide long-term family care alternatives in countries where adoption is prohibited,[1] are excluded.[2] On the other hand, 'simple' adoptions which do not completely sever the legal ties between the natural family and the adopted child are included.

14.20   The Hague Convention does not, however, affect any law of a State of origin which requires that the adoption of a child habitually resident within that State takes place within that State or which prohibits the child's placement in or transfer to the receiving State prior to adoption.[3]

Requirements for intercountry adoptions

14.21   The Hague Convention shares the responsibilities between the authorities in the two States dealing with the intercountry adoption. Under Art 4, the State of origin must ensure that:

(1)   the child is adoptable;[4]
(2)   due consideration is given to the possibilities of the placement of the child within the State of origin;[5]
(3)   adoption is in the child's best interests;[6]
(4)   the consents have been freely given, ie:

---

1   Adoption is generally prohibited in Islamic countries.
2   W Duncan 'The Hague Convention on Protection of Children and Co-operation in Respect of Intercountry Adoption' in P Selman (ed) *Intercountry Adoptions. Developments, Trends and Perspectives* (BAAF, 2000) at p 50.
3   Article 28.
4   Article 4(a).
5   Article 4(b).
6   Ibid.

(i)   the persons whose consent is necessary for the adoption have been counselled and informed of the effects of their consent, in particular whether or not an adoption will result in the termination of the legal relationship between the child and his or her family of origin;

(ii)   such persons have given their consent freely, in the required legal form and expressed or evidenced in writing;

(iii) the consents have not been induced by payment or compensation of any kind and have not been withdrawn;

(iv)   the consent of the mother has been given only after the birth of the child;[1]

(5)   having regard to the age and degree of maturity of the child, consideration has been given to the child's wishes and opinions and he or she has been counselled, informed of the effects of the adoption and of his or her consent to the adoption (such consent to be freely given, in the required form, in writing and not induced by payment of any kind).[2]

14.22   Under Art 5, further key requirements are imposed on the receiving State. The competent authorities of the receiving State must ensure that: (i) the prospective adopters are eligible and suitable to adopt; (ii) they have been counselled;[3] and (iii) the child is authorised to enter and reside permanently in that State.[4]

14.23   Moreover, there must be no unsupervised contact between the prospective adopters and the natural parents until the essential requirements of Arts 4(a)–(c) and 5(a) have been met.[5] This is intended to prevent the natural parents being placed under any form of pressure by the prospective adopters.

Subsidiarity

14.24   Article 4(b) provides that a Convention adoption 'shall take place only if the competent authorities of the State of origin ... have determined, *after the possibilities for placement of the child within the State of origin have been given due consideration,* that an intercountry adoption is in the child's best interests'.[6]

14.25   As has been seen, the source for Art 4(b) is to be found in the principle of subsidiarity in Art 21(b) of the UN Convention, which states that Member States are required to consider intercountry adoption only 'if the child cannot be placed in a foster or an adoptive family or cannot be cared for in the child's country of origin'.

14.26   It is implicit in the principle of subsidiarity in both Conventions that 'State of origin' placements are necessarily to be preferred over intercountry solutions. This preference reflects one of the principal concerns underlying the growth of intercountry adoptions. This was to ensure that children abandoned in developing countries should, if at all possible, be placed with families within their own communities and intercountry adoption only considered when all the possibilities in the child's State of origin had been exhausted. It has been explained as follows:

1   Article 4(c).
2   Article 4(d).
3   Article 5(a) and (b).
4   Article 5(c).
5   Article 29.
6   Emphasis added.

'In intercountry adoptions, there is concern lest the principle of giving priority to the child's interests be used as an excuse for social engineering, that is to justify a more generalised transfer of children from poor to wealthy parents or form developing to rich economies.'[1]

14.27 The objective of the Hague Convention is, therefore, not just to 'facilitate' intercountry adoption but to 'regulate' it in a manner which best protects and promotes the interests of children.[2] One of its side effects, however, is to create a tension between the 'subsidiarity' principle and the 'best interests' principle.[3] In the context of Art 4(b), the 'best interests' principle does not hold the 'paramount' position and, arguably, is subordinated to the principle of 'subsidiarity'. This places it in potential conflict with the approach under the ACA 2002, where the paramountcy principle supersedes all other considerations.

14.28 This tension flows from a conceptual fault line running through the surface of Art 21 of the UN Convention which juxtaposes the paramountcy principle and the principle of 'subsidiarity'. It is a fault line which finds its way into the ACA 2002 through its absorption of the Hague Convention. Although conceptually a surface crack could open up between the two principles, in practice, however, UK courts are likely to bridge the gap by giving weight to the matters in s 1(4)(c), (f) and (5) of the ACA 2002 in the welfare balance. In any event, it is suggested that it would prove a seismic shift in thinking, even if it were jurisprudentially possible under the ACA 2002, to contemplate dislodging the fundamental alignment between the CA 1989 and the ACA 2002 by giving precedence to the principle of subsidiarity over the child's best interests.

Procedural requirements

14.29 Articles 14 to 22 set out the procedural requirements. Those wishing to adopt a child habitually resident in another Contracting State must apply to the Central Authority in the State of their habitual residence[4] (the receiving State). If satisfied that the applicants are eligible and suited to adopt, the Central Authority for the receiving State must prepare for transmission to the State of origin a report which includes information about:

(a) the identity of the applicants;
(b) their eligibility and suitability to adopt;
(c) their background;
(d) their family and medical history;
(e) their social environment;
(f) their reasons for adoption;
(g) their ability to undertake an intercountry adoption; and
(h) the characteristics of the children for whom they are qualified to care.[5]

14.30 If satisfied that the child is adoptable, the Central Authority of the State of origin must:

---

1 W Duncan 'Regulating Intercountry Adoption – an International Perspective' in A Bainham et al (eds) *Frontiers of Family Law* (John Wiley & Co, 1995), p 42.
2 Ibid, at p 51.
3 This potential tension is illustrated by the decision in *Re C (Adoption: Legality)* [1999] 1 FLR 370.
4 Article 14.
5 Article 15.

(a)   prepare a report, including information about his or her:
    (i)   adoptability;
    (ii)   background;
    (iii) social environment;
    (iv)   family history; and
    (v)   any special needs;
(b)   give due consideration to the child's upbringing and to his or her ethnic, religious and cultural background;
(c)   ensure that consents have been obtained in accordance with Art 4;
(d)   determine whether the placement is in the best interests of the child, particularly on the basis of both reports.[1]

In addition, it must transmit (i) proof that the necessary consents have been obtained, and (ii) the reasons for the determination on the placement, without disclosing the identity of the birth parents, if so required.[2]

14.31   The State of origin may decide to entrust a child to prospective adoptive parents only if:

(a)   it has ensured that the prospective parents agree;
(b)   the receiving State has approved the decision;
(c)   both States have agreed that the adoption may proceed; and
(d)   Art 5 has been complied with.[3]

14.32   Only once the requirements in **14.31** have been satisfied, may a transfer of the child to the receiving State take place.[4] There are reciprocal duties on both Central Authorities to keep each other informed about the adoption process,[5] and Art 21 provides a procedure for the protection of the child in the event that the continued placement appears not to be in the child's best interests.

14.33   Article 22(e) of the UN Convention requires Member States to ensure 'that the placement of the child in another country is carried out by competent authorities or organs'. This proved to be one of the problematic areas leading up to the implementation of the Hague Convention. The question which arose was whether independent persons, such as lawyers, should be permitted to be a lawful instrument in making the arrangements for an intercountry adoption. In some States of the USA, for example, this is allowed, but in others there is a prohibition upon anyone other than non-profit authorised agencies providing the essential objectivity to protect the interests of children within the adoption process.[6]

14.34   Article 22 of the Hague Convention represents a compromise. It provides that a Contracting State may permit the involvement of non-accredited persons in making arrangements for intercountry adoption, subject to supervision and provided that such persons 'meet the requirements of integrity, professional competence, experience and

---

1   Article 16(1)(a)–(d).
2   Article 16(2).
3   Article 17.
4   Article 19.
5   Article 20.
6   W Duncan 'The Hague Convention' in Peter Selman (ed) *Intercountry Adoption* (BAAF, 2000).

accountability of that State and are qualified by their ethical standards and by training or experience to work in the field of intercountry adoption'.

Recognition and effects

14.35   The main objective of Arts 23–27 of the Hague Convention is to guarantee that all adoptions certified under the Convention are recognised by the other Contracting States. One of the aims is to avoid 'repeat' adoptions under the domestic law of the receiving country, save on exceptional grounds of public policy.

14.36   This whole area of 'recognition and effects' caused controversy from the outset and is the product of a complicated compromise between the interests of the States of origin and the receiving States.

> 'The States of origin were interested in the adoption in the receiving States having the same effects as in the State of origin. The receiving States, on the other hand, wanted the effect of an adoption taking place in the State of origin to follow the law of the receiving State . . . It was only a few days before the end of the conference (at The Hague) that under great pressure of time a compromise proposal was accepted.'[1]

14.37   Following this inauspicious beginning, the topic has continued to be the subject of controversy and academic criticism.[2] Lying at the heart of the academic criticism is the assumption made in the Convention that recognition and effect can be differentiated, with the consequence that an order can be recognised without it necessarily being given the same effects in the receiving State as in the State of origin.

Recognition and public policy

14.38   Article 23 regulates the recognition of a certified Convention adoption by operation of law in other Contracting States, which under Art 24 may only be refused if the adoption is 'manifestly contrary to public policy, taking into account the best interests of the child'.[3]

14.39   The relevant paragraphs provide as follows:

'*Article 23*

(1)   An adoption certified by the competent authority of the State of the adoption as having been made in accordance with the Convention shall be recognised by operation of law in the other Contracting States . . .

(2)   Each Contracting State shall, at the time of signature, ratification, acceptance, approval or accession, notify the depository of the Convention of the identity and the functions of the authority or the authorities which, in that State, are competent to make the certification. It shall also notify the depository of any modification in the designation of these authorities.

---

1   R Frank 'The Recognition of Intercountry Adoptions in the Light of the 1993 Hague Convention on Intercountry Adoptions' in N Lowe and G Douglas (eds) *Families Across Frontiers* (Kluwer Academic Publishers, 1996), p 591.

2   Ibid. See also J Murphy 'Rhetoric and Reality in Inter-country Adoptions: Divergent Principles and Stratified Status' in J Murphy (ed) *Ethnic Minorities: Their Families and the Law* (Hart Publishing, 2000).

3   Article 24.

Article 24

The recognition of an adoption may be refused in a Contracting State only if the adoption is manifestly contrary to its public policy, taking into account the best interests of the child.'

14.40   Whether the adoption is made 'in accordance with the Hague Convention', therefore, turns upon a 'simple' certification by the State of origin. Where the requirements of the Convention are not complied with and, thus, the certification is in fact incorrect, recognition can be refused, but only in the exceptional circumstances in Art 24. The justification for this simplicity of process is founded upon a basis of reciprocal trust and confidence between the Contracting States to the Hague Convention.

14.41   Although Art 23(2) requires every Contracting State to notify the depository of the Convention as to the identity and the functions of the authority which is competent to make the certification, it does not specify that the competent authority must be a court. It seems, therefore, that a certification by a competent authority other than a court would still be recognised under Art 23(1) by operation of law. This neutrality as to whether a 'competent authority' should be an administrative or a judicial body is an inevitable consequence of the Hague Convention's compromising approach aimed at accommodating the multifarious types of adoption worldwide.

14.42   The 'public policy' exception under Art 24, however, does leave the door slightly ajar to the possibility that the receiving State or a third Convention country may refuse to recognise an adoption obtained in the State of origin, even where it has been certified.

14.43   Article 24 is, however, itself not without its difficulties. One of the consequences for the child, for example, could be that he or she falls in an adoptive black hole with the adoption recognised in his or her State of origin and unrecognised in the receiving State. On the other hand, if the child has been living with the adoptive parents in the receiving State for some time, then the 'best interests of the child' are likely to outweigh the public policy issues and enable the adoption to be recognised, notwithstanding that the certification may have been flawed.

Full and simple adoptions

14.44   Adoption law in the United Kingdom recognises only one form of adoption, ie 'full adoption', whereby a new and irrevocable legal relationship between the child and the adopters is created which severs all ties with the natural parents. The USA, Australia, the Nordic countries (Norway, Sweden, Denmark and Finland) and Italy, in general, recognise only a full adoption. However, the clean-break model of adoption is not universal.[1] Other countries, for example France, Belgium, Portugal, Bulgaria, Romania, Japan, most of the South American countries and some African countries (eg Senegal, Madagascar, Mauritius), have 'simple adoptions' which do not have the effect of severing completely all ties with the natural parents.

---

1   See W Duncan 'Regulating Intercountry Adoption – an International Perspective' in A Bainham, DS Pearl and R Pickford (eds) *Frontiers of Family Law* (2nd edn, John Wiley & Sons, 1995) at p 44.

14.45   In France,[1] the original *Code civil*[2] followed the traditional form of civil law adoption. It provided for adoption only in respect of adults and its purpose was to provide an heir for a childless person as a means of ensuring the continuation of the family line, particularly for passing on property. In 1923, due to the number of children orphaned in the First World War, adoption was extended to include persons under the age of 21. The *tribunal de grande instance* (the French equivalent of the High Court) may now order either *adoption simple* or *adoption plénière* (Arts 343–370 of the *Code civil*). *Adoption simple*, while creating a new relationship with the adopter, does not alter the connection which the adoptee has with his or her birth family. For example, the adoptee retains the succession rights which stem from his or her birth family and acquires additional succession rights from the adopter.

14.46   *Adoption plénière* is a full adoption in the English sense; its principal effect being the substitution of a new family for the birth family with the adoptee acquiring full succession rights as if he or she were the legitimate child of the adopter. The adopter must be over 30 years old or have been married for more than 5 years, and the adoptee should be at least 15 years younger, unless he or she is the child of the adopter's spouse in which case he or she can be any age (Arts 343–344). The adoptee must be less than 15 years of age unless he or she is the subject of an *adoption simple* and if aged 13 or more his or her consent is a pre-requisite to the adoption. The consent of the birth family is required and can be withdrawn during the following 3-month period.

The effects of recognition

14.47   Article 26 deals with the question of what effects a Convention adoption has in the domestic law of the receiving State and in other Contracting States and provides for the recognition of both full adoptions[3] and simple adoptions.[4]

ARTICLE 26(1)

14.48   Article 26(1) states that the 'recognition of an adoption' includes recognition of:

(a)   the legal parent–child relationship between the child and his or her adoptive parents;
(b)   the parental responsibility of the adoptive parents for the child;
(c)   the termination of a pre-existing legal relationship between the child and his or her mother and father 'if the adoption has this effect in the Contracting State where it is made'.

14.49   Under Art 26(1)(c), only the State of origin which makes the adoption can decide whether the legal relationship between the child and the birth parents can be legally severed. Sub-paragraph (1)(c) also regulates whether or not the relationship between the child and other natural relatives, such as siblings and grandparents, is

---

1   See B Dickson *Introduction to French Law* (Financial Times Pitman Publishing) at pp 225–226.
2   *Code Napoléon* of 1804.
3   Article 26(1)(a) and (b).
4   Article 26(1)(c).

terminated.[1] The basis for this is an assumption that a termination of the legal relationship between the child and parents would also necessarily terminate the relationship between the child and other relatives. This assumption does not, however, operate in every Contracting State.[2]

14.50   Article 26(1) is also not without conceptual difficulty. For example, it merely allows for the recognition of the adoptive parent–child relationship and parental responsibility among other Contracting States. It fails to specify whether it is the law of the State of origin or that of the receiving State which governs the relationship and the scope of parental responsibility. This may lead to confusion where, for example, the adoption in the State of origin was a simple adoption which did not sever the natural parents' relationship with the child.

ARTICLE 26(2)

14.51   Article 26(2) provides:

> 'In the case of an adoption having the effect of terminating a pre-existing legal parent–child relationship, the child shall enjoy in the receiving State and in any other Contracting State where the adoption is recognised, rights equivalent to those resulting from adoptions having this effect in each such State.'

14.52   Article 26(2) is intended to cater for those States where there are two different types of adoption, such as France. In those cases where the child has been fully adopted in the State of origin, it prescribes for 'equivalent rights' in the receiving State, ie the child is not restricted to the effect of an *adoption simple*.

14.53   The rights to be enjoyed are 'equivalent' rights and not 'identical' rights. It follows that it is not the law of the State of origin but the law of the receiving State which determines the content of the legal relationship between the child and adoptive family. Under Art 26(2), therefore, notwithstanding that the adoption obtained in the State of origin terminates the parent–child legal relationship, it is for the receiving State to determine, with respect to the legal status of the child, the extent to which he or she is legally integrated into his or her adoptive family.

14.54   Circumstances may well arise under Art 26(2), therefore, which lead to confusion as to the precise legal relationship between the child and the adopters in the receiving State. By way of illustration, whereas under the law of the State of origin the child would have a completely new adoptive family, under the law of the receiving State the child may have new parents but existing grandparents. In the USA, for example, some of the State laws provide for the legal relationship between an adopted step-child and the relatives of the deceased natural parent after the remarriage of the other parent to continue.[3] Another anomaly which could arise is where an adoption which was

---

1   R Frank, 'The Recognition of Intercountry Adoptions in the Light of the 1993 Hague Convention on Intercountry Adoptions' in N Lowe and G Douglas (eds) *Families Across Frontiers* (Kluwer Academic Publishers, 1996), at p 598.

2   For example, under German law in an adoption by relatives, old parents are substituted for new parents, but without otherwise changing the child's family relationship: 1756 para I Civil Code. See R Frank, op cit, at p 598.

3   Eg Arkansas, Alaska, Connecticut, Montana, New Mexico, New York, North Dakota, Ohio, Wisconsin.

irrevocable under the law of the State of origin was revocable in the receiving State. It follows that Art 26(2) has the potential in the hands of the receiving State to undermine one of the pivots of adoption, namely certainty.[1]

14.55   The confusion may be further compounded by the provision in Art 26(2) for the child's enjoyment of equivalent rights in any other Contracting State. This could lead to the child's rights having a peripatetic, rather than a static, effect. By way of example, the adoptive parents may have adopted the child in the child's State of origin in accordance with the Hague Convention and, after living in the receiving State for some years, may then have taken up habitual residence with the child in another Contracting State. Under Art 26(2), the content of the legal relationship between the child and the adopters would initially be governed by the law of the receiving State but, immediately upon moving to the other Contracting State, would have to be re-assessed under the law of that State, where the adoption may have different legal consequences from those of the receiving State. Such confusion cannot be conducive to the child's best interests.

14.56   Another difficulty is that Art 26(2) does not apply where the adoption in the State of origin is a full adoption but the law of the receiving State recognises only 'simple' adoptions. Although sub-paras (1)(a) and (b) deal with the creation of the new parent–child relationship and provide for the adoptive parents to have parental responsibility, the Article does not identify the child's legal status in those circumstances. As Art 27 applies only where an adoption granted in the State of origin does not have the effect of terminating a pre-existing legal parent–child relationship, it does not provide a remedy in this situation.

ARTICLE 26(3)

14.57   A solution may perhaps be found in the wording of Art 26(3), which provides that recognition under Art 26(1) does not prejudice the application of any legal provision in force in the Contracting State if it is more favourable to the child.[2] However, it is not made clear how the comparative exercise envisaged under Art 26(3) is intended to work in practice.

Conversion

14.58   Article 27(1) provides:

> 'Where an adoption granted in the State of origin does not have the effect of terminating a pre-existing legal parent-child relationship, it may, in the receiving State which recognises the adoption under the Convention, be converted into an adoption having such an effect:
>
> (a)   if the law of the receiving State so permits; and
> (b)   if the consents referred to in Art 4(c) and (d) have been or are given for the purpose of such an adoption.'

14.59   Article 27, therefore, allows a receiving State to convert a simple adoption into a full adoption, if its law so permits and provided that the birth parents and relevant parties

---

1   See J Murphy 'Rhetoric and Reality in Inter-Country Adoptions: Divergent Principles and Stratified Status' in J Murphy (ed) *Ethnic Minorities: Their Families and the Law* (Hart Publishing, 2000).
2   Article 26(3).

under Art 4 have given their consent to a full adoption. A certified 'converted' adoption is recognised by operation of law in other Contracting States.[1]

14.60   As the Convention is silent as to whether repeat adoptions are permissible other than under Art 27, it is probable that the repetition of an intercountry adoption domestically in the receiving State is intended to be excluded where the adoption leads to a termination of the natural parent–child relationship. This follows from Convention's objective of reducing the repetitions of intercountry adoptions in receiving States and other Contracting countries. Therefore, a repeat adoption under Art 27 in the case of a simple adoption should be regarded as being the only exception to the general rule that it is the adoption in the State of origin which has effect.[2]

General provisions

14.61   The preservation and access to information relating to the child's origin, including information concerning the identity of the natural parents and medical history, are governed by Arts 30 and 31. The obligation is upon the competent authorities to ensure that the information is preserved and that the child or his or her representative has access, subject to this being under appropriate guidance and so far as is permitted by the State's law.

14.62   Article 32 provides that 'no one shall derive improper financial or other gain from an activity related to an intercountry adoption, save for costs and expenses, including reasonable professional fees of persons involved in the adoption'.

14.63   Under Art 35, an obligation is placed upon the competent authorities of the Contracting States to 'act expeditiously in the process of adoption'. It follows that delay is regarded as just as inimical to the interests of the child under the Hague Convention as under s 1(3) of the ACA 2002 and s 1(2) of the CA 1989.

14.64   Articles 36–38 deal with the position where there are two or more systems of law applicable in different territorial units or to different categories of persons.

14.65   Under Art 41, the Convention is applicable in every case where an application under Art 14 has been received after the Convention has entered into force in the receiving State and the State of origin.

ADOPTION (INTERCOUNTRY ASPECTS) ACT 1999

14.66   It was against this backdrop that the Adoption (Intercountry Aspects) Act 1999 (A(IA)A 1999) was in part implemented to make way for the ratification of the Hague Convention in respect of intercountry adoption in England, Wales and Scotland.

14.67   Sections 1, 2 and 7 of, and Sch 1 to, the A(IA)A 1999 are to remain but the other provisions, so far as they apply to England and Wales and amend the AA 1976, have been incorporated into the ACA 2002. Section 1 of the A(IA)A 1999 provides for the

---

1   Article 27(2).
2   J Murphy, op cit, at p 125.

Secretary of State to make regulations[1] to give effect to the Convention (the material parts of which are set out in Sch 1 to the Act). Section 144(1) of the ACA 2002 defines a 'Convention adoption order' as an adoption order made by virtue of regulations made under s 1 of the A(IA)A 1999.

Central Authority

14.68   Section 2 of the A(IA)A 1999 provides for the setting up of a Central Authority (in accordance with Art 6(1) of the Hague Convention), which is responsible for implementing the Hague Convention. This body is to act as the focal point for Great Britain for any communication relating to the Hague Convention (Art 6(2)).

14.69   The Central Authority for England will be the Department of Health. Wales will have as its Central Authority the National Assembly for Wales, Scotland the Scottish Executive and Northern Ireland the Department of Health, Social Services and Public Safety. The Central Authority's duties are specified under Arts 6–22 of the Hague Convention.

Accredited body

14.70   Section 2(3) of the A(IA)A 1999 implements Arts 9–11 of the Hague Convention and makes provision for an accredited body (ie a body approved by the Central Authority to carry out work under the Convention).

14.71   Adoption societies approved by the Secretary of State to provide Convention adoption services will be automatically accredited for the purposes of the Convention.[2] A Voluntary Adoption Agency (VAA) in respect of which a person is registered under Part 2 of the CSA 2000 will be an accredited body.[3] Local authorities, as public authorities, will have responsibility for providing a Convention adoption service, but do not require accreditation.

Functions

14.72   The functions[4] to be discharged by local authorities or accredited bodies on behalf of the Central Authority are:

(1)   to collect, preserve and exchange information about the situation of the child and prospective adoptive parents, so far as is necessary to complete the adoption;[5]

---

1   Draft Intercountry Adoption (Hague Convention) Regulations 2002 have been issued for consultation. They will set out the procedural requirements to be followed in respect of Convention adoptions. Also note the Adoption of Children from Overseas Regulations 2001, SI 2001/1251 (in force from 30 April 2001) which imposed requirements with which a person who is habitually resident in the British Islands must comply before and after bringing a child who is habitually resident outside those Islands into the United Kingdom for the purpose of adoption and specify the procedure to be followed by the adoption agency and adoption panel in relation to assessment and approval of a person wishing to adopt a child from overseas.
2   A(IA)A 1999, s 2(3).
3   Ibid, s 2(2A) inserted by CSA 2000, s 116, Sch 4, para 27(a).
4   Ibid, s 2(4).
5   Article 9(a) of the Hague Convention.

(2)   to facilitate, follow and expedite proceedings with a view to obtaining the adoption;[1] and

(3)   to promote the development of adoption counselling and post-adoption services.[2]

Acquisition of British citizenship

14.73   Section 7 of the A(IA)A 1999 makes an important amendment to s 1(5) of the British Nationality Act 1981, which provides that, where an order authorising the adoption of a minor who is not a British citizen is made by a court in the United Kingdom, he or she becomes a citizen as from the date on which the order is made, if the adopter or one of the adopters is a British citizen on that date.

14.74   Section 7 of the A(IA)A 1999 provides that, if a child who does not have British nationality is adopted, whether in any UK court or outside the British Isles under the Hague Convention, he or she will be able to acquire British nationality automatically. This is subject to the proviso that at least one of the adoptive parents is a British citizen at the time the adoption order is made and, in the case of a Convention adoption, that the adopter or (in the case of an adoption by a married couple) are habitually resident in the United Kingdom.[3]

14.75   This amendment implements Art 26 of the Hague Convention and ensures that the adopted child enjoys the same status from the making of a Convention order as he or she would if the adoption were made in the United Kingdom.

THE ADOPTION AND CHILDREN ACT 2002

14.76   Upon enactment, the ACA 2002[4] largely replaces the A(IA)A 1999. It provides the statutory basis for the regulation of intercountry adoption in England, Wales and Scotland. It sets out to embrace the Hague Convention into domestic law and to reform the deficiencies under the AA 1976 which have been exploited in the context of illicit intercountry adoptions.

14.77   The key provisions of the ACA 2002 are:

(1)   to enable the United Kingdom to ratify the Hague Convention;
(2)   to place a duty on local authorities to provide an intercountry adoption service;
(3)   to provide for VAAs to apply to operate an intercountry adoption service;
(4)   to review the 'designated list' so as to ensure that in future overseas adoptions will be recognised in the United Kingdom only when the systems in the overseas country meet certain prescribed criteria (including ensuring that proper consents have been given by the birth parents, that the prospective adopters have been assessed and approved as suitable to adopt and that no profit has been made from the process);

---

1   Article 9(b) of the Hague Convention.
2   Ibid, Art 9(c).
3   'United Kingdom' includes the Channel Islands and the Isle of Man.
4   It incorporates the reforms foreshadowed in the A(IA)A 1999.

(5) to incorporate the restriction in the A(IA)A 1999[1] on bringing a child into the United Kingdom for the purpose of adoption by a British resident without complying with prescribed procedures; including a restriction which makes it an offence for a child who has been adopted overseas by a British resident within the last 6 months to be brought into the United Kingdom without prescribed procedures being complied with;[2]

(6) to extend the penalties when someone is found guilty of bringing a child into the United Kingdom without complying with the prescribed procedures.[3]

Omissions from the Adoption and Children Act 2002

14.78   There are, however, some notable omissions from the ACA 2002, which have particular relevance to intercountry adoptions.

Protected status

14.79   Under s 32(1) of the AA 1976, when notice was given to the local authority of the intention to adopt as required under s 22(1), the child became a protected child and ceased to be a privately fostered child under CA 1989, Sch 8, para 5(b). A duty was imposed on the local authority to secure that protected children were visited by officers of the authority to satisfy themselves as to their well-being.[4] Provision was made for notice to be given to the local authority of any changes of permanent address.[5] Failures to give the requisite notice or information or refusals to allow the visiting of the child were criminal offences.[6]

14.80   This protected status for the prospective adoptee has not been reproduced in the ACA 2002. As has been seen, the 'looked-after' provisions of the CA 1989 apply to a child who is placed or authorised to be placed for adoption with prospective adopters by a local authority.[7] In circumstances where a foreign child is brought into the United Kingdom by a British resident, s 83(6) will make provision (through regulations) for a notice of intention to adopt to be given to the local authority. The Government has emphasised that, where such a notice of intent has been given to the local authority, certain functions will be imposed upon the authority, such as visiting the child.[8] Otherwise, safeguards for the child can be found in the private fostering arrangements under ss 66 and 67 of the CA 1989, and the Children (Private Arrangements for Fostering) Regulations 1991.[9] The local authority will continue to have duties under s 17 of the CA 1989 in respect of children in need and in relation to s 47 child protection inquiries and can, if appropriate, take action under Parts IV or V of the CA 1989.

---

1   Section 14 of which inserted a new s 56A into the AA 1976.
2   Paragraph 12 of Sch 4 to the ACA 2002 inserts a new s 56A into the AA 1976 which reflects s 83 (restriction on bringing children in), and para 14 inserts new subs (1A) into s 58 of the AA 1976 (restrictions on advertisements), which reflects s 123 of the ACA 2002; thus enabling implementation in advance of the Act.
3   See fn 2 above.
4   AA 1976, s 33.
5   Ibid, s 36.
6   Ibid, s 38.
7   CA 1989, s 18(3).
8   HC Deb, vol 386, no 150, col 24, per Ms Jacqui Smith.
9   SI 1991/2050. This is dealt with in more detail at **14.100–14.104**.

The restrictions under s 24(2) of the AA 1976

14.81　Under s 24(2) of the AA 1976, the court was restricted from making an adoption order where there had been a contravention of s 57 (which prohibited certain payments for an adoption, an agreement for adoption, placement for adoption or the making of arrangements for adoption). Section 57 has been replicated and expanded in s 95 of the ACA 2002, but the court is no longer precluded from making an adoption order in the event of contravention. Given that one of the objectives underlying the ACA 2002 is to strengthen the court's policing of illicit intercountry adoptions, the deletion of the former restriction is surprising.

Practice

14.82　Under s 2 of the ACA 2002, local authorities are under a duty to establish and maintain an adoption service. This service now includes 'the adoption of persons, wherever they may be habitually resident, effected under the law of any country or territory, whether within or outside the British Islands'.[1] It therefore covers both domestic and intercountry adoptions.[2] Local authorities also have a specific responsibility for establishing and maintaining a Convention adoption service. They may commission approved VAAs to provide an intercountry adoption service in their area, provided they supervise such work.

14.83　The intercountry adoption process in England and Wales requires that the same adoption practice and standards be applied to intercountry and domestic adoptions. This reflects the principle enshrined in Art 21(c) of the UN Convention, whereby States which recognise and permit the system of adoption must ensure that the child who is the subject of intercountry adoption enjoys safeguards and standards equivalent to those existing in the case of national adoption.

14.84　The key elements of the intercountry adoption service are:

(1)　the provision of information and advice about overseas adoption procedures;
(2)　the provision of counselling and advice to those wishing to adopt a child from overseas and to people adopted from overseas;
(3)　the written assessment of the applicants' suitability to be adoptive parents (to the same standards as for domestic adoptions);
(4)　the supervision of the adoptive placements, the preparation of reports and the provision of recommendations to the courts where appropriate; and
(5)　the arranging of adoption services.

14.85　The Department of Health has commissioned the production of National Standards for Intercountry Adoption which it published for consultation during 2002.[3]

1　ACA 2002, s 2(7).
2　This expanded service commenced on 30 April 2001 by virtue of the Adoption of Children from Overseas Regulations 2001 made under the A(IA)A 1999.
3　Additional information will be posted on the Department of Health website at www.doh.gov.uk/ adoption. This site contains information on both domestic and intercountry adoption. There is also a DoH Helpline on 020 7972 4014. The Home Office leaflet 'Intercountry Adoption' provides information on immigration requirements in relation to intercountry adoption and can be found on www.ind.homeoffice.gov.uk.

The Department of Health has also issued for consultation Draft Regulations and Guidance for Implementing the Adoption (Intercountry Aspects) Act 1999.

14.86 The Guidance will replace the *Intercountry Adoption Guide – Practice and Procedures* (April 2001) and, although designed for councils with social services responsibilities and approved VAAs, it will be a very useful tool for practitioners generally.[1] Its forerunner[2] was commended by Bracewell J in *Re R (Inter-country Adoptions: Practice)*[3] as a 'document which should be readily available and accessible for all adoption agencies, local authorities, guardians ad litem, judges, court staff, barristers, solicitors and anyone who has to consider the appropriate procedure'. It is revised from time to time and may be further updated upon the implementation of the ACA 2002. *Re R (Inter-country Adoptions: Practice)* itself gives detailed guidance as to practice in intercountry adoption, which should be considered together with the Intercountry Adoption Guide.[4]

Immigration law and nationality

14.87 The adoption of a foreign minor by a British citizen has, in the context of its relationship with the immigration law, two significant effects. First, it confers on the adopted child British citizenship as from the date of the adoption order under s 1(5) of the British Nationality Act 1981. Secondly, it confers on the adopted child *the right of abode* in the United Kingdom for the purpose of s 1(1) of the Immigration Act 1971.[5]

14.88 Without such right of abode, the foreign minor would be subject to all the restrictions imposed by the Immigration Act 1971 ('the 1971 Act'), in particular:

(a) he or she may only live, work and settle in the United Kingdom by permission and subject to such regulation of his or her entry into, stay in and departure from the United Kingdom as is imposed by the 1971 Act (s 1(2));

(b) he or she may not enter the United Kingdom without leave (s 3(1)(a)), which may be subject to limitations as to time (s 3(1)(b)) or other conditions (s 3(1)(c));

(c) the conditions attached to his or her leave to enter may be varied (s 3(3));

(d) he or she may be liable to deportation (s 3(5)).

14.89 Thus it can be seen that the adoption of a foreign minor by a British citizen makes a very substantial alteration to his position *vis-à-vis* his or her right to live, work and settle in the United Kingdom.

14.90 The administration of immigration control under the 1971 Act is conferred on immigration officers and the Secretary of State by s 4, while ss 13 and 14 of the 1971 Act lay down procedures for appeal against refusal of leave to enter the United Kingdom, and against the conditions upon which leave to enter has been granted.

---

1   It will provide essential step-by-step advice and information (including helpful background Annexes) for local authorities, VAAs and practitioners.

2   *A Guide to Intercountry Adoption (Practice and Procedures)* (May 1997).

3   [1999] 1 FLR 1042 at 1044G–H.

4   *Adoption Proceedings – A New Approach:* Guidance issued by the President of the Family Division with the approval of the Lord Chancellor, under the heading 'The First Directions Hearing', para (vi).

5   Immigration Act 1971, s 2(1)(a).

14.91   The Secretary of State has laid down a Statement of Rules as to the practice to be followed in the administration of the 1971 Act. The current rules are contained in HC 395, as amended, in particular:

(1)   rr 310–316C set out the requirements for leave to enter or remain with a view to settlement as an adopted child;[1]

(2)   rr 297–303 relate to the admission for settlement of a child who is the dependent of a person who is present and settled in the United Kingdom or being admitted for settlement here;

(3)   rr 320–322 set out the general grounds for the refusal of entry clearance, leave to enter or variation of leave to enter or remain in the United Kingdom.

14.92   When bringing a child to live in the United Kingdom, adopters must seek entry clearance[2] for the child. Where the adoption order has been made in one of the designated[3] countries, the adoption order is recognised under UK law. If the Entry Clearance Officer (ECO) is satisfied that the immigration requirements have been met, then a visa for indefinite leave to remain will be granted. The requirements are set out in the Home Office leaflet on intercountry adoption.[4] The ECO may on occasion refer the case to the Joint Entry Clearance Unit in London.

14.93   When the United Kingdom does not recognise an adoption order made under the law of the adopters' home country (ie it is a non-designated country), or the child is coming to the United Kingdom for adoption, the ECO must not only be satisfied that the immigration requirements referred to above are met, but must also seek the advice of the relevant home health department as to the likelihood of an adoption order being made. That department will require to see additional documentation. Once satisfied, the ECO will issue an entry clearance visa which gives leave to enter for 12 months.

14.94   Where children are brought illegally into the country, an offence under s 25 of the Immigration Act 1971 is committed. It carries a maximum sentence of 7 years' imprisonment. Referral to the police in such circumstances should be routine.[5]

14.95   In *Re R (Inter-country Adoptions: Practice)* Bracewell J stipulated guidelines for whenever a child who is a non-European foreign national arrives at the UK port of entry and is not going to stay with a relative in the United Kingdom. They cover the situations not only where there is an intention to adopt, but also where there is an initial (false) denial that the entry is for the purpose of adoption.

14.96   Where the applicants have circumvented the usual procedures for adopting a child overseas, then an application should be made immediately for the adoption application to be transferred to the High Court.[6] The adoption application should be

---

1   Under the rules there are four categories of application in relation to an adopted child. There are currently no specific rules relating to applicants seeking leave to enter for the purposes of adoption.

2   An entry clearance is a visa or entry certificate issued for the purpose of travel to the United Kingdom. Applications for entry clearance must be made to the British Embassy, High Commission or other Diplomatic Mission (collectively known as British Diplomatic Posts) which is nearest to the child's normal place of residence and designated to issue entry clearance.

3   See **15.8** for the proposed review of the 'designated countries'.

4   The documents must be in the original form and accompanied by certified translations.

5   *Re R (Inter-country Adoptions: Practice)* [1999] 1 FLR 1042 at 1054A–B.

6   Ibid, at 1051B–D and 1052A–C.

listed as a matter of urgency[1] before the High Court judge for preliminary directions as to the investigation of the circumstances in which the child was brought to the United Kingdom and the natural parents' attitude to the adoption application.[2] In the case of a non-agency intercountry application to adopt, the court must be vigilant at all times to ensure full, prompt and appropriate investigation.[3]

14.97 In reaching any decision about whether an adoption order should be made or any other question relating to the child, the court is under a duty to apply the paramountcy principle in s 1 of the ACA 2002. Under s 109 of the ACA 2002, it must draw up a timetable with a view to determining such questions without delay and giving such directions for the purpose of ensuring that the timetable is adhered to. In advance of such directions hearing, the prospective adopter should be required to file and serve an affidavit setting out the full details of the circumstances in which the child was brought to the United Kingdom and of the natural parents' attitude to the adoption application and compliance with the Department of Health procedures, and further should exhibit the child's passport.[4]

14.98 CAFCASS should be invited to act on behalf of the child.[5]

14.99 If the child did not receive entry clearance, the local authority should notify the Home Office of the application for an adoption order so that the Home Secretary can consider whether to be made a party to the proceedings, and should thereafter keep the Home Office informed of the progress of the application, as the child remains subject to immigration control until the adoption order has been granted.[6] The prospective adopters, the local authority and an officer of CAFCASS should be required to attend the directions hearing. The Home Office, whether it decides to apply to be a party or not, should be invited to attend by a representative with knowledge of the circumstances in which permission to enter the United Kingdom was granted. CAFCASS and the local authority should be permitted to cross-examine the prospective adopters if deemed appropriate.[7]

Status

14.100 The 'protected status' under s 32 of the AA 1976 is not replicated in the ACA 2002. Unless the child is placed for adoption by a local authority (in which case the 'looked-after' provisions of CA 1989 apply), the child's status is, therefore, governed by the private fostering arrangements under ss 66 and 67 of the CA 1989, and Children

---

1   *Re R (Inter-country Adoptions: Practice)* [1999] 1 FLR 1042 at 1051E–F, Bracewell J criticised r 21 of the Adoption Rules 1984 which provides that the court shall list the case for hearing before a judge on notice to the parties as soon as practicable after the application has been filed. In the case of non-agency cases, this had to be not less than 3 months after the date on which notice of intention was given to the local authority. She said that 'r 21 does not import sufficient urgency in listing non-agency . . . cases and further consideration may be appropriate in respect of the President's Practice Direction of 23 November 1993 on the transfer of inter-country adoptions between the county court and the High Court'.
2   Ibid, at 1051B–C.
3   Ibid, at 1051G–H.
4   Ibid at 1052C–D.
5   Ibid, at 1052B and 1053F–H.
6   Department of Health, *Intercountry Adoption Guide – Practice and Procedures* (April 2001), p 9.
7   *Re R (Inter-country Adoptions: Practice)* [1999] 1 FLR 1042 at 1052D–E.

(Private Arrangements for Fostering) Regulations 1991 ('Fostering Regs 1991'), regs 2(2) and 4.

14.101   There is a duty on a prospective adopter under reg 4 of the Fostering Regs 1991 to notify the local authority in advance, save in the case of an emergency, that he or she proposes to foster privately.

14.102   The local authority has duties under s 67 of the CA 1989 to satisfy itself that the child's welfare is being satisfactorily safeguarded and promoted and to secure advice for the carers. If not satisfied, it has a duty to consider steps to secure a family placement or to exercise its powers under s 67(5).

14.103   Regulation 2(2) of the Fostering Regs 1991 sets out the matters in respect of which the local authority must satisfy itself: including under (a) the purpose and duration of the fostering arrangement; under (c) whether the child's religious, racial, cultural and linguistic needs are being met; under (k) whether contact between the child and his or her parents is satisfactory; under (l) whether the child's parents are exercising parental responsibility; and under (m) the child's wishes.

14.104   In *Re R (Inter-country Adoptions: Practice)* it was emphasised that the local authority has a pivotal role in responsibility for the welfare of the child at various stages.[1] Upon being notified of the child's presence, the local authority, therefore, must strictly comply with its duties under s 67 of the CA 1989.

---

1   [1999] 1 FLR 1042 at 1049E–1050C.

Chapter 15

RECOGNITION OF INTERNATIONAL ADOPTIONS

CONVENTION ADOPTIONS

15.1   Section 66 of the ACA 2002 defines 'adoption' as including a Convention adoption.[1] The effect is to enable Convention adoptions to be recognised automatically by operation of law, and the adopted person's status to be conferred by s 66 of the ACA 2002, thus obviating the need for a repeat adoption domestically.

15.2   Under s 66, all Convention adoptions are to be recognised as full adoptions, subject to s 88 of the ACA 2002, which provides a mechanism whereby the High Court may give a direction with regard to a child's status if this is more favourable to the child. Unless an application is made for a s 88 direction, the adoption is to be treated as a full adoption in accordance with Art 26(3) of the Hague Convention.

Simple adoptions

15.3   Section 88 grapples with the dichotomy between full and simple adoptions. It provides that where the High Court, on application, is satisfied that the conditions set out in s 88(2) are met, it may direct that s 67(3) (which specifies the status conferred by adoption) does not apply or does not apply to any extent which may be specified in the direction.

15.4   The conditions are threefold,[2] namely that:

(1)   under the law of the country in which the adoption was effected the adoption is not a full adoption;
(2)   the consents referred to in Art 4(c) and (d) of the Hague Convention have not been given for a full adoption, or that the United Kingdom is not the receiving State;
(3)   it would be more favourable to the adopted child for a direction to be given under s 88(1).

15.5   The reasoning behind this provision is that (i) the adoption law of the United Kingdom recognises only full adoption, and (ii) s 67(3) provides that an adopted child is

---

1   ACA 2002, s 66(1)(c), and s 144(1) defines 'the Convention' as meaning the Hague Convention on Protection of Children and Co-operation in respect of Intercountry Adoptions 1993 and a 'Convention adoption order' as 'an adoption order which by virtue of regulations under the Intercountry Act 1999 [is made as a Convention adoption order]'. 'Convention country' means a country or territory in which the Convention is in force. Section 137 extends the Hague Convention to British Overseas territories and makes consequential amendments to the British Nationality Act 1981.
2   ACA 2002, s 88(2).

to be treated in law as not being the child of any person other than the adopters (which is echoed in s 88(3)).

15.6 As has been seen, Art 26 of the Hague Convention provides for the recognition of full and simple adoptions, and Art 27 allows a receiving State to convert a simple adoption into a full adoption *if its law so permits* and provided that the natural parents and relevant parties under Art 4 have given their consent to a full adoption. The three conditions in s 88(2) of the ACA 2002, therefore, are intended to filter out simple adoptions which fail to satisfy the consent requirements of Art 4 of the Hague Convention and the 'more favourable' test in s 88(2) of the ACA 2002.

15.7 Where the receiving State is England and Wales, the Central Authority will ensure that in all cases the birth parents are informed of the effects of a simple adoption in England and Wales and will seek to obtain their consent to a full adoption prior to a Convention adoption being made in a country outside the British Isles or a Convention adoption being made in England and Wales.

15.8 Where the receiving State is not England and Wales, it is possible that the child may be brought to this country in circumstances where simple adoptions are recognised both in the State of origin and the receiving State. The result is that no consent to full adoption has in fact been given. In these circumstances, the adoption will still be treated as a full adoption by operation of law. However, if any issue of status arises where it is felt it would be more favourable to the child to treat the adoption otherwise than as a full adoption, then s 88(2)(c) will bite and an application may be made to the High Court.

15.9 Section 88, therefore, provides a new legal mechanism for the High Court to give a direction[1] whether and to what extent a child adopted under a simple adoption under the Convention should be treated as if he or she were not the child of any person other than the adopters or adopter. It only arises where: (i) the adoption is not a full adoption; (ii) the consents to a full adoption were not given or the United Kingdom is not the receiving State; and (iii) it is more favourable to the adopted child for the direction to be given. The cases where a court may be required to make such a direction are likely to be exceptional, such as where the birth parents win the lottery or otherwise receive an unexpected windfall.[2]

15.10 Rules of court will be made as to the parties to any such application and the court may involve the Attorney-General.

Annulment

15.11 ACA 2002, s 89 makes provision for the High Court to annul by order a Convention adoption or Convention adoption order on the ground that the adoption is contrary to public policy. The effect of such an order will be that the Convention order ceases to have effect in the United Kingdom.

15.12 This implements Art 24 of the Hague Convention, which provides that 'the recognition of an adoption may be refused in a Contracting State only if the adoption is

---

1 In relation to a direction under this section and an application for it, ss 59 and 60 of the Family Law Act 1986 (declarations under that Act as to marital status) apply.
2 Explanatory Notes to Adoption (Intercountry Aspects) Act 1999, paras 34 and 35.

manifestly contrary to its public policy, taking into account the best interests of the child'. As under the ACA 2002, the best interests of the child are paramount under s 1 and this is the overarching principle throughout the Act, it follows that any public policy issue which arises under s 89 must be subservient to the welfare principle. It should also be noted that Art 24, by the use of such words as 'only if' and 'manifestly', signals that refusal should be viewed as a very exceptional event, as otherwise it would undermine the whole ethos of the Convention which operates upon a basis of mutual confidence between Contracting States.[1]

15.13   Section 89(4) makes it clear that, subject to the circumstances in s 89(1), the validity of a Convention adoption or Convention adoption order cannot be called into question in proceedings in any court in England and Wales.

15.14   An application for an order under s 89(1) must be made in the prescribed manner and within any prescribed period[2] and cannot be made unless, immediately before the application is made, (a) the person adopted, or (b) the adopter or (in the case of a married couple) both of them, habitually resides in England and Wales.[3]

Determinations

15.15   Section 91(1) and (2) of the ACA 2002 provide for the recognition of determinations made by any authority of a Convention country (other than the United Kingdom)[4] (a) authorising or reviewing an adoption, or (b) revoking or annulling such an order ('s 91 determination').[5] The High Court may, on an application under s 89(2), by order: (a) impugn a s 91 determination on two grounds – (i) it is contrary to public policy, or (ii) the authority was not competent to entertain the case – or (b) decide the extent to which a s 9 determination has been affected by a subsequent s 9 determination. Otherwise, the validity of the s 91 determination cannot be called in question. As to the competency of the authority to entertain the particular case, the court is bound by any finding of fact made by the authority and stated by the authority to be so made to that effect.[6]

OVERSEAS ADOPTIONS

Definition

15.16   Section 66(1) of the ACA 2002 defines 'adoption' as including 'an overseas adoption'.[7] For an adoption to qualify as an 'overseas adoption':

---

1   'Public policy' is discussed in more detail at **15.25** et seq.
2   ACA 2002, s 90(1). 'Prescribed' means prescribed by rules.
3   Ibid, s 90(2).
4   Also the Channel Islands, the Isle of Man or any colony: s 91(1).
5   ACA 2002, s 91(2) is subject to s 89 and to any subsequent determination having effect under that subsection: s 91(3).
6   Ibid, s 90(3).
7   Ibid, s 66(1)(d).

–   it must meet the description specified by order made by the Secretary of State, being
     a 'description of adoptions effected under the law of any country or territory outside
     the British Islands'; and
–   it must not be a Convention adoption.[1]

15.17   Under the AA 1976, the specification for an overseas adoption had been made
by the Adoption (Designation of Overseas Adoptions) Order 1973 ('the 1973 Overseas
Order').[2] It provided that an adoption was an overseas adoption if it was effected under
the law in force in a place which forms part of a country or territory described in Part I
(namely 39 Commonwealth countries (exceptions include India and Bangladesh) and
UK-dependent territories) or Part II (namely 22 other countries including the USA, the
People's Republic of China, all Western European countries, Greece, Turkey, Yugoslavia
and South Africa)[3] of the Schedule to the Order.[4]

15.18   Section 87 of the ACA 2002[5] allows arrangements to be put in place for the
recognition in England and Wales of overseas adoptions. The policy intention is to
review which overseas countries' adoptions will be recognised in the future and to
produce a revised 'designated list' following the ratification of the Hague Convention and
as soon as possible following the enactment of the ACA 2002. Having completed the
review, the Secretary of State will make an order that adoptions made in those countries
from the date that the order is made are to be 'overseas adoption' for the purposes of the
AA 1976[6] and the ACA 2002.

15.19   The section, therefore, permits the Secretary of State to make an order specifying
the adoption orders to be included and enables him to make regulations setting out the
criteria that an overseas adoption must meet to be included.[7] The criteria are likely to
include:

(a)   confirming that the law in the overseas country ensures that the child has been freely
      given up for adoption and that this has not been induced by payment or
      compensation of any kind;
(b)   confirming that the overseas country has made attempts to place the child in a
      family in that country;
(c)   confirming that intercountry adoption is in the child's best interests;
(d)   requiring that the domestic and intercountry adoption arrangements are the same;
      and

---

1   ACA 2002, s 87(1).
2   SI 1973/19, as amended by SI 1993/690. The order came into effect on February 1973 and applies
     to adoptions made before and after that date: art 3(2); see *Secretary of State for the Home Department v
     Lofthouse* [1981] Imm AR 166.
3   1973 Overseas Order, art 3(2A).
4   Ibid, art 3(1) and (2). Under art 3(3), the adoption order must: (i) have been made in a country or
     territory designated in the Order; (ii) have been effected under statutory law and not customary law;
     and (iii) relate to a person, who, at the time when the application for adoption was made had not
     attained the age of 18 years and had not been married.
5   ACA 2002, s 134 makes similar provision to s 87 for Scotland.
6   Ibid, s 87(4).
7   Ibid, s 87(2) and (3).

(e) ensuring that profit is not made from the process.[1]

15.20 The review will involve bilateral discussions with countries to decide which ones should be included in the list on the basis that their adoptions are likely to meet the requirements set out in the regulations. This will be a time-consuming exercise, as the review cannot happen without changes in primary legislation which ensure that the removal of a country from the list does not automatically remove the recognition of adoptions made prior to the review of the designated list. This would undermine the status of children and adults adopted in the past from countries included in the list. Therefore, it is to be assumed that legislation will ensure that the status afforded by an adoption recognised by the 1973 Overseas Order is preserved. As the review is unlikely to be completed by the time the ACA 2002 comes fully into force, the aim of the section is to provide flexibility to continue to recognise adoptions from those countries currently on the designated list which have not yet reached the review process.[2]

Recognition of an overseas adoption

15.21 By its inclusion in the definition of 'adoption' in s 66 of the ACA 2002, an 'overseas adoption' is automatically recognised as an adoption order in England and Wales and does not need to be repeated domestically in the UK courts. Its status as a valid adoption, therefore, does not need to be established in any court proceedings.

15.22 However, automatic recognition of the adoption order does not necessarily confer UK citizenship upon the child, as the 'status' conferred by adoption under s 67 of the ACA 2002 does not apply for the purposes of the British Nationality Act 1981.[3] The amendments to s 1(5) of the British Nationality Act 1981 effected by s 7 of the A(IA)A 1999 do not apply to overseas adoptions.[4]

Evidence

15.23 The Secretary of State will make provision for the manner in which evidence of any overseas adoption may be given.[5] In respect of an overseas adoption under the 1973 Overseas Order,[6] evidence that it had been effected was given by the production of:

(a) a certified copy of an entry made, in accordance with the law of the country or territory concerned, in a public register relating to the recording of adoptions showing that the adoption has been effected; or

---

1   HC Deb, 20 May 2002, vol 386, no 150, col 25, per Ms Jacqui Smith. These examples are given in the Draft Regulations and Guidance *Implementing the Adoption (Intercountry Aspects) Act 1999*, at para 35 of the Introduction.

2   HC Deb, 20 May 2002, vol 386, no 150, cols 23 and 25. See also the Draft Regulations and Guidance *Implementing the Adoption (Intercountry Aspects) Act 1999*, paras 32 and 34 of the Introduction.

3   ACA 2002, s 74(2)(a).

4   For the relevance of 'overseas adoptions' for immigration purposes, see *R v Secretary of State for the Home Office, ex p Tahid* [1990] TLR 651, CA.

5   ACA 2002, s 87(5).

6   Other proof that an overseas adoption has been effected may be received: art 4(3) of the 1973 Overseas Order.

(b)　a certificate that the adoption has been effected, signed or purporting to be signed by a person authorised by the law of the country or territory concerned or a certified copy of such certificate.[1] Where the document produced was not in English, the Registrar General required an English translation.[2] (This may continue to be relevant in respect of those overseas adoptions which pre-date the ACA 2002.)

Annulment

15.24　Under s 89(2)(a) of the ACA 2002 an overseas adoption may be impugned[3] by an order of the High Court on two grounds:

(a)　that the adoption is contrary to public policy; or
(b)　that the authority which purported to authorise the adoption was not competent to authorise the case.

Otherwise an overseas adoption cannot be called into question in any proceedings in England and Wales.[4]

Public policy

15.25　In *Re Valentine's Settlement*,[5] the Court of Appeal left it open to domestic courts to refuse to recognise a foreign adoption on the grounds of public policy. This was a response in general principle to the fact that the laws of some foreign countries may differ widely from UK law. In *Bedinger v Graybill's Executor*,[6] for example, the Kentucky Court of Appeals held that a husband could adopt his wife in order that she might qualify as a 'child' under his mother's will, whereas in *Wende v Victoria (County) Official Administrator*[7] the court refused to recognise a German adoption by an 83-year-old man of a 44-year-old woman with whom he had cohabited as man and wife for more than 15 years.

15.26　It is submitted that the domestic court should, however, be reluctant to impugn an overseas adoption save in exceptional circumstances. Examples of what may constitute 'exceptional circumstances' may include: (i) where an overseas adoption is being employed to further some immoral or financial advantage for the adopter; (ii) where a child habitually resident outside the British Islands has been brought into the United Kingdom illegally for adoption, contrary to s 83 of the ACA 2002; or (iii) where a child has been illegally removed from England and Wales and taken abroad to be adopted, contrary to s 85 of the ACA 2002.

15.27　The test of 'public policy' is, therefore, a high one.[8] It is also provided for in Art 24 of the Hague Convention which states:

1　1973 Overseas Order, art 4(1)(a), (b).
2　Ibid, art 4(2).
3　ACA 2002, s 89(3).
4　Ibid, s 89(4).
5　[1965] Ch 831 at 842F–G, per Lord Denning MR, and at 854F–G, per Salmon LJ.
6　302 SW 2d 594 (1957), cited in *Dicey and Morris on the Conflict of Laws* (13th edn, Sweet & Maxwell), at p 898, para 20–123.
7　[1998] 7 WWR 480 (BC) cited in ibid.
8　HC Special Standing Committee, 11 December 2001, cols 533–534, per Ms Jacqui Smith.

'The recognition of an adoption may be refused in a Contracting State only if the adoption is manifestly contrary to its public policy, taking into account the best interests of the child.'

It follows that the High Court must be convinced that to recognise an adoption would offend basic moral principles before impugning the adoption order.

15.28   Where a foreign order is made in accordance with the proper procedures of the foreign law and there is no fraud or other delinquency, the domestic court should only reject the decree if the foreign law is so offensive to the English conception that it would constitute an infraction of the rules of natural justice in the eye of the English court.[1] In analogous situations, misrepresentation has not necessarily invalidated the recognition of a decree[2] and, even where there has been fraud, recognition has been given in England and Wales jurisprudence to an innocent party being afforded relief.[3]

COMITY

15.29   Important considerations of comity also come into play. By way of analogy,[4] in *Igra v Igra* (which concerned the validity of a decree of divorce) Pearce J said:[5]

'... [the court of domicile's] decisions should, as far as reasonably possible, be acknowledged by other countries in the interests of comity. Different countries have different personal laws, different standards of justice and different practice. The interests of comity are not served if one country is too reluctant to recognise decrees that are valid by the law of domicile.'

15.30   In *Travers v Holley*[6] the notion of comity was expressed in the following terms of reciprocity:

'... it seems that where it is found that municipal law is not peculiar to the forum of one country but corresponds with a law of a second country, such municipal law cannot be said to trench upon the interests of that country. I would say that where ... there is in substance reciprocity, it would be contrary to principle and inconsistent with comity if the courts of this country were to refuse to recognise a jurisdiction which *mutates mutandis* they claim for themselves.'

15.31   Lord Denning in *Re Valentine's Settlement*[7] applied considerations of international comity in the context of the status of adoption. He said:

'... when is the status of adoption duly constituted? Clearly it is so when it is constituted in another country in similar circumstances as we claim for ourselves. Our courts should recognise a jurisdiction which *mutates mutandis* they claim for themselves: see *Travers v Holley*. We claim jurisdiction to make an adoption order when the adopting parents are domiciled in this country and the child is resident here. So also, out of the comity of nations, we should recognise an adoption order made by another country when the adopting parents are domiciled there and the child is resident here.'

---

1   *Armitage v Nanchen* (1983) 4 FLR 293 at 300, per Sir John Arnold P.
2   *Puttick v AG* [1980] Fam 1; *Eroglu v Eroglu* [1994] 2 FLR 287, where it was held that it was not contrary to public policy to recognise a foreign decree of divorce, pronounced by a foreign court in good faith, upon the fraudulent evidence of the parties to the marriage.
3   *Whiston v Whiston* [1995] Fam 198 at 207E–F.
4   See also *Société Nationale Industrielle Aérospatiale v Lee Kui Jak* [1987] 1 AC 871 at 895G–H; *Butler v Butler (Nos 1 and 2)* [1997] 2 FLR 311 at 318B–F, per Thorpe LJ.
5   [1951] P 404 at 412.
6   [1953] P 246 at 257, per Hodson LJ, citing the principle in *Le Mesurier v Le Mesurier* [1895] AC 517 at 528, per Lord Watson.
7   [1965] 1 Ch 831 at 842B–C.

DISTINCTION BETWEEN STATUS AND EFFECT

15.32 It is important to distinguish between recognising the status of a foreign adoption and giving effect to its consequences. It has been suggested[1] that:

> 'the facts would have to be extreme before public policy demanded the total non-recognition of a foreign adoption for all purposes ... the fact that an adopted person was over the age of 18, or that the adoption was not made by court order should not prevent recognition. A system of law which is prepared to recognise polygamous marriages and extra-judicial divorces should not be too squeamish about recognising foreign adoptions.'

Competency

15.33 An overseas adoption can also be impugned where the overseas authority which granted the adoption order had no jurisdiction to do so.

15.34 The question of the jurisdiction of a foreign court to enter an adoption decree arose in *Flintshire County Council v K*[2] (which became known as the 'Internet twins' case). On 22 December 2000, Mr and Mrs K, a British couple resident in North Wales, had obtained an interlocutory decree of adoption from the Probate Court of Pulaski County, Arkansas, in relation to the twin girls of US parents, Mr and Mrs W, both residents of Missouri. On 22 January 2001, a judge in the Missouri Circuit Court (St Louis City) made an interim custody order in respect in favour of Mr W. A further complication was that the twins had been initially placed for adoption by the mother, Mrs W, with Mr and Mrs A in California, and Mr and Mrs A were also indicating that they might seek to involve themselves in the proceedings and assert a claim to the twins. Kirkwood J said:[3]

> '... a question of English law of potential importance was identified, namely what relationship, in law, did Mr and Mrs K have with the twins? Was the interlocutory decree of adoption an overseas adoption within the meaning of Part IV and s 72 of the Adoption Act 1976 [now s 87 of the ACA 2002]? If so, then it accorded to Mr and Mrs K and the twins exactly the same status as an English adoption order. But there are doubts.
>
> It does not appear to be a final order. On the other hand, the Supreme Court of Arkansas has held:
>
> > "Understandably, confusion now exists among the members of the bar about when an adoption order is final and may be appealed ... In order to put an end to confusion, we shall prospectively construe any decree of adoption to be a final order, no matter whether it is interlocutory or final, if no subsequent hearing is required by the terms of that decree."
>
> [*In the matter of Appeals for Adoption orders*, 227A 520, 642 SW 2d 573 (1982)]
>
> The Court of Appeal of Arkansas has held "Once an interlocutory decree of adoption is entered, it is to be construed as a final decree, if no subsequent hearing is required under the terms of that decree" (*Maybury v Flowers* (2000) 69 Ark Ap 307).
>
> But the Arkansas Statutes Annotated, s 9–9–213, provides:

---

1   D McClean *Morris: The Conflict of Laws* (5th edn, Sweet & Maxwell, 2000) at pp 316–317.
2   [2001] 2 FLR 476. The facts are dealt with at **16.14–16.17**.
3   Ibid, at 483G–484D.

"... an interlocutory decree of adoption ... does not become final until the minor to be adopted has lived in the adoptive home for at least six months after the petition for adoption is filed."

Foreign law is not a matter for this court save to the extent of any findings of fact it can make as to what that law is. Given that the twins have not lived with Mr and Mrs K since 18 January 2001 and were by this court's order to remain away from their home for longer than that, it looked difficult to reconcile the practical facts of the case with the interlocutory decree of adoption of 22 December 2000 being a final adoption order or becoming a final adoption order on 1 June 2001 in accordance with its internal terms and also in accordance with the Arkansas statute.'

15.35   In the event, on 6 March 2001 the judge in the Probate Court of Pulaski County, Arkansas, who had made the interlocutory decree of adoption, held, on review, that the adoption had been defective because, contrary to the provisions of the Arkansas code, jurisdictional requirements did not appear on the record so that his court did not in fact have jurisdiction to enter an adoption in the case. He accordingly set aside and cancelled the interlocutory decree of adoption made on 22 December 2000 and Kirkwood J held that, as a result, Mr and Mrs K did not have parental rights in respect of the twins in the USA.

15.36   The question of jurisdiction of an overseas court will generally be for an independent expert in the law of that country. Where an application is made to the High Court under s 89(2) of the ACA 2002 and the jurisdiction of the overseas authority is in question, it is an appropriate role for CAFCASS, who, particularly given the international aspect, are likely to be invited to act on behalf of the child to obtain the relevant expert evidence to assist the High Court to determine such issue. This was the course adopted by Kirkwood J in the Internet twins case. Kirkwood J said:[1]

'The profound concerns of this court from the outset, when considering any possible order for the return of the twins to the US were: to which State should they be sent? who would look after them? which State courts may be receiving claims? which court should decide the future of the twins? and how long would it all take?

With those matters in mind, I appointed the Official Solicitor to assist the court in a neutral way with a view to his liaising with judicial and administrative authorities in the US in an endeavour to answer the questions ...

All authorities have throughout been at pains to seek the best outcome for the twins, and it has been a feature of the conduct of this case, that this court has been able, through the Official Solicitor, to keep the authorities in the US informed of the work in and the conduct of the case, and they in turn have kept this court fully informed. All parties have been kept fully informed of the detail of all communications.'

ADOPTIONS IN THE BRITISH ISLES

15.37   Under s 66 of the ACA 2002, adoption is defined as including 'adoption by a Scottish or Northern Irish adoption order'[2] and 'by an order made in the Isle of Man or

---

1   [2001] 2 FLR 476 at 483E–484G.
2   ACA 2002, s 66(1)(a).

any of the Channel Islands'.[1] These, therefore, are automatically recognised without the need for further domestic court proceedings.

FOREIGN ADOPTIONS RECOGNISED AT COMMON LAW

15.38   The definition of 'adoption' in s 66 of the ACA 2002 includes 'an adoption recognised by the law of England and Wales and effected under the law of any other country'.[2] This provides for the recognition of a foreign adoption by common law rules where, for example:

(1)   the adoption order is not made in the British Isles nor in a Hague Convention country nor in a country specified as an 'overseas adoption'; or
(2)   although made in a country designated in the 1973 Overseas Order, the adoption was effected under the customary or common law rather than under statutory law or involved the adoption of an adult.

15.39   Given that the numbers of designated 'overseas' countries are extensive and those of the Hague Convention are annually increasing, there is diminishing scope for the operation of common law. Nevertheless, it remains relevant in such countries as India, Pakistan, Japan, some Eastern European countries, Middle Eastern countries (other than Turkey and Israel) and some of the countries in Central and Southern America.

Recognition rules at common law

15.40   The majority of the Court of Appeal in *Re Valentine's Settlement*[3] held that the domestic courts would only recognise an adoption in another country if the adopting parents were domiciled there.[4] Lord Denning said:

> 'Apart from international comity, we reach the same result on principle. When a court of any country makes an adoption order for an infant child, it does two things: (i) it destroys the legal relationship thereto existing between the child and its natural parents, be it legitimate or illegitimate; (ii) it creates the legal relationship of parent and child between the child and its adopting parents, making it their legitimate child. Now it has long been settled that questions affecting status are determined by the law of the domicile. This new status of parent and child, in order to be recognised everywhere, must be validly created by the law of the domicile of the adopting parent. You do not look to the domicile of the child; for that has no separate domicile of his or her own. The child takes his or her parents' domicile . . . If you find that a legitimate relationship of parent and child has been validly created by the law of the parents'

---

1   ACA 2002, s 66(1)(b).
2   Ibid, s 66(1)(e).
3   [1965] Ch 831 at 843A–C, per Lord Denning MR.
4   Although Lord Denning referred at 843B–C also to a requirement that the child should ordinarily be resident in the foreign country, this was based upon the fact that, at the time, residence of the child in England was a precondition for the adoption jurisdiction of the English courts to operate. Since the Children Act 1975 there has been no such jurisdictional requirement and, therefore, it is very unlikely that the ordinary residence of the child in the foreign country will be required for the recognition of a foreign adoption at common law: see *Morris: The Conflict of Laws*, op cit, p 316. Danckwerts LJ expressed some doubt at the time in *Re Valentine* at 846F–G, when he said that he was 'not sure' whether the ordinary residence of the child was a requirement.

domicile at the time the relationship is created, then the status so created should be universally recognised throughout the civilised world ...'[1]

15.41   By way of analogy with the recognition at common law of foreign divorces,[2] it has been suggested that the common law principle in relation to foreign adoptions may be widened by extending the recognition to include recognition in the country in which the adopters are domiciled.[3]

15.42   Further, since *Re Valentine's Settlement* was decided, the Domicile and Matrimonial Proceedings Act 1973 has been enacted, enabling a wife to have a different domicile from her husband. As s 49(2) of the ACA 2002 requires only that one of the applicant couple should be domiciled in this jurisdiction, it is, therefore, arguable that the domicile of only one of the adopters may suffice for recognition at common law.

15.43   The words 'effected under the law of any country' are wide enough to encompass adoptions other than by court order, for example by deed, contract or religious ceremony.[4]

15.44   Where adopters have obtained a foreign adoption order which does not qualify for automatic recognition as a Convention adoption or overseas adoption but which satisfies the common law rules, their best course is to apply for a declaration in the High Court to that effect, relying upon expert evidence as to the applicable adoption law and procedure in the country of domicile and as to their compliance with that law and procedure.[5] The questions to the experts should be posed in such a way that the court can consider, if it decides that the orders are ones that should be recognised, their effect under English law.[6] Copies of the relevant orders should be obtained and filed together with translations.

Public policy

15.45   In this context, there is, of course, no statutory public policy ground for setting aside the order, as in the case of overseas and Convention adoptions. Lord Denning in *Re Valentine's Settlement*, however, after citing the proposition set out at **15.40** above, added the following proviso:[7]

> 'If you find that a legitimate relationship of parent and child has been validly created by the law of the parent's domicile ... then the status so created should be universally recognised ... *provided always that there is nothing contrary to public policy in so recognising it.*'

15.46   As 'welfare' is the 'paramount consideration' and no longer the 'first consideration' and the words 'all the circumstances' have been deleted from s 1 of the ACA 2002 (both of which enabled policy considerations to be weighed in the balance along with welfare), does this exclude public policy under the ACA 2002, apart from

---

1   [1965] Ch 831 at 842B–G.
2   *Armitage v AG* [1906] P 135.
3   D McClean *Morris: The Conflict of Laws*, op cit, at p 316.
4   See *Re Wilby* [1956] P 174 (adoption by deed in Burma); and the other cases cited in *Dicey & Morris: The Conflict of Laws*, op cit, at p 897, para 20–121, n 87.
5   *Re AMR (Adoption: Procedure)* [1999] 2 FLR 807 at 817C–D, per HHJ David Gee (sitting as a deputy judge of the High Court).
6   Ibid, at 817D.
7   [1965] Ch 831 at 842F–G. (Emphasis added.)

where it is expressly provided for by the statute? Although public policy considerations are plainly diminished, it is nevertheless arguable that they are not excluded. Inter-country adoption encompasses private international law and public policy considerations can still be generated by the private international law context. However, now that the paramountcy principle is the prime consideration, the reality is that welfare will normally override public policy.

REQUIREMENT FOR A DOMESTIC ADOPTION WHERE A FOREIGN CHILD IS INVOLVED

15.47   An application for a domestic adoption order, where a foreign child is involved, will be required in the following circumstances (which are not exhaustive):

(1)   where a foreign adoption has been obtained but does not qualify for automatic recognition as a Convention adoption or overseas adoption nor for recognition at common law:
(2)   where a foreign child is being adopted by a relative domiciled in England or Wales;
(3)   where a foreign child is brought to this jurisdiction by prospective adopters (previously unconnected with the child) for the specific purpose of adoption in England and Wales.

15.48   In intercountry adoptions which arise in the circumstances listed above, the proposed adopters must apply for an adoption order in this jurisdiction and must comply with (a) the emigration and adoption law and procedure applicable in the child's country of origin, and (b) UK immigration law, adoption law and procedure. Certain aspects of procedure which raised points of law under the former legislation and which are likely to recur under the new legislation are considered below.

Parental agreement

15.49   An area which arose for consideration under the former law related to whether the agreement of foreign natural parents to a domestic English adoption order was required.

15.50   In *Re G (Foreign Adoption: Consent)*,[1] which concerned a Paraguayan child with respect to whom the Paraguayan court had made a simple adoption order, Johnson J held that the agreement referred to in s 16 of the AA 1976 was an agreement to an adoption order under that Act and the mother's agreement to the Paraguayan adoption was not effective for the purposes of s 16. He found that, while consent may be given and agreement expressed orally,[2] the mother had only agreed to the Paraguayan order and nothing she had done or said in the Paraguayan court could be construed as an agreement to an adoption order made in England. Although this approach has been the subject of

1   [1995] 2 FLR 534.
2   *Re T (A Minor) (Adoption: Validity of Order)* [1986] Fam 160, [1986] 2 FLR 31.

debate,[1] the absorption of the 1993 Hague Convention with its strict requirements as to consent into our law is likely to generate a jurisprudential climate for the decision in *Re G* to take root under the new legislation.

15.51　In *Re AMR (Adoption: Procedure)*,[2] a family court in Poland had deprived the natural parents of their parental responsibility and appointed the great-grandmother as the child's guardian. The great-grandmother brought the child to England to live with another relative, who then sought to adopt her. One of the questions which arose was whether the consent of the natural parents was required to the adoption.

15.52　Applying the principles in *Re Valentine,* the court recognised the Polish order for the purpose of the domestic adoption proceedings and held that, as the Polish order deprived the parents of parental responsibility, it had the effect of depriving them of parental responsibility under English law and that, consequently, their consent was not required. The same principles will apply under the new legislation.

Dispensing with service

15.53　In *Re R (Adoption)*[3] Buckley J found that in a case where there were no practical means of communicating with a person whose agreement to an adoption order was required, then that 'person cannot be found' and is 'incapable of giving agreement' within the meaning of s 16(2)(a) of the AA 1976. This approach was followed in *Re An Adoption Application*,[4] which concerned a child from El Salvador, where there was doubt as to the identity of the true natural mother, and neither of the persons named as the mother could be found in El Salvador despite the personal efforts of the British consul.[5]

15.54　In contrast, in *Re G (Foreign Adoption: Consent)*,[6] Johnson J held that it was not a case for dispensing with service as the mother's probable whereabouts were known and therefore there was no proper basis for departing from the ordinary requirement of service upon the natural mother. He ordered that the mother be made a respondent to the proceedings and be properly served. In the circumstances, the Official Solicitor was to ask the British consul in Paraguay to speak with the mother with a view to ensuring she agreed to the making of an adoption order in England.[7]

1　*Re A (Adoption of Russian Child)* [2000] 1 FLR 539 at 543C–D. Charles J expressed the view (*per curiam*) that there was force in the argument that, despite *Re G*, valid parental agreement could consist in agreement to the adoption in the country of origin and did not have to include specific agreement to an English adoption.

2　[1999] 2 FLR 807; see also *Adoption Application 96 AO 147* (unreported, 31 January 1997) which is cited by Cazalet J in *Re AGN (Adoption: Foreign Adoption)* [2000] 2 FLR 431 at 436H–437F.

3　[1967] 1 WLR 34.

4　[1992] 1 FLR 341 at 347H.

5　Ibid, at 345D–E.

6　[1995] 2 FLR 534.

7　See also *Re WM (Adoption: Non-Patrial)* [1997] 1 FLR 132, where the mother had consented to an adoption order in El Salvador, but, unlike in *Re G,* there was evidence via a letter from the ambassador to El Salvador that the mother was aware that there would be adoption proceedings in England and gave her consent for the purpose of the English proceedings. Johnson J was satisfied on the evidence that the mother had given her consent freely and with full understanding to the English adoption.

15.55   However, in *Re S (Adoption)*,[1] the Court of Session in Scotland, applying *Re F (R) (An Infant)*,[2] stated that before it can be held that a person cannot be found for the purposes of adoption proceedings all reasonable steps must be taken to find him and if even only one reasonable step is not taken, one cannot say that the person cannot be found.

15.56   In *Re A (Adoption of Russian Child)*,[3] Charles J found that the interpretations of the phrase 'cannot be found' in the two cases were not in conflict. He said:

> 'The first refers to "no *practical* means" and the second to "all *reasonable* steps" ... It is important to note that, in my judgment correctly, neither case refers to *possible* means or steps. They are therefore authority that all practical means must be employed and all reasonable steps must be taken to find and communicate with the relevant person. What is "reasonable" and what is "practical" are not necessarily the same but will often overlap. In my judgment any potential difference does not give rise to difficulty.'

15.57   Section 16(2)(a) of the AA 1976 has now become s 52(1)(a) of the ACA 2002 and similar considerations will apply under the new law.

The meaning of 'guardian'

15.58   Under s 72(1) of the AA 1976, 'guardian' for the purposes of the AA 1976 was defined as having the same meaning as in the CA 1989 'unless the context otherwise requires'. Section 105(1) of the CA 1989 provides that 'a guardian of the child' means 'a guardian (other than a guardian of the estate of a child) appointed in accordance with the provisions of s 5'. Section 5(13) of the CA 1989 provides: 'A guardian of a child may only be appointed in accordance with the provision of this section'.

15.59   In *Re D (Adoption: Foreign Guardianship)*[4] the question arose as to whether a Romanian institution (the United Hospital Alesd) where the child had been living was a guardian whose agreement to the adoption was required. Holman J adopted a strict construction of s 16 and concluded that 'guardian' under s 16 was necessarily limited to a guardian appointed under s 5 of the CA 1989. He, therefore, held that the Romanian institution was not a guardian for the purpose of giving agreement under s 16 of the AA 1976.

15.60   *Re AMR (Adoption: Procedure)*[5] his Honour Judge Gee, sitting as a deputy High Court judge, had to consider the effect and consequences of the order of the Polish court appointing the great-grandmother as guardian. He adopted a broader approach:

> 'I do not interpret the word "require" [in s 72(1) of the AA 1976] in the narrow and restricted sense adopted by Holman J. Respectfully, I take the view that "the context" means the entire context of the case. I think I can and should look at the full background to this case, including its international aspects and decide whether the context does require a different definition to be applied to the word "guardian". Taking all these factors into account I conclude that the context does so require and that the great-grandmother is a guardian for the purpose of the Adoption Act and that her consent is required or must be dispensed with.'

1   [1999] 2 FLR 374 at 379A–C.
2   [1970] 1 QB 358.
3   [2000] 1 FLR 539 at 547D–G.
4   [1999] 2 FLR 865 at 869–870.
5   [1999] 2 FLR 807 at 816F–817A.

15.61   In *Re AGN (Adoption: Foreign Adoption)*[1] where a Romanian adoption had been preceded by a declaration of abandonment declaring that parental rights should be transferred to the orphanage where the child was living, the question again arose as to whether the agreement of the orphanage as guardian of the child under Romanian law was required. Cazelet J followed the rationale of the case of *Re AMR (Adoption: Procedure)* and adopted a broader approach.[2] He accepted:

(1)   the line of authority running through *Di Savini v Lousada*[3] and *Monaco v Monaco*[4] to the effect that English law will recognise a foreign guardianship order provided that it is made by a court of competent jurisdiction;

(2)   that, until the amendment brought in by the CA 1989 requiring a guardian to be appointed under s 5(13), a guardian appointed by a foreign court of competent jurisdiction was a guardian within the meaning of s 72(1) of the AA 1976. Had Parliament intended that such a guardian should be excluded, such a fundamental change would only have been put in place by a significantly more specific definition;

(3)   that the preamble to the definition, 'unless the context otherwise requires', can include a foreign guardian;

(4)   that, where there is a foreign guardian in whom parental rights have been vested by a foreign court of competent jurisdiction, then the whole spirit of the adoption legislation requires that such a person should be made a party to the proceedings.

15.62   *Re J (Adoption: Consent of Foreign Public Authority)*[5] followed the trend of adopting a broad and flexible approach as to whether a foreign authority or institution could be construed as guardian, taking into account the whole context. A child who had been abandoned shortly before birth was admitted to an orphanage in Jordan and shortly thereafter was brought to England by a British couple who proposed to adopt him. They had complied with all the required procedures both in England and in Jordan. The child was placed by the orphanage into the prospective adopters' care a week before coming to England. The Jordanian Ministry of Social Development had issued documents approving of the child's removal, including his passport. In Jordan, Sharia law applies. Under Sharia law, while fostering is allowed, adoption is prohibited. The question which arose was whether the child had a guardian whose consent had been given or dispensed with. Charles J, in making the adoption order, held that when considering whether a person in another jurisdiction is to be treated as a guardian, the court should consider: (i) the extent to which that person's duties, rights and responsibilities equate to those of a person who has parental responsibility in English law and whose consent has been given or is dispensed with; and (ii) whether in all the circumstances that person's consent should be given or dispensed with before the adoption is made. He found that the consent of the Jordanian authority was not required, as a pubic authority in Jordan could not consent to an adoption, and fostering in Jordan did not give the public authority parental responsibility carrying with it the ability to consent to adoption. He went on to find that

---

1   [2000] 2 FLR 431.
2   This extension of the definition of the term 'guardian' in the AA 1976, where the international context in relation to a foreign child and foreign guardian so required, was approved by way of analogy in the Court of Appeal decision of *Re S (Freeing for Adoption)* [2002] EWCA Civ 798, [2002] 2 FLR 681.
3   (1870) 18 WR 425.
4   (1937) 157 LT 231.
5   [2002] 2 FLR 618.

if his conclusion was wrong, the consent of the Jordanian authority could be dispensed with because it was incapable of giving agreement, being prevented under Sharia law from consenting to adoption. The consent of the parents was dispensed with on the ground that they could not be found.

15.63   Central to his Honour Judge Gee's reasoning had been the scope which the preamble to s 72(1) of the AA 1976, 'unless the context otherwise requires', gave him in looking at the full background, including the international aspects. However, under the new interpretation section, s 144(1) of the ACA 2002, there is no such preamble. The definition of 'guardian' is that it has 'the same meaning' as in the CA 1989 and 'includes a special guardian within the meaning of that Act'. At first blush, the omission of the preamble from the definition appears to support the strict construction enunciated by Holman J in *Re D (Adoption: Foreign Guardianship)*.[1]

15.64   As, however, a strict interpretation flies in the face of the history and the spirit of domestic and international adoption law (as the other compelling arguments ((1), (2) and (4) in *Re AGN (Adoption: Foreign Adoption)*[2] show),[3] it may still be arguable that a broader purposive construction should be adopted for the definition of 'guardian' under the ACA 2002 rather than a literal construction.

IMMIGRATION LAW AND PUBLIC POLICY

The balancing exercise under the former law

15.65   In *Re H (A Minor) (Adoption: Non-Patrial)*[4] Hollings J highlighted 'the conflict or even collision which can occur, and seems bound to occur from time to time, between immigration policy and procedures and adoption law and procedures'.

15.66   Hollings J went on to hold that the court should take into account considerations of public policy in relation to the effect of an adoption order on nationality and the right of abode and should carry out the balancing act between welfare (being then the first consideration) and public policy relating to immigration. He was concerned with a boy who was aged nearly 16 and who, before coming to England, had been turned out of his home in Pakistan and was destitute. His application for leave to settle in this country had been refused by the Home Office and the appeal procedures against that refusal had been exhausted. Hollings J said:[5]

> 'What then should the approach of this court be in applications of this nature? Clearly, it must pay great regard to the "immigration decision" and in particular considerations of public policy and, where relevant, national security. It must be on its guard against the possibility of abuse; but the mere fact that nationality or patriality would result is not

---

1   [1999] 2 FLR 865. Holman J did not have the advantage of full argument.
2   See **15.61**.
3   In *Re S (Freeing for Adoption)* [2002] EWCA Civ 798, [2002] 2 FLR 681, although not directly in point, *Re AMR (Adoption: Procedure)* [1999] 2 FLR 807, and *Re AGN (Adoption: Foreign Adoption)* [2002] 2 FLR 431 were cited with approval as illustrations of a broad judicial construction which reflected the desire to achieve a sensible outcome and advance the welfare of the child.
4   [1982] Fam 121 at 126H; (1983) 4 FLR 85 at 91B.
5   Ibid, at 133C–E; cited with approval by Balcombe LJ in *Re W (A Minor) (Adoption: Non-Patrial)* [1986] Fam 54 at 61D–62A and 63B–C; also [1986] 1 FLR 179.

conclusive. It must treat welfare as the first consideration, outweighing any one other factor but not all factors. If the court considers on the evidence and the information before it that the true motive of the application is based upon the desire to achieve nationality and the right of abode rather than the general welfare of the minor, then an adoption order should not be made. If on the other hand part of the motive – or it may be at least as much – is to achieve real emotional or psychological, social and legal benefits[1] . . . of adoption, then an adoption order may be proper, notwithstanding that this has the effect of overriding an immigration decision or even an immigration rule. In every case it is a matter of balancing welfare against public policy and the wider the implications of the public policy aspect the less weight may be attached to the aspect of the particular individual.'[2]

15.67 In *Re W (A Minor) (Adoption: Non-Patrial)*[3] (which approved *Re H (A Minor) (Adoption: Non-Patrial)*[4]) Balcombe LJ, in a further important passage,[5] set out the considerations which were to apply when an application was made by a British citizen to adopt a foreign child, which included the following:

(1)   When the court comes to consider the application on its merits it must, of course, give first consideration to the need to safeguard and promote the welfare of the child throughout his or her childhood. If only a short period of that childhood remains, then clearly this factor carries less weight.[6]

(2)   The court should also consider whether the welfare of the child would be better, or as well, promoted by another type of order which does not have the same effect on nationality and immigration as an adoption order.[7]

(3)   In any event the court should take into account those considerations of public policy in relation to the effect of an adoption order on nationality and the right of abode to which we have already referred and should carry out the balancing act between welfare (being the first consideration) and public policy to which Hollings J referred *In Re H (A Minor)*.[8]

---

1   As to 'legal benefits', he excluded the benefit of British nationality under what would now be s 1(5) of the British Nationality Act 1971. However, this must be now read in the light of the judgment of Lord Hoffmann in *Re B (Adoption Order: Nationality)* [1999] 1 FLR 907, in which he held that legal benefits such as a right of abode should not necessarily be excluded from the balancing exercise.

2   In *Re K (A Minor) Adoption Order: Nationality)* [1995] Fam 38 at 43G, [1994] 2 FLR 557 at 561C–D, Hollings J's judgment was elevated into a two-stage approach: (i) to consider the motive of the application; and (ii) if satisfied that the true motive was not to achieve British nationality and the right of abode rather than welfare, to carry out a balancing exercise between public policy and welfare. Subsequently the two-stage test, which had become rigid practice, was rejected as unnecessarily complicating the judicial task: *Re H (Adoption: Non-Patrial)* [1996] 2 FLR 187 at 192H–193A, per Thorpe LJ.

3   [1986] Fam 54.

4   [1982] Fam 121, (1983) 4 FLR 85.

5   [1986] Fam 54 at 62–63.

6   This has now to be viewed against the background of the new paramountcy principle in s 1 of the ACA 2002 which extends 'throughout life' (which is discussed at **15.75**).

7   Balcombe LJ suggested a custodianship under Part II of the CA 1975. This could be updated to special guardianship under the ACA 2002. This is in line with s 1(6) of the ACA 2002.

8   This consideration has now to be viewed in the light of the House of Lords decision in *Re B (Adoption Order: Nationality)* [1999] 1 FLR 907.

The benefits flowing from the acquisition of British nationality

15.68   In *Re K (A Minor) (Adoption Order: Nationality)*,[1] Balcombe LJ had said:

> '... both on principle and on authority, in carrying out the balancing exercise ... the court should not take into account those benefits which flow from the acquisition of British nationality.'

The role of immigration policy in adoption was, however, re-cast by the House of Lords in *Re B (Adoption Order: Nationality)*.[2] In *Re B*, the prospective adopters who were British citizens applied for an adoption order with respect to their 16-year-old Jamaican granddaughter. She had originally been granted 6 months' leave to visit but this was not extended by the Home Office who were insisting that she return to Jamaica. Her father in Jamaica had died and her mother was living in impoverished circumstances. She had been doing well at her local school in the United Kingdom and her grandparents wanted her to finish her education in the United Kingdom.

15.69   Although there were only 2 years left of her minority, the judge at first instance made the order, which was discharged on appeal, only to be reinstated by the House of Lords. The Home Secretary had argued that 'the court should ignore the benefits which solely result from a change in immigration status when determining whether the child's welfare calls for adoption'. This was decisively rejected by the House of Lords as being contrary to the AA 1976. Lord Hoffmann said:[3]

> 'Section 6 requires the judge to have regard to "all the circumstances" and to treat the welfare of the child "throughout his childhood" as the first consideration. I do not see how, consistently with this language, the court could simply ignore the considerable benefits which would have accrued to [the grandchild] during the remainder of her childhood. *That the order would enable her to enjoy those benefits was a fact that the court had to take into account. No doubt the views of the Home Office on immigration policy were also a circumstance which the court was entitled to take into account, although it is not easy to see what weight they could be given.* Parliament has not provided ... that adoption of a non-British child should require the consent of the Home Secretary. On the contrary, it has provided that the making of an adoption order automatically takes the child out of the reach of the Home Secretary's powers of immigration control. The decision whether to make the order is entirely one for the judge ... *In cases in which it appears to the judge that adoption would confer real benefits upon the child during its childhood, it is very unlikely that general considerations of "maintaining an effective and consistent immigration policy" could justify the refusal of an order. The two kinds of consideration are hardly commensurable so as to be capable of being weighed in the balance against each other.*'

15.70   Lord Hoffmann, however, accepted two 'modest' propositions:[4]

---

1   [1995] Fam 38 at 45C; [1994] 2 FLR 557 at 562H.
2   [1999] 1 FLR 907.
3   Ibid, at 910A–D (emphasis added).
4   Ibid, at 910D.

(1)   The court will not make an 'accommodation'[1] adoption order; that is, when the adopters do not intend to exercise any parental responsibility, but merely wish to assist the child to acquire a right to abode.[2]

(2)   The court will rarely make an order when it confers no benefits upon the child during his or her childhood but gives a right of abode for the rest of his or her life.[3] In such a case there are no welfare benefits during the childhood to constitute the 'first consideration'.

15.71   *Re K (A Minor) (Adoption Order: Nationality)*[4] was cited as a striking case in the second category. In *Re K*, in setting aside an adoption order in favour of a British citizen in relation to her niece which was made 8 days before the child's eighteenth birthday, Hobhouse LJ said:[5]

> '[The judge] infringed the public policy of not allowing an application for an adoption order to be a substitute for the criteria and procedures under the Immigration Act 1971. Because of the age of K there were no substantial welfare considerations which could be invoked to justify the adoption order.'

15.72   Unlike in *Re K*, Lord Hoffmann in *Re B (Adoption Order: Nationality)* did not exclude from consideration any circumstances which would follow from the adoption, such as a right of abode or the possibility of succession, whether they were matters which would occur during childhood or afterwards. Where he drew the exclusionary line was in respect of those benefits which accrued only after the end of childhood. He said:[6] 'If a right of abode will be of benefit only when the child becomes an adult, that benefit will ordinarily have to give way to the public policy of not usurping the Home Secretary's discretion'.

15.73   *Re B (Adoption Order: Nationality)* was a ground-breaking decision which significantly broadened the approach to s 6 of the AA 1976. Benefits flowing from a change of immigration status were no longer to be discounted and, indeed, had to be given 'first consideration' when they had effect before a child reached the age of majority. The decision implicitly recognised that nationality can be an important element of a person's identity. Since the 'private life' provisions under Art 8 of the European Convention on Human Rights include 'the right to develop one's own personality',[7]

---

1   The term 'accommodation' adoption was coined by Cross J in *Re A (An Infant)* [1963] 1 WLR 231 at 236. Cross J refused to make an adoption order in respect of a French boy aged 20, having found that the applicants wished to adopt him so that he would acquire British nationality. He pointed out that the benefit to the boy would flow from the fact that he was being adopted, not from the fact that he was being adopted by particular adopters. The basic objection was that the applicants were not *in loco parentis* to the boy.

2   *Re B* (above) at 910D–E.

3   Ibid, at 910E–F.

4   [1995] Fam 38, [1994] 2 FLR 557.

5   Ibid, at 50 and 567G, respectively; see also *Re W (A Minor) (Adoption: Non-Patrial)* [1986] Fam 54 at 63C–D, per Balcombe LJ.

6   [1999] 1 FLR 907 at 911C.

7   *Niemitz v Germany* (1993) 16 EHRR 97.

denial of citizenship would arguably interfere with the child's right to respect for private life, even if there are no practical consequences for family life.[1]

Under the Adoption and Children Act 2002

15.74   Although under the ACA 2002 there may still be a balancing exercise between welfare (which now will be the paramount consideration) and public policy, it is very unlikely in practice that, where there are real welfare benefits to the child from adoption, public policy relating to immigration will carry anything other than minimal 'token' weight. This was largely foreshadowed by Lord Hoffmann in *Re B (Adoption Order: Nationality)*[2] (under the former law, when welfare was only the 'first consideration'), when he said: 'The two kinds of consideration are hardly commensurable so as to be capable of being weighed in the balance against each other'.

15.75   One of the questions which arises under the ACA 2002 is where (if at all), in the light of the paramountcy principle in s 1, should the exclusionary line be drawn with respect to Lord Hoffmann's second proposition. As has been seen, the language of s 1 of the ACA 2002 differs significantly from that of s 6 of the AA 1976. First, s 1 of the ACA 2002 does not require the judge to have regard to 'all the circumstances'. Secondly, it does require the child's welfare to be treated as the paramount consideration 'throughout his life'. It appears to follow from the wording of s 1 that, as the scope of s 1 extends 'throughout his life', even those benefits including the right of abode which accrue *only* after the end of childhood, cannot now be excluded and, moreover, will normally override the public policy issues relating to immigration/nationality. The new Act again seems to provide even less of a toehold in the balance for immigration policy than its predecessor.

15.76   Does Lord Hoffmann's first proposition relating to 'accommodation' adoptions survive the ACA 2002? Where the application is demonstrated to be a sham application or an application of convenience solely designed to achieve legal status, the answer is no longer an obvious 'no'. By applying *Re B* in the context of the new welfare provision, where there is no 'cut-off' point at 'the end of childhood', and with an eye to the private life provision of Art 8 of the European Convention on Human Rights, it is at least arguable that the 'welfare benefits' arising from nationality, even if the sole benefits, should prevail as the paramount consideration, notwithstanding the taint of 'sham' or 'convenience'. It is, however, suggested that this argument is flawed in that there is no real intention on the part of the adopters to exercise parental responsibility, which is such a fundamental element of adoption that it cannot be simply dismissed as illusory or otiose.

---

1   *Karassev v Finland* (Application No 31414/96) 12 January 1999, ECtHR. In *The Queen on the Application of Montana v Secretary of State for the Home Office* [2001] 1 FLR 449 at [18]–[19] the Court of Appeal accepted the Secretary of State's arguments that the refusal of British citizenship in itself could not be an interference with family life. Any interference with family life can only arise incidentally from withholding citizenship. The appellant's relationship and contact with his illegitimate son (in respect of whom he had applied for registration as a British citizen) would not be affected for the foreseeable future by their different nationalities. 'Common citizenship was not a necessary component of family life'. See also *The Queen on the Application of Mahmood v Secretary of State for the Home Department* [2001] 1 FLR 756.

2   [1999] 1 FLR 907.

15.77 However, it will remain important to distinguish between sham applications and real applications which are tainted by deception in their history but which nevertheless create a psychological relationship of parent and child. In the latter case, under the former law, the welfare consideration generally outweighed the immigration irregularities[1] and this is more than likely to be the case under the new law, given the pre-eminence of the welfare principle.

Immigration irregularities

15.78 In *Re H (Adoption: Non-Patrial)*[2] Thorpe LJ made a strong statement with respect to abuses of the immigration procedures:

> 'Although not referred to in the section [s 6 of the AA 1976], it is an important consideration that immigration regulations and policies should be upheld. A misuse of the right to apply for adoption as a device to circumvent immigration controls will always be fatal to an adoption application. Quite apart from immigration policy considerations, adults exposed in that way are likely to have forfeited the confidence in their maturity and responsibility which the judge must hold before committing to them a child on such an irrevocable basis. Nor can I conceive that in a case of blatant abuse the application might be rescued by the argument that the subsequent delay has resulted in the development of circumstances justifying a submission that the refusal of the application would be contrary to the welfare consideration. In such circumstances even if the applicants have redeemed themselves to some extent as potential parents, the public policy consideration is likely to outweigh the welfare consideration.'

15.79 The ease, however, with which determined illicit adopters have abused the immigration system is demonstrated by a number of the reported authorities. By way of example, in *Re An Adoption Application*[3] the El Salvador court made an adoption order with respect to a baby girl and a notarial document was obtained, signifying the mother's consent to the adoption. On receipt of these documents, the husband applicant flew to El Salvador and returned to England the following day. The natural mother had brought the child to the airport and there handed her over to the husband, together with the child's passport. The wife was waiting at Heathrow and met the child for the first time on the English side of immigration. No entry clearance certificate had previously been obtained from the immigration authorities in respect of the child, but, on arrival at Heathrow, the child was given leave to enter and to stay for a certain period. The period was thereafter extended from time to time, so that the child was allowed by the immigration authorities to stay in England pending the result of the proceedings. The absence of an entry clearance certificate in advance of arrival meant that there had been no opportunity for the ECO at the British Embassy in El Salvador to make any necessary enquiries or report.[4]

15.80 Another striking example is provided by the facts in *Re R (No 1) (Inter-country Adoption)*.[5] The applicants, who at all times intended to adopt a 5-year-old Romanian child, duped the natural parents into obtaining a passport for the child, claiming that all

---

1   *Re J (Adoption: Non-Patrial)* [1998] 1 FLR 225.
2   [1996] 2 FLR 187 at 193B–C.
3   [1992] 1 FLR 341.
4   See also *Re C (Adoption: Legality)* [1999] 1 FLR 370 at 373C–D and 376D–F which is discussed in detail below.
5   [1999] 1 FLR 1014.

that was intended was a visit for 3 months for medical treatment. The applicants attended the British Embassy in Bucharest in order to obtain entry clearance. The wife was interviewed by the ECO and stated that she was going to the United Kingdom for a few weeks' holiday and that the child was coming with her. She made no reference to medical treatment. When she was asked in terms whether she had any other intentions such as adoption, she gave the answer 'no'. Having obtained entry clearance, the wife travelled by aeroplane with the child to the United Kingdom and informed the immigration officer that she lived in Romania and was only staying in the United Kingdom for a holiday for one month. In consequence, a standard 6-month entry visa was granted. Shortly thereafter, the child was registered in a local school and the applicants began the adoption process, obtaining extensions from the immigration authorities as necessary. In deceiving the immigration authorities, the applicants had committed an offence under s 26 of the Immigration Act 1971. In this case the applicants withdrew their application for adoption, but the child continued to be a ward and, notwithstanding the immigration irregularities, the illegality and the deception, the applicants retained care and control of the child as the welfare considerations prevailed.

15.81   Bracewell J, in determining the complex issue of the child's future, said:[1]

> 'That issue [of the child's future] cannot be resolved merely by looking at the illegality of the [applicants'] conduct and resolving that no one should benefit from their own misconduct thereby rewarding the deception perpetrated on the birth parents. Issues of public policy and deception of natural parents are highly relevant to determining adoption applications, and early in this hearing the [applicants] began to realise there was no prospect of any court making an adoption order which dispensed with the consent of the birth parents.
>
> These deficits and deceits do have a relevance to welfare placement as well, in that consideration must be given to whether it is in the interests of a child to have a personal history based on deception, illegality and injustice to her own family. It is part of the balancing equation. However much this court regrets what has happened and wishes the clock could be turned back several years, the reality is that it cannot be and therefore I have to determine the question of placement in accordance with the welfare of [the child] ...
>
> The crucial overwhelming consideration which tilts the balance is that now it is simply too late to remove her and to do so would constitute a second wrong ...'

15.82   Clearly, the detailed judgment of Bracewell J in *Re R (Inter-country Adoptions: Practice)*[2] addresses many of the abuses of the immigration system, but cannot eradicate them all. For example, the recommendation that the child should be afforded entry clearance for only the minimum period remains vulnerable to future applications for extensions on bogus but plausible claims about the child's health requiring special medical care in this country. Immigration officers may also find it difficult to refuse entry if the child is brought into this country with an official document recording an overseas adoption which may eventually not be recognised by UK courts.[3]

15.83   Once the prospective adoptee has entered the United Kingdom and been settled in the jurisdiction for a period of time with the adopters, notwithstanding the strong

---

1   [1999] 1 FLR 1014 at 1036G–1037B, and 1040G.
2   [1999] 1 FLR 1042, which is set out in detail at **14.95** et seq.
3   See J Murphy 'Rhetoric and Reality in Inter-country Adoptions: Divergent Principles and Stratified Status' in J Murphy (ed) *Ethnic Minorities: Their Families and the Law* (Hart Publishing, 2000) p 120.

statement of Thorpe LJ referred to above, then in practice under the former law,[1] irrespective of any immigration irregularities, adoption has been almost a *fait accompli*, the child's welfare generally predominating. As this was the case under the AA 1976, where welfare was the *first* consideration, it is even more likely to be the case under the ACA 2002 where welfare is the *paramount* consideration.

---

1   *Re An Adoption Application* [1992] 1 FLR 341; *Re C (Adoption: Legality)* [1999] 1 FLR 370.

Chapter 16

ILLEGAL TRANSFERS, PLACEMENTS AND TRANSACTIONS

UNDER THE FORMER LAW

16.1 It was particularly in the context of intercountry adoptions that the prohibitions on illegal transactions under the former legislation were exposed as having no real bite. The courts' approach was to overlook the taint of illegality resulting from breaches of s 11[1] and s 57[2] of the AA 1976, where an adoption order would promote the welfare of the child, and to hold that breaches in these circumstances did not constitute an absolute bar to obtaining an adoption order.

16.2 In the case of s 57 of the AA 1976, this was in the face of what appeared to be the clear statutory bar in s 24(2) of the AA 1976, which provided that: 'The court shall not make an adoption order in relation to a child unless it is satisfied that the applicants have not, as respects the child, contravened s 57'. However, s 57(3) of the AA 1976 was interpreted as giving the court retrospective power to authorise any payment or reward[3] and, with welfare the first consideration under s 6 of the AA 1976, the balance in most cases came down heavily in favour of adoption so as to justify the court retrospectively authorising the payment. In this way, the court was able to circumvent the bar in s 24(2).

16.3 This approach was exemplified in *Re Adoption Application (Non-Patrial: Breach of Procedures)*.[4] Douglas Brown J, after rejecting the existence of a retrospective power vested in the court either to dispense with or authorise a breach of s 11, went on to say:[5]

'it would be a most undesirable thing if there was no possibility of intervention by the court, if there was a proved breach of s 11 . . .

The approach of the court to decisions in adoption cases is governed by s 6 . . . Whereas the first consideration must be given to the welfare question, the circumstances include considerations of public policy. The question for the court, bearing in mind s 6, is: does public policy require that the applicants should be refused the order they seek because of their criminal conduct? The court, still bearing in mind the guidance contained in s 6, must conduct a balancing exercise

. . . that decision must be a decision relating to the adoption of the child. Similarly, because of the prohibition on the making of an adoption order in s 24(2), a decision under s 57(3)

---

1   Restriction on arranging adoptions and placing children.
2   Prohibition on certain payments in connection with adoption.
3   *In re Adoption Application (Payment for Adoption)* [1987] Fam 81 at 87, per Latey J.
4   [1993] Fam 125, [1993] 1 FLR 947.
5   [1993] Fam 125 at 133H–135D; [1993] 1 FLR 947 at 955G–957B.

whether to authorise a breach of s 57 must also be a decision relating to the adoption of a child
...

Applying those principles to the facts of this case, I was in no doubt that an adoption order should be made. The welfare considerations were very powerful with no indication pointing away from such an order.'

16.4   This approach was endorsed by the Court of Appeal in *Re G (Adoption: Illegal Placement)*[1] and finds its most striking illustration in the first instance decision of Johnson J in *Re C (Adoption: Legality)*.[2]

The two-tier system

16.5   In *Re C (Adoption: Legality)* the applicant was aged 39, recently separated and 'desperate and determined to become the mother of a child'. She had approached various social services seeking to adopt a child, without success. There were several reasons for her being rejected, including the recent breakdown of her marriage, her weight (19 stones) and the view that she needed more time to recover from the breakdown of her marriage and her ill-health. She approached Parents for Children, an adoption agency dealing with the placement of children with special needs, but was ultimately rejected as an adopter of a child with special needs.

16.6   She sought help from the Guatemalan Support Group (a group of UK families who have themselves adopted a child from Guatemala and provide support for each other and advice for others). The group put her in touch with a contact in Guatemala who was actively involved in finding overseas adoptive families. She appointed a Guatemalan lawyer to act in the Guatemalan adoption process. She obtained a home study report for which she paid £300, which was described as 'striking in its superficiality' and an adoption order was made in her absence. The birth mother gave her consent and the adoption order provided that the child was to continue to bear his first names.

16.7   The applicant had neither seen the child nor been to Guatemala and no one in Guatemala had seen the applicant. The handover took place at the Amsterdam airport where the mother first met the child. She brought him to England through Heathrow in the early hours of the morning and merely explained to the immigration officer her intention to apply for adoption. Within 2 days of the child's arrival in England the applicant notified the relevant social services department of her intention to adopt and issued her application. Contrary to the Guatemalan adoption order, the applicant proposed that the child be known by two European names.

16.8   At the adoption hearing, both the local authority and the guardian supported the making of an adoption order on the basis that the alternatives would be more damaging. The court held that:

(1)   the applicant had blatantly sought to achieve her objective in disregard of the legal processes in place under the AA 1976;
(2)   in arranging to have the home study report prepared, instructing lawyers and giving information for the purposes of the Guatemalan adoption, the applicant was making arrangements to facilitate the adoption in breach of s 11 of the AA 1976 and

---

1   [1995] 1 FLR 403.
2   [1999] 1 FLR 370.

was guilty of a criminal offence. The author who prepared the home study report and received a fee had also committed a criminal offence under s 11;

(3) in paying the Guatemalan lawyers a fee, the applicant was also in breach of s 57 of the AA 1976.

16.9 Notwithstanding the applicant's breaches of due process and criminality and the serious concerns about her ability to meet the entirety of the child's needs, Johnson J accepted that her acts did not represent an absolute bar to the making of an adoption order and concluded that, in terms of welfare, all these concerns were outweighed by the considerable disadvantage that might accrue to the child if the adoption order were not made.

16.10 The facts of this case graphically highlight the dilemma facing the courts where there has been a deliberate and criminal disregard of adoption procedures and yet the welfare of the child dictates that the adoption order be made. After referring to the appalling conditions in which some children are brought up in some foreign countries, Johnson J stated that: 'there is an immediate humanitarian instinct to disregard the niceties of the statutory procedures'. In the overwhelming majority of reported cases, the welfare considerations have indeed prevailed over the breaches of procedure.[1]

16.11 The problem with this approach, which Johnson J recognised,[2] was that it led inexorably to the creation of a two-tier adoption service with a lower standard applying to a foreign adoption.[3] It also came perilously close to falling into the trap of 'social engineering' (which the principle of subsidiarity in the UN Convention is intended to avoid) by placing greater emphasis upon the advantages of being in the United Kingdom than upon the deficiencies of the proposed adopters.

16.12 Although Johnson J speculated upon the potential deterrent effect of the criminal sanctions in ss 11 and 57 of the AA 1976,[4] the reality is that the deterrent effect has been minimal.[5] As John Murphy has pointed out:

'Taken together, the frequency of judicial condonation, the absence of a bar to subsequent adoption, the concern not to do direct harm to the child by prosecuting, the short limitation

---

1   *Re C (Adoption: Legality)* [1999] 1 FLR 370 at 377B–C. Note also 382D–E: 'Except for the very unusual case where there is a claim for the return of the child to the natural family, in all the reported cases the welfare considerations seem to have led the court to authorise or waive whatever breaches have occurred in the particular case'. Subsequent to *Re C*, the court has declined to make an adoption order in one reported case only: *Re R (No 1) (Intercountry Adoption)* [1999] 1 FLR 1014, but even here the child, who was made a ward of court, ended up in the care and control of the applicants who had sought the adoption order. See also *Re Adoption Application (Non-Patrial: Breach of Procedures)* [1993] 2 WLR 110.

2   *Re C (Adoption: Legality)* (above) at 382A–C.

3   In consequence, it flew in the face of the DoH's *A Guide to Intercountry Adoption Practice and Procedure* (1997) which stated that '... there can be no question of operating a two tier adoption service, applying a lower standard to overseas adoption. A person who cannot be recommended as suitable to adopt a child living in the United Kingdom cannot be recommended to adopt a child living overseas'.

4   *Re C (Adoption: Legality)* (above) at 382E–G.

5   For a guide as to some of the reported cases, see K O'Donnell 'Illegal Placements in Adoption' [1994] *Journal of Child Law* 115.

period (6 months) and the summary nature of the offences, do little to deter childless couples from illicit inter-country adoptions.'[1]

16.13   The question immediately set by the ACA 2002 is whether its new provisions and amendments on illegal transfer and placement will, in reality, redress the current balance in favour of adoption notwithstanding the taint of illegality. Will the new Act provide a deterrent for those childless couples who have failed to satisfy the strict requirements for adoption in this jurisdiction and nevertheless remain desperate to adopt a child, whatever the risks?

UNDER THE ADOPTION AND CHILDREN ACT 2002

16.14   'The need for improved safeguards was highlighted by the high profile Internet twins case in 2001'.[2] In the Internet twins case Mr and Mrs K, UK citizens living in North Wales, had two boys born of their marriage but wanted more children. Having unsuccessfully followed medical advice and having explored surrogacy, they decided on an overseas adoption. They commissioned in England, and paid for, a home study report. They contacted adoption organisations in the USA whose details they found on the Internet. In February or March 2000 they contacted a private adoption agency in California called 'A Caring Heart'.

16.15   The US parents of the twins, who were resident in Missouri, had agreed before their birth that they should be given up for adoption, using the same private adoption agency trading under the name of 'An Angel's Touch'. The twins, Belinda and Kimberley, were born prematurely in June 2000. In July 2000 Mr and Mrs K signed an 'Adoption Co-ordination Contract' and paid a fee of $12,500 in respect of a child in North Carolina, but that proposal fell through. In October 2000 the twins were placed by the US agency with prospective adopters in California. The mother, apparently influenced by a cheque which had bounced, removed the twins from the Californian couple, ostensibly for a farewell visit.

16.16   Meanwhile, Mr and Mrs K had been told that the twins were available for adoption in California. On 1 December 2000, Mr and Mrs K flew to San Diego and paid a further $1200, allegedly to cover the mother's expenses, and spent 2 December 2000 with the twins. On 3 December 2000, the family of the Californian couple caused a commotion outside the hotel where Mr and Mrs K were staying, which involved the police. Mr and Mrs K, the mother and the twins drove 2000 miles, arriving in Little Rock, Arkansas, on 7 December 2000. The mother had not in fact lived in Arkansas at any material time.

16.17   The next day Mr and Mrs K met an attorney specialising in Arkansas law and over the next few days the mother made a statement giving unconditional consent to the adoption of the twins, and the father signed an identical consent in Missouri. On 19 December 2000, a petition for adoption was filed at the Probate Court of Pulaski County, Arkansas, which contained no reference to the residence of the mother or the

---

1   J Murphy 'Rhetoric and Reality in Intercountry Adoptions: Divergent Principles and Stratified Status' in J Murphy (ed) *Ethnic Minorities: Their Families and the Law* (Hart Publishing, 2000), at p 121.

2   HC Special Standing Committee, Second Sitting, 20 November 2001, col 6, para 19, referring to *Flintshire County Council v K* [2001] 2 FLR 476.

twins. On 22 December 2000, an interlocutory decree of adoption was made, which recited that the mother was 'a resident of Pulaski County' and was so at the time she executed her consent. Mr and Mrs K then travelled to Chicago to obtain passports for the twins, which were issued on 26 December 2000. They flew back to the United Kingdom with the twins, arriving on 29 December 2000. Although no prior Home Office immigration clearance had been obtained, they were allowed entry into the United Kingdom. By mid-January 2001, Mr and Mrs K had given a story to the newspapers and the twins had become the subject of extensive and intense media interest. The local authority made inquiries about the well-being of the twins and their concerns led to emergency protection orders and the removal of the twins into foster care. In March 2001 the Arkansas court reviewed the adoption order and held it to be defective, because the jurisdictional requirements as to the mother's residence had not been met. In April 2001, Kirkwood J made a care order, approving plans for the twins to return Missouri where, under a court order made in Missouri, protective custody and control of the twins were given to the Division of Family Services pending a resolution of matters before that court.

16.18 This 'alarming story'[1] of the Internet twins and the universal public outcry which broke out in response caused the Government to set as one of the key objectives of the ACA 2002 the stamping out of international trafficking in children. With the facts of the Internet twins case clearly in the forefront of Government thinking, the Act has been shaped to achieve this by:

(1) re-introducing the prohibition on bringing overseas children into the United Kingdom[2] (first brought into effect under the A(IA)A 1999)[3] and extending it to include bringing into the United Kingdom a child adopted under an external adoption effected within the previous 6 months;[4]

(2) making the offences under s 83 (restrictions on bringing a child into the United Kingdom) and s 85 (restrictions on taking a child out of the United Kingdom) indictable (as well as summary) with a maximum penalty on conviction on indictment of 12 months' imprisonment, an unlimited fine or both;[5]

(3) extending and reinforcing the former prohibitions on illegal placements under the AA 1976,[6] and on advertising,[7] including tougher penalties for those seeking to circumvent these safeguards, and by introducing criminal sanctions in relation to the preparation and submission of reports which fall outside certain prescribed personnel and circumstances.[8]

---

1   *Flintshire County Council v K* [2001] 2 FLR 476 at 482C, per Kirkwood J; and see also the judgment of Munby J in *Re M (Adoption: International Adoption Trade)* [2003] EWHC 219 (Fam).

2   ACA 2002, s 83(1)(a).

3   Section 14 of the A(IA)A 1999, which inserted a new s 56A into the AA 1976 making it an offence for anyone habitually resident in the British Islands to bring a child into the United Kingdom for the purpose of adoption (other than adoption by a parent, guardian or relative) unless they meet the requirements in the Adoption of Children from Overseas Regulations 2001, SI 2001/1251. Section 56A was further amended: see **16.26–16.27**.

4   ACA 2002, s 83(1)(b). Under ACA 2002, Sch 4, para 4, the expanded restriction is to be substituted for s 56A of the AA 1976 prior to implementation of the ACA 2002.

5   ACA 2002, ss 83(8) and 85(6).

6   Ibid, ss 92–97, ss 123–124.

7   Ibid, ss 123–124. Under ACA 2002, Sch 4, para 14, a new s 58(1A) of the AA 1976 is to be inserted which reflects ss 123–124 of the ACA 2002 before the Act is implemented.

8   Ibid, s 94.

Prohibitions on the transfer of children

Bringing overseas children into the United Kingdom

16.19   Section 83 of the ACA 2002[1] applies where a British resident (ie a person habitually resident in the British Islands):

(a)   brings[2] into the United Kingdom a child who is habitually resident outside the United Kingdom for the purpose of adoption[3] by the British resident;[4] or

(b)   at any time brings[5] into the United Kingdom a child adopted by the British resident under an external adoption effected within the preceding 6 months.[6]

16.20   An 'external adoption' means an adoption of a child effected under the law of any country or territory outside the British islands, whether or not the adoption is (i) an adoption within the meaning of Chapter 4 or (ii) a full adoption under s 88(3) (ie an adoption by virtue of which the child is to be treated in law as not being the child of any person other than the adopters or adopter).[7] It excludes a Convention adoption.[8]

16.21   The Adoption of Children from Overseas Regulations 2001 already make it a requirement that prospective adopters apply to a local authority or voluntary adoption agency to be assessed and approved under similar procedures to those followed in domestic adoptions and have a certificate of eligibility issued by the Secretary of State. In addition, the prescribed requirements will include taking the following steps:

–   the prospective adopters are to provide as much information as requested by the agency, while going through the assessment process;[9]
–   they must consent to police and medical checks;
–   the case is referred to the adoption panel;
–   a home study assessment and such other information as is required by the overseas authority is sent to the Central Authority, so that it can check that the proper procedures have been followed and all the relevant information collected before a certificate of eligibility is issued on behalf of the Secretary of State and sent on to the relevant overseas authority;
–   notice of intention to adopt must be given to the local authority in whose area the prospective adopters reside within 14 days of arrival in the United Kingdom with a child they intend to adopt.

16.22   The effect of these provisions is that the prospective adopters must first be assessed and approved as suitable to adopt in the United Kingdom before adopting

---

1   ACA 2002, s 133 makes similar provision for Scotland.
2   'or causes to bring'.
3   References to 'adoption' and to a child 'adopted' include a reference to adoption or to a child adopted by the British resident and another person: s 83(1).
4   ACA 2002, s 83(1)(a).
5   'or causes to bring'.
6   ACA 2002, s 83(1)(b).
7   Ibid, s 83(3)(a) and (b).
8   Ibid, s 83(3).
9   Ibid, s 83(4) provides for regulations requiring a person intending to bring a child into the UK in circumstances where s 83 applies (i) to apply to an adoption agency for an assessment of his or her suitability to adopt the child, and (ii) to give the agency any information it may require for the purpose of the assessment.

overseas. If they fail to undergo assessment and obtain approval, then they will be guilty of an offence.[1] A person is liable[2] (a) on summary conviction, to imprisonment for a term not exceeding 6 months or a fine not exceeding the statutory maximum, or both, or (b) on conviction on indictment, to imprisonment for a term not exceeding 12 months or an unlimited fine, or both. There is no time limit in respect of this offence.

16.23 Section 83 also makes provision for Chapter 3 of the ACA 2002 to apply (with modifications) or not to apply.[3] It is intended to modify the provisions to provide that, where the proper procedures have been followed, children brought to the United Kingdom for adoption spend at least 6 months living with their prospective adopters prior to an application being made for an adoption order; and at least 12 months, where the procedures have not been followed.[4] Where s 83 does not apply, the standard residence periods set out in s 42 will apply. The intention is that s 83 will apply to all but a very limited group of people. The exceptions are likely to be, for example, parents in prescribed circumstances. Regulation-making powers[5] have been taken to enable provisions to be prescribed setting out the circumstances in which the restrictions on bringing in a child are not to apply (or where necessary, to apply with modification) to parents, relatives and step-parents. These powers will be used to specify the time that a child must live with a parent, relative, guardian or step-parent in intercountry adoption cases. The intention is to ensure that children who are to be adopted from overseas by parents, relatives, guardians and step-parents are properly safeguarded. This is in recognition that such children are potentially vulnerable, that they need to be protected and that their relatives may well need the same assessment of their suitability and/or help to prepare for adoption as would be the case in relation to a stranger planning to adopt a child from overseas.[6]

16.24 A further objective is to ensure that children adopted from overseas are able to obtain access to information that the agency holds about them, although the exact nature of such information will vary depending upon the procedures in the child's State of origin.[7] Where a notice of intent to adopt has been given, regulations will impose certain functions upon the local authority in respect of the child brought into the country for the purposes of adoption.[8] These are likely to require a local authority: (i) to visit the child; (ii) to inspect premises; (iii) to require specified information in respect of the child and prospective adopters; and (iv) to monitor the child.[9]

16.25 Section 83, however, has no application where the child is intended to be adopted under a Convention adoption order.[10]

---

1   ACA 2002, s 83(7).
2   Ibid, s 83(8)(a) and (b).
3   Ibid, s 83(6)(a).
4   HL Deb, 30 October 2002, col 214, per Lord McIntosh of Haringey. See also s 13 of the AA 1976, as amended by para 10 of Sch 4 to the ACA 2002.
5   ACA 2002, s 86. Note also s 56 of the AA 1976 and para 11 of Sch 4 to the ACA 2002.
6   HL Deb, 30 October 2002, cols 214–216, per Lord McIntosh of Haringey.
7   HC Deb, 20 May 2002, vol 386, no 150, col 23.
8   ACA 2002, s 83(6).
9   HC Deb, 20 May 2002, vol 386, no 150, col 24, per Ms Jacqui Smith.
10 ACA 2002, s 83(2).

16.26 This section replaces and strengthens s 56A of the AA 1976 (which was inserted by s 14 of the Intercountry Act 1999 and came into effect as from 30 April 2001).[1] Section 56A was a new provision and was rushed into effect when the wave of worldwide media interest engendered by the Internet twins case first hit the public conscience. Simultaneously, the Adoption of Children from Overseas Regulations 2001 ('the Overseas Regs 2001')[2] came into effect, the aim of which was to deter people from bringing children into the United Kingdom for the purpose of adoption unless the proposed adopters have been first assessed and approved by a local authority or a VAA and had their suitability endorsed. It has been further amended by the transitional provisions contained in para 12 of Sch 4 to the ACA 2002.

16.27 The Government clearly benefited from the opportunity to reflect further upon the Internet twins case and has made the earlier s 56A measures much tougher so as to send out a clear message of intent that the tide of illicit intercountry adoptions is to be stemmed before it reaches the coast of the United Kingdom and to be diverted into approved channels. It has also made provision for a strengthened s 56A to be inserted in the AA 1976 in advance of the implementation of the ACA 2002.[3]

Taking children out of the United Kingdom

16.28 Under s 85, restrictions which carry criminal sanctions are imposed upon removing from the United Kingdom children who are Commonwealth citizens or who are habitually resident in the United Kingdom for the purpose of adoption unless the proposed adopters have parental responsibility under s 84.[4] Regulation-making powers have been taken in s 86 to enable provisions to be prescribed setting out the circumstances in which restrictions on removing a child are not to apply (or are to apply with modifications) to parents, relatives and step-parents.

16.29 'Removing a child' includes[5] arranging to do so where the person:

- enters into an arrangement for the purpose of facilitating removal;
- initiates or takes part in negotiations for the purpose of concluding such an arrangement; or
- causes another person to take such a step.

16.30 Under s 84 of the ACA 2002, the High Court may make an order giving parental responsibility for a child to prospective adopters who are not domiciled or habitually resident in England and Wales but who, it is satisfied, intend to adopt the child outside the British Islands.[6] The requirements which are to be satisfied in such a case will be prescribed by regulations.[7] The rules must provide for a CAFCASS officer to be

---

1   Note the amendments to s 56A of the AA 1976 effected by the transitional provisions in para 12 of Sch 4 to the ACA 2002.
2   The Overseas Regs 2001 cover some of the essential features which are likely to be reflected in the regulations supporting s 81 of the ACA 2001.
3   ACA 2002, Sch 4, para 12.
4   Ibid, s 85(1) and (2). It also includes 'removing a child under the authority of an order under s 49 of the Adoption (Scotland) Act 1978 or Art 57 of the Adoption (Northern Ireland) Order 1987': s 85(2)(a) and (b); see **16.30** et seq.
5   ACA 2002, s 84(3)(a)–(c). 'Arrangement' includes an agreement (whether enforceable or not).
6   Ibid, s 84(1).
7   Ibid, s 84(3), (6) and (7).

appointed and to act on behalf of the child, with the duty of safeguarding the child's interests, in an application for the transfer of parental responsibility prior to an adoption abroad.[1] An application for an order may not be made unless the child's home has been with the applicants at all times during the preceding 10 weeks.[2] Nor can an order be made where the prospective adopters meet the requirements of domicile or habitual residence to allow an adoption order to be made in the England and Wales.[3] Section 46(2)–(4) has the same effect in relation to this order as in relation to adoption orders.

16.31   To remove a child from the United Kingdom is an offence punishable[4] (a) on summary conviction, by imprisonment not exceeding 6 months or a fine not exceeding the statutory maximum, or both, or (b) on conviction on indictment, with imprisonment for a term not exceeding 12 months or an unlimited fine, or both. No time limit has been imposed for this offence. However, a person is not guilty of an offence of causing a person to enter into an arrangement or to initiate or take part in negotiations for removal of a child unless he knew or had reason to suspect that the step taken would contravene s 85(1).[5] This only applies if sufficient evidence is adduced to raise an issue as to whether the person had the knowledge or reason mentioned.[6] This has been included to ensure that the section complies with Art 6 of the European Convention on Human Rights, which states:

> 'Everyone charged with a criminal offence shall be presumed innocent until proved guilty according to law.'

16.32   It changes the legal burden in the defence provision to an evidential burden. If there is sufficient evidence that a defence provision may apply to the case before the court, it will be for the prosecution to prove (to the criminal standard of proof) that it does not.[7]

Illegal placements

16.33   The ACA 2002 reaffirms and strengthens the safeguards existing under the AA 1976, which permitted only adoption agencies to make arrangements for adoption and to advertise about adoption. In the light of the Internet twins case, the ACA 2002 has expanded the restrictions on advertising to include both traditional media and electronic means, including the Internet.[8] It has also imposed for the first time express restrictions on the preparation and submission of reports.[9]

16.34   The restrictions imposed by ss 92–97 and ss 123–124 of the ACA 2002 apply to both domestic and intercountry adoptions. They are discussed here, as most of the

---

1   ACA 2002, s 102(1)(a), (3) and (6)(d).

2   Ibid, s 83(4).

3   Ibid, s 83(2).

4   Ibid, s 84(4) and (6).

5   Ibid, s 84(5).

6   Ibid, s 84(5).

7   HC Deb, 20 May 2002, vol 386, no 150, col 235, per Ms Jacqui Smith. The words 'did not know and had no reason to suspect' were substituted for 'did not know or have reasonable cause to believe' as a higher test, so as to provide a counterbalance to the change in the evidential burden. See *R v Lambert* [2001] UKHL 37, [2001] 3 WLR 206.

8   ACA 2002, s 123(4)(a).

9   Ibid, s 94.

jurisprudence generated by their predecessor sections under the AA 1976 was in the field of intercountry adoptions.

Prohibition upon making arrangements

16.35 Section 92 of the ACA 2002 sets out the restrictions in relation to arranging an adoption imposed on persons who are neither an adoption agency nor acting in pursuance of an order of the High Court. It marks a substantial overhaul of its forerunner, s 11 of the AA 1976.

16.36 The nine steps which must not be taken are:[1]

(1) asking a person other than an adoption agency[2] to provide a child for adoption;
(2) asking a person other than an adoption agency to provide prospective adopters for a child;
(3) offering to find a child for adoption;
(4) offering a child for adoption to a person other than an adoption agency;
(5) handing over a child for adoption to any person other than an agency;
(6) receiving a child handed over to him in contravention of (5);
(7) entering into an agreement[3] with any person for the adoption of a child or for the purpose of facilitating the adoption of a child, where no adoption agency is acting on behalf of the child in the adoption;
(8) initiating or taking part in negotiations of which the purpose is the conclusion of an agreement with (7);
(9) causing any other person to take any of the steps mentioned in (1) to (8).

Where the prospective adopters are parents, relatives, guardians or one of them is a partner of a parent of the child, steps (4), (5), (7), (8) and (9) do not apply.[4]

16.37 These nine steps considerably expand s 92's predecessor, s 72(3) of the AA 1976, and are designed to cover: (i) making contact with birth parents on behalf of prospective adopters; (ii) obtaining the birth parents' consent to adoption; and (iii) taking forward agreed matches between children and adoptive families by placing a child for adoption. For example, where one person says to another that he or she can locate a child for that person to adopt, he or she will be caught by s 92(2)(c). When a person, a parent of a child or an intermediary, who has already identified a child to be adopted, offers that child to another for adoption, the person who makes the offer would be caught by s 92(2)(d). If that person were to hand over a child for adoption to the person who would adopt that child or to someone else who would pass the child to the adopter, he or she would be caught by s 92(2)(e). If he or she entered into an agreement for the purpose of facilitating the adoption of a child, he or she would be caught by s 92(2)(g). If he or she initiated or took part in negotiations intended to lead to an agreement within subs (g) for

---

1   ACA 2002, s 92(2).
2   References to 'an adoption agency' in s 92(2) include 'a prescribed person outside the United Kingdom exercising functions corresponding to those of an adoption agency': s 92(5). 'Prescribed' means 'prescribed by regulations made by the Secretary of State after consultation with the Assembly': s 92(7)(b).
3   'Agreement' includes an arrangement (whether enforceable or not): s 92(7)(a).
4   ACA 2002, s 92(3) and (4). Regulations will set out who should be treated as an adoption agency in respect of intercountry adoption for the purpose of this provision: s 92(5).

the adoption of a child or an agreement to facilitate the adoption of a child, he or she would be caught by subs (h). In relation to causing another person to take any of those steps, he or she would be caught by subs (i).

16.38 A contravention of s 92 is a summary offence punishable with imprisonment for a term not exceeding 6 months or a fine not exceeding £10,000 or both.[1] Under s 138 of the ACA 2002, the prosecution may be brought within 6 months from the date on which the prosecutor has sufficient evidence to do so and must not be brought more than 6 years after the commission of the offence. It thus extends the usual time limit for a prosecution.[2] This new time limit of 6 years also applies to offences under ss 94 and 95.[3] Although the expectation is that these offences will be discovered within the 6-month time limit, the 6-year time limit is aimed at catching those offences which may go unnoticed by the adoption agency or other authorities where, for example, the agency is not involved in making the arrangements for the adoption. It is therefore intended that there will be enough scope to bring prosecutions against those who arrange or facilitate private adoption.[4]

16.39 The clear intention is that these much tougher penalties will provide a deterrent to illicit adopters. Where the culprit is an adoption society, the offence also catches within its net the person who manages the society.[5]

16.40 There are certain defences available. Where a person is charged with receiving a child handed over to him or her under s 92(2)(f), that person is not guilty unless it is proved that he or she knew or had reason to suspect that the child was handed over to him or her rather than to an adoption agency.[6] A similar defence is available to someone in contravention of s 92 by causing a person to take any of the steps set out above.[7] In each case the defence only applies if he or she adduces sufficient evidence to raise the issue as to whether he or she had the specified knowledge or reason.[8]

16.41 Under the AA 1976, it was established[9] that there was no power in the court to authorise retrospectively a placement in breach of s 11 and this is likely to remain the position under the new legislation. Under the former law, however, the courts adopted an approach to 'illegal placements' by which a breach of s 11 was not necessarily fatal to an adoption order being made.[10] Notwithstanding the greater scope and tougher penalties of ss 92 and 93 of the ACA 2002, as welfare is now the paramount consideration, one cannot rule out the court taking a similar approach under the new law where the child has become settled in an illegal placement, but the disruption of that placement would be contrary to the child's welfare under the s 1 principles.

---

1   ACA 2002, s 93(1) and (4).

2   The usual time limit for a prosecution is 6 months after the offence is committed: s 127(1) of the Magistrates' Courts Act 1980. This extended time limit applies in respect of the proceedings for offences by virtue of ss 9, 59, 93, 94, 95 and 129 of the ACA 2002: s 138.

3   See **16.43–16.50**.

4   HC Deb, 20 May 2002, vol 386, no 150, col 37, per Ms Jacqui Smith.

5   ACA 2002, s 93(1).

6   Ibid, s 93(2).

7   Ibid, s 93(3).

8   Ibid, s 93(4).

9   *Re G (Adoption: Illegal Placement)* [1995] 1 FLR 403 at 407, per Balcombe LJ.

10   Ibid; *Re C (Adoption: Legality)* [1999] 1 FLR 370.

16.42 In *Re G (Adoption: Illegal Placement)*[1] the Court of Appeal held that where there had been an illegal placement, the adoption application is 'appropriate for determination in the High Court' and should be commenced or transferred to that court. There is unlikely to be any change to this practice under the new legislation.

Prohibitions on reports

16.43 In the Internet twins case[2] Mr and Mrs K did not seek a Social Services Department home study report, which would have accorded with UK requirements[3] and US requirements, but commissioned and paid for a report privately. Kirkwood J in a strong judgment highlighted the hazard of such a practice to children.[4]

16.44 Section 94 is a new provision which imposes restrictions on the preparation of certain reports in connection with adoption. It is intended to ensure that only professionally qualified staff carry out the necessary assessments and the preparation of reports and, thus, aims at eradicating the hazard which arose from privately commissioned home study reports.

16.45 Under s 94(1) of the ACA 2002, a person who does not fall within a prescribed description and certain prescribed circumstances may not prepare a report about the suitability of a child for adoption or of a person to adopt or about the adoption or placement for adoption of a child. To do so constitutes a summary offence punishable with imprisonment for a term not exceeding 6 months or a fine not exceeding level 5 (£5000) or both.[5] Additional offenders include someone who causes a person to prepare a report or submits to anyone a report prepared in contravention of s 94(1)[6] and, if the person concerned works for an adoption society, the manager of the society.[7] A person is not guilty of an offence of causing someone to prepare a report in contravention of s 94(1) unless it is proved that he or she knew or had reasonable cause to suspect that the report had been so prepared.[8] This applies only if sufficient evidence is adduced by him or her to raise an issue as to whether he or she had the requisite knowledge or reason.[9]

1   [1995] 1 FLR 403 at 409H–410A, per Balcombe LJ; see also *Re S (Arrangements for Adoption)* [1985] FLR 579 at 583, per Slade LJ; *Re Adoption Application (Non-Patrial: Breach of Procedures)* [1993] Fam 125, [1993] 1 FLR 947, per Douglas Brown J.
2   *Flintshire County Council v K* [2001] 2 FLR 476.
3   As advocated in Department of Health *A Guide to Intercountry Adoption (Practice and Procedure)* (May 1997).
4   *Flintshire County Council v K* (above) at 486C–487D; see also *Re C (Adoption: Legality)* [1999] 1 FLR 370 at 375D–G and *Re JS (Private International Adoption)* [2000] 2 FLR 638 at 640E–F per Johnson J. See also *Re M (Adoption: International Adoption Trade)* [2003] EWHC 219 (Fam).
5   ACA 2002, s 94(2)(a) and (5). The proceedings may be brought more than 6 years after the commission of the offence but subject to that may be brought within a period of 6 months from the date on which evidence, sufficient in the opinion of the prosecutor (procurator fiscal in Scotland) to warrant the proceedings, came to his knowledge: s 138.
6   Ibid, s 94(2)(b).
7   Ibid, s 94(3)(a) and (b).
8   Ibid, s 94(4).
9   Ibid, s 94(4).

Prohibition on payments

16.46 Section 95 of the ACA 2002[1] prohibits certain payments or rewards[2] in connection with the adoption of a child. It is an offence[3] for a person: (a) to make any such payment or reward; (b) to agree or offer to make such payment; or (c) to receive or agree to receive or to attempt to obtain such payment[4] for:[5]

– the adoption of a child;
– the giving of any consent required in connection with the adoption of a child;
– removing from the United Kingdom a child who is a Commonwealth citizen or who is habitually resident in the United Kingdom to a place outside for the purpose of adoption;
– the taking of any step prohibited in s 92(2) (where the person is neither an adoption agency nor acting in pursuance of a High Court order);
– the preparing or submitting a report in contravention of s 94(1).

16.47 The prohibition does not apply to certain 'excepted payments' which are defined in s 96 as those made:

– by virtue of or in accordance with the provisions made by or under the ACA 2002;[6]
– to a registered adoption society by a parent or an adopter or proposed adopter in respect of expenses reasonably incurred by the society in connection with the adoption or proposed adoption;[7]
– in respect of any legal or medical expenses incurred in connection with a court application for an adoption order, placement order or an order under s 26 (contact) or s 84 (giving of parental responsibility prior to adoption abroad);[8]
– in respect of the removal of a child from the United Kingdom for the purpose of adoption[9] where: (a) the proposed adopters are (i) parents, relatives or guardians,[10] or (ii) one of them is a step-parent, or (iii) they have parental responsibility under s 84;[11] and (b) the payment is in respect of travel and accommodation expenses reasonably incurred in removing the child from the United Kingdom.[12]

16.48 The intention is to prohibit money changing hands in relation to the adoption of a child, while still permitting payment of the legitimate expenses of adoption agencies and persons applying or proposing to apply for adoption or transfer of parental responsibility orders.

---

1   ACA 2002, s 95 replaces s 57 of the AA 1976.
2   Ibid, s 97(b).
3   Ibid, s 95(4); it is a summary offence punishable with imprisonment for a term not exceeding 6 months or a fine not exceeding £10,000 or both. The time limit for prosecution has been extended: s 138.
4   Ibid, s 95(3).
5   Ibid, s 95(1)(a)–(e).
6   Ibid, s 96(1). It also includes the Adoption (Scotland) Act 1978 and the Adoption (Northern Ireland) Order 1987.
7   ACA 2002, s 96(2).
8   Ibid, s 96(3).
9   Ibid, s 96(1)(c).
10 'or one of them'.
11 'or the child is removed under the authority of an order under s 49 of the Adoption (Scotland) Act 1978 or Art 57 of the Adoption (Northern Ireland) Order 1987': s 85(2)(b).
12 ACA 2002, s 96(4)(a) and (b).

16.49   Although, under the former law, provision was made for retrospective authorisation of payments by the court,[1] a similar discretion has not been expressly given to the court under the ACA 2002. This may be deliberate omission to preclude retrospective authorisation and to give the prohibition more bite. Alternatively, it may be arguable that s 96(1), which sanctions payments made 'by virtue of or in accordance with the Act', enables the practice of retrospective authorisation by the court to continue.

16.50   In ss 92–96, references to 'adoption' are to the adoption of persons, wherever they may be habitually resident, effected under the law of any country or territory, whether within or outside the British Isles.[2] Under s 2(1), a local authority or registered adoption society is an adoption agency and in ss 92–96 a Scottish or Irish adoption agency is included. The definition of 'adoption agency' does not include adoption agencies abroad and payments to a foreign agency do not fall within the exception for permitted payments. Such payments, therefore, require the sanction of the court.[3]

Prohibition on advertisements

16.51   Section 123 imposes restrictions, carrying criminal sanctions, on publishing or distributing[4] an advertisement or information indicating that:

–   the parent wants his or her child to be adopted; or
–   a person wants to adopt a child; or
–   a person[5] is willing to take any step in arranging for the adoption of a child as specified in s 92(2)(a)–(e), (g)–(i); or
–   a person[6] willing to receive a child handed over to him with a view to the child's adoption by him or another;[7]
–   a person willing to remove a child from the United Kingdom for the purposes of adoption.[8]

16.52   'Information' includes: (i) information about how to do anything, which if done would constitute an offence under s 85 (restriction on taking children out) or s 93 (restrictions on arranging adoptions),[9] whether or not the information contains a warning that it may constitute an offence; and (ii) information about a particular child as a child available for adoption.[10] 'Publishing or distributing' means doing so 'to the public'[11] and covers all forms of publication and distribution including electronic means

---

1   Adoption Act 1958, s 50(2); AA 1976, s 57(3); see *Re Adoption Application (Payment for Adoption)* [1987] Fam 81; [1987] 2 FLR 291, per Latey J, and *Re WM (Adoption: Non-Patrial)* [1997] 1 FLR 132 at 135B, per Johnson J.
2   ACA 2002, s 97(c).
3   *Re A (Adoption Placement)* [1988] 2 FLR 133 at 137.
4   'or causing such advertisements or information to be published or distributed': s 118(1)(b).
5   'other than an adoption agency': s 123(2)(c).
6   'other than an adoption agency': s 123(2)(d).
7   ACA 2002, s 123(2)(d).
8   Ibid, s 123(2)(e).
9   Ibid, s 123(3)(a) also includes offences under s 11 or s 50 of the Adoption (Scotland) Act 1978 or Art 11 or Art 58 of the Adoption (Northern Ireland) Order 1987.
10   ACA 2002, s 123(3)(b).
11   'The public' includes 'selected members of the public as well as the public generally or any section of the public': ACA 2002, s 123(4)(b).

(for example, by means of the internet).[1] However, s 123(1) does not apply to publication or distribution by or on behalf of an adoption agency, which may include a person outside the United Kingdom exercising functions corresponding to those of an adoption agency.[2] Subsection (7) provides a regulation-making power to enable the Secretary of State to consider whether a body outside the United Kingdom corresponds in its functions to a UK adoption agency. It may not be an adoption agency as such, as some countries do not have adoption agencies. However, if it provides the necessary protection, the Secretary of State may use the power to prescribe that the body is, for the purposes of s 123, to be treated as a UK adoption agency. As a consequence, such a body would not be considered to act in contravention of s 123 if it were to advertise in the United Kingdom. It will, therefore, make it possible for a body established in another country that corresponds to a UK adoption agency to advertise its services to the United Kingdom. This may be helpful to prospective intercountry adopters who may be able to obtain information advertised or distributed in the United Kingdom, if such a body has been prescribed as corresponding to a UK agency. By requiring that the body must correspond to a UK adoption agency, the Secretary of State must satisfy himself that such bodies are properly regulated in the country in which they are established.[3] Such a pre-condition is essential to ensure that proper safeguards are in place to protect the welfare of children.

16.53   Section 124 makes a contravention of s 123(1) a summary criminal offence[4] for anyone who publishes or distributes an advertisement or information in breach of the section. The following defence is available. A person is not guilty of an offence under s 123(1) unless it is proved that he knew or had reason to suspect that the section applied to the advertisement or information. It applies only if sufficient evidence is adduced to raise the issue of knowledge or reason.

16.54   Section 123 restates and amends s 58 of the AA 1976. It goes considerably further than its predecessor and is another example of tighter controls which have been put in place to 'police' intercountry adoptions in the light of the Internet twins case.

16.55   Section 123 is, however, a UK-wide provision and although it makes explicit reference to the Internet, given the nature of the Internet it is difficult to restrict information which flows from a website hosted by an Internet Service Provider (ISP) located in another country. In August 2002, the Government implemented the e-commerce Directive. The objective of the Directive is to remove obstacles which act as a barrier to the growth and competitiveness of e-commerce within the European Community. An obligation is placed on each Member State to ensure that the providers of information society services (such as those of ISPs) established on its territory comply with national law. In short, each Member State will be prohibited from restricting the freedom to provide information society services from another Member State. It further

---

1   The Secretary of State may by order make amendments to this section as a result of developments in
     technology , following consultation: s 123(6) and (8).
2   ACA 2002, s 123(7). The functions have to be exercised in the circumstances prescribed by
     regulations. An adoption agency also includes a Scottish or Northern Irish adoption agency:
     s 123(9)(a).
3   HL Deb, 30 October 2002, col 245, per Lord McIntosh of Haringey.
4   ACA 2002, s 124(1). The penalty is imprisonment not exceeding 3 months or a fine not exceeding
     level 5 on the standard scale or both: s 124(3).

limits the liability of intermediaries (such as ISPs) to circumstances in which there is actual knowledge of illegal activity and where corrective action is not taken expeditiously.

16.56   The Directive is binding on the United Kingdom and there is, therefore, an obligation to ensure that the restrictions in the ACA 2002 are compatible with the e-commerce Directive. The intention is to use a regulation-making power contained in the European Communities Act 1972, and it is recognised that the liability of ISPs has to be provided for in a way which is consistent with the Directive.[1] If there were, however, concerns for the welfare of children, then the first resort would be the assistance of the authorities in the particular country. Failing that, then the second resort would be an application for a derogation under the e-commerce Directive, if the ISP were located in a Member State. An intention to provide for derogations through regulations made under the European Communities Act 1972 has been signalled should such circumstances arise.[2] If a person were to see information on the Internet and then act upon it by bringing a child into the United Kingdom for adoption, then the ACA 2002 is, nevertheless, intended to provide the means to penalise that person if he or she fails to comply with the conditions in s 83.

Extra-territorial effect

16.57   One of the key issues which arises in relation to the above prohibitions is whether they have extra-territorial effect. Clearly, if they do not, this seriously weakens their impact in deterring illicit intercountry adoptions.

UNDER THE ADOPTION ACT 1976

16.58   There were a number of conflicting first instance decisions on the question whether ss 11 and 57 of the AA 1976 had extra-territorial effect.[3] In *Re Adoption Application (Non-Patrial: Breach of Procedures)*[4] Douglas Brown J held that neither s 11 nor s 57 had extra-territorial effect. His reasoning[5] included the following points.

(1)   In the first place, there is an established presumption that, in the absence of clear and specific words to the contrary, a statute does not make conduct outside the jurisdiction a criminal offence.[6]

(2)   Secondly, in the AA 1976 there are positive provisions excluding extra-territorial effect. The extent of the statute is dealt with in s 74(3) which provides that the Act extends to England and Wales only. Section 72(3) expressly refers to adoption 'in Great Britain or elsewhere' but does not apply those words to 'agreement or arrangement'.

---

1   HL Deb, 30 October 2002, vol 640, no 196, col 246. Note the transitional provisions relating to advertising contained in paras 14–16 of Sch 4 to the ACA 2002.
2   HL Deb, 30 October 2002, vol 640, no 196, col 245, per Lord McIntosh of Haringey.
3   Contrast (i) *Re A (Adoption Placement)* [1988] 2 FLR 133, per Anthony Lincoln J; *Re F* (unreported) 6 December 1988, per Hollings J; *Re AW (Adoption Application)* [1993] 1 FLR 62, per Bracewell J (which held no extra-territorial effect), with: (ii) *Re An Adoption Application* [1992] 1 FLR 341, per Hollings J; *Re WM (Adoption: Non-Patrial)* [1997] 1 FLR 132, per Johnson J; *Re C (Adoption: Legality)* [1999] 1 FLR 370, per Johnson J (which held extra-territorial effect).
4   [1993] Fam 125, [1993] 1 FLR 947.
5   [1993] 1 FLR 947 at 954E–H.
6   See *Air India v Wiggins* 71 Cr App R 213 (see **16.61**).

He further relied upon the preponderance of judicial opinion which at 1993 clearly favoured non-extraterritorial effect.[1]

16.59   In the later 1990s, however, the needle of the judicial compass swung round more towards extra-territoriality. For example, in *Re WM (Adoption: Non-Patrial)*[2] the child concerned was born in El Salvador and for economic reasons his mother decided that she would give him up for adoption. The applicants, an English couple who were unable to have more children, were put in touch with a lawyer in El Salvador with a view to adopting the child. They went to El Salvador and paid the lawyer £5000 and he arranged for them to adopt the child under the law of El Salvador. Although the payment was outside the jurisdiction, Johnson J held even in those circumstances that there was a breach of s 57, but went on to exercise his discretion to authorise retrospectively the payment to the lawyer, following the decision of Latey J in *Re Adoption Application (Payment for Adoption)*.[3]

UNDER THE ADOPTION AND CHILDREN ACT 2002

16.60   The extent of the ACA 2002 is dealt with in s 149(2), which provides that the Act extends to England and Wales only.[4] It therefore mirrors s 74(3) of the AA 1976. Section 97, the interpretation section for ss 92–96 of the ACA 2002, and s 123(9)(b), specifically provide that 'references to adoption of persons, wherever they may be habitually resident, effected under the law of any country or territory whether within or outside the British Islands'. Therefore, 'extra-territorial effect' is clearly intended to apply to 'adoption'. However, there is no comparable section in respect of, for example, the definition of 'agreement' in s 92(7)(a). 'Agreement' is there simply defined as including 'an arrangement (whether or not enforceable)'. Arguably, extra-territoriality applies to 'adoption' but not to 'agreement'.

16.61   This exclusionary interpretation is consistent with the approach under criminal law, where the primary basis of English criminal jurisdiction is territorial and, statutory exceptions apart, UK domestic criminal courts are generally not concerned with conduct abroad. In *Cox v Army Council*,[5] Viscount Simonds said: '... the whole body of the criminal law of England deals only with acts committed in England'. In *Air India v Wiggins*,[6] Lord Diplock enunciated the following presumption with respect to statutory construction:

> '... in construing Acts of Parliament there is a well-established presumption that, in the absence of clear and specific words to the contrary, an "offence-creating section" of an Act of Parliament ... was not intended to make conduct taking place outside the territorial jurisdiction of the Crown an offence triable in an English criminal court ...'

---

1   Although, arguably, the whole judgment of Douglas Brown J met with the approval of the Court of Appeal in *Re G (Adoption: Illegal Placement)* [1995] 1 FLR 403 at 409D–E, per Balcombe LJ, it is also arguable that, as the court's focus was upon whether the placement of a child in breach of s 11 constituted a bar to the making of an adoption order, its approval should be confined to this aspect of his judgment.

2   [1997] 1 FLR 132.

3   [1987] Fam 81, sub nom *Re Adoption Application AA212/86 (Adoption: Payment)* [1987] 2 FLR 291.

4   The exception is s 137 which extends the Hague Convention to British overseas territories.

5   [1963] AC 48 at 67.

6   71 Cr App R 213 at 217.

16.62   As there appears to be nothing in the wording of the ACA 2002 which rebuts that presumption, it is arguable that Douglas Brown J's reasoning under the AA 1976 equally applies to the prohibitions under the new Act. On this strict interpretation, therefore, these prohibitions would have no extra-territorial effect.

16.63   However, what is the position where the conduct in question takes place partly outside the jurisdiction and partly within it, or where the conduct is without the jurisdiction but the consequences fall within (as is often the case)? For example, in *Re C (Adoption: Legality)*[1] the applicant was asked to make payments to her Guatemalan lawyers, which she transmitted from the United Kingdom; the question which arose was whether there was a breach of s 57 of the AA 1976. Johnson J, in finding that there was a breach, rejected the submission that a payment was not made until it was received and inclined to the view that, for the purpose of this section, a payment was 'made' when it was dispatched. Although Douglas Brown J in *Re Adoption Application (Non-Patrial: Breach of Procedures)*[2] held that payments to a foreign lawyer were 'clearly caught by s 57', he made this subject to the question of extra-territoriality. If Douglas Brown J is right, then the prohibitions would be largely ineffective and constitute no deterrent to illicit intercountry adopters.

16.64   The traditional common law view,[3] where the definition of an offence includes (i) the conduct of the accused, and (ii) the consequences resulting from such conduct, is that an offence is committed within the jurisdiction if the essence or gist of the offence occurred within the jurisdiction. For example, in the offence of obtaining by deception, the essence of the offence is the obtaining and, therefore, if the property was obtained without the jurisdiction, the English court has no jurisdiction to try the offence, even though the deception was made within this jurisdiction.[4]

16.65   In *Treacy v DPP*[5] Lord Diplock, in an *obiter* decision, canvassed a more expansive approach ('the *Treacy* approach'):

> 'When Parliament, as in the Theft Act 1968, defines new crimes in words which, as a matter of language do not contain any geographical limitation either as to where a person's punishable conduct took place or, when the definition requires that the conduct shall be followed by specified consequences, as to where those consequences took effect, what reason have we to suppose that Parliament intended any geographical limitation to be understood?
>
> The only relevant reason, now that the technicalities of venue have long since been abolished, is to be found in the international rules of comity, which, in the absence of express provision to the contrary, it is presumed that Parliament did not intend to break. It would be an unjustifiable interference with the sovereignty of other nations over the conduct of persons in their own territories if we were to punish persons for conduct which did not take place in the United Kingdom and had no harmful consequences there. But I see no reason in comity for

---

1   [1999] 1 FLR 370 at 380G–381C.
2   [1993] Fam 125, [1993] 1 FLR 947.
3   For a discussion on territorial effect in criminal law (which lies outside the ambit of this book), see *Archbold: Criminal Pleading, Evidence & Practice 2003* (Sweet & Maxwell), paras 2–33 and 2–34.
4   *R v Harden* [1963] 1 QB 8; in *R v Manning* [1998] 2 Cr App R 461, in which the Court of Appeal referred to the rule in *R v Harden* as 'the last act' rule, the court expressed a preference for the rule in *Harden* over earlier decisions which had preferred the approach in the *obiter* opinion of Lord Diplock in *Treacy v DPP* [1971] AC 537 at 561E–562E; 564C–F.
5   [1971] AC 537 at 561E–F, 562B.

requiring any wider limitation than that upon the exercise by Parliament of its legislative power in the field of criminal law ...

Nor ... can I see any reason in comity to prevent Parliament from rendering liable to punishment, if they subsequently come to England, persons who have done outside the United Kingdom physical acts which have had harmful consequences upon victims in England.'

16.66   In the context of offences against the Theft Act 1968, in *Somchai Liangsiriprasert v Government of the United States of America*[1] the Privy Council, following the *obiter* decision of Lord Diplock in *Treacy v DPP*,[2] recognised that crime has ceased to be largely local in origin and effect and the common law must now face this new reality. It held that there is nothing in precedent, comity or good sense to inhibit the common law from regarding as justiciable in England inchoate crimes committed abroad which are intended to result in the commission of criminal offences in England. In *R v Sansom*[3] Taylor LJ (as he then was) said that the principle propounded in *Somchai* should be regarded as the law of England and did not refer only to the common law.

16.67   It may, therefore, be arguable that in the specialised statutory context of intercountry adoptions (with their extra-territorial component) the *Treacy* approach provides a way through the jurisdictional complexities, so as to enable it to be sufficient to constitute an offence if either the conduct or the consequences take place in England and Wales. The *Treacy* approach, however, has not been universally adopted. In *R v Manning*[4] the Court of Appeal applied 'the last act' rule in preference to the *Treacy* approach. Consequently, the definitive answer to the issue of extra-territoriality in relation to the prohibitions in ss 92–96 and ss 123–124 of the ACA 2002 awaits a decision of the higher courts.

16.68   However, if a person abroad commits an offence in England through the agency of another, he or she is clearly liable in this country.[5]

CONCLUSION

16.69   There is little doubt that the ACA 2002 has sought to address the shortcomings of the former law in respect of illegal trafficking. It has made breaches of ss 83 and 85 (which regulate the bringing in and taking out of children in the United Kingdom) indictable offences (with no time limit for prosecution) and increased the maximum penalty to 12 months' imprisonment; it has extended the time for prosecution for offences under ss 93–95,[6] extended the scope of the prohibitions against illegal placements and transactions, and generally stiffened the penalties; it has introduced criminal sanctions in respect of privately commissioned reports.

---

1   [1991] 1 AC 225 at 251C–D, per Lord Griffiths.
2   [1971] AC 537.
3   [1991] 2 QB 130 at 137H–138A.
4   [1998] 2 Cr App R 461.
5   *R v Baxter* [1972] QB 1; *DPP v Stonehouse* [1978] AC 55.
6   ACA 2002, s 135.

16.70   These sanctions will undoubtedly provide a deterrent to a number of prospective illicit adopters but whether they will deter the hard core of individuals or couples desperate for a child remains to be seen. A maximum sentence of 7 years' imprisonment for an offence of assisting illegal entry into the United Kingdom under s 25 of the Immigration Act 1971 did not deter either Mr and Mrs K in *Flintshire County Council v K*[1] or the applicant in *Re C (Adoption: Legality)*.[2] Much will turn upon whether the breaches are in fact prosecuted and, if so, whether the criminal courts are prepared to impose sentences of imprisonment. Once a child becomes established with the adopters or prospective adopters in the United Kingdom, then one can envisage a similar reluctance, as under the former law, to embark upon a prosecution or to pass a sentence of imprisonment upon the adopters where the result would be likely to cause harm to the child. Even though the extension of the time limit to 6 years for bringing proceedings under ss 93–95 is to provide a longer time scale for the authorities to bring prosecutions against those arranging private adoptions, the Government has acknowledged that it remains up to the prosecuting authorities 'to decide that, if no harm has come to the child, it is not in the public interest to prosecute the parents'.[3] As welfare is the paramount consideration, it is difficult to see the court treating illegality as an absolute bar to adoption, where an application of the s 1 principles requires an adoption in the child's best interests.

1   [2001] 2 FLR 476.
2   [1999] 1 FLR 370.
3   HC Deb, 20 May 2002, vol 386, no 150, col 37, per Ms Jacqui Smith.

Appendix

ADOPTION AND CHILDREN ACT 2002

Chapter number—2002 c 38.

Long title—An Act to restate and amend the law relating to adoption; to make further amendments of the law relating to children; to amend section 93 of the Local Government Act 2000; and for connected purposes.

Royal Assent— 7 November 2002.

Commencement—This Act is not yet in force except where otherwise stated.

PART 1

ADOPTION

Chapter 1

Introductory

1 Considerations applying to the exercise of powers

(1) This section applies whenever a court or adoption agency is coming to a decision relating to the adoption of a child.

(2) The paramount consideration of the court or adoption agency must be the child's welfare, throughout his life.

(3) The court or adoption agency must at all times bear in mind that, in general, any delay in coming to the decision is likely to prejudice the child's welfare.

(4) The court or adoption agency must have regard to the following matters (among others) –

    (a) the child's ascertainable wishes and feelings regarding the decision (considered in the light of the child's age and understanding),

    (b) the child's particular needs,

    (c) the likely effect on the child (throughout his life) of having ceased to be a member of the original family and become an adopted person,

    (d) the child's age, sex, background and any of the child's characteristics which the court or agency considers relevant,

    (e) any harm (within the meaning of the Children Act 1989) which the child has suffered or is at risk of suffering,

    (f) the relationship which the child has with relatives, and with any other person in relation to whom the court or agency considers the relationship to be relevant, including –

        (i) the likelihood of any such relationship continuing and the value to the child of its doing so,

(ii)   the ability and willingness of any of the child's relatives, or of any such person, to provide the child with a secure environment in which the child can develop, and otherwise to meet the child's needs,

(iii) the wishes and feelings of any of the child's relatives, or of any such person, regarding the child.

(5) In placing the child for adoption, the adoption agency must give due consideration to the child's religious persuasion, racial origin and cultural and linguistic background.

(6) The court or adoption agency must always consider the whole range of powers available to it in the child's case (whether under this Act or the Children Act 1989); and the court must not make any order under this Act unless it considers that making the order would be better for the child than not doing so.

(7) In this section, 'coming to a decision relating to the adoption of a child', in relation to a court, includes –

(a)   coming to a decision in any proceedings where the orders that might be made by the court include an adoption order (or the revocation of such an order), a placement order (or the revocation of such an order) or an order under section 26 (or the revocation or variation of such an order),

(b)   coming to a decision about granting leave in respect of any action (other than the initiation of proceedings in any court) which may be taken by an adoption agency or individual under this Act,

but does not include coming to a decision about granting leave in any other circumstances.

(8) For the purposes of this section –

(a)   references to relationships are not confined to legal relationships,

(b)   references to a relative, in relation to a child, include the child's mother and father.

Chapter 2

The Adoption Service

The Adoption Service

2 Basic definitions

(1) The services maintained by local authorities under section 3(1) may be collectively referred to as 'the Adoption Service', and a local authority or registered adoption society may be referred to as an adoption agency.

(2) In this Act, 'registered adoption society' means a voluntary organisation which is an adoption society registered under Part 2 of the Care Standards Act 2000; but in relation to the provision of any facility of the Adoption Service, references to a registered adoption society or to an adoption agency do not include an adoption society which is not registered in respect of that facility.

(3) A registered adoption society is to be treated as registered in respect of any facility of the Adoption Service unless it is a condition of its registration that it does not provide that facility.

(4) No application for registration under Part 2 of the Care Standards Act 2000 may be made in respect of an adoption society which is an unincorporated body.

(5) In this Act –

'the 1989 Act' means the Children Act 1989,

'adoption society' means a body whose functions consist of or include making arrangements for the adoption of children,

'voluntary organisation' means a body other than a public or local authority the activities of which are not carried on for profit.

(6) In this Act, 'adoption support services' means –

(a) counselling, advice and information, and
(b) any other services prescribed by regulations,

in relation to adoption.

(7) The power to make regulations under subsection (6)(b) is to be exercised so as to secure that local authorities provide financial support.

(8) In this Chapter, references to adoption are to the adoption of persons, wherever they may be habitually resident, effected under the law of any country or territory, whether within or outside the British Islands.

Commencement—Subsections (6)–(8) in force from 10 March 2003 (England only) for the purposes of Sch 4, para 3 in relation to the making of regulations (SI 2003/366).

3 Maintenance of Adoption Service

(1) Each local authority must continue to maintain within their area a service designed to meet the needs, in relation to adoption, of –

(a) children who may be adopted, their parents and guardians,
(b) persons wishing to adopt a child, and
(c) adopted persons, their parents, natural parents and former guardians;

and for that purpose must provide the requisite facilities.

(2) Those facilities must include making, and participating in, arrangements –

(a) for the adoption of children, and
(b) for the provision of adoption support services.

(3) As part of the service, the arrangements made for the purposes of subsection (2)(b) –

(a) must extend to the provision of adoption support services to persons who are within a description prescribed by regulations,
(b) may extend to the provision of those services to other persons.

(4) A local authority may provide any of the requisite facilities by securing their provision by –

(a) registered adoption societies, or
(b) other persons who are within a description prescribed by regulations of persons who may provide the facilities in question.

(5) The facilities of the service must be provided in conjunction with the local authority's other social services and with registered adoption societies in their area, so that help may be given in a co-ordinated manner without duplication, omission or avoidable delay.

(6) The social services referred to in subsection (5) are the functions of a local authority which are social services functions within the meaning of the Local Authority Social Services Act 1970 (which include, in particular, those functions in so far as they relate to children).

4 Assessments etc for adoption support services

(1) A local authority must at the request of –

- (a) any of the persons mentioned in paragraphs (a) to (c) of section 3(1), or
- (b) any other person who falls within a description prescribed by regulations (subject to subsection (7)(a)),

carry out an assessment of that person's needs for adoption support services.

(2) A local authority may, at the request of any person, carry out an assessment of that person's needs for adoption support services.

(3) A local authority may request the help of the persons mentioned in paragraph (a) or (b) of section 3(4) in carrying out an assessment.

(4) Where, as a result of an assessment, a local authority decide that a person has needs for adoption support services, they must then decide whether to provide any such services to that person.

(5) If –

- (a) a local authority decide to provide any adoption support services to a person, and
- (b) the circumstances fall within a description prescribed by regulations,

the local authority must prepare a plan in accordance with which adoption support services are to be provided to the person and keep the plan under review.

(6) Regulations may make provision about assessments, preparing and reviewing plans, the provision of adoption support services in accordance with plans and reviewing the provision of adoption support services.

(7) The regulations may in particular make provision –

- (a) as to the circumstances in which a person mentioned in paragraph (b) of subsection (1) is to have a right to request an assessment of his needs in accordance with that subsection,
- (b) about the type of assessment which, or the way in which an assessment, is to be carried out,
- (c) about the way in which a plan is to be prepared,
- (d) about the way in which, and time at which, a plan or the provision of adoption support services is to be reviewed,
- (e) about the considerations to which a local authority are to have regard in carrying out an assessment or review or preparing a plan,
- (f) as to the circumstances in which a local authority may provide adoption support services subject to conditions,
- (g) as to the consequences of conditions imposed by virtue of paragraph (f) not being met (including the recovery of any financial support provided by a local authority),
- (h) as to the circumstances in which this section may apply to a local authority in respect of persons who are outside that local authority's area,
- (i) as to the circumstances in which a local authority may recover from another local authority the expenses of providing adoption support services to any person.

(8) A local authority may carry out an assessment of the needs of any person under this section at the same time as an assessment of his needs is made under any other enactment.

(9) If at any time during the assessment of the needs of any person under this section, it appears to a local authority that –

- (a) there may be a need for the provision of services to that person by a Primary Care Trust (in Wales, a Health Authority or Local Health Board), or

(b) there may be a need for the provision to him of any services which fall within the functions of a local education authority (within the meaning of the Education Act 1996),

the local authority must notify that Primary Care Trust, Health Authority, Local Health Board or local education authority.

(10) Where it appears to a local authority that another local authority could, by taking any specified action, help in the exercise of any of their functions under this section, they may request the help of that other local authority, specifying the action in question.

(11) A local authority whose help is so requested must comply with the request if it is consistent with the exercise of their functions.

Commencement—Subsections (6) and (7)(b)–(i) in force from 10 March 2003 (England only) for the purposes of Sch 4, para 3, in relation to the making of regulations (SI 2003/366).

5 Local authority plans for adoption services

(1) Each local authority must prepare a plan for the provision of the services maintained under section 3(1) and secure that it is published.

(2) The plan must contain information of a description prescribed by regulations (subject to subsection (4)(b)).

(3) The regulations may make provision requiring local authorities –

   (a) to review any plan,
   (b) in the circumstances prescribed by the regulations, to modify that plan and secure its publication or to prepare a plan in substitution for that plan and secure its publication.

(4) The appropriate Minister may direct –

   (a) that a plan is to be included in another document specified in the direction,
   (b) that the requirements specified in the direction as to the description of information to be contained in a plan are to have effect in place of the provision made by regulations under subsection (2).

(5) Directions may be given by the appropriate Minister for the purpose of making provision in connection with any duty imposed by virtue of this section including, in particular, provision as to –

   (a) the form and manner in which, and the time at which, any plan is to be published,
   (b) the description of persons who are to be consulted in the preparation of any plan,
   (c) the time at which any plan is to be reviewed.

(6) Subsections (2) to (5) apply in relation to a modified or substituted plan (or further modified or substituted plan) as they apply in relation to a plan prepared under subsection (1).

(7) Directions given under this section may relate –

   (a) to a particular local authority,
   (b) to any class or description of local authorities, or
   (c) except in the case of a direction given under subsection (4)(b), to local authorities generally,

and accordingly different provision may be made in relation to different local authorities or classes or descriptions of local authorities.

6 Arrangements on cancellation of registration

Where, by virtue of the cancellation of its registration under Part 2 of the Care Standards Act 2000, a body has ceased to be a registered adoption society, the appropriate Minister may direct the body to make such arrangements as to the transfer of its functions relating to children and other transitional matters as seem to him expedient.

7 Inactive or defunct adoption societies etc

(1) This section applies where it appears to the appropriate Minister that –

(a) a body which is or has been a registered adoption society is inactive or defunct, or
(b) a body which has ceased to be a registered adoption society by virtue of the cancellation of its registration under Part 2 of the Care Standards Act 2000 has not made such arrangements for the transfer of its functions relating to children as are specified in a direction given by him.

(2) The appropriate Minister may, in relation to such functions of the society as relate to children, direct what appears to him to be the appropriate local authority to take any such action as might have been taken by the society or by the society jointly with the authority.

(3) A local authority are entitled to take any action which –

(a) apart from this subsection the authority would not be entitled to take, or would not be entitled to take without joining the society in the action, but
(b) they are directed to take under subsection (2).

(4) The appropriate Minister may charge the society for expenses necessarily incurred by him or on his behalf in securing the transfer of its functions relating to children.

(5) Before giving a direction under subsection (2) the appropriate Minister must, if practicable, consult both the society and the authority.

8 Adoption support agencies

(1) In this Act, 'adoption support agency' means an undertaking the purpose of which, or one of the purposes of which, is the provision of adoption support services; but an undertaking is not an adoption support agency –

(a) merely because it provides information in connection with adoption other than for the purpose mentioned in section 98(1), or
(b) if it is excepted by virtue of subsection (2).

'Undertaking' has the same meaning as in the Care Standards Act 2000.

(2) The following are excepted –

(a) a registered adoption society, whether or not the society is registered in respect of the provision of adoption support services,
(b) a local authority,
(c) a local education authority (within the meaning of the Education Act 1996),
(d) a Special Health Authority, Primary Care Trust (in Wales, a Health Authority or Local Health Board) or NHS trust,
(e) the Registrar General,
(f) any person, or description of persons, excepted by regulations.

(3) In section 4 of the Care Standards Act 2000 (basic definitions) –

(a) after subsection (7) there is inserted –

'(7A) "Adoption support agency" has the meaning given by section 8 of the Adoption and Children Act 2002.',

(b) in subsection (9)(a) (construction of references to descriptions of agencies), for 'or a voluntary adoption agency' there is substituted 'a voluntary adoption agency or an adoption support agency'.

Regulations

9 General power to regulate adoption etc agencies

(1) Regulations may make provision for any purpose relating to –

(a) the exercise by local authorities or voluntary adoption agencies of their functions in relation to adoption, or
(b) the exercise by adoption support agencies of their functions in relation to adoption.

(2) The extent of the power to make regulations under this section is not limited by sections 10 to 12, 45, 54, 56 to 65 and 98 or by any other powers exercisable in respect of local authorities, voluntary adoption agencies or adoption support agencies.

(3) Regulations may provide that a person who contravenes or fails to comply with any provision of regulations under this section is to be guilty of an offence and liable on summary conviction to a fine not exceeding level 5 on the standard scale.

(4) In this section and section 10, 'voluntary adoption agency' means a voluntary organisation which is an adoption society.

10 Management etc of agencies

(1) In relation to local authorities, voluntary adoption agencies and adoption support agencies, regulations under section 9 may make provision as to –

(a) the persons who are fit to work for them for the purposes of the functions mentioned in section 9(1),
(b) the fitness of premises,
(c) the management and control of their operations,
(d) the number of persons, or persons of any particular type, working for the purposes of those functions,
(e) the management and training of persons working for the purposes of those functions,
(f) the keeping of information.

(2) Regulations made by virtue of subsection (1)(a) may, in particular, make provision for prohibiting persons from working in prescribed positions unless they are registered in, or in a particular part of, one of the registers maintained under section 56(1) of the Care Standards Act 2000 (registration of social care workers).

(3) In relation to voluntary adoption agencies and adoption support agencies, regulations under section 9 may –

(a) make provision as to the persons who are fit to manage an agency, including provision prohibiting persons from doing so unless they are registered in, or in a particular part of, one of the registers referred to in subsection (2),
(b) impose requirements as to the financial position of an agency,
(c) make provision requiring the appointment of a manager,

(d) in the case of a voluntary adoption agency, make provision for securing the welfare of children placed by the agency, including provision as to the promotion and protection of their health,

(e) in the case of an adoption support agency, make provision as to the persons who are fit to carry on the agency.

(4) Regulations under section 9 may make provision as to the conduct of voluntary adoption agencies and adoption support agencies, and may in particular make provision –

(a) as to the facilities and services to be provided by an agency,

(b) as to the keeping of accounts,

(c) as to the notification to the registration authority of events occurring in premises used for the purposes of an agency,

(d) as to the giving of notice to the registration authority of periods during which the manager of an agency proposes to be absent, and specifying the information to be given in such a notice,

(e) as to the making of adequate arrangements for the running of an agency during a period when its manager is absent,

(f) as to the giving of notice to the registration authority of any intended change in the identity of the manager,

(g) as to the giving of notice to the registration authority of changes in the ownership of an agency or the identity of its officers,

(h) requiring the payment of a prescribed fee to the registration authority in respect of any notification required to be made by virtue of paragraph (g),

(i) requiring arrangements to be made for dealing with complaints made by or on behalf of those seeking, or receiving, any of the services provided by an agency and requiring the agency or manager to take steps for publicising the arrangements.

11 Fees

(1) Regulations under section 9 may prescribe –

(a) the fees which may be charged by adoption agencies in respect of the provision of services to persons providing facilities as part of the Adoption Service (including the Adoption Services in Scotland and Northern Ireland),

(b) the fees which may be paid by adoption agencies to persons providing or assisting in providing such facilities.

(2) Regulations under section 9 may prescribe the fees which may be charged by local authorities in respect of the provision of prescribed facilities of the Adoption Service where the following conditions are met.

(3) The conditions are that the facilities are provided in connection with –

(a) the adoption of a child brought into the United Kingdom for the purpose of adoption, or

(b) a Convention adoption, an overseas adoption or an adoption effected under the law of a country or territory outside the British Islands.

(4) Regulations under section 9 may prescribe the fees which may be charged by adoption agencies in respect of the provision of counselling, where the counselling is provided in connection with the disclosure of information in relation to a person's adoption.

12 Independent review of determinations

(1) Regulations under section 9 may establish a procedure under which any person in respect of whom a qualifying determination has been made by an adoption agency may apply to a panel constituted by the appropriate Minister for a review of that determination.

(2) The regulations must make provision as to the description of determinations which are qualifying determinations for the purposes of subsection (1).

(3) The regulations may include provision as to –

(a) the duties and powers of a panel (including the power to recover the costs of a review from the adoption agency by which the determination reviewed was made),
(b) the administration and procedures of a panel,
(c) the appointment of members of a panel (including the number, or any limit on the number, of members who may be appointed and any conditions for appointment),
(d) the payment of expenses of members of a panel,
(e) the duties of adoption agencies in connection with reviews conducted under the regulations,
(f) the monitoring of any such reviews.

(4) The appropriate Minister may make an arrangement with an organisation under which functions in relation to the panel are performed by the organisation on his behalf.

(5) If the appropriate Minister makes such an arrangement with an organisation, the organisation is to perform its functions under the arrangement in accordance with any general or special directions given by the appropriate Minister.

(6) The arrangement may include provision for payments to be made to the organisation by the appropriate Minister.

(7) Where the appropriate Minister is the Assembly, subsections (4) and (6) also apply as if references to an organisation included references to the Secretary of State.

(8) In this section, 'organisation' includes a public body and a private or voluntary organisation.

Supplemental

13 Information concerning adoption

(1) Each adoption agency must give to the appropriate Minister any statistical or other general information he requires about –

(a) its performance of all or any of its functions relating to adoption,
(b) the children and other persons in relation to whom it has exercised those functions.

(2) The following persons –

(a) the justices' chief executive for each magistrates' court,
(b) the relevant officer of each county court,
(c) the relevant officer of the High Court,

must give to the appropriate Minister any statistical or other general information he requires about the proceedings under this Act of the court in question.

(3) In subsection (2), 'relevant officer', in relation to a county court or the High Court, means the officer of that court who is designated to act for the purposes of that subsection by a direction given by the Lord Chancellor.

(4) The information required to be given to the appropriate Minister under this section must be given at the times, and in the form, directed by him.

(5) The appropriate Minister may publish from time to time abstracts of the information given to him under this section.

14 Default power of appropriate Minister

(1) If the appropriate Minister is satisfied that any local authority have failed, without reasonable excuse, to comply with any of the duties imposed on them by virtue of this Act or of section 1 or 2(4) of the Adoption (Intercountry Aspects) Act 1999, he may make an order declaring that authority to be in default in respect of that duty.

(2) An order under subsection (1) must give the appropriate Minister's reasons for making it.

(3) An order under subsection (1) may contain such directions as appear to the appropriate Minister to be necessary for the purpose of ensuring that, within the period specified in the order, the duty is complied with.

(4) Any such directions are enforceable, on the appropriate Minister's application, by a mandatory order.

15 Inspection of premises etc

(1) The appropriate Minister may arrange for any premises in which –

   (a) a child is living with a person with whom the child has been placed by an adoption agency, or
   (b) a child in respect of whom a notice of intention to adopt has been given under section 44 is, or will be, living,

to be inspected from time to time.

(2) The appropriate Minister may require an adoption agency –

   (a) to give him any information, or
   (b) to allow him to inspect any records (in whatever form they are held),

relating to the discharge of any of its functions in relation to adoption which the appropriate Minister specifies.

(3) An inspection under this section must be conducted by a person authorised by the appropriate Minister.

(4) An officer of a local authority may only be so authorised with the consent of the authority.

(5) A person inspecting any premises under subsection (1) may –

   (a) visit the child there,
   (b) make any examination into the state of the premises and the treatment of the child there which he thinks fit.

(6) A person authorised to inspect any records under this section may at any reasonable time have access to, and inspect and check the operation of, any computer (and associated apparatus) which is being or has been used in connection with the records in question.

(7) A person authorised to inspect any premises or records under this section may –

   (a) enter the premises for that purpose at any reasonable time,
   (b) require any person to give him any reasonable assistance he may require.

(8) A person exercising a power under this section must, if required to do so, produce a duly authenticated document showing his authority.

(9) Any person who intentionally obstructs another in the exercise of a power under this section is guilty of an offence and liable on summary conviction to a fine not exceeding level 3 on the standard scale.

16 Distribution of functions in relation to registered adoption societies

After section 36 of the Care Standards Act 2000 there is inserted –

'36A Voluntary adoption agencies: distribution of functions

(1) This section applies to functions relating to voluntary adoption agencies conferred on the registration authority by or under this Part or under Chapter 2 of Part 1 of the Adoption and Children Act 2002.

(2) Subject to the following provisions, functions to which this section applies are exercisable –

(a) where the principal office of an agency is in England, by the Commission,
(b) where the principal office of an agency is in Wales, by the Assembly.

(3) So far as those functions relate to the imposition, variation or removal of conditions of registration, they may only be exercised after consultation with the Assembly or (as the case may be) the Commission.

(4) But –

(a) where such a function as is mentioned in subsection (3) is exercisable by the Commission in relation to an agency which has a branch in Wales, it is exercisable only with the agreement of the Assembly,
(b) where such a function as is mentioned in subsection (3) is exercisable by the Assembly in relation to an agency which has a branch in England, it is exercisable only with the agreement of the Commission.

(5) The functions conferred on the registration authority by sections 31 and 32 of this Act in respect of any premises of a voluntary adoption agency are exercisable –

(a) where the premises are in England, by the Commission, ∗
(b) where the premises are in Wales, by the Assembly.

(6) In spite of subsections (2) to (5), regulations may provide for any function to which this section applies to be exercisable by the Commission instead of the Assembly, or by the Assembly instead of the Commission, or by one concurrently with the other, or by both jointly or by either with the agreement of or after consultation with the other.

(7) In this section, "regulations" means regulations relating to England and Wales.'

Commencement—Section 16 in force from 1 February 2003 (Wales only) (SI 2003/181), and from 25 February 2003 (England) so far as it inserts Care Standards Act 2000, s 36A(1)–(4) in relation to functions conferred under Part II of that Act, and under the Adoption Act 1976, and from 30 April 2003 (England) otherwise in relation to those functions (SI 2003/366).

17 Inquiries

(1) The appropriate Minister may cause an inquiry to be held into any matter connected with the functions of an adoption agency.

(2) Before an inquiry is begun, the appropriate Minister may direct that it is to be held in private.

(3) Where no direction has been given, the person holding the inquiry may if he thinks fit hold it, or any part of it, in private.

(4) Subsections (2) to (5) of section 250 of the Local Government Act 1972 (powers in relation to local inquiries) apply in relation to an inquiry under this section as they apply in relation to a local inquiry under that section.

Chapter 3

Placement for Adoption and Adoption Orders

Placement of children by adoption agency for adoption

18 Placement for adoption by agencies

(1) An adoption agency may –

- (a) place a child for adoption with prospective adopters, or
- (b) where it has placed a child with any persons (whether under this Part or not), leave the child with them as prospective adopters,

but, except in the case of a child who is less than six weeks old, may only do so under section 19 or a placement order.

(2) An adoption agency may only place a child for adoption with prospective adopters if the agency is satisfied that the child ought to be placed for adoption.

(3) A child who is placed or authorised to be placed for adoption with prospective adopters by a local authority is looked after by the authority.

(4) If an application for an adoption order has been made by any persons in respect of a child and has not been disposed of –

- (a) an adoption agency which placed the child with those persons may leave the child with them until the application is disposed of, but
- (b) apart from that, the child may not be placed for adoption with any prospective adopters.

'Adoption order' includes a Scottish or Northern Irish adoption order.

(5) References in this Act (apart from this section) to an adoption agency placing a child for adoption –

- (a) are to its placing a child for adoption with prospective adopters, and
- (b) include, where it has placed a child with any persons (whether under this Act or not), leaving the child with them as prospective adopters;

and references in this Act (apart from this section) to a child who is placed for adoption by an adoption agency are to be interpreted accordingly.

(6) References in this Chapter to an adoption agency being, or not being, authorised to place a child for adoption are to the agency being or (as the case may be) not being authorised to do so under section 19 or a placement order.

(7) This section is subject to sections 30 to 35 (removal of children placed by adoption agencies).

19 Placing children with parental consent

(1) Where an adoption agency is satisfied that each parent or guardian of a child has consented to the child –

- (a) being placed for adoption with prospective adopters identified in the consent, or
- (b) being placed for adoption with any prospective adopters who may be chosen by the agency,

and has not withdrawn the consent, the agency is authorised to place the child for adoption accordingly.

(2) Consent to a child being placed for adoption with prospective adopters identified in the consent may be combined with consent to the child subsequently being placed for adoption with any prospective adopters who may be chosen by the agency in circumstances where the child is removed from or returned by the identified prospective adopters.

(3) Subsection (1) does not apply where –

    (a) an application has been made on which a care order might be made and the application has not been disposed of, or

    (b) a care order or placement order has been made after the consent was given.

(4) References in this Act to a child placed for adoption under this section include a child who was placed under this section with prospective adopters and continues to be placed with them, whether or not consent to the placement has been withdrawn.

(5) This section is subject to section 52 (parental etc consent).

20 Advance consent to adoption

(1) A parent or guardian of a child who consents to the child being placed for adoption by an adoption agency under section 19 may, at the same or any subsequent time, consent to the making of a future adoption order.

(2) Consent under this section –

    (a) where the parent or guardian has consented to the child being placed for adoption with prospective adopters identified in the consent, may be consent to adoption by them, or

    (b) may be consent to adoption by any prospective adopters who may be chosen by the agency.

(3) A person may withdraw any consent given under this section.

(4) A person who gives consent under this section may, at the same or any subsequent time, by notice given to the adoption agency –

    (a) state that he does not wish to be informed of any application for an adoption order, or

    (b) withdraw such a statement.

(5) A notice under subsection (4) has effect from the time when it is received by the adoption agency but has no effect if the person concerned has withdrawn his consent.

(6) This section is subject to section 52 (parental etc consent).

21 Placement orders

(1) A placement order is an order made by the court authorising a local authority to place a child for adoption with any prospective adopters who may be chosen by the authority.

(2) The court may not make a placement order in respect of a child unless –

    (a) the child is subject to a care order,

    (b) the court is satisfied that the conditions in section 31(2) of the 1989 Act (conditions for making a care order) are met, or

    (c) the child has no parent or guardian.

(3) The court may only make a placement order if, in the case of each parent or guardian of the child, the court is satisfied –

(a) that the parent or guardian has consented to the child being placed for adoption with any prospective adopters who may be chosen by the local authority and has not withdrawn the consent, or

(b) that the parent's or guardian's consent should be dispensed with.

This subsection is subject to section 52 (parental etc consent).

(4) A placement order continues in force until –

(a) it is revoked under section 24,
(b) an adoption order is made in respect of the child, or
(c) the child marries or attains the age of 18 years.

'Adoption order' includes a Scottish or Northern Irish adoption order.

22 Applications for placement orders

(1) A local authority must apply to the court for a placement order in respect of a child if –

(a) the child is placed for adoption by them or is being provided with accommodation by them,
(b) no adoption agency is authorised to place the child for adoption,
(c) the child has no parent or guardian or the authority consider that the conditions in section 31(2) of the 1989 Act are met, and
(d) the authority are satisfied that the child ought to be placed for adoption.

(2) If –

(a) an application has been made (and has not been disposed of) on which a care order might be made in respect of a child, or
(b) a child is subject to a care order and the appropriate local authority are not authorised to place the child for adoption,

the appropriate local authority must apply to the court for a placement order if they are satisfied that the child ought to be placed for adoption.

(3) If –

(a) a child is subject to a care order, and
(b) the appropriate local authority are authorised to place the child for adoption under section 19,

the authority may apply to the court for a placement order.

(4) If a local authority –

(a) are under a duty to apply to the court for a placement order in respect of a child, or
(b) have applied for a placement order in respect of a child and the application has not been disposed of,

the child is looked after by the authority.

(5) Subsections (1) to (3) do not apply in respect of a child –

(a) if any persons have given notice of intention to adopt, unless the period of four months beginning with the giving of the notice has expired without them applying for an adoption order or their application for such an order has been withdrawn or refused, or
(b) if an application for an adoption order has been made and has not been disposed of.

'Adoption order' includes a Scottish or Northern Irish adoption order.

(6) Where –

    (a) an application for a placement order in respect of a child has been made and has not been disposed of, and

    (b) no interim care order is in force,

the court may give any directions it considers appropriate for the medical or psychiatric examination or other assessment of the child; but a child who is of sufficient understanding to make an informed decision may refuse to submit to the examination or other assessment.

(7) The appropriate local authority –

    (a) in relation to a care order, is the local authority in whose care the child is placed by the order, and

    (b) in relation to an application on which a care order might be made, is the local authority which makes the application.

23 Varying placement orders

(1) The court may vary a placement order so as to substitute another local authority for the local authority authorised by the order to place the child for adoption.

(2) The variation may only be made on the joint application of both authorities.

24 Revoking placement orders

(1) The court may revoke a placement order on the application of any person.

(2) But an application may not be made by a person other than the child or the local authority authorised by the order to place the child for adoption unless –

    (a) the court has given leave to apply, and

    (b) the child is not placed for adoption by the authority.

(3) The court cannot give leave under subsection (2)(a) unless satisfied that there has been a change in circumstances since the order was made.

(4) If the court determines, on an application for an adoption order, not to make the order, it may revoke any placement order in respect of the child.

(5) Where –

    (a) an application for the revocation of a placement order has been made and has not been disposed of, and

    (b) the child is not placed for adoption by the authority,

the child may not without the court's leave be placed for adoption under the order.

25 Parental responsibility

(1) This section applies while –

    (a) a child is placed for adoption under section 19 or an adoption agency is authorised to place a child for adoption under that section, or

    (b) a placement order is in force in respect of a child.

(2) Parental responsibility for the child is given to the agency concerned.

(3) While the child is placed with prospective adopters, parental responsibility is given to them.

(4) The agency may determine that the parental responsibility of any parent or guardian, or of prospective adopters, is to be restricted to the extent specified in the determination.

26 Contact

(1) On an adoption agency being authorised to place a child for adoption, or placing a child for adoption who is less than six weeks old, any provision for contact under the 1989 Act ceases to have effect.

(2) While an adoption agency is so authorised or a child is placed for adoption –

    (a) no application may be made for any provision for contact under that Act, but

    (b) the court may make an order under this section requiring the person with whom the child lives, or is to live, to allow the child to visit or stay with the person named in the order, or for the person named in the order and the child otherwise to have contact with each other.

(3) An application for an order under this section may be made by –

    (a) the child or the agency,

    (b) any parent, guardian or relative,

    (c) any person in whose favour there was provision for contact under the 1989 Act which ceased to have effect by virtue of subsection (1),

    (d) if a residence order was in force immediately before the adoption agency was authorised to place the child for adoption or (as the case may be) placed the child for adoption at a time when he was less than six weeks old, the person in whose favour the order was made,

    (e) if a person had care of the child immediately before that time by virtue of an order made in the exercise of the High Court's inherent jurisdiction with respect to children, that person,

    (f) any person who has obtained the court's leave to make the application.

(4) When making a placement order, the court may on its own initiative make an order under this section.

(5) This section does not prevent an application for a contact order under section 8 of the 1989 Act being made where the application is to be heard together with an application for an adoption order in respect of the child.

(6) In this section, 'provision for contact under the 1989 Act' means a contact order under section 8 of that Act or an order under section 34 of that Act (parental contact with children in care).

27 Contact: supplementary

(1) An order under section 26 –

    (a) has effect while the adoption agency is authorised to place the child for adoption or the child is placed for adoption, but

    (b) may be varied or revoked by the court on an application by the child, the agency or a person named in the order.

(2) The agency may refuse to allow the contact that would otherwise be required by virtue of an order under that section if –

    (a) it is satisfied that it is necessary to do so in order to safeguard or promote the child's welfare, and

    (b) the refusal is decided upon as a matter of urgency and does not last for more than seven days.

(3) Regulations may make provision as to –

    (a) the steps to be taken by an agency which has exercised its power under subsection (2),

(b) the circumstances in which, and conditions subject to which, the terms of any order under section 26 may be departed from by agreement between the agency and any person for whose contact with the child the order provides,

(c) notification by an agency of any variation or suspension of arrangements made (otherwise than under an order under that section) with a view to allowing any person contact with the child.

(4) Before making a placement order the court must –

(a) consider the arrangements which the adoption agency has made, or proposes to make, for allowing any person contact with the child, and

(b) invite the parties to the proceedings to comment on those arrangements.

(5) An order under section 26 may provide for contact on any conditions the court considers appropriate.

28 Further consequences of placement

(1) Where a child is placed for adoption under section 19 or an adoption agency is authorised to place a child for adoption under that section –

(a) a parent or guardian of the child may not apply for a residence order unless an application for an adoption order has been made and the parent or guardian has obtained the court's leave under subsection (3) or (5) of section 47,

(b) if an application has been made for an adoption order, a guardian of the child may not apply for a special guardianship order unless he has obtained the court's leave under subsection (3) or (5) of that section.

(2) Where –

(a) a child is placed for adoption under section 19 or an adoption agency is authorised to place a child for adoption under that section, or

(b) a placement order is in force in respect of a child,

then (whether or not the child is in England and Wales) a person may not do either of the following things, unless the court gives leave or each parent or guardian of the child gives written consent.

(3) Those things are –

(a) causing the child to be known by a new surname, or

(b) removing the child from the United Kingdom.

(4) Subsection (3) does not prevent the removal of a child from the United Kingdom for a period of less than one month by a person who provides the child's home.

29 Further consequences of placement orders

(1) Where a placement order is made in respect of a child and either –

(a) the child is subject to a care order, or

(b) the court at the same time makes a care order in respect of the child,

the care order does not have effect at any time when the placement order is in force.

(2) On the making of a placement order in respect of a child, any order mentioned in section 8(1) of the 1989 Act, and any supervision order in respect of the child, ceases to have effect.

(3) Where a placement order is in force –

(a) no prohibited steps order, residence order or specific issue order, and

(b) no supervision order or child assessment order,

may be made in respect of the child.

(4) Subsection (3)(a) does not apply in respect of a residence order if –

(a) an application for an adoption order has been made in respect of the child, and

(b) the residence order is applied for by a parent or guardian who has obtained the court's leave under subsection (3) or (5) of section 47 or by any other person who has obtained the court's leave under this subsection.

(5) Where a placement order is in force, no special guardianship order may be made in respect of the child unless –

(a) an application has been made for an adoption order, and

(b) the person applying for the special guardianship order has obtained the court's leave under this subsection or, if he is a guardian of the child, has obtained the court's leave under section 47(5).

(6) Section 14A(7) of the 1989 Act applies in respect of an application for a special guardianship order for which leave has been given as mentioned in subsection (5)(b) with the omission of the words 'the beginning of the period of three months ending with'.

(7) Where a placement order is in force –

(a) section 14C(1)(b) of the 1989 Act (special guardianship: parental responsibility) has effect subject to any determination under section 25(4) of this Act,

(b) section 14C(3) and (4) of the 1989 Act (special guardianship: removal of child from UK etc) does not apply.

Removal of children who are or may be placed by adoption agencies

30 General prohibitions on removal

(1) Where –

(a) a child is placed for adoption by an adoption agency under section 19, or

(b) a child is placed for adoption by an adoption agency and either the child is less than six weeks old or the agency has at no time been authorised to place the child for adoption,

a person (other than the agency) must not remove the child from the prospective adopters.

(2) Where –

(a) a child who is not for the time being placed for adoption is being provided with accommodation by a local authority, and

(b) the authority have applied to the court for a placement order and the application has not been disposed of,

only a person who has the court's leave (or the authority) may remove the child from the accommodation.

(3) Where subsection (2) does not apply, but –

(a) a child who is not for the time being placed for adoption is being provided with accommodation by an adoption agency, and

(b) the agency is authorised to place the child for adoption under section 19 or would be so authorised if any consent to placement under that section had not been withdrawn, a person (other than the agency) must not remove the child from the accommodation.

(4) This section is subject to sections 31 to 33 but those sections do not apply if the child is subject to a care order.

(5) This group of sections (that is, this section and those sections) apply whether or not the child in question is in England and Wales.

(6) This group of sections does not affect the exercise by any local authority or other person of any power conferred by any enactment, other than section 20(8) of the 1989 Act (removal of children from local authority accommodation).

(7) This group of sections does not prevent the removal of a child who is arrested.

(8) A person who removes a child in contravention of this section is guilty of an offence and liable on summary conviction to imprisonment for a term not exceeding three months, or a fine not exceeding level 5 on the standard scale, or both.

31 Recovery by parent etc where child not placed or is a baby

(1) Subsection (2) applies where –

(a) a child who is not for the time being placed for adoption is being provided with accommodation by an adoption agency, and
(b) the agency would be authorised to place the child for adoption under section 19 if consent to placement under that section had not been withdrawn.

(2) If any parent or guardian of the child informs the agency that he wishes the child to be returned to him, the agency must return the child to him within the period of seven days beginning with the request unless an application is, or has been, made for a placement order and the application has not been disposed of.

(3) Subsection (4) applies where –

(a) a child is placed for adoption by an adoption agency and either the child is less than six weeks old or the agency has at no time been authorised to place the child for adoption, and
(b) any parent or guardian of the child informs the agency that he wishes the child to be returned to him,

unless an application is, or has been, made for a placement order and the application has not been disposed of.

(4) The agency must give notice of the parent's or guardian's wish to the prospective adopters who must return the child to the agency within the period of seven days beginning with the day on which the notice is given.

(5) A prospective adopter who fails to comply with subsection (4) is guilty of an offence and liable on summary conviction to imprisonment for a term not exceeding three months, or a fine not exceeding level 5 on the standard scale, or both.

(6) As soon as a child is returned to an adoption agency under subsection (4), the agency must return the child to the parent or guardian in question.

32 Recovery by parent etc where child placed and consent withdrawn

(1) This section applies where –

(a) a child is placed for adoption by an adoption agency under section 19, and

    (b) consent to placement under that section has been withdrawn,

unless an application is, or has been, made for a placement order and the application has not been disposed of.

(2) If a parent or guardian of the child informs the agency that he wishes the child to be returned to him –

    (a) the agency must give notice of the parent's or guardian's wish to the prospective adopters, and

    (b) the prospective adopters must return the child to the agency within the period of 14 days beginning with the day on which the notice is given.

(3) A prospective adopter who fails to comply with subsection (2)(b) is guilty of an offence and liable on summary conviction to imprisonment for a term not exceeding three months, or a fine not exceeding level 5 on the standard scale, or both.

(4) As soon as a child is returned to an adoption agency under this section, the agency must return the child to the parent or guardian in question.

(5) Where a notice under subsection (2) is given, but –

    (a) before the notice was given, an application for an adoption order (including a Scottish or Northern Irish adoption order), special guardianship order or residence order, or for leave to apply for a special guardianship order or residence order, was made in respect of the child, and

    (b) the application (and, in a case where leave is given on an application to apply for a special guardianship order or residence order, the application for the order) has not been disposed of,

the prospective adopters are not required by virtue of the notice to return the child to the agency unless the court so orders.

33 Recovery by parent etc where child placed and placement order refused

(1) This section applies where –

    (a) a child is placed for adoption by a local authority under section 19,
    (b) the authority have applied for a placement order and the application has been refused, and
    (c) any parent or guardian of the child informs the authority that he wishes the child to be returned to him.

(2) The prospective adopters must return the child to the authority on a date determined by the court.

(3) A prospective adopter who fails to comply with subsection (2) is guilty of an offence and liable on summary conviction to imprisonment for a term not exceeding three months, or a fine not exceeding level 5 on the standard scale, or both.

(4) As soon as a child is returned to the authority, they must return the child to the parent or guardian in question.

34 Placement orders: prohibition on removal

(1) Where a placement order in respect of a child –

    (a) is in force, or
    (b) has been revoked, but the child has not been returned by the prospective adopters or remains in any accommodation provided by the local authority,

a person (other than the local authority) may not remove the child from the prospective adopters or from accommodation provided by the authority.

(2) A person who removes a child in contravention of subsection (1) is guilty of an offence.

(3) Where a court revoking a placement order in respect of a child determines that the child is not to remain with any former prospective adopters with whom the child is placed, they must return the child to the local authority within the period determined by the court for the purpose; and a person who fails to do so is guilty of an offence.

(4) Where a court revoking a placement order in respect of a child determines that the child is to be returned to a parent or guardian, the local authority must return the child to the parent or guardian as soon as the child is returned to the authority or, where the child is in accommodation provided by the authority, at once.

(5) A person guilty of an offence under this section is liable on summary conviction to imprisonment for a term not exceeding three months, or a fine not exceeding level 5 on the standard scale, or both.

(6) This section does not affect the exercise by any local authority or other person of a power conferred by any enactment, other than section 20(8) of the 1989 Act.

(7) This section does not prevent the removal of a child who is arrested.

(8) This section applies whether or not the child in question is in England and Wales.

35 Return of child in other cases

(1) Where a child is placed for adoption by an adoption agency and the prospective adopters give notice to the agency of their wish to return the child, the agency must –

    (a) receive the child from the prospective adopters before the end of the period of seven days beginning with the giving of the notice, and

    (b) give notice to any parent or guardian of the child of the prospective adopters' wish to return the child.

(2) Where a child is placed for adoption by an adoption agency, and the agency –

    (a) is of the opinion that the child should not remain with the prospective adopters, and

    (b) gives notice to them of its opinion,

the prospective adopters must, not later than the end of the period of seven days beginning with the giving of the notice, return the child to the agency.

(3) If the agency gives notice under subsection (2)(b), it must give notice to any parent or guardian of the child of the obligation to return the child to the agency.

(4) A prospective adopter who fails to comply with subsection (2) is guilty of an offence and liable on summary conviction to imprisonment for a term not exceeding three months, or a fine not exceeding level 5 on the standard scale, or both.

(5) Where –

    (a) an adoption agency gives notice under subsection (2) in respect of a child,

    (b) before the notice was given, an application for an adoption order (including a Scottish or Northern Irish adoption order), special guardianship order or residence order, or for leave to apply for a special guardianship order or residence order, was made in respect of the child, and

(c) the application (and, in a case where leave is given on an application to apply for a special guardianship order or residence order, the application for the order) has not been disposed of,

prospective adopters are not required by virtue of the notice to return the child to the agency unless the court so orders.

(6) This section applies whether or not the child in question is in England and Wales.

Removal of children in non-agency cases

36 Restrictions on removal

(1) At any time when a child's home is with any persons ('the people concerned') with whom the child is not placed by an adoption agency, but the people concerned –

(a) have applied for an adoption order in respect of the child and the application has not been disposed of,
(b) have given notice of intention to adopt, or
(c) have applied for leave to apply for an adoption order under section 42(6) and the application has not been disposed of,

a person may remove the child only in accordance with the provisions of this group of sections (that is, this section and sections 37 to 40).

The reference to a child placed by an adoption agency includes a child placed by a Scottish or Northern Irish adoption agency.

(2) For the purposes of this group of sections, a notice of intention to adopt is to be disregarded if –

(a) the period of four months beginning with the giving of the notice has expired without the people concerned applying for an adoption order, or
(b) the notice is a second or subsequent notice of intention to adopt and was given during the period of five months beginning with the giving of the preceding notice.

(3) For the purposes of this group of sections, if the people concerned apply for leave to apply for an adoption order under section 42(6) and the leave is granted, the application for leave is not to be treated as disposed of until the period of three days beginning with the granting of the leave has expired.

(4) This section does not prevent the removal of a child who is arrested.

(5) Where a parent or guardian may remove a child from the people concerned in accordance with the provisions of this group of sections, the people concerned must at the request of the parent or guardian return the child to the parent or guardian at once.

(6) A person who –

(a) fails to comply with subsection (5), or
(b) removes a child in contravention of this section,

is guilty of an offence and liable on summary conviction to imprisonment for a term not exceeding three months, or a fine not exceeding level 5 on the standard scale, or both.

(7) This group of sections applies whether or not the child in question is in England and Wales.

37 Applicants for adoption

If section 36(1)(a) applies, the following persons may remove the child –

(a) a person who has the court's leave,

(b) a local authority or other person in the exercise of a power conferred by any enactment, other than section 20(8) of the 1989 Act.

38 Local authority foster parents

(1) This section applies if the child's home is with local authority foster parents.

(2) If –

(a) the child has had his home with the foster parents at all times during the period of five years ending with the removal and the foster parents have given notice of intention to adopt, or

(b) an application has been made for leave under section 42(6) and has not been disposed of,

the following persons may remove the child.

(3) They are –

(a) a person who has the court's leave,

(b) a local authority or other person in the exercise of a power conferred by any enactment, other than section 20(8) of the 1989 Act.

(4) If subsection (2) does not apply but –

(a) the child has had his home with the foster parents at all times during the period of one year ending with the removal, and

(b) the foster parents have given notice of intention to adopt,

the following persons may remove the child.

(5) They are –

(a) a person with parental responsibility for the child who is exercising the power in section 20(8) of the 1989 Act,

(b) a person who has the court's leave,

(c) a local authority or other person in the exercise of a power conferred by any enactment, other than section 20(8) of the 1989 Act.

39 Partners of parents

(1) This section applies if a child's home is with a partner of a parent and the partner has given notice of intention to adopt.

(2) If the child's home has been with the partner for not less than three years (whether continuous or not) during the period of five years ending with the removal, the following persons may remove the child –

(a) a person who has the court's leave,

(b) a local authority or other person in the exercise of a power conferred by any enactment, other than section 20(8) of the 1989 Act.

(3) If subsection (2) does not apply, the following persons may remove the child –

(a) a parent or guardian,

(b) a person who has the court's leave,

(c) a local authority or other person in the exercise of a power conferred by any enactment, other than section 20(8) of the 1989 Act.

40 Other non-agency cases

(1) In any case where sections 37 to 39 do not apply but –

(a) the people concerned have given notice of intention to adopt, or
(b) the people concerned have applied for leave under section 42(6) and the application has not been disposed of,

the following persons may remove the child.

(2) They are –

(a) a person who has the court's leave,
(b) a local authority or other person in the exercise of a power conferred by any enactment, other than section 20(8) of the 1989 Act.

Breach of restrictions on removal

41 Recovery orders

(1) This section applies where it appears to the court –

(a) that a child has been removed in contravention of any of the preceding provisions of this Chapter or that there are reasonable grounds for believing that a person intends to remove a child in contravention of those provisions, or
(b) that a person has failed to comply with section 31(4), 32(2), 33(2), 34(3) or 35(2).

(2) The court may, on the application of any person, by an order –

(a) direct any person who is in a position to do so to produce the child on request to any person mentioned in subsection (4),
(b) authorise the removal of the child by any person mentioned in that subsection,
(c) require any person who has information as to the child's whereabouts to disclose that information on request to any constable or officer of the court,
(d) authorise a constable to enter any premises specified in the order and search for the child, using reasonable force if necessary.

(3) Premises may only be specified under subsection (2)(d) if it appears to the court that there are reasonable grounds for believing the child to be on them.

(4) The persons referred to in subsection (2) are –

(a) any person named by the court,
(b) any constable,
(c) any person who, after the order is made under that subsection, is authorised to exercise any power under the order by an adoption agency which is authorised to place the child for adoption.

(5) A person who intentionally obstructs a person exercising a power of removal conferred by the order is guilty of an offence and liable on summary conviction to a fine not exceeding level 3 on the standard scale.

(6) A person must comply with a request to disclose information as required by the order even if the information sought might constitute evidence that he had committed an offence.

(7) But in criminal proceedings in which the person is charged with an offence (other than one mentioned in subsection (8)) –

(a) no evidence relating to the information provided may be adduced, and
(b) no question relating to the information may be asked,

by or on behalf of the prosecution, unless evidence relating to it is adduced, or a question relating to it is asked, in the proceedings by or on behalf of the person.

(8) The offences excluded from subsection (7) are –

(a) an offence under section 2 or 5 of the Perjury Act 1911 (false statements made on oath otherwise than in judicial proceedings or made otherwise than on oath),
(b) an offence under section 44(1) or (2) of the Criminal Law (Consolidation) (Scotland) Act 1995 (false statements made on oath or otherwise than on oath).

(9) An order under this section has effect in relation to Scotland as if it were an order made by the Court of Session which that court had jurisdiction to make.

Preliminaries to adoption

42 Child to live with adopters before application

(1) An application for an adoption order may not be made unless –

(a) if subsection (2) applies, the condition in that subsection is met,
(b) if that subsection does not apply, the condition in whichever is applicable of subsections (3) to (5) applies.

(2) If –

(a) the child was placed for adoption with the applicant or applicants by an adoption agency or in pursuance of an order of the High Court, or
(b) the applicant is a parent of the child,

the condition is that the child must have had his home with the applicant or, in the case of an application by a couple, with one or both of them at all times during the period of ten weeks preceding the application.

(3) If the applicant or one of the applicants is the partner of a parent of the child, the condition is that the child must have had his home with the applicant or, as the case may be, applicants at all times during the period of six months preceding the application.

(4) If the applicants are local authority foster parents, the condition is that the child must have had his home with the applicants at all times during the period of one year preceding the application.

(5) In any other case, the condition is that the child must have had his home with the applicant or, in the case of an application by a couple, with one or both of them for not less than three years (whether continuous or not) during the period of five years preceding the application.

(6) But subsections (4) and (5) do not prevent an application being made if the court gives leave to make it.

(7) An adoption order may not be made unless the court is satisfied that sufficient opportunities to see the child with the applicant or, in the case of an application by a couple, both of them together in the home environment have been given –

(a) where the child was placed for adoption with the applicant or applicants by an adoption agency, to that agency,
(b) in any other case, to the local authority within whose area the home is.

(8) In this section and sections 43 and 44(1) –

(a) references to an adoption agency include a Scottish or Northern Irish adoption agency,
(b) references to a child placed for adoption by an adoption agency are to be read accordingly.

43 Reports where child placed by agency

Where an application for an adoption order relates to a child placed for adoption by an adoption agency, the agency must –

(a) submit to the court a report on the suitability of the applicants and on any other matters relevant to the operation of section 1, and
(b) assist the court in any manner the court directs.

44 Notice of intention to adopt

(1) This section applies where persons (referred to in this section as 'proposed adopters') wish to adopt a child who is not placed for adoption with them by an adoption agency.

(2) An adoption order may not be made in respect of the child unless the proposed adopters have given notice to the appropriate local authority of their intention to apply for the adoption order (referred to in this Act as a 'notice of intention to adopt').

(3) The notice must be given not more than two years, or less than three months, before the date on which the application for the adoption order is made.

(4) Where –

(a) if a person were seeking to apply for an adoption order, subsection (4) or (5) of section 42 would apply, but
(b) the condition in the subsection in question is not met,

the person may not give notice of intention to adopt unless he has the court's leave to apply for an adoption order.

(5) On receipt of a notice of intention to adopt, the local authority must arrange for the investigation of the matter and submit to the court a report of the investigation.

(6) In particular, the investigation must, so far as practicable, include the suitability of the proposed adopters and any other matters relevant to the operation of section 1 in relation to the application.

(7) If a local authority receive a notice of intention to adopt in respect of a child whom they know was (immediately before the notice was given) looked after by another local authority, they must, not more than seven days after the receipt of the notice, inform the other local authority in writing that they have received the notice.

(8) Where –

(a) a local authority have placed a child with any persons otherwise than as prospective adopters, and
(b) the persons give notice of intention to adopt,

the authority are not to be treated as leaving the child with them as prospective adopters for the purposes of section 18(1)(b).

(9) In this section, references to the appropriate local authority, in relation to any proposed adopters, are –

(a) in prescribed cases, references to the prescribed local authority,

(b) in any other case, references to the local authority for the area in which, at the time of giving the notice of intention to adopt, they have their home,

and 'prescribed' means prescribed by regulations.

45 Suitability of adopters

(1) Regulations under section 9 may make provision as to the matters to be taken into account by an adoption agency in determining, or making any report in respect of, the suitability of any persons to adopt a child.

(2) In particular, the regulations may make provision for the purpose of securing that, in determining the suitability of a couple to adopt a child, proper regard is had to the need for stability and permanence in their relationship.

The making of adoption orders

46 Adoption orders

(1) An adoption order is an order made by the court on an application under section 50 or 51 giving parental responsibility for a child to the adopters or adopter.

(2) The making of an adoption order operates to extinguish –

(a) the parental responsibility which any person other than the adopters or adopter has for the adopted child immediately before the making of the order,

(b) any order under the 1989 Act or the Children (Northern Ireland) Order 1995 (SI 1995/755 (NI 2)),

(c) any order under the Children (Scotland) Act 1995 other than an excepted order, and

(d) any duty arising by virtue of an agreement or an order of a court to make payments, so far as the payments are in respect of the adopted child's maintenance or upbringing for any period after the making of the adoption order.

'Excepted order' means an order under section 9, 11(1)(d) or 13 of the Children (Scotland) Act 1995 or an exclusion order within the meaning of section 76(1) of that Act.

(3) An adoption order –

(a) does not affect parental responsibility so far as it relates to any period before the making of the order, and

(b) in the case of an order made on an application under section 51(2) by the partner of a parent of the adopted child, does not affect the parental responsibility of that parent or any duties of that parent within subsection (2)(d).

(4) Subsection (2)(d) does not apply to a duty arising by virtue of an agreement –

(a) which constitutes a trust, or

(b) which expressly provides that the duty is not to be extinguished by the making of an adoption order.

(5) An adoption order may be made even if the child to be adopted is already an adopted child.

(6) Before making an adoption order, the court must consider whether there should be arrangements for allowing any person contact with the child; and for that purpose the court must consider any existing or proposed arrangements and obtain any views of the parties to the proceedings.

47 Conditions for making adoption orders

(1) An adoption order may not be made if the child has a parent or guardian unless one of the following three conditions is met; but this section is subject to section 52 (parental etc consent).

(2) The first condition is that, in the case of each parent or guardian of the child, the court is satisfied –

   (a) that the parent or guardian consents to the making of the adoption order,
   (b) that the parent or guardian has consented under section 20 (and has not withdrawn the consent) and does not oppose the making of the adoption order, or
   (c) that the parent's or guardian's consent should be dispensed with.

(3) A parent or guardian may not oppose the making of an adoption order under subsection (2)(b) without the court's leave.

(4) The second condition is that –

   (a) the child has been placed for adoption by an adoption agency with the prospective adopters in whose favour the order is proposed to be made,
   (b) either –
      (i)   the child was placed for adoption with the consent of each parent or guardian and the consent of the mother was given when the child was at least six weeks old, or
      (ii) the child was placed for adoption under a placement order, and
   (c) no parent or guardian opposes the making of the adoption order.

(5) A parent or guardian may not oppose the making of an adoption order under the second condition without the court's leave.

(6) The third condition is that the child is free for adoption by virtue of an order made –

   (a) in Scotland, under section 18 of the Adoption (Scotland) Act 1978, or
   (b) in Northern Ireland, under Article 17(1) or 18(1) of the Adoption (Northern Ireland) Order 1987 (SI 1987/2203 (NI 22)).

(7) The court cannot give leave under subsection (3) or (5) unless satisfied that there has been a change in circumstances since the consent of the parent or guardian was given or, as the case may be, the placement order was made.

(8) An adoption order may not be made in relation to a person who is or has been married.

(9) An adoption order may not be made in relation to a person who has attained the age of 19 years.

48 Restrictions on making adoption orders

(1) The court may not hear an application for an adoption order in relation to a child, where a previous application to which subsection (2) applies made in relation to the child by the same persons was refused by any court, unless it appears to the court that, because of a change in circumstances or for any other reason, it is proper to hear the application.

(2) This subsection applies to any application –

   (a) for an adoption order or a Scottish or Northern Irish adoption order, or
   (b) for an order for adoption made in the Isle of Man or any of the Channel Islands.

49 Applications for adoption

(1) An application for an adoption order may be made by –

   (a) a couple, or

(b) one person,

but only if it is made under section 50 or 51 and one of the following conditions is met.

(2) The first condition is that at least one of the couple (in the case of an application under section 50) or the applicant (in the case of an application under section 51) is domiciled in a part of the British Islands.

(3) The second condition is that both of the couple (in the case of an application under section 50) or the applicant (in the case of an application under section 51) have been habitually resident in a part of the British Islands for a period of not less than one year ending with the date of the application.

(4) An application for an adoption order may only be made if the person to be adopted has not attained the age of 18 years on the date of the application.

(5) References in this Act to a child, in connection with any proceedings (whether or not concluded) for adoption, (such as 'child to be adopted' or 'adopted child') include a person who has attained the age of 18 years before the proceedings are concluded.

50 Adoption by couple

(1) An adoption order may be made on the application of a couple where both of them have attained the age of 21 years.

(2) An adoption order may be made on the application of a couple where –

(a) one of the couple is the mother or the father of the person to be adopted and has attained the age of 18 years, and
(b) the other has attained the age of 21 years.

51 Adoption by one person

(1) An adoption order may be made on the application of one person who has attained the age of 21 years and is not married.

(2) An adoption order may be made on the application of one person who has attained the age of 21 years if the court is satisfied that the person is the partner of a parent of the person to be adopted.

(3) An adoption order may be made on the application of one person who has attained the age of 21 years and is married if the court is satisfied that –

(a) the person's spouse cannot be found,
(b) the spouses have separated and are living apart, and the separation is likely to be permanent, or
(c) the person's spouse is by reason of ill-health, whether physical or mental, incapable of making an application for an adoption order.

(4) An adoption order may not be made on an application under this section by the mother or the father of the person to be adopted unless the court is satisfied that –

(a) the other natural parent is dead or cannot be found,
(b) by virtue of section 28 of the Human Fertilisation and Embryology Act 1990 , there is no other parent, or
(c) there is some other reason justifying the child's being adopted by the applicant alone,

and, where the court makes an adoption order on such an application, the court must record that it is satisfied as to the fact mentioned in paragraph (a) or (b) or, in the case of paragraph (c), record the reason.

Placement and adoption: general

52 Parental etc consent

(1) The court cannot dispense with the consent of any parent or guardian of a child to the child being placed for adoption or to the making of an adoption order in respect of the child unless the court is satisfied that –

  (a) the parent or guardian cannot be found or is incapable of giving consent, or
  (b) the welfare of the child requires the consent to be dispensed with.

(2) The following provisions apply to references in this Chapter to any parent or guardian of a child giving or withdrawing –

  (a) consent to the placement of a child for adoption, or
  (b) consent to the making of an adoption order (including a future adoption order).

(3) Any consent given by the mother to the making of an adoption order is ineffective if it is given less than six weeks after the child's birth.

(4) The withdrawal of any consent to the placement of a child for adoption, or of any consent given under section 20, is ineffective if it is given after an application for an adoption order is made.

(5) 'Consent' means consent given unconditionally and with full understanding of what is involved; but a person may consent to adoption without knowing the identity of the persons in whose favour the order will be made.

(6) 'Parent' (except in subsections (9) and (10) below) means a parent having parental responsibility.

(7) Consent under section 19 or 20 must be given in the form prescribed by rules, and the rules may prescribe forms in which a person giving consent under any other provision of this Part may do so (if he wishes).

(8) Consent given under section 19 or 20 must be withdrawn –

  (a) in the form prescribed by rules, or
  (b) by notice given to the agency.

(9) Subsection (10) applies if –

  (a) an agency has placed a child for adoption under section 19 in pursuance of consent given by a parent of the child, and
  (b) at a later time, the other parent of the child acquires parental responsibility for the child.

(10) The other parent is to be treated as having at that time given consent in accordance with this section in the same terms as those in which the first parent gave consent.

53 Modification of 1989 Act in relation to adoption

(1) Where –

  (a) a local authority are authorised to place a child for adoption, or
  (b) a child who has been placed for adoption by a local authority is less than six weeks old,

regulations may provide for the following provisions of the 1989 Act to apply with modifications, or not to apply, in relation to the child.

(2) The provisions are –

(a) section 22(4)(b), (c) and (d) and (5)(b) (duty to ascertain wishes and feelings of certain persons),

(b) paragraphs 15 and 21 of Schedule 2 (promoting contact with parents and parents' obligation to contribute towards maintenance).

(3) Where a registered adoption society is authorised to place a child for adoption or a child who has been placed for adoption by a registered adoption society is less than six weeks old, regulations may provide –

(a) for section 61 of that Act to have effect in relation to the child whether or not he is accommodated by or on behalf of the society,

(b) for subsections (2)(b) to (d) and (3)(b) of that section (duty to ascertain wishes and feelings of certain persons) to apply with modifications, or not to apply, in relation to the child.

(4) Where a child's home is with persons who have given notice of intention to adopt, no contribution is payable (whether under a contribution order or otherwise) under Part 3 of Schedule 2 to that Act (contributions towards maintenance of children looked after by local authorities) in respect of the period referred to in subsection (5).

(5) That period begins when the notice of intention to adopt is given and ends if –

(a) the period of four months beginning with the giving of the notice expires without the prospective adopters applying for an adoption order, or

(b) an application for such an order is withdrawn or refused.

(6) In this section, 'notice of intention to adopt' includes notice of intention to apply for a Scottish or Northern Irish adoption order.

54 Disclosing information during adoption process

Regulations under section 9 may require adoption agencies in prescribed circumstances to disclose in accordance with the regulations prescribed information to prospective adopters.

55 Revocation of adoptions on legitimation

(1) Where any child adopted by one natural parent as sole adoptive parent subsequently becomes a legitimated person on the marriage of the natural parents, the court by which the adoption order was made may, on the application of any of the parties concerned, revoke the order.

(2) In relation to an adoption order made by a magistrates' court, the reference in subsection (1) to the court by which the order was made includes a court acting for the same petty sessions area.

Disclosure of information in relation to a person's adoption

56 Information to be kept about a person's adoption

(1) In relation to an adopted person, regulations may prescribe –

(a) the information which an adoption agency must keep in relation to his adoption,

(b) the form and manner in which it must keep that information.

(2) Below in this group of sections (that is, this section and sections 57 to 65), any information kept by an adoption agency by virtue of subsection (1)(a) is referred to as section 56 information.

(3) Regulations may provide for the transfer in prescribed circumstances of information held, or previously held, by an adoption agency to another adoption agency.

57 Restrictions on disclosure of protected etc information

(1) Any section 56 information kept by an adoption agency which –

    (a) is about an adopted person or any other person, and
    (b) is or includes identifying information about the person in question,

may only be disclosed by the agency to a person (other than the person the information is about) in pursuance of this group of sections.

(2) Any information kept by an adoption agency –

    (a) which the agency has obtained from the Registrar General on an application under section 79(5) and any other information which would enable the adopted person to obtain a certified copy of the record of his birth, or
    (b) which is information about an entry relating to the adopted person in the Adoption Contact Register,

may only be disclosed to a person by the agency in pursuance of this group of sections.

(3) In this group of sections, information the disclosure of which to a person is restricted by virtue of subsection (1) or (2) is referred to (in relation to him) as protected information.

(4) Identifying information about a person means information which, whether taken on its own or together with other information disclosed by an adoption agency, identifies the person or enables the person to be identified.

(5) This section does not prevent the disclosure of protected information in pursuance of a prescribed agreement to which the adoption agency is a party.

(6) Regulations may authorise or require an adoption agency to disclose protected information to a person who is not an adopted person.

58 Disclosure of other information

(1) This section applies to any section 56 information other than protected information.

(2) An adoption agency may for the purposes of its functions disclose to any person in accordance with prescribed arrangements any information to which this section applies.

(3) An adoption agency must, in prescribed circumstances, disclose prescribed information to a prescribed person.

59 Offence

Regulations may provide that a registered adoption society which discloses any information in contravention of section 57 is to be guilty of an offence and liable on summary conviction to a fine not exceeding level 5 on the standard scale.

60 Disclosing information to adopted adult

(1) This section applies to an adopted person who has attained the age of 18 years.

(2) The adopted person has the right, at his request, to receive from the appropriate adoption agency –

    (a) any information which would enable him to obtain a certified copy of the record of his birth, unless the High Court orders otherwise,

(b) any prescribed information disclosed to the adopters by the agency by virtue of section 54.

(3) The High Court may make an order under subsection (2)(a), on an application by the appropriate adoption agency, if satisfied that the circumstances are exceptional.

(4) The adopted person also has the right, at his request, to receive from the court which made the adoption order a copy of any prescribed document or prescribed order relating to the adoption.

(5) Subsection (4) does not apply to a document or order so far as it contains information which is protected information.

61 Disclosing protected information about adults

(1) This section applies where –

(a) a person applies to the appropriate adoption agency for protected information to be disclosed to him, and
(b) none of the information is about a person who is a child at the time of the application.

(2) The agency is not required to proceed with the application unless it considers it appropriate to do so.

(3) If the agency does proceed with the application it must take all reasonable steps to obtain the views of any person the information is about as to the disclosure of the information about him.

(4) The agency may then disclose the information if it considers it appropriate to do so.

(5) In deciding whether it is appropriate to proceed with the application or disclose the information, the agency must consider –

(a) the welfare of the adopted person,
(b) any views obtained under subsection (3),
(c) any prescribed matters,

and all the other circumstances of the case.

(6) This section does not apply to a request for information under section 60(2) or to a request for information which the agency is authorised or required to disclose in pursuance of regulations made by virtue of section 57(6).

62 Disclosing protected information about children

(1) This section applies where –

(a) a person applies to the appropriate adoption agency for protected information to be disclosed to him, and
(b) any of the information is about a person who is a child at the time of the application.

(2) The agency is not required to proceed with the application unless it considers it appropriate to do so.

(3) If the agency does proceed with the application, then, so far as the information is about a person who is at the time a child, the agency must take all reasonable steps to obtain –

(a) the views of any parent or guardian of the child, and
(b) the views of the child, if the agency considers it appropriate to do so having regard to his age and understanding and to all the other circumstances of the case,

as to the disclosure of the information.

(4) And, so far as the information is about a person who has at the time attained the age of 18 years, the agency must take all reasonable steps to obtain his views as to the disclosure of the information.

(5) The agency may then disclose the information if it considers it appropriate to do so.

(6) In deciding whether it is appropriate to proceed with the application, or disclose the information, where any of the information is about a person who is at the time a child –

(a) if the child is an adopted child, the child's welfare must be the paramount consideration,
(b) in the case of any other child, the agency must have particular regard to the child's welfare.

(7) And, in deciding whether it is appropriate to proceed with the application or disclose the information, the agency must consider –

(a) the welfare of the adopted person (where subsection (6)(a) does not apply),
(b) any views obtained under subsection (3) or (4),
(c) any prescribed matters,

and all the other circumstances of the case.

(8) This section does not apply to a request for information under section 60(2) or to a request for information which the agency is authorised or required to disclose in pursuance of regulations made by virtue of section 57(6).

63 Counselling

(1) Regulations may require adoption agencies to give information about the availability of counselling to persons –

(a) seeking information from them in pursuance of this group of sections,
(b) considering objecting or consenting to the disclosure of information by the agency in pursuance of this group of sections, or
(c) considering entering with the agency into an agreement prescribed for the purposes of section 57(5).

(2) Regulations may require adoption agencies to make arrangements to secure the provision of counselling for persons seeking information from them in prescribed circumstances in pursuance of this group of sections.

(3) The regulations may authorise adoption agencies –

(a) to disclose information which is required for the purposes of such counselling to the persons providing the counselling,
(b) where the person providing the counselling is outside the United Kingdom, to require a prescribed fee to be paid.

(4) The regulations may require any of the following persons to provide counselling for the purposes of arrangements under subsection (2) –

(a) a local authority, a council constituted under section 2 of the Local Government etc (Scotland) Act 1994 or a Health and Social Services Board established under Article 16 of the Health and Personal Social Services (Northern Ireland) Order 1972 (SI 1972/1265 (NI 14)),
(b) a registered adoption society, an organisation within section 144(3)(b) or an adoption society which is registered under Article 4 of the Adoption (Northern Ireland) Order 1987 (SI 1987/2203 (NI 22)),
(c) an adoption support agency in respect of which a person is registered under Part 2 of the Care Standards Act 2000.

(5) For the purposes of subsection (4), where the functions of a Health and Social Services Board are exercisable by a Health and Social Services Trust, the reference in sub-paragraph (a) to a Board is to be read as a reference to the Health and Social Services Trust.

64 Other provision to be made by regulations

(1) Regulations may make provision for the purposes of this group of sections, including provision as to –

(a) the performance by adoption agencies of their functions,
(b) the manner in which information may be received, and
(c) the matters mentioned below in this section.

(2) Regulations may prescribe –

(a) the manner in which agreements made by virtue of section 57(5) are to be recorded,
(b) the information to be provided by any person on an application for the disclosure of information under this group of sections.

(3) Regulations may require adoption agencies –

(a) to give to prescribed persons prescribed information about the rights or opportunities to obtain information, or to give their views as to its disclosure, given by this group of sections,
(b) to seek prescribed information from, or give prescribed information to, the Registrar General in prescribed circumstances.

(4) Regulations may require the Registrar General –

(a) to disclose to any person (including an adopted person) at his request any information which the person requires to assist him to make contact with the adoption agency which is the appropriate adoption agency in the case of an adopted person specified in the request (or, as the case may be, in the applicant's case),
(b) to disclose to the appropriate adoption agency any information which the agency requires about any entry relating to the adopted person on the Adoption Contact Register.

(5) Regulations may provide for the payment of a prescribed fee in respect of the disclosure in prescribed circumstances of any information in pursuance of section 60, 61 or 62; but an adopted person may not be required to pay any fee in respect of any information disclosed to him in relation to any person who (but for his adoption) would be related to him by blood (including half-blood) or marriage.

(6) Regulations may provide for the payment of a prescribed fee by an adoption agency obtaining information under subsection (4)(b).

65 Sections 56 to 65: interpretation

(1) In this group of sections –

'appropriate adoption agency', in relation to an adopted person or to information relating to his adoption, means –

(a) if the person was placed for adoption by an adoption agency, that agency or (if different) the agency which keeps the information in relation to his adoption,
(b) in any other case, the local authority to which notice of intention to adopt was given,

'prescribed' means prescribed by subordinate legislation,

'regulations' means regulations under section 9,

'subordinate legislation' means regulations or, in relation to information to be given by a court, rules.

(2) But –

    (a) regulations under section 63(2) imposing any requirement on a council constituted under section 2 of the Local Government etc (Scotland) Act 1994 , or an organisation within section 144(3)(b), are to be made by the Scottish Ministers,

    (b) regulations under section 63(2) imposing any requirement on a Health and Social Services Board established under Article 16 of the Health and Personal Social Services (Northern Ireland) Order 1972 (SI 1972/1265 (NI 14)), or an adoption society which is registered under Article 4 of the Adoption (Northern Ireland) Order 1987 (SI 1987/2203 (NI 22)), are to be made by the Department of Health, Social Services and Public Safety.

(3) The power of the Scottish Ministers or of the Department of Health, Social Services and Public Safety to make regulations under section 63(2) includes power to make –

    (a) any supplementary, incidental or consequential provision,

    (b) any transitory, transitional or saving provision,

which the person making the regulations considers necessary or expedient.

(4) Regulations prescribing any fee by virtue of section 64(6) require the approval of the Chancellor of the Exchequer.

(5) Regulations making any provision as to the manner in which any application is to be made for the disclosure of information by the Registrar General require his approval.

Chapter 4

Status of Adopted Children

66 Meaning of adoption in Chapter 4

(1) In this Chapter 'adoption' means –

    (a) adoption by an adoption order or a Scottish or Northern Irish adoption order,

    (b) adoption by an order made in the Isle of Man or any of the Channel Islands,

    (c) an adoption effected under the law of a Convention country outside the British Islands, and certified in pursuance of Article 23(1) of the Convention (referred to in this Act as a 'Convention adoption'),

    (d) an overseas adoption, or

    (e) an adoption recognised by the law of England and Wales and effected under the law of any other country;

and related expressions are to be interpreted accordingly.

(2) But references in this Chapter to adoption do not include an adoption effected before the day on which this Chapter comes into force (referred to in this Chapter as 'the appointed day').

(3) Any reference in an enactment to an adopted person within the meaning of this Chapter includes a reference to an adopted child within the meaning of Part 4 of the Adoption Act 1976.

67 Status conferred by adoption

(1) An adopted person is to be treated in law as if born as the child of the adopters or adopter.

(2) An adopted person is the legitimate child of the adopters or adopter and, if adopted by –

(a) a couple, or

(b) one of a couple under section 51(2),

is to be treated as the child of the relationship of the couple in question.

(3) An adopted person –

(a) if adopted by one of a couple under section 51(2), is to be treated in law as not being the child of any person other than the adopter and the other one of the couple, and

(b) in any other case, is to be treated in law, subject to subsection (4), as not being the child of any person other than the adopters or adopter;

but this subsection does not affect any reference in this Act to a person's natural parent or to any other natural relationship.

(4) In the case of a person adopted by one of the person's natural parents as sole adoptive parent, subsection (3)(b) has no effect as respects entitlement to property depending on relationship to that parent, or as respects anything else depending on that relationship.

(5) This section has effect from the date of the adoption.

(6) Subject to the provisions of this Chapter and Schedule 4, this section –

(a) applies for the interpretation of enactments or instruments passed or made before as well as after the adoption, and so applies subject to any contrary indication, and

(b) has effect as respects things done, or events occurring, on or after the adoption.

68 Adoptive relatives

(1) A relationship existing by virtue of section 67 may be referred to as an adoptive relationship, and –

(a) an adopter may be referred to as an adoptive parent or (as the case may be) as an adoptive father or adoptive mother,

(b) any other relative of any degree under an adoptive relationship may be referred to as an adoptive relative of that degree.

(2) Subsection (1) does not affect the interpretation of any reference, not qualified by the word 'adoptive', to a relationship.

(3) A reference (however expressed) to the adoptive mother and father of a child adopted by –

(a) a couple of the same sex, or

(b) a partner of the child's parent, where the couple are of the same sex,

is to be read as a reference to the child's adoptive parents.

69 Rules of interpretation for instruments concerning property

(1) The rules of interpretation contained in this section apply (subject to any contrary indication and to Schedule 4) to any instrument so far as it contains a disposition of property.

(2) In applying section 67(1) and (2) to a disposition which depends on the date of birth of a child or children of the adoptive parent or parents, the disposition is to be interpreted as if –

(a) the adopted person had been born on the date of adoption,

(b) two or more people adopted on the same date had been born on that date in the order of their actual births;

but this does not affect any reference to a person's age.

(3) Examples of phrases in wills on which subsection (2) can operate are –

1. Children of A 'living at my death or born afterwards'.
2. Children of A 'living at my death or born afterwards before any one of such children for the time being in existence attains a vested interest and who attain the age of 21 years'.
3. As in example 1 or 2, but referring to grandchildren of A instead of children of A.
4. A for life 'until he has a child', and then to his child or children.

Note. Subsection (2) will not affect the reference to the age of 21 years in example 2.

(4) Section 67(3) does not prejudice –

(a) any qualifying interest, or
(b) any interest expectant (whether immediately or not) upon a qualifying interest.

'Qualifying interest' means an interest vested in possession in the adopted person before the adoption.

(5) Where it is necessary to determine for the purposes of a disposition of property effected by an instrument whether a woman can have a child –

(a) it must be presumed that once a woman has attained the age of 55 years she will not adopt a person after execution of the instrument, and
(b) if she does so, then (in spite of section 67) that person is not to be treated as her child or (if she does so as one of a couple) as the child of the other one of the couple for the purposes of the instrument.

(6) In this section, 'instrument' includes a private Act settling property, but not any other enactment.

70 Dispositions depending on date of birth

(1) Where a disposition depends on the date of birth of a person who was born illegitimate and who is adopted by one of the natural parents as sole adoptive parent, section 69(2) does not affect entitlement by virtue of Part 3 of the Family Law Reform Act 1987 (dispositions of property).

(2) Subsection (1) applies for example where –

(a) a testator dies in 2001 bequeathing a legacy to his eldest grandchild living at a specified time,
(b) his unmarried daughter has a child in 2002 who is the first grandchild,
(c) his married son has a child in 2003,
(d) subsequently his unmarried daughter adopts her child as sole adoptive parent.

In that example the status of the daughter's child as the eldest grandchild of the testator is not affected by the events described in paragraphs (c) and (d).

71 Property devolving with peerages etc

(1) An adoption does not affect the descent of any peerage or dignity or title of honour.

(2) An adoption does not affect the devolution of any property limited (expressly or not) to devolve (as nearly as the law permits) along with any peerage or dignity or title of honour.

(3) Subsection (2) applies only if and so far as a contrary intention is not expressed in the instrument, and has effect subject to the terms of the instrument.

72 Protection of trustees and personal representatives

(1) A trustee or personal representative is not under a duty, by virtue of the law relating to trusts or the administration of estates, to enquire, before conveying or distributing any property, whether any adoption has been effected or revoked if that fact could affect entitlement to the property.

(2) A trustee or personal representative is not liable to any person by reason of a conveyance or distribution of the property made without regard to any such fact if he has not received notice of the fact before the conveyance or distribution.

(3) This section does not prejudice the right of a person to follow the property, or any property representing it, into the hands of another person, other than a purchaser, who has received it.

73 Meaning of disposition

(1) This section applies for the purposes of this Chapter.

(2) A disposition includes the conferring of a power of appointment and any other disposition of an interest in or right over property; and in this subsection a power of appointment includes any discretionary power to transfer a beneficial interest in property without the furnishing of valuable consideration.

(3) This Chapter applies to an oral disposition as if contained in an instrument made when the disposition was made.

(4) The date of death of a testator is the date at which a will or codicil is to be regarded as made.

(5) The provisions of the law of intestate succession applicable to the estate of a deceased person are to be treated as if contained in an instrument executed by him (while of full capacity) immediately before his death.

74 Miscellaneous enactments

(1) Section 67 does not apply for the purposes of –

  (a) the table of kindred and affinity in Schedule 1 to the Marriage Act 1949,
  (b) sections 10 and 11 of the Sexual Offences Act 1956 (incest), or
  (c) section 54 of the Criminal Law Act 1977 (inciting a girl to commit incest).

(2) Section 67 does not apply for the purposes of any provision of –

  (a) the British Nationality Act 1981,
  (b) the Immigration Act 1971,
  (c) any instrument having effect under an enactment within paragraph (a) or (b), or
  (d) any other provision of the law for the time being in force which determines British citizenship, British overseas territories citizenship, the status of a British National (Overseas) or British Overseas citizenship.

75 Pensions

Section 67(3) does not affect entitlement to a pension which is payable to or for the benefit of a person and is in payment at the time of the person's adoption.

76 Insurance

(1) Where a child is adopted whose natural parent has effected an insurance with a friendly society or a collecting society or an industrial insurance company for the payment on the death of the child of money for funeral expenses, then –

(a) the rights and liabilities under the policy are by virtue of the adoption transferred to the adoptive parents, and

(b) for the purposes of the enactments relating to such societies and companies, the adoptive parents are to be treated as the person who took out the policy.

(2) Where the adoption is effected by an order made by virtue of section 51(2), the references in subsection (1) to the adoptive parents are to be read as references to the adopter and the other one of the couple.

Chapter 5

The Registers

Adopted Children Register etc

77 Adopted Children Register

(1) The Registrar General must continue to maintain in the General Register Office a register, to be called the Adopted Children Register.

(2) The Adopted Children Register is not to be open to public inspection or search.

(3) No entries may be made in the Adopted Children Register other than entries –

(a) directed to be made in it by adoption orders, or
(b) required to be made under Schedule 1.

(4) A certified copy of an entry in the Adopted Children Register, if purporting to be sealed or stamped with the seal of the General Register Office, is to be received as evidence of the adoption to which it relates without further or other proof.

(5) Where an entry in the Adopted Children Register contains a record –

(a) of the date of birth of the adopted person, or
(b) of the country, or the district and sub-district, of the birth of the adopted person,

a certified copy of the entry is also to be received, without further or other proof, as evidence of that date, or country or district and sub-district, (as the case may be) in all respects as if the copy were a certified copy of an entry in the registers of live-births.

(6) Schedule 1 (registration of adoptions and the amendment of adoption orders) is to have effect.

78 Searches and copies

(1) The Registrar General must continue to maintain at the General Register Office an index of the Adopted Children Register.

(2) Any person may –

(a) search the index,
(b) have a certified copy of any entry in the Adopted Children Register.

(3) But a person is not entitled to have a certified copy of an entry in the Adopted Children Register relating to an adopted person who has not attained the age of 18 years unless the applicant has provided the Registrar General with the prescribed particulars.

'Prescribed' means prescribed by regulations made by the Registrar General with the approval of the Chancellor of the Exchequer.

(4) The terms, conditions and regulations as to payment of fees, and otherwise, applicable under the Births and Deaths Registration Act 1953, and the Registration Service Act 1953, in respect of –

(a) searches in the index kept in the General Register Office of certified copies of entries in the registers of live-births,
(b) the supply from that office of certified copies of entries in those certified copies,

also apply in respect of searches, and supplies of certified copies, under subsection (2).

79 Connections between the register and birth records

(1) The Registrar General must make traceable the connection between any entry in the registers of live-births or other records which has been marked 'Adopted' and any corresponding entry in the Adopted Children Register.

(2) Information kept by the Registrar General for the purposes of subsection (1) is not to be open to public inspection or search.

(3) Any such information, and any other information which would enable an adopted person to obtain a certified copy of the record of his birth, may only be disclosed by the Registrar General in accordance with this section.

(4) In relation to a person adopted before the appointed day the court may, in exceptional circumstances, order the Registrar General to give any information mentioned in subsection (3) to a person.

(5) On an application made in the prescribed manner by the appropriate adoption agency in respect of an adopted person a record of whose birth is kept by the Registrar General, the Registrar General must give the agency any information relating to the adopted person which is mentioned in subsection (3).

'Appropriate adoption agency' has the same meaning as in section 65.

(6) In relation to a person adopted before the appointed day, Schedule 2 applies instead of subsection (5).

(7) On an application made in the prescribed manner by an adopted person a record of whose birth is kept by the Registrar General and who –

(a) is under the age of 18 years, and
(b) intends to be married,

the Registrar General must inform the applicant whether or not it appears from information contained in the registers of live-births or other records that the applicant and the person whom the applicant intends to marry may be within the prohibited degrees of relationship for the purposes of the Marriage Act 1949.

(8) Before the Registrar General gives any information by virtue of this section, any prescribed fee which he has demanded must be paid.

(9) In this section –

'appointed day' means the day appointed for the commencement of sections 56 to 65,
'prescribed' means prescribed by regulations made by the Registrar General with the approval of the Chancellor of the Exchequer.

Adoption Contact Register

80 Adoption Contact Register

(1) The Registrar General must continue to maintain at the General Register Office in accordance with regulations a register in two Parts to be called the Adoption Contact Register.

(2) Part 1 of the register is to contain the prescribed information about adopted persons who have given the prescribed notice expressing their wishes as to making contact with their relatives.

(3) The Registrar General may only make an entry in Part 1 of the register for an adopted person –

- (a) a record of whose birth is kept by the Registrar General,
- (b) who has attained the age of 18 years, and
- (c) who the Registrar General is satisfied has such information as is necessary to enable him to obtain a certified copy of the record of his birth.

(4) Part 2 of the register is to contain the prescribed information about persons who have given the prescribed notice expressing their wishes, as relatives of adopted persons, as to making contact with those persons.

(5) The Registrar General may only make an entry in Part 2 of the register for a person –

- (a) who has attained the age of 18 years, and
- (b) who the Registrar General is satisfied is a relative of an adopted person and has such information as is necessary to enable him to obtain a certified copy of the record of the adopted person's birth.

(6) Regulations may provide for –

- (a) the disclosure of information contained in one Part of the register to persons for whom there is an entry in the other Part,
- (b) the payment of prescribed fees in respect of the making or alteration of entries in the register and the disclosure of information contained in the register.

81 Adoption Contact Register: supplementary

(1) The Adoption Contact Register is not to be open to public inspection or search.

(2) In section 80, 'relative', in relation to an adopted person, means any person who (but for his adoption) would be related to him by blood (including half-blood) or marriage.

(3) The Registrar General must not give any information entered in the register to any person except in accordance with subsection (6)(a) of that section or regulations made by virtue of section 64(4)(b).

(4) In section 80, 'regulations' means regulations made by the Registrar General with the approval of the Chancellor of the Exchequer, and 'prescribed' means prescribed by such regulations.

General

82 Interpretation

(1) In this Chapter –

'records' includes certified copies kept by the Registrar General of entries in any register of births,
'registers of live-births' means the registers of live-births made under the Births and Deaths Registration Act 1953.

(2) Any register, record or index maintained under this Chapter may be maintained in any form the Registrar General considers appropriate; and references (however expressed) to entries in such a register, or to their amendment, marking or cancellation, are to be read accordingly.

Chapter 6

Adoptions with a Foreign Element

Bringing children into and out of the United Kingdom

83 Restriction on bringing children in

(1) This section applies where a person who is habitually resident in the British Islands (the 'British resident') –

    (a) brings, or causes another to bring, a child who is habitually resident outside the British Islands into the United Kingdom for the purpose of adoption by the British resident, or

    (b) at any time brings, or causes another to bring, into the United Kingdom a child adopted by the British resident under an external adoption effected within the period of six months ending with that time.

The references to adoption, or to a child adopted, by the British resident include a reference to adoption, or to a child adopted, by the British resident and another person.

(2) But this section does not apply if the child is intended to be adopted under a Convention adoption order.

(3) An external adoption means an adoption, other than a Convention adoption, of a child effected under the law of any country or territory outside the British Islands, whether or not the adoption is –

    (a) an adoption within the meaning of Chapter 4, or

    (b) a full adoption (within the meaning of section 88(3)).

(4) Regulations may require a person intending to bring, or to cause another to bring, a child into the United Kingdom in circumstances where this section applies –

    (a) to apply to an adoption agency (including a Scottish or Northern Irish adoption agency) in the prescribed manner for an assessment of his suitability to adopt the child, and

    (b) to give the agency any information it may require for the purpose of the assessment.

(5) Regulations may require prescribed conditions to be met in respect of a child brought into the United Kingdom in circumstances where this section applies.

(6) In relation to a child brought into the United Kingdom for adoption in circumstances where this section applies, regulations may –

    (a) provide for any provision of Chapter 3 to apply with modifications or not to apply,

    (b) if notice of intention to adopt has been given, impose functions in respect of the child on the local authority to which the notice was given.

(7) If a person brings, or causes another to bring, a child into the United Kingdom at any time in circumstances where this section applies, he is guilty of an offence if –

    (a) he has not complied with any requirement imposed by virtue of subsection (4), or

    (b) any condition required to be met by virtue of subsection (5) is not met,

before that time, or before any later time which may be prescribed.

(8) A person guilty of an offence under this section is liable –

(a) on summary conviction to imprisonment for a term not exceeding six months, or a fine not exceeding the statutory maximum, or both,

(b) on conviction on indictment, to imprisonment for a term not exceeding twelve months, or a fine, or both.

(9) In this section, 'prescribed' means prescribed by regulations and 'regulations' means regulations made by the Secretary of State, after consultation with the Assembly.

84 Giving parental responsibility prior to adoption abroad

(1) The High Court may, on an application by persons who the court is satisfied intend to adopt a child under the law of a country or territory outside the British Islands, make an order giving parental responsibility for the child to them.

(2) An order under this section may not give parental responsibility to persons who the court is satisfied meet those requirements as to domicile, or habitual residence, in England and Wales which have to be met if an adoption order is to be made in favour of those persons.

(3) An order under this section may not be made unless any requirements prescribed by regulations are satisfied.

(4) An application for an order under this section may not be made unless at all times during the preceding ten weeks the child's home was with the applicant or, in the case of an application by two people, both of them.

(5) Section 46(2) to (4) has effect in relation to an order under this section as it has effect in relation to adoption orders.

(6) Regulations may provide for any provision of this Act which refers to adoption orders to apply, with or without modifications, to orders under this section.

(7) In this section, 'regulations' means regulations made by the Secretary of State, after consultation with the Assembly.

85 Restriction on taking children out

(1) A child who –

(a) is a Commonwealth citizen, or
(b) is habitually resident in the United Kingdom,

must not be removed from the United Kingdom to a place outside the British Islands for the purpose of adoption unless the condition in subsection (2) is met.

(2) The condition is that –

(a) the prospective adopters have parental responsibility for the child by virtue of an order under section 84, or
(b) the child is removed under the authority of an order under section 49 of the Adoption (Scotland) Act 1978 or Article 57 of the Adoption (Northern Ireland) Order 1987 (SI 1987/2203 (NI 22)).

(3) Removing a child from the United Kingdom includes arranging to do so; and the circumstances in which a person arranges to remove a child from the United Kingdom include those where he –

(a) enters into an arrangement for the purpose of facilitating such a removal of the child,

(b) initiates or takes part in any negotiations of which the purpose is the conclusion of an arrangement within paragraph (a), or

(c) causes another person to take any step mentioned in paragraph (a) or (b).

An arrangement includes an agreement (whether or not enforceable).

(4) A person who removes a child from the United Kingdom in contravention of subsection (1) is guilty of an offence.

(5) A person is not guilty of an offence under subsection (4) of causing a person to take any step mentioned in paragraph (a) or (b) of subsection (3) unless it is proved that he knew or had reason to suspect that the step taken would contravene subsection (1).

But this subsection only applies if sufficient evidence is adduced to raise an issue as to whether the person had the knowledge or reason mentioned.

(6) A person guilty of an offence under this section is liable –

(a) on summary conviction to imprisonment for a term not exceeding six months, or a fine not exceeding the statutory maximum, or both,

(b) on conviction on indictment, to imprisonment for a term not exceeding twelve months, or a fine, or both.

(7) In any proceedings under this section –

(a) a report by a British consular officer or a deposition made before a British consular officer and authenticated under the signature of that officer is admissible, upon proof that the officer or the deponent cannot be found in the United Kingdom, as evidence of the matters stated in it, and

(b) it is not necessary to prove the signature or official character of the person who appears to have signed any such report or deposition.

86 Power to modify sections 83 and 85

(1) Regulations may provide for section 83 not to apply if –

(a) the adopters or (as the case may be) prospective adopters are natural parents, natural relatives or guardians of the child in question (or one of them is), or

(b) the British resident in question is a partner of a parent of the child,

and any prescribed conditions are met.

(2) Regulations may provide for section 85(1) to apply with modifications, or not to apply, if –

(a) the prospective adopters are parents, relatives or guardians of the child in question (or one of them is), or

(b) the prospective adopter is a partner of a parent of the child,

and any prescribed conditions are met.

(3) On the occasion of the first exercise of the power to make regulations under this section –

(a) the statutory instrument containing the regulations is not to be made unless a draft of the instrument has been laid before, and approved by a resolution of, each House of Parliament, and

(b) accordingly section 140(2) does not apply to the instrument.

(4) In this section, 'prescribed' means prescribed by regulations and 'regulations' means regulations made by the Secretary of State after consultation with the Assembly.

Overseas adoptions

87 Overseas adoptions

(1) In this Act, 'overseas adoption' –

   (a) means an adoption of a description specified in an order made by the Secretary of State, being a description of adoptions effected under the law of any country or territory outside the British Islands, but
   (b) does not include a Convention adoption.

(2) Regulations may prescribe the requirements that ought to be met by an adoption of any description effected after the commencement of the regulations for it to be an overseas adoption for the purposes of this Act.

(3) At any time when such regulations have effect, the Secretary of State must exercise his powers under this section so as to secure that subsequently effected adoptions of any description are not overseas adoptions for the purposes of this Act if he considers that they are not likely within a reasonable time to meet the prescribed requirements.

(4) In this section references to this Act include the Adoption Act 1976.

(5) An order under this section may contain provision as to the manner in which evidence of any overseas adoption may be given.

(6) In this section –

   'adoption' means an adoption of a child or of a person who was a child at the time the adoption was applied for,
   'regulations' means regulations made by the Secretary of State after consultation with the Assembly.

Commencement—Subsections (1)(b) and (4) in force from 1 June 2003 (SI 2003/366).

Miscellaneous

88 Modification of section 67 for Hague Convention adoptions

(1) If the High Court is satisfied, on an application under this section, that each of the following conditions is met in the case of a Convention adoption, it may direct that section 67(3) does not apply, or does not apply to any extent specified in the direction.

(2) The conditions are –

   (a) that under the law of the country in which the adoption was effected, the adoption is not a full adoption,
   (b) that the consents referred to in Article 4(c) and (d) of the Convention have not been given for a full adoption or that the United Kingdom is not the receiving State (within the meaning of Article 2 of the Convention),
   (c) that it would be more favourable to the adopted child for a direction to be given under subsection (1).

(3) A full adoption is an adoption by virtue of which the child is to be treated in law as not being the child of any person other than the adopters or adopter.

(4) In relation to a direction under this section and an application for it, sections 59 and 60 of the Family Law Act 1986 (declarations under Part 3 of that Act as to marital status) apply as they apply in relation to a direction under that Part and an application for such a direction.

89 Annulment etc of overseas or Hague Convention adoptions

(1) The High Court may, on an application under this subsection, by order annul a Convention adoption or Convention adoption order on the ground that the adoption is contrary to public policy.

(2) The High Court may, on an application under this subsection –

 (a) by order provide for an overseas adoption or a determination under section 91 to cease to be valid on the ground that the adoption or determination is contrary to public policy or that the authority which purported to authorise the adoption or make the determination was not competent to entertain the case, or
 (b) decide the extent, if any, to which a determination under section 91 has been affected by a subsequent determination under that section.

(3) The High Court may, in any proceedings in that court, decide that an overseas adoption or a determination under section 91 is to be treated, for the purposes of those proceedings, as invalid on either of the grounds mentioned in subsection (2)(a).

(4) Subject to the preceding provisions, the validity of a Convention adoption, Convention adoption order or overseas adoption or a determination under section 91 cannot be called in question in proceedings in any court in England and Wales.

90 Section 89: supplementary

(1) Any application for an order under section 89 or a decision under subsection (2)(b) or (3) of that section must be made in the prescribed manner and within any prescribed period.

 'Prescribed' means prescribed by rules.

(2) No application may be made under section 89(1) in respect of an adoption unless immediately before the application is made –

 (a) the person adopted, or
 (b) the adopters or adopter,

habitually reside in England and Wales.

(3) In deciding in pursuance of section 89 whether such an authority as is mentioned in section 91 was competent to entertain a particular case, a court is bound by any finding of fact made by the authority and stated by the authority to be so made for the purpose of determining whether the authority was competent to entertain the case.

91 Overseas determinations and orders

(1) Subsection (2) applies where any authority of a Convention country (other than the United Kingdom) or of the Channel Islands, the Isle of Man or any British overseas territory has power under the law of that country or territory –

 (a) to authorise, or review the authorisation of, an adoption order made in that country or territory, or
 (b) to give or review a decision revoking or annulling such an order or a Convention adoption.

(2) If the authority makes a determination in the exercise of that power, the determination is to have effect for the purpose of effecting, confirming or terminating the adoption in question or, as the case may be, confirming its termination.

(3) Subsection (2) is subject to section 89 and to any subsequent determination having effect under that subsection.

Chapter 7

Miscellaneous

Restrictions

92 Restriction on arranging adoptions etc

(1) A person who is neither an adoption agency nor acting in pursuance of an order of the High Court must not take any of the steps mentioned in subsection (2).

(2) The steps are –

  (a) asking a person other than an adoption agency to provide a child for adoption,
  (b) asking a person other than an adoption agency to provide prospective adopters for a child,
  (c) offering to find a child for adoption,
  (d) offering a child for adoption to a person other than an adoption agency,
  (e) handing over a child to any person other than an adoption agency with a view to the child's adoption by that or another person,
  (f) receiving a child handed over to him in contravention of paragraph (e),
  (g) entering into an agreement with any person for the adoption of a child, or for the purpose of facilitating the adoption of a child, where no adoption agency is acting on behalf of the child in the adoption,
  (h) initiating or taking part in negotiations of which the purpose is the conclusion of an agreement within paragraph (g),
  (i) causing another person to take any of the steps mentioned in paragraphs (a) to (h).

(3) Subsection (1) does not apply to a person taking any of the steps mentioned in paragraphs (d), (e), (g), (h) and (i) of subsection (2) if the following condition is met.

(4) The condition is that –

  (a) the prospective adopters are parents, relatives or guardians of the child (or one of them is), or
  (b) the prospective adopter is the partner of a parent of the child.

(5) References to an adoption agency in subsection (2) include a prescribed person outside the United Kingdom exercising functions corresponding to those of an adoption agency, if the functions are being exercised in prescribed circumstances in respect of the child in question.

(6) The Secretary of State may, after consultation with the Assembly, by order make any amendments of subsections (1) to (4), and any consequential amendments of this Act, which he considers necessary or expedient.

(7) In this section –

  (a) 'agreement' includes an arrangement (whether or not enforceable),
  (b) 'prescribed' means prescribed by regulations made by the Secretary of State after consultation with the Assembly.

93 Offence of breaching restrictions under section 92

(1) If a person contravenes section 92(1), he is guilty of an offence; and, if that person is an adoption society, the person who manages the society is also guilty of the offence.

(2) A person is not guilty of an offence under subsection (1) of taking the step mentioned in paragraph (f) of section 92(2) unless it is proved that he knew or had reason to suspect that the child was handed over to him in contravention of paragraph (e) of that subsection.

(3) A person is not guilty of an offence under subsection (1) of causing a person to take any of the steps mentioned in paragraphs (a) to (h) of section 92(2) unless it is proved that he knew or had reason to suspect that the step taken would contravene the paragraph in question.

(4) But subsections (2) and (3) only apply if sufficient evidence is adduced to raise an issue as to whether the person had the knowledge or reason mentioned.

(5) A person guilty of an offence under this section is liable on summary conviction to imprisonment for a term not exceeding six months, or a fine not exceeding £10,000, or both.

94 Restriction on reports

(1) A person who is not within a prescribed description may not, in any prescribed circumstances, prepare a report for any person about the suitability of a child for adoption or of a person to adopt a child or about the adoption, or placement for adoption, of a child.

'Prescribed' means prescribed by regulations made by the Secretary of State after consultation with the Assembly.

(2) If a person –

  (a) contravenes subsection (1), or
  (b) causes a person to prepare a report, or submits to any person a report which has been prepared, in contravention of that subsection,

he is guilty of an offence.

(3) If a person who works for an adoption society –

  (a) contravenes subsection (1), or
  (b) causes a person to prepare a report, or submits to any person a report which has been prepared, in contravention of that subsection,

the person who manages the society is also guilty of the offence.

(4) A person is not guilty of an offence under subsection (2)(b) unless it is proved that he knew or had reason to suspect that the report would be, or had been, prepared in contravention of subsection (1).

But this subsection only applies if sufficient evidence is adduced to raise an issue as to whether the person had the knowledge or reason mentioned.

(5) A person guilty of an offence under this section is liable on summary conviction to imprisonment for a term not exceeding six months, or a fine not exceeding level 5 on the standard scale, or both.

95 Prohibition of certain payments

(1) This section applies to any payment (other than an excepted payment) which is made for or in consideration of –

  (a) the adoption of a child,
  (b) giving any consent required in connection with the adoption of a child,
  (c) removing from the United Kingdom a child who is a Commonwealth citizen, or is habitually resident in the United Kingdom, to a place outside the British Islands for the purpose of adoption,
  (d) a person (who is neither an adoption agency nor acting in pursuance of an order of the High Court) taking any step mentioned in section 92(2),

(e) preparing, causing to be prepared or submitting a report the preparation of which contravenes section 94(1).

(2) In this section and section 96, removing a child from the United Kingdom has the same meaning as in section 85.

(3) Any person who –

(a) makes any payment to which this section applies,
(b) agrees or offers to make any such payment, or
(c) receives or agrees to receive or attempts to obtain any such payment,

is guilty of an offence.

(4) A person guilty of an offence under this section is liable on summary conviction to imprisonment for a term not exceeding six months, or a fine not exceeding £10,000, or both.

96 Excepted payments

(1) A payment is an excepted payment if it is made by virtue of, or in accordance with provision made by or under, this Act, the Adoption (Scotland) Act 1978 or the Adoption (Northern Ireland) Order 1987 (SI 1987/2203 (NI 22)).

(2) A payment is an excepted payment if it is made to a registered adoption society by –

(a) a parent or guardian of a child, or
(b) a person who adopts or proposes to adopt a child,

in respect of expenses reasonably incurred by the society in connection with the adoption or proposed adoption of the child.

(3) A payment is an excepted payment if it is made in respect of any legal or medical expenses incurred or to be incurred by any person in connection with an application to a court which he has made or proposes to make for an adoption order, a placement order, or an order under section 26 or 84.

(4) A payment made as mentioned in section 95(1)(c) is an excepted payment if –

(a) the condition in section 85(2) is met, and
(b) the payment is made in respect of the travel and accommodation expenses reasonably incurred in removing the child from the United Kingdom for the purpose of adoption.

97 Sections 92 to 96: interpretation

In sections 92 to 96 –

(a) 'adoption agency' includes a Scottish or Northern Irish adoption agency,
(b) 'payment' includes reward,
(c) references to adoption are to the adoption of persons, wherever they may be habitually resident, effected under the law of any country or territory, whether within or outside the British Islands.

Information

98 Pre-commencement adoptions: information

(1) Regulations under section 9 may make provision for the purpose of –

(a) assisting persons adopted before the appointed day who have attained the age of 18 to obtain information in relation to their adoption, and
(b) facilitating contact between such persons and their relatives.

(2) For that purpose the regulations may confer functions on –

(a) registered adoption support agencies,
(b) the Registrar General,
(c) adoption agencies.

(3) For that purpose the regulations may –

(a) authorise or require any person mentioned in subsection (2) to disclose information,
(b) authorise or require the disclosure of information contained in records kept under section 8 of the Public Records Act 1958 (court records),

and may impose conditions on the disclosure of information, including conditions restricting its further disclosure.

(4) The regulations may authorise the charging of prescribed fees by any person mentioned in subsection (2) or in respect of the disclosure of information under subsection (3)(b).

(5) An authorisation or requirement to disclose information by virtue of subsection (3)(a) has effect in spite of any restriction on the disclosure of information in Chapter 5.

(6) The making of regulations by virtue of subsections (2) to (4) which relate to the Registrar General requires the approval of the Chancellor of the Exchequer.

(7) In this section –

'appointed day' means the day appointed for the commencement of sections 56 to 65,
'registered adoption support agency' means an adoption support agency in respect of which a person is registered under Part 2 of the Care Standards Act 2000,
'relative', in relation to an adopted person, means any person who (but for his adoption) would be related to him by blood (including half-blood) or marriage.

Proceedings

99 Proceedings for offences

Proceedings for an offence by virtue of section 9 or 59 may not, without the written consent of the Attorney General, be taken by any person other than the National Care Standards Commission or the Assembly.

100 Appeals

In section 94 of the 1989 Act (appeals under that Act), in subsections (1)(a) and (2), after 'this Act' there is inserted 'or the Adoption and Children Act 2002'.

101 Privacy

(1) Proceedings under this Act in the High Court or a County Court may be heard and determined in private.

(2) In section 12 of the Administration of Justice Act 1960 (publication of information relating to proceedings in private), in subsection (1)(a)(ii), after '1989' there is inserted 'or the Adoption and Children Act 2002'.

(3) In section 97 of the 1989 Act (privacy for children involved in certain proceedings), after 'this Act' in subsections (1) and (2) there is inserted 'or the Adoption and Children Act 2002'.

The Children and Family Court Advisory and Support Service

102 Officers of the Service

(1) For the purposes of –

(a) any relevant application,
(b) the signification by any person of any consent to placement or adoption,

rules must provide for the appointment in prescribed cases of an officer of the Children and Family Court Advisory and Support Service ('the Service').

(2) The rules may provide for the appointment of such an officer in other circumstances in which it appears to the Lord Chancellor to be necessary or expedient to do so.

(3) The rules may provide for the officer –

(a) to act on behalf of the child upon the hearing of any relevant application, with the duty of safeguarding the interests of the child in the prescribed manner,
(b) where the court so requests, to prepare a report on matters relating to the welfare of the child in question,
(c) to witness documents which signify consent to placement or adoption,
(d) to perform prescribed functions.

(4) A report prepared in pursuance of the rules on matters relating to the welfare of a child must –

(a) deal with prescribed matters (unless the court orders otherwise), and
(b) be made in the manner required by the court.

(5) A person who –

(a) in the case of an application for the making, varying or revocation of a placement order, is employed by the local authority which made the application,
(b) in the case of an application for an adoption order in respect of a child who was placed for adoption, is employed by the adoption agency which placed him, or
(c) is within a prescribed description,

is not to be appointed under subsection (1) or (2).

(6) In this section, 'relevant application' means an application for –

(a) the making, varying or revocation of a placement order,
(b) the making of an order under section 26, or the varying or revocation of such an order,
(c) the making of an adoption order, or
(d) the making of an order under section 84.

(7) Rules may make provision as to the assistance which the court may require an officer of the Service to give to it.

103 Right of officers of the Service to have access to adoption agency records

(1) Where an officer of the Service has been appointed to act under section 102(1), he has the right at all reasonable times to examine and take copies of any records of, or held by, an adoption agency

which were compiled in connection with the making, or proposed making, by any person of any application under this Part in respect of the child concerned.

(2) Where an officer of the Service takes a copy of any record which he is entitled to examine under this section, that copy or any part of it is admissible as evidence of any matter referred to in any –

    (a) report which he makes to the court in the proceedings in question, or

    (b) evidence which he gives in those proceedings.

(3) Subsection (2) has effect regardless of any enactment or rule of law which would otherwise prevent the record in question being admissible in evidence.

Evidence

104 Evidence of consent

(1) If a document signifying any consent which is required by this Part to be given is witnessed in accordance with rules, it is to be admissible in evidence without further proof of the signature of the person by whom it was executed.

(2) A document signifying any such consent which purports to be witnessed in accordance with rules is to be presumed to be so witnessed, and to have been executed and witnessed on the date and at the place specified in the document, unless the contrary is proved.

Scotland, Northern Ireland and the Islands

105–108 (*not reproduced*)

General

109 Avoiding delay

(1) In proceedings in which a question may arise as to whether an adoption order or placement order should be made, or any other question with respect to such an order, the court must (in the light of any rules made by virtue of subsection (2)) –

    (a) draw up a timetable with a view to determining such a question without delay, and

    (b) give such directions as it considers appropriate for the purpose of ensuring that the timetable is adhered to.

(2) Rules may –

    (a) prescribe periods within which prescribed steps must be taken in relation to such proceedings, and

    (b) make other provision with respect to such proceedings for the purpose of ensuring that such questions are determined without delay.

110 Service of notices etc

Any notice or information required to be given by virtue of this Act may be given by post.

PART 2

AMENDMENTS OF THE CHILDREN ACT 1989

111   Parental responsibility of unmarried father

(1) Section 4 of the 1989 Act (acquisition of responsibility by the father of a child who is not married to the child's mother) is amended as follows.

(2) In subsection (1) (cases where parental responsibility is acquired), for the words after 'birth' there is substituted ', the father shall acquire parental responsibility for the child if –

- (a) he becomes registered as the child's father under any of the enactments specified in subsection (1A);
- (b) he and the child's mother make an agreement (a 'parental responsibility agreement') providing for him to have parental responsibility for the child; or
- (c) the court, on his application, orders that he shall have parental responsibility for the child.'

(3) After that subsection there is inserted –

'(1A) The enactments referred to in subsection (1)(a) are –

- (a) paragraphs (a), (b) and (c) of section 10(1) and of section 10A(1) of the Births and Deaths Registration Act 1953;
- (b) paragraphs (a), (b)(i) and (c) of section 18(1), and sections 18(2)(b) and 20(1)(a) of the Registration of Births, Deaths and Marriages (Scotland) Act 1965; and
- (c) sub-paragraphs (a), (b) and (c) of Article 14(3) of the Births and Deaths Registration (Northern Ireland) Order 1976.

(1B) The Lord Chancellor may by order amend subsection (1A) so as to add further enactments to the list in that subsection.'

(4) For subsection (3) there is substituted –

'(2A) A person who has acquired parental responsibility under subsection (1) shall cease to have that responsibility only if the court so orders.

(3) The court may make an order under subsection (2A) on the application –

- (a) of any person who has parental responsibility for the child; or
- (b) with the leave of the court, of the child himself,

subject, in the case of parental responsibility acquired under subsection (1)(c), to section 12(4).'

(5) Accordingly, in section 2(2) of the 1989 Act (a father of a child who is not married to the child's mother shall not have parental responsibility for the child unless he acquires it in accordance with the provisions of the Act), for the words from 'shall not' to 'acquires it' there is substituted 'shall have parental responsibility for the child if he has acquired it (and has not ceased to have it)'.

(6) In section 104 of the 1989 Act (regulations and orders) –

- (a) in subsection (2), after 'section' there is inserted '4(1B),', and
- (b) in subsection (3), after 'section' there is inserted '4(1B) or'.

(7) Paragraph (a) of section 4(1) of the 1989 Act, as substituted by subsection (2) of this section, does not confer parental responsibility on a man who was registered under an enactment referred to in paragraph (a), (b) or (c) of section 4(1A) of that Act, as inserted by subsection (3) of this section, before the commencement of subsection (3) in relation to that paragraph.

112 Acquisition of parental responsibility by step-parent

After section 4 of the 1989 Act there is inserted –

'4A Acquisition of parental responsibility by step-parent

(1) Where a child's parent ("parent A") who has parental responsibility for the child is married to a person who is not the child's parent ("the step-parent") –

    (a) parent A or, if the other parent of the child also has parental responsibility for the child, both parents may by agreement with the step-parent provide for the step-parent to have parental responsibility for the child; or

    (b) the court may, on the application of the step-parent, order that the step-parent shall have parental responsibility for the child.

(2) An agreement under subsection (1)(a) is also a "parental responsibility agreement", and section 4(2) applies in relation to such agreements as it applies in relation to parental responsibility agreements under section 4.

(3) A parental responsibility agreement under subsection (1)(a), or an order under subsection (1)(b), may only be brought to an end by an order of the court made on the application –

    (a) of any person who has parental responsibility for the child; or

    (b) with the leave of the court, of the child himself.

(4) The court may only grant leave under subsection (3)(b) if it is satisfied that the child has sufficient understanding to make the proposed application.'

113 Section 8 orders: local authority foster parents

In section 9 of the 1989 Act (restrictions on making section 8 orders) –

    (a) in subsection (3)(c), for 'three years' there is substituted 'one year', and

    (b) subsection (4) is omitted.

114 Residence orders: extension to age of 18

(1) In section 12 of the 1989 Act (residence orders and parental responsibility), after subsection (4) there is inserted –

    '(5) The power of a court to make a residence order in favour of any person who is not the parent or guardian of the child concerned includes power to direct, at the request of that person, that the order continue in force until the child reaches the age of eighteen (unless the order is brought to an end earlier); and any power to vary a residence order is exercisable accordingly.

    (6) Where a residence order includes such a direction, an application to vary or discharge the order may only be made, if apart from this subsection the leave of the court is not required, with such leave'.

(2) In section 9 of that Act (restrictions on making section 8 orders), at the beginning of subsection (6) there is inserted 'Subject to section 12(5)'.

(3) In section 91 of that Act (effect and duration of orders), in subsection (10), after '9(6)' there is inserted 'or 12(5)'.

115 Special guardianship

(1) After section 14 of the 1989 Act there is inserted –

'Special guardianship

14A Special guardianship orders

(1) A "special guardianship order" is an order appointing one or more individuals to be a child's "special guardian" (or special guardians).

(2) A special guardian –

  (a) must be aged eighteen or over; and
  (b) must not be a parent of the child in question,

and subsections (3) to (6) are to be read in that light.

(3) The court may make a special guardianship order with respect to any child on the application of an individual who –

  (a) is entitled to make such an application with respect to the child; or
  (b) has obtained the leave of the court to make the application,

or on the joint application of more than one such individual.

(4) Section 9(3) applies in relation to an application for leave to apply for a special guardianship order as it applies in relation to an application for leave to apply for a section 8 order.

(5) The individuals who are entitled to apply for a special guardianship order with respect to a child are –

  (a) any guardian of the child;
  (b) any individual in whose favour a residence order is in force with respect to the child;
  (c) any individual listed in subsection (5)(b) or (c) of section 10 (as read with subsection (10) of that section);
  (d) a local authority foster parent with whom the child has lived for a period of at least one year immediately preceding the application.

(6) The court may also make a special guardianship order with respect to a child in any family proceedings in which a question arises with respect to the welfare of the child if –

  (a) an application for the order has been made by an individual who falls within subsection (3)(a) or (b) (or more than one such individual jointly); or
  (b) the court considers that a special guardianship order should be made even though no such application has been made.

(7) No individual may make an application under subsection (3) or (6)(a) unless, before the beginning of the period of three months ending with the date of the application, he has given written notice of his intention to make the application –

  (a) if the child in question is being looked after by a local authority, to that local authority, or
  (b) otherwise, to the local authority in whose area the individual is ordinarily resident.

(8) On receipt of such a notice, the local authority must investigate the matter and prepare a report for the court dealing with –

  (a) the suitability of the applicant to be a special guardian;

(b) such matters (if any) as may be prescribed by the Secretary of State; and

(c) any other matter which the local authority consider to be relevant.

(9) The court may itself ask a local authority to conduct such an investigation and prepare such a report, and the local authority must do so.

(10) The local authority may make such arrangements as they see fit for any person to act on their behalf in connection with conducting an investigation or preparing a report referred to in subsection (8) or (9).

(11) The court may not make a special guardianship order unless it has received a report dealing with the matters referred to in subsection (8).

(12) Subsections (8) and (9) of section 10 apply in relation to special guardianship orders as they apply in relation to section 8 orders.

(13) This section is subject to section 29(5) and (6) of the Adoption and Children Act 2002.

14B Special guardianship orders: making

(1) Before making a special guardianship order, the court must consider whether, if the order were made –

(a) a contact order should also be made with respect to the child, and

(b) any section 8 order in force with respect to the child should be varied or discharged.

(2) On making a special guardianship order, the court may also –

(a) give leave for the child to be known by a new surname;

(b) grant the leave required by section 14C(3)(b), either generally or for specified purposes.

14C Special guardianship orders: effect

(1) The effect of a special guardianship order is that while the order remains in force –

(a) a special guardian appointed by the order has parental responsibility for the child in respect of whom it is made; and

(b) subject to any other order in force with respect to the child under this Act, a special guardian is entitled to exercise parental responsibility to the exclusion of any other person with parental responsibility for the child (apart from another special guardian).

(2) Subsection (1) does not affect –

(a) the operation of any enactment or rule of law which requires the consent of more than one person with parental responsibility in a matter affecting the child; or

(b) any rights which a parent of the child has in relation to the child's adoption or placement for adoption.

(3) While a special guardianship order is in force with respect to a child, no person may –

(a) cause the child to be known by a new surname; or

(b) remove him from the United Kingdom,

without either the written consent of every person who has parental responsibility for the child or the leave of the court.

(4) Subsection (3)(b) does not prevent the removal of a child, for a period of less than three months, by a special guardian of his.

(5) If the child with respect to whom a special guardianship order is in force dies, his special guardian must take reasonable steps to give notice of that fact to –

(a) each parent of the child with parental responsibility; and
(b) each guardian of the child,

but if the child has more than one special guardian, and one of them has taken such steps in relation to a particular parent or guardian, any other special guardian need not do so as respects that parent or guardian.

(6) This section is subject to section 29(7) of the Adoption and Children Act 2002.

14D Special guardianship orders: variation and discharge

(1) The court may vary or discharge a special guardianship order on the application of –

(a) the special guardian (or any of them, if there are more than one);
(b) any parent or guardian of the child concerned;
(c) any individual in whose favour a residence order is in force with respect to the child;
(d) any individual not falling within any of paragraphs (a) to (c) who has, or immediately before the making of the special guardianship order had, parental responsibility for the child;
(e) the child himself; or
(f) a local authority designated in a care order with respect to the child.

(2) In any family proceedings in which a question arises with respect to the welfare of a child with respect to whom a special guardianship order is in force, the court may also vary or discharge the special guardianship order if it considers that the order should be varied or discharged, even though no application has been made under subsection (1).

(3) The following must obtain the leave of the court before making an application under subsection (1) –

(a) the child;
(b) any parent or guardian of his;
(c) any step-parent of his who has acquired, and has not lost, parental responsibility for him by virtue of section 4A;
(d) any individual falling within subsection (1)(d) who immediately before the making of the special guardianship order had, but no longer has, parental responsibility for him.

(4) Where the person applying for leave to make an application under subsection (1) is the child, the court may only grant leave if it is satisfied that he has sufficient understanding to make the proposed application under subsection (1).

(5) The court may not grant leave to a person falling within subsection (3)(b)(c) or (d) unless it is satisfied that there has been a significant change in circumstances since the making of the special guardianship order.

14E Special guardianship orders: supplementary

(1) In proceedings in which any question of making, varying or discharging a special guardianship order arises, the court shall (in the light of any rules made by virtue of subsection (3)) –

(a) draw up a timetable with a view to determining the question without delay; and
(b) give such directions as it considers appropriate for the purpose of ensuring, so far as is reasonably practicable, that the timetable is adhered to.

(2) Subsection (1) applies also in relation to proceedings in which any other question with respect to a special guardianship order arises.

(3) The power to make rules in subsection (2) of section 11 applies for the purposes of this section as it applies for the purposes of that.

(4) A special guardianship order, or an order varying one, may contain provisions which are to have effect for a specified period.

(5) Section 11(7) (apart from paragraph (c)) applies in relation to special guardianship orders and orders varying them as it applies in relation to section 8 orders.

14F Special guardianship support services

(1) Each local authority must make arrangements for the provision within their area of special guardianship support services, which means –

  (a) counselling, advice and information; and
  (b) such other services as are prescribed,

in relation to special guardianship.

(2) The power to make regulations under subsection (1)(b) is to be exercised so as to secure that local authorities provide financial support.

(3) At the request of any of the following persons –

  (a) a child with respect to whom a special guardianship order is in force;
  (b) a special guardian;
  (c) a parent;
  (d) any other person who falls within a prescribed description,

a local authority may carry out an assessment of that person's needs for special guardianship support services (but, if the Secretary of State so provides in regulations, they must do so if he is a person of a prescribed description, or if his case falls within a prescribed description, or if both he and his case fall within prescribed descriptions).

(4) A local authority may, at the request of any other person, carry out an assessment of that person's needs for special guardianship support services.

(5) Where, as a result of an assessment, a local authority decide that a person has needs for special guardianship support services, they must then decide whether to provide any such services to that person.

(6) If –

  (a) a local authority decide to provide any special guardianship support services to a person, and
  (b) the circumstances fall within a prescribed description,

the local authority must prepare a plan in accordance with which special guardianship support services are to be provided to him, and keep the plan under review.

(7) The Secretary of State may by regulations make provision about assessments, preparing and reviewing plans, the provision of special guardianship support services in accordance with plans and reviewing the provision of special guardianship support services.

(8) The regulations may in particular make provision –

(a) about the type of assessment which is to be carried out, or the way in which an assessment is to be carried out;

(b) about the way in which a plan is to be prepared;

(c) about the way in which, and the time at which, a plan or the provision of special guardianship support services is to be reviewed;

(d) about the considerations to which a local authority are to have regard in carrying out an assessment or review or preparing a plan;

(e) as to the circumstances in which a local authority may provide special guardianship support services subject to conditions (including conditions as to payment for the support or the repayment of financial support);

(f) as to the consequences of conditions imposed by virtue of paragraph (e) not being met (including the recovery of any financial support provided);

(g) as to the circumstances in which this section may apply to a local authority in respect of persons who are outside that local authority's area;

(h) as to the circumstances in which a local authority may recover from another local authority the expenses of providing special guardianship support services to any person.

(9) A local authority may provide special guardianship support services (or any part of them) by securing their provision by –

(a) another local authority; or

(b) a person within a description prescribed in regulations of persons who may provide special guardianship support services,

and may also arrange with any such authority or person for that other authority or that person to carry out the local authority's functions in relation to assessments under this section.

(10) A local authority may carry out an assessment of the needs of any person for the purposes of this section at the same time as an assessment of his needs is made under any other provision of this Act or under any other enactment.

(11) Section 27 (co-operation between authorities) applies in relation to the exercise of functions of a local authority under this section as it applies in relation to the exercise of functions of a local authority under Part 3.

14G Special guardianship support services: representations

(1) Every local authority shall establish a procedure for considering representations (including complaints) made to them by any person to whom they may provide special guardianship support services about the discharge of their functions under section 14F in relation to him.

(2) Regulations may be made by the Secretary of State imposing time limits on the making of representations under subsection (1).

(3) In considering representations under subsection (1), a local authority shall comply with regulations (if any) made by the Secretary of State for the purposes of this subsection.'

(2) The 1989 Act is amended as follows.

(3) In section 1 (welfare of the child), in subsection (4)(b), after 'discharge' there is inserted 'a special guardianship order or'.

(4) In section 5 (appointment of guardians) –

(a) in subsection (1) –

(i) in paragraph (b), for 'or guardian' there is substituted ', guardian or special guardian', and

(ii)   at the end of paragraph (b) there is inserted '; or

(c)   paragraph (b) does not apply, and the child's only or last surviving special guardian dies.',

(b)   in subsection (4), at the end there is inserted '; and a special guardian of a child may appoint another individual to be the child's guardian in the event of his death', and

(c)   in subsection (7), at the end of paragraph (b) there is inserted 'or he was the child's only (or last surviving) special guardian'.

116 Accommodation of children in need etc

(1) In section 17 of the 1989 Act (provision of services for children in need, their families and others), in subsection (6) (services that may be provided in exercise of the functions under that section) after 'include' there is inserted 'providing accommodation and'.

(2) In section 22 of that Act (general duty of local authority in relation to children looked after by them), in subsection (1) (looked after children include those provided with accommodation, with exceptions) before '23B' there is inserted '17'.

(3) In section 24A of that Act (advice and assistance for certain children and young persons aged 16 or over), in subsection (5), for 'or, in exceptional circumstances, cash' there is substituted 'and, in exceptional circumstances, assistance may be given –

(a)   by providing accommodation, if in the circumstances assistance may not be given in respect of the accommodation under section 24B, or

(b)   in cash'.

Commencement—7 November 2002 (Royal Assent).

117 Inquiries by local authorities into representations

(1) In section 24D of the 1989 Act (representations: sections 23A to 24B), after subsection (1) there is inserted –

'(1A) Regulations may be made by the Secretary of State imposing time limits on the making of representations under subsection (1).'

(2) Section 26 of that Act (procedure for considering other representations) is amended as follows.

(3) In subsection (3) (which makes provision as to the persons by whom, and the matters in respect of which, representations may be made), for 'functions under this Part' there is substituted 'qualifying functions'.

(4) After that subsection there is inserted –

'(3A) The following are qualifying functions for the purposes of subsection (3) –

(a)   functions under this Part,

(b)   such functions under Part 4 or 5 as are specified by the Secretary of State in regulations.

(3B) The duty under subsection (3) extends to representations (including complaints) made to the authority by –

(a)   any person mentioned in section 3(1) of the Adoption and Children Act 2002 (persons for whose needs provision is made by the Adoption Service) and any other person to whom arrangements for the provision of adoption support services (within the meaning of that Act) extend,

(b) such other person as the authority consider has sufficient interest in a child who is or may be adopted to warrant his representations being considered by them,

about the discharge by the authority of such functions under the Adoption and Children Act 2002 as are specified by the Secretary of State in regulations.'

(5) In subsection (4) (procedure to require involvement of independent person), after paragraph (b) there is inserted –

'but this subsection is subject to subsection (5A).'

(6) After that subsection there is inserted –

'(4A) Regulations may be made by the Secretary of State imposing time limits on the making of representations under this section.'

(7) After subsection (5) there is inserted –

'(5A) Regulations under subsection (5) may provide that subsection (4) does not apply in relation to any consideration or discussion which takes place as part of a procedure for which provision is made by the regulations for the purpose of resolving informally the matters raised in the representations.'

118 Review of cases of looked after children

(1) In section 26 of the 1989 Act (review of cases of looked after children, etc), in subsection (2) (regulations as to reviews) –

- (a) in paragraph (e), 'to consider' is omitted and after 'their care' there is inserted –
    - '(i) to keep the section 31A plan for the child under review and, if they are of the opinion that some change is required, to revise the plan, or make a new plan, accordingly,
    - (ii) to consider',
- (b) in paragraph (f), 'to consider' is omitted and after the second mention of 'the authority' there is inserted –
    - '(i) if there is no plan for the future care of the child, to prepare one,
    - (ii) if there is such a plan for the child, to keep it under review and, if they are of the opinion that some change is required, to revise the plan or make a new plan, accordingly,
    - (iii) to consider',
- (c) after paragraph (j) there is inserted –

    '(k) for the authority to appoint a person in respect of each case to carry out in the prescribed manner the functions mentioned in subsection (2A) and any prescribed function'.

(2) After that subsection there is inserted –

'(2A) The functions referred to in subsection (2)(k) are –

- (a) participating in the review of the case in question,
- (b) monitoring the performance of the authority's functions in respect of the review,
- (c) referring the case to an officer of the Children and Family Court Advisory and Support Service, if the person appointed under subsection (2)(k) considers it appropriate to do so.

(2B) A person appointed under subsection (2)(k) must be a person of a prescribed description.

(2C) In relation to children whose cases are referred to officers under subsection (2A)(c), the Lord Chancellor may by regulations –

(a) extend any functions of the officers in respect of family proceedings (within the meaning of section 12 of the Criminal Justice and Court Services Act 2000) to other proceedings,

(b) require any functions of the officers to be performed in the manner prescribed by the regulations.'

119 Advocacy services

After section 26 of the 1989 Act there is inserted –

'26A Advocacy services

(1) Every local authority shall make arrangements for the provision of assistance to –

(a) persons who make or intend to make representations under section 24D; and
(b) children who make or intend to make representations under section 26.

(2) The assistance provided under the arrangements shall include assistance by way of representation.

(3) The arrangements –

(a) shall secure that a person may not provide assistance if he is a person who is prevented from doing so by regulations made by the Secretary of State; and
(b) shall comply with any other provision made by the regulations in relation to the arrangements.

(4) The Secretary of State may make regulations requiring local authorities to monitor the steps that they have taken with a view to ensuring that they comply with regulations made for the purposes of subsection (3).

(5) Every local authority shall give such publicity to their arrangements for the provision of assistance under this section as they consider appropriate.'

120 Meaning of 'harm' in the 1989 Act

In section 31 of the 1989 Act (care and supervision orders), at the end of the definition of 'harm' in subsection (9) there is inserted 'including, for example, impairment suffered from seeing or hearing the ill-treatment of another'.

121 Care plans

(1) In section 31 of the 1989 Act (care and supervision orders), after subsection (3) there is inserted –

'(3A) No care order may be made with respect to a child until the court has considered a section 31A plan.'

(2) After that section there is inserted –

'31A Care orders: care plans

(1) Where an application is made on which a care order might be made with respect to a child, the appropriate local authority must, within such time as the court may direct, prepare a plan ("a care plan") for the future care of the child.

(2) While the application is pending, the authority must keep any care plan prepared by them under review and, if they are of the opinion some change is required, revise the plan, or make a new plan, accordingly.

(3) A care plan must give any prescribed information and do so in the prescribed manner.

(4) For the purposes of this section, the appropriate local authority, in relation to a child in respect of whom a care order might be made, is the local authority proposed to be designated in the order.

(5) In section 31(3A) and this section, references to a care order do not include an interim care order.

(6) A plan prepared, or treated as prepared, under this section is referred to in this Act as a "section 31A plan".'

(3) If –

(a) before subsection (2) comes into force, a care order has been made in respect of a child and a plan for the future care of the child has been prepared in connection with the making of the order by the local authority designated in the order, and

(b) on the day on which that subsection comes into force the order is in force, or would be in force but for section 29(1) of this Act,

the plan is to have effect as if made under section 31A of the 1989 Act.

122 Interests of children in proceedings

(1) In section 41 of the 1989 Act (specified proceedings) –

(a) in subsection (6), after paragraph (h) there is inserted –

'(hh) on an application for the making or revocation of a placement order (within the meaning of section 21 of the Adoption and Children Act 2002);',

(b) after that subsection there is inserted –

'(6A) The proceedings which may be specified under subsection (6)(i) include (for example) proceedings for the making, varying or discharging of a section 8 order.'

(2) In section 93 of the 1989 Act (rules of court), in subsection (2), after paragraph (b) there is inserted –

'(bb) for children to be separately represented in relevant proceedings,'.

PART 3

MISCELLANEOUS AND FINAL PROVISIONS

Chapter 1

Miscellaneous

Advertisements in the United Kingdom

123 Restriction on advertisements etc

(1) A person must not –

(a) publish or distribute an advertisement or information to which this section applies, or

(b) cause such an advertisement or information to be published or distributed.

(2) This section applies to an advertisement indicating that –

(a) the parent or guardian of a child wants the child to be adopted,
(b) a person wants to adopt a child,
(c) a person other than an adoption agency is willing to take any step mentioned in paragraphs (a) to (e), (g) and (h) and (so far as relating to those paragraphs) (i) of section 92(2),
(d) a person other than an adoption agency is willing to receive a child handed over to him with a view to the child's adoption by him or another, or
(e) a person is willing to remove a child from the United Kingdom for the purposes of adoption.

(3) This section applies to –

(a) information about how to do anything which, if done, would constitute an offence under section 85 or 93, section 11 or 50 of the Adoption (Scotland) Act 1978 or Article 11 or 58 of the Adoption (Northern Ireland) Order 1987 (SI 1987/2203 (NI 22)) (whether or not the information includes a warning that doing the thing in question may constitute an offence),
(b) information about a particular child as a child available for adoption.

(4) For the purposes of this section and section 124 –

(a) publishing or distributing an advertisement or information means publishing it or distributing it to the public and includes doing so by electronic means (for example, by means of the internet),
(b) the public includes selected members of the public as well as the public generally or any section of the public.

(5) Subsection (1) does not apply to publication or distribution by or on behalf of an adoption agency.

(6) The Secretary of State may by order make any amendments of this section which he considers necessary or expedient in consequence of any developments in technology relating to publishing or distributing advertisements or other information by electronic or electro-magnetic means.

(7) References to an adoption agency in this section include a prescribed person outside the United Kingdom exercising functions corresponding to those of an adoption agency, if the functions are being exercised in prescribed circumstances.

'Prescribed' means prescribed by regulations made by the Secretary of State.

(8) Before exercising the power conferred by subsection (6) or (7), the Secretary of State must consult the Scottish Ministers, the Department of Health, Social Services and Public Safety and the Assembly.

(9) In this section –

(a) 'adoption agency' includes a Scottish or Northern Irish adoption agency,
(b) references to adoption are to the adoption of persons, wherever they may be habitually resident, effected under the law of any country or territory, whether within or outside the British Islands.

124 Offence of breaching restriction under section 123

(1) A person who contravenes section 123(1) is guilty of an offence.

(2) A person is not guilty of an offence under this section unless it is proved that he knew or had reason to suspect that section 123 applied to the advertisement or information.

But this subsection only applies if sufficient evidence is adduced to raise an issue as to whether the person had the knowledge or reason mentioned.

(3) A person guilty of an offence under this section is liable on summary conviction to imprisonment for a term not exceeding three months, or a fine not exceeding level 5 on the standard scale, or both.

Adoption and Children Act Register

125 Adoption and Children Act Register

(1) Her Majesty may by Order in Council make provision for the Secretary of State to establish and maintain a register, to be called the Adoption and Children Act Register, containing –

(a) prescribed information about children who are suitable for adoption and prospective adopters who are suitable to adopt a child,
(b) prescribed information about persons included in the register in pursuance of paragraph (a) in respect of things occurring after their inclusion.

(2) For the purpose of giving assistance in finding persons with whom children may be placed for purposes other than adoption, an Order under this section may –

(a) provide for the register to contain information about such persons and the children who may be placed with them, and
(b) apply any of the other provisions of this group of sections (that is, this section and sections 126 to 131), with or without modifications.

(3) The register is not to be open to public inspection or search.

(4) An Order under this section may make provision about the retention of information in the register.

(5) Information is to be kept in the register in any form the Secretary of State considers appropriate.

126 Use of an organisation to establish the register

(1) The Secretary of State may make an arrangement with an organisation under which any function of his under an Order under section 125 of establishing and maintaining the register, and disclosing information entered in, or compiled from information entered in, the register to any person is performed wholly or partly by the organisation on his behalf.

(2) The arrangement may include provision for payments to be made to the organisation by the Secretary of State.

(3) If the Secretary of State makes an arrangement under this section with an organisation, the organisation is to perform the functions exercisable by virtue of this section in accordance with any directions given by the Secretary of State and the directions may be of general application (or general application in any part of Great Britain) or be special directions.

(4) An exercise of the Secretary of State's powers under subsection (1) or (3) requires the agreement of the Scottish Ministers (if the register applies to Scotland) and of the Assembly (if the register applies to Wales).

(5) References in this group of sections to the registration organisation are to any organisation for the time being performing functions in respect of the register by virtue of arrangements under this section.

127 Use of an organisation as agency for payments

(1) An Order under section 125 may authorise an organisation with which an arrangement is made under section 126 to act as agent for the payment or receipt of sums payable by adoption agencies to other adoption agencies and may require adoption agencies to pay or receive such sums through the organisation.

(2) The organisation is to perform the functions exercisable by virtue of this section in accordance with any directions given by the Secretary of State; and the directions may be of general application (or general application in any part of Great Britain) or be special directions.

(3) An exercise of the Secretary of State's power to give directions under subsection (2) requires the agreement of the Scottish Ministers (if any payment agency provision applies to Scotland) and of the Assembly (if any payment agency provision applies to Wales).

128 Supply of information for the register

(1) An Order under section 125 may require adoption agencies to give prescribed information to the Secretary of State or the registration organisation for entry in the register.

(2) Information is to be given to the Secretary of State or the registration organisation when required by the Order and in the prescribed form and manner.

(3) An Order under section 125 may require an agency giving information which is entered on the register to pay a prescribed fee to the Secretary of State or the registration organisation.

(4) But an adoption agency is not to disclose any information to the Secretary of State or the registration organisation –

    (a) about prospective adopters who are suitable to adopt a child, or persons who were included in the register as such prospective adopters, without their consent,

    (b) about children suitable for adoption, or persons who were included in the register as such children, without the consent of the prescribed person.

(5) Consent under subsection (4) is to be given in the prescribed form.

129 Disclosure of information

(1) Information entered in the register, or compiled from information entered in the register, may only be disclosed under subsection (2) or (3).

(2) Prescribed information entered in the register may be disclosed by the Secretary of State or the registration organisation –

    (a) where an adoption agency is acting on behalf of a child who is suitable for adoption, to the agency to assist in finding prospective adopters with whom it would be appropriate for the child to be placed,

    (b) where an adoption agency is acting on behalf of prospective adopters who are suitable to adopt a child, to the agency to assist in finding a child appropriate for adoption by them.

(3) Prescribed information entered in the register, or compiled from information entered in the register, may be disclosed by the Secretary of State or the registration organisation to any prescribed person for use for statistical or research purposes, or for other prescribed purposes.

(4) An Order under section 125 may prescribe the steps to be taken by adoption agencies in respect of information received by them by virtue of subsection (2).

(5) Subsection (1) does not apply –

(a) to a disclosure of information with the authority of the Secretary of State, or
(b) to a disclosure by the registration organisation of prescribed information to the Scottish Ministers (if the register applies to Scotland) or the Assembly (if the register applies to Wales).

(6) Information disclosed to any person under subsection (2) or (3) may be given on any prescribed terms or conditions.

(7) An Order under section 125 may, in prescribed circumstances, require a prescribed fee to be paid to the Secretary of State or the registration organisation –

(a) by a prescribed adoption agency in respect of information disclosed under subsection (2), or
(b) by a person to whom information is disclosed under subsection (3).

(8) If any information entered in the register is disclosed to a person in contravention of subsection (1), the person disclosing it is guilty of an offence.

(9) A person guilty of an offence under subsection (8) is liable on summary conviction to imprisonment for a term not exceeding three months, or a fine not exceeding level 5 on the standard scale, or both.

130 Territorial application

(1) In this group of sections, 'adoption agency' means –

(a) a local authority in England,
(b) a registered adoption society whose principal office is in England.

(2) An Order under section 125 may provide for any requirements imposed on adoption agencies in respect of the register to apply –

(a) to Scottish local authorities and to voluntary organisations providing a registered adoption service,
(b) to local authorities in Wales and to registered adoption societies whose principal offices are in Wales,

and, in relation to the register, references to adoption agencies in this group of sections include any authorities or societies mentioned in paragraphs (a) and (b) to which an Order under that section applies those requirements.

(3) For the purposes of this group of sections, references to the register applying to Scotland or Wales are to those requirements applying as mentioned in paragraph (a) or, as the case may be, (b) of subsection (2).

(4) An Order under section 125 may apply any provision made by virtue of section 127 –

(a) to Scottish local authorities and to voluntary organisations providing a registered adoption service,
(b) to local authorities in Wales and to registered adoption societies whose principal offices are in Wales.

(5) For the purposes of this group of sections, references to any payment agency provision applying to Scotland or Wales are to provision made by virtue of section 127 applying as mentioned in paragraph (a) or, as the case may be, (b) of subsection (4).

131 Supplementary

(1) In this group of sections –

    (a) 'organisation' includes a public body and a private or voluntary organisation,

    (b) 'prescribed' means prescribed by an Order under section 125,

    (c) 'the register' means the Adoption and Children Act Register,

    (d) 'Scottish local authority' means a local authority within the meaning of the Regulation of Care (Scotland) Act 2001,

    (e) 'voluntary organisation providing a registered adoption service' has the same meaning as in section 144(3).

(2) For the purposes of this group of sections –

    (a) a child is suitable for adoption if an adoption agency is satisfied that the child ought to be placed for adoption,

    (b) prospective adopters are suitable to adopt a child if an adoption agency is satisfied that they are suitable to have a child placed with them for adoption.

(3) Nothing authorised or required to be done by virtue of this group of sections constitutes an offence under section 93, 94 or 95.

(4) No recommendation to make an Order under section 125 is to be made to Her Majesty in Council unless a draft has been laid before and approved by resolution of each House of Parliament.

(5) If any provision made by an Order under section 125 would, if it were included in an Act of the Scottish Parliament, be within the legislative competence of that Parliament, no recommendation to make the Order is to be made to Her Majesty in Council unless a draft has been laid before, and approved by resolution of, the Parliament.

(6) No recommendation to make an Order under section 125 containing any provision in respect of the register is to be made to Her Majesty in Council if the register applies to Wales or the Order would provide for the register to apply to Wales, unless a draft has been laid before, and approved by resolution of, the Assembly.

(7) No recommendation to make an Order under section 125 containing any provision by virtue of section 127 is to be made to Her Majesty in Council if any payment agency provision applies to Wales or the Order would provide for any payment agency provision to apply to Wales, unless a draft has been laid before, and approved by resolution of, the Assembly.

Other miscellaneous provisions

132 Amendment of Adoption (Scotland) Act 1978: contravention of sections 30 to 36 of this Act

After section 29 of the Adoption (Scotland) Act 1978 there is inserted –

'29A Contravention of sections 30 to 36 of Adoption and Children Act 2002

(1) A person who contravenes any of the enactments specified in subsection (2) is guilty of an offence and liable on summary conviction to imprisonment for a term not exceeding three months, or a fine not exceeding level 5 on the standard scale, or both.

(2) Those enactments are –

    (a) section 30(1), (2) and (3) (removal of child placed or who may be placed for adoption),

    (b) sections 32(2)(b), 33(2) and 35(2) (return of child by prospective adopters),

(c) section 34(1) (removal of child in contravention of placement order),
(d) section 36(1) (removal of child in non-agency case), and
(e) section 36(5) (return of child to parent or guardian),

of the Adoption and Children Act 2002.'

133 Scottish restriction on bringing children into or out of United Kingdom

(1) In section 50 of the Adoption (Scotland) Act 1978 (restriction on removal of children for adoption outside Great Britain) –

(a) in subsection (1), 'not being a parent or guardian or relative of the child' is omitted,
(b) after subsection (3) there is inserted –

'(4) The Scottish Ministers may by regulations provide for subsection (1) to apply with modifications, or not to apply, if –

(a) the prospective adopters are parents, relatives or guardians of the child (or one of them is), or
(b) the prospective adopter is a step-parent of the child,

and any conditions prescribed by the regulations are met.

(5) On the occasion of the first exercise of the power to make regulations under subsection (4) –

(a) the regulations shall not be made unless a draft of the regulations has been approved by a resolution of the Scottish Parliament, and
(b) accordingly section 60(2) does not apply to the statutory instrument containing the regulations.'

(2) For section 50A of that Act (restriction on bringing children into the United Kingdom for adoption) there is substituted –

'50A Restriction on bringing children into the United Kingdom

(1) This section applies where a person who is habitually resident in the British Islands (the "British resident") –

(a) brings, or causes another to bring, a child who is habitually resident outside the British Islands into the United Kingdom for the purpose of adoption by the British resident; or
(b) at any time brings, or causes another to bring, into the United Kingdom a child adopted by the British resident under an external adoption effected within the period of six months ending with that time.

(2) In subsection (1) above the references to adoption, or to a child adopted, by the British resident include a reference to adoption, or to a child adopted, by the British resident and another person.

(3) This section does not apply if the child is intended to be adopted under a Convention adoption order.

(4) An external adoption means an adoption, other than a Convention adoption, of a child effected under the law of any country or territory outside the British Islands, whether or not the adoption is –

(a) an adoption within the meaning of Part IV; or

(b) a full adoption (as defined in section 39(2A)).

(5) Regulations may require a person intending to bring, or to cause another to bring, a child into the United Kingdom in circumstances where this section applies –

(a) to apply to an adoption agency in the prescribed manner for an assessment of his suitability to adopt the child; and

(b) to give the agency any information it may require for the purpose of the assessment.

(6) Regulations may require prescribed conditions to be met in respect of a child brought into the United Kingdom in circumstances where this section applies.

(7) In relation to a child brought into the United Kingdom for adoption in circumstances where this section applies, regulations may provide for any provision of Part II of this Act to apply with modifications or not to apply.

(8) If a person brings, or causes another to bring, a child into the United Kingdom at any time in circumstances where this section applies, he is guilty of an offence if –

(a) he has not complied with any requirement imposed by virtue of subsection (5); or

(b) any condition required to be met by virtue of subsection (6) is not met,

before that time, or before any later time which may be prescribed.

(9) A person guilty of an offence under this section is liable –

(a) on summary conviction to imprisonment for a term not exceeding six months, or a fine not exceeding the statutory maximum, or both;

(b) on conviction on indictment, to imprisonment for a term not exceeding twelve months, or a fine, or both.

(10) Regulations may provide for this section not to apply if –

(a) the adopters or (as the case may be) prospective adopters are natural parents (whether or not they have parental responsibilities or parental rights in relation to the child), natural relatives or guardians of the child in question (or one of them is), or

(b) the British resident in question is a step-parent of the child,

and any prescribed conditions are met.

(11) On the occasion of the first exercise of the power to make regulations under subsection (10) –

(a) the regulations shall not be made unless a draft of the regulations has been approved by a resolution of the Scottish Parliament, and

(b) accordingly section 60(2) does not apply to the statutory instrument containing the regulations.

(12) In this section, "prescribed" means prescribed by regulations and "regulations" means regulations made by the Scottish Ministers.'

(3) In section 65 of that Act (interpretation), in subsection (1), in the definition of 'adoption agency', for 'and 27' there is substituted ', 27 and 50A'.

134 Amendment of Adoption (Scotland) Act 1978: overseas adoptions

In section 65 of the Adoption (Scotland) Act 1978 (interpretation), for subsection (2) there is substituted –

'(2) In this Act, "overseas adoption" –

(a) means an adoption of a description specified in an order made by the Scottish
    Ministers, being a description of adoptions effected under the law of any country or
    territory outside the British Islands, but
(b) does not include a Convention adoption.

(2A) The Scottish Ministers may by regulations prescribe the requirements that ought to be
met by an adoption of any description effected after the commencement of the regulations for
it to be an overseas adoption for the purposes of this Act.

(2B) At any time when such regulations have effect, the Scottish Ministers must exercise their
power under subsection (2) so as to secure that subsequently effected adoptions of any
description are not overseas adoptions for the purposes of this Act if they consider that such
adoptions are not likely within a reasonable time to meet the prescribed requirements.

(2C) An order under subsection (2) may contain provision as to the manner in which evidence
of any overseas adoption may be given.

(2D) In subsections (2) to (2C), "adoption" means the adoption of a child or of a person who
was a child at the time the adoption was applied for.'

135 Adoption and fostering: criminal records

(1) Part 5 of the Police Act 1997 (certificates of criminal records) is amended as follows.

(2) In section 113 (criminal record certificates), in subsection (3A), for 'his suitability' there is
substituted 'the suitability of the applicant, or of a person living in the same household as the
applicant, to be a foster parent or'.

(3) In section 115 (enhanced criminal record certificates), in subsection (6A), for 'his suitability'
there is substituted 'the suitability of the applicant, or of a person living in the same household as
the applicant, to be a foster parent or'.

Commencement—1 June 2003 (England and Wales only) (SI 2003/366).

136 Payment of grants in connection with welfare services

(1) Section 93 of the Local Government Act 2000 (payment of grants for welfare services) is
amended as follows.

(2) In subsection (1) (payment of grants by the Secretary of State), for the words from 'in providing'
to the end there is substituted –

'(a) in providing, or contributing to the provision of, such welfare services as may be
     determined by the Secretary of State, or
(b) in connection with any such welfare services.'

(3) In subsection (2) (payment of grants by the Assembly), for the words from 'in providing' to the
end there is substituted –

'(a) in providing, or contributing to the provision of, such welfare services as may be
     determined by the Assembly, or
(b) in connection with any such welfare services.'

(4) After subsection (6) there is inserted –

'(6A) Before making any determination under subsection (3) or (5) the Secretary of State must
obtain the consent of the Treasury.'

Commencement—7 November 2002 (Royal Assent).

137 Extension of the Hague Convention to British overseas territories

(1) Her Majesty may by Order in Council provide for giving effect to the Convention in any British overseas territory.

(2) An Order in Council under subsection (1) in respect of any British overseas territory may, in particular, make any provision corresponding to provision which in relation to any part of Great Britain is made by the Adoption (Intercountry Aspects) Act 1999 or may be made by regulations under section 1 of that Act.

(3) The British Nationality Act 1981 is amended as follows.

(4) In section 1 (acquisition of British citizenship by birth or adoption) –

    (a) in subsection (5), at the end of paragraph (b) there is inserted 'effected under the law of a country or territory outside the United Kingdom',

    (b) at the end of subsection (5A)(b) there is inserted 'or in a designated territory',

    (c) in subsection (8), the words following 'section 50' are omitted.

(5) In section 15 (acquisition of British overseas territories citizenship) –

    (a) after subsection (5) there is inserted –

  '(5A) Where –

      (a) a minor who is not a British overseas territories citizen is adopted under a Convention adoption,

      (b) on the date on which the adoption is effected –

        (i) the adopter or, in the case of a joint adoption, one of the adopters is a British overseas territories citizen, and

        (ii) the adopter or, in the case of a joint adoption, both of the adopters are habitually resident in a designated territory, and

      (c) the Convention adoption is effected under the law of a country or territory outside the designated territory,

  the minor shall be a British overseas territories citizen as from that date.',

    (b) in subsection (6), after 'order' there is inserted 'or a Convention adoption'.

(6) In section 50 (interpretation), in subsection (1) –

    (a) after the definition of 'company' there is inserted –

  '"Convention adoption" means an adoption effected under the law of a country or territory in which the Convention is in force, and certified in pursuance of Article 23(1) of the Convention',

    (b) after the definition of 'Crown service under the government of the United Kingdom' there is inserted –

  '"designated territory" means a qualifying territory, or the Sovereign Base Areas of Akrotiri and Dhekelia, which is designated by Her Majesty by Order in Council under subsection (14)'.

(7) After subsection (13) of that section there is inserted –

  '(14) For the purposes of the definition of "designated territory" in subsection (1), an Order in Council may –

    (a) designate any qualifying territory, or the Sovereign Base Areas of Akrotiri and Dhekelia, if the Convention is in force there, and

    (b) make different designations for the purposes of section 1 and section 15;

and, for the purposes of this subsection and the definition of "Convention adoption" in subsection (1), "the Convention" means the Convention on the Protection of Children and Co-operation in respect of Intercountry Adoption, concluded at the Hague on 29th May 1993.

An Order in Council under this subsection shall be subject to annulment in pursuance of a resolution of either House of Parliament.'

138 Proceedings in Great Britain

Proceedings for an offence by virtue of section 9, 59, 93, 94, 95 or 129 –

    (a) may not be brought more than six years after the commission of the offence but, subject to that,

    (b) may be brought within a period of six months from the date on which evidence sufficient in the opinion of the prosecutor to warrant the proceedings came to his knowledge.

[*Words apply to Scotland only.*]

Amendments etc

139 Amendments, transitional and transitory provisions, savings and repeals

(1) Schedule 3 (minor and consequential amendments) is to have effect.

(2) Schedule 4 (transitional and transitory provisions and savings) is to have effect.

(3) The enactments set out in Schedule 5 are repealed to the extent specified.

Chapter 2

Final provisions

140 Orders, rules and regulations

(1) Any power to make subordinate legislation conferred by this Act on the Lord Chancellor, the Secretary of State, the Scottish Ministers, the Assembly or the Registrar General is exercisable by statutory instrument.

(2) A statutory instrument containing subordinate legislation made under any provision of this Act (other than section 14 or 148 or an instrument to which subsection (3) applies) is to be subject to annulment in pursuance of a resolution of either House of Parliament.

(3) A statutory instrument containing subordinate legislation –

    (a) under section 9 which includes provision made by virtue of section 45(2),

    (b) under section 92(6), 94 or 123(6), or

    (c) which adds to, replaces or omits any part of the text of an Act,

is not to be made unless a draft of the instrument has been laid before, and approved by resolution of, each House of Parliament.

(4) Subsections (2) and (3) do not apply to an Order in Council or to subordinate legislation made –

    (a) by the Scottish Ministers, or

(b) by the Assembly, unless made jointly by the Secretary of State and the Assembly.

(5) A statutory instrument containing regulations under section 63(2) made by the Scottish Ministers is to be subject to annulment in pursuance of a resolution of the Scottish Parliament.

(6) The power of the Department of Health, Social Services and Public Safety to make regulations under section 63(2) is to be exercisable by statutory rule for the purposes of the Statutory Rules (Northern Ireland) Order 1979 (SI 1979/1573 (NI 12)); and any such regulations are to be subject to negative resolution within the meaning of section 41(6) of the Interpretation Act (Northern Ireland) 1954 as if they were statutory instruments within the meaning of that Act.

(7) Subordinate legislation made under this Act may make different provision for different purposes.

(8) A power to make subordinate legislation under this Act (as well as being exercisable in relation to all cases to which it extends) may be exercised in relation to –

(a) those cases subject to specified exceptions, or
(b) a particular case or class of case.

(9) In this section, 'subordinate legislation' does not include a direction.

Commencement—7 November 2002 (Royal Assent).

141 Rules of procedure

(1) The Lord Chancellor may make rules in respect of any matter to be prescribed by rules made by virtue of this Act and dealing generally with all matters of procedure.

(2) Subsection (1) does not apply in relation to proceedings before magistrates' courts, but the power to make rules conferred by section 144 of the Magistrates' Courts Act 1980 includes power to make provision in respect of any of the matters mentioned in that subsection.

(3) In the case of an application for a placement order, for the variation or revocation of such an order, or for an adoption order, the rules must require any person mentioned in subsection (4) to be notified –

(a) of the date and place where the application will be heard, and
(b) of the fact that, unless the person wishes or the court requires, the person need not attend.

(4) The persons referred to in subsection (3) are –

(a) in the case of a placement order, every person who can be found whose consent to the making of the order is required under subsection (3)(a) of section 21 (or would be required but for subsection (3)(b) of that section) or, if no such person can be found, any relative prescribed by rules who can be found,
(b) in the case of a variation or revocation of a placement order, every person who can be found whose consent to the making of the placement order was required under subsection (3)(a) of section 21 (or would have been required but for subsection (3)(b) of that section),
(c) in the case of an adoption order –
  (i) every person who can be found whose consent to the making of the order is required under subsection (2)(a) of section 47 (or would be required but for subsection (2)(c) of that section) or, if no such person can be found, any relative prescribed by rules who can be found,
  (ii) every person who has consented to the making of the order under section 20 (and has not withdrawn the consent) unless he has given a notice under subsection (4)(a) of that section which has effect,

(iii) every person who, if leave were given under section 47(5), would be entitled to oppose the making of the order.

(5) Rules made in respect of magistrates' courts may provide –

    (a) for enabling any fact tending to establish the identity of a child with a child to whom a document relates to be proved by affidavit, and

    (b) for excluding or restricting in relation to any facts that may be so proved the power of a justice of the peace to compel the attendance of witnesses.

Commencement—7 November 2002 (Royal Assent).

142 Supplementary and consequential provision

(1) The appropriate Minister may by order make –

    (a) any supplementary, incidental or consequential provision,

    (b) any transitory, transitional or saving provision,

which he considers necessary or expedient for the purposes of, in consequence of or for giving full effect to any provision of this Act.

(2) For the purposes of subsection (1), where any provision of an order extends to England and Wales, and Scotland or Northern Ireland, the appropriate Minister in relation to the order is the Secretary of State.

(3) Before making an order under subsection (1) containing provision which would, if included in an Act of the Scottish Parliament, be within the legislative competence of that Parliament, the appropriate Minister must consult the Scottish Ministers.

(4) Subsection (5) applies to any power of the Lord Chancellor, the Secretary of State or the Assembly to make regulations, rules or an order by virtue of any other provision of this Act or of Her Majesty to make an Order in Council by virtue of section 125.

(5) The power may be exercised so as to make –

    (a) any supplementary, incidental or consequential provision,

    (b) any transitory, transitional or saving provision,

which the person exercising the power considers necessary or expedient.

(6) The provision which may be made under subsection (1) or (5) includes provision modifying Schedule 4 or amending or repealing any enactment or instrument.

In relation to an Order in Council, 'enactment' in this subsection includes an enactment comprised in, or in an instrument made under, an Act of the Scottish Parliament.

(7) The power of the Registrar General to make regulations under Chapter 5 of Part 1 may, with the approval of the Chancellor of the Exchequer, be exercised so as to make –

    (a) any supplementary, incidental or consequential provision,

    (b) any transitory, transitional or saving provision,

which the Registrar General considers necessary or expedient.

Commencement—7 November 2002 (Royal Assent).

143 Offences by bodies corporate and unincorporated bodies

(1) Where an offence under this Act committed by a body corporate is proved to have been committed with the consent or connivance of, or to be attributable to any neglect on the part of, any director, manager, secretary or other similar officer of the body, or a person purporting to act in any such capacity, that person as well as the body is guilty of the offence and liable to be proceeded against and punished accordingly.

(2) Where the affairs of a body corporate are managed by its members, subsection (1) applies in relation to the acts and defaults of a member in connection with his functions of management as it applies to a director of a body corporate.

(3) Proceedings for an offence alleged to have been committed under this Act by an unincorporated body are to be brought in the name of that body (and not in that of any of its members) and, for the purposes of any such proceedings in England and Wales or Northern Ireland, any rules of court relating to the service of documents have effect as if that body were a corporation.

(4) A fine imposed on an unincorporated body on its conviction of an offence under this Act is to be paid out of the funds of that body.

(5) If an unincorporated body is charged with an offence under this Act –

    (a) in England and Wales, section 33 of the Criminal Justice Act 1925 and Schedule 3 to the Magistrates' Courts Act 1980 (procedure on charge of an offence against a corporation),

    (b) in Northern Ireland, section 18 of the Criminal Justice Act (Northern Ireland) 1945 and Schedule 4 to the Magistrates' Courts (Northern Ireland) Order 1981 (SI 1981/1675 (NI 26)) (procedure on charge of an offence against a corporation),

have effect in like manner as in the case of a corporation so charged.

(6) Where an offence under this Act committed by an unincorporated body (other than a partnership) is proved to have been committed with the consent or connivance of, or to be attributable to any neglect on the part of, any officer of the body or any member of its governing body, he as well as the body is guilty of the offence and liable to be proceeded against and punished accordingly.

(7) Where an offence under this Act committed by a partnership is proved to have been committed with the consent or connivance of, or to be attributable to any neglect on the part of, a partner, he as well as the partnership is guilty of the offence and liable to be proceeded against and punished accordingly.

Commencement—7 November 2002 (Royal Assent).

144 General interpretation etc

(1) In this Act –

'appropriate Minister' means –

    (a) in relation to England, Scotland or Northern Ireland, the Secretary of State,

    (b) in relation to Wales, the Assembly,

and in relation to England and Wales means the Secretary of State and the Assembly acting jointly,

'the Assembly' means the National Assembly for Wales,

'body' includes an unincorporated body,

'by virtue of' includes 'by' and 'under',

'child', except where used to express a relationship, means a person who has not attained the age of 18 years, 'the Convention' means the Convention on Protection of Children and Co-operation in respect of Intercountry Adoption, concluded at the Hague on 29th May 1993,

'Convention adoption order' means an adoption order which, by virtue of regulations under section 1 of the Adoption (Intercountry Aspects) Act 1999 (regulations giving effect to the Convention), is made as a Convention adoption order,

'Convention country' means a country or territory in which the Convention is in force,

'court' means, subject to any provision made by virtue of Part 1 of Schedule 11 to the 1989 Act, the High Court, a county court or a magistrates' court,

'enactment' includes an enactment comprised in subordinate legislation,

'fee' includes expenses,

'guardian' has the same meaning as in the 1989 Act and includes a special guardian within the meaning of that Act,

'information' means information recorded in any form,

'local authority' means any unitary authority, or any county council so far as they are not a unitary authority,

'Northern Irish adoption agency' means an adoption agency within the meaning of Article 3 of the Adoption (Northern Ireland) Order 1987 (SI 1987/2203 (NI 22)),

'Northern Irish adoption order' means an order made, or having effect as if made, under Article 12 of the Adoption (Northern Ireland) Order 1987,

'notice' means a notice in writing,

'registration authority' (in Part 1) has the same meaning as in the Care Standards Act 2000,

'regulations' means regulations made by the appropriate Minister, unless they are required to be made by the Lord Chancellor, the Secretary of State or the Registrar General,

'relative', in relation to a child, means a grandparent, brother, sister, uncle or aunt, whether of the full blood or half-blood or by marriage,

'rules' means rules made under section 141(1) or made by virtue of section 141(2) under section 144 of the Magistrates' Courts Act 1980,

'Scottish adoption order' means an order made, or having effect as if made, under section 12 of the Adoption (Scotland) Act 1978,

'subordinate legislation' has the same meaning as in the Interpretation Act 1978,

'unitary authority' means –

(a) the council of any county so far as they are the council for an area for which there are no district councils,

(b) the council of any district comprised in an area for which there is no county council,

(c) the council of a county borough,

(d) the council of a London borough,

(e) the Common Council of the City of London.

(2) Any power conferred by this Act to prescribe a fee by Order in Council or regulations includes power to prescribe –

(a) a fee not exceeding a prescribed amount,

(b) a fee calculated in accordance with the Order or, as the case may be, regulations,

(c) a fee determined by the person to whom it is payable, being a fee of a reasonable amount.

(3) In this Act, 'Scottish adoption agency' means –

(a) a local authority, or

(b) a voluntary organisation providing a registered adoption service;

but in relation to the provision of any particular service, references to a Scottish adoption agency do not include a voluntary organisation unless it is registered in respect of that service or a service which, in Scotland, corresponds to that service.

Expressions used in this subsection have the same meaning as in the Regulation of Care (Scotland) Act 2001 and 'registered' means registered under Part 1 of that Act.

(4) In this Act, a couple means –

(a) a married couple, or
(b) two people (whether of different sexes or the same sex) living as partners in an enduring family relationship.

(5) Subsection (4)(b) does not include two people one of whom is the other's parent, grandparent, sister, brother, aunt or uncle.

(6) References to relationships in subsection (5) –

(a) are to relationships of the full blood or half blood or, in the case of an adopted person, such of those relationships as would exist but for adoption, and
(b) include the relationship of a child with his adoptive, or former adoptive, parents,

but do not include any other adoptive relationships.

(7) For the purposes of this Act, a person is the partner of a child's parent if the person and the parent are a couple but the person is not the child's parent.

Commencement—7 November 2002 (Royal Assent).

145 Devolution: Wales

(1) The references to the Adoption Act 1976 and to the 1989 Act in Schedule 1 to the National Assembly for Wales (Transfer of Functions) Order 1999 (SI 1999/672) are to be treated as referring to those Acts as amended by virtue of this Act.

(2) This section does not affect the power to make further Orders varying or omitting those references.

(3) In Schedule 1 to that Order, in the entry for the Adoption Act 1976, '9' is omitted.

(4) The functions exercisable by the Assembly under sections 9 and 9A of the Adoption Act 1976 (by virtue of paragraphs 4 and 5 of Schedule 4 to this Act) are to be treated for the purposes of section 44 of the Government of Wales Act 1998 (parliamentary procedures for subordinate legislation) as if made exercisable by the Assembly by an Order in Council under section 22 of that Act.

Commencement—7 November 2002 (Royal Assent).

146 Expenses

There shall be paid out of money provided by Parliament –

(a) any expenditure incurred by a Minister of the Crown by virtue of this Act,
(b) any increase attributable to this Act in the sums payable out of money so provided under any other enactment.

Commencement—7 November 2002 (Royal Assent).

147 Glossary

Schedule 6 (glossary) is to have effect.

Commencement—7 November 2002 (Royal Assent).

148 Commencement

(1) This Act (except sections 116 and 136, this Chapter and the provisions mentioned in subsections (5) and (6)) is to come into force on such day as the Secretary of State may by order appoint.

(2) Before making an order under subsection (1) (other than an order bringing paragraph 53 of Schedule 3 into force) the Secretary of State must consult the Assembly.

(3) Before making an order under subsection (1) bringing sections 123 and 124 into force, the Secretary of State must also consult the Scottish Ministers and the Department of Health, Social Services and Public Safety.

(4) Before making an order under subsection (1) bringing sections 125 to 131 into force, the Secretary of State must also consult the Scottish Ministers.

(5) The following are to come into force on such day as the Scottish Ministers may by order appoint –

    (a) section 41(5) to (9), so far as relating to Scotland,
    (b) sections 132 to 134,
    (c) paragraphs 21 to 35 and 82 to 84 of Schedule 3,
    (d) paragraphs 15 and 23 of Schedule 4,
    (e) the entries in Schedule 5, so far as relating to the provisions mentioned in paragraphs (c) and (d),
    (f) section 139, so far as relating to the provisions mentioned in the preceding paragraphs.

(6) Sections 2(6), 3(3) and (4), 4 to 17, 27(3), 53(1) to (3), 54, 56 to 65 and 98, paragraphs 13, 65, 66 and 111 to 113 of Schedule 3 and paragraphs 3 and 5 of Schedule 4 are to come into force on such day as the appropriate Minister may by order appoint.

Commencement—7 November 2002 (Royal Assent).

149 Extent

(1) The amendment or repeal of an enactment has the same extent as the enactment to which it relates.

(2) Subject to that and to the following provisions, this Act except section 137 extends to England and Wales only.

(3) The following extend also to Scotland and Northern Ireland –

    (a) sections 63(2) to (5), 65(2)(a) and (b) and (3), 123 and 124,
    (b) this Chapter, except sections 141 and 145.

(4) The following extend also to Scotland –

    (a) section 41(5) to (9),
    (b) sections 125 to 131,
    (c) section 138,
    (d) section 139, so far as relating to provisions extending to Scotland.

(5) In Schedule 4, paragraph 23 extends only to Scotland.

Commencement—7 November 2002 (Royal Assent).

150 Short title

This Act may be cited as the Adoption and Children Act 2002.

_____

Commencement—7 November 2002 (Royal Assent).

SCHEDULES

SCHEDULE 1
REGISTRATION OF ADOPTIONS

Registration of adoption orders

1 (1) Every adoption order must contain a direction to the Registrar General to make in the Adopted Children Register an entry in the form prescribed by regulations made by the Registrar General with the approval of the Chancellor of the Exchequer.

(2) Where, on an application to a court for an adoption order in respect of a child, the identity of the child with a child to whom an entry in the registers of live-births or other records relates is proved to the satisfaction of the court, any adoption order made in pursuance of the application must contain a direction to the Registrar General to secure that the entry in the register or, as the case may be, record in question is marked with the word 'Adopted'.

(3) Where an adoption order is made in respect of a child who has previously been the subject of an adoption order made by a court in England or Wales under Part 1 of this Act or any other enactment –

(a) sub-paragraph (2) does not apply, and
(b) the order must contain a direction to the Registrar General to mark the previous entry in the Adopted Children Register with the word 'Re-adopted'.

(4) Where an adoption order is made, the prescribed officer of the court which made the order must communicate the order to the Registrar General in the prescribed manner; and the Registrar General must then comply with the directions contained in the order.

'Prescribed' means prescribed by rules.

Registration of adoptions in Scotland, Northern Ireland, the Isle of Man and the Channel Islands

2 (1) Sub-paragraphs (2) and (3) apply where the Registrar General is notified by the authority maintaining a register of adoptions in a part of the British Islands outside England and Wales that an order has been made in that part authorising the adoption of a child.

(2) If an entry in the registers of live-births or other records (and no entry in the Adopted Children Register) relates to the child, the Registrar General must secure that the entry is marked with –

(a) the word 'Adopted', followed by
(b) the name, in brackets, of the part in which the order was made.

(3) If an entry in the Adopted Children Register relates to the child, the Registrar General must mark the entry with –

(a) the word 'Re-adopted', followed by

(b) the name, in brackets, of the part in which the order was made.

(4) Where, after an entry in either of the registers or other records mentioned in sub-paragraphs (2) and (3) has been so marked, the Registrar General is notified by the authority concerned that –

(a) the order has been quashed,
(b) an appeal against the order has been allowed, or
(c) the order has been revoked,

the Registrar General must secure that the marking is cancelled.

(5) A copy or extract of an entry in any register or other record, being an entry the marking of which is cancelled under sub-paragraph (4), is not to be treated as an accurate copy unless both the marking and the cancellation are omitted from it.

Registration of other adoptions

3 (1) If the Registrar General is satisfied, on an application under this paragraph, that he has sufficient particulars relating to a child adopted under a registrable foreign adoption to enable an entry to be made in the Adopted Children Register for the child he must make the entry accordingly.

(2) If he is also satisfied that an entry in the registers of live-births or other records relates to the child, he must –

(a) secure that the entry is marked 'Adopted', followed by the name, in brackets, of the country in which the adoption was effected, or
(b) where appropriate, secure that the overseas registers of births are so marked.

(3) An application under this paragraph must be made, in the prescribed manner, by a prescribed person and the applicant must provide the prescribed documents and other information.

(4) An entry made in the Adopted Children Register by virtue of this paragraph must be made in the prescribed form.

(5) In this Schedule 'registrable foreign adoption' means an adoption which satisfies prescribed requirements and is either –

(a) adoption under a Convention adoption, or
(b) adoption under an overseas adoption.

(6) In this paragraph –

(a) 'prescribed' means prescribed by regulations made by the Registrar General with the approval of the Chancellor of the Exchequer,
(b) 'overseas register of births' includes –
    (i) a register made under regulations made by the Secretary of State under section 41(1)(g), (h) or (i) of the British Nationality Act 1981,
    (ii) a record kept under an Order in Council made under section 1 of the Registration of Births, Deaths and Marriages (Special Provisions) Act 1957 (other than a certified copy kept by the Registrar General).

Amendment of orders and rectification of Registers and other records

4 (1) The court by which an adoption order has been made may, on the application of the adopter or the adopted person, amend the order by the correction of any error in the particulars contained in it.

(2) The court by which an adoption order has been made may, if satisfied on the application of the adopter or the adopted person that within the period of one year beginning with the date of the order any new name –

(a) has been given to the adopted person (whether in baptism or otherwise), or
(b) has been taken by the adopted person,

either in place of or in addition to a name specified in the particulars required to be entered in the Adopted Children Register in pursuance of the order, amend the order by substituting or, as the case may be, adding that name in those particulars.

(3) The court by which an adoption order has been made may, if satisfied on the application of any person concerned that a direction for the marking of an entry in the registers of live-births, the Adopted Children Register or other records included in the order in pursuance of paragraph 1(2) or (3) was wrongly so included, revoke that direction.

(4) Where an adoption order is amended or a direction revoked under sub-paragraphs (1) to (3), the prescribed officer of the court must communicate the amendment in the prescribed manner to the Registrar General.

'Prescribed' means prescribed by rules.

(5) The Registrar General must then –

(a) amend the entry in the Adopted Children Register accordingly, or
(b) secure that the marking of the entry in the registers of live-births, the Adopted Children Register or other records is cancelled,

as the case may be.

(6) Where an adoption order is quashed or an appeal against an adoption order allowed by any court, the court must give directions to the Registrar General to secure that –

(a) any entry in the Adopted Children Register, and
(b) any marking of an entry in that Register, the registers of live-births or other records as the case may be, which was effected in pursuance of the order,

is cancelled.

(7) Where an adoption order has been amended, any certified copy of the relevant entry in the Adopted Children Register which may be issued pursuant to section 78(2)(b) must be a copy of the entry as amended, without the reproduction of –

(a) any note or marking relating to the amendment, or
(b) any matter cancelled in pursuance of it.

(8) A copy or extract of an entry in any register or other record, being an entry the marking of which has been cancelled, is not to be treated as an accurate copy unless both the marking and the cancellation are omitted from it.

(9) If the Registrar General is satisfied –

(a) that a registrable foreign adoption has ceased to have effect, whether on annulment or otherwise, or
(b) that any entry or mark was erroneously made in pursuance of paragraph 3 in the Adopted Children Register, the registers of live-births, the overseas registers of births or other records,

he may secure that such alterations are made in those registers or other records as he considers are required in consequence of the adoption ceasing to have effect or to correct the error.

'Overseas register of births' has the same meaning as in paragraph 3.

(10) Where an entry in such a register is amended in pursuance of sub-paragraph (9), any copy or extract of the entry is not to be treated as accurate unless it shows the entry as amended but without indicating that it has been amended.

Marking of entries on re-registration of birth on legitimation

5 (1) Without prejudice to paragraphs 2(4) and 4(5), where, after an entry in the registers of live-births or other records has been marked in accordance with paragraph 1 or 2, the birth is re-registered under section 14 of the Births and Deaths Registration Act 1953 (re-registration of births of legitimated persons), the entry made on the re-registration must be marked in the like manner.

(2) Without prejudice to paragraph 4(9), where an entry in the registers of live-births or other records is marked in pursuance of paragraph 3 and the birth in question is subsequently re-registered under section 14 of that Act, the entry made on re-registration must be marked in the like manner.

Cancellations in registers on legitimation

6 (1) This paragraph applies where an adoption order is revoked under section 55(1).

(2) The prescribed officer of the court must communicate the revocation in the prescribed manner to the Registrar General who must then cancel or secure the cancellation of –

(a) the entry in the Adopted Children Register relating to the adopted person, and
(b) the marking with the word 'Adopted' of any entry relating to the adopted person in the registers of live-births or other records.

'Prescribed' means prescribed by rules.

(3) A copy or extract of an entry in any register or other record, being an entry the marking of which is cancelled under this paragraph, is not to be treated as an accurate copy unless both the marking and the cancellation are omitted from it.

SCHEDULE 2
DISCLOSURE OF BIRTH RECORDS BY REGISTRAR GENERAL

1 On an application made in the prescribed manner by an adopted person –

(a) a record of whose birth is kept by the Registrar General, and
(b) who has attained the age of 18 years,

the Registrar General must give the applicant any information necessary to enable the applicant to obtain a certified copy of the record of his birth.

'Prescribed' means prescribed by regulations made by the Registrar General with the approval of the Chancellor of the Exchequer.

2 (1) Before giving any information to an applicant under paragraph 1, the Registrar General must inform the applicant that counselling services are available to the applicant –

(a) from a registered adoption society, an organisation within section 144(3)(b) or an adoption society which is registered under Article 4 of the Adoption (Northern Ireland) Order 1987 (SI 1987/2203 (NI 22)),

(b) if the applicant is in England and Wales, at the General Register Office or from any local authority or registered adoption support agency,

(c) if the applicant is in Scotland, from any council constituted under section 2 of the Local Government etc (Scotland) Act 1994 ,

(d) if the applicant is in Northern Ireland, from any Board.

(2) In sub-paragraph (1)(b), 'registered adoption support agency' means an adoption support agency in respect of which a person is registered under Part 2 of the Care Standards Act 2000.

(3) In sub-paragraph (1)(d), 'Board' means a Health and Social Services Board established under Article 16 of the Health and Personal Social Services (Northern Ireland) Order 1972 (SI 1972/1265 (NI 14)); but where the functions of a Board are exercisable by a Health and Social Services Trust, references in that sub-paragraph to a Board are to be read as references to the Health and Social Services Trust.

(4) If the applicant chooses to receive counselling from a person or body within sub-paragraph (1), the Registrar General must send to the person or body the information to which the applicant is entitled under paragraph 1.

3 (1) Where an adopted person who is in England and Wales –

(a) applies for information under paragraph 1 or Article 54 of the Adoption (Northern Ireland) Order 1987, or

(b) is supplied with information under section 45 of the Adoption (Scotland) Act 1978,

the persons and bodies mentioned in sub-paragraph (2) must, if asked by the applicant to do so, provide counselling for the applicant.

(2) Those persons and bodies are –

(a) the Registrar General,

(b) any local authority,

(c) a registered adoption society, an organisation within section 144(3)(b) or an adoption society which is registered under Article 4 of the Adoption (Northern Ireland) Order 1987.

4 (1) Where a person –

(a) was adopted before 12th November 1975, and

(b) applies for information under paragraph 1,

the Registrar General must not give the information to the applicant unless the applicant has attended an interview with a counsellor arranged by a person or body from whom counselling services are available as mentioned in paragraph 2.

(2) Where the Registrar General is prevented by sub-paragraph (1) from giving information to a person who is not living in the United Kingdom, the Registrar General may give the information to any body which –

(a) the Registrar General is satisfied is suitable to provide counselling to that person, and

(b) has notified the Registrar General that it is prepared to provide such counselling.

SCHEDULE 3
MINOR AND CONSEQUENTIAL AMENDMENTS

The Marriage Act 1949

1 Section 3 of the Marriage Act 1949 (marriage of person aged under eighteen) is amended as follows.

2 In subsection (1), for 'person or persons specified in subsection (1A) of this section' there is substituted 'appropriate persons'.

3 For subsection (1A) there is substituted –

'(1A) The appropriate persons are –

(a) if none of paragraphs (b) to (h) apply, each of the following –
  (i) any parent of the child who has parental responsibility for him; and
  (ii) any guardian of the child;
(b) where a special guardianship order is in force with respect to a child, each of the child's special guardians, unless any of paragraphs (c) to (g) applies;
(c) where a care order has effect with respect to the child, the local authority designated in the order, and each parent, guardian or special guardian (in so far as their parental responsibility has not been restricted under section 33(3) of the Children Act 1989), unless paragraph (e) applies;
(d) where a residence order has effect with respect to the child, the persons with whom the child lives, or is to live, as a result of the order, unless paragraph (e) applies;
(e) where an adoption agency is authorised to place the child for adoption under section 19 of the Adoption and Children Act 2002, that agency or, where a care order has effect with respect to the child, the local authority designated in the order;
(f) where a placement order is in force with respect to the child, the appropriate local authority;
(g) where a child has been placed for adoption with prospective adopters, the prospective adopters (in so far as their parental responsibility has not been restricted under section 25(4) of the Adoption and Children Act 2002), in addition to those persons specified in paragraph (e) or (f);
(h) where none of paragraphs (b) to (g) apply but a residence order was in force with respect to the child immediately before he reached the age of sixteen, the persons with whom he lived, or was to live, as a result of the order.'

4 For subsection (1B) there is substituted –

'(1B) In this section –

"guardian of a child", "parental responsibility", "residence order", "special guardian", "special guardianship order" and "care order" have the same meaning as in the Children Act 1989;
"adoption agency", "placed for adoption", "placement order" and "local authority" have the same meaning as in the Adoption and Children Act 2002;
"appropriate local authority" means the local authority authorised by the placement order to place the child for adoption.'

5 In subsection (2), for 'The last foregoing subsection' there is substituted 'Subsection (1)'.

The Births and Deaths Registration Act 1953

6 In section 10 of the Births and Deaths Registration Act 1953 (registration of father where parents not married) –

(a) in subsection (1)(d)(i), for 'a parental responsibility agreement made between them in relation to the child' there is substituted 'any agreement made between them under section 4(1)(b) of the Children Act 1989 in relation to the child',
(b) in subsection (1)(d)(ii), for 'the Children Act 1989' there is substituted 'that Act',
(c) in subsection (3), the words following 'the Family Law Reform Act 1987' are omitted.

7 In section 10A of the Births and Deaths Registration Act 1953 (re-registration of father where parents not married) –

(a) in subsection (1)(d)(i), for 'a parental responsibility agreement made between them in relation to the child' there is substituted 'any agreement made between them under section 4(1)(b) of the Children Act 1989 in relation to the child',

(b) in subsection (1)(d)(ii), for 'the Children Act 1989' there is substituted 'that Act'.

The Sexual Offences Act 1956

8 In section 28 of the Sexual Offences Act 1956 (causing or encouraging prostitution of, intercourse with, or indecent assault on, girl under sixteen), in subsection (4), the 'or' at the end of paragraph (a) is omitted, and after that paragraph there is inserted –

'(aa) a special guardianship order under that Act is in force with respect to her and he is not her special guardian; or'.

The Health Services and Public Health Act 1968

9 The Health Services and Public Health Act 1968 is amended as follows.

10 In section 64 (financial assistance by the Secretary of State to certain voluntary organisations), in subsection (3)(a)(xviii), for 'the Adoption Act 1976' there is substituted 'the Adoption and Children Act 2002'.

11 In section 65 (financial and other assistance by local authorities to certain voluntary organisations), in subsection (3)(b), for 'the Adoption Act 1976' there is substituted 'the Adoption and Children Act 2002'.

The Local Authority Social Services Act 1970

12 The Local Authority Social Services Act 1970 is amended as follows.

13 In section 7D (default powers of Secretary of State as respects social services functions of local authorities), in subsection (1), after 'the Children Act 1989' there is inserted 'section 1 or 2(4) of the Adoption (Intercountry Aspects) Act 1999 or the Adoption and Children Act 2002'.

14 In Schedule 1 (enactments conferring functions assigned to social services committee) –

(a) the entry relating to the Adoption Act 1976 is omitted,

(b) in the entry relating to the Children Act 1989, after 'Consent to application for residence order in respect of child in care' there is inserted 'Functions relating to special guardianship orders',

(c) in the entry relating to the Adoption (Intercountry Aspects) Act 1999 –
  (i) in the first column, for 'Section' there is substituted 'Sections 1 and',
  (ii) in the second column, for 'Article 9(a) to (c) of' there is substituted 'regulations made under section 1 giving effect to' and at the end there is inserted 'and functions under Article 9(a) to (c) of the Convention',

and at the end of the Schedule there is inserted –

'Adoption and Children Act 2002	Maintenance of Adoption Service; functions of local authority as adoption agency.'

The Immigration Act 1971

15 In section 33(1) of the Immigration Act 1971 (interpretation) –

(a) in the definition of 'Convention adoption', after '1978' there is inserted 'or in the Adoption and Children Act 2002',
(b) in the definition of 'legally adopted', for 'section 72(2) of the Adoption Act 1976' there is substituted 'section 87 of the Adoption and Children Act 2002'.

The Legitimacy Act 1976

16 The Legitimacy Act 1976 is amended as follows.

17 In section 4 (legitimation of adopted child) –

(a) in subsection (1), after '1976' there is inserted 'or section 67 of the Adoption and Children Act 2002',
(b) in subsection (2) –
 (i) in paragraph (a), after '39' there is inserted 'or subsection (3)(b) of the said section 67',
 (ii) in paragraph (b), after '1976' there is inserted 'or section 67, 68 or 69 of the Adoption and Children Act 2002'.

18 In section 6 (dispositions depending on date of birth), at the end of subsection (2) there is inserted 'or section 69(2) of the Adoption and Children Act 2002'.

The Adoption Act 1976

19 In section 38 of the Adoption Act 1976 (meaning of 'adoption' in Part 4), in subsection (2), after '1975' there is inserted 'but does not include an adoption of a kind mentioned in paragraphs (c) to (e) of subsection (1) effected on or after the day which is the appointed day for the purposes of Chapter 4 of Part 1 of the Adoption and Children Act 2002'.

The National Health Service Act 1977

20 In section 124A(3) of the National Health Service Act 1977 (information provided by the Registrar General to the Secretary of State), the 'or' at the end of paragraph (a) is omitted and after that paragraph there is inserted –

'(aa) entered in the Adopted Children Register maintained by the Registrar General under the Adoption and Children Act 2002; or'.

The Adoption (Scotland) Act 1978

21 The Adoption (Scotland) Act 1978 is amended as follows.

22 In section 11 (restriction on arranging adoptions and placing of children) –

(a) in subsection (2) –
 (i) for paragraph (a) there is substituted –

 '(a) a registered adoption society (within the meaning of section 2(2) of the Adoption and Children Act 2002)'; and

 (ii) for 'section 1' there is substituted 'section 3(1)', and
(b) after subsection (2) there is inserted –

'(2A) In relation to the provision of any particular service by an adoption society, the reference in subsection (2)(a) to a registered adoption society does not include a voluntary organisation unless it is registered under Part 2 of the Care Standards Act 2000 in respect of that service or a service which, in England, corresponds to that service.'

23 In section 16 (parental agreement to adoption order) –

(a) in subsection (1), after paragraph (a) there is inserted –

'(aa) each parent or guardian of the child has consented under section 20 of the Adoption and Children Act 2002 (advance consent to adoption), has not withdrawn the consent and does not oppose the making of the adoption order;

(ab) subsection (3A) applies and no parent or guardian of the child opposes the making of the adoption order', and

(b) after subsection (3) there is inserted –

'(3A) This subsection applies where –

(a) the child has been placed for adoption by an adoption agency (within the meaning of section 2(1) of the Adoption and Children Act 2002) with the prospective adopters in whose favour the adoption order is proposed to be made; and

(b) the child was placed for adoption –

(i) under section 19 of that Act (placing children with parental consent) with the consent of each parent or guardian and the consent of the mother was given when the child was at least six weeks old; or

(ii) under an order made under section 21 of that Act (placement orders) and the child was at least six weeks old when that order was made.

(3B) A parent or guardian may not oppose the making of an adoption order under subsection (1)(aa) or (ab) without the leave of the court.

(3C) The court shall not give leave under subsection (3B) unless satisfied that there has been a change of circumstances since the consent of the parent or guardian was given or, as the case may be, the order under section 21 of that Act was made.

(3D) The withdrawal of –

(a) any consent to the placement of a child for adoption –

(i) under section 19; or

(ii) under an order made under section 21,

of the Adoption and Children Act 2002; or

(b) any consent given under section 20 of that Act,

is ineffective if it is given after an application for an adoption order is made.'

24 In section 29 (return of children taken away in breach of section 27 or 28) –

(a) in subsection (1), for 'section 27 or 28 of the Adoption Act 1976' there is substituted 'section 30, 34, 35 or 36 of the Adoption and Children Act 2002', and

(b) in subsection (2), for 'section 27 or 28 of the Adoption Act 1976', in both places where those words occur, there is substituted 'section 30, 34, 35 or 36 of the Adoption and Children Act 2002'.

25 In section 45 (Adopted Children Register) –

(a) in subsection (6)(d), for sub-paragraph (ii) there is substituted –

'(ii) registered under Part II of the Care Standards Act 2000;';

(b) in subsection (6A)(b), for sub-paragraph (i) there is substituted –

      '(i)   Schedule 2 to the Adoption and Children Act 2002;'.

26 In section 47 (annulment etc of overseas adoptions), in subsection (4), for 'section 53 of the Adoption Act 1976' there is substituted 'section 89(2) of the Adoption and Children Act 2002'.

27 In section 50 (restriction on removal of children for adoption outside Great Britain), in subsection (1), for 'section 55 of the Adoption Act 1976' there is substituted 'section 84 of the Adoption and Children Act 2002'.

28 Section 52 (restriction on advertisements) is omitted.

29 In section 53 (effect of determination and orders made in England and Wales and overseas in adoption proceedings), in subsection (2), the words 'England and Wales or' are omitted.

30 After section 53 there is inserted –

'53A Effect of certain orders made in England and Wales

(1) An adoption order (within the meaning of section 46(1) of the Adoption and Children Act 2002) has effect in Scotland as it has in England and Wales but as if any reference to the parental responsibility for the child were to the parental responsibilities and parental rights in relation to the child.

(2) An order made under section 21 of that Act (placement orders), and the variation or revocation of such an order under section 23 or 24 of that Act, have effect in Scotland as they have in England and Wales but as if any reference to the parental responsibility for the child were to the parental responsibilities and parental rights in relation to the child.

53B Effect of placing for adoption etc under Adoption and Children Act 2002

(1) If –

    (a) a child is placed for adoption under section 19 of the Adoption and Children Act 2002 (placing children with parental consent); or
    (b) an adoption agency is authorised to place a child for adoption under that section,

sections 25 (parental responsibility) and 28(2) to (4) (further consequences of placement) of that Act have effect in Scotland as they have in England and Wales but with the modifications specified in subsection (2).

(2) Those modifications are –

    (a) in section 25, any reference to the parental responsibility for the child is to be read as a reference to the parental responsibilities and parental rights in relation to the child; and
    (b) in section 28(2), the reference to the court is to be read as a reference to the authorised court.

53C Further consequences of placement and placement orders

(1) Subsection (2) applies where –

    (a) a child is placed for adoption under section 19 of the Adoption and Children Act 2002 (placing children with parental consent); or
    (b) an adoption agency is authorised to place the child for adoption under that section.

(2) No order under subsection (1) of section 11 of the Children (Scotland) Act 1995 (court orders relating to parental responsibilities etc) of a kind referred to in subsection (2)(c) (residence orders) of that section may be made in respect of the child.

(3) On the making of an order under section 21 of the Adoption and Children Act 2002 (a 'placement order') in respect of a child, any order under subsection (1) of section 11 of the Children (Scotland) Act 1995 of a kind referred to in subsection (2)(c) to (f) (residence orders, contact orders, specific issue orders and interdicts in relation to parental responsibilities) of that section in respect of the child ceases to have effect.

(4) Where a placement order is in force –

(a) no such order as is referred to in subsection (3) of this section; and

(b) no order under section 55 of the Children (Scotland) Act 1995 (child assessment orders),

may be made in respect of the child.'

31 In section 54 (evidence of adoption in England, Wales and Northern Ireland), in paragraph (a), for 'section 50(2) of the Adoption Act 1976' there is substituted 'section 77(4) and (5) of the Adoption and Children Act 2002'.

32 In section 56 (authorised courts), in subsection (3), for 'Great Britain' there is substituted 'Scotland'.

33 In section 59 (rules of procedure) –

(a) in subsection (2) –
(i)   for the words from 'in relation to' to 'adoption', where it secondly occurs, there is substituted '(except where an order has been made freeing the child for adoption)'; and
(ii) for the words from 'every' to 'Act' there is substituted 'any person mentioned in subsection (2A)'; and
(b) after subsection (2) there is inserted –

'(2A) The persons referred to in subsection (2) are –

(a) every person who can be found and whose agreement or consent to the making of the order is required to be given or dispensed with under this Act or, if no such person can be found, any relative prescribed by rules who can be found;
(b) every person who has consented to the making of the order under section 20 of the Adoption and Children Act 2002 (and has not withdrawn the consent) unless he has given a notice under subsection (4)(a) of that section which has effect;
(c) every person who, if leave were given under section 16(3B), would be entitled to oppose the making of the order.'

34 In section 60 (orders, rules and regulations), after subsection (3) there is inserted –

'(3A) An order under section 65(2) shall be subject to annulment in pursuance of a resolution of the Scottish Parliament.'

35 In section 65 (interpretation), in subsection (1) –

(a) in the definition of 'adoption agency', for 'section 1 of the Adoption Act 1976' there is substituted 'section 2(1) of the Adoption and Children Act 2002',
(b) in the definition of 'adoption order' –
(i)   in paragraph (b), for 'section 12 of the Adoption Act 1976' there is substituted 'section 46 of the Adoption and Children Act 2002',

(ii)   in paragraph (c), for 'section 55 of the Adoption Act 1976' there is substituted 'section 84 of the Adoption and Children Act 2002', and

(c)   in the definition of 'order freeing a child for adoption', paragraph (a) and the word 'and' immediately following that paragraph are omitted.

The Magistrates' Courts Act 1980

36 The Magistrates' Courts Act 1980 is amended as follows.

37 In section 65 (meaning of family proceedings), in subsection (1), for paragraph (h) there is substituted –

'(h) the Adoption and Children Act 2002;'.

38 In section 69 (sitting of magistrates' courts for family proceedings), in subsections (2) and (3), for 'the Adoption Act 1976' there is substituted 'the Adoption and Children Act 2002'.

39 In section 71 (newspaper reports of family proceedings) –

(a)   in subsection (1), '(other than proceedings under the Adoption Act 1976)' is omitted,
(b)   in subsection (2) –
    (i)   for 'the Adoption Act 1976' there is substituted 'the Adoption and Children Act 2002',
    (ii)   the words following '(a) and (b)' are omitted.

40 In Part 1 of Schedule 6 (fees to be taken by justices' chief executives), in the entry relating to family proceedings –

(a)   for 'the Adoption Act 1976, except under section 21 of that Act', there is substituted 'the Adoption and Children Act 2002, except under section 23 of that Act',
(b)   in paragraph (c), for 'section 21 of the Adoption Act 1976' there is substituted 'section 23 of the Adoption and Children Act 2002'.

The Mental Health Act 1983

41 In section 28 of the Mental Health Act 1983 (nearest relative of minor under guardianship, etc), in subsection (3), after '"guardian"' there is inserted 'includes a special guardian (within the meaning of the Children Act 1989), but'.

The Child Abduction Act 1984

42 (1) Section 1 of the Child Abduction Act 1984 (offence of abduction of child by parent, etc) is amended as follows.

(2) In subsection (2), after paragraph (c) there is inserted –

'(ca) he is a special guardian of the child; or'.

(3) In subsection (3)(a), after sub-paragraph (iii) there is inserted –

'(iiia) any special guardian of the child;'.

(4) In subsection (4), for paragraphs (a) and (b) there is substituted –

'(a)   he is a person in whose favour there is a residence order in force with respect to the child, and he takes or sends the child out of the United Kingdom for a period of less than one month; or
(b)   he is a special guardian of the child and he takes or sends the child out of the United Kingdom for a period of less than three months.'

(5) In subsection (5A), the 'or' at the end of sub-paragraph (i) of paragraph (a) is omitted, and after that sub-paragraph there is inserted –

'(ia) who is a special guardian of the child; or'.

(6) In subsection (7)(a), after ' "guardian of a child," ' there is inserted ' "special guardian," '.

43 (1) The Schedule to that Act (modifications of section 1 for children in certain cases) is amended as follows.

(2) In paragraph 3 (adoption and custodianship), for sub-paragraphs (1) and (2) there is substituted –

'(1) This paragraph applies where –

(a) a child is placed for adoption by an adoption agency under section 19 of the Adoption and Children Act 2002, or an adoption agency is authorised to place the child for adoption under that section; or

(b) a placement order is in force in respect of the child; or

(c) an application for such an order has been made in respect of the child and has not been disposed of; or

(d) an application for an adoption order has been made in respect of the child and has not been disposed of; or

(e) an order under section 84 of the Adoption and Children Act 2002 (giving parental responsibility prior to adoption abroad) has been made in respect of the child, or an application for such an order in respect of him has been made and has not been disposed of.

(2) Where this paragraph applies, section 1 of this Act shall have effect as if –

(a) the reference in subsection (1) to the appropriate consent were –

(i) in a case within sub-paragraph (1)(a) above, a reference to the consent of each person who has parental responsibility for the child or to the leave of the High Court;

(ii) in a case within sub-paragraph (1)(b) above, a reference to the leave of the court which made the placement order;

(iii) in a case within sub-paragraph (1)(c) or (d) above, a reference to the leave of the court to which the application was made;

(iv) in a case within sub-paragraph (1)(e) above, a reference to the leave of the court which made the order or, as the case may be, to which the application was made;

(b) subsection (3) were omitted;

(c) in subsection (4), in paragraph (a), for the words from 'in whose favour' to the first mention of 'child' there were substituted 'who provides the child's home in a case falling within sub-paragraph (1)(a) or (b) of paragraph 3 of the Schedule to this Act'; and

(d) subsections (4A), (5), (5A) and (6) were omitted.'

(3) In paragraph 5 (interpretation), in sub-paragraph (a), for the words from 'and "adoption order" ' to the end there is substituted ', "adoption order", "placed for adoption by an adoption agency" and "placement order" have the same meaning as in the Adoption and Children Act 2002; and'.

The Matrimonial and Family Proceedings Act 1984

44 In section 40 of the Matrimonial and Family Proceedings Act 1984 (family proceedings rules), in subsection (2), in paragraph (a), after 'the Adoption Act 1968' the 'or' is omitted and after 'the Adoption Act 1976' there is inserted 'or section 141(1) of the Adoption and Children Act 2002'.

The Child Abduction and Custody Act 1985

45 In Schedule 3 to the Child Abduction and Custody Act 1985 (custody orders), in paragraph 1, the 'and' at the end of paragraph (b) is omitted and after that paragraph there is inserted –

'(bb) a special guardianship order (within the meaning of the Act of 1989); and',

and paragraph (c)(v) is omitted.

The Family Law Act 1986

46 The Family Law Act 1986 is amended as follows.

47 In section 1 (orders to which Part 1 applies), in subsection (1), after paragraph (a) there is inserted –

'(aa) a special guardianship order made by a court in England and Wales under the Children Act 1989;

(ab) an order made under section 26 of the Adoption and Children Act 2002 (contact), other than an order varying or revoking such an order'.

48 In section 2 (jurisdiction: general), after subsection (2) there is inserted –

'(2A) A court in England and Wales shall not have jurisdiction to make a special guardianship order under the Children Act 1989 unless the condition in section 3 of this Act is satisfied.

(2B) A court in England and Wales shall not have jurisdiction to make an order under section 26 of the Adoption and Children Act 2002 unless the condition in section 3 of this Act is satisfied.'

49 In section 57 (declarations as to adoptions effected overseas) –

(a) for subsection (1)(a) there is substituted –

'(a) a Convention adoption, or an overseas adoption, within the meaning of the Adoption and Children Act 2002, or',

(b) in subsection (2)(a), after '1976' there is inserted 'or section 67 of the Adoption and Children Act 2002'.

The Family Law Reform Act 1987

50 The Family Law Reform Act 1987 is amended as follows.

51 In section 1 (general principle), for paragraph (c) of subsection (3) there is substituted –

'(c) is an adopted person within the meaning of Chapter 4 of Part 1 of the Adoption and Children Act 2002'.

52 In section 19 (dispositions of property), in subsection (5), after '1976' there is inserted 'or section 69 of the Adoption and Children Act 2002'.

The Adoption (Northern Ireland) Order 1987 (SI 1987/2203 (NI 22))

53 In Article 2(2) (interpretation), in the definition of 'prescribed', for 'Articles 54' there is substituted 'Articles 53(3B) and (3D), 54'.

Commencement—3 February 2003 (SI 2003/288).

The Children Act 1989

54 The Children Act 1989 is amended as follows.

55 In section 8 (residence, contact and other orders with respect to children), in subsection (4), for paragraph (d) there is substituted –

'(d) the Adoption and Children Act 2002;'.

56 In section 10 (power of court to make section 8 orders) –

(a) in subsection (4)(a), for 'or guardian' there is substituted ', guardian or special guardian',
(b) after subsection (4)(a) there is inserted –

'(aa) any person who by virtue of section 4A has parental responsibility for the child;',

(c) after subsection (5) there is inserted –

'(5A) A local authority foster parent is entitled to apply for a residence order with respect to a child if the child has lived with him for a period of at least one year immediately preceding the application.',

(d) after subsection (7) there is inserted –

'(7A) If a special guardianship order is in force with respect to a child, an application for a residence order may only be made with respect to him, if apart from this subsection the leave of the court is not required, with such leave.'

57 In section 12 (residence orders and parental responsibility), in subsection (3) –

(a) paragraph (a) is omitted,
(b) in paragraph (b), for 'section 55 of the Act of 1976' there is substituted 'section 84 of the Adoption and Children Act 2002'.

58 In section 16 (family assistance orders), in subsection (2)(a), for 'or guardian' there is substituted ', guardian or special guardian'.

59 In section 20 (provision of accommodation for children: general), in subsection (9), the 'or' at the end of paragraph (a) is omitted and after that paragraph there is inserted –

'(aa) who is a special guardian of the child; or'.

60 In section 24 (persons qualifying for advice and assistance) –

(a) for subsection (1) there is substituted –

'(1) In this Part 'a person qualifying for advice and assistance' means a person to whom subsection (1A) or (1B) applies.

(1A) This subsection applies to a person –

(a) who has reached the age of sixteen but not the age of twenty-one;
(b) with respect to whom a special guardianship order is in force (or, if he has reached the age of eighteen, was in force when he reached that age); and
(c) who was, immediately before the making of that order, looked after by a local authority.

(1B) This subsection applies to a person to whom subsection (1A) does not apply, and who –

(a) is under twenty-one; and

(b) at any time after reaching the age of sixteen but while still a child was, but is no longer, looked after, accommodated or fostered.',

(b) in subsection (2), for 'subsection (1)(b)' there is substituted 'subsection (1B)(b)',
(c) in subsection (5), before paragraph (a) there is inserted –

'(za) in the case of a person to whom subsection (1A) applies, a local authority determined in accordance with regulations made by the Secretary of State;'.

61 In section 24A (advice and assistance for qualifying persons) –

(a) in subsection (2)(b), after 'a person' there is inserted 'to whom section 24(1A) applies, or to whom section 24(1B) applies and',
(b) in subsection (3)(a), after 'if' there is inserted 'he is a person to whom section 24(1A) applies, or he is a person to whom section 24(1B) applies and'.

62 In section 24B (assistance with employment, education and training), in each of subsections (1) and (3)(b), after 'of' there is inserted 'section 24(1A) or'.

63 In section 33 (effect of care order) –

(a) in subsection (3)(b), for 'a parent or guardian of the child' there is substituted '–
   (i)   a parent, guardian or special guardian of the child; or
   (ii) a person who by virtue of section 4A has parental responsibility for the child,',

(b) in subsection (5), for 'a parent or guardian of the child who has care of him' there is substituted 'a person mentioned in that provision who has care of the child',
(c) in subsection (6)(b) –
   (i)   sub-paragraph (i) is omitted,
   (ii) in sub-paragraph (ii), for 'section 55 of the Act of 1976' there is substituted 'section 84 of the Adoption and Children Act 2002',
(d) in subsection (9), for 'a parent or guardian of the child' there is substituted 'a person mentioned in that provision'.

64 In section 34 (parental contact etc with children in care) –

(a) in subsection (1)(b), after 'guardian' there is inserted 'or special guardian', and
(b) after subsection (1)(b) there is inserted –

'(ba) any person who by virtue of section 4A has parental responsibility for him;'.

65 In section 80 (inspection of children's homes by persons authorised by Secretary of State), in subsection (1), paragraphs (e) and (f) are omitted.

66 In section 81 (inquiries), in subsection (1), paragraph (b) is omitted.

67 In section 88 (amendments of adoption legislation), subsection (1) is omitted.

68 In section 91 (effect and duration of orders, etc) –

(a) after subsection (5) there is inserted –

'(5A) The making of a special guardianship order with respect to a child who is the subject of –

   (a) a care order; or
   (b) an order under section 34,

discharges that order.',

(b) in subsection (7), after '4(1)' there is inserted '4A(1)',

(c) in subsection (8)(a), after '4' there is inserted 'or 4A'.

69 In section 102 (power of constable to assist in exercise of certain powers to search for children or inspect premises), in subsection (6), paragraph (c) is omitted.

70 In section 105 (interpretation), in subsection (1) –

(a) in the definition of 'adoption agency', for 'section 1 of the Adoption Act 1976' there is substituted 'section 2 of the Adoption and Children Act 2002',
(b) at the appropriate place there is inserted –

'"section 31A plan" has the meaning given by section 31A(6);',

(c) in the definition of 'parental responsibility agreement', for 'section 4(1)' there is substituted 'sections 4(1) and 4A(2)',
(d) the definition of 'protected child' is omitted,
(e) after the definition of 'special educational needs' there is inserted –

'"special guardian" and "special guardianship order" have the meaning given by section 14A;'.

71 In Schedule 1 (financial provision for children) –

(a) in paragraph 1 (orders for financial relief against parents) –
   (i) in sub-paragraph (1), for 'or guardian' there is substituted ', guardian or special guardian', and
   (ii) in sub-paragraph (6), after 'order' there is inserted 'or a special guardianship order',
(b) in paragraph 6 (variation etc of orders for periodical payments), in sub-paragraph (8), after 'guardian' there is inserted 'or special guardian',
(c) in paragraph 8 (financial relief under other enactments), in sub-paragraph (1) and in sub-paragraph (2)(b), after 'residence order' there is inserted 'or a special guardianship order',
(d) in paragraph 14 (financial provision for child resident in country outside England and Wales), in sub-paragraph (1)(b), after 'guardian' there is inserted 'or special guardian'.

72 In Schedule 2, in paragraph 19 (arrangements by local authorities to assist children to live abroad) –

(a) in sub-paragraph (4) (arrangements to assist children to live abroad), after 'guardian,' there is inserted 'special guardian,',
(b) in sub-paragraph (6), for the words from the beginning to 'British subject)' there is substituted 'Section 85 of the Adoption and Children Act 2002 (which imposes restrictions on taking children out of the United Kingdom)',
(c) after sub-paragraph (8) there is inserted –

'(9) This paragraph does not apply to a local authority placing a child for adoption with prospective adopters.'

73 In Schedule 8 (privately fostered children), in paragraph 5, for sub-paragraphs (a) and (b) there is substituted 'he is placed in the care of a person who proposes to adopt him under arrangements made by an adoption agency within the meaning of –

(a) section 2 of the Adoption and Children Act 2002;
(b) section 1 of the Adoption (Scotland) Act 1978; or
(c) Article 3 of the Adoption (Northern Ireland) Order 1987'.

74 Part 1 of Schedule 10 is omitted.

75 In Schedule 11 (jurisdiction), in paragraphs 1 and 2, for the words 'the Adoption Act 1976', wherever they occur, there is substituted 'the Adoption and Children Act 2002'.

The Human Fertilisation and Embryology Act 1990

76 The Human Fertilisation and Embryology Act 1990 is amended as follows.

77 In section 27 (meaning of mother), in subsection (2), for 'child of any person other than the adopter or adopters' there is substituted 'woman's child'.

78 In section 28 (meaning of father), in subsection (5)(c), for 'child of any person other than the adopter or adopters' there is substituted 'man's child'.

79 In section 30 (parental orders in favour of gamete donors), in subsection (10) for 'Adoption Act 1976' there is substituted 'Adoption and Children Act 2002'.

The Courts and Legal Services Act 1990

80 In section 58A of the Courts and Legal Services Act 1990 (conditional fee agreements: supplementary), in subsection (2), for paragraph (b) there is substituted –

'(b) the Adoption and Children Act 2002;'.

The Child Support Act 1991

81 In section 26 of the Child Support Act 1991 (disputes about parentage), in subsection (3), after '1976' there is inserted 'or Chapter 4 of Part 1 of the Adoption and Children Act 2002'.

The Children (Scotland) Act 1995

82 Section 86 of the Children (Scotland) Act 1995 (parental responsibilities order: general) is amended as follows.

83 In subsection (3), in paragraph (a), for 'section 18 (freeing for adoption) or 55 (adoption abroad) of the Adoption Act 1976' there is substituted 'section 19 (placing children with parental consent) or 84 (giving parental responsibility prior to adoption abroad) of the Adoption and Children Act 2002'.

84 In subsection (6), in paragraph (b), for the words from the beginning to 'Adoption Act 1976' there is substituted –

'(b)   he becomes the subject of an adoption order within the meaning of the Adoption (Scotland) Act 1978;
(bb) an adoption agency, within the meaning of section 2 of the Adoption and Children Act 2002, is authorised to place him for adoption under section 19 of that Act (placing children with parental consent) or he becomes the subject of an order under section 21 of that Act (placement orders) or under section 84 of that Act (giving parental responsibility prior to adoption abroad)'.

The Family Law Act 1996

85 The Family Law Act 1996 is amended as follows.

86 In section 62 (meaning of 'relevant child' etc) –

(a) in subsection (2), in paragraph (b), after 'the Adoption Act 1976' there is inserted ', the Adoption and Children Act 2002',
(b) in subsection (5), for the words from 'has been freed' to '1976' there is substituted 'falls within subsection (7)'.

87 At the end of that section there is inserted –

'(7) A child falls within this subsection if –

(a) an adoption agency, within the meaning of section 2 of the Adoption and Children Act 2002, has power to place him for adoption under section 19 of that Act (placing children with parental consent) or he has become the subject of an order under section 21 of that Act (placement orders), or

(b) he is freed for adoption by virtue of an order made –
   (i) in England and Wales, under section 18 of the Adoption Act 1976,
   (ii) in Scotland, under section 18 of the Adoption (Scotland) Act 1978, or
   (iii) in Northern Ireland, under Article 17(1) or 18(1) of the Adoption (Northern Ireland) Order 1987.'

88 In section 63 (interpretation of Part 4) –

(a) in subsection (1), for the definition of 'adoption order', there is substituted –

'"adoption order" means an adoption order within the meaning of section 72(1) of the Adoption Act 1976 or section 46(1) of the Adoption and Children Act 2002;',

(b) in subsection (2), after paragraph (h) there is inserted –

'(i) the Adoption and Children Act 2002.'

The Housing Act 1996

89 Section 178 of the Housing Act 1996 (meaning of associated person) is amended as follows.

90 In subsection (2), for the words from 'has been freed' to '1976' there is substituted 'falls within subsection (2A)'.

91 After that subsection there is inserted –

'(2A) A child falls within this subsection if –

(a) an adoption agency, within the meaning of section 2 of the Adoption and Children Act 2002, is authorised to place him for adoption under section 19 of that Act (placing children with parental consent) or he has become the subject of an order under section 21 of that Act (placement orders), or

(b) he is freed for adoption by virtue of an order made –
   (i) in England and Wales, under section 18 of the Adoption Act 1976,
   (ii) in Scotland, under section 18 of the Adoption (Scotland) Act 1978, or
   (iii) in Northern Ireland, under Article 17(1) or 18(1) of the Adoption (Northern Ireland) Order 1987.'

92 In subsection (3), for the definition of 'adoption order', there is substituted –

'"adoption order" means an adoption order within the meaning of section 72(1) of the Adoption Act 1976 or section 46(1) of the Adoption and Children Act 2002;'.

The Police Act 1997

93 In section 115 of the Police Act 1997 (enhanced criminal records), in subsection (5)(h), for 'section 11 of the Adoption Act 1976' there is substituted 'section 2 of the Adoption and Children Act 2002'.

The Protection of Children Act 1999

94 In section 2B of the Protection of Children Act 1999 (individuals named in the findings of certain inquiries), in subsection (7), after paragraph (a) there is inserted –

'(vi) section 17 of the Adoption and Children Act 2002;'.

The Adoption (Intercountry Aspects) Act 1999

95 The following provisions of the Adoption (Intercountry Aspects) Act 1999 cease to have effect in relation to England and Wales: sections 3, 6, 8, 9 and 11 to 13.

96 Section 2 of that Act (accredited bodies) is amended as follows.

97 In subsection (2A) –

(a) for the words from the beginning to '2000' there is substituted 'A registered adoption society',

(b) for 'agency' there is substituted 'society'.

98 For subsection (5) there is substituted –

'(5) In this section, "registered adoption society" has the same meaning as in section 2 of the Adoption and Children Act 2002 (basic definitions); and expressions used in this section in its application to England and Wales which are also used in that Act have the same meanings as in that Act.'

99 In subsection (6) –

(a) the words 'in its application to Scotland' are omitted,

(b) after 'expressions' there is inserted 'used in this section in its application to Scotland'.

100 Section 14 (restriction on bringing children into the United Kingdom for adoption) is omitted.

101 In section 16(1) (devolution: Wales), the words ', or section 17 or 56A of the 1976 Act,' are omitted.

The Access to Justice Act 1999

102 In Schedule 2 to the Access to Justice Act 1999 (Community Legal Service: excluded services), in paragraph 2(3)(c) –

(a) for 'section 27 or 28 of the Adoption Act 1976' there is substituted 'section 36 of the Adoption and Children Act 2002',

(b) for 'an order under Part II or section 29 or 55' there is substituted 'a placement order or adoption order (within the meaning of the Adoption and Children Act 2002) or an order under section 41 or 84'.

The Care Standards Act 2000

103 The Care Standards Act 2000 is amended as follows.

104 In section 4 (basic definitions), in subsection (7), for 'the Adoption Act 1976' there is substituted 'the Adoption and Children Act 2002'.

105 At the end of section 5 (registration authorities) there is inserted –

'(2) This section is subject to section 36A.'

Commencement—25 February 2003 (England only) for the purposes of s 16 of this Act insofar as that section was brought into force on that date by SI 2003/366, and 30 April 2003 (otherwise) (SI 2003/366).

106 In section 11 (requirement to register), in subsection (3), for 'reference in subsection (1) to an agency does' there is substituted 'references in subsections (1) and (2) to an agency do'.

Commencement—25 February 2003 (England only) for the purposes of s 16 of this Act insofar as that section was brought into force on that date by SI 2003/366, and 30 April 2003 (otherwise) (SI 2003/366).

107 In section 14 (2) (offences conviction of which may result in cancellation of registration), for paragraph (d) there is substituted –

> '(d) an offence under regulations under section 1(3) of the Adoption (Intercountry Aspects) Act 1999,
> (e) an offence under the Adoption and Children Act 2002 or regulations made under it'.

108 In section 16(2) (power to make regulations providing that no application for registration may be made in respect of certain agencies which are unincorporated bodies), 'or a voluntary adoption agency' is omitted.

109 In section 22(10) (disapplication of power to make regulations in the case of voluntary adoption agencies), at the end there is inserted 'or adoption support agencies'.

110 In section 23 (standards), at the end of subsection (4)(d) there is inserted 'or proceedings against a voluntary adoption agency for an offence under section 9(4) of the Adoption Act 1976 or section 9 of the Adoption and Children Act 2002'.

Commencement—30 April 2003 (England only) (SI 2003/366).

111 In section 31 (inspections by authorised persons), in subsection (3)(b), for 'section 9(2) of the Adoption Act 1976' there is substituted 'section 9 of the Adoption and Children Act 2002'.

112 In section 43 (introductory), in subsection (3)(a) –

> (a) for 'the Adoption Act 1976' there is substituted 'the Adoption and Children Act 2002',
> (b) after 'children' there is inserted 'or the provision of adoption support services (as defined in section 2(6) of the Adoption and Children Act 2002)'.

113 In section 46 (inspections: supplementary), in subsection (7)(c), for 'section 9(3) of the Adoption Act 1976' there is substituted 'section 9 of the Adoption and Children Act 2002'.

114 In section 48 (regulation of fostering functions), at the end of subsection (1) there is inserted –

> '(f) as to the fees or expenses which may be paid to persons assisting local authorities in making decisions in the exercise of such functions'.

115 In section 55(2)(b) (definition of 'social care worker'), for 'or a voluntary adoption agency' there is substituted ', a voluntary adoption agency or an adoption support agency'.

116 In section 121 (general interpretation) –

> (a) in subsection (1), in the definition of 'voluntary organisation', for 'the Adoption Act 1976' there is substituted 'the Adoption and Children Act 2002',
> (b) in subsection (13), in the appropriate place in the table there is inserted –

'Adoption support agency	Section 4'

117 In Schedule 4 (minor and consequential amendments), paragraph 27(b) is omitted.

The Criminal Justice and Court Services Act 2000

118 In section 12(5) of the Criminal Justice and Court Services Act 2000 (meaning of 'family proceedings' in relation to CAFCASS), paragraph (b) (supervision orders under the 1989 Act) and the preceding 'and' are omitted.

SCHEDULE 4
TRANSITIONAL AND TRANSITORY PROVISIONS AND SAVINGS

General rules for continuity

1 (1) Any reference (express or implied) in Part 1 or any other enactment, instrument or document to –

    (a) any provision of Part 1, or
    (b) things done or falling to be done under or for the purposes of any provision of Part 1,

must, so far as the nature of the reference permits, be construed as including, in relation to the times, circumstances or purposes in relation to which the corresponding provision repealed by this Act had effect, a reference to that corresponding provision or (as the case may be) to things done or falling to be done under or for the purposes of that corresponding provision.

(2) Any reference (express or implied) in any enactment, instrument or document to –

    (a) a provision repealed by this Act, or
    (b) things done or falling to be done under or for the purposes of such a provision,

must, so far as the nature of the reference permits, be construed as including, in relation to the times, circumstances or purposes in relation to which the corresponding provision of Part 1 has effect, a reference to that corresponding provision or (as the case may be) to things done or falling to be done under or for the purposes of that corresponding provision.

General rule for old savings

2 (1) The repeal by this Act of an enactment previously repealed subject to savings does not affect the continued operation of those savings.

(2) The repeal by this Act of a saving made on the previous repeal of an enactment does not affect the operation of the saving in so far as it is not specifically reproduced in this Act but remains capable of having effect.

Adoption support services

3 *(1) The facilities to be provided by local authorities as part of the service maintained under section 1(1) of the Adoption Act 1976 include such arrangements as the authorities may be required by regulations to make for the provision of adoption support services to prescribed persons.*

(2) Regulations under sub-paragraph (1) may require a local authority –

    (a) at the request of a prescribed person, to carry out an assessment of his needs for adoption support services,
    (b) if, as a result of the assessment, the authority decide that he has such needs, to decide whether to provide any such services to him,
    (c) if the authority decide to provide any such services to a person, and the circumstances fall within a description prescribed by the regulations, to prepare a plan in accordance with which the services are to be provided to him and keep the plan under review.

(3) Subsections (6) and (7) (except paragraph (a)) of section 4 of this Act apply to regulations under sub-paragraph (1) as they apply to regulations made by virtue of that section.

(4) Section 57(1) of the Adoption Act 1976 (prohibited payments) does not apply to any payment made in accordance with regulations under sub-paragraph (1).

Commencement—10 March 2003 (England only) for the purpose of making regulations (SI 2003/366).

Prospective amendment—Paragraph in italics prospectively repealed by Adoption and Children Act 2002, s 139(3), Sch 5, from a date to be appointed.

Regulation of adoption agencies

4 (1) In section 9 of the Adoption Act 1976 –

   (a) for 'Secretary of State' in subsections (2) and (3) there is substituted 'appropriate Minister', and
   (b) at the end of that section there is inserted –

     '(5) In this section and section 9A, "the appropriate Minister" means –

      (a) in relation to England, the Secretary of State,
      (b) in relation to Wales, the National Assembly for Wales,

     and in relation to England and Wales, means the Secretary of State and the Assembly acting jointly.'

(2) Until the commencement of the repeal by this Act of section 9(2) of the Adoption Act 1976, section 36A of the Care Standards Act 2000 (inserted by section 16 of this Act) is to have effect as if, after '2002', there were inserted 'or under section 9(2) of the Adoption Act 1976'.

Commencement—Subsection (1) in force from 3 February 2003 (SI 2003/288); subs (2) in force from 25 February 2003 (SI 2003/366).

Prospective amendment—Paragraph in italics prospectively repealed by Adoption and Children Act 2002, s 139(3), Sch 5, from a date to be appointed.

Independent review mechanism

5 After section 9 of the Adoption Act 1976 there is inserted –

'9A Independent review of determinations

(1) Regulations under section 9 may establish a procedure under which any person in respect of whom a qualifying determination has been made by an adoption agency may apply to a panel constituted by the appropriate Minister for a review of that determination.

(2) The regulations must make provision as to the description of determinations which are qualifying determinations for the purposes of subsection (1).

(3) The regulations may include provision as to –

   (a) the duties and powers of a panel (including the power to recover the costs of a review from the adoption agency by which the determination reviewed was made),
   (b) the administration and procedures of a panel,
   (c) the appointment of members of a panel (including the number, or any limit on the number, of members who may be appointed and any conditions for appointment),
   (d) the payment of expenses of members of a panel,
   (e) the duties of adoption agencies in connection with reviews conducted under the regulations,
   (f) the monitoring of any such reviews.

(4) The appropriate Minister may make an arrangement with an organisation under which functions in relation to the panel are performed by the organisation on his behalf.

(5) If the appropriate Minister makes such an arrangement with an organisation, the organisation is to perform its functions under the arrangement in accordance with any general or special directions given by the appropriate Minister.

(6) The arrangement may include provision for payments to be made to the organisation by the appropriate Minister.

(7) Where the appropriate Minister is the National Assembly for Wales, subsections (4) and (6) also apply as if references to an organisation included references to the Secretary of State.

(8) In this section, "organisation" includes a public body and a private or voluntary organisation.'

Prospective amendment—Paragraph in italics prospectively repealed by Adoption and Children Act 2002, s 139(3), Sch 5, from a date to be appointed.

Pending applications for freeing orders

6 Nothing in this Act affects any application for an order under section 18 of the Adoption Act 1976 (freeing for adoption) where –

(a) the application has been made and has not been disposed of immediately before the repeal of that section, and
(b) the child in relation to whom the application is made has his home immediately before that repeal with a person with whom he has been placed for adoption by an adoption agency.

Freeing orders

7 (1) Nothing in this Act affects any order made under section 18 of the Adoption Act 1976 and –

(a) sections 19 to 21 of that Act are to continue to have effect in relation to such an order, and
(b) Part 1 of Schedule 6 to the Magistrates' Courts Act 1980 is to continue to have effect for the purposes of an application under section 21 of the Adoption Act 1976 in relation to such an order.

(2) Section 20 of that Act, as it has effect by virtue of this paragraph, is to apply as if, in subsection (3)(c) after '1989' there were inserted –

'(iia) any care order, within the meaning of that Act'.

(3) Where a child is free for adoption by virtue of an order made under section 18 of that Act, the third condition in section 47(6) is to be treated as satisfied.

Pending applications for adoption orders

8 Nothing in this Act affects any application for an adoption order under section 12 of the Adoption Act 1976 where –

(a) the application has been made and has not been disposed of immediately before the repeal of that section, and
(b) the child in relation to whom the application is made has his home immediately before that repeal with a person with whom he has been placed for adoption by an adoption agency.

Notification of adoption applications

9 Where a notice given in respect of a child by the prospective adopters under section 22(1) of the Adoption Act 1976 is treated by virtue of paragraph 1(1) as having been given for the purposes of section 44(2) in respect of an application to adopt the child, section 42(3) has effect in relation to their application for an adoption order as if for 'six months' there were substituted 'twelve months'.

Adoptions with a foreign element

10 *In section 13 of the Adoption Act 1976 (child to live with adopters before order is made) –*

(a) in subsection (1)(a), at the beginning there is inserted '(subject to subsection (1A))',

(b) after subsection (1) there is inserted –

'(1A) Where an adoption is proposed to be effected by a Convention adoption order, the order shall not be made unless at all times during the preceding six months the child had his home with the applicants or one of them.',

(c) in subsection (2), after 'subsection (1)' there is inserted 'or (1A)',

(d) subsection (4) is omitted.

Commencement—1 June 2003 (SI 2003/366).

Prospective amendment—Paragraph in italics prospectively repealed by Adoption and Children Act 2002, s 139(3), Sch 5, from a date to be appointed.

11 *In section 56 of the Adoption Act 1976 (restriction on removal of children for adoption outside Great Britain) –*

(a) in subsection (1), 'not being a parent or guardian or relative of the child' is omitted,

(b) at the end of that section there is inserted –

'(4) Regulations may provide for subsection (1) to apply with modifications, or not to apply, if –

(a) the prospective adopters are parents, relatives or guardians of the child in question (or one of them is), or

(b) the prospective adopter is a step-parent of the child,

and any prescribed conditions are met.

(5) On the occasion of the first exercise of the power to make regulations under subsection (4) –

(a) the regulations shall not be made unless a draft of the regulations has been approved by a resolution of each House of Parliament, and

(b) accordingly section 67(2) does not apply to the statutory instrument containing the regulations.

(6) In this section, "prescribed" means prescribed by regulations and "regulations" means regulations made by the Secretary of State, after consultation with the National Assembly for Wales.'

Commencement—Subparagraph (a) in force from 1 June 2003 (SI 2003/366).

Prospective amendment—Paragraph in italics prospectively repealed by Adoption and Children Act 2002, s 139(3), Sch 5, from a date to be appointed.

12 *For section 56A of the Adoption Act 1976 there is substituted –*

'**56A** *Restriction on bringing children into the United Kingdom*

(1) This section applies where a person who is habitually resident in the British Islands (the "British resident") –

(a) brings, or causes another to bring, a child who is habitually resident outside the British Islands into the United Kingdom for the purpose of adoption by the British resident, or

(b) at any time brings, or causes another to bring, into the United Kingdom a child adopted by the British resident under an external adoption effected within the period of six months ending with that time.

The references to adoption, or to a child adopted, by the British resident include a reference to adoption, or to a child adopted, by the British resident and another person.

(2) But this section does not apply if the child is intended to be adopted under a Convention adoption order.

(3) An external adoption means an adoption, other than a Convention adoption, of a child effected under the law of any country or territory outside the British Islands, whether or not the adoption is –

> *(a) an adoption within the meaning of Part IV of this Act, or*
> *(b) a full adoption (within the meaning of section 39(3A)).*

(4) Regulations may require a person intending to bring, or to cause another to bring, a child into the United Kingdom in circumstances where this section applies –

> *(a) to apply to an adoption agency (including an adoption agency within the meaning of section 1 of the Adoption (Scotland) Act 1978 or Article 3 of the Adoption (Northern Ireland) Order 1987) in the prescribed manner for an assessment of his suitability to adopt the child, and*
> *(b) to give the agency any information it may require for the purpose of the assessment.*

(5) Regulations may require prescribed conditions to be met in respect of a child brought into the United Kingdom in circumstances where this section applies.

(6) In relation to a child brought into the United Kingdom for adoption in circumstances where this section applies, regulations may provide for any provision of Part II to apply with modifications or not to apply.

(7) If a person brings, or causes another to bring, a child into the United Kingdom at any time in circumstances where this section applies, he is guilty of an offence if –

> *(a) he has not complied with any requirement imposed by virtue of subsection (4), or*
> *(b) any condition required to be met by virtue of subsection (5) is not met,*

before that time, or before any later time which may be prescribed.

(8) A person guilty of an offence under this section is liable –

> *(a) on summary conviction to imprisonment for a term not exceeding six months, or a fine not exceeding the statutory maximum, or both,*
> *(b) on conviction on indictment, to imprisonment for a term not exceeding twelve months, or a fine, or both.*

(9) Regulations may provide for the preceding provisions of this section not to apply if –

> *(a) the adopters or (as the case may be) prospective adopters are natural parents, natural relatives or guardians of the child in question (or one of them is), or*
> *(b) the British resident in question is a step-parent of the child,*

and any prescribed conditions are met.

(10) On the occasion of the first exercise of the power to make regulations under subsection (9) –

> *(a) the regulations shall not be made unless a draft of the regulations has been approved by a resolution of each House of Parliament, and*
> *(b) accordingly section 67(2) does not apply to the statutory instrument containing the regulations.*

(11) In this section, "prescribed" means prescribed by regulations and "regulations" means regulations made by the Secretary of State, after consultation with the National Assembly for Wales.'

Commencement—1 April 2003 for the purpose of making regulations, except insofar as inserts Adoption Act 1976, s 56A(9), (10); 1 June 2003 otherwise, except as above (SI 2003/366).

Prospective amendment—Paragraph in italics prospectively repealed by Adoption and Children Act 2002, s 139(3), Sch 5, from a date to be appointed.

13 In section 72 of the Adoption Act 1976 (interpretation), subsection (3B) is omitted.

Commencement—1 June 2003 (SI 2003/366).

Prospective amendment—Paragraph in italics prospectively repealed by Adoption and Children Act 2002, s 139(3), Sch 5, from a date to be appointed.

Advertising

14 In section 58 of the Adoption Act 1976 (restrictions on advertisements) –

(a) after subsection (1) there is inserted –

'(1A) Publishing an advertisement includes doing so by electronic means (for example, by means of the internet).',

(b) in subsection (2), for the words following 'conviction' there is substituted 'to imprisonment for a term not exceeding three months, or a fine not exceeding level 5 on the standard scale, or both'.

Commencement—1 June 2003 (SI 2003/366).

Prospective amendment—Paragraph in italics prospectively repealed by Adoption and Children Act 2002, s 139(3), Sch 5, from a date to be appointed.

15 In section 52 of the Adoption (Scotland) Act 1978 (restriction on advertisements) –

(a) after subsection (1) there is inserted –

'(1A) Publishing an advertisement includes doing so by electronic means (for example, by means of the internet).',

(b) in subsection (2), for the words following 'conviction' there is substituted 'to imprisonment for a term not exceeding three months, or a fine not exceeding level 5 on the standard scale, or both'.

Prospective amendment—Paragraph in italics prospectively repealed by Adoption and Children Act 2002, s 139(3), Sch 5, from a date to be appointed.

16 (1) The Secretary of State may make regulations providing for the references to an adoption agency in –

(a) section 58(1)(c) of the Adoption Act 1976, and
(b) section 52(1)(c) of the Adoption (Scotland) Act 1978,

to include a prescribed person outside the United Kingdom exercising functions corresponding to those of an adoption agency, if the functions are being exercised in prescribed circumstances.

'Prescribed' means prescribed by the regulations.

(2) Before exercising the power conferred by sub-paragraph (1) in relation to the Adoption (Scotland) Act 1978, the Secretary of State must consult the Scottish Ministers.

Prospective amendment—Paragraph in italics prospectively repealed by Adoption and Children Act 2002, s 139(3), Sch 5, from a date to be appointed.

Status

17 (1) Section 67 –

    (a) does not apply to a pre-1976 instrument or enactment in so far as it contains a disposition of property, and

    (b) does not apply to any public general Act in its application to any disposition of property in a pre-1976 instrument or enactment.

(2) Section 73 applies in relation to this paragraph as if this paragraph were contained in Chapter 4 of Part 1; and an instrument or enactment is a pre-1976 instrument or enactment for the purposes of this Schedule if it was passed or made at any time before 1st January 1976.

18 Section 69 does not apply to a pre-1976 instrument.

19 In section 70(1), the reference to Part 3 of the Family Law Reform Act 1987 includes Part 2 of the Family Law Reform Act 1969.

Registration of adoptions

20 (1) The power of the court under paragraph 4(1) of Schedule 1 to amend an order on the application of the adopter or adopted person includes, in relation to an order made before 1st April 1959, power to make any amendment of the particulars contained in the order which appears to be required to bring the order into the form in which it would have been made if paragraph 1 of that Schedule had applied to the order.

(2) In relation to an adoption order made before the commencement of the Adoption Act 1976, the reference in paragraph 4(3) of that Schedule to paragraph 1(2) or (3) is to be read –

    (a) in the case of an order under the Adoption of Children Act 1926, as a reference to section 12(3) and (4) of the Adoption of Children Act 1949,

    (b) in the case of an order under the Adoption Act 1950, as a reference to section 18(3) and (4) of that Act,

    (c) in the case of an order under the Adoption Act 1958, as a reference to section 21(4) and (5) of that Act.

The Child Abduction Act 1984

21 Paragraph 43 of Schedule 3 does not affect the Schedule to the Child Abduction Act 1984 in its application to a child who is the subject of –

    (a) an order under section 18 of the Adoption Act 1976 freeing the child for adoption,

    (b) a pending application for such an order, or

    (c) a pending application for an order under section 12 of that Act.

The Courts and Legal Services Act 1990

22 Paragraph 80 of Schedule 3 does not affect section 58A(2)(b) of the Courts and Legal Services Act 1990 in its application to proceedings under the Adoption Act 1976.

The Children (Scotland) Act 1995

23 *[Applies to Scotland only]*

SCHEDULE 5
REPEALS

Short title and chapter	Extent of repeal
Births and Deaths Registration Act 1953 (c 20).	In section 10(3), the words following 'the Family Law Reform Act 1987'.
Sexual Offences Act 1956 (c 69).	In section 28(4), the 'or' at the end of paragraph (a).
Local Authority Social Services Act 1970 (c 42).	In Schedule 1, the entry relating to the Adoption Act 1976.
Adoption Act 1976 (c 36).	The whole Act, except Part 4 and paragraph 6 of Schedule 2.
Criminal Law Act 1977 (c 45).	In Schedule 12, the entries relating to the Adoption Act 1976.
National Health Service Act 1977 (c 49).	In section 124A(3), the 'or' at the end of paragraph (a).
Domestic Proceedings and Magistrates' Courts Act 1978 (c 22).	Sections 73(2), 74(2) and 74(4).
Adoption (Scotland) Act 1978 (c 28).	In section 50, the words 'not being a parent or guardian or relative of the child'. Section 52. In section 53(2), the words 'England and Wales or'. In section 65(1), in the definition of 'order freeing a child for adoption', paragraph (a) and the word 'and' immediately following that paragraph.
Magistrates' Courts Act 1980 (c 43).	In section 71(1) the words '(other than proceedings under the Adoption Act 1976)'. In section 71(2) the words following '(a) and (b)'. In Schedule 7, paragraphs 141 and 142.
British Nationality Act 1981 (c 61).	In section 1(8), the words following 'section 50'.
Mental Health Act 1983 (c 20).	In Schedule 4, paragraph 45.
Health and Social Services and Social Security Adjudications Act 1983 (c 41).	In Schedule 2, paragraphs 29 to 33, 35 and 36. In Schedule 9, paragraph 19.
County Courts Act 1984 (c 28).	In Schedule 2, paragraph 58.
Child Abduction Act 1984 (c 37).	In section 1(5A)(a), the 'or' at the end of sub-paragraph (i).

Short title and chapter	Extent of repeal
Matrimonial and Family Proceedings Act 1984 (c 42).	In section 40(2)(a), after 'the Adoption Act 1968', the word 'or'. In Schedule 1, paragraph 20.
Child Abduction and Custody Act 1985 (c 60).	In Schedule 3, in paragraph 1, the 'and' at the end of paragraph (b). In Schedule 3, in paragraph 1(c), paragraph (v).
Family Law Reform Act 1987 (c 42).	In Schedule 3, paragraphs 2 to 5.
Children Act 1989 (c 41).	Section 9(4). Section 12(3)(a). In section 20(9), the 'or' at the end of paragraph (a). In section 26(2)(e) and (f), the words 'to consider'. Section 33(6)(b)(i). Section 80(1)(e) and (f). Section 81(1)(b). Section 88(1). Section 102(6)(c). In section 105(1), the definition of 'protected child'. In Schedule 10, Part 1.
National Health Service and Community Care Act 1990 (c 19).	In Schedule 9, paragraph 17.
Human Fertilisation and Embryology Act 1990 (c 37).	In Schedule 4, paragraph 4.
Courts and Legal Services Act 1990 (c 41).	In Schedule 16, paragraph 7.
Local Government (Wales) Act 1994 (c 19).	In Schedule 10, paragraph 9.
Health Authorities Act 1995 (c 17).	In Schedule 1, paragraph 101.
Adoption (Intercountry Aspects) Act 1999 (c 18).	In section 2(6), the words 'in its application to Scotland'. Section 7(3). Section 14. In section 16(1), the words ', or section 17 or 56A of the 1976 Act,'. In Schedule 2, paragraph 3.
Access to Justice Act 1999 (c 22).	In Schedule 13, paragraph 88.
Care Standards Act 2000 (c 14).	In section 16(2), the words 'or a voluntary adoption agency'. In Schedule 4, paragraphs 5 and 27(b).
Local Government Act 2000 (c 22).	In Schedule 5, paragraph 16.

Short title and chapter	Extent of repeal
Criminal Justice and Court Services Act 2000 (c 43).	Section 12(5)(b) and the preceding 'and'. In Schedule 7, paragraphs 51 to 53.
This Act.	In Schedule 4, paragraphs 3 to 5 and 10 to 16.

SCHEDULE 6
GLOSSARY

In this Act, the expressions listed in the left-hand column below have the meaning given by, or are to be interpreted in accordance with, the provisions of this Act or (where stated) of the 1989 Act listed in the right-hand column.

Expression	Provision
the 1989 Act	section 2(5)
Adopted Children Register	section 77
Adoption and Children Act Register	section 125
adoption (in relation to Chapter 4 of Part 1)	section 66
adoption agency	section 2(1)
adoption agency placing a child for adoption	section 18(5)
Adoption Contact Register	section 80
adoption order	section 46(1)
Adoption Service	section 2(1)
adoption society	section 2(5)
adoption support agency	section 8
adoption support services	section 2(6)
appointed day (in relation to Chapter 4 of Part 1)	section 66(2)
appropriate Minister	section 144
Assembly	section 144
body	section 144
by virtue of	section 144
care order	section 105(1) of the 1989 Act
child	sections 49(5) and 144
child assessment order	section 43(2) of the 1989 Act
child in the care of a local authority	section 105(1) of the 1989 Act
child looked after by a local authority	section 22 of the 1989 Act

Expression	Provision
child placed for adoption by an adoption agency	section 18(5)
child to be adopted, adopted child	section 49(5)
consent (in relation to making adoption orders or placing for adoption)	section 52
the Convention	section 144
Convention adoption	section 66(1)(c)
Convention adoption order	section 144
Convention country	section 144
couple	section 144(4)
court	section 144
disposition (in relation to Chapter 4 of Part 1)	section 73
enactment	section 144
fee	section 144
guardian	section 144
information	section 144
interim care order	section 38 of the 1989 Act
local authority	section 144
local authority foster parent	section 23(3) of the 1989 Act
Northern Irish adoption agency	section 144
Northern Irish adoption order	section 144
notice	section 144
notice of intention to adopt	section 44(2)
overseas adoption	section 87
parental responsibility	section 3 of the 1989 Act
partner, in relation to a parent of a child	section 144(7)
placement order	section 21
placing, or placed, for adoption	sections 18(5) and 19(4)
prohibited steps order	section 8(1) of the 1989 Act
records (in relation to Chapter 5 of Part 1)	section 82
registered adoption society	section 2(2)
registers of live-births (in relation to Chapter 5 of Part 1)	section 82
registration authority (in Part 1)	section 144

Expression	Provision
regulations	section 144
relative	section 144, read with section 1(8)
residence order	section 8(1) of the 1989 Act
rules	section 144
Scottish adoption agency	section 144(3)
Scottish adoption order	section 144
specific issue order	section 8(1) of the 1989 Act
subordinate legislation	section 144
supervision order	section 31(11) of the 1989 Act
unitary authority	section 144
voluntary organisation	section 2(5)

Commencement—7 November 2002 (Royal Assent).

Index

References are to paragraph numbers.